Embedded Linux Primer, Second Edition

Embedded Linux Primer, Second Edition

A Practical, Real-World Approach

Christopher Hallinan

PRENTICE
HALL

Prentice Hall Professional Technical Reference
Upper Saddle River, NJ · Boston · Indianapolis · San Francisco
New York · Toronto · Montreal · London · Munich · Paris · Madrid
Capetown · Sydney · Tokyo · Singapore · Mexico City

Many of the designations used by manufacturers and sellers to distinguish their products are claimed as trademarks. Where those designations appear in this book, and the publisher was aware of a trademark claim, the designations have been printed with initial capital letters or in all capitals.

The author and publisher have taken care in the preparation of this book, but make no expressed or implied warranty of any kind and assume no responsibility for errors or omissions. No liability is assumed for incidental or consequential damages in connection with or arising out of the use of the information or programs contained herein.

The publisher offers excellent discounts on this book when ordered in quantity for bulk purchases or special sales, which may include electronic versions and/or custom covers and content particular to your business, training goals, marketing focus, and branding interests. For more information, please contact:

U.S. Corporate and Government Sales
(800) 382-3419
corpsales@pearsontechgroup.com

For sales outside the United States, please contact:

International Sales
international@pearson.com

Visit us on the Web: informit.com/aw

Library of Congress Cataloging-in-Publication Data:

Hallinan, Christopher.
 Embedded Linux primer : a practical real-world approach / Christopher Hallinan.
   p. cm.
 ISBN 978-0-13-701783-6 (hardback : alk. paper) 1. Linux. 2. Operating systems (Computers) 3. Embedded computer systems--Programming. I. Title.

QA76.76.O63H34462 2011
005.4'32--dc22

2010032891

ISBN-13: 978-0-137-01783-6
ISBN-10: 0-137-01783-9

Text printed in the United States on recycled paper at Courier in Westford, Massachusetts.
Fourth printing   March 2014

Editor-in-Chief: Mark L. Taub
Executive Acquisitions Editor: Debra Williams Cauley
Development Editor: Michael Thurston
Managing Editor: Kristy Hart
Project Editors: Alexandra Maurer and Jovana San Nicolas-Shirley
Copy Editor: Gayle Johnson
Indexer: Heather McNeill
Proofreader: Sarah Kearns
Technical Reviewers: Robert P.J. Day, Kurt Lloyd, Jon Masters, Sandra Terrace, and Mark A. Yoder
Publishing Coordinator: Kim Boedigheimer
Cover Designer: Alan Clements
Compositor: Tricia Bronkella

To my grandmother Edythe Diorio Ricciuti, who, at one hundred and five and counting, continues to provide inspiration to her loving family through her deep faith, unshakable moral compass, and selfless dedication to others.

Contents

Foreword for the First Edition xxv

Foreword for the Second Edition xxvi

Preface xxvii

Acknowledgments for the First Edition xxxiii

Acknowledgments for the Second Edition xxxv

About the Author xxxvi

Chapter 1   Introduction 1

1.1   Why Linux? 2

1.2   Embedded Linux Today 3

1.3   Open Source and the GPL 3

   1.3.1   Free Versus Freedom 4

1.4   Standards and Relevant Bodies 5

   1.4.1   Linux Standard Base 5

   1.4.2   Linux Foundation 6

   1.4.3   Carrier-Grade Linux 6

   1.4.4   Mobile Linux Initiative: Moblin 7

   1.4.5   Service Availability Forum 7

1.5   Summary 8

   1.5.1   Suggestions for Additional Reading 8

Chapter 2   The Big Picture 9

2.1   Embedded or Not? 10

   2.1.1   BIOS Versus Bootloader 11

2.2   Anatomy of an Embedded System 12

   2.2.1   Typical Embedded Linux Setup 13

   2.2.2   Starting the Target Board 14

   2.2.3   Booting the Kernel 16

   2.2.4   Kernel Initialization: Overview 18

   2.2.5   First User Space Process: `init` 19

2.3   Storage Considerations 20

   2.3.1   Flash Memory 20

   2.3.2   NAND Flash 22

   2.3.3   Flash Usage 23

   2.3.4   Flash File Systems 24

   2.3.5   Memory Space 25

   2.3.6   Execution Contexts 26

   2.3.7   Process Virtual Memory 28

   2.3.8   Cross-Development Environment 30

2.4   Embedded Linux Distributions 32

   2.4.1   Commercial Linux Distributions 33

   2.4.2   Do-It-Yourself Linux Distributions 33

2.5   Summary 34

   2.5.1   Suggestions for Additional Reading 35

Chapter 3   Processor Basics 37

3.1   Stand-Alone Processors 38

   3.1.1   IBM 970FX 39

   3.1.2   Intel Pentium M 39

3.1.3   Intel Atom™ 40

3.1.4   Freescale MPC7448 40

3.1.5   Companion Chipsets 41

3.2   Integrated Processors: Systems on Chip 43

3.2.1   Power Architecture 44

3.2.2   Freescale Power Architecture 44

3.2.3   Freescale PowerQUICC I 45

3.2.4   Freescale PowerQUICC II 46

3.2.5   PowerQUICC II Pro 47

3.2.6   Freescale PowerQUICC III 48

3.2.7   Freescale QorIQ™ 48

3.2.8   AMCC Power Architecture 50

3.2.9   MIPS 53

3.2.10   Broadcom MIPS 54

3.2.11   Other MIPS 55

3.2.12   ARM 55

3.2.13   TI ARM 56

3.2.14   Freescale ARM 58

3.2.15   Other ARM Processors 59

3.3   Other Architectures 59

3.4   Hardware Platforms 60

3.4.1   CompactPCI 60

3.4.2   ATCA 60

3.5   Summary 61

3.5.1   Suggestions for Additional Reading 62

Chapter 4   The Linux Kernel: A Different Perspective 63

4.1   Background 64

    4.1.1   Kernel Versions 65

    4.1.2   Kernel Source Repositories 67

    4.1.3   Using `git` to Download a Kernel 68

4.2   Linux Kernel Construction 68

    4.2.1   Top-Level Source Directory 69

    4.2.2   Compiling the Kernel 69

    4.2.3   The Kernel Proper: `vmlinux` 72

    4.2.4   Kernel Image Components 73

    4.2.5   Subdirectory Layout 77

4.3   Kernel Build System 78

    4.3.1   The Dot-Config 78

    4.3.2   Configuration Editor(s) 80

    4.3.3   Makefile Targets 83

4.4   Kernel Configuration 89

    4.4.1   Custom Configuration Options 91

    4.4.2   Kernel Makefiles 95

4.5   Kernel Documentation 96

4.6   Obtaining a Custom Linux Kernel 96

    4.6.1   What Else Do I Need? 97

4.7   Summary 97

    4.7.1   Suggestions for Additional Reading 98

Chapter 5   Kernel Initialization 99

5.1   Composite Kernel Image: Piggy and Friends 100

    5.1.1   The `Image` Object 103

    5.1.2   Architecture Objects 104

5.1.3   Bootstrap Loader 105

5.1.4   Boot Messages.. 106

5.2   Initialization Flow of Control.. 109

5.2.1   Kernel Entry Point: `head.o`.. 111

5.2.2   Kernel Startup: `main.c` 113

5.2.3   Architecture Setup 114

5.3   Kernel Command-Line Processing 115

5.3.1   The `__setup` Macro 116

5.4   Subsystem Initialization.. 122

5.4.1   The `*__initcall` Macros 122

5.5   The `init` Thread.. 125

5.5.1   Initialization Via `initcalls`.. 126

5.5.2   `initcall_debug`.. 127

5.5.3   Final Boot Steps... 127

5.6   Summary.. 129

5.6.1   Suggestions for Additional Reading.. 130

Chapter 6   User Space Initialization **131**

6.1   Root File System 132

6.1.1   FHS: File System Hierarchy Standard 133

6.1.2   File System Layout... 133

6.1.3   Minimal File System 134

6.1.4   The Embedded Root FS Challenge 136

6.1.5   Trial-and-Error Method 137

6.1.6   Automated File System Build Tools... 137

6.2   Kernel's Last Boot Steps.. 137

   6.2.1   First User Space Program 139

   6.2.2   Resolving Dependencies... 139

   6.2.3   Customized Initial Process 140

6.3   The init Process.. 140

   6.3.1   inittab.. 143

   6.3.2   Sample Web Server Startup Script... 145

6.4   Initial RAM Disk 146

   6.4.1   Booting with initrd... 147

   6.4.2   Bootloader Support for initrd... 148

   6.4.3   initrd Magic: linuxrc 150

   6.4.4   The initrd Plumbing... 151

   6.4.5   Building an initrd Image.. 152

6.5   Using initramfs... 153

   6.5.1   Customizing initramfs... 154

6.6   Shutdown... 156

6.7   Summary... 156

   6.7.1   Suggestions for Additional Reading.. 157

Chapter 7   Bootloaders 159

7.1   Role of a Bootloader... 160

7.2   Bootloader Challenges.. 161

   7.2.1   DRAM Controller 161

   7.2.2   Flash Versus RAM... 162

   7.2.3   Image Complexity.. 162

   7.2.4   Execution Context 165

7.3   A Universal Bootloader: Das U-Boot 166

    7.3.1   Obtaining U-Boot 166

    7.3.2   Configuring U-Boot 167

    7.3.3   U-Boot Monitor Commands 169

    7.3.4   Network Operations 170

    7.3.5   Storage Subsystems 173

    7.3.6   Booting from Disk 174

7.4   Porting U-Boot 174

    7.4.1   EP405 U-Boot Port 175

    7.4.2   U-Boot Makefile Configuration Target 176

    7.4.3   EP405 First Build 177

    7.4.4   EP405 Processor Initialization 178

    7.4.5   Board-Specific Initialization 181

    7.4.6   Porting Summary 184

    7.4.7   U-Boot Image Format 185

7.5   Device Tree Blob (Flat Device Tree) 187

    7.5.1   Device Tree Source 189

    7.5.2   Device Tree Compiler 192

    7.5.3   Alternative Kernel Images Using DTB 193

7.6   Other Bootloaders 194

    7.6.1   Lilo 194

    7.6.2   GRUB 195

    7.6.3   Still More Bootloaders 197

7.7   Summary 197

    7.7.1   Suggestions for Additional Reading 198

Chapter 8 Device Driver Basics **201**

8.1   Device Driver Concepts 202

    8.1.1   Loadable Modules.. 203

    8.1.2   Device Driver Architecture 204

    8.1.3   Minimal Device Driver Example... 204

    8.1.4   Module Build Infrastructure 205

    8.1.5   Installing a Device Driver 209

    8.1.6   Loading a Module.. 210

    8.1.7   Module Parameters 211

8.2   Module Utilities 212

    8.2.1   `insmod` 212

    8.2.2   `lsmod` 213

    8.2.3   `modprobe`.. 213

    8.2.4   `depmod` 214

    8.2.5   `rmmod` 215

    8.2.6   `modinfo`.. 216

8.3   Driver Methods.. 217

    8.3.1   Driver File System Operations 217

    8.3.2   Allocation of Device Numbers 220

    8.3.3   Device Nodes and `mknod`.. 220

8.4   Bringing It All Together.. 222

8.5   Building Out-of-Tree Drivers 223

8.6   Device Drivers and the GPL.. 224

8.7   Summary.. 225

    8.7.1   Suggestions for Additional Reading....................................... 226

Chapter 9   File Systems..**227**

9.1   Linux File System Concepts 228

    9.1.1   Partitions 229

9.2   ext2 230

    9.2.1   Mounting a File System 232

    9.2.2   Checking File System Integrity 233

9.3   ext3 235

9.4   ext4 237

9.5   ReiserFS 238

9.6   JFFS2 239

    9.6.1   Building a JFFS2 Image 240

9.7   *cramfs* 242

9.8   Network File System 244

    9.8.1   Root File System on NFS... 246

9.9   Pseudo File Systems... 248

    9.9.1   /proc File System... 249

    9.9.2   sysfs 252

9.10   Other File Systems 255

9.11   Building a Simple File System 256

9.12   Summary.. 258

    9.12.1   Suggestions for Additional Reading..................................... 259

Chapter 10   MTD Subsystem **261**

10.1   MTD Overview 262

    10.1.1   Enabling MTD Services.. 263

    10.1.2   MTD Basics... 265

    10.1.3   Configuring MTD on Your Target....................................... 267

10.2   MTD Partitions 267

    10.2.1   Redboot Partition Table Partitioning.............................. 269

    10.2.2   Kernel Command-Line Partitioning 273

    10.2.3   Mapping Driver.. 274

    10.2.4   Flash Chip Drivers.. 276

    10.2.5   Board-Specific Initialization 276

10.3   MTD Utilities... 279

    10.3.1   JFFS2 Root File System 281

10.4   UBI File System 284

    10.4.1   Configuring for UBIFS... 284

    10.4.2   Building a UBIFS Image.. 284

    10.4.3   Using UBIFS as the Root File System 287

10.5   Summary.. 287

    10.5.1   Suggestions for Additional Reading............................... 288

Chapter 11   BusyBox 289

11.1   Introduction to BusyBox.. 290

    11.1.1   BusyBox Is Easy 291

11.2   BusyBox Configuration 291

    11.2.1   Cross-Compiling BusyBox... 293

11.3   BusyBox Operation 293

    11.3.1   BusyBox `init`.. 297

    11.3.2   Sample `rcs` Initialization Script 299

    11.3.3   BusyBox Target Installation.. 300

    11.3.4   BusyBox Applets 302

11.4   Summary.. 303

    11.4.1   Suggestions for Additional Reading.............................. 304

Chapter 12   Embedded Development Environment 305

12.1   Cross-Development Environment 306

12.1.1   "Hello World" Embedded 307

12.2   Host System Requirements... 311

12.2.1   Hardware Debug Probe 311

12.3   Hosting Target Boards.. 312

12.3.1   TFTP Server 312

12.3.2   BOOTP/DHCP Server.. 313

12.3.3   NFS Server 316

12.3.4   Target NFS Root Mount 318

12.3.5   U-Boot NFS Root Mount Example 320

12.4   Summary.. 322

12.4.1   Suggestions for Additional Reading.. 323

Chapter 13   Development Tools 325

13.1   GNU Debugger (GDB) 326

13.1.1   Debugging a Core Dump 327

13.1.2   Invoking GDB... 329

13.1.3   Debug Session in GDB.. 331

13.2   Data Display Debugger 333

13.3   `cbrowser/cscope`... 335

13.4   Tracing and Profiling Tools.. 337

13.4.1   `strace`... 337

13.4.2   `strace` Variations... 341

13.4.3   `ltrace`... 343

13.4.4   `ps`.. 344

13.4.5   `top`... 346

13.4.6 `mtrace` 348

13.4.7 `dmalloc` 350

13.4.8 Kernel Oops 353

13.5 Binary Utilities 355

13.5.1 `readelf` 355

13.5.2 Examining Debug Information Using `readelf` 357

13.5.3 `objdump` 359

13.5.4 `objcopy` 360

13.6 Miscellaneous Binary Utilities 361

13.6.1 `strip` 361

13.6.2 `addr2line` 361

13.6.3 `strings` 362

13.6.4 `ldd` 362

13.6.5 `nm` 363

13.6.6 `prelink` 364

13.7 Summary 364

13.7.1 Suggestions for Additional Reading 365

Chapter 14   Kernel Debugging Techniques 367

14.1 Challenges to Kernel Debugging 368

14.2 Using KGDB for Kernel Debugging 369

14.2.1 KGDB Kernel Configuration 371

14.2.2 Target Boot with KGDB Support 372

14.2.3 Useful Kernel Breakpoints 376

14.2.4 Sharing a Console Serial Port with KGDB 377

14.2.5 Debugging Very Early Kernel Code 379

14.2.6 KGDB Support in the Mainline Kernel 380

14.3   Kernel Debugging Techniques 381

14.3.1   gdb Remote Serial Protocol 382

14.3.2   Debugging Optimized Kernel Code 385

14.3.3   GDB User-Defined Commands 392

14.3.4   Useful Kernel GDB Macros 393

14.3.5   Debugging Loadable Modules 402

14.3.6   printk Debugging 407

14.3.7   Magic SysReq Key 409

14.4   Hardware-Assisted Debugging 410

14.4.1   Programming Flash Using a JTAG Probe 411

14.4.2   Debugging with a JTAG Probe 413

14.5   When It Doesn't Boot 417

14.5.1   Early Serial Debug Output 417

14.5.2   Dumping the printk Log Buffer 417

14.5.3   KGDB on Panic 420

14.6   Summary 421

14.6.1   Suggestions for Additional Reading 422

Chapter 15   Debugging Embedded Linux Applications 423

15.1   Target Debugging 424

15.2   Remote (Cross) Debugging 424

15.2.1   gdbserver 427

15.3   Debugging with Shared Libraries 429

15.3.1   Shared Library Events in GDB 431

15.4   Debugging Multiple Tasks 435

15.4.1   Debugging Multiple Processes 435

15.4.2   Debugging Multithreaded Applications 438

15.4.3   Debugging Bootloader/Flash Code 441

15.5   Additional Remote Debug Options... 442

   15.5.1   Debugging Using a Serial Port 442

   15.5.2   Attaching to a Running Process 442

15.6   Summary.. 443

   15.6.1   Suggestions for Additional Reading............................... 444

Chapter 16   Open Source Build Systems **445**

16.1   Why Use a Build System?... 446

16.2   Scratchbox.. 447

   16.2.1   Installing Scratchbox... 447

   16.2.2   Creating a Cross-Compilation Target............................ 448

16.3   Buildroot... 451

   16.3.1   Buildroot Installation... 451

   16.3.2   Buildroot Configuration 451

   16.3.3   Buildroot Build... 452

16.4   OpenEmbedded 454

   16.4.1   OpenEmbedded Composition 455

   16.4.2   BitBake Metadata... 456

   16.4.3   Recipe Basics.. 456

   16.4.4   Metadata Tasks... 460

   16.4.5   Metadata Classes.. 461

   16.4.6   Configuring OpenEmbedded 462

   16.4.7   Building Images 463

16.5   Summary.. 464

   16.5.1   Suggestions for Additional Reading............................... 464

Chapter 17   Linux and Real Time..**465**

17.1   What Is Real Time? 466

17.1.1   Soft Real Time 466

17.1.2   Hard Real Time 467

17.1.3   Linux Scheduling... 467

17.1.4   Latency 467

17.2   Kernel Preemption 469

17.2.1   Impediments to Preemption... 469

17.2.2   Preemption Models... 471

17.2.3   SMP Kernel 472

17.2.4   Sources of Preemption Latency 473

17.3   Real-Time Kernel Patch... 473

17.3.1   Real-Time Features 475

17.3.2   O(1) Scheduler 476

17.3.3   Creating a Real-Time Process... 477

17.4   Real-Time Kernel Performance Analysis 478

17.4.1   Using Ftrace for Tracing... 478

17.4.2   Preemption Off Latency Measurement............................. 479

17.4.3   Wakeup Latency Measurement 481

17.4.4   Interrupt Off Timing 483

17.4.5   Soft Lockup Detection... 484

17.5   Summary.. 485

17.5.1   Suggestion for Additional Reading................................... 485

Chapter 18   Universal Serial Bus **487**

18.1   USB Overview 488

18.1.1   USB Physical Topology... 488

18.1.2   USB Logical Topology 490

18.1.3 USB Revisions 491

18.1.4 USB Connectors 492

18.1.5 USB Cable Assemblies 494

18.1.6 USB Modes 494

18.2 Configuring USB 495

18.2.1 USB Initialization 497

18.3 sysfs and USB Device Naming 500

18.4 Useful USB Tools 502

18.4.1 USB File System 502

18.4.2 Using usbview 504

18.4.3 USB Utils (lsusb) 507

18.5 Common USB Subsystems 508

18.5.1 USB Mass Storage Class 508

18.5.2 USB HID Class 511

18.5.3 USB CDC Class Drivers 512

18.5.4 USB Network Support 515

18.6 USB Debug 516

18.6.1 usbmon 517

18.6.2 Useful USB Miscellanea 518

18.7 Summary 519

18.7.1 Suggestions for Additional Reading 519

Chapter 19 udev 521

19.1 What Is udev? 522

19.2 Device Discovery 523

19.3 Default udev Behavior 525

19.4 Understanding udev Rules.. 527

    19.4.1 Modalias 530

    19.4.2 Typical udev Rules Configuration 533

    19.4.3 Initial System Setup for udev 535

19.5 Loading Platform Device Drivers 538

19.6 Customizing udev Behavior... 540

    19.6.1 udev Customization Example: USB Automounting 540

19.7 Persistent Device Naming.. 541

    19.7.1 udev Helper Utilities.. 542

19.8 Using udev with busybox 545

    19.8.1 busybox mdev.. 545

    19.8.2 Configuring mdev... 547

19.9 Summary.. 548

    19.9.1 Suggestions for Additional Reading... 548

Appendix A GNU Public License... **549**

Preamble 550

Terms and Conditions for Copying, Distribution, and Modification............. 551

No Warranty 555

Appendix B U-Boot Configurable Commands **557**

Appendix C BusyBox Commands.. **561**

Appendix D SDRAM Interface Considerations 571

D.1 SDRAM Basics 572

    D.1.1 SDRAM Refresh... 573

D.2 Clocking 574

D.3   SDRAM Setup.. 575

D.4   Summary 580

   D.4.1   Suggestions for Additional Reading... 580

Appendix E   Open Source Resources **581**

Source Repositories and Developer Information... 582

Mailing Lists 582

Linux News and Developments... 583

Open Source Legal Insight and Discussion... 583

Appendix F   Sample BDI-2000 Configuration File **585**

Index..**593**

Foreword for the First Edition

Computers are everywhere.

This fact, of course, is no surprise to anyone who hasn't been living in a cave during the past 25 years or so. And you probably know that computers aren't just on our desktops, in our kitchens, and, increasingly, in our living rooms, holding our music collections. They're also in our microwave ovens, our regular ovens, our cell phones, and our portable digital music players.

And if you're holding this book, you probably know a lot, or are interested in learning more about, these embedded computer systems.

Until not too long ago, embedded systems were not very powerful, and they ran special-purpose, proprietary operating systems that were very different from industry-standard ones. (Plus, they were much harder to develop for.) Today, embedded computers are as powerful as, if not more powerful than, a modern home computer. (Consider the high-end gaming consoles, for example.)

Along with this power comes the capability to run a full-fledged operating system such as Linux. Using a system such as Linux for an embedded product makes a lot of sense. A large community of developers are making this possible. The development environment and the deployment environment can be surprisingly similar, which makes your life as a developer much easier. And you have both the security of a protected address space that a virtual memory-based system gives you and the power and flexibility of a multiuser, multi-process system. That's a good deal all around.

For this reason, companies all over the world are using Linux on many devices such as PDAs, home entertainment systems, and even, believe it or not, cell phones!

I'm excited about this book. It provides an excellent "guide up the learning curve" for the developer who wants to use Linux for his or her embedded system. It's clear, well-written, and well-organized; Chris's knowledge and understanding show through at every turn. It's not only informative and helpful; it's also enjoyable to read.

I hope you learn something and have fun at the same time. I know I did.

Arnold Robbins
Series Editor

Foreword for the Second Edition

Smart phones. PDAs. Home routers. Smart televisions. Smart Blu-ray players. Smart yo-yos. OK, maybe not. More and more of the everyday items in our homes and offices, used for work and play, have computers embedded in them. And those computers are running GNU/Linux.

You may be a GNU/Linux developer used to working on desktop (or notebook) Intel Architecture systems. Or you may be an embedded systems developer used to more traditional embedded and/or real-time operating systems. Whatever your background, if you're entering the world of embedded Linux development, Dorothy's "Toto, I've a feeling we're not in Kansas anymore" applies to you. Welcome to the adventure!

Dorothy had a goal, and some good friends, but no *guide*. You, however, are better off, since you're holding an amazing field guide to the world of embedded Linux development. Christopher Hallinan lays it all out for you—the how, the where, the why, and also the "what not to do." This book will keep you out of the school of hard knocks and get you going easily and quickly on the road to building your product.

It is no surprise that this book has been a leader in its market. This new edition is even better. It is up to date and brings all the author's additional experience to bear on the subject.

I am very proud to have this book in my series. But what's more important is that you will be proud of yourself for having built a better product because you read it! Enjoy!

Arnold Robbins
Series Editor

Preface

Although many good books cover Linux, this one brings together many dimensions of information and advice specifically targeted to the embedded Linux developer. Indeed, some very good books have been written about the Linux kernel, Linux system administration, and so on. This book refers to many of the ones I consider to be at the top of their categories.

Much of the material presented in this book is motivated by questions I've received over the years from development engineers in my capacity as an embedded Linux consultant and from my direct involvement in the commercial embedded Linux market.

Embedded Linux presents the experienced software engineer with several unique challenges. First, those with many years of experience with legacy real-time operating systems (RTOSs) find it difficult to transition their thinking from those environments to Linux. Second, experienced application developers often have difficulty understanding the relative complexities of a cross-development environment.

Although this is a primer, intended for developers new to embedded Linux, I am confident that even developers who are experienced in embedded Linux will benefit from the useful tips and techniques I have learned over the years.

PRACTICAL ADVICE FOR THE PRACTICING EMBEDDED DEVELOPER

This book describes my view of what an embedded engineer needs to know to get up to speed fast in an embedded Linux environment. Instead of focusing on Linux kernel internals, the kernel chapters in this book focus on the project nature of the kernel and leave the internals to the other excellent texts on the subject. You will learn the organization and layout of the kernel source tree. You will discover the binary components that make up a kernel image, how they are loaded, and what purpose they serve on an embedded system.

In this book, you will learn how the Linux kernel build system works and how to incorporate your own custom changes that are required for your projects. You will learn the details of Linux system initialization, from the kernel to user space initialization. You will learn many useful tips and tricks for your embedded project, from bootloaders, system initialization, file systems, and Flash memory to advanced kernel- and application-debugging techniques. This second edition features much new and updated content, as well as new chapters on open source build systems, USB and udev, highlighting how to configure and use these complex systems on your embedded Linux project.

INTENDED AUDIENCE

This book is intended for programmers who have working knowledge of programming in C. I assume that you have a rudimentary understanding of local area networks and the Internet. You should understand and recognize an IP address and how it is used on a simple local area network. I also assume that you understand hexadecimal and octal numbering systems and their common usage in a book such as this.

Several advanced concepts related to C compiling and linking are explored, so you will benefit from having at least a cursory understanding of the role of the linker in ordinary C programming. Knowledge of the GNU make operation and semantics also will prove beneficial.

WHAT THIS BOOK IS NOT

This book is not a detailed hardware tutorial. One of the difficulties the embedded developer faces is the huge variety of hardware devices in use today. The user manual for a modern 32-bit processor with some integrated peripherals can easily exceed 3,000 pages. There are no shortcuts. If you need to understand a hardware device from a programmer's point of view, you need to spend plenty of hours in your favorite reading chair with hardware data sheets and reference guides, and many more hours writing and testing code for these hardware devices!

This is also not a book about the Linux kernel or kernel internals. In this book, you won't learn about the intricacies of the Memory Management Unit (MMU) used to implement Linux's virtual memory-management policies and procedures; there are already several good books on this subject. You are encouraged to take advantage of the "Suggestions for Additional Reading" sections found at the end of every chapter.

Conventions Used

Filenames, directories, utilities, tools, commands, and code statements are presented in a `monospace` font. Commands that the user enters appear in bold monospace. New terms or important concepts are presented in italics.

When you see a pathname preceded by three dots, this refers to a well-known but unspecified top-level directory. The top-level directory is context-dependent but almost universally refers to a top-level Linux source directory. For example, `.../arch/powerpc/kernel/setup_32.c` refers to the `setup_32.c` file located in the architecture branch of a Linux source tree. The actual path might be something like `~/sandbox/linux.2.6.33/arch/power/kernel/setup_32.c`.

How This Book Is Organized

Chapter 1, "Introduction," provides a brief look at the factors driving the rapid adoption of Linux in the embedded environment. Several important standards and organizations relevant to embedded Linux are introduced.

Chapter 2, "The Big Picture," introduces many concepts related to embedded Linux upon which later chapters are built.

Chapter 3, "Processor Basics," presents a high-level look at the more popular processors and platforms that are being used to build embedded Linux systems. We examine selected products from many of the major processor manufacturers. All the major architecture families are represented.

Chapter 4, "The Linux Kernel: A Different Perspective," examines the Linux kernel from a slightly different perspective. Instead of kernel theory or internals, we look at its structure, layout, and build construction so that you can begin learning your way around this large software project and, more important, learn where your own customization efforts must be focused. This includes detailed coverage of the kernel build system.

Chapter 5, "Kernel Initialization," details the Linux kernel's initialization process. You will learn how the architecture- and bootloader-specific image components are concatenated to the image of the kernel proper for downloading to Flash and booting by an embedded bootloader. The knowledge you gain here will help you customize the Linux kernel to your own embedded application requirements.

Chapter 6, "User Space Initialization," continues the detailed examination of the initialization process. When the Linux kernel has completed its own initialization, application programs continue the initialization process in a predetermined manner. Upon completing Chapter 6, you will have the necessary knowledge to customize your own userland application startup sequence.

Chapter 7, "Bootloaders," is dedicated to the bootloader and its role in an embedded Linux system. We examine the popular open-source bootloader U-Boot and present a porting example. We briefly introduce additional bootloaders in use today so that you can make an informed choice about your particular requirements.

Chapter 8, "Device Driver Basics," introduces the Linux device driver model and provides enough background to launch into one of the great texts on device drivers, listed in "Suggestions for Additional Reading" at the end of the chapter.

Chapter 9, "File Systems," describes the more popular file systems being used in embedded systems today. We include coverage of the JFFS2, an important embedded file system used on Flash memory devices. This chapter includes a brief introduction to building your own file system image, one of the more difficult tasks the embedded Linux developer faces.

Chapter 10, "MTD Subsystem," explores the Memory Technology Devices (MTD) subsystem. MTD is an extremely useful abstraction layer between the Linux file system and hardware memory devices, primarily Flash memory.

Chapter 11, "BusyBox," introduces BusyBox, one of the most useful utilities for building small embedded systems. We describe how to configure and build BusyBox for your particular requirements, along with detailed coverage of system initialization unique to a BusyBox environment. Appendix C, "BusyBox Commands," lists the available BusyBox commands from a recent BusyBox release.

Chapter 12, "Embedded Development Environment," takes a detailed look at the unique requirements of a typical cross-development environment. Several techniques are presented to enhance your productivity as an embedded developer, including the powerful NFS root mount development configuration.

Chapter 13, "Development Tools," examines many useful development tools. Debugging with gdb is introduced, including coverage of core dump analysis. Many more tools are presented and explained, with examples including strace, ltrace, top, and ps, and the memory profilers mtrace and dmalloc. The chapter concludes with an introduction to the more important binary utilities, including the powerful readelf utility.

Chapter 14, "Kernel Debugging Techniques," provides a detailed examination of many debugging techniques useful for debugging inside the Linux kernel. We introduce the use of the kernel debugger KGDB and present many useful debugging techniques using the combination of gdb and KGDB as debugging tools. Included is an introduction to using hardware JTAG debuggers and some tips for analyzing failures when the kernel won't boot.

Chapter 15, "Debugging Embedded Linux Applications," moves the debugging context from the kernel to your application programs. We continue to build on the gdb examples from the previous two chapters, and we present techniques for multi-threaded and multiprocess debugging.

Chapter 16, "Open Source Build Systems," replaces the kernel porting chapter from the first edition. That chapter had become hopelessly outdated, and proper treatment of that topic in modern kernels would take a book of its own. I think you will be pleased with the new Chapter 16, which covers the popular build systems available for building complete embedded Linux distributions. Among other systems, we introduce OpenEmbedded, a build system that has gained significant traction in commercial and other open source projects.

Chapter 17, "Linux and Real Time," introduces one of the more interesting challenges in embedded Linux: configuring for real time via the PREEMPT_RT option. We cover the features available with RT and how they can be used in a design. We also present techniques for measuring latency in your application configuration.

Chapter 18, "Universal Serial Bus," describes the USB subsystem in easy-to-understand language. We introduce concepts and USB topology and then present several examples of USB configuration. We take a detailed look at the role of sysfs and USB to help you understand this powerful facility. We also present several tools that are useful for understanding and troubleshooting USB.

Chapter 19, "udev," takes the mystery out of this powerful system configuration utility. We examine udev's default behavior as a foundation for understanding how to customize it. Several real-world examples are presented. For BusyBox users, we examine BusyBox's mdev utility.

The appendixes cover the GNU Public License, U-Boot configurable commands, BusyBox commands, SDRAM interface considerations, resources for the open source developer, and a sample configuration file for one of the more popular hardware JTAG debuggers, the BDI-2000.

FOLLOW ALONG

You will benefit most from this book if you can divide your time between this book and your favorite Linux workstation. Grab an old x86 computer to experiment on an embedded system. Even better, if you have access to a single-board computer based on another architecture, use that. The BeagleBoard makes an excellent low-cost platform for experimentation. Several examples in this book are based on that platform. You will benefit from learning the layout and organization of a very large code base (the Linux kernel), and you will gain significant knowledge and experience as you poke around the kernel and learn by doing.

Look at the code and try to understand the examples produced in this book. Experiment with different settings, configuration options, and hardware devices. You can gain much in terms of knowledge, and besides, it's loads of fun. If you are so inclined, please log on and contribute to the website dedicated to this book, www.embeddedlinuxprimer.com. Feel free to create an account, add content and comments to other contributions, and share your own successes and solutions as you gain experience in this growing segment of the Linux community. Your input will help others as they learn. It is a work in progress, and your contributions will help it become a valuable community resource.

GPL COPYRIGHT NOTICE

Portions of open-source code reproduced in this book are copyrighted by a large number of individual and corporate contributors. The code reproduced here has been licensed under the terms of the GNU Public License (GPL).

Appendix A contains the text of the GNU Public License.

Acknowledgments for the First Edition

I am constantly amazed by the graciousness of open source developers. I am humbled by the talent in our community that often far exceeds my own. During the course of this project, I reached out to many people in the Linux and open source community with questions. Most often my questions were answered quickly and with encouragement. In no particular order, I'd like to express my gratitude to the following members of the Linux and open source community who contributed answers to my questions:

Dan Malek provided inspiration for some of the contents of Chapter 2.

Dan Kegel and Daniel Jacobowitz patiently answered my toolchain questions.

Scott Anderson provided the original ideas for the gdb macros presented in Chapter 14.

Brad Dixon continues to challenge and expand my technical vision through his own.

George Davis answered my ARM questions.

Jim Lewis provided comments and suggestions on the MTD coverage.

Cal Erickson answered my gdb use questions.

John Twomey advised me on Chapter 3.

Lee Revell, Sven-Thorsten Dietrich, and Daniel Walker advised me on real-time Linux content. Klaas van Gend provided excellent feedback and ideas for my development tools and debugging content.

Many thanks to AMCC, Embedded Planet, Ultimate Solutions, and United Electronic Industries for providing hardware for the examples. Many thanks to my employer, Monta Vista Software, for tolerating the occasional distraction and for providing software for some of the examples. Many others contributed ideas, encouragement, and support over the course of the project. To them I am also grateful.

I offer my sincere appreciation to my primary review team, who promptly read each chapter and provided excellent feedback, comments, and ideas. Thanks to Arnold Robbins, Sandy Terrace, Kurt Lloyd, and Rob Farber. Thanks also to David Brief, who reviewed the proposal and provided valuable input on the book's organization. Many thanks to Arnold for helping this newbie learn the ropes of writing a technical book. Although I have made every attempt to eliminate mistakes, those that remain are solely my own.

I want to thank Mark L. Taub for bringing this project to fruition and for his encouragement and infinite patience. I want to thank the production team, including Kristy Hart, Jennifer Cramer, Krista Hansing, and Cheryl Lenser.

Finally, a very special and heartfelt thank-you to Cary Dillman, who read each chapter as it was written, and for her constant encouragement and occasional sacrifice throughout the project.

Acknowledgments for the Second Edition

First I must acknowledge the guidance, experience, and endless patience of Debra Williams Cauley, Executive Acquisitions Editor, without whom this project would never have happened.

Many thanks to my dedicated primary review team: Robert P.J. Day, Sandy Terrace, Kurt Lloyd, Jon Masters, and series editor Arnold Robbins. I cannot say enough about the value of their individual contributions to the quality of this book.

Thanks also to Professor Mark A. Yoder and his embedded Linux class for giving the manuscript a thorough classroom test.

A special thanks to Freescale Semiconductor for providing hardware that served as the basis for many of the examples in this book. I would not have enjoyed this support without the efforts of Kalpesh Gala, who facilitated these arrangements.

Thanks also to Embedded Planet and Tim Van de Walle, who provided hardware for some of the examples.

Several individuals were especially helpful with advice and answers to questions during the project. In no particular order, my appreciation and thanks are extended to Cedric Hombourger, Klaas van Gend, George Davis, Sven-Thorsten Dietrich, Jason Wessels, and Dave Anders.

I also want to thank the production team who endured my sometimes-hectic schedule. They include Alexandra Maurer, Michael Thurston, Jovana San Nicolas-Shirley, Gayle Johnson, Heather McNeill, Tricia Bronkella, and Sarah Kearns.

With every project of this magnitude, countless people provide input in the form of an answer to a quick question, or perhaps an idea from a conversation. They are too numerous to mention but nonetheless deserve credit for their willing and sometimes unknowing support.

In the first edition, I specifically thanked Cary Dillman for her tireless efforts to review my chapters as they were written. She is now my lovely wife, Cary Hallinan. Cary continued her support by providing much-needed inspiration, patience, and occasional sacrifice throughout the second-edition project.

About the Author

Christopher Hallinan is a technical marketing engineer for the Embedded Systems Division of Mentor Graphics, living and working in Florida. He has spent more than 25 years in the networking and communications industry, mostly in various product development, management, and marketing roles, where he developed a strong background in the space where hardware meets software. Prior to joining Mentor Graphics, he spent nearly seven years as a field applications engineer for Monta Vista Software. Before that, Hallinan spent four years as an independent Linux consultant, providing custom Linux board ports, device drivers, and bootloaders. His introduction to the open source community was through contributions to the popular U-Boot bootloader. When not messing about with Linux, he is often found singing and playing a Taylor or Martin.

Chapter 1

Introduction

In This Chapter

■ 1.1 Why Linux?   2

■ 1.2 Embedded Linux Today   3

■ 1.3 Open Source and the GPL   3

■ 1.4 Standards and Relevant Bodies   5

■ 1.5 Summary   8

The move away from proprietary embedded operating systems is causing quite a stir in the corporate boardrooms of many traditional embedded operating system (OS) companies. For many well-founded reasons, Linux is being adopted as the operating system in many products beyond its traditional stronghold in server applications. Examples of these embedded systems include cellular phones, DVD players, video games, digital cameras, network switches, and wireless networking gear. It is quite likely that Linux is already in your home or automobile. Linux has been commonly selected as the embedded operating system in devices including set-top boxes, high-definition televisions, Blu-ray DVD players, automobile infotainment centers, and many other devices encountered in everyday life.

1.1 Why Linux?

Because of the numerous economic and technical benefits, we are seeing strong growth in the adoption of Linux for embedded devices. This trend has crossed virtually all markets and technologies. Linux has been adopted for embedded products in the worldwide public switched telephone network, global data networks, and wireless cellular handsets, as well as radio node controllers and backhaul infrastructure that operates these networks. Linux has enjoyed success in automobile applications, consumer products such as games and PDAs, printers, enterprise switches and routers, and many other products. Tens of millions of cell phones are now shipping worldwide with Linux as the operating system of choice. The adoption rate of embedded Linux continues to grow, with no end in sight.

Here are some of the reasons for the growth of embedded Linux:

- Linux supports a vast variety of hardware devices, probably more than any other OS.
- Linux supports a huge variety of applications and networking protocols.
- Linux is scalable, from small consumer-oriented devices to large, heavy-iron, carrier-class switches and routers.

- Linux can be deployed without the royalties required by traditional proprietary embedded operating systems.

- Linux has attracted a huge number of active developers, enabling rapid support of new hardware architectures, platforms, and devices.

- An increasing number of hardware and software vendors, including virtually all the top-tier chip manufacturers and independent software vendors (ISVs), now support Linux.

For these and other reasons, we are seeing an accelerated adoption rate of Linux in many common household items, ranging from high-definition televisions to cellular handsets.

1.2   Embedded Linux Today

It may come as no surprise that Linux has experienced significant growth in the embedded space. Indeed, the fact that you are reading this book indicates that Linux has touched your life. It is difficult to estimate the market size, because many companies continue to build their own embedded Linux distributions.

LinuxDevices.com, the popular news and information portal founded by Rick Lehrbaum, now owned by Ziff Davis, conducts an annual survey of the embedded Linux market. In its latest survey, it reports that Linux has emerged as the dominant operating system used in thousands of new designs each year. In fact, nearly half the respondents reported using Linux in an embedded design. The next most popular operating system reportedly was used by only about one in eight respondents. Commercial operating systems that once dominated the embedded market were reportedly used by fewer than one in ten respondents. Even if you find reason to dispute these results, no one can ignore the momentum in the embedded Linux marketplace today.

1.3   Open Source and the GPL

One of the fundamental factors driving the adoption of Linux is the fact that it is open source. For a fascinating and insightful look at the history and culture of the open source movement, read Eric S. Raymond's book, referenced at the end of this chapter.

The Linux kernel is licensed under the terms of the GNU GPL[1] (General Public License), which leads to the popular myth that Linux is free. In fact, the second

---

[1] See http://www.gnu.org/licenses/gpl.html for complete text of the license.

paragraph of the GNU GPL Version 3 declares: "When we speak of free software, we are referring to freedom, not price." Most professional development managers agree: You can download Linux without charge, but development and deployment with any OS on an embedded platform carries an (often substantial) cost. Linux is no different in this regard.

The GPL is remarkably short and easy to read. Here are some of its most important characteristics:

- The license is self-perpetuating.
- The license grants the user freedom to run the program.
- The license grants the user the right to study and modify the source code.
- The license grants the user permission to distribute the original code and his modifications.
- The license is viral. In other words, it grants these same rights to anyone to whom you distribute GPL software.

When software is released under the terms of the GPL, it must forever carry that license.[2] Even if the code is highly modified, which is allowed and even encouraged by the license, the GPL mandates that it must be released under the same license. The intent of this feature is to guarantee freedom of access to the software, including modified versions of the software (or derived works, as they are commonly called).

No matter how the software was obtained, the GPL grants the licensee unlimited distribution rights, without the obligation to pay royalties or per-unit fees. This does not mean that vendors can't charge for their GPL software—this is a reasonable and common business practice. It means that once in possession of GPL software, it is permissible to modify and redistribute it, whether or not it is a derived (modified) work. However, as dictated by the GPL, the authors of the modified work are obligated to release the work under the terms of the GPL if they decide to do so. Any distribution of a derived work, such as shipment to a customer, triggers this obligation.

1.3.1   Free Versus Freedom

Two popular phrases are often repeated in the discussion about the free nature of open source: "free as in freedom" and "free as in beer." (The author is particularly fond of the latter.) The GPL exists to guarantee "free as in freedom" of a particular body of

---

[2] If all the copyright holders agreed, the software could in theory be released under a new license. This would be a very unlikely scenario indeed, especially for a large software base with thousands of contributors.

software. It guarantees your freedom to use it, study it, and change it. It also guarantees these freedoms for anyone to whom you distribute your modified code. This concept has become fairly widely understood.

One of the misconceptions frequently heard is that Linux is "free as in beer." You can obtain Linux free of cost. You can download a Linux kernel in a few minutes. However, as any professional development manager understands, certain costs are associated with any software to be incorporated into a design. These include the costs of acquisition, integration, modification, maintenance, and support. Add to that the cost of obtaining and maintaining a properly configured toolchain, libraries, application programs, and specialized cross-development tools compatible with your chosen architecture, and you can quickly see that it is a nontrivial exercise to develop the needed software components and development environment necessary to develop and deploy your embedded Linux-based system.

1.4 Standards and Relevant Bodies

As Linux continues to gain market share in the desktop, enterprise, and embedded market segments, new standards and organizations have emerged to help influence the use and acceptance of Linux. This section introduces the standards you might want to familiarize yourself with.

1.4.1 Linux Standard Base

Probably the single most relevant standard for a Linux distribution maintainer is the Linux Standard Base (LSB). The goal of the LSB is to establish a set of standards designed to enhance the interoperability of applications among different Linux distributions. Currently, the LSB spans several architectures, including IA32/64, Power Architecture 32- and 64-bit, AMD64, and others. The standard is divided into a core component and the individual architectural components.

The LSB specifies common attributes of a Linux distribution, including object format, standard library interfaces, a minimum set of commands and utilities and their behavior, file system layout, system initialization, and so on.

You can learn more about the LSB at the link given at the end of this chapter.

1.4.2   Linux Foundation

According to its website, the Linux Foundation "is a non-profit consortium dedicated to fostering the growth of Linux." The Linux Foundation sponsors the work of Linus Torvalds, the creator of Linux. The Linux Foundation sponsors several working groups to define standards and participate in the development of features targeting many important Linux platform attributes. The next two sections introduce some of these initiatives.

1.4.3   Carrier-Grade Linux

A significant number of the world's largest networking and telecommunications equipment manufacturers are either developing or shipping carrier-class equipment running Linux as the operating system. Significant features of carrier-class equipment include high reliability, high availability, and rapid serviceability. These vendors design products using redundant hot-swap architectures, fault-tolerant features, clustering, and often real-time performance.

The Linux Foundation Carrier Grade Linux workgroup has produced a specification defining a set of requirements for carrier-class equipment. The current version of the specification covers seven functional areas:

- **Availability**—Requirements that provide enhanced availability, including online maintenance operations, redundancy, and status monitoring
- **Clusters**—Requirements that facilitate redundant services, such as cluster membership management and data checkpointing
- **Serviceability**—Requirements for remote servicing and maintenance, such as SNMP and diagnostic monitoring of fans and power supplies
- **Performance**—Requirements to define performance and scalability, symmetric multiprocessing, latencies, and more
- **Standards**—Requirements that define standards to which CGL-compliant equipment shall conform
- **Hardware**—Requirements related to high-availability hardware, such as blade servers and hardware-management interfaces
- **Security**—Requirements to improve overall system security and protect the system from various external threats

1.4.4 Mobile Linux Initiative: Moblin

Several mobile handsets (cellular phones) available on the worldwide market have been built around embedded Linux. It has been widely reported that tens of millions of handsets have been shipped with Linux as the operating system platform. The only certainty is that more are coming. This promises to be one of the most explosive market segments for what was formerly the role of a proprietary real-time operating system. This speaks volumes about the readiness of Linux for commercial embedded applications.

The Linux Foundation sponsors a workgroup originally called the Mobile Linux Initiative, now referred to as Moblin. Its purpose is to accelerate the adoption of Linux on next-generation mobile handsets and other converged voice/data portable devices, according to the Linux Foundation website. The areas of focus for this working group include development tools, I/O and networking, memory management, multimedia, performance, power management, security, and storage. The Moblin website can be found at http://moblin.org. You can try out a Moblin release, such as Fedora/Moblin, found at http://fedoraproject.org/wiki/Features/FedoraMoblin, or the Ubuntu Moblin remix found on the author's Dell Mini 10 Netbook.

The embedded Linux landscape is continuously evolving. As this second edition was being prepared, the Moblin and Maemo project merged to become MeeGo. You can learn more about MeeGo, and even download a MeeGo image to try out, at http://meego.com/.

1.4.5 Service Availability Forum

If you are engaged in building products for environments in which high reliability, availability, and serviceability (RAS) are important, you should be aware of the Service Availability Forum (SA Forum). This organization is playing a leading role in defining a common set of interfaces for use in carrier-grade and other commercial equipment for system management. The SA Forum website is at www.saforum.org.

1.5   Summary

Embedded Linux has won the race. Indeed, you probably have embedded Linux in your car or home. This chapter examined the reasons why and developed a perspective for the material to come:

- Adoption of Linux among developers and manufacturers of embedded products continues to accelerate.
- Use of Linux in embedded devices continues to grow at an exciting pace.
- Many factors are driving the growth of Linux in the embedded market.
- Several standards and relevant organizations are influencing embedded Linux.

1.5.1   Suggestions for Additional Reading

The Cathedral and the Bazaar
Eric S. Raymond
O'Reilly Media, Inc., 2001

Linux Standard Base Project
http://www.linuxfoundation.org/collaborate/workgroups/lsb

Linux Foundation
http://www.linuxfoundation.org/

Chapter 2

The Big Picture

In This Chapter

■ 2.1 Embedded or Not? 10

■ 2.2 Anatomy of an Embedded System 12

■ 2.3 Storage Considerations 20

■ 2.4 Embedded Linux Distributions 32

■ 2.5 Summary 34

O ften the best path to understanding a given task is to have a good grasp of the big picture. Many fundamental concepts can present challenges to the newcomer to embedded systems development. This chapter takes you on a tour of a typical embedded system and the development environment with specific emphasis on the concepts and components that make developing these systems unique and often challenging.

2.1   Embedded or Not?

Several key attributes are associated with embedded systems. You wouldn't necessarily call your desktop PC an embedded system. But consider a desktop PC hardware platform in a remote data center that performs a critical monitoring and alarm task. Assume that this data center normally is not staffed. This imposes a different set of requirements on this hardware platform. For example, if power is lost and then restored, you would expect this platform to resume its duties without operator intervention.

Embedded systems come in a variety of shapes and sizes, from the largest multiple-rack data storage or networking powerhouses to tiny modules such as your personal MP3 player or cellular handset. Following are some of the usual characteristics of an embedded system:

- Contains a processing engine, such as a general-purpose microprocessor.
- Typically designed for a specific application or purpose.
- Includes a simple (or no) user interface, such as an automotive engine ignition controller.
- Often is resource-limited. For example, it might have a small memory footprint and no hard drive.
- Might have power limitations, such as a requirement to operate from batteries.
- Not typically used as a general-purpose computing platform.
- Generally has application software built in, not user-selected.

- Ships with all intended application hardware and software preintegrated.
- Often is intended for applications without human intervention.

Most commonly, embedded systems are resource-constrained compared to the typical desktop PC. Embedded systems often have limited memory, small or no hard drives, and sometimes no external network connectivity. Frequently, the only user interface is a serial port and some LEDs. These and other issues can present challenges to the embedded system developer.

2.1.1 BIOS Versus Bootloader

When power is first applied to the desktop computer, a software program called the BIOS immediately takes control of the processor. (Historically, BIOS was an acronym meaning Basic Input/Output Software, but the term has taken on a meaning of its own as the functions it performs have become much more complex than the original implementations.) The BIOS might actually be stored in Flash memory (described shortly) to facilitate field upgrade of the BIOS program itself.

The BIOS is a complex set of system-configuration software routines that have knowledge of the low-level details of the hardware architecture. Most of us are unaware of the extent of the BIOS and its functionality, but it is a critical piece of the desktop computer. The BIOS first gains control of the processor when power is applied. Its primary responsibility is to initialize the hardware, especially the memory subsystem, and load an operating system from the PC's hard drive.

In a typical embedded system (assuming that it is not based on an industry-standard x86 PC hardware platform), a bootloader is the software program that performs the equivalent functions. In your own custom embedded system, part of your development plan must include the development of a bootloader specific to your board. Luckily, several good open source bootloaders are available that you can customize for your project. These are introduced in Chapter 7, "Bootloaders."

Here are some of the more important tasks your bootloader performs on power-up:

- Initializes critical hardware components, such as the SDRAM controller, I/O controllers, and graphics controllers.
- Initializes system memory in preparation for passing control to the operating system.
- Allocates system resources such as memory and interrupt circuits to peripheral controllers, as necessary.

- Provides a mechanism for locating and loading your operating system image.

- Loads and passes control to the operating system, passing any required startup information. This can include total memory size, clock rates, serial port speeds, and other low-level hardware-specific configuration data.

This is a simplified summary of the tasks that a typical embedded-system bootloader performs. The important point to remember is this: If your embedded system will be based on a custom-designed platform, these bootloader functions must be supplied by you, the system designer. If your embedded system is based on a commercial off-the-shelf (COTS) platform such as an ATCA chassis,[1] the bootloader (and often the Linux kernel) typically is included on the board. Chapter 7 discusses bootloaders in more detail.

2.2   Anatomy of an Embedded System

Figure 2-1 is a block diagram of a typical embedded system. This is a simple example of a high-level hardware architecture that might be found in a wireless access point. The system is architected around a 32-bit RISC processor. Flash memory is used for nonvolatile program and data storage. Main memory is synchronous dynamic random-access memory (SDRAM) and might contain anywhere from a few megabytes to hundreds of megabytes, depending on the application. A real-time clock module, often backed up by battery, keeps the time of day (calendar/wall clock, including date). This example includes an Ethernet and USB interface, as well as a serial port for console access via RS-232. The 802.11 chipset or module implements the wireless modem function.

Often the processor in an embedded system performs many functions beyond the traditional core instruction stream processing. The hypothetical processor shown in Figure 2-1 contains an integrated UART for a serial interface and integrated USB and Ethernet controllers. Many processors contain integrated peripherals. Sometimes they are referred to as system on chip (SOC). We look at several examples of integrated processors in Chapter 3, "Processor Basics."

---

[1] ATCA platforms are introduced in Chapter 3.

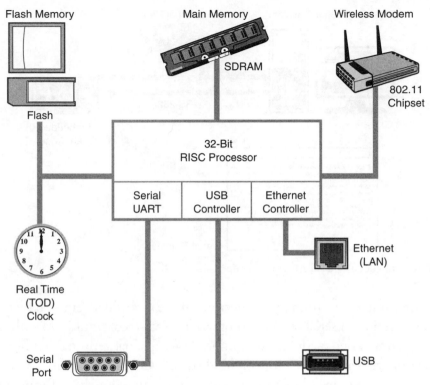

FIGURE 2-1   Embedded system

2.2.1   Typical Embedded Linux Setup

Often the first question posed by the newcomer to embedded Linux is, just what do you need to begin development? To answer that question, Figure 2-2 shows a typical embedded Linux development setup.

Figure 2-2 is a common arrangement. It shows a host development system, running your favorite desktop Linux distribution, such as Red Hat, SUSE, or Ubuntu Linux. The embedded Linux target board is connected to the development host via an RS-232 serial cable. You plug the target board's Ethernet interface into a local Ethernet hub or switch, to which your development host is also attached via Ethernet. The development host contains your development tools and utilities along with target files, which normally are obtained from an embedded Linux distribution.

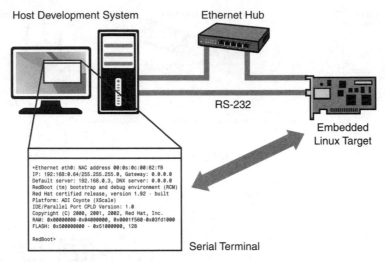

Host Development System   Ethernet Hub

RS-232

Embedded
Linux Target

```
+Ethernet eth0: NAC address 00:0s:0c:00:82:fB
IP: 192:168:0.64/255.255.255.0, Gateway: 0.0.0.0
Default server: 192.168.0.3, DNX server: 0.0.0.0
RedBoot (tm) bootstrap and debug environment (RCM)
Red Hat certified release, version 1.92 - built
Platform: ADI Coyote (XScale)
IDE/Parallel Port CPLD Version: 1.0
Copyright (C) 2000, 2001, 2002, Red Hat, Inc.
RAM: 0x00000000-0x04000000, 0x0001f560-0x03fd1000
FLASH: 0x50000000 - 0x51000000, 128

RedBoot>
```

Serial Terminal

FIGURE 2-2   Embedded Linux development setup

For this example, our primary connection to the embedded Linux target is via the RS-232 connection. A serial terminal program is used to communicate with the target board. Minicom is one of the most commonly used serial terminal applications and is available on virtually all desktop Linux distributions.[2] The author has switched to using `screen` as his terminal of choice, replacing the functionality of minicom. It offers much more flexibility, especially for capturing traces, and it's more forgiving of serial line garbage often encountered during system bringup or troubleshooting. To use `screen` in this manner on a USB-attached serial dongle, simply invoke it on your serial terminal and specify the speed:

```
$ screen /dev/ttyUSB0 115200
```

2.2.2   Starting the Target Board

When power is first applied, a bootloader supplied with your target board takes immediate control of the processor. It performs some very low-level hardware initialization, including processor and memory setup, initialization of the UART controlling the serial port, and initialization of the Ethernet controller. Listing 2-1 displays the characters received from the serial port, resulting from power being applied to the target.

---

[2] You may have to install minicom from your distribution's repository. On Ubuntu, for example, you would execute `sudo apt-get install minicom` to install minicom on your desktop.

For this example, we have chosen a target board from Freescale Semiconductor, the PowerQUICC III MPC8548 Configurable Development System (CDS). It contains the MPC8548 PowerQUICC III processor. It ships from Freescale with the U-Boot bootloader preinstalled.

LISTING 2-1   Initial Bootloader Serial Output

```
U-Boot 2009.01 (May 20 2009 - 09:45:35)

CPU:   8548E, Version: 2.1, (0x80390021)
Core:  E500, Version: 2.2, (0x80210022)
Clock Configuration:
       CPU:990  MHz, CCB:396  MHz,
       DDR:198  MHz (396 MT/s data rate), LBC:49.500 MHz
L1:    D-cache 32 kB enabled
       I-cache 32 kB enabled
Board: CDS Version 0x13, PCI Slot 1
CPU Board Revision 0.0 (0x0000)
I2C:   ready
DRAM:  Initializing
   SDRAM: 64 MB
   DDR: 256 MB
FLASH: 16 MB
L2:    512 KB enabled
Invalid ID (ff ff ff ff)
   PCI: 64 bit, unknown MHz, async, host, external-arbiter
             Scanning PCI bus 00
PCI on bus 00 - 02

   PCIE connected to slot as Root Complex (base address e000a000)
PCIE on bus 3 - 3
In:    serial
Out:   serial
Err:   serial
Net:   eTSEC0, eTSEC1, eTSEC2, eTSEC3
=>
```

When power is applied to the MPC8548CDS board, U-Boot performs some low-level hardware initialization, which includes configuring a serial port. It then prints a banner line, as shown in the first line of Listing 2-1. Next the CPU and core are displayed, followed by some configuration data describing clocks and cache configuration. This is followed by a text string describing the board.

When the initial hardware configuration is complete, U-Boot configures any hardware subsystems as directed by its static configuration. Here we see I2C, DRAM, FLASH, L2 cache, PCI, and network subsystems being configured by U-Boot. Finally, U-Boot waits for input from the console over the serial port, as indicated by the => prompt.

2.2.3   Booting the Kernel

Now that U-Boot has initialized the hardware, serial port, and Ethernet network interfaces, it has only one job left in its short but useful life span: to load and boot the Linux kernel. All bootloaders have a command to load and execute an operating system image. Listing 2-2 shows one of the more common ways U-Boot is used to manually load and boot a Linux kernel.

LISTING 2-2   Loading the Linux Kernel

```
=> tftp 600000 uImage
Speed: 1000, full duplex
Using eTSEC0 device
TFTP from server 192.168.0.103; our IP address is 192.168.0.18
Filename 'uImage'.
Load address: 0x600000
Loading: #################################################################
         ###########################################################
done
Bytes transferred = 1838553 (1c0dd9 hex)
=> tftp c00000 dtb
Speed: 1000, full duplex
Using eTSEC0 device
TFTP from server 192.168.0.103; our IP address is 192.168.0.18
Filename 'dtb'.
Load address: 0xc00000
Loading: ##
done
Bytes transferred = 16384 (4000 hex)
=> bootm 600000 - c00000
## Booting kernel from Legacy Image at 00600000 ...
   Image Name:    MontaVista Linux 6/2.6.27/freesc
   Image Type:    PowerPC Linux Kernel Image (gzip compressed)
   Data Size:     1838489 Bytes =  1.8 MB
   Load Address:  00000000
   Entry Point:   00000000
```

LISTING 2-2 Continued

```
   Verifying Checksum ... OK
## Flattened Device Tree blob at 00c00000
   Booting using the fdt blob at 0xc00000
   Uncompressing Kernel Image ... OK
   Loading Device Tree to 007f9000, end 007fffff ... OK
Using MPC85xx CDS machine description
Memory CAM mapping: CAM0=256Mb, CAM1=0Mb, CAM2=0Mb residual: 0Mb

...
< Lots of Linux kernel boot messages, removed for clarity >
...

freescale-8548cds login:  <<--- Linux login prompt
```

The `tftp` command at the start of Listing 2-2 instructs U-Boot to load the kernel image `uImage` into memory over the network using the TFTP[3] protocol. The kernel image, in this case, is located on the development workstation (usually the same machine that has the serial port connected to the target board). The `tftp` command is passed an address that is the physical address in the target board's memory where the kernel image will be loaded. Don't worry about the details now; Chapter 7 covers U-Boot in much greater detail.

The second invocation of the `tftp` command loads a board configuration file called a *device tree*. It is referred to by other names, including *flat device tree* and *device tree binary* or dtb. You will learn more about this file in Chapter 7. For now, it is enough for you to know that this file contains board-specific information that the kernel requires in order to boot the board. This includes things such as memory size, clock speeds, onboard devices, buses, and Flash layout.

Next, the `bootm` (boot from memory image) command is issued, to instruct U-Boot to boot the kernel we just loaded from the address specified by the `tftp` command. In this example of using the `bootm` command, we instruct U-Boot to load the kernel that we put at `0x600000` and pass the device tree binary (dtb) we loaded at `0xc00000` to the kernel. This command transfers control to the Linux kernel. Assuming that your kernel is properly configured, this results in booting the Linux kernel to a console command prompt on your target board, as shown by the login prompt.

Note that the `bootm` command is the death knell for U-Boot. This is an important concept. Unlike the BIOS in a desktop PC, most embedded systems are architected

---

[3] This and other servers you will be using are covered in detail in Chapter 12, "Embedded Development Environment."

in such a way that when the Linux kernel takes control, the bootloader ceases to exist. The kernel claims any memory and system resources that the bootloader previously used. The only way to pass control back to the bootloader is to reboot the board.

One final observation is worth noting. All the serial output in Listing 2-2 up to and including this line is produced by the U-Boot bootloader:

```
Loading Device Tree to 007f9000, end 007fffff ... OK
```

The rest of the boot messages are produced by the Linux kernel. We'll have much more to say about this later, but it is worth noting where U-Boot leaves off and where the Linux kernel image takes over.

2.2.4   Kernel Initialization: Overview

When the Linux kernel begins execution, it spews out numerous status messages during its rather comprehensive boot process. In the example being discussed here, the Linux kernel displayed approximately 200 printk[4] lines before it issues the login prompt. (We omitted them from the listing to clarify the point being discussed.) Listing 2-3 reproduces the last several lines of output before the login prompt. The goal of this exercise is not to delve into the details of the kernel initialization (this is covered in Chapter 5, "Kernel Initialization"). The goal is to gain a high-level understanding of what is happening and what components are required to boot a Linux kernel on an embedded system.

LISTING 2-3   Linux Final Boot Messages

```
...
Looking up port of RPC 100005/1 on 192.168.0.9
VFS: Mounted root (nfs filesystem).
Freeing unused kernel memory: 152k init
INIT: version 2.86 booting
...

freescale-8548cds login:
```

Shortly before issuing a login prompt on the serial terminal, Linux *mounts* a *root file system*. In Listing 2-3, Linux goes through the steps required to mount its root file system remotely (via Ethernet) from an NFS[5] server on a machine with the IP

---

[4] printk() is the function in the kernel responsible for displaying messages to the system console.

[5] NFS and other required servers are covered in Chapter 12.

address 192.168.0.9. Usually, this is your development workstation. The root file system contains the application programs, system libraries, and utilities that make up a Linux system.

The important point in this discussion should not be understated: *Linux requires a file system.* Many legacy embedded operating systems did not require a file system. This fact is a frequent surprise to engineers making the transition from legacy embedded OSs to embedded Linux. A file system consists of a predefined set of system directories and files in a specific layout on a hard drive or other medium that the Linux kernel *mounts* as its root file system.

Note that Linux can mount a root file system from other devices. The most common, of course, is to mount a partition from a hard drive as the root file system, as is done on your Linux laptop or workstation. Indeed, NFS is pretty useless when you ship your embedded Linux widget out the door and away from your development environment. However, as you progress through this book, you will come to appreciate the power and flexibility of NFS root mounting as a development environment.

2.2.5 First User Space Process: `init`

Another important point should be made before we move on. Notice in Listing 2-3 this line:

```
INIT: version 2.86 booting
```

Until this point, the kernel itself was executing code, performing the numerous initialization steps in a context known as *kernel context.* In this operational state, the kernel owns all system memory and operates with full authority over all system resources. The kernel has access to all physical memory and to all I/O subsystems. It executes code in kernel virtual address space, using a stack created and owned by the kernel itself.

When the Linux kernel has completed its internal initialization and mounted its root file system, the default behavior is to spawn an application program called `init`. When the kernel starts `init`, it is said to be running in *user space* or user space context. In this operational mode, the user space process has restricted access to the system and must use kernel system calls to request kernel services such as device and file I/O. These user space processes, or programs, operate in a virtual memory space picked at random[6] and managed by the kernel. The kernel, in cooperation with specialized memory-management hardware in the processor, performs virtual-to-physical address translation for the user space process. The single biggest benefit of this architecture is that an

---

[6] It's not actually random, but for purposes of this discussion, it might as well be. This topic will be covered in more detail later.

error in one process can't trash the memory space of another. This is a common pitfall in legacy embedded OSs that can lead to bugs that are some of the most difficult to track down.

Don't be alarmed if these concepts seem foreign. The objective of this section is to paint a broad picture from which you will develop more detailed knowledge as you progress through the book. These and other concepts are covered in great detail in later chapters.

2.3   Storage Considerations

One of the most challenging aspects of embedded Linux development is that most embedded systems have limited physical resources. Although the Core™ 2 Duo machine on your desktop might have 500GB of hard drive space, it is not uncommon to find embedded systems with a fraction of that amount. In many cases, the hard drive typically is replaced by smaller and less expensive nonvolatile storage devices. Hard drives are bulky, have rotating parts, are sensitive to physical shock, and require multiple power supply voltages, which makes them unsuitable for many embedded systems.

2.3.1   Flash Memory

Nearly everyone is familiar with Compact Flash and SD cards used in a wide variety of consumer devices, such as digital cameras and PDAs (both great examples of embedded systems). These modules, based on *Flash* memory technology, can be thought of as solid-state hard drives, capable of storing many megabytes—and even gigabytes—of data in a tiny footprint. They contain no moving parts, are relatively rugged, and operate on a single common power supply voltage.

Several manufacturers of Flash memory exist. Flash memory comes in a variety of electrical formats, physical packages, and capacities. It is not uncommon to see embedded systems with as little as 4MB or 8MB of nonvolatile storage. More typical storage requirements for embedded Linux systems range from 16MB to 256MB or more. An increasing number of embedded Linux systems have nonvolatile storage into the gigabyte range.

Flash memory can be written to and erased under software control. Rotational hard drive technology remains the fastest writable medium. Flash writing and erasing speeds have improved considerably over time, although Flash write and erase time is still considerably slower. You must understand some fundamental differences between hard drive and Flash memory technology to properly use the technology.

Flash memory is divided into relatively large erasable units, referred to as erase blocks. One of the defining characteristics of Flash memory is how data in Flash is written and erased. In a typical NOR[7] Flash memory chip, data can be changed from a binary 1 to a binary 0 under software control using simple data writes directly to the cell's address, one bit or word at a time. However, to change a bit from a 0 back to a 1, an entire *erase block* must be erased using a special sequence of control instructions to the Flash chip.

A typical NOR Flash memory device contains many erase blocks. For example, a 4MB Flash chip might contain 64 erase blocks of 64KB each. Flash memory is also available with nonuniform erase block sizes, to facilitate flexible data-storage layouts. These are commonly called boot block or boot sector Flash chips. Often the bootloader is stored in the smaller blocks, and the kernel and other required data are stored in the larger blocks. Figure 2-3 illustrates the block size layout for a typical top boot Flash.

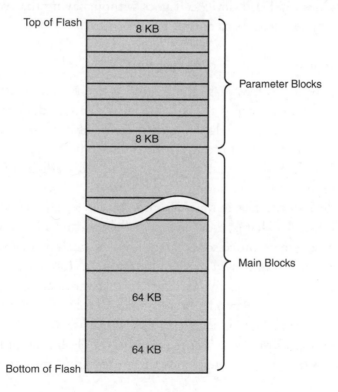

FIGURE 2-3   Boot block Flash architecture

---

[7] There are several types of Flash technologies. NOR Flash is one of the most commonly used in small embedded systems.

To modify data stored in a Flash memory array, the block in which the modified data resides must be completely erased. Even if only 1 byte in a block needs to be changed, the entire block must be erased and rewritten.[8] Flash block sizes are relatively large compared to traditional hard-drive sector sizes. In comparison, a typical high-performance hard drive has writable sectors of 512 or 1024 bytes. The ramifications of this might be obvious: Write times for updating data in Flash memory can be many times that of a hard drive, due in part to the relatively large quantity of data that must be erased and written back to the Flash for each update. In the worst case, these write cycles can take several seconds.

Another limitation of Flash memory that must be considered is Flash memory cell write lifetime. A NOR Flash memory cell has a limited number of write cycles before failure. Although the number of cycles is fairly large (100,000 cycles per block is typical), it is easy to imagine a poorly designed Flash storage algorithm (or even a bug) that can quickly destroy Flash devices. It goes without saying that you should avoid configuring your system loggers to output to a Flash-based device.

2.3.2   NAND Flash

NAND Flash is a relatively new Flash technology. When NAND Flash hit the market, traditional Flash memory such as that described in the preceding section was called NOR Flash. These distinctions relate to the internal Flash memory cell architecture. NAND Flash devices improve on some of the limitations of traditional (NOR) Flash by offering smaller block sizes, resulting in faster and more efficient writes and generally more efficient use of the Flash array.

NOR Flash devices interface to the microprocessor in a fashion similar to many microprocessor peripherals. That is, they have a parallel data and address bus that are connected directly[9] to the microprocessor data/address bus. Each byte or word in the Flash array can be individually addressed in a random fashion. In contrast, NAND devices are accessed serially through a complex interface that varies among vendors. NAND devices present an operational model more similar to that of a traditional hard drive and associated controller. Data is accessed in serial bursts, which are far smaller than NOR Flash block size. Write cycle lifetime for NAND Flash is an order of magnitude greater than for NOR Flash, although erase times are significantly smaller.

---

[8] Remember, you can change a 1 to a 0 a byte at a time, but you must erase the entire block to change any bit from a 0 to a 1.

[9] Directly in the logical sense. The actual circuitry may contain bus buffers or bridge devices and so on.

In summary, NOR Flash can be directly accessed by the microprocessor, and code can even be executed directly out of NOR Flash. (However, for performance reasons, this is rarely done, and then only on systems in which resources are extremely scarce.) In fact, many processors cannot cache instruction accesses to Flash, as they can with DRAM. This further degrades execution speed. In contrast, NAND Flash is more suitable for bulk storage in file system format than raw binary executable code and data storage.

2.3.3   Flash Usage

An embedded system designer has many options in the layout and use of Flash memory. In the simplest of systems, in which resources are not overly constrained, raw binary data (perhaps compressed) can be stored on the Flash device. When booted, a file system image stored in Flash is read into a Linux ramdisk block device, mounted as a file system, and accessed only from RAM. This is often a good design choice when the data in Flash rarely needs to be updated. Any data that does need to be updated is relatively small compared to the size of the ramdisk. It is important to realize that any changes to files in the ramdisk are lost upon reboot or power cycle.

Figure 2-4 illustrates a common Flash memory organization that is typical of a simple embedded system in which nonvolatile storage requirements of dynamic data are small and infrequent.

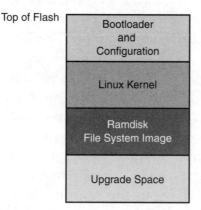

FIGURE 2-4   Typical Flash memory layout

The bootloader is often placed in the top or bottom of the Flash memory array. Following the bootloader, space is allocated for the Linux kernel image and the ramdisk file system image,[10] which holds the root file system. Typically, the Linux kernel and ramdisk file system images are compressed, and the bootloader handles the decompression task during the boot cycle.

For dynamic data that needs to be saved between reboots and power cycles, another small area of Flash can be dedicated, or another type of nonvolatile storage[11] can be used. This is a typical configuration for embedded systems that have requirements to store configuration data, as might be found in a wireless access point aimed at the consumer market, for example.

2.3.4   Flash File Systems

The limitations of the simple Flash layout scheme just described can be overcome by using a Flash file system to manage data on the Flash device in a manner similar to how data is organized on a hard drive. Early implementations of file systems for Flash devices consisted of a simple block device layer that emulated the 512-byte sector layout of a common hard drive. These simple emulation layers allowed access to data in file format rather than unformatted bulk storage, but they had some performance limitations.

One of the first enhancements to Flash file systems was the incorporation of wear leveling. As discussed earlier, Flash blocks are subject to a finite write lifetime. Wear-leveling algorithms are used to distribute writes evenly over the physical erase blocks of the Flash memory in order to extend the life of the Flash memory chip.

Another limitation that arises from the Flash architecture is the risk of data loss during a power failure or premature shutdown. Consider that the Flash block sizes are relatively large and that average file sizes being written are often much smaller relative to the block size. You learned previously that Flash blocks must be written one block at a time. Therefore, to write a small 8KB file, you must erase and rewrite an entire Flash block, perhaps 64KB or 128KB in size; in the worst case, this can take several seconds to complete. This opens a significant window to risk of data loss due to power failure.

One of the more popular Flash file systems in use today is JFFS2, or Journaling Flash File System 2. It has several important features aimed at improving overall performance, increasing Flash lifetime, and reducing the risk of data loss in the case of power failure. The more significant improvements in the latest JFFS2 file system include improved wear leveling, compression and decompression to squeeze more data

---

[10] We discuss ramdisk file systems in more detail in Chapter 9, "File Systems."

[11] Real-time clock modules and serial EEPROMs are often choices for nonvolatile storage of small amounts of data.

into a given Flash size, and support for Linux hard links. This topic is covered in detail in Chapter 9 and in Chapter 10, "MTD Subsystem," when we discuss the Memory Technology Device (MTD) subsystem.

2.3.5 Memory Space

Virtually all legacy embedded operating systems view and manage system memory as a single large, flat address space. That is, a microprocessor's address space exists from 0 to the top of its physical address range. For example, if a microprocessor had 24 physical address lines, its top of memory would be 16MB. Therefore, its hexadecimal address would range from `0x00000000` to `0x00ffffff`. Hardware designs commonly place DRAM starting at the bottom of the range, and Flash memory from the top down. Unused address ranges between the top of DRAM and bottom of Flash would be allocated for addressing of various peripheral chips on the board. This design approach is often dictated by the choice of microprocessor. Figure 2-5 shows a typical memory layout for a simple embedded system.

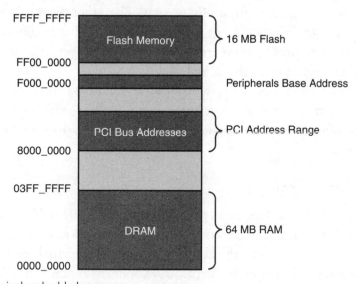

FIGURE 2-5   Typical embedded system memory map

In traditional embedded systems based on legacy operating systems, the OS and all the tasks[12] had equal access rights to all resources in the system. A bug in one process could wipe out memory contents anywhere in the system, whether it belonged to itself, the OS, another task, or even a hardware register somewhere in the address space. Although this approach had simplicity as its most valuable characteristic, it led to bugs that could be challenging to diagnose.

High-performance microprocessors contain complex hardware engines called Memory Management Units (MMUs). Their purpose is to enable an operating system to exercise a high degree of management and control over its address space and the address space it allocates to processes. This control comes in two primary forms: *access rights* and *memory translation*. Access rights allow an operating system to assign specific memory-access privileges to specific tasks. Memory translation allows an operating system to virtualize its address space, which has many benefits.

The Linux kernel takes advantage of these hardware MMUs to create a *virtual memory* operating system. One of the biggest benefits of virtual memory is that it can make more efficient use of physical memory by presenting the appearance that the system has more memory than is physically present. The other benefit is that the kernel can enforce access rights to each range of system memory that it allocates to a task or process, to prevent one process from errantly accessing memory or other resources that belong to another process or to the kernel itself.

The next section examines in more detail how this works. A tutorial on the complexities of virtual memory systems is beyond the scope of this book.[13] Instead, we examine the ramifications of a virtual memory system as it appears to an embedded systems developer.

2.3.6   Execution Contexts

One of the very first chores that Linux performs is to configure the hardware MMU on the processor and the data structures used to support it, and to enable address translation. When this step is complete, the kernel runs in its own virtual memory space. The virtual kernel address selected by the kernel developers in recent Linux kernel versions defaults to `0xC0000000`. In most architectures, this is a configurable parameter.[14] If we

---

[12] In this discussion, the word task is used to denote any thread of execution, regardless of the mechanism used to spawn, manage, or schedule it.

[13] Many good books cover the details of virtual memory systems. See the last section of this chapter for recommendations.

[14] However, there is seldom a good reason to change it.

looked at the kernel's symbol table, we would find kernel symbols linked at an address starting with 0xC0xxxxxx. As a result, any time the kernel executes code in kernel space, the processor's instruction pointer (program counter) contains values in this range.

In Linux, we refer to two distinctly separate operational contexts, based on the environment in which a given thread[15] is executing. Threads executing entirely within the kernel are said to be operating in *kernel context*. Application programs are said to operate in *user space context*. A user space process can access only memory it owns, and it is required to use kernel system calls to access privileged resources such as file and device I/O. An example might make this more clear.

Consider an application that opens a file and issues a read request, as shown in Figure 2-6. The read function call begins in user space, in the C library read() function. The C library then issues a read request to the kernel. The read request results in a context switch from the user's program to the kernel, to service the request for the file's data. Inside the kernel, the read request results in a hard-drive access requesting the sectors containing the file's data.

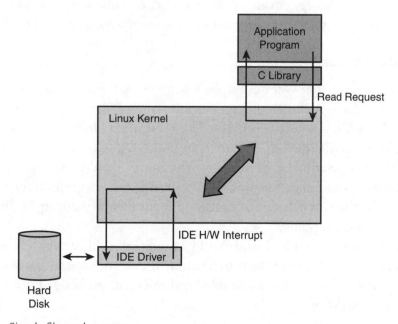

FIGURE 2-6   Simple file read request

---

[15] The term *thread* is used here in the generic sense to indicate any sequential flow of instructions.

Usually the hard-drive read request is issued asynchronously to the hardware itself. That is, the request is posted to the hardware, and when the data is ready, the hardware interrupts the processor. The application program waiting for the data is *blocked* on a wait queue until the data is available. Later, when the hard disk has the data ready, it posts a hardware interrupt. (This description is intentionally simplified for the purposes of this illustration.) When the kernel receives the hardware interrupt, it suspends whatever process was executing and proceeds to read the waiting data from the drive.

To summarize this discussion, we have identified two general execution contexts—user space and kernel space. When an application program executes a system call that results in a context switch and enters the kernel, it is executing kernel code on behalf of a process. You will often hear this referred to as *process context* within the kernel. In contrast, the interrupt service routine (ISR) handling the IDE drive (or any other ISR, for that matter) is kernel code that is not executing on behalf of any particular process. This is typically called *interrupt context*.

Several limitations exist in this operational context, including the limitation that the ISR cannot block (sleep) or call any kernel functions that might result in blocking. For further reading on these concepts, consult the references at the end of this chapter.

2.3.7 Process Virtual Memory

When a process is spawned—for example, when the user types `ls` at the Linux command prompt—the kernel allocates memory for the process and assigns a range of virtual-memory addresses to the process. The resulting address values bear no fixed relationship to those in the kernel, nor to any other running process. Furthermore, there is no direct correlation between the physical memory addresses on the board and the virtual memory as seen by the process. In fact, it is not uncommon for a process to occupy multiple different physical addresses in main memory during its lifetime as a result of paging and swapping.

Listing 2-4 is the venerable "Hello World," modified to illustrate the concepts just discussed. The goal of this example is to illustrate the address space that the kernel assigns to the process. This code was compiled and run on an embedded system containing 256MB of DRAM memory.

LISTING 2-4   Hello World, Embedded Style

```
#include <stdio.h>

int bss_var;          /* Uninitialized global variable */

int data_var = 1;    /* Initialized global variable */

int main(int argc, char **argv)
{
  void *stack_var;                /* Local variable on the stack */

  stack_var = (void *)main;    /* Don't let the compiler */
                               /* optimize it out */

  printf("Hello, World! Main is executing at %p\n", stack_var);
  printf("This address (%p) is in our stack frame\n", &stack_var);

  /* bss section contains uninitialized data */
  printf("This address (%p) is in our bss section\n", &bss_var);

  /* data section contains initializated data */
  printf("This address (%p) is in our data section\n", &data_var);

  return 0;
}
```

Listing 2-5 shows the console output that this program produces. Notice that the process called `hello` thinks it is executing somewhere in high RAM just above the 256MB boundary (`0x10000418`). Notice also that the stack address is roughly halfway into a 32-bit address space, well beyond our 256MB of RAM (`0x7ff8ebb0`). How can this be? DRAM is usually contiguous in systems like these. To the casual observer, it appears that we have nearly 2GB of DRAM available for our use. These *virtual addresses* were assigned by the kernel and are backed by physical RAM somewhere within the 256MB range of available memory on our embedded board.

LISTING 2-5   Hello Output

```
root@192.168.4.9:~# ./hello
Hello, World! Main is executing at 0x10000418
This address (0x7ff8ebb0) is in our stack frame
This address (0x10010a1c) is in our bss section
This address (0x10010a18) is in our data section
root@192.168.4.9:~#
```

One of the characteristics of a virtual memory system is that when available physical RAM goes below a designated threshold, the kernel can swap out memory pages to a bulk storage medium, usually a hard disk drive (if available). The kernel examines its active memory regions, determines which areas in memory have been least recently used, and swaps out these memory regions to disk to free them for the current process. Developers of embedded systems often disable swapping on embedded systems because of performance or resource constraints. For example, it would be ridiculous in most cases to use a relatively slow Flash memory device with limited write life cycles as a swap device. Without a swap device, you must carefully design your applications to exist within the limitations of your available physical memory.

2.3.8   Cross-Development Environment

Before we can develop applications and device drivers for an embedded system, we need a set of tools (compiler, utilities, and so on) that will generate binary executables in the proper format for the target system. Consider a simple application written on your desktop PC, such as the traditional "Hello World" example. After you have created the source code on your desktop, you invoke the compiler that came with your desktop system (usually GNU `gcc`) to generate a binary executable image. That image file is properly formatted to execute on the machine on which it was compiled. This is referred to as *native* compilation. In other words, using compilers on your desktop system, you generate code that will execute on that desktop system.

Note that *native* does not imply an architecture. Indeed, if you have a toolchain that runs on your target board, you can natively compile applications for your target's architecture. In fact, one great way to stress-test a new embedded kernel and custom board is to repeatedly compile the Linux kernel on it.

Developing software in a cross-development environment requires that the compiler running on your development host output a binary executable that is incompatible with the desktop development workstation on which it was compiled. The primary reason these tools exist is that it is often impractical or impossible to develop and compile software natively on the embedded system because of resource (typically memory and CPU horsepower) constraints.

Numerous hidden traps to this approach often catch the unwary newcomer to embedded development. When a given program is compiled, the compiler often knows how to find include files, and where to find libraries that might be required for the compilation to succeed. To illustrate these concepts, let's look again at the "Hello

World" program. The example reproduced in Listing 2-4 was compiled with the following command line:

```
gcc -Wall -o hello hello.c
```

In Listing 2-4, we see an include file, `stdio.h`. This file does not reside in the same directory as the `hello.c` file specified on the `gcc` command line. So how does the compiler find them? Also, the `printf()` function is not defined in the file `hello.c`. Therefore, when `hello.c` is compiled, it will contain an unresolved reference for this symbol. How does the linker resolve this reference at link time?

Compilers have built-in defaults for locating include files. When the reference to the include file is encountered, the compiler searches its default list of locations to find the file. A similar process exists for the linker to resolve the reference to the external symbol `printf()`. The linker knows by default to search the C library (`libc-*`) for unresolved references, and it knows where to find the reference on your system. Again, this default behavior is built into the toolchain.

Now assume you are building an application targeting a Power Architecture embedded system. Obviously, you will need a cross-compiler to generate binary executables compatible with the Power Architecture processor. If you issue a similar compilation command using your cross-compiler to compile the preceding `hello.c` example, it is possible that your binary executable could end up being accidentally linked with an x86 version of the C library on your development system, attempting to resolve the reference to `printf()`. Of course, the results of running this bogus hybrid executable, containing a mix of Power Architecture and x86 binary instructions,[16] are predictable: crash!

The solution to this predicament is to instruct the cross-compiler to look in nonstandard locations to pick up the header files and target specific libraries. We cover this topic in much more detail in Chapter 12. The intent of this example was to illustrate the differences between a native development environment and a development environment targeted at cross-compilation for embedded systems. This is but one of the complexities of a cross-development environment. The same issue and solutions apply to cross-debugging, as you will see starting in Chapter 14, "Kernel Debugging Techniques." A proper cross-development environment is crucial to your success and involves much more than just compilers, as you will see in Chapter 12.

---

[16] In fact, it wouldn't even compile or link, much less run. We're just trying to illustrate the point!

2.4   Embedded Linux Distributions

What exactly is a Linux distribution? After the Linux kernel boots, it expects to find and mount a root file system. When a suitable root file system has been mounted, start-up scripts launch a number of programs and utilities that the system requires. These programs often invoke other programs to do specific tasks, such as spawn a login shell, initialize network interfaces, and launch a user's applications. Each of these programs has specific requirements (often called dependencies) that must be satisfied by other components in the system. Most Linux application programs depend on one or more system libraries. Other programs require configuration and log files, and so on. In summary, even a small embedded Linux system needs many dozens of files populated in an appropriate directory structure on a *root file system*.

Full-blown desktop systems have many thousands of files on the root file system. These files come from *packages* that are usually grouped by functionality. The packages typically are installed and managed using a package manager. Red Hat's Package Manager (rpm) is a popular example and is widely used to install, remove, and update packages on a Linux system. If your Linux workstation is based on Red Hat, including the Fedora series, typing rpm -qa at a command prompt lists all the packages installed on your system. If you are using a distribution based on Debian, such as Ubuntu, typing dpkg -l has the same result.

A package can consist of many files; indeed, some packages contain hundreds of files. A complete Linux distribution can contain hundreds or even thousands of packages. These are some examples of packages you might find on an embedded Linux distribution, and their purpose:

- initscripts contains basic system startup and shutdown scripts.
- apache implements the popular Apache web server.
- telnet-server contains files necessary to implement telnet server functionality, which allows you to establish telnet sessions to your embedded target.
- glibc implements the Standard C library.
- busybox contains compact versions of dozens of popular command-line utilities commonly found on UNIX/Linux systems.[17]

This is the purpose of a Linux *distribution*, as the term has come to be used. A typical Linux distribution comes with several CD-ROMs full of useful programs, libraries,

---

[17] This package is important enough to warrant its own chapter. Chapter 11, "BusyBox," covers BusyBox in detail.

tools, utilities, and documentation. Installation of a distribution typically leaves the user with a fully functional system based on a reasonable set of default configuration options, which can be tailored to suit a particular set of requirements. You may be familiar with one of the popular desktop Linux distributions, such as Red Hat or Ubuntu.

A Linux distribution for embedded targets differs in several significant ways. First, the executable target binaries from an embedded distribution will not run on your PC, but are targeted to the architecture and processor of your embedded system. (Of course, if your embedded Linux distribution targets the x86 architecture, this statement does not necessarily apply.) A desktop Linux distribution tends to have many GUI tools aimed at the typical desktop user, such as fancy graphical clocks, calculators, personal time-management tools, e-mail clients, and more. An embedded Linux distribution typically omits these components in favor of specialized tools aimed at developers, such as memory analysis tools, remote debug facilities, and many more.

Another significant difference between desktop and embedded Linux distributions is that an embedded distribution typically contains cross tools, as opposed to native tools. For example, the gcc toolchain that ships with an embedded Linux distribution runs on your x86 desktop PC but produces binary code that runs on your target system, often a non-x86 architecture. Many of the other tools in the toolchain are similarly configured: They run on the development host (usually an x86 PC) but are designed to emit or manipulate objects targeted at foreign architectures such as ARM or Power Architecture.

2.4.1 Commercial Linux Distributions

Several vendors of commercial embedded Linux distributions exist. The leading embedded Linux vendors have been shipping embedded Linux distributions for years. It is relatively easy to find information on the leading embedded Linux vendors. A quick Internet search for "embedded Linux distributions" points to several compilations. One particularly good compilation can be found at http://elinux.org/Embedded_Linux_Distributions.

2.4.2 Do-It-Yourself Linux Distributions

You can choose to assemble all the components you need for your embedded project on your own. You have to decide whether the risks are worth the effort. If you find yourself involved with embedded Linux purely for the pleasure of it, such as for a hobby or college project, this approach might be a good one. However, plan to spend a significant amount of time assembling all the tools and utilities your project needs and making sure they all interoperate.

For starters, you need a toolchain. `gcc` and `binutils` are available from www.fsf.org and other mirrors around the world. Both are required to compile the kernel and user-space applications for your project. These are distributed primarily in source code form, and you must compile the tools to suit your particular cross-development environment. Patches are often required to the most recent "stable" source trees of these utilities, especially when they will be used beyond the x86/IA32 architecture. The patches usually can be found at the same location as the base packages. The challenge is to discover which collections of patches you need for your particular problem or architecture.

As soon as your toolchain is working, you need to download and compile many application packages along with the dependencies they require. This can be a formidable challenge, since many packages even today do not lend themselves to cross-compiling. Many still have build or other issues when moved away from their native x86 environment where they were developed.

Beyond these challenges, you might want to assemble a competent development environment, containing tools such as graphical debuggers, memory analysis tools, system tracing and profiling tools, and more. You can see from this discussion that building your own embedded Linux distribution can be quite challenging.

2.5   Summary

This chapter covered many subjects in a broad fashion. Now you have a proper perspective for the material to follow. In later chapters, this perspective will be expanded to help you develop the skills and knowledge required to be successful in your next embedded project.

- Embedded systems share some common attributes. Often resources are limited, and user interfaces are simple or nonexistent and are often designed for a specific purpose.

- The bootloader is a critical component of a typical embedded system. If your embedded system is based on a custom-designed board, you must provide a bootloader as part of your design. Often this is just a porting effort of an existing bootloader.

- Several software components are required to boot a custom board, including the bootloader and the kernel and file system image.
- Flash memory is widely used as a storage medium in embedded Linux systems. This chapter introduced the concept of Flash memory. Chapters 9 and 10 expand on this coverage.
- An application program, also called a process, lives in its own virtual memory space assigned by the kernel. Application programs are said to run in user space.
- A properly equipped and configured cross-development environment is crucial to the embedded developer. Chapter 12 is devoted to this important subject.
- You need an embedded Linux distribution to begin developing your embedded target. Embedded distributions contain many components, compiled and optimized for your chosen architecture.

2.5.1 Suggestions for Additional Reading

Linux Kernel Development, 3rd Edition
Robert Love
Addison-Wesley, 2010

Understanding the Linux Kernel
Daniel P. Bovet and Marco Cesati
O'Reilly & Associates, Inc., 2002

Understanding the Linux Virtual Memory Manager
Bruce Perens
Prentice Hall, 2004

Chapter 3

Processor Basics

In This Chapter

- 3.1 Stand-Alone Processors   38
- 3.2 Integrated Processors: Systems on Chip   43
- 3.3 Other Architectures   59
- 3.4 Hardware Platforms   60
- 3.5 Summary   61

This chapter presents some basic information to help you navigate the huge array of embedded processor choices. We look at some of the processors on the market and the types of features they contain. Stand-alone processors are highlighted first. These tend to be the most powerful processors and require external chipsets to form complete systems. Next we present some of the many integrated processors that are supported under Linux. Finally, we look at some of the common hardware platforms in use today.

Dozens of embedded processors are available to choose from in a given embedded design. For the purposes of this chapter, we limit the discussion to those that contain a hardware memory-management unit and, of course, to those that are supported under Linux. One of the fundamental architectural design aspects of Linux is that it is a virtual memory operating system.[1] Employing Linux on a processor that does not contain an MMU gives up one of the more valuable architectural features of the kernel and is beyond the scope of this book.

3.1 Stand-Alone Processors

Stand-alone processors are processor chips that are dedicated exclusively to the processing function. As opposed to integrated processors, stand-alone processors require additional support circuitry for their basic operation. In many cases, this means a chipset or custom logic surrounding the processor to handle functions such as DRAM controller, system bus addressing configuration, and external peripheral devices such as keyboard controllers and serial ports. Stand-alone processors often offer the highest overall CPU performance.

Numerous processors exist in both 32-bit and 64-bit implementations[2] that have seen widespread use in embedded systems. These include the IBM Power Architecture 970/970FX, the Intel Pentium M, and the Freescale MPC74xx Host Processors,

---

[1] Linux supports some basic processors that do not contain MMUs, but this is not considered a mainstream use of Linux.

[2] 32-bit and 64-bit refer to the native width of the processor's main facilities, such as its execution units, register file, and address bus.

among others. The Intel Atom family of processors has found a niche in embedded applications.

The following sections describe processors from each of the major manufacturers of stand-alone processors. These processors are well supported under Linux and have been used in many embedded Linux designs.

3.1.1 IBM 970FX

The IBM 970FX processor core is a high-performance 64-bit-capable stand-alone processor. The 970FX is a superscalar architecture. This means that the core can fetch, issue, and obtain results from more than one instruction at a time. This is done through a pipelining architecture, which provides the effect of multiple streams of instruction simultaneously under ideal circumstances. The IBM 970FX contains up to 25 stages of pipelining, depending on the instruction stream and operations contained therein.

Some of the key features of the 970FX are as follows:

- A 64-bit implementation of the popular Power Architecture
- Deeply pipelined design, for very-high-performance computing applications
- Static and dynamic power-management features
- Multiple sleep modes, to minimize power requirements and maximize battery life
- Dynamically adjustable clock rates, supporting lower-power modes
- Optimized for high-performance, low-latency storage management

The IBM 970FX has been incorporated into a number of high-end server blades and computing platforms, including IBM's own Blade Server platform.

3.1.2 Intel Pentium M

Certainly one of the most popular architectures, x86 in both 32- and 64-bit flavors has been employed for embedded devices in a variety of applications. In the most common form, these platforms are based on a variety of commercial off-the-shelf (COTS) hardware implementations. Numerous manufacturers supply IA32/64 single-board computers and complete platforms in a variety of form factors. Section 3.2 discusses the more common platforms in use today.

The Intel Pentium M has been used in a wide variety of laptop computers and has found a niche in embedded products. Like the IBM 970FX processor, the Pentium M is a superscalar architecture. These characteristics make it attractive in embedded applications:

- The Pentium M is based on the popular x86 architecture and thus is widely supported by a large ecosystem of hardware and software vendors.
- It consumes less power than other x86 processors.
- Advanced power-management features enable low-power operating modes and multiple sleep modes.
- Dynamic clock speed capability enhances battery-powered operations such as standby.
- On-chip thermal monitoring enables automatic transition to lower power modes to reduce power consumption in overtemperature conditions.
- Multiple frequency and voltage operating points (dynamically selectable) are designed to maximize battery life in portable equipment.

Many of these features are especially useful for embedded applications. It is not uncommon for embedded products to require portable or battery-powered configurations. The Pentium M has enjoyed popularity in this application space because of its power- and thermal-management features.

3.1.3   Intel Atom™

The Intel Atom™ has enjoyed success in Netbooks and a range of embedded systems. The Intel Atom™ family of processors features low power consumption and binary compatibility with older 32-bit Intel processors, enabling a wide range of off-the-shelf software solutions. Like the other stand-alone processors described in this section, the Atom™ is paired with companion chipset(s) to build a complete solution. The N270 and Z5xx series of processors have been widely used in low-power products. The author's Dell Mini 10, on which portions of this second-edition manuscript were written, contains the Intel Atom™ Z530 processor.

More information about Intel Atom™ processors can be found via the URL given in the last section of this chapter.

3.1.4   Freescale MPC7448

The Freescale MPC7448 contains what is referred to as a fourth-generation Power Architecture core, commonly called G4.[3] This high-performance 32-bit processor is

---

[3] Freescale literature now refers to the G4 core as the e600 core.

commonly found in networking and telecommunications applications. Several companies manufacture blades that conform to ATCA, an industry-standard platform specification, including this and other similar stand-alone Freescale processors. Section 3.3 examines these platforms.

The MPC7448 has enjoyed popularity in a wide variety of signal-processing and networking applications because of its advanced feature set:

- Operating clock rates in excess of 1.5GHz
- 1MB onboard L2 cache
- Advanced power-management capabilities, including multiple sleep modes
- Advanced AltiVec vector-execution unit
- Voltage scaling for reduced-power configurations

The MPC7448 contains a Freescale technology called AltiVec to enable very fast algorithmic computations and other data-crunching applications. The AltiVec unit consists of a register file containing 32 very wide (128-bit) registers. Each value within one of these AltiVec registers can be considered a vector of multiple elements. AltiVec defines a set of instructions to manipulate this vector data effectively in parallel with core CPU instruction processing. AltiVec operations include such computations as sum-across, multiply-sum, simultaneous data distribute (store), and data gather (load) instructions.

Programmers have used the AltiVec hardware to enable very fast software computations commonly found in signal-processing and network elements. Examples include fast Fourier Transform, digital signal processing such as filtering, MPEG video encoding and decoding, and fast generation of encryption protocols such as DES, MD5, and SHA1.

Other chips in the Freescale lineup of stand-alone processors include the MPC7410, MPC7445, MPC7447, MPC745x, and MPC7xx family.

3.1.5 Companion Chipsets

Stand-alone processors such as those just described require support logic to connect to and enable external peripheral devices such as main system memory (DRAM), ROM or Flash memory, system buses such as PCI, and other peripherals, such as keyboard controllers, serial ports, IDE interfaces, and the like. This support logic often is accomplished by companion *chipsets*, which may even be purpose-designed specifically for a family of processors.

For example, the Pentium M is supported by one such chipset, called the 855GM. The 855GM chipset is the primary interface to graphics and memory—thus the suffix GM. The 855GM has been optimized as a companion to the Pentium M. Figure 3-1 illustrates the relationship between the processor and chipsets in this type of hardware design.

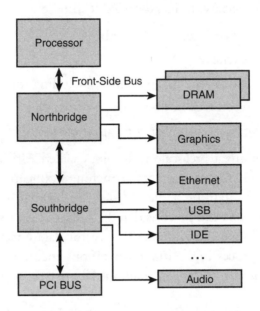

FIGURE 3-1   Processor/chipset relationship

Note the terminology that has become common for describing these chipsets. The Intel 855GM is an example of what is commonly referred to as a *northbridge* chip because it is directly connected to the processor's high-speed front-side bus (FSB). Another companion chip that provides I/O and PCI bus connectivity is similarly referred to as the *southbridge* chip because of its position in the architecture. The southbridge chip (actually, an I/O controller) in these hardware architectures is responsible for providing interfaces such as those shown in Figure 3-1, including Ethernet, USB, IDE, audio, keyboard, and mouse controllers.

On the Power Architecture side, the Tundra Tsi110 Host Bridge for Power Architecture is an example of a chipset that supports the stand-alone Power Architecture processors. The Tsi110 supports several interface functions for many common stand-alone Power Architecture processors. The Tundra chip supports the Freescale MPC74xx and the IBM PPC 750xx family of processors. These processors can use the

Tundra chip to provide direct interfaces to the following peripherals:

- Dual data rate (DDR) DRAM, integrated memory controller
- Ethernet (the Tundra provides four Gigabit Ethernet ports)
- PCI Express (supports two PCI Express ports)
- PCI/X (PCI 2.3, PCI-X, and Compact PCI [cPCI])
- Serial ports
- I2C
- Programmable interrupt controller
- Parallel port

Many manufacturers of chipsets exist, including VIA Technologies, Marvell, Tundra (now IDT), nVidia, Intel, and others. Marvell and Tundra primarily serve the Power Architecture market, whereas the others specialize in Intel architectures. Hardware designs based on one of the many stand-alone processors, such as Intel x86, IBM, or Freescale Power Architecture, need to have a companion chipset to interface with system devices.

One of the advantages of Linux as an embedded OS is rapid support of new chipsets. Linux currently supports the chipsets mentioned here, as well as many others. Consult the Linux source code and configuration utility for information on your chosen chipset.

3.2 Integrated Processors: Systems on Chip

The preceding section highlighted stand-alone processors. Although they are used for many applications, including some high-horsepower processing engines, the vast majority of smaller embedded systems employ some type of integrated processor, or system on chip (SOC). Scores of SOCs exist to choose from. This section examines a few from the industry leaders and looks at some of the features that set each group apart.

Several major processor architectures exist, and each architecture has examples of integrated SOCs. Power Architecture has been a traditional leader in many networking- and telecommunications-related embedded applications, and MIPS may have the market lead in lower-end consumer-grade equipment.[4] ARM is used in many cellular phones. These architectures and, of course, IA32/64 represent the major architectures

---

[4] These are the author's opinions and are based on market observation, not scientific data.

in widespread use in embedded Linux systems. However, as you will see in Chapter 4, "The Linux Kernel: A Different Perspective," Linux supports more than 20 different hardware architectures today.

3.2.1   Power Architecture

Power Architecture is the modern term that refers to the family of technology and products conforming to the various versions of the Power Architecture Instruction Set Architecture. Many good documents describe Power Architecture in great detail. Consult the last section of this chapter as a starting point.

Power Architecture processors have found their way into embedded products of every description. From automotive, consumer, and networking applications to the largest data and telecommunications switches, Power Architecture is one of the most popular and successful architectures for embedded applications. Because of this popularity, there exists a large array of hardware and software solutions from numerous manufacturers targeted at Power Architecture.

3.2.2   Freescale Power Architecture

Freescale Semiconductor has a large range of Power Architecture processors with integrated peripherals. Freescale Power Architecture processors have enjoyed enormous success in the networking market segment. This lineup of processors has wide appeal in a large variety of network equipment, from the low end to the high end of the product space.

By anyone's measure, Freescale has enjoyed tremendous success in the embedded market. Part of this success goes as far back as the venerable 68K family of products, which still capture market share today in the form of Coldfire processors. More recently, Freescale has enjoyed success with its PowerQUICC product line. The PowerQUICC architecture has been shipping for more than a decade. It is based on a Power Architecture core of a particular version integrated with a QUICC engine (also called a communications processor module or CPM in the Freescale literature). The QUICC engine is an independent RISC processor designed to offload the communications processing from the main Power Architecture core, thus freeing the Power Architecture core to focus on control and management applications. The QUICC engine is a complex but highly flexible communications peripheral controller.

In its current incarnation, PowerQUICC encompasses five general groups. Although somewhat dated, the PowerQUICC I family (8xx) lives on. PowerQUICC II (82xx) is still quite popular, as is PowerQUICC II Pro (83xx). PowerQUICC III (85xx) is hugely popular in networking and other gear.

PowerQUICC III gave rise to the new QorIQ family of processors, which employ the high-performance e500 core in single-core and multicore implementations. QorIQ processors promise to be market-leading multicore processing engines with powerful features that make them suitable for high-speed networking and other commercial and industrial applications.

3.2.3   Freescale PowerQUICC I

The PowerQUICC I family includes the original Power Architecture-based Power-QUICC implementations and consists of the MPC8xx family of processors. These integrated communications processors operate at 50 to 133MHz and feature the embedded Power Architecture 8xx core. The PowerQUICC I family has been used for ATM and Ethernet edge devices, such as routers for the small office/home office (SOHO) market, residential gateways, ADSL and cable modems, and similar applications.

The CPM or QUICC engine incorporates two unique and powerful communications controllers. The Serial Communication Controller (SCC) is a flexible serial interface that can implement many serial-based communications protocols, including Ethernet, HDLC/SDLC, AppleTalk, synchronous and asynchronous UARTs, IrDA, and other bitstream data.

The Serial Management Controller (SMC) is a module capable of similar serial-communications protocols. It includes support for ISDN, serial UART, and SPI protocols.

Using a combination of these SCCs and SMCs, you can create flexible I/O combinations. An internal time-division multiplexer even allows these interfaces to implement channelized communications such as T1 and E1 I/O.

Table 3-1 summarizes a small sampling of the PowerQUICC I product line.

TABLE 3-1   Freescale PowerQUICC I Highlights

Feature	MPC850	MPC860	MPC875	MPC885
Core	PPC 8xx	PPC 8xx	PPC 8xx	PPC 8xx
Clock rates	Up to 80MHz	Up to 80MHz	Up to 133MHz	Up to 133MHz
DRAM controller	Yes	Yes	Yes	Yes
USB	Yes	No	Yes	Yes
SPI controller	Yes	Yes	Yes	Yes
I2C controller	Yes	Yes	Yes	Yes
SCC controllers	2	4	1	3
SMC controllers	2	2	1	1
Security engine	No	No	Yes	Yes
Dedicated Fast Ethernet controller	No	No	2	2

3.2.4   Freescale PowerQUICC II

The next step up in the Freescale Power Architecture product line is PowerQUICC II. PowerQUICC II incorporates the company's G2 Power Architecture core derived from the 603e embedded Power Architecture core. These integrated communications processors operate at 133 to 450MHz and feature multiple 10/100Mbps Ethernet interfaces, security engines, ATM and PCI support, and more. The PowerQUICC II encompasses the MPC82xx products.

PowerQUICC II adds two new types of controllers to the QUICC engine. The FCC is a full-duplex fast serial communications controller. The FCC supports high-speed communications such as 100Mbps Ethernet and T3/E3 up to 45Mbps. The MCC is a multichannel controller capable of 128KB 64KB channelized data.

Table 3-2 summarizes the highlights of selected PowerQUICC II processors.

TABLE 3-2   Freescale PowerQUICC II Highlights

Feature	MPC8250	MPC8260	MPC8272	MPC8280
Core	G2/603e	G2/603e	G2/603e	G2/603e
Clock rates	150 to 200MHz	100 to 300MHz	266 to 400MHz	266 to 400MHz
DRAM controller	Yes	Yes	Yes	Yes
USB	No	No	Yes	Via SCC4
SPI controller	Yes	Yes	Yes	Yes
I2C controller	Yes	Yes	Yes	Yes
SCC controllers	4	4	3	4

TABLE 3-2   Continued

Feature	MPC8250	MPC8260	MPC8272	MPC8280
SMC controllers	2	2	2	2
FCC controllers	3	3	2	3
MCC controllers	1	2	0	2

3.2.5 PowerQUICC II Pro

Based on the Freescale Power Architecture e300 core (evolved from the G2/603e), the PowerQUICC II Pro family operates at 266 to 667MHz and features support for Gigabit Ethernet, DDR SDRAM controllers, PCI, high-speed USB, security acceleration, and more. These are the MPC83xx family of processors. The PowerQUICC II and PowerQUICC II Pro families of processors have been designed into a wide variety of equipment, such as LAN and WAN switches, hubs and gateways, PBX systems, and many other systems with similar complexity and performance requirements.

The PowerQUICC II Pro contains three family members without the QUICC engine and two that are based on an updated version of the QUICC engine. The MPC8358E and MPC8360E both add a new Universal Communications Controller, which supports a variety of protocols.

Table 3-3 summarizes the highlights of selected members of the PowerQUICC II Pro family.

TABLE 3-3   Freescale PowerQUICC II Pro Highlights

Feature	MPC8343E	MPC8347E	MPC8349E	MPC8360E
Core	e300	e300	e300	e300
Clock rates	266 to 400MHz	266 to 667MHz	400 to 667MHz	266 to 667MHz
DRAM controller	Y-DDR	Y-DDR	Y-DDR	Y-DDR
USB	Yes	2	2	Yes
SPI controller	Yes	Yes	Yes	Yes
I2C controller	2	2	2	2
Ethernet 10/100/1000	2	2	2	Via UCC
UART	2	2	2	2
PCI controller	Yes	Yes	Yes	Yes
Security engine	Yes	Yes	Yes	Yes
MCC	0	0	0	1
UCC	0	0	0	8

3.2.6   Freescale PowerQUICC III

At the top of the PowerQUICC family are the PowerQUICC III processors. These operate between 600MHz and 1.5GHz. They are based on the e500 core and support Gigabit Ethernet, DDR SDRAM, RapidIO, PCI and PCI/X, ATM, HDLC, and more. This family incorporates the MPC85xx product line. These processors have found their way into high-end products such as wireless base station controllers, optical edge switches, central office switches, and similar equipment.

Table 3-4 highlights some of the PowerQUICC III family members.

TABLE 3-4   Freescale PowerQUICC III Highlights

Feature	MPC8540	MPC8548E	MPC8555E	MPC8560
Core	e500	e500	e500	e500
Clock rates	Up to 1.0GHz	Up to 1.5GHz	Up to 1.0GHz	Up to 1.0GHz
DRAM controller	Y-DDR	Y-DDR	Y-DDR	Y-DDR
USB	No	No	Via SCC	No
SPI controller	No	No	Yes	Yes
I2C controller	Yes	Yes	Yes	Yes
Ethernet 10/100	1	Via Gigabit Ethernet	Via SCC	Via SCC
Gigabit Ethernet	2	4	2	2
UART	2	2	2	Via SCC
PCI controller	PCI/PCI-X	PCI/PCI-X	PCI	PCI/PCI-X
RapidIO	Yes	Yes	No	Yes
Security engine	No	Yes	Yes	No
SCC	—	—	3	4
FCC	—	—	2	3
SMC	—	—	2	0
MCC	—	—	0	2

3.2.7   Freescale QorIQ™

Pronounced "core eye queue," QorIQ is Freescale's newest technology based on Power Architecture. Many chips in the QorIQ family are multicore processors based on the e500 and e500mc cores. Freescale currently describes three platforms in the QorIQ family on its public website.[5] That information is summarized here.

---

[5] www.freescale.com/QorIQ

The P1 series includes the P1011/P1020 and the P1013/P1022. These processors contain the e500 Power Architecture core, and each has a specialized set of peripherals aimed at the networking, communications, and control plane applications. They have one or two cores, and they have a remarkably low power profile capable of roughly 3.5 watts. Table 3-5 summarizes the major highlights of the P1 series.

TABLE 3-5   Freescale QorIQ P1 Series Highlights

Feature	P1011	P1020	P1013	P1022
Core	e500	e500	e500	e500
Clock rates	Up to 800MHz	Up to 800MHz	Up to 1055MHz	Up to 1055MHz
Number of cores	1	2	1	2
USB	2.0	2.0	2.0	2.0
SPI controller	Yes	Yes	Yes	Yes
I2C controller	Yes	Yes	Yes	Yes
Ethernet	3 × Gigabit Ethernet	3 × Gigabit Ethernet	2 × Gigabit Ethernet	2 × Gigabit Ethernet
DUART	2	2	2	2
PCI	2 × PCI Express	2 × PCI Express	3 × PCI Express	3 × PCI Express
SATA	—	—	2 × SATA	2 × SATA
Security engine	Yes	Yes	Yes	Yes
SD/MMC	Yes	Yes	Yes	Yes

The P2 series consists of the P2010 and P2020. This series also contains one or two cores. They offer a higher level of performance than the P1 series, with core speeds up to 1.2 GHz, and they have larger cache arrays. They have typical power requirements in the 6-watt range. Table 3-6 lists the highlights of the P2 series.

TABLE 3-6   Freescale QorIQ P2 Series Highlights

Feature	P2010	P2020
Core	e500	e500
Core speed	Up to 1.2GHz	Up to 1.2GHz
Number of cores	1	2
USB	2.0	2.0
SPI controller	Yes	Yes
I2C controller	Yes	Yes
Ethernet	3 × Gigabit Ethernet	3 × Gigabit Ethernet
DUART	2	2
PCI	3 × PCI Express	3 × PCI Express

TABLE 3-6   Continued

Feature	P2010	P2020
Serial RapidIO	2 × SRIO	2 × SRIO
Security engine	Optional	Optional
SD/MMC	Yes	Yes

The P4 series consists of the P4040 and P4080. This series has processors up to eight cores, and it is based on a special multicore optimized e500 core called e500mc. These cores have hardware support for a hypervisor, private back-side caches, and floating point support. Unique to this family is the Data Path Acceleration Architecture (DPAA) for very-high-speed data plane applications. This family of processors also has enhanced debug and tracing capabilities. Table 3-7 shows the highlights from the P4 series.

TABLE 3-7   Freescale QorIQ P4 Series Highlights

Feature	P4040	P4080
Core	e500mc	e500mc
Core speed	Up to 1.5GHz	Up to 1.5GHz
Number of cores	4	8
USB	2 × 2.0	2 × 2.0
SPI controller	Yes	Yes
I2C controller	Yes	Yes
Ethernet	8 × 10/100/1000	8 × 10/100/1000
10 Gigabit Ethernet	2	—
DUART	2	2
PCI	3 × PCI Express V2	3 × PCI Express V2
Serial RapidIO	2	2
Security engine	Yes	Yes
SD/MMC	Yes	Yes

3.2.8   AMCC Power Architecture

Some of the examples later in this book are based on the AMCC Power Architecture 440EP Embedded Processor. The 440EP is a popular integrated processor found in many networking and communications products. The following list highlights some of the features of the 440EP:

- On-chip dual data rate (DDR) SDRAM controller
- Integrated NAND Flash controller
- PCI bus interface
- Dual 10/100Mbps Ethernet ports
- On-chip USB 2.0 interface
- Up to four user-configurable serial ports
- Dual I2C controllers
- Programmable Interrupt Controller
- Serial Peripheral Interface (SPI) controller
- Programmable timers
- JTAG interface for debugging

This is indeed a complete SOC. Figure 3-2 is a block diagram of the AMCC Power Architecture 440EP Embedded Processor. With the addition of memory chips and physical I/O hardware, a complete high-end embedded system can be built around this integrated microprocessor with minimal interface circuitry.

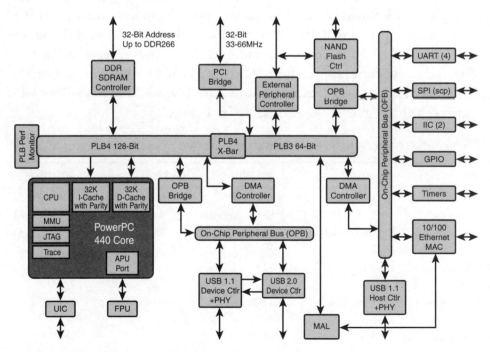

Courtesy AMCC Corporation

FIGURE 3-2   AMCC PPC 440EP Embedded Processor

Many manufacturers offer reference hardware platforms to enable a developer to explore the capabilities of the processor or other hardware. The examples in Chapter 14, "Kernel Debugging Techniques," and Chapter 15, "Debugging Embedded Linux Applications," were executed on the AMCC Yosemite board, which is the company's reference platform containing the 440EP, shown in Figure 3-2.

Numerous product configurations are available with Power Architecture processors. As shown in Figure 3-2, the AMCC 440EP contains sufficient I/O interfaces for many common products, with very little additional circuitry. Because this processor contains an integrated floating-point unit (FPU), it is ideally suited for products such as network-attached imaging systems, general industrial control, and networking equipment.

AMCC's Power Architecture product lineup includes several configurations powered by two proven cores. Its 405 core products are available in configurations with and without Ethernet controllers. All 405 core configurations include integrated SDRAM controllers, dual UARTs for serial ports, I2C for low-level onboard management communications, general-purpose I/O pins, and integral timers. The AMCC 405 core integrated processors provide economical performance on a proven core for a wide range of applications that do not require a hardware FPU.

The AMCC 440-based core products raise the performance level and add peripherals. The 440EP featured in some of our examples includes a hardware FPU. The 440GX adds two triple-speed 10/100/1000Mbps Ethernet interfaces (in addition to the two 10/100Mbps Ethernet ports) and TCP/IP hardware acceleration for high-performance networking applications. The 440SP adds hardware acceleration for RAID 5/6 applications. All these processors have mature Linux support. Table 3-8 summarizes the highlights of the AMCC 405xx family.

TABLE 3-8   AMCC Power Architecture 405xx Highlights

Feature	405CR	405EP	405GP	405GPr
Core	PPC 405	PPC 405	PPC 405	PPC 405
Core speeds	133 to 266MHz	133 to 333MHz	133 to 266MHz	266 to 400MHz
DRAM controller	SDRAM/133	SDRAM/133	SDRAM/133	SDRAM/133
Ethernet 10/100	No	2	1	1
GPIO lines	23	32	24	24
UARTs	2	2	2	2
DMA controller	4 channel	4 channel	4 channel	4 channel
I2C controller	Yes	Yes	Yes	Yes
PCI host controller	No	Yes	Yes	Yes
Interrupt controller	Yes	Yes	Yes	Yes

See the AMCC website, www.amcc.com/embedded, for complete details.

Table 3-9 summarizes the features of the AMCC 440xx family of processors.

TABLE 3-9 AMCC Power Architecture 440xx Highlights

Feature	440EP	440GP	440GX	440SP
Core	PPC 440	PPC 440	PPC 440	PPC 440
Core speeds	333 to 667MHz	400 to 500MHz	533 to 800MHz	533 to 667MHz
DRAM controller	DDR	DDR	DDR	DDR
Ethernet 10/100	2	2	2	Via Gigabit Ethernet
Gigabit Ethernet	No	No	2	1
GPIO lines	64	32	32	32
UARTs	4	2	2	3
DMA controller	4 channel	4 channel	4 channel	3 channel
I2C controller	2	2	2	2
PCI host controller	Yes	PCI-X	PCI-X	3 PCI-X
SPI controller	Yes	No	No	No
Interrupt controller	Yes	Yes	Yes	Yes

3.2.9 MIPS

You might be surprised to learn that 32-bit processors based on the MIPS architecture have been shipping for more than 20 years. The MIPS architecture was designed in 1981 by a Stanford University engineering team led by Dr. John Hennessey, who later went on to form MIPS Computer Systems, Inc. That company has morphed into the present-day MIPS Technologies, whose primary role is the design and subsequent licensing of MIPS architecture and cores.

The MIPS core has been licensed by many companies, several of which have become powerhouses in the embedded processor market. MIPS is a Reduced Instruction Set Computing (RISC) architecture with both 32-bit and 64-bit implementations shipping in many popular products. MIPS processors are found in a large variety of products, from high-end to consumer devices. It is public knowledge that MIPS processors power many popular, well-known consumer products, such as Sony high-definition television sets, Linksys wireless access points, and the popular Sony PlayStation game console.

The MIPS Technology website lists 73 licensees that currently are engaged in manufacturing products using MIPS processor cores. Some of these companies are household names, including Sony, Texas Instruments, Cisco's Scientific Atlanta (a leading manufacturer of cable TV set-top boxes), Motorola, and others. One of the largest and most successful of these is Broadcom Corporation.

3.2.10   Broadcom MIPS

Broadcom is a leading supplier of SOC solutions for markets such as cable TV set-top boxes, cable modems, HDTV, wireless networks, Gigabit Ethernet, and Voice over IP (VoIP). Broadcom's SOCs have been very popular in these markets. We mentioned earlier that you likely have Linux in your home even if you don't know it. If you do, it probably is running on a Broadcom MIPS-based SOC.

In 2000, Broadcom acquired SiByte Inc., which resulted in the communications processor product lineup the company is currently marketing. These processors currently ship in single-core, dual-core, and quad-core configurations. The company still refers to them as SiByte processors.

The single-core SiByte processors include the BCM1122 and BCM1125H. They are both based on the MIPS64 core and operate at clock speeds of 400 to 900MHz. They include on-chip peripheral controllers such as the DDR SDRAM controller, 10/100Mbps Ethernet, and the PCI host controller. Both include an SMBus serial configuration interface, PCMCIA, and two UARTs for serial port connections. The BCM1125H includes a triple-speed 10/100/1000Mbps Ethernet controller. One of the more striking features of these processors is their power dissipation. Both feature a 4W operating budget at 400MHz operation.

The dual-core SiByte processors include the BCM1250, BCM1255, and BCM1280. Also based on the MIPS64 core, these processors operate at clock rates from 600MHz (BCM1250) to as high as 1.2GHz (BCM1255 and BCM1280). These dual-core chips include integrated peripheral controllers such as DDR SDRAM controllers; various combinations of Gigabit Ethernet controllers; 64-bit PCI-X interfaces; and SMBus, PCMCIA, and multiple UART interfaces. Like their single-core cousins, these dual-core implementations feature low power dissipation. For example, the BCM1255 features a 13W power budget at 1GHz operation.

The quad-core SiByte processors include the BCM1455 and BCM1480 communications processors. As with the other SiByte processors, these are based on the MIPS64 core. The cores can be run from 800MHz to 1.2GHz. These SOCs include integrated DDR SDRAM controllers, four separate Gigabit Ethernet MAC controllers, and 64-bit PCI-X host controllers. They also contain SMBus, PCMCIA, and four serial UARTs.

Table 3-10 summarizes selected Broadcom SiByte processors.

TABLE 3-10   Broadcom SiByte Processor Highlights

Feature	BCM1125H	BCM1250	BCM1280	BCM1480
Core	SB-1 MIPS64	Dual SB-1 MIPS64	Dual SB-1 MIPS64	Quad SB-1 MIPS64
Core speeds	400 to 900 MHz	600 to 1000 MHz	800 to 1200 MHz	800 to 1200 MHz
DRAM controller	Y-DDR	Y-DDR	Y-DDR	Y-DDR
Serial interface	2 to 55Mbps	2 to 55Mbps	4 UART	4 UART
SMBus interface	2	2	2	2
PCMCIA	Yes	Yes	Yes	Yes
Gigabit Ethernet (10/100/1000Mbps)	2	3	4	4
PCI controller	Yes	Yes	PCI/PCI-X	PCI/PCI-X
Security engine	No	No	No	—
High-speed I/O (HyperTransport)	1	1	3	3

3.2.11   Other MIPS

As we pointed out earlier, nearly 100 current MIPS licensees are shown on the MIPS Technologies licensees web page, at www.mips.com/content/Licensees/ProductCatalog/licensees. Unfortunately, it is not possible to cover them all here. Start your search at the MIPS technologies website for a good cross-section of the MIPS processor vendors.

For example, ATI Technologies uses a MIPS core in its Xilleon set-top box family of chipsets. Cavium Networks' Octeon family uses MIPS64 cores in a variety of multicore processor implementations. Integrated Device Technology, Inc. (IDT), has a family of integrated communications processors called Interprise, based on the MIPS architecture. PMC-Sierra, NEC, Toshiba, and others have integrated processors based on MIPS. All of these and more are well supported under Linux.

3.2.12   ARM

The ARM architecture has achieved a very large market share in the consumer electronics marketplace. Many popular and now ubiquitous products contain ARM cores. Some well-known examples include the Sony PlayStation Portable (PSP), Apple iPhone, Blackberry Storm, TomTom GO 300 GPS, and the Motorola Droid mobile phone. Processors containing ARM cores power the majority of the world's digital cellular phones, according to the ARM Corporate Backgrounder at www.arm.com/miscPDFs/3822.pdf.

The ARM architecture was developed by ARM Holdings, plc and is licensed to semiconductor manufacturers around the globe. Many of the world's leading semiconductor companies have licensed ARM technology and currently are shipping integrated processors based on one of several ARM cores.

3.2.13 TI ARM

Texas Instruments uses ARM cores in the DaVinci, OMAP, and other families of integrated processors. These processors contain many integrated peripherals intended to be used as single-chip solutions for various consumer products, such as cellular handsets, PDAs, and similar multimedia platforms. In addition to the interfaces commonly found on integrated processors, such as UARTs and I2C, the OMAP devices contain a wide range of special-purpose interfaces, including the following:

- LCD screen and backlight controllers
- Buzzer driver
- Camera interface
- MMC/SD card controller
- Battery-management hardware
- USB client/host interfaces
- Radio modem interface logic
- Integrated 2D or 3D graphics accelerators
- Integrated security accelerator
- S-Video outputs
- IrDA controller
- DACs for direct TV (PAL/NTSC) video output
- Integrated DSPs for video and audio processing

Many popular cellular handsets and PDA devices have been marketed based on the TI OMAP platform. Because they are based on an ARM core, these processors are supported by Linux today. Table 3-11 compares some of the more recent ARM-based processors from TI.

TABLE 3-11   TI ARM Highlights

Feature	OMAP-L138	DaVinci 6467	OMAP3515/03	OMAP3530
ARM core	ARM926EJ-S	ARM926EJ-S	ARM Cortex A8	ARM Cortex A8
Clock rates	300MHz	Up to 365MHz	Up to 720MHz	550MHz
DRAM controller	DDR2	DDR2	DDR2	Yes
Onboard DSP	300MHz C674x	300MHz C64X+	—	C64X+ Video/image accelerator subsystem
UARTs	3	3	3	3
USB	USB 1.1 host USB 2.0 OTG	USB 2.0 host USB 2.0 client	USB 2.0 host USB 2.0 client	USB 2.0 host USB 2.0 client
I2C controller/bus	2	1	Yes	Yes
MMC-SD interface	2	—	Yes	Yes
Camera interface	See video ports	See video ports	Yes	Yes
Video ports	2 in, 2 out	2 in, 2 out	S-Video or CVBS	S-Video or CVBS
Video acceleration hardware	—	2 HD video-imaging coprocessors	POWERVR SGX display controller	Imaging Video Accelerator (IVA 2+)
Audio codec support	AC97[6] interface	AC97 interface	Via DSP	Via DSP
LCD controller	Yes	Yes	Yes	Yes
Display controllers	LCD Controller and Video in/out	LCD Controller and Video in/out	Dual output 3-layer display processor	Dual output 3-layer display processor

3.2.13.1   BeagleBoard

If you have been around embedded Linux for any length of time, you have undoubtedly heard of the BeagleBoard. Its popularity stems from its low price point, easy availability, and broad community support. The popular U-Boot bootloader is supported on the board, making kernel integration easier. The BeagleBoard is based on the TI OMAP3530. It has provisions to connect keyboard and display, SD cards for kernel and root file system, a serial connection for a console, and a dual-mode USB 2.0 port.

The BeagleBoard is a great platform for experimentation and learning, as well as a perfect development platform for various OMAP-related development projects. The only drawback of the BeagleBoard was the lack of an Ethernet port. Fortunately, this problem was remedied by a company called Tin Can Tools. It developed a companion board called the BeagleBuddy Zippy Ethernet Combo Board. In addition to adding an Ethernet port, it adds another SD/MMC interface, a battery-backed real-time clock, an I2C expansion interface, and another serial port. You can find more information at www.tincantools.com/product.php?productid=16147&cat=255&page=1.

---

[6] These chips have internal support for connection to AC97 audio streams. Beyond that, realize that the integrated DSPs can run a wide variety of audio and video codecs.

3.2.14   Freescale ARM

The success of the ARM architecture is made more evident by the fact that leading manufacturers of competing architectures have licensed ARM technology. As a prime example, Freescale Semiconductor has licensed ARM technology for its line of i.MX application processors. These popular ARM-based integrated processors have achieved widespread industry success in multimedia consumer devices such as portable game platforms, PDAs, and cellular handsets.

The Freescale ARM product portfolio currently includes nine families of application processors. They range from the i.MX21 through the i.MX51 series. All the i.MX products can be found at www.freescale.com/webapp/sps/site/homepage.jsp?code=IMX_HOME.

The i.MX21 features an ARM9 core, and the i.MX31 has an ARM11 core. Like their TI counterparts, these SOCs contain many integrated peripherals required by portable consumer electronics devices with multimedia requirements. The i.MX21/31 contains some of the following integrated interfaces:

- Graphics accelerator
- MPEG-4 encoder
- Keypad and LCD controllers
- Camera interface
- Audio multiplexer
- IrDA infrared I/O
- SD/MMC interface
- Numerous external I/O, such as PCMCIA, USB, DRAM controllers, and UARTs for serial port connection

The i.MX35 family of processors is used in automotive, consumer, and industrial applications. They feature ARM11 cores running at 532 MHz with many integrated features similar to the i.MX21/31 families. Here are some examples of i.MX35 integrated peripherals:

- LCD controller (all but i.MX351)
- OpenVG graphics accelerator (i.MX356/7)
- High-speed Ethernet controller
- CAN bus controller
- USB 2.0 host and OTG plus PHY

- SD/MMC interface
- I2C controller
- UARTs, SPI, and SSI/I2S

The i.MX37 family of processors currently consists of the single i.MX37 Applications Processor. It is ideally suited for portable multimedia applications. The i.MX37 features the ARM1176JZF-S ARM core; an image-processing unit; and integrated support for H.264, VC-1, MPEG-2, and MPEG-4 decoders. It has all the usual connectivity, including SD/MMC, USB, UART, audio in/out, GPIO, keypad controller, and more. More information on this processor is available at www.freescale.com/web app/sps/site/taxonomy.jsp?code=IMX37_FAMILY.

The i.MX51 family of processors currently consists of five products, ranging from the i.MX512 to the i.MX516. According to Freescale's summary page for i.MX51, these processors are targeted at consumer, industrial, and automotive applications. They feature CPU speeds from 600MHz to 800MHz. These chips, like their brethren, have a high level of integration. They feature various hardware accelerators such as integrated video accelerators, integrated hardware-based codecs, and security accelerators. These processors all contain some combination of the usual array of I/O, including USB, Ethernet, video in/out, SD/MMC, and UARTS.

3.2.15 Other ARM Processors

More than 100 semiconductor companies are developing integrated solutions based on ARM technology—far too many to list here. Many offer specialized application processors serving vertical markets such as the handset market, storage area networking, network processing, the automotive market, and many more. These companies include Altera, PMC-Sierra, Samsung Electronics, Philips Semiconductor, Fujitsu, and more. See the ARM Technologies website at www.arm.com for additional ARM licensees and information.

3.3 Other Architectures

We have covered the major architectures in widespread use in embedded Linux systems. However, for completeness, you should be aware of other architectures that Linux supports. A recent Linux snapshot revealed over 20 architecture branches (subdirectories).

The Linux source tree contains ports for Sun Sparc and the Xtensa from Tensilica, to name a couple. Spend a few minutes looking through the architecture branch of the

Linux kernel to see the range of architectures for which Linux has been ported. Beware, however, that not all these architectures might be up to date in any given snapshot. You can be reasonably certain that the major architectures are fairly current, but the only way to be certain is to follow the development in the Linux community or to consult with your favorite embedded Linux vendor. Appendix E, "Open Source Resources," contains a list of resources you can consult to help stay current with Linux developments.

3.4   Hardware Platforms

The idea of a common hardware reference platform is not new. The venerable PC/104 and VMEbus are two examples of hardware platforms that have withstood the test of time in the embedded market.[7] More recent successful platforms include CompactPCI and its derivatives.

3.4.1   CompactPCI

The CompactPCI (cPCI) hardware platform is based on PCI electrical standards and Eurocard physical specifications. cPCI has the following general features:

- Vertical cards of 3U or 6U heights
- A latch system for securing and ejecting cards
- Front- or rear-panel I/O connections are supported
- High-density backplane connector
- Staggered power pins for hot-swap support
- Support by many vendors
- Compatibility with standard PCI chipsets

You can view highlights of and obtain specifications for the cPCI architecture at the PCI Industrial Computer Manufacturers Group (PICMG) cPCI web page at www.picmg.org/compactpci.stm.

3.4.2   ATCA

A successor to the successful cPCI, Advanced Telecommunications Computing Architecture is the name given to the architecture and platforms designed around the PICMG 3.*x* series of specifications. Many top-tier hardware manufacturers are shipping or

---

[7] VMEbus isn't really a hardware reference platform per se, but based on Eurocard physical standards, its level of compatibility among multiple vendors qualifies it for the label.

developing new ATCA-based platforms. The primary applications for ATCA platforms are carrier-class telecommunications switching and transport equipment, and high-end data-center server and storage equipment.

ATCA platforms are leading the industry trend away from in-house proprietary hardware and software platforms. Many of the largest equipment manufacturers in the telecommunications and networking markets have been slowly moving away from custom, in-house-designed hardware platforms. This trend is also evident in the software platforms, from operating systems to so-called middleware such as high-availability and protocol stack solutions. Downsizing and time-to-market pressures are two key factors driving this trend.

ATCA is defined by several PICMG specifications, summarized in Table 3-12.

TABLE 3-12   ATCA PICMG 3.x Specification Summary

Specification	Description
PICMG 3.0	Mechanical specifications, including interconnects, power, cooling, and base system management
PICMG 3.1	Ethernet and Fiber Channel switching fabric interface
PICMG 3.2	Infiniband switching fabric interface
PICMG 3.3	StarFabric interface
PICMG 3.4	PCI Express interface
PICMG 3.5	RapidIO interface

The platforms described in this section are the most relevant in any discussion of embedded Linux platforms today. Especially with ATCA, the industry is increasingly moving toward COTS technology. Both ATCA and Linux are playing increasingly important roles in this industry trend.

3.5   Summary

- Linux supports many stand-alone processors. The most widely supported are IA32/IA64 and Power Architecture. These stand-alone processors are used as building blocks to create very-high-performance computing engines. This chapter presented several examples from Intel, IBM, and Freescale.

- Integrated processors, or systems on chip (SOCs), dominate the embedded Linux landscape. Many vendors and several popular architectures are used in embedded Linux designs. Several of the most popular were presented in this chapter by architecture and manufacturer.

- An increasingly popular trend in larger systems is to move away from proprietary hardware and software platforms and toward commercial off-the-shelf (COTS) solutions. Two popular platforms in widespread use in embedded Linux systems are cPCI and ATCA.

3.5.1   Suggestions for Additional Reading

PowerPC 32-bit architecture reference manual
Programming Environments Manual for 32-Bit Implementations of the PowerPC Architecture—Revision 2
Freescale Semiconductor, Inc.
www.freescale.com/files/product/doc/MPCFPE32B.pdf

PowerPC 64-bit architecture reference manual
Programming Environments Manual for 64-Bit Microprocessors—Version 3.0
International Business Machines, Inc.
https://www-01.ibm.com/chips/techlib/techlib.nsf/techdocs/F7E732FF811F783187
256FDD004D3797/$file/pem_64bit_v3.0.2005jul15.pdf

Short summary of Power Architecture
A Developer's Guide to the POWER Architecture
Brett Olsson, Processor Architect, IBM Corp.
Anthony Marsala, Software Engineer, IBM Corp.
http://www-128.ibm.com/developerworks/linux/library/l-powarch

Intel XScale overview page
www.intel.com/design/intelxscale/

Intel Atom overview page
www.intel.com/design/intarch/atom/index.htm

Power.org home page
www.power.org/home

BeagleBoard resources
www.beagleboard.org

Chapter 4

The Linux Kernel: A Different Perspective

In This Chapter

- 4.1 Background   64
- 4.2 Linux Kernel Construction   68
- 4.3 Kernel Build System   78
- 4.4 Kernel Configuration   89
- 4.5 Kernel Documentation   96
- 4.6 Obtaining a Custom Linux Kernel   96
- 4.7 Summary   97

If you want to learn about kernel internals, many good books on kernel design and operation are available. Several are presented in the last section, in this as well as other chapters. However, very little has been written about how the kernel is organized and structured from a project perspective. What if you're looking for the right place to add some custom support for your new embedded project? How do you know which files are important for your architecture?

At first glance, it might seem an almost impossible task to understand the Linux kernel and how to configure it for a specific platform or application. In a recent Linux kernel snapshot, the Linux kernel source tree consists of more than 28,000[1] files that contain somewhere between 10 and 11 million[2] lines of code, depending on how you count actual lines of code.[3] And that's just the beginning. You still need tools (the most obvious being a compiler) and a root file system containing many Linux applications to build a usable system.

This chapter introduces the Linux kernel and covers kernel organization and how the source tree is structured. We then examine the components that make up the kernel image and discuss the kernel source tree layout. Following this, we present the details of the kernel build system and the files that drive the kernel configuration and build system. The chapter concludes by examining the requirements for a complete embedded Linux system.

4.1 Background

Linus Torvalds wrote the original version of Linux while he was a student at the University of Helsinki in Finland. His work began in 1991. In August of that year, Torvalds posted this now-famous announcement on `comp.os.minix`:

---

[1] Interestingly, that is 8,000 more files than were present during the preparation of the first edition of this book!

[2] That is 4 million more lines of code than reported in the first edition!

[3] Roughly, this number was derived by counting raw lines from header files, C and assembler source, makefiles, and Kconfig files. Scripts were not included.

```
From: torvalds@klaava.Helsinki.FI (Linus Benedict Torvalds)
Newsgroups: comp.os.minix
Subject: What would you like to see most in minix?
Summary: small poll for my new operating system
Message-ID: <1991Aug25.205708.9541@klaava.Helsinki.FI>
Date: 25 Aug 91 20:57:08 GMT
Organization: University of Helsinki


Hello everybody out there using minix -

I'm doing a (free) operating system (just a hobby, won't be big and profession-
al like gnu) for 386(486) AT clones.  This has been brewing since april, and is
starting to get ready.  I'd like any feedback on things people like/dislike in
minix, as my OS resembles it somewhat(same physical layout of the file-system (due
to practical reasons) among other things).

I've currently ported bash(1.08) and gcc(1.40), and things seem to work. This im-
plies that I'll get something practical within a few months, and I'd like to know
what features most people would want.  Any suggestions are welcome, but I won't
promise I'll implement them :-)

            Linus (torvalds@kruuna.helsinki.fi)

PS.  Yes - it's free of any minix code, and it has a multi-threaded fs.
It is NOT protable (uses 386 task switching etc), and it probably never
will support anything other than AT-harddisks, as that's all I have :-(.
```

Since that initial release, Linux has matured into a full-featured operating system with robustness, reliability, and high-end features that rival those of the best commercial operating systems. By some estimates, more than half of the Internet servers on the Web are powered by Linux servers. It is no secret that the online search giant Google uses a large collection of low-cost PCs running a fault-tolerant version of Linux to implement its popular search engine.

4.1.1 Kernel Versions

You can obtain the source code for a Linux kernel and complementary components in numerous places. Your local bookstore might have several versions as companion CD-ROMs in books about Linux. You can also download the kernel itself or even complete Linux distributions from numerous locations on the Internet. The official home for the Linux kernel is www.kernel.org. You will often hear the terms mainline source or mainline kernel, referring to the source trees found at kernel.org.

For quite some time now, Linux version 2.6 has been the current version. Early in the development cycle, the developers chose a numbering system designed to differentiate between kernel source trees intended for development and experimentation and source trees intended to be stable, production-ready kernels. The numbering scheme contains a major version number, a minor version number, and a sequence number. Before Linux version 2.6, if the minor version number is even, it denotes a production kernel; if it is odd, it denotes a development kernel. For example:

- **Linux 2.4.x**—Production kernel
- **Linux 2.5.x**—Experimental (development)
- **Linux 2.6.x**—Production kernel

Currently, the Linux 2.6 kernel has no separate development branch. All new features, enhancements, and bug fixes are funneled through a series of gatekeepers who ultimately filter and push changes to the top-level Linux source trees maintained by Andrew Morton and Linus Torvalds.

It is easy to tell what kernel version you are working with. The first few lines of the top-level *makefile*[4] in a kernel source tree detail the exact kernel version represented by a given instance. It looks like this for the 2.6.30 kernel release:

```
VERSION = 2
PATCHLEVEL = 6
SUBLEVEL = 30
EXTRAVERSION =
NAME=Man-Eating Seals of Antiquity
```

Later in the same makefile, these macros are used to form a version-level macro, like this:

```
KERNELVERSION=$(VERSION).$(PATCHLEVEL).$(SUBLEVEL)$(EXTRAVERSION)
```

This macro is used in several places in the kernel build system to indicate the kernel version. Its use has diminished in more recent kernels to a few locations in the scripts directory. It has been replaced by a more complete descriptive string called KERNELRELEASE. This string contains the kernel version as well as a tag that correlates to a source control revision level that comes from git, the source control system adopted for Linux.

---

[4] We'll talk about the kernel build system and makefiles shortly.

KERNELRELEASE is used in several places within the kernel source tree. This macro is also built into the kernel image so that it can be queried from the console. You can check the kernel release string from a command prompt on a running Linux system like this:

```
$ cat /proc/version
Linux version 2.6.13 (chris@pluto) (gcc version 4.0.0 (DENX ELDK 4.0
4.0.0)) #2 Thu Feb 16 19:30:13 EST 2006
```

One final note about kernel versions: You can make it easy to keep track of the kernel version in your own kernel project by customizing the EXTRAVERSION field. For example, if you are developing enhancements for some new kernel feature, you might set EXTRAVERSION to something like this:

```
EXTRAVERSION=-foo
```

Later, when you use cat /proc/version, you would see Linux version 2.6.13-foo, and this would help you distinguish between development versions of your own kernel.

4.1.2 Kernel Source Repositories

The official home of the Linux kernel source code is www.kernel.org. There you can find both current and historical versions of the Linux kernel, as well as numerous patches. The primary FTP repository, found at ftp.kernel.org, contains subdirectories going all the way back to Linux version 1.0. kernel.org is the primary focus of the on-going development activities within the Linux kernel.

If you download a recent Linux kernel from kernel.org, you will find files in the source tree for over 20 different architectures and subarchitectures. Several other development trees support the major architectures. One of the reasons is simply the sheer volume of developers and changes to the kernel. If every developer on every architecture submitted patches to a single source tree, the maintainers would be inundated with changes and patch management and would never get to do any feature development. As anyone involved with kernel development will tell you, it's already very busy!

Several other public source trees exist outside the mainline kernel.org source, mostly for architecture-specific development. For example, a developer working on the MIPS architecture might find a suitable kernel at www.linux-mips.org. Normally, work done in an architecture tree is eventually submitted to the mainline kernel maintainers. Most architecture developers try to sync with the mainline kernel often, to keep up with new developments whenever possible. However, it is not always straightforward to get one's patches included in the mainline kernel. Indeed, there will always be differences between architecture kernel trees and mainline at any given point in time.

If you are wondering how to find a kernel for your particular application, the best way to proceed is to obtain the latest stable Linux source tree. Check to see if support for your particular processor exists, and then search the Linux kernel mailing lists for any patches or issues related to your application. Also find the mailing list that most closely matches your interest, and search that archive as well.

Appendix E, "Open Source Resources," contains several good references and sources of information related to kernel source repositories, mailing lists, and more.

4.1.3   Using `git` to Download a Kernel

The simplest way to download the latest Linux kernel is to use `git`. This utility has become the tool of choice for source control management in the Linux kernel community. The repositories of most modern desktop distributions contain a version of `git`. For example, on Ubuntu,[5] enter the following command to install `git` on your desktop or laptop PC:

```
$ sudo apt-get install git-core⁶
```

After `git` has been properly installed on your system, you can use the `git clone` command to *clone* a `git` source tree:

```
$ git clone
git://git.kernel.org/pub/scm/linux/kernel/git/torvalds/linux-2.6.git linux-2.6
```

This results in a new directory beneath the current directory where this command was entered, named `linux-2.6`. It contains the *cloned* tree from kernel.org. Many good tutorials and web pages are devoted to learning `git`. You might start with this tutorial on Jeff Garzik's website: http://linux.yyz.us/git-howto.html.

4.2   Linux Kernel Construction

The next few sections explore the layout, organization, and construction of the Linux kernel. Armed with this knowledge, you will find it much easier to navigate this large,

---

[5] Consult the documentation for your Linux distribution for how to install `git` on your system.

[6] Note that your distribution might call it something different. Unfortunately, the name `git` conflicts with another package of the same name, the GNU Interactive Tools!

complex source code base. Over time, significant improvements have been made to the organization of the source tree, especially in the architecture branch, which contains support for numerous architectures and machine types.

4.2.1 Top-Level Source Directory

This book often refers to the top-level source directory. In every case, we are referring to the highest-level directory contained in the kernel source tree. On any given machine, it might be located anywhere, but on a desktop Linux workstation, it is often found in `/usr/src/linux-x.y.z`, where `x.y.z` represents the kernel version. Throughout the book, we use the shorthand `.../` to represent the top-level kernel source directory.

The top-level kernel source directory contains the following subdirectories. (We have omitted the nondirectory entries in this listing, as well as directories used for source control, for clarity and brevity.)

```
arch/           firmware/   kernel/   scripts/
block/          fs/         lib/      security/
crypto/         include/    mm/       sound/
Documentation/  init/       net/      usr/
drivers/        ipc/        samples/  virt/
```

Many of these directories contain several additional levels of subdirectories containing source code, makefiles, and configuration files. By far the largest branch of the Linux kernel source tree is found under `.../drivers`. Here you can find support for the various Ethernet network cards, USB controllers, and the numerous hardware devices that the Linux kernel supports. As you might imagine, the `.../arch` subdirectory is the next largest, containing support for more than 20 unique processor architectures.

Additional files found in the top-level Linux subdirectory include the top-level makefile, a hidden configuration file (*dot-config*, introduced in Section 4.3.1, "The Dot-Config"), and various other informational files not involved in the build itself. Finally, two important build targets are found in the top-level kernel source tree after a successful build: `System.map` and the kernel proper, `vmlinux`. Both are described in the next section.

4.2.2 Compiling the Kernel

Understanding a large body of software such as Linux can be a daunting task. It is too large to simply "step through" the code to follow what is happening. Multithreading and preemption add to the complexity of analysis. In fact, even locating the entry point (the first line of code to be executed upon entry to the kernel) can be challenging. One of the more useful ways to understand the structure of a large binary image is to examine its build components.

The output of the kernel build system produces several common files, as well as one or more architecture-specific binary modules. Common files are always built regardless of the architecture. Two of the common files are System.map and vmlinux. The former is useful during kernel debug and is particularly interesting. It contains a human-readable list of the kernel symbols and their respective addresses. The latter is an architecture-specific *ELF*[7] file in executable format. It is produced by the top-level kernel makefile for every architecture. If the kernel was compiled with symbolic debug information, it will be contained in the vmlinux image. In practice, although it is an ELF executable, this file is virtually *never* booted directly, as you will see shortly.

Listing 4-1 is a snippet of output resulting from executing make in a recent kernel tree configured for the ARM XScale architecture. The kernel source tree was configured for the ADI Engineering Coyote reference board based on the Intel IXP425 network processor using the following command:

```
$ make ARCH=arm CROSS_COMPILE=xscale_be- ixp4xx_defconfig
```

This command does not build the kernel; it prepares the kernel source tree for the XScale architecture, including an initial default configuration for this architecture and processor. It builds a default configuration (the dot-config file) that drives the kernel build, based on the defaults found in the ixp4xx_defconfig file. We have more to say about the configuration process in Section 4.3, "Kernel Build System."

In Listing 4-1, only the first few and last few lines of the build output are shown for this discussion.

LISTING 4-1   Kernel Build Output

```
$ make ARCH=arm CROSS_COMPILE=xscale_be- zImage
  CHK     include/linux/version.h
  UPD     include/linux/version.h
  Generating include/asm-arm/mach-types.h
  CHK     include/linux/utsrelease.h
  UPD     include/linux/utsrelease.h
  SYMLINK include/asm -> include/asm-arm
```

---

[7] Executable and Linking Format, a de facto standard format for binary executable files.

LISTING 4-1 Continued

```
CC      kernel/bounds.s
GEN     include/linux/bounds.h
CC      arch/arm/kernel/asm-offsets.s
.
. <hundreds of lines of output omitted here>
.
LD      vmlinux
SYSMAP  System.map
SYSMAP  .tmp_System.map
OBJCOPY arch/arm/boot/Image
Kernel: arch/arm/boot/Image is ready
AS      arch/arm/boot/compressed/head.o
GZIP    arch/arm/boot/compressed/piggy.gz
AS      arch/arm/boot/compressed/piggy.o
CC      arch/arm/boot/compressed/misc.o
AS      arch/arm/boot/compressed/head-xscale.o
AS      arch/arm/boot/compressed/big-endian.o
LD      arch/arm/boot/compressed/vmlinux
OBJCOPY arch/arm/boot/zImage
Kernel: arch/arm/boot/zImage is ready

...
```

To begin, notice the invocation of the build. Both the desired architecture (ARCH=arm) and the toolchain[8] (CROSS_COMPILE=xscale_be-) are specified on the command line. This forces the make utility to use the XScale toolchain[9] to build the kernel image and to use the arm-specific branch of the kernel source tree for architecture-dependent portions of the build. We also specify a target called zImage. This target is common to many architectures and is described in Chapter 5, "Kernel Initialization." Modern kernels today build the proper default targets without specifying the make target, so you might not need to specify zImage or any other targets.

The next thing you might notice is that the actual commands used for each step have been hidden and replaced with a shorthand notation. The motivation behind this was to clean up the build output to draw more attention to intermediate build issues, particularly compiler warnings. In earlier kernel source trees, each compilation or link command was output to the console verbosely, which often required several lines for

---

[8] Of course, your toolchain prefix might be different.

[9] Actually, this simply prepends the value of CROSS_COMPILE to CC, LD, AR, and so on in the makefiles.

each step. The end result was virtually unreadable, and compiler warnings slipped by unnoticed in the noise. The new system is definitely an improvement, because any anomaly in the build process is easily spotted. If you want or need to see the complete build step, you can force verbose output by defining V=1 on the make command line:

```
$ make ARCH=arm CROSS_COMPILE=xscale_be- V=1 zImage
```

We have omitted most of the actual compilation and link steps in Listing 4-1 for clarity. (This particular build contained more than 1,000 individual compile, link, and other commands. That would have made for a long listing indeed.) After all the intermediate files and library archives have been built and compiled, they are put together in one large ELF build target called vmlinux. Although it is architecture-specific, vmlinux is a common target. It is produced for all supported Linux architectures, and it lands in the top-level kernel source directory for easy reference.

4.2.3   The Kernel Proper: vmlinux

Notice this line in Listing 4-1:

```
LD vmlinux
```

The vmlinux file is the actual *kernel proper*. It is a fully stand-alone, monolithic ELF image. That is, the vmlinux binary contains no unresolved external references.. When caused to execute in the proper context (by a bootloader designed to boot the Linux kernel), it boots the board on which it is running, leaving a completely functional kernel. (Actually, this vmlinux ELF target is rarely used directly. It is almost always used in compressed form, which is produced from the final steps shown in Listing 4-1. We will have much more to say about this soon.)

In keeping with the philosophy that to understand a system you must first understand its parts, let's look at the construction of the vmlinux kernel object. Listing 4-2 reproduces the actual link stage of the build process that resulted in the vmlinux ELF object. We have formatted it with line breaks (indicated by the UNIX line-continuation character, \) to make it more readable, but otherwise it is the exact output produced by the vmlinux link step in the build process from Listing 4-1. If you were building the kernel by hand, this is the link command you would issue from the command line.

LISTING 4-2   Link Stage: `vmlinux`

```
$ xscale_be-ld -EB  -p --no-undefined -X  -o vmlinux \
-T arch/arm/kernel/vmlinux.lds     \
arch/arm/kernel/head.o             \
arch/arm/kernel/init_task.o        \
init/built-in.o                    \
--start-group                      \
  usr/built-in.o                   \
  arch/arm/kernel/built-in.o       \
  arch/arm/mm/built-in.o           \
  arch/arm/common/built-in.o       \
  arch/arm/mach-ixp4xx/built-in.o \
  arch/arm/nwfpe/built-in.o        \
  kernel/built-in.o                \
  mm/built-in.o                    \
  fs/built-in.o                    \
  ipc/built-in.o                   \
  security/built-in.o              \
  crypto/built-in.o                \
  block/built-in.o                 \
  arch/arm/lib/lib.a               \
  lib/lib.a                        \
  arch/arm/lib/built-in.o          \
  lib/built-in.o                   \
  drivers/built-in.o               \
  sound/built-in.o                 \
  firmware/built-in.o              \
  net/built-in.o                   \
--end-group                        \
.tmp_kallsyms2.o
```

4.2.4   Kernel Image Components

From Listing 4-2, you can see that the `vmlinux` image consists of several composite binary images. Right now, it is not important to understand the purpose of each component. What is important is to understand the top-level view of what components make up the kernel. The first line of the link command in Listing 4-2 specifies the output file (`-o vmlinux`). The second line specifies the *linker script* file (`-T vmlinux.lds`), a detailed recipe for how the kernel binary image should be linked.[10]

---

[10] The linker script file has a peculiar syntax. The details can be found in the documentation for the GNU linker.

The third and subsequent lines in Listing 4-2 specify the object modules that form the resulting binary image. Notice that the first object specified is `head.o`. This object was assembled from `.../arch/arm/kernel/head.S`, an architecture-specific assembly language source file that performs very low-level kernel initialization. If you were searching for the first line of code to be executed by the kernel, it would make sense to start your search here, because it will ultimately be the first code found in the binary image created by this link stage. We examine kernel initialization in detail in Chapter 5.

The next object, `init_task.o`, sets up initial thread and task structures that the kernel requires. Following this is a large collection of object modules, each having a common name: `built-in.o`. You will notice, however, that each `built-in.o` object comes from a specific part of the kernel source tree, as indicated by the path component preceding the `built-in.o` object name. These are the binary objects that are included in the kernel image. An illustration might help make this more clear.

Figure 4-1 illustrates the binary makeup of the `vmlinux` image. It contains a section for each line of the link stage. It is not to scale because of space considerations, but you can see the relative sizes of each functional component. Some components are tiny. For example, sound and firmware are each 8 bytes in this build, because they are empty object files. (Sound is compiled as modules, and this build has no firmware.)

It might come as no surprise that the three largest binary components are the file system code, network code, and all the built-in drivers. If you take the kernel code and the architecture-specific kernel code together, this is the next-largest binary component. Here you find the scheduler, process and thread management, timer management, and other core kernel functionality. Naturally, the kernel contains some architecture-specific functionality, such as low-level context switching, hardware-level interrupt and timer processing, processor exception handling, and more. This is found in `.../arch/arm/kernel`.

Bear in mind that we are looking at a specific example of a kernel build. In this particular example, we are building a kernel specific to the ARM XScale architecture and, more specifically, the Intel IXP425 network processor on the ADI Engineering reference board. You can see the machine-specific binary components in Figure 4-1 as `arch/arm/mach-ixp4xx`. Each architecture and machine type (processor/reference board) has different elements in the architecture-specific portions of the kernel, so the makeup of the `vmlinux` image is slightly different. When you understand one example, you will find it easy to navigate others.

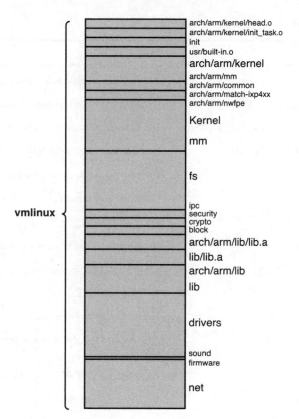

FIGURE 4-1 vmlinux image components

To help you understand the breakdown of functionality in the kernel source tree, Table 4-1 lists each component in Figure 4-1 and describes each binary element that makes up the vmlinux image.

TABLE 4-1 vmlinux **Image Components**

Component	Description
arch/arm/kernel/head.o	Kernel-architecture-specific startup code.
arch/arm/kernel/init_task.o	Initial thread and task structs required by the kernel.
init/built-in.o	Main kernel initialization code. See Chapter 5.
usr/built-in.o	Built-in initramfs image. See Chapter 6.
arch/arm/kernel/built-in.o	Architecture-specific kernel code.

TABLE 4-1   Continued

Component	Description
`arch/arm/mm/built-in.o`	Architecture-specific memory-management code.
`arch/arm/common/built-in.o`	Architecture-specific generic code. Varies by architecture.
`arch/arm/mach-ixp4xx/built-in.o`	Machine-specific code, usually initialization.
`arch/arm/nwfpe/built-in.o`	Architecture-specific floating-point emulation code.
`kernel/built-in.o`	Common components of the kernel itself.
`mm/built-in.o`	Common components of memory-management code.
`fs/built-in.o`	File system code.
`ipc/built-in.o`	Interprocess communications, such as SysV IPC.
`security/built-in.o`	Linux security components.
`crypto/built-in.o`	Cryptographic API.
`block/built-in.o`	Kernel block layer core code.
`arch/arm/lib/lib.a`	Architecture-specific common facilities. Varies by architecture.
`lib/lib.a`	Common kernel helper functions.
`arch/arm/lib/built-in.o`	Architecture-specific helper routines.
`lib/built-in.o`	Common library functions.
`drivers/built-in.o`	All the built-in drivers. Does not include loadable modules.
`sound/built-in.o`	Sound drivers.
`firmware/built-in.o`	Driver firmware objects.
`net/built-in.o`	Linux networking.
`.tmp_kallsyms2.o`	Kernel Symbol table.

When we speak of the kernel proper, this `vmlinux` image (found at the top-level kernel directory) is being referenced. As mentioned earlier, very few platforms boot this image directly. For one thing, the image that we use to boot is almost universally compressed. At a bare minimum, a bootloader must decompress the image. Many platforms require some type of stub bolted onto the image to perform the decompression. In Chapter 5, you will learn how this image is packaged for different architectures, machine types, and bootloaders, and the requirements for booting it.

4.2.5   Subdirectory Layout

Now that you've seen the components that make up the kernel image, let's take a look at a representative kernel subdirectory. Listing 4-3 details the contents of the `mach-ixp4xx` subdirectory. This directory exists under the `.../arch/arm` architecture-specific branch of the source tree.

LISTING 4-3   Kernel Subdirectory

```
$ ls -l ./arch/arm/mach-ixp4xx
total 204
-rw-r--r-- 1 chris chris  1817 2009-11-19 17:12 avila-pci.c
-rw-r--r-- 1 chris chris  4610 2009-11-19 17:12 avila-setup.c
-rw-r--r-- 1 chris chris 11812 2009-11-19 17:12 common.c
-rw-r--r-- 1 chris chris 12979 2009-11-19 17:12 common-pci.c
-rw-r--r-- 1 chris chris  1459 2009-11-19 17:12 coyote-pci.c
-rw-r--r-- 1 chris chris  3158 2009-11-19 17:12 coyote-setup.c
-rw-r--r-- 1 chris chris  1898 2009-11-19 17:12 dsmg600-pci.c
-rw-r--r-- 1 chris chris  7030 2009-11-19 17:12 dsmg600-setup.c
-rw-r--r-- 1 chris chris  1625 2009-11-19 17:12 fsg-pci.c
-rw-r--r-- 1 chris chris  6622 2009-11-19 17:12 fsg-setup.c
-rw-r--r-- 1 chris chris  1490 2009-11-19 17:12 gateway7001-pci.c
-rw-r--r-- 1 chris chris  2646 2009-11-19 17:12 gateway7001-setup.c
-rw-r--r-- 1 chris chris 12280 2009-11-19 17:12 goramo_mlr.c
-rw-r--r-- 1 chris chris  2623 2009-11-19 17:12 gtwx5715-pci.c
-rw-r--r-- 1 chris chris  3935 2009-11-19 17:12 gtwx5715-setup.c
drwxr-xr-x 3 chris chris  4096 2009-11-19 17:12 include
-rw-r--r-- 1 chris chris  1794 2009-11-19 17:12 ixdp425-pci.c
-rw-r--r-- 1 chris chris  7430 2009-11-19 17:12 ixdp425-setup.c
-rw-r--r-- 1 chris chris  1354 2009-11-19 17:12 ixdpg425-pci.c
-rw-r--r-- 1 chris chris 21560 2009-11-19 17:12 ixp4xx_npe.c
-rw-r--r-- 1 chris chris  9350 2009-11-19 17:12 ixp4xx_qmgr.c
-rw-r--r-- 1 chris chris  6422 2009-11-19 17:12 Kconfig
-rw-r--r-- 1 chris chris  1319 2009-11-19 17:12 Makefile
-rw-r--r-- 1 chris chris    57 2009-11-19 17:12 Makefile.boot
-rw-r--r-- 1 chris chris  1751 2009-11-19 17:12 nas100d-pci.c
-rw-r--r-- 1 chris chris  7764 2009-11-19 17:12 nas100d-setup.c
-rw-r--r-- 1 chris chris  1561 2009-11-19 17:12 nslu2-pci.c
-rw-r--r-- 1 chris chris  6732 2009-11-19 17:12 nslu2-setup.c
-rw-r--r-- 1 chris chris  1468 2009-11-19 17:12 wg302v2-pci.c
-rw-r--r-- 1 chris chris  2585 2009-11-19 17:12 wg302v2-setup.c
```

The directory contents shown in Listing 4-3 have common components found in many kernel source subdirectories: `Makefile` and `Kconfig`. These two files drive the kernel configuration and build process. Let's look at how that works.

4.3   Kernel Build System

The Linux kernel configuration and build system is rather complicated, as you would expect of software projects containing more than 10 million lines of code! This section covers the foundation of the kernel build system in case you need to customize your build environment.

A recent Linux kernel snapshot showed more than 1,200 makefiles[11] in the kernel source tree. (The first edition of this book reported only 800 makefiles. This is a 50% increase from the days of Linux 2.6.10!) This might sound like a rather large number, but it might not seem so big when you understand the structure and operation of the build system. The Linux kernel build system has been significantly updated since the days of Linux 2.4 and earlier. If you're familiar with the older kernel build system, we're sure you'll find the new Kbuild system to be a huge improvement.

4.3.1   The Dot-Config

Introduced earlier, the dot-config file is the configuration blueprint for building a Linux kernel image. You will likely spend significant effort at the start of your Linux project building a configuration that is appropriate for your embedded platform. Several editors, both text-based and graphical, are designed to edit your kernel configuration. The output of this configuration exercise is written to a configuration file named `.config`, located in the top-level Linux source directory that drives the kernel build.

You have likely invested a significant amount of time in perfecting your kernel configuration, so you will want to protect it. Several `make` commands delete this configuration file without warning. The most common is `make distclean`. This `make` target is designed to return the kernel source tree to its pristine, unconfigured state. This includes removing all configuration data from the source tree—and, yes, it deletes your preexisting `.config`.

As you might know, any filename in a Linux file system preceded by a dot is a hidden file in Linux. It is unfortunate that such an important file is marked as hidden; this has brought considerable grief to more than one developer. If you execute `make distclean` or `make mrproper` without having a backup copy of your `.config` file, you too will share our grief. (You have been warned—back up your `.config` file!)

---

[11] Not all these makefiles are directly involved in building the kernel. Some, for example, build documentation files.

The .config file is a collection of definitions with a simple format. Listing 4-4 shows a snippet of a .config from a recent Linux kernel release.

LISTING 4-4   Snippet from Linux 2.6 .config

```
...
# USB support
#
CONFIG_USB=m
# CONFIG_USB_DEBUG is not set

# Miscellaneous USB options
#
CONFIG_USB_DEVICEFS=y
# CONFIG_USB_BANDWIDTH is not set
# CONFIG_USB_DYNAMIC_MINORS is not set

# USB Host Controller Drivers
#
CONFIG_USB_EHCI_HCD=m
# CONFIG_USB_EHCI_SPLIT_ISO is not set
# CONFIG_USB_EHCI_ROOT_HUB_TT is not set
CONFIG_USB_OHCI_HCD=m
CONFIG_USB_UHCI_HCD=m
...
```

To understand the .config file, you need to understand a fundamental aspect of the Linux kernel. Linux has a monolithic structure. In other words, the entire kernel is compiled and linked as a single statically linked executable. However, it is possible to compile and *incrementally link*[12] a set of sources into a single object module suitable for dynamic insertion into a running kernel. This is the usual method for supporting most common device drivers. In Linux, these are called *loadable modules*. They are also generically called device drivers. After the kernel is booted, a special application program is invoked to insert the loadable module into a running kernel.

Armed with that knowledge, let's look again at Listing 4-4. This snippet of the configuration file (.config) shows a portion of the USB subsystem configuration. The first configuration option, CONFIG_USB=m, declares that the USB subsystem is to be

---

[12] Incremental linking is a technique used to generate an object module that is intended to be linked again into another object. In this way, unresolved symbols that remain after incremental linking do not generate errors—they are resolved at the next link stage.

included in this kernel configuration and that it will be compiled as a *dynamically loadable module* (=m), to be loaded sometime after the kernel has booted. The other choice would have been =y, in which case the USB module would be compiled and statically linked as part of the kernel image itself. It would end up in the .../drivers/built-in.o composite binary that you saw in Listing 4-2 and Figure 4-1. The astute reader will realize that if a driver is configured as a loadable module, its code is not included in the kernel proper, but rather exists as a stand-alone object module, a *loadable module*, to be inserted into the running kernel after boot.

Notice in Listing 4-4 the CONFIG_USB_DEVICEFS=y declaration. This configuration option behaves in a slightly different manner. In this case, USB_DEVICEFS (as configuration options are commonly abbreviated) is not a stand-alone module, but rather a feature to be enabled or disabled in the USB driver. It does not necessarily result in a module that is compiled into the kernel proper (=y). Instead, it enables one or more features, often represented as additional object modules to be included in the overall USB device driver module. Usually, the help text in the configuration editor, or the hierarchy presented by the configuration editor, makes this distinction clear.

4.3.2   Configuration Editor(s)

Early kernels used a simple command-line-driven script to configure the kernel. This was cumbersome even for early kernels, in which the number of configuration parameters was much smaller. This command-line-style interface is still supported, but using it is tedious, to say the least. A typical configuration from a recent kernel requires you to answer more than 900 questions from the command line. You enter your choice and then press Enter for each query in the script. Furthermore, if you make a mistake, there is no way to back up; you must start from the beginning. That can be profoundly frustrating if you make a mistake on the 899th entry!

In some situations, such as building a kernel on an embedded system without graphics, using the command-line configuration utility may be unavoidable, but this author would go to great lengths to find a way around it.

The kernel configuration subsystem has several configuration targets. In fact, a recent Linux kernel release included 11 such configuration targets. They are summarized here, from text taken from the output of make help:

- config—Update current config using a line-oriented program
- menuconfig—Update current config using a menu-based program
- xconfig—Update current config using a QT-based front end

- gconfig—Update current config using a GTK-based front end
- oldconfig—Update current config using a provided .config as the base
- silentoldconfig—Same as oldconfig but silently
- randconfig—New config with random answer to all options
- defconfig—New config with default answer to all options
- allmodconfig—New config that selects modules, when possible
- allyesconfig—New config in which all options are accepted with yes
- allnoconfig—New minimal config

The first four of these makefile configuration targets invoke a form of configuration editor, as described in the list. Because of space considerations, we focus our discussion in this chapter and the rest of this book only on the GTK-based graphical front end. Realize that you can use the configuration editor of your choice with the same results.

You invoke the configuration editor by entering the command make gconfig from the top-level kernel directory.[13] Figure 4-2 shows the top-level configuration menu presented to the developer when gconfig is run. From here, you can access every available configuration parameter to generate a custom kernel configuration.

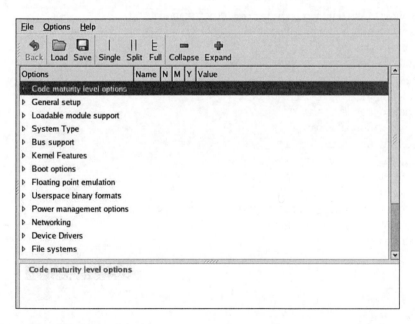

FIGURE 4-2   Top-level kernel configuration

---

[13] As mentioned, you can use the configuration editor of your choice, such as make xconfig or make menuconfig.

When you exit the configuration editor, you are prompted to save your changes. If you elect to save your changes, the global configuration file .config is updated (or created, if it does not already exist). This .config file, introduced earlier, drives the kernel build via the top-level makefile.

Most kernel software modules also read the configuration indirectly via the .config file as follows. During the build process, the .config file is processed into a C header file found in the .../include/linux directory, called autoconf.h. This file is generated automatically. You should never edit it directly, because edits are lost each time a configuration is changed and a new build is started. Many kernel source files include this file directly using the #include preprocessor directive. Listing 4-5 reproduces a section of this header file related to USB support. The kernel build files include this autoconf.h file into every kernel compile command line, using the -include gcc directive as follows:

```
gcc ... -include include/linux/autoconf.h ... <somefile.c>
```

This is how the kernel config is accessed by various kernel modules.

LISTING 4-5   Linux autoconf.h

```
$ cat include/linux/autoconf.h | grep CONFIG_USB
#define CONFIG_USB_ARCH_HAS_EHCI 1
#define CONFIG_USB_HID 1
#define CONFIG_USB_EHCI_BIG_ENDIAN_DESC 1
#define CONFIG_USB_ARCH_HAS_OHCI 1
#define CONFIG_USB_EHCI_BIG_ENDIAN_MMIO 1
#define CONFIG_USB_STORAGE 1
#define CONFIG_USB_SUPPORT 1
#define CONFIG_USB_EHCI_HCD 1
#define CONFIG_USB_DEVICEFS 1
#define CONFIG_USB_OHCI_HCD 1
#define CONFIG_USB_UHCI_HCD 1
#define CONFIG_USB_OHCI_LITTLE_ENDIAN 1
#define CONFIG_USB_ARCH_HAS_HCD 1
#define CONFIG_USB 1
```

If you haven't already done so, execute `make gconfig` in your top-level kernel source directory, and poke around this configuration utility to see the large number of subsections and configuration options available to the Linux developer. As long as you don't explicitly save your changes, they will be lost when you exit the configuration editor, so you can safely explore without modifying your kernel configuration.[14] Many configuration parameters contain helpful explanatory text, which can add to your understanding of the various configuration options.

4.3.3 Makefile Targets

If you type `make help` at the top-level Linux source directory, you are presented with a list of targets that can be generated from the source tree. The most common use of `make` is to specify no target. This generates the kernel ELF file `vmlinux` and the default binary image for your chosen architecture (for example, `bzImage` for x86). Specifying `make` with no target also builds all the device driver modules (kernel loadable modules) specified by the configuration.

Many architectures and machine types require binary targets specific to the architecture and bootloader in use. One of the more common architecture-specific targets is `zImage`. In many architectures, this is the default target image that can be loaded and run on the target embedded system. One of the common mistakes that newcomers make is to specify `bzImage` as the `make` target. The `bzImage` target is specific to the x86/PC architecture. Contrary to popular myth, the `bzImage` is not a `bzip2`-compressed image. It is a big `zImage`. Without going into the details of legacy PC architecture, it is enough for you to know that a `bzImage` is suitable only for PC-compatible machines with an industry-standard PC-style BIOS.

Listing 4-6 contains the output from `make help` from a recent Linux kernel. You can see from the listing that many targets are available. Each is listed, along with a short description of its use. It is important to realize that even the `help make` target (as in `make help`) is architecture-specific. You get a different list of architecture-specific targets depending on the architecture you specify on the `make` invocation. Listing 4-6 illustrates an invocation that specifies the ARM architecture, as you can see from the command line.

---

[14] Better yet, make a backup copy of your `.config` file.

LISTING 4-6   Makefile Targets

```
$ make ARCH=arm help
Cleaning targets:
  clean           - Remove most generated files but keep the config and
                      enough build support to build external modules
  mrproper        - Remove all generated files + config + various backup files
  distclean       - mrproper + remove editor backup and patch files

Configuration targets:
  config          - Update current config utilising a line-oriented program
  menuconfig      - Update current config utilising a menu based program
  xconfig         - Update current config utilising a QT based front-end
  gconfig         - Update current config utilising a GTK based front-end
  oldconfig       - Update current config utilising a provided .config as base
  silentoldconfig - Same as oldconfig, but quietly
  randconfig      - New config with random answer to all options
  defconfig       - New config with default answer to all options
  allmodconfig    - New config selecting modules when possible
  allyesconfig    - New config where all options are accepted with yes
  allnoconfig     - New config where all options are answered with no

Other generic targets:
  all             - Build all targets marked with [*]
* vmlinux         - Build the bare kernel
* modules         - Build all modules
  modules_install - Install all modules to INSTALL_MOD_PATH (default: /)
  firmware_install- Install all firmware to INSTALL_FW_PATH
                      (default: $(INSTALL_MOD_PATH)/lib/firmware)
  dir/            - Build all files in dir and below
  dir/file.[ois]  - Build specified target only
  dir/file.ko     - Build module including final link
  modules_prepare - Set up for building external modules
  tags/TAGS       - Generate tags file for editors
  cscope          - Generate cscope index
  kernelrelease   - Output the release version string
  kernelversion   - Output the version stored in Makefile
  headers_install - Install sanitised kernel headers to INSTALL_HDR_PATH
                      (default: /home/chris/temp/linux-2.6/usr)

Static analysers
  checkstack      - Generate a list of stack hogs
  namespacecheck  - Name space analysis on compiled kernel
  versioncheck    - Sanity check on version.h usage
```

LISTING 4-6   Continued

```
   includecheck     - Check for duplicate included header files
   export_report    - List the usages of all exported symbols
   headers_check    - Sanity check on exported headers
   headerdep        - Detect inclusion cycles in headers

Kernel packaging:
  rpm-pkg           - Build both source and binary RPM kernel packages
  binrpm-pkg        - Build only the binary kernel package
  deb-pkg           - Build the kernel as an deb package
  tar-pkg           - Build the kernel as an uncompressed tarball
  targz-pkg         - Build the kernel as a gzip compressed tarball
  tarbz2-pkg        - Build the kernel as a bzip2 compressed tarball

Documentation targets:
 Linux kernel internal documentation in different formats:
  htmldocs          - HTML
  pdfdocs           - PDF
  psdocs            - Postscript
  xmldocs           - XML DocBook
  mandocs           - man pages
  installmandocs    - install man pages generated by mandocs
  cleandocs         - clean all generated DocBook files

Architecture specific targets (arm):
* zImage            - Compressed kernel image (arch/arm/boot/zImage)
  Image             - Uncompressed kernel image (arch/arm/boot/Image)
* xipImage          - XIP kernel image, if configured (arch/arm/boot/xipImage)
  uImage            - U-Boot wrapped zImage
  bootpImage        - Combined zImage and initial RAM disk
                      (supply initrd image via make variable INITRD=<path>)
  install           - Install uncompressed kernel
  zinstall          - Install compressed kernel
                      Install using (your) ~/bin/installkernel or
                      (distribution) /sbin/installkernel or
                      install to $(INSTALL_PATH) and run lilo

  acs5k_defconfig        - Build for acs5k
  acs5k_tiny_defconfig   - Build for acs5k_tiny
  afeb9260_defconfig     - Build for afeb9260
  am200epdkit_defconfig  - Build for am200epdkit
  ams_delta_defconfig    - Build for ams_delta
  assabet_defconfig      - Build for assabet
```

LISTING 4-6   Continued

```
at91cap9adk_defconfig      - Build for at91cap9adk
at91rm9200dk_defconfig     - Build for at91rm9200dk
at91rm9200ek_defconfig     - Build for at91rm9200ek
at91sam9260ek_defconfig    - Build for at91sam9260ek
at91sam9261ek_defconfig    - Build for at91sam9261ek
at91sam9263ek_defconfig    - Build for at91sam9263ek
at91sam9g20ek_defconfig    - Build for at91sam9g20ek
at91sam9rlek_defconfig     - Build for at91sam9rlek
ateb9200_defconfig         - Build for ateb9200
badge4_defconfig           - Build for badge4
cam60_defconfig            - Build for cam60
carmeva_defconfig          - Build for carmeva
cerfcube_defconfig         - Build for cerfcube
cm_x2xx_defconfig          - Build for cm_x2xx
cm_x300_defconfig          - Build for cm_x300
colibri_pxa270_defconfig   - Build for colibri_pxa270
colibri_pxa300_defconfig   - Build for colibri_pxa300
collie_defconfig           - Build for collie
corgi_defconfig            - Build for corgi
csb337_defconfig           - Build for csb337
csb637_defconfig           - Build for csb637
davinci_all_defconfig      - Build for davinci_all
ebsa110_defconfig          - Build for ebsa110
ecbat91_defconfig          - Build for ecbat91
edb7211_defconfig          - Build for edb7211
em_x270_defconfig          - Build for em_x270
ep93xx_defconfig           - Build for ep93xx
eseries_pxa_defconfig      - Build for eseries_pxa
ezx_defconfig              - Build for ezx
footbridge_defconfig       - Build for footbridge
fortunet_defconfig         - Build for fortunet
h3600_defconfig            - Build for h3600
h5000_defconfig            - Build for h5000
h7201_defconfig            - Build for h7201
h7202_defconfig            - Build for h7202
hackkit_defconfig          - Build for hackkit
integrator_defconfig       - Build for integrator
iop13xx_defconfig          - Build for iop13xx
iop32x_defconfig           - Build for iop32x
iop33x_defconfig           - Build for iop33x
ixp2000_defconfig          - Build for ixp2000
ixp23xx_defconfig          - Build for ixp23xx
```

LISTING 4-6 **Continued**

```
ixp4xx_defconfig             - Build for ixp4xx
jornada720_defconfig         - Build for jornada720
kafa_defconfig               - Build for kafa
kb9202_defconfig             - Build for kb9202
kirkwood_defconfig           - Build for kirkwood
ks8695_defconfig             - Build for ks8695
lart_defconfig               - Build for lart
littleton_defconfig          - Build for littleton
loki_defconfig               - Build for loki
lpd270_defconfig             - Build for lpd270
lpd7a400_defconfig           - Build for lpd7a400
lpd7a404_defconfig           - Build for lpd7a404
lubbock_defconfig            - Build for lubbock
lusl7200_defconfig           - Build for lusl7200
magician_defconfig           - Build for magician
mainstone_defconfig          - Build for mainstone
msm_defconfig                - Build for msm
mv78xx0_defconfig            - Build for mv78xx0
mx1ads_defconfig             - Build for mx1ads
mx1_defconfig                - Build for mx1
mx27_defconfig               - Build for mx27
mx31pdk_defconfig            - Build for mx31pdk
mx3_defconfig                - Build for mx3
n770_defconfig               - Build for n770
neocore926_defconfig         - Build for neocore926
neponset_defconfig           - Build for neponset
netwinder_defconfig          - Build for netwinder
netx_defconfig               - Build for netx
ns9xxx_defconfig             - Build for ns9xxx
omap_2430sdp_defconfig       - Build for omap_2430sdp
omap_3430sdp_defconfig       - Build for omap_3430sdp
omap3_beagle_defconfig       - Build for omap3_beagle
omap3_pandora_defconfig      - Build for omap3_pandora
omap_apollon_2420_defconfig - Build for omap_apollon_2420
omap_generic_1510_defconfig - Build for omap_generic_1510
omap_generic_1610_defconfig - Build for omap_generic_1610
omap_generic_1710_defconfig - Build for omap_generic_1710
omap_generic_2420_defconfig - Build for omap_generic_2420
omap_h2_1610_defconfig       - Build for omap_h2_1610
omap_h4_2420_defconfig       - Build for omap_h4_2420
omap_innovator_1510_defconfig - Build for omap_innovator_1510
omap_innovator_1610_defconfig - Build for omap_innovator_1610
```

LISTING 4-6   Continued

```
omap_ldp_defconfig        - Build for omap_ldp
omap_osk_5912_defconfig   - Build for omap_osk_5912
omap_perseus2_730_defconfig - Build for omap_perseus2_730
onearm_defconfig          - Build for onearm
orion5x_defconfig         - Build for orion5x
overo_defconfig           - Build for overo
palmte_defconfig          - Build for palmte
palmtt_defconfig          - Build for palmtt
palmz71_defconfig         - Build for palmz71
palmz72_defconfig         - Build for palmz72
pcm027_defconfig          - Build for pcm027
picotux200_defconfig      - Build for picotux200
pleb_defconfig            - Build for pleb
pnx4008_defconfig         - Build for pnx4008
pxa168_defconfig          - Build for pxa168
pxa255-idp_defconfig      - Build for pxa255-idp
pxa910_defconfig          - Build for pxa910
qil-a9260_defconfig       - Build for qil-a9260
realview_defconfig        - Build for realview
realview-smp_defconfig    - Build for realview-smp
rpc_defconfig             - Build for rpc
rx51_defconfig            - Build for rx51
s3c2410_defconfig         - Build for s3c2410
s3c6400_defconfig         - Build for s3c6400
sam9_19260_defconfig      - Build for sam9_19260
shannon_defconfig         - Build for shannon
shark_defconfig           - Build for shark
simpad_defconfig          - Build for simpad
spitz_defconfig           - Build for spitz
sx1_defconfig             - Build for sx1
tct_hammer_defconfig      - Build for tct_hammer
trizeps4_defconfig        - Build for trizeps4
usb-a9260_defconfig       - Build for usb-a9260
usb-a9263_defconfig       - Build for usb-a9263
versatile_defconfig       - Build for versatile
viper_defconfig           - Build for viper
w90p910_defconfig         - Build for w90p910
y19200_defconfig          - Build for y19200
zylonite_defconfig        - Build for zylonite


make V=0|1 [targets] 0 => quiet build (default), 1 => verbose build
make V=2   [targets] 2 => give reason for rebuild of target
```

LISTING 4-6   Continued

```
make O=dir [targets] Locate all output files in "dir", including .config
make C=1   [targets] Check all c source with $CHECK (sparse by default)
make C=2   [targets] Force check of all c source with $CHECK

Execute "make" or "make all" to build all targets marked with [*]
For further info see the ./README file
```

Many of these targets you might never use. However, it is good to know that they exist. As you can see from Listing 4-6, the targets listed with an asterisk are built by default. Notice the numerous default configurations, listed as *_defconfig. Recall from Section 4.2.2, "Compiling the Kernel," the command we used to preconfigure a pristine kernel source tree: We invoked make with an architecture and a default configuration. The default configuration was ixp4xx_defconfig, which appears in this list of ARM targets. This is a good way to discover all the default configurations available for a particular kernel release and architecture.

4.4 Kernel Configuration

Kconfig (or a file with a similar root followed by an extension, such as Kconfig.ext) exists in almost 300 kernel subdirectories. Kconfig drives the configuration process for the features contained within its subdirectory. The contents of Kconfig are parsed by the configuration subsystem, which presents configuration choices to the user and contains help text associated with a given configuration parameter.

The configuration utility (such as gconf, presented earlier) reads the Kconfig files starting from the arch subdirectory's Kconfig file. It is invoked from the Kconfig makefile with an entry that looks like this:

```
ifdef KBUILD_KCONFIG
Kconfig := $(KBUILD_KCONFIG)
else
Kconfig := arch/$(SRCARCH)/Kconfig
endif
...
gconfig: $(obj)/gconf
        $< $(Kconfig)
```

Depending on which architecture you are building, gconf reads this architecture-specific Kconfig as the top-level configuration definition. Contained within Kconfig are a number of lines that look like this:

```
source  "drivers/pci/Kconfig"
```

This directive tells the configuration editor utility to read in another Kconfig file from another location within the kernel source tree. Each architecture contains many such Kconfig files; taken together, these determine the complete set of menu options presented to the user when configuring the kernel. Each Kconfig file is free to source additional Kconfig files in different parts of the source tree. The configuration utility—gconf, in this case—recursively reads the Kconfig file chain and builds the configuration menu structure.

Listing 4-7 is a partial tree view of the Kconfig files associated with the ARM architecture. In a recent Linux 2.6 source tree from which this example was taken, the kernel configuration was defined by 473 separate Kconfig files. This listing omits most of those for the sake of space and clarity; the idea is to show the overall structure. Listing them all in this tree view would take several pages.

LISTING 4-7   Partial Listing of Kconfig for ARM Architecture

```
arch/arm/Kconfig <<<<<< (top level Kconfig)
 |->  init/Kconfig
 |  ...
 |->  arch/arm/mach-iop3xx/Kconfig
 |->  arch/arm/mach-ixp4xx/Kconfig
 |     ...
 |->  net/Kconfig
 |    |-->  net/ipv4/Kconfig
 |    |     |-->  net/ipv4/ipvs/Kconfig
 |    ...
 |->  drivers/pci/Kconfig
 |    ...
 |->  drivers/usb/Kconfig
 |    |-->  drivers/usb/core/Kconfig
 |    |-->  drivers/usb/host/Kconfig
 | ...
 |->  lib/Kconfig
```

Looking at Listing 4-7, the file . . ./arch/arm/Kconfig would contain a line like this:

```
source  "net/Kconfig"
```

The file net/Kconfig would contain a line like this:

```
source "net/ipv4/Kconfig"
```

and so on.

As mentioned earlier, these Kconfig files taken together determine the configuration menu structure and configuration options presented to the user during kernel configuration. Figure 4-3 is an example of the configuration utility (gconf) for the ARM architecture.

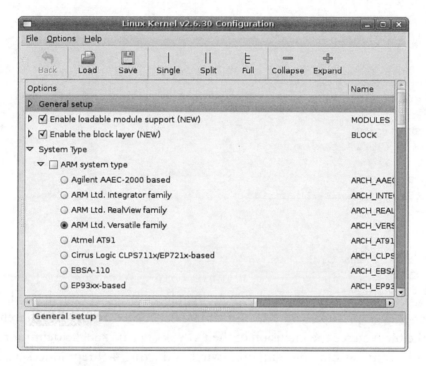

FIGURE 4-3   gconf configuration screen

4.4.1   Custom Configuration Options

Many embedded developers add feature support to the Linux kernel to support their particular custom hardware. The configuration management architecture just described makes it easy to customize and add features. A quick peek into a typical Kconfig file shows the structure of the configuration script language. As an example, assume that you have two hardware platforms based on the IXP425 network processor, and that your engineering team has dubbed them Vega and Constellation. Each board has specialized hardware that must be initialized early during the kernel boot phase. Let's see how easy it is to add these configuration options to the set of choices presented to the developer during kernel configuration. Listing 4-8 is a snippet from the top-level ARM Kconfig file.

LISTING 4-8   Snippet from . . . /arch/arm/Kconfig

```
source "init/Kconfig"

menu "System Type"

choice
        prompt "ARM system type"
        default ARCH_RPC

config ARCH_CLPS7500
        bool "Cirrus-CL-PS7500FE"

config ARCH_CLPS711X
        bool "CLPS711x/EP721x-based"

...

source "arch/arm/mach-ixp4xx/Kconfig"
```

In this Kconfig snippet, you see the menu item System Type being defined. After the ARM System type prompt, you see a list of choices related to the ARM architecture. Later in the file, you see the inclusion of the IXP4xx-specific Kconfig definitions. In this file, you add your custom configuration switches. Listing 4-9 reproduces a snippet of this file. Again, for readability and convenience, we've omitted irrelevant text, as indicated by the ellipsis.

LISTING 4-9   Snippet from . . . /arch/arm/mach-ixp4xx/Kconfig

```
menu "Intel IXP4xx Implementation Options"

comment "IXP4xx Platforms"

config ARCH_AVILA
```

LISTING 4-9   Continued

```
        bool "Avila"
        help
          Say 'Y' here if you want your kernel to support...

config ARCH_ADI_COYOTE
        bool "Coyote"
        help
           Say 'Y' here if you want your kernel to support
         the ADI Engineering Coyote...

# (These are our new custom options)
config ARCH_VEGA
        bool "Vega"
        help
          Select this option for "Vega" hardware support

config ARCH_CONSTELLATION
        bool "Constellation"
        help
          Select this option for "Constellation"
          hardware support
. . .
```

Figure 4-4 shows the result of these changes as it appears when you run the gconf utility (via make ARCH=arm gconfig). As a result of these simple changes, the configuration editor now includes options for our two new hardware platforms.[15] Shortly, you'll see how you can use this configuration information in the source tree to conditionally select objects that contain support for your new boards.

After the configuration editor (gconf in these examples) is run and you select support for one of your custom hardware platforms, the .config file introduced earlier contains macros for your new options. As with all kernel-configuration options, each is preceded with CONFIG_ to identify it as a kernel-configuration option. As a result, two new configuration options have been defined, and their state has been recorded in the .config file. Listing 4-10 shows the new .config file with your new configuration options.

---

[15] We removed many options under ARM system type and Intel IXP4*xx* Implementation Options to fit the figure on the page.

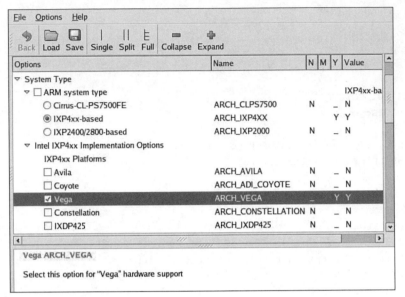

FIGURE 4-4   Custom configuration options

LISTING 4-10   Customized .config File Snippet

```
...
#
# IXP4xx Platforms
#
# CONFIG_ARCH_AVILA is not set
# CONFIG_ARCH_ADI_COYOTE is not set
CONFIG_ARCH_VEGA=y
# CONFIG_ARCH_CONSTELLATION is not set
# CONFIG_ARCH_IXDP425 is not set
# CONFIG_ARCH_PRPMC1100 is not set
...
```

Notice two new configuration options related to your Vega and Constellation hardware platforms. As shown in Figure 4-4, you selected support for Vega; in the .config file, you can see that the new CONFIG_ option representing the Vega board is selected and set to the value y. Notice also that the CONFIG_ option related to Constellation is present but not selected.

4.4.2 Kernel Makefiles

When building the kernel, the makefiles scan the configuration and decide what sub-directories to descend into and what source files to compile for a given configuration. To complete the example of adding support for two custom hardware platforms, Vega and Constellation, let's look at the makefile that would read this configuration and take some action based on customizations.

Because you're dealing with hardware-specific options in this example, assume that the customizations are represented by two hardware-setup modules called `vega_setup.c` and `constellation_setup.c`. We've placed these C source files in the `.../arch/arm/mach-ixp4xx` subdirectory of the kernel source tree. Listing 4-11 contains the complete makefile for this directory from a recent Linux release.

LISTING 4-11   Makefile from `.../arch/arm/mach-ixp4xx` Kernel Subdirectory

```
#
# Makefile for the linux kernel.
#


obj-y    += common.o common-pci.o

obj-$(CONFIG_ARCH_IXDP4XX)      += ixdp425-pci.o ixdp425-setup.o
obj-$(CONFIG_MACH_IXDPG425)     += ixdpg425-pci.o coyote-setup.o
obj-$(CONFIG_ARCH_ADI_COYOTE)   += coyote-pci.o coyote-setup.o
obj-$(CONFIG_MACH_GTWX5715)     += gtwx5715-pci.o gtwx5715-setup.o
```

You might be surprised by the simplicity of this makefile. Much work has gone into the development of the kernel build system for just this reason. For the average developer who simply needs to add support for his custom hardware, the design of the kernel build system makes these kinds of customizations very straightforward.[16]

Looking at this makefile, it might be obvious what must be done to introduce new hardware setup routines conditionally based on your configuration options. Simply add the following two lines at the bottom of the makefile, and you're done:

```
obj-$(CONFIG_ARCH_VEGA)    += vega_setup.o
obj-$(CONFIG_ARCH_CONSTELLATION)   += costellation_setup.o
```

These steps complete the simple addition of setup modules specific to the hypothetical sample custom hardware. Using similar logic, you should now be able to make your own modifications to the kernel configuration/build system.

---

[16] In actuality, the kernel build system is complicated, but most of the complexity is cleverly hidden from the average developer. As a result, it is relatively easy to add, modify, or delete configurations without having to be an expert.

4.5   Kernel Documentation

A wealth of information is available in the Linux source tree. It would be difficult to read it all, because the ... /Documentation directory contains nearly 1,300 documentation files in 118 subdirectories. Be cautious in reading this material: Given the rapid pace of kernel development and release, this documentation tends to become outdated quickly. Nonetheless, it often provides a great starting point from which you can form a foundation of knowledge on a particular kernel subsystem or concept.

Do not neglect the Linux Documentation Project, found at www.tldp.org, where you might find the most up-to-date version of a particular document or man page.[17] Of particular interest to the previous discussion is the Kbuild documentation, found in the kernel ... /Documentation/kbuild subdirectory.

No discussion of kernel documentation would be complete without mentioning Google. One day soon, Google will appear in Merriam-Webster's as a verb! Chances are, many problems you might have and questions you might ask have been addressed and answered. Spend some time becoming proficient in searching the Internet for answers to questions. You will discover numerous mailing lists and other information repositories full of invaluable information related to your specific project or problem. Appendix E contains a useful list of open-source resources.

4.6   Obtaining a Custom Linux Kernel

In general, you can obtain an embedded Linux kernel for your hardware platform in three ways: You can purchase a suitable commercial embedded Linux distribution; you can download a free embedded distribution that supports your particular hardware platform, if you can find one suitable for your particular architecture and processor; or you can find the closest open-source Linux kernel to your application and port it yourself.

Although porting an open source kernel to your custom board is not necessarily difficult, it represents a significant investment in engineering/development resources. This approach gives you access to free software, but deploying Linux in your development project is far from free, as we discussed in Chapter 1, "Introduction." Even for a small system with minimal application requirements, you need many more components than just a Linux kernel.

---

[17] Always assume that features advance faster than the corresponding documentation, so treat the docs as a guide rather than indisputable facts.

4.6.1 What Else Do I Need?

This chapter has focused on the layout and construction of the Linux kernel itself. As you might have discovered, Linux is only a small component of an embedded system based on Linux. In addition to the Linux kernel, you need the following components to develop, test, and launch your embedded Linux widget:

- A bootloader ported to and configured for your specific hardware platform
- A cross-compiler and associated toolchain for your chosen architecture
- A file system containing many packages—binary executables and libraries compiled for your native hardware architecture/processor
- Device drivers for any custom devices on your board
- A development environment, including host tools and utilities
- A Linux kernel source tree enabled for your particular processor and board

These are the components of an embedded Linux distribution.

4.7 Summary

This chapter covered the kernel build system and the process of modifying the build system to facilitate modifications. We leave it to other great books to describe the theory and operation of the Linux kernel. Here we discussed how it is built and identified the components that make up the image. Breaking the kernel into understandable pieces is the key to learning how to navigate this large software project.

- The Linux kernel is almost 20 years old and has become a mainstream, well-supported operating system for many architectures.
- The Linux open source home is found at www.kernel.org. Virtually every release version of the kernel is available there, going all the way back to Linux 1.0.
- Several kernel configuration editors exist. We chose one and examined how it is driven and how to modify the menus and menu items within. These concepts apply to all the graphical front ends.
- The kernel itself comes with an entire directory structure full of useful kernel documentation. This is a helpful resource for understanding and navigating the kernel and its operation.

- This chapter concluded with a brief introduction to the options available for obtaining an embedded Linux distribution.

4.7.1   Suggestions for Additional Reading

Linux Kernel HOWTO
www.linuxdocs.org/HOWTOs/Kernel-HOWTO.html

Kernel Kbuild documentation
Linux kernel source tree
```
.../Documentation/kbuild/*
```

The Linux Documentation Project:
www.tldp.org

Tool Interface Standard (TIS) Executable and Linking Format (ELF) Specification, Version 1.2
TIS Committee, May 1995
http://refspecs.freestandards.org/elf/elf.pdf

Linux kernel source tree
```
.../Documentation/kbuild/makefiles.txt
```

Linux kernel source tree
```
.../Documentation/kbuild/kconfig-language.txt
```

Linux Kernel Development, 3rd Edition
Robert Love
Addison-Wesley, 2010

Chapter 5

Kernel Initialization

In This Chapter

- 5.1 Composite Kernel Image: Piggy and Friends   100
- 5.2 Initialization Flow of Control   109
- 5.3 Kernel Command-Line Processing   115
- 5.4 Subsystem Initialization   122
- 5.5 The init Thread   125
- 5.6 Summary   129

When the power is applied to an embedded Linux system, a complex sequence of events is started. After a few tens of seconds, the Linux kernel is operational and has spawned a series of application programs as specified by the system init scripts. A significant portion of these activities are governed by system configuration and are under the control of the embedded developer.

This chapter examines the initial sequence of events in the Linux kernel. We take a detailed look at the mechanisms and processes used during kernel initialization. We then describe the Linux kernel command line and its use to customize the Linux environment on startup. With this knowledge, you will be able to customize and control the initialization sequence to meet the requirements of your particular embedded system.

5.1 Composite Kernel Image: Piggy and Friends

Upon power-on, the bootloader in an embedded system is the first software to get processor control. After the bootloader has performed some low-level hardware initialization, control is passed to the Linux kernel. This can be a manual sequence of events to facilitate the development process (for example, the user types interactive load/boot commands at the bootloader prompt), or it can be an automated startup sequence typical of a production environment. We have dedicated Chapter 7, "Bootloaders," to this subject, so we defer any detailed bootloader discussion to that chapter.

In Chapter 4, "The Linux Kernel: A Different Perspective," we examined the components that make up the Linux kernel image. Recall that one of the common files built for every architecture is the ELF binary named vmlinux. This binary file is the monolithic kernel itself, or what we have been calling the *kernel proper*. In fact, when we looked at its construction in the link stage of vmlinux, we pointed out where we might look to see where the first line of code might be found. In most architectures, it is found in an assembly language source file called head.s or a similar filename. In the Power Architecture (powerpc) branch of the kernel, several versions of head.s are present, depending on the processor. For example, the AMCC 440 series processors are initialized from a file called head_44x.S.

Some architectures and bootloaders can directly boot the `vmlinux` kernel image. For example, platforms based on Power Architecture and the U-Boot bootloader usually can boot the `vmlinux` image directly[1] (after conversion from ELF to binary, as you will see shortly). In other combinations of architecture and bootloader, additional functionality might be needed to set up the proper context and provide the necessary utilities to load and boot the kernel.

Listing 5-1 details the final sequence of steps in the kernel build process for a hardware platform based on the ADI Engineering Coyote Reference Platform, which contains an Intel IXP425 network processor. This listing uses the quiet form of output from the kernel build system, which is the default. As pointed out in Chapter 4, it is a useful shorthand notation, allowing more of a focus on errors and warnings during the build process.

LISTING 5-1   Final Kernel Build Sequence: ARM/IXP425 (Coyote)

```
$ make ARCH=arm CROSS_COMPILE=xscale_be- zImage
...   < many build steps omitted for clarity>
  LD      vmlinux
  SYSMAP  System.map
  SYSMAP  .tmp_System.map
  OBJCOPY arch/arm/boot/Image
  Kernel: arch/arm/boot/Image is ready
  AS      arch/arm/boot/compressed/head.o
  GZIP    arch/arm/boot/compressed/piggy.gz
  AS      arch/arm/boot/compressed/piggy.o
  CC      arch/arm/boot/compressed/misc.o
  AS      arch/arm/boot/compressed/head-xscale.o
  AS      arch/arm/boot/compressed/big-endian.o
  LD      arch/arm/boot/compressed/vmlinux
  OBJCOPY arch/arm/boot/zImage
  Kernel: arch/arm/boot/zImage is ready
```

In the third line of Listing 5-1, the `vmlinux` image (the kernel proper) is linked. Following that, a number of additional object modules are processed. These include

---

[1] The kernel image is nearly always stored in compressed format, unless boot time is a critical issue. In this case, the image might be called `uImage`, a compressed `vmlinux` file with a U-Boot header. See Chapter 7.

`head.o`, `piggy.o`,[2] and the architecture-specific `head-xscale.o`, among others. (The tags identify what is happening on each line. For example, `AS` indicates that the assembler is invoked, `GZIP` indicates compression, and so on.) In general, these object modules are specific to a given architecture (ARM/XScale in this example) and contain low-level utility routines needed to boot the kernel on this particular architecture. Table 5-1 details the components from Listing 5-1.

TABLE 5-1   ARM/XScale Low-Level Architecture Objects

Component	Description
vmlinux	Kernel proper, in ELF format, including symbols, comments, debug info (if compiled with -g), and architecture-generic components.
System.map	Text-based kernel symbol table for the `vmlinux` module.
.tmp_System.map	Generated only to sanity-check `System.map`; otherwise, not used in the final build image.
Image	Binary kernel module, stripped of symbols, notes, and comments.
head.o	ARM-specific startup code generic to ARM processors. This object is passed control by the bootloader.
piggy.gz	The file `Image` compressed with `gzip`.
piggy.o	The file `piggy.gz` in assembly language format so that it can be linked with a subsequent object, `misc.o` (see the text).
misc.o	Routines used to decompress the kernel image (`piggy.gz`) and the source of the familiar boot message `Uncompressing Linux . . . Done` on some architectures.
head-xscale.o	Processor initialization specific to the XScale processor family.
big-endian.o	Tiny assembly language routine to switch the XScale processor into big-endian mode.
vmlinux	Composite kernel image. This is an unfortunate choice of names, because it duplicates the name for the kernel proper; the two are not the same. This binary image is the result when the kernel proper is linked with the objects in this table. See the text for an explanation.
zImage	Final composite kernel image loaded by bootloader. See the following text.

An illustration will help you understand this structure and the following discussion. Figure 5-1 shows the image components and their metamorphosis during the build process leading up to a bootable kernel image. The following sections describe the components and process in detail.

---

[2] The term *piggy* was originally used to describe a "piggyback" concept. In this case, the binary kernel image is piggybacked onto the bootstrap loader to produce the composite kernel image.

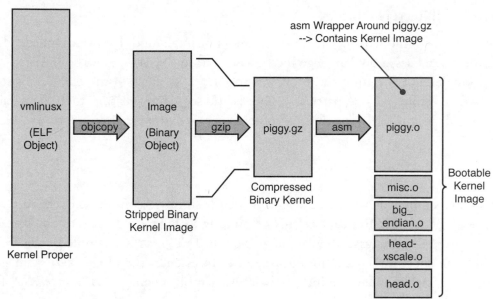

FIGURE 5-1   Composite kernel image construction

5.1.1   The `Image` Object

After the `vmlinux` kernel ELF file has been built, the kernel build system continues to process the targets described in Table 5-1. The `Image` object is created from the `vmlinux` object. `Image` is basically the `vmlinux` ELF file stripped of redundant sections (notes and comments) and also stripped of any debugging symbols that might have been present. The following command is used for this purpose:

```
xscale_be-objcopy -O binary -R .note -R .note.gnu.build-id -R .comment -S
 vmlinux arch/arm/boot/Image
```

The `-O` option tells `objcopy` to generate a binary file; the `-R` option removes the ELF sections named `.note`, `.note.gnu.build-id`, and `.comment`; and the `-S` option is the flag to strip debugging symbols. Notice that `objcopy` takes the `vmlinux` ELF image as input and generates the target binary file called `Image`. In summary, `Image` is nothing more than the kernel proper converted from ELF to binary form and stripped of debug symbols and the aforementioned `.note*` and `.comment` sections.

5.1.2   Architecture Objects

Following the build sequence further, a number of small modules are compiled. These include several assembly language files (`head.o`, `head-xscale.o`, and so on) that perform low-level architecture and processor-specific tasks. Each of these objects is summarized in Table 5-1. Of particular note is the sequence creating the object called `piggy.o`. First, the `Image` file (binary kernel image) is compressed using this `gzip` command:

```
cat Image | gzip -f -9 > piggy.gz
```

This creates a new file called `piggy.gz`, which is simply a compressed version of the binary kernel `Image`. You can see this graphically in Figure 5-1. What comes next is rather interesting. An assembly language file called `piggy.s` is assembled, which contains a reference to the compressed `piggy.gz`. In essence, the binary kernel image is being piggybacked as payload into a low-level assembly language *bootstrap loader*.[3] This bootstrap loader initializes the processor and required memory regions, decompresses the binary kernel image, and loads it into the proper place in system memory before passing control to it. Listing 5-2 reproduces `.../arch/arm/boot/compressed/piggy.S` in its entirety.

LISTING 5-2   Assembly File `Piggy.S`

```
  .section  .piggydata,#alloc
  .globl    input_data
input_data:
  .incbin   "arch/arm/boot/compressed/piggy.gz"
  .globl    input_data_end
input_data_end:
```

This small assembly-language file is simple yet produces a complexity that is not immediately obvious. The purpose of this file is to cause the compressed binary kernel image to be emitted by the assembler as an ELF section called `.piggydata`. It is triggered by the `.incbin` assembler preprocessor directive, which can be viewed as the assembler's version of an `#include` file, except that it expects binary data. In summary, the net result of this assembly language file is to contain the compressed binary ker-

---

[3] Not to be confused with the bootloader, a bootstrap loader can be considered a second-stage loader, and the bootloader itself can be thought of as a first-stage loader.

nel image as a payload within another image—the bootstrap loader. Notice the labels `input_data` and `input_data_end`. The bootstrap loader uses these to identify the boundaries of the binary payload—the kernel image itself.

5.1.3   Bootstrap Loader

Not to be confused with a bootloader, many architectures use a *bootstrap loader* (or second-stage loader) to load the Linux kernel image into memory. Some bootstrap loaders perform checksum verification of the kernel image, and most decompress and relocate the kernel image. The difference between a bootloader and a bootstrap loader in this context is simple: The bootloader controls the board upon power-up and does not rely on the Linux kernel in any way. In contrast, the bootstrap loader's primary purpose is to act as the *glue* between a bare metal bootloader and the Linux kernel. It is the bootstrap loader's responsibility to provide a proper context for the kernel to run in, as well as perform the necessary steps to decompress and relocate the kernel binary image. It is similar to the concept of a primary and secondary loader found in the PC architecture.

Figure 5-2 makes this concept clear. The bootstrap loader is concatenated to the kernel image for loading.

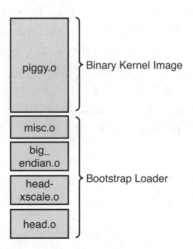

FIGURE 5-2   Composite kernel image for ARM XScale

In the example we have been studying, the bootstrap loader consists of the binary images shown in Figure 5-2. The functions performed by this bootstrap loader include the following:

- Low-level assembly language processor initialization, which includes support for enabling the processor's internal instruction and data caches, disabling interrupts, and setting up a C runtime environment. These include `head.o` and `head-xscale.o`.

- Decompression and relocation code, embodied in `misc.o`.

- Other processor-specific initialization, such as `big-endian.o`, which enables big endian mode for this particular processor.

It is worth noting that the details we have been examining are specific to the ARM/ XScale kernel implementation. Each architecture has different details, although the concepts are similar. Using an analysis similar to that presented here, you can learn the requirements of your own architecture.

5.1.4   Boot Messages

Perhaps you've seen a PC workstation booting a desktop Linux distribution such as Red Hat or SUSE Linux. After the PC's own BIOS messages, you see Linux display a flurry of console messages as it initializes the various kernel subsystems. Significant portions of the output are common across disparate architectures and machines. Two of the more interesting early boot messages are the kernel version string and the *kernel command line*, which is described shortly. Listing 5-3 reproduces the kernel boot messages for the ADI Engineering Coyote Reference Platform booting Linux on the Intel XScale IXP425 processor. The listing has been formatted with line numbers for easy reference.

LISTING 5-3   Linux Boot Messages on IPX425

```
1   Using base address 0x01000000 and length 0x001ce114
2   Uncompressing Linux....... done, booting the kernel.
3   Linux version 2.6.32-07500-g8bea867 (chris@brutus2) (gcc version 4.2.0
20070126 (prerelease) (MontaVista 4.2.0-3.0.0.0702771 2007-03-10)) #12 Wed Dec 16
23:07:01 EST 2009
4   CPU: XScale-IXP42x Family [690541c1] revision 1 (ARMv5TE), cr=000039ff
5   CPU: VIVT data cache, VIVT instruction cache
6   Machine: ADI Engineering Coyote
7   Memory policy: ECC disabled, Data cache writeback
```

LISTING 5-3   Continued

```
 8  Built 1 zonelists in Zone order, mobility grouping on.  Total pages: 16256
 9  Kernel command line: console=ttyS0,115200 root=/dev/nfs ip=dhcp
10  PID hash table entries: 256 (order: -2, 1024 bytes)
11  Dentry cache hash table entries: 8192 (order: 3, 32768 bytes)
12  Inode-cache hash table entries: 4096 (order: 2, 16384 bytes)
13  Memory: 64MB = 64MB total
14  Memory: 61108KB available (3332K code, 199K data, 120K init, 0K highmem)
15  SLUB: Genslabs=11, HWalign=32, Order=0-3, MinObjects=0, CPUs=1, Nodes=1
16  Hierarchical RCU implementation.
17  RCU-based detection of stalled CPUs is enabled.
18  NR_IRQS:64
19  Calibrating delay loop... 532.48 BogoMIPS (lpj=2662400)
20  Mount-cache hash table entries: 512
21  CPU: Testing write buffer coherency: ok
22  NET: Registered protocol family 16
23  IXP4xx: Using 16MiB expansion bus window size
24  PCI: IXP4xx is host
25  PCI: IXP4xx Using direct access for memory space
26  PCI: bus0: Fast back to back transfers enabled
27  SCSI subsystem initialized
28  usbcore: registered new interface driver usbfs
29  usbcore: registered new interface driver hub
30  usbcore: registered new device driver usb
31  NET: Registered protocol family 8
32  NET: Registered protocol family 20
33  NET: Registered protocol family 2
34  IXP4xx Queue Manager initialized.
35  NetWinder Floating Point Emulator V0.97 (double precision)
36  JFFS2 version 2.2. (NAND) (c) 2001-2006 Red Hat, Inc.
37  io scheduler noop registered
38  io scheduler deadline registered
39  io scheduler cfq registered (default)
40  Serial: 8250/16550 driver, 2 ports, IRQ sharing disabled
41  serial8250.0: ttyS0 at MMIO 0xc8001000 (irq = 13) is a XScale
42  console [ttyS0] enabled
43  Uniform Multi-Platform E-IDE driver
44  ide-gd driver 1.18
45  IXP4XX-Flash.0: Found 1 x16 devices at 0x0 in 16-bit bank
46   Intel/Sharp Extended Query Table at 0x0031
47   Intel/Sharp Extended Query Table at 0x0031
48  Using buffer write method
49  Searching for RedBoot partition table in IXP4XX-Flash.0 at offset 0xfe0000
```

LISTING 5-3   Continued

```
50   5 RedBoot partitions found on MTD device IXP4XX-Flash.0
51   Creating 5 MTD partitions on "IXP4XX-Flash.0":
52   0x000000000000-0x000000060000 : "RedBoot"
53   0x000000100000-0x000000260000 : "MyKernel"
54   0x000000300000-0x000000900000 : "RootFS"
55   0x000000fc0000-0x000000fc1000 : "RedBoot config"
56   0x000000fe0000-0x000001000000 : "FIS directory"
57   e100: Intel(R) PRO/100 Network Driver, 3.5.24-k2-NAPI
58   e100: Copyright(c) 1999-2006 Intel Corporation
59   ehci_hcd: USB 2.0 'Enhanced' Host Controller (EHCI) Driver
60   ohci_hcd: USB 1.1 'Open' Host Controller (OHCI) Driver
61   uhci_hcd: USB Universal Host Controller Interface driver
62   Initializing USB Mass Storage driver...
63   usbcore: registered new interface driver usb-storage
64   USB Mass Storage support registered.
65   IXP4xx Watchdog Timer: heartbeat 60 sec
66   usbcore: registered new interface driver usbhid
67   usbhid: USB HID core driver
68   TCP cubic registered
69   NET: Registered protocol family 17
70   XScale DSP coprocessor detected.
71   drivers/rtc/hctosys.c: unable to open rtc device (rtc0)
72   e100 0000:00:0f.0: firmware: using built-in firmware e100/d101m_ucode.bin
73   e100: eth0 NIC Link is Up 100 Mbps Full Duplex
74   IP-Config: Complete:
75       device=eth0, addr=192.168.0.29, mask=255.255.255.0, gw=255.255.255.255,
76       host=coyote1, domain=, nis-domain=(none),
77       bootserver=192.168.0.103, rootserver=192.168.0.103, rootpath=
78   Looking up port of RPC 100003/2 on 192.168.0.103
79   Looking up port of RPC 100005/1 on 192.168.0.103
80   VFS: Mounted root (nfs filesystem) on device 0:11.
81   Freeing init memory: 120K
82   INIT: version 2.86 booting
83   ... <some userland init messages omitted>
84   coyote1 login:
```

The kernel produces much useful information during startup, as shown in Listing 5-3. We study this output in some detail in the next few sections. Line 1 is produced by the Redboot bootloader on the board. Line 2 is produced by the bootstrap loader we presented earlier in this chapter. This message was produced by the decompression loader found in .../arch/arm/boot/compressed/misc.c, in a function called decompress_kernel().

Line 3 of Listing 5-3 is the kernel version string. It is the first line of output from the kernel itself. One of the first lines of C code executed by the kernel (in `.../init/main.c`) upon entering `start_kernel()` is as follows:

```
printk(KERN_NOTICE "%s", linux_banner);
```

This line produces the output just described—the kernel version string, line 3 of Listing 5-3. This version string contains a number of pertinent data points related to the kernel image:

- Kernel version: Linux version 2.6.32-07500-g8bea867[4]
- Username/machine name where the kernel was compiled
- Toolchain info: gcc version 4.2.0, supplied by MontaVista Software
- Build number
- Date and time the kernel image was compiled

This is useful information both during development and later in production. All but one of the entries are self-explanatory. The *build number* is simply a tool that the developers added to the version string to indicate that something more substantial than the date and time changed from one build to the next. It is a way for developers to keep track of the build in a generic and automatic fashion. You will notice in this example that this was the twelfth build in this series, as indicated by the #12 on line 3 of Listing 5-3. The build number is stored in a hidden file in the top-level Linux directory and is called `.version`. It is automatically incremented by a build script found in `.../scripts/mkversion`. In short, it is a numeric string tag that is automatically incremented whenever anything substantial in the kernel is rebuilt. Note that it is reset to #1 on execution of `make mrproper`.

5.2   Initialization Flow of Control

Now that you understand the structure and components of the composite kernel image, let's examine the flow of control from the bootloader to the kernel in a complete boot cycle. As we discussed in Chapter 2, "The Big Picture," the bootloader is the low-level component that resides in system nonvolatile memory (Flash or ROM). It takes control immediately after the power has been applied. It is typically a small, simple

---

[4] The numbers following 2.6.32 are tags placed on the version string from the build system; they are not relevant for the current discussion. Chapter 4, Section 4.1.1, explains this mechanism.

set of routines designed primarily to do low-level initialization, operating system image loading, and system diagnostics. It might contain memory dump and fill routines for examining and modifying the contents of memory. It might also contain low-level board self-test routines, including memory and I/O tests. Finally, a bootloader contains logic for loading and passing control to another program, usually an operating system such as Linux.

The ARM XScale platform used as a basis for the examples in this chapter contains the Redboot bootloader. When power is first applied, this bootloader is invoked and proceeds to load the operating system (OS). When the bootloader locates and loads the OS image (which could be resident locally in Flash, on a hard drive, or via a local area network or other device), control is passed to that image.

On this particular XScale platform, the bootloader passes control to our `head.o` module at the label `start` in the bootstrap loader, as shown in Figure 5-3.

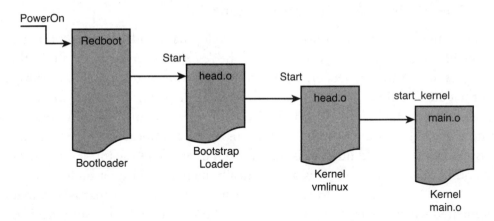

FIGURE 5-3   ARM boot control flow

As discussed earlier, the bootstrap loader prepended to the kernel image has a single primary responsibility: to create the proper environment to decompress and relocate the kernel and pass control to it. Control is passed from the bootstrap loader directly to the kernel proper, to a module called `head.o` for most architectures. It is an unfortunate historical artifact that both the bootstrap loader and the kernel proper contain a module called `head.o`, because it is a source of confusion for the new embedded Linux developer. The `head.o` module in the bootstrap loader might be more appropriately called `kernel_bootstrap_loader_head.o`, although I doubt that the kernel developers would accept this patch! In fact, a recent Linux 2.6 source tree contains more than

25 source files named `head.s` and almost 70 named `head*.s` This is another reason why you need to know your way around the kernel source tree.

Refer to Figure 5-3 for a graphical view of the flow of control. When the bootstrap loader has completed its job, control is passed to the kernel proper's `head.o`, and from there to `start_kernel()` in `main.c`.

5.2.1   Kernel Entry Point: `head.o`

The intention of the kernel developers was to keep the architecture-specific `head.o` module very generic, without any specific machine[5] dependencies. This module, derived from the assembly language file `head.s`, is located at `.../arch/<ARCH>/kernel/head.s`, where `<ARCH>` is replaced by the given architecture. The examples in this chapter are based on the ARM/XScale, as you have seen, with `<ARCH>=arm`.

The `head.o` module performs architecture- and often CPU-specific initialization in preparation for the main body of the kernel. CPU-specific tasks are kept as generic as possible across processor families. Machine-specific initialization is performed elsewhere, as you will discover shortly. Among other low-level tasks, `head.o` does the following:

- Checks for valid processor and architecture
- Creates initial page table entries
- Enables the processor's memory management unit (MMU)
- Establishes limited error detection and reporting
- Jumps to the start of the kernel proper, `start_kernel()` in `main.c`

These functions contain some hidden complexities. Many novice embedded developers have tried to single-step through parts of this code, only to find that the debugger becomes hopelessly lost. Although a discussion of the complexities of assembly language and the hardware details of virtual memory is beyond the scope of this book, a few things are worth noting about this complicated module.

When control is first passed to the kernel's `head.o` from the bootstrap loader, the processor is operating in what we used to call real mode in x86 terminology. In effect, the logical address contained in the processor's *program counter*[6] (or any other register, for that matter) is the actual physical address driven onto the processor's electrical

---

[5] The term *machine* as used here refers to a specific hardware platform.

[6] Often called Instruction Pointer, the register that holds the address of the next machine instruction in memory.

memory address pins. Soon after the processor's registers and kernel data structures are initialized to enable memory translation, the processor's MMU is turned on. Suddenly, the address space as seen by the processor is yanked from beneath it and replaced by an arbitrary virtual addressing scheme determined by the kernel developers. This creates a complexity that can really be understood only by a detailed analysis of both the assembly language constructs and logical flow, as well as a detailed knowledge of the CPU and its hardware address translation mechanism. In short, physical addresses are replaced by logical addresses the moment the MMU is enabled. That is why a debugger can't single-step through this portion of code, as with ordinary code.

The second point worth noting is the limited available mapping at this early stage of the kernel boot process. Many developers have stumbled into this limitation while trying to modify `head.o` for their particular platform.[7] One such scenario might go like this. Let's say you have a hardware device that needs a firmware load very early in the boot cycle. One possible solution is to compile the necessary firmware statically into the kernel image and then reference it via a pointer to download it to your device. However, because of the limited memory mapping done at this point, it is quite possible that your firmware image will exist beyond the range that has been mapped at this early stage in the boot cycle. When your code executes, it generates a page fault, because you have attempted to access a memory region for which no valid mapping has been created inside the processor. Worse yet, a page fault handler has not yet been installed at this early stage, so all you get is an unexplained system crash. At this early stage in the boot cycle, you are pretty much guaranteed *not* to have any error messages to help you figure out what's wrong.

You are wise to consider delaying any custom hardware initialization until after the kernel has booted, if at all possible. In this manner, you can rely on the well-known device driver model for access to custom hardware instead of trying to customize the much more complicated assembly language startup code. Numerous undocumented techniques are used at this level. One common example of this is to work around hardware errata that may or may not be documented. A much higher price will be paid in development time, cost, and complexity if you must make changes to the early startup assembly language code. Hardware and software engineers should discuss these facts during early stages of hardware development, when often a minor hardware change can lead to significant savings in software development time.

---

[7] Modifying `head.S` for your custom platform is highly discouraged. There is almost always a better way.

It is important to recognize the constraints placed on the developer in a virtual memory environment. Many experienced embedded developers have little or no experience in this environment, and the scenario just presented is but one small example of the pitfalls that await the developer new to virtual memory architectures. Nearly all modern 32-bit and larger microprocessors have memory-management hardware used to implement virtual memory architectures. One of the most significant advantages of virtual memory machines is that they help separate teams of developers writing large, complex applications, while protecting other software modules, and the kernel itself, from programming errors.

5.2.2 Kernel Startup: `main.c`

The final task performed by the kernel's own `head.o` module is to pass control to the primary kernel startup file written in C. We spend a good portion of the rest of this chapter on this important file.

Each architecture has a different syntax and methodology, but every architecture's `head.o` module has a similar construct for passing control to the kernel proper. For the ARM architecture, it looks as simple as this:

```
b       start_kernel[8]
```

For Power Architecture, it looks similar to this:

```
lis     r4,start_kernel@h
ori     r4,r4,start_kernel@l
lis     r3,MSR_KERNEL@h
ori     r3,r3,MSR_KERNEL@l
mtspr   SRR0,r4
mtspr   SRR1,r3
rfi
```

Without going into the details of the specific assembly language syntax, both of these examples result in the same thing. Control is passed from the kernel's first object module (`head.o`) to the C language routine `start_kernel()` located in `.../init/main.c`. Here the kernel begins to develop a life of its own.

---

[8] Modern Linux kernels separate out some common code in `head-common.S`, which is incorporated into `head.S` using an `include` directive. This is where the call to `start_kernel()` is found.

The file `main.c` should be studied carefully by anyone seeking a deeper understanding of the Linux kernel, what components make it up, and how they are initialized and/or instantiated. `main.c` does the bulk of the post-assembly-language startup work for the Linux kernel, from initializing the first kernel thread all the way to mounting a root file system and executing the very first user space Linux application program.

The function `start_kernel()` is by far the largest function in `main.c`. Most of the Linux kernel initialization takes place in this routine. Our purpose here is to highlight the particular elements that will prove useful in the context of embedded systems development. It is worth repeating that studying `main.c` is a great way to spend your time if you want to develop a better understanding of the Linux kernel as a system.

5.2.3   Architecture Setup

Among the first few things that happen in `.../init/main.c` in the `start_kernel()` function is the call to `setup_arch()` found in `.../arch/arm/kernel/setup.c`. This function takes a single parameter—a pointer to the kernel command line (introduced earlier and detailed in the next section):

```
setup_arch(&command_line);
```

This statement calls an architecture-specific setup routine responsible for performing initialization tasks common across each major architecture. Among other functions, `setup_arch()` calls functions that identify the specific CPU and provides a mechanism for calling high-level CPU-specific initialization routines. One such function, called directly by `setup_arch()`, is `setup_processor()`, found in `.../arch/arm/kernel/setup.c`. This function verifies the CPU ID and revision, calls CPU-specific initialization functions, and displays several lines of information on the console during boot.

An example of this output can be found in Listing 5-3, lines 4 through 6, reproduced here for your convenience:

```
4   CPU: XScale-IXP42x Family [690541c1] revision 1 (ARMv5TE), cr=000039ff
5   CPU: VIVT data cache, VIVT instruction cache
6   Machine: ADI Engineering Coyote
```

Here you can see the CPU type, ID string, and revision read directly from the processor core. This is followed by details of the processor cache and machine type. In this example, the IXP425-based Coyote board has an XScale-IXP42x revision 1 processor, ARMv5TE architecture, virtually indexed, virtually tagged (VIVT) data, and instruction caches.

One of the final actions of the architecture setup routines is to perform any ma-chine-dependent initialization. The exact mechanism for this varies across different architectures. For ARM, you will find machine-specific initialization in the ...`/arch/ arm/mach-*` series of directories, depending on your machine type. MIPS architecture also contains directories specific to supported reference platforms. With Power Archi-tecture, a `platforms` directory contains machine-specific routines.

5.3   Kernel Command-Line Processing

Following the architecture setup, `main.c` performs generic early kernel initialization and then displays the kernel command line. Line 9 of Listing 5-3 is reproduced here for your convenience:

```
Kernel command line: console=ttyS0,115200 root=/dev/nfs ip=dhcp
```

In this simple example, the kernel being booted is instructed to open a console de-vice on serial port device `ttyS0` (usually the first serial port) at a baud rate of 115Kbps. It is being instructed to obtain its initial IP address information from a DHCP server and to mount a root file system via the NFS protocol. (We cover DHCP in Chapter 12, "Embedded Development Environment," and NFS in Chapter 9, "File Systems," and Chapter 12. For now, we limit the discussion to the kernel command-line mecha-nism.)

Linux typically is launched by a bootloader (or bootstrap loader) with a series of parameters that have come to be called the *kernel command line*. Although you don't actually invoke the kernel using a command prompt from a shell, many bootloaders can pass parameters to the kernel in a fashion that resembles this well-known model. On some platforms whose bootloaders are not Linux-aware, the kernel command line can be defined at compile time and becomes hard-coded as part of the kernel binary image. On other platforms (such as a desktop PC running Red Hat Linux), the user can modify the command line without having to recompile the kernel. The bootstrap loader (Grub or Lilo in the desktop PC case) builds the kernel command line from a configuration file and passes it to the kernel during the boot process. These command-line parameters are a boot mechanism to set the initial configuration necessary for proper boot on a given machine.

Numerous command-line parameters are defined throughout the kernel. The ...`/Documentation` subdirectory in the kernel source contains a file called `kernel-parameters.txt` containing a list of kernel command-line parameters in dictionary order. Remember the previous warning about kernel documentation: The kernel changes far faster than the documentation. Use this file as a guide, but not a definitive reference. Hundreds of distinct kernel command-line parameters are documented in this file, but it cannot be considered a comprehensive list. For that, you must refer directly to the source code.

The basic syntax for kernel command-line parameters is fairly simple and mostly evident from the example in line 9 of Listing 5-3. Kernel command-line parameters can be either a single text word, a *key=value* pair, or a *key=value1,value2,...* key and multivalue format. It is up to the consumer of this information to process the data as delivered. The command line is available globally and is processed by as many modules as needed. As noted earlier, `setup_arch()` in `main.c` is called with the kernel command line as its only argument. This is to pass architecture-specific parameters and configuration directives to the relevant portions of architecture- and machine-specific code.

Device driver writers and kernel developers can add additional kernel command-line parameters for their own specific needs. Let's take a look at the mechanism. Unfortunately, some complications are involved in using and processing kernel command-line parameters. The first of these is that the original mechanism is being deprecated in favor of a much more robust implementation. The second complication is that you need to comprehend the complexities of a linker script file to fully understand the mechanism.[9]

5.3.1   The `__setup` Macro

As an example of the use of kernel command-line parameters, consider the specification of the console device. We want a console initialized early in the boot cycle so that we have a destination for messages during boot. This initialization takes place in a kernel object called `printk.o`. The C source file for this module is found in `.../kernel/printk.c`. The console initialization routine is called `console_setup()` and takes the kernel command-line parameter string as its only argument.

The challenge is to communicate the console parameters specified on the kernel command line to the setup and device driver routines that require this data in a modular and general fashion. Further complicating the issue is that typically the command-line

---

[9] It's not necessarily all that complex, but most of us never need to understand a linker script file. The embedded engineer does. It is well documented in the GNU LD manual referenced at the end of this chapter.

parameters are required early, before (or in time for) the modules that need them. The startup code in `main.c`, where the main processing of the kernel command line takes place, cannot possibly know the destination functions for each of hundreds of kernel command-line parameters without being hopelessly polluted with knowledge from every consumer of these parameters. What is needed is a flexible and generic way to pass these kernel command-line parameters to their consumers.

A special macro defined in `.../include/linux/init.h` is used to associate a portion of the kernel command-line string with a function that will act on that portion of the string. We now demonstrate how the `__setup` macro works using the kernel command line from Listing 5-3 as an example.

From the previous kernel command line (line 9 of Listing 5-3), this is the first complete command-line parameter passed to the kernel:

```
console=ttyS0,115200
```

For the purposes of this example, the actual meaning of the parameters is irrelevant. Our goal here is to illustrate the mechanism, so don't be concerned if you don't understand the argument or its values.

Listing 5-4 is a snippet of code from `.../kernel/printk.c`. The body of the function has been stripped because it is not relevant to the discussion. The most relevant part of Listing 5-4 is the last line, the invocation of the `__setup` macro. This macro expects two arguments; in this case, it is passed a string literal and a function pointer. It is no coincidence that the string literal passed to the `__setup` macro is the same as the first eight characters of the kernel command line related to the console: `console=`.

LISTING 5-4 Console Setup Code Snippet

```
/*
 *    Setup a list of consoles. Called from init/main.c
 */
static int __init console_setup(char *str)
{
    char buf[sizeof(console_cmdline[0].name) + 4]; /* 4 for index */
    char *s, *options, *brl_options = NULL;
    int idx;

    ...
    <body omitted for clarity...>
    ...
```

LISTING 5-4   Continued

```
    return 1;
}


__setup("console=", console_setup);
```

You can think of the __setup macro as a registration function for the kernel command-line console parameter. In effect, it says: When the console= string is encountered on the kernel command line, invoke the function represented by the second
__setup macro argument—in this case, the console_setup() function. But how is
this information communicated to the early setup code, outside this module, which
has no knowledge of the console functions? The mechanism is both clever and somewhat complicated, and it relies on lists built by the linker.

The details are hidden in a set of macros designed to conceal the syntactical tedium
of adding section attributes (and other attributes) to a portion of object code. The objective is to build a static list of string literals associated with function pointers. This list
is emitted by the compiler in a separately named ELF section in the final vmlinux ELF
image. It is important to understand this technique; it is used in several places within
the kernel for special-purpose processing.

Let's now examine how this is done for the __setup macro case. Listing 5-5 is a
portion of code from the header file .../include/linux/init.h defining the __setup
family of macros.

LISTING 5-5   Family of __setup Macro Definitions from init.h

```
...
#define __setup_param(str, unique_id, fn, early)            \
    static const char __setup_str_##unique_id[] __initconst \
        __aligned(1) = str; \
    static struct obs_kernel_param __setup_##unique_id  \
        __used __section(.init.setup)            \
        __attribute__((aligned((sizeof(long)))))     \
        = { __setup_str_##unique_id, fn, early }

#define __setup(str, fn)                    \
    __setup_param(str, fn, fn, 0)
...
```

Listing 5-5 is the author's definition of syntactical tedium! Recall from Listing 5-4 that our invocation of the original __setup macro looked like this:

```
__setup("console=", console_setup);
```

With some slight simplification, here is what the compiler's preprocessor produces after macro expansion:

```
static const char __setup_str_console_setup[] __initconst \
__aligned(1) = "console=";

static struct obs_kernel_param __setup_console_setup __used  \
__section(.init.setup) __attribute__ ((aligned((sizeof(long))))) \
= { __setup_str_console_setup, console_setup, early};
```

To make this more readable, we have split the lines, as indicated by the UNIX line-continuation character (\).

Several macros are in use here, which we will describe only briefly. The __used macro tells the compiler to emit the function or variable, even if the optimizer determines that it is unused.[10] __attribute__ ((aligned)) tells the compiler to align the structures on a specific boundary—in this case, sizeof(long). If we remove these for simplification, we are left with this:

```
static struct obs_kernel_param __setup_console_setup \
__section(.init.setup) = { __setup_str_console_setup, console_setup, early};
```

What we have left after simplification is the heart of the mechanism. First, the compiler generates an array of characters (a string pointer) called __setup_str_console_setup[] initialized to contain the string console=. Next, the compiler generates a structure that contains three members: a pointer to the kernel command-line string (the array just declared), a pointer to the setup function itself, and a simple flag. The key to the magic here is the section attribute attached to the structure. This attribute instructs the compiler to emit this structure into a special section within the ELF object module, called .init.setup. During the link stage, all the structures defined using the __setup macro are collected and placed in this .init.setup section, in effect creating an array of these structures. Listing 5-6, a snippet from .../init/main.c, shows how this data is accessed and used.

---

[10] Normally, the compiler complains if a variable is defined static and is never referenced in the compilation unit. Because these variables are not explicitly referenced, the warning would be emitted without this directive.

LISTING 5-6   Kernel Command-Line Processing

```
1   extern struct obs_kernel_param __setup_start[], __setup_end[];
2
3   static int __init obsolete_checksetup(char *line)
4   {
5       struct obs_kernel_param *p;
6       int had_early_param = 0;
7
8       p = __setup_start;
9       do {
10          int n = strlen(p->str);
11          if (!strncmp(line, p->str, n)) {
12              if (p->early) {
13                  /* Already done in parse_early_param?
14                   * (Needs exact match on param part).
15                   * Keep iterating, as we can have early
16                   * params and __setups of same names 8( */
17                  if (line[n] == '\0' || line[n] == '=')
18                      had_early_param = 1;
19              } else if (!p->setup_func) {
20                  printk(KERN_WARNING "Parameter %s is obsolete,"
21                          " ignored\n", p->str);
22                  return 1;
23              } else if (p->setup_func(line + n))
24                  return 1;
25          }
26          p++;
27      } while (p < __setup_end);
28
29      return had_early_param;
30  }
31
```

Examination of this code should be fairly straightforward, with a couple of explanations. The function is called with a single argument, the kernel command line, parsed in .../kernel/params.c. In the example we've been discussing, `line` would point to the string "console=ttyS0", which is part of the kernel command line. The two external structure pointers `__setup_start` and `__setup_end` are defined in a linker script file, not in a C source or header file. These labels mark the start and end of the array of `obs_kernel_param` structures that were placed in the `.init.setup` section of the object file.

The code in Listing 5-6 scans all these structures via the pointer p to find a match for this particular kernel command-line parameter. In this case, the code is searching for the string console= and finds a match. From the relevant structure, the function pointer element returns a pointer to the console_setup() function, which is called with the balance of the parameter (the string ttyS0,115200) as its only argument. This process is repeated for every element in the kernel command line until the kernel command line has been exhausted.

The technique just described, collecting objects into lists in uniquely named ELF sections, is used in many places in the kernel. Another example of this technique is the use of the __init family of macros to place one-time initialization routines into a common section in the object file. Their cousin __initconst, used to mark one-time-use data items, is used by the __setup macro. Functions and data marked as initialization using these macros are collected into specially named ELF sections. Later, after these one-time initialization functions and data objects have been used, the kernel frees the memory occupied by these items. You might have seen the familiar kernel message near the final part of the boot process saying Freeing init memory: 296K. Your mileage may vary, but a third of a megabyte is well worth the effort of using the __init family of macros. This is exactly the purpose of the __initconst macro in the earlier declaration of __setup_str_console_setup[].

You might have been wondering about the use of symbol names preceded with obsolete_. This is because the kernel developers are replacing the kernel command-line processing mechanism with a more generic mechanism for registering both boot time and loadable module parameters. Currently, hundreds of parameters are declared with the __setup macro. However, new development is expected to use the family of functions defined by the kernel header file .../include/linux/moduleparam.h—most notably, the family of module_param* macros. These are explained in more detail in Chapter 8, "Device Driver Basics," when we introduce device drivers.

The new mechanism maintains backward compatibility by including an unknown function pointer argument in the parsing routine. Thus, parameters that are unknown to the module_param* infrastructure are considered unknown, and the processing falls back to the old mechanism under control of the developer. This is easily understood by examining the well-written code in .../kernel/params.c and the parse_args() calls in .../init/main.c.

The last point worth mentioning is the purpose of the flag member of the obs_kernel_param structure created by the __setup macro. Examination of the code in Listing 5-6 should make it clear. The flag in the structure, called early, is used to indicate whether this particular command-line parameter was already consumed earlier in the boot process. Some command-line parameters are intended for consumption very early in the boot process, and this flag provides a mechanism for an early parsing algorithm. You will find a function in `main.c` called `do_early_param()` that traverses the linker-generated array of `__setup`-generated structures and processes, each one marked for early consumption. This gives the developer some control over when in the boot process this processing is done.

5.4   Subsystem Initialization

Many kernel subsystems are initialized by the code found in `main.c`. Some are initialized explicitly, as with the calls to `init_timers()` and `console_init()`, which need to be called very early. Others are initialized using a technique very similar to that described earlier for the `__setup` macro. In short, the linker builds lists of function pointers to various initialization routines, and a simple loop is used to execute each in turn. Listing 5-7 shows how this works.

LISTING 5-7   Sample Initialization Routine

```
static int __init customize_machine(void)
{
    /* customizes platform devices, or adds new ones */
    if (init_machine)
        init_machine();
    return 0;
}
arch_initcall(customize_machine);
```

This code snippet comes from `.../arch/arm/kernel/setup.c`. It is a simple routine designed to provide a customization hook for a particular board.

5.4.1   The *`__initcall` Macros

Notice two important things about the initialization routine shown in Listing 5-7. First, it is defined with the `__init` macro. As we saw earlier, this macro applies a `section` attribute to declare that this function gets placed in a section called `.init.text` in the `vmlinux` ELF file. Recall that the purpose of placing this function in a special section of the object file is so that the memory space it occupies can be reclaimed when it is no longer needed.

The second thing to notice is the macro immediately following the definition of the function: `arch_initcall(customize_machine)`. This macro is part of a family of macros defined in `.../include/linux/init.h`. These macros are reproduced here as Listing 5-8.

LISTING 5-8   `initcall` **Family of Macros**

```
#define __define_initcall(level,fn,id) \
    static initcall_t __initcall_##fn##id __used \
    __attribute__((__section__(".initcall" level ".init"))) = fn


/*
 * Early initcalls run before initializing SMP.
 *
 * Only for built-in code, not modules.
 */
#define early_initcall(fn)        __define_initcall("early",fn,early)


/*
 * A "pure" initcall has no dependencies on anything else, and purely
 * initializes variables that couldn't be statically initialized.
 *
 * This only exists for built-in code, not for modules.
 */
#define pure_initcall(fn)         __define_initcall("0",fn,0)


#define core_initcall(fn)         __define_initcall("1",fn,1)
#define core_initcall_sync(fn)      __define_initcall("1s",fn,1s)
#define postcore_initcall(fn)        __define_initcall("2",fn,2)
#define postcore_initcall_sync(fn)  __define_initcall("2s",fn,2s)
#define arch_initcall(fn)         __define_initcall("3",fn,3)
#define arch_initcall_sync(fn)       __define_initcall("3s",fn,3s)
#define subsys_initcall(fn)       __define_initcall("4",fn,4)
#define subsys_initcall_sync(fn)     __define_initcall("4s",fn,4s)
#define fs_initcall(fn)           __define_initcall("5",fn,5)
#define fs_initcall_sync(fn)         __define_initcall("5s",fn,5s)
#define rootfs_initcall(fn)         __define_initcall("rootfs",fn,rootfs)
#define device_initcall(fn)         __define_initcall("6",fn,6)
#define device_initcall_sync(fn)     __define_initcall("6s",fn,6s)
#define late_initcall(fn)         __define_initcall("7",fn,7)
#define late_initcall_sync(fn)       __define_initcall("7s",fn,7s)


#define __initcall(fn) device_initcall(fn)
...
```

In a similar fashion to the __setup macro described earlier, these macros declare a data item based on the function's name. They also use the section attribute to place this data item in a uniquely named section of the vmlinux ELF file. The benefit of this approach is that main.c can call an arbitrary initialization function for a subsystem that it has no knowledge of. The only other option, as mentioned earlier, is to pollute main.c with knowledge of every subsystem in the kernel.

You can derive the section names from Listing 5-8. The name of the section is .initcall*N*.init, where *N* is the level defined, between 1 and 7. Notice also that there is a section named for each of the seven levels with an s appended. This is intended to be a synchronous initcall. The data item is assigned the address of the function being named in the macro. In the example defined by Listings 5-7 and 5-8, the data item would be as follows (simplified by omitting the section attribute):

```
static initcall_t __initcall_customize_machine = customize_machine;
```

This data item is placed in the kernel's object file in a section called .initcall3. init.

The level (*N*) is used to provide an ordering of initialization calls. Functions declared using the core_initcall() macro are called before all others. Functions declared using the postcore_initcall() macros are called next, and so on, and those declared with late_initcall() are the last initialization functions to be called.

In a fashion similar to the __setup macro, you can think of this family of *_initcall macros as registration functions for kernel subsystem initialization routines that need to be run once at kernel startup and never used again. These macros provide a mechanism for causing the initialization routine to be executed during system startup and a mechanism to discard the code and reclaim the memory after the routine has been executed. The developer is also provided up to seven levels of when to perform the initialization routines.[11] Therefore, if you have a subsystem that relies on another subsystem's being available, you can enforce this ordering using these levels. If you grep (search) the kernel for the string [a-z]*_initcall, you will see that this family of macros is used extensively.

One final note about the *_initcall family of macros: The use of multiple levels was introduced during the development of the 2.6 kernel series. Earlier kernel versions used the __initcall() macro for this purpose. This macro is still in widespread use, especially in device drivers. To maintain backward compatibility, this macro has been defined to device_initcall(), which has been defined as a level 6 initcall.

---

[11] Seven variations of each level also are marked synchronous.

5.5 The init Thread

The code found in .../init/main.c is responsible for bringing the kernel to life. After start_kernel() performs some basic kernel initialization, calling early initialization functions explicitly by name, the very first kernel thread is spawned. This thread eventually becomes the kernel thread called init(), with a process ID (PID) of 1. As you will learn, init() becomes the parent of all Linux processes in user space. At this point in the boot sequence, two distinct threads are running: that represented by start_kernel(), and now init(). The former goes on to become the idle process, having completed its work. The latter becomes the init process. This is shown in Listing 5-9.

LISTING 5-9   Creation of Kernel init Thread

```
static noinline void __init_refok rest_init(void)
    __releases(kernel_lock)
{
    int pid;

    rcu_scheduler_starting();
    kernel_thread(kernel_init, NULL, CLONE_FS | CLONE_SIGHAND);
    numa_default_policy();
    pid = kernel_thread(kthreadd, NULL, CLONE_FS | CLONE_FILES);
    kthreadd_task = find_task_by_pid_ns(pid, &init_pid_ns);
    unlock_kernel();

    /*
     * The boot idle thread must execute schedule()
     * at least once to get things moving:
     */
    init_idle_bootup_task(current);
    preempt_enable_no_resched();
    schedule();
    preempt_disable();

    /* Call into cpu_idle with preempt disabled */
    cpu_idle();
}
```

The start_kernel() function calls rest_init(), reproduced in Listing 5-9. The kernel's init process is spawned by the call to kernel_thread(), with the function kernel_init as its first parameter. init goes on to complete the rest of the system initialization, while the thread of execution started by `start_kernel()` loops forever in the call to `cpu_idle()`.

The reason for this structure is interesting. You might have noticed that `start_kernel()`, a relatively large function, was marked with the `__init` macro. This means that the memory it occupies will be reclaimed during the final stages of kernel initialization. It is necessary to exit this function and the address space it occupies before reclaiming its memory. The answer to this is for `start_kernel()` to call `rest_init()`, shown in Listing 5-9, a much smaller piece of memory that becomes the idle process.

5.5.1 Initialization Via `initcalls`

When `kernel_init()` is spawned, it eventually calls `do_initcalls()`, which is the function responsible for calling most of the initialization functions registered with the `*_initcall` family of macros. The code is reproduced in Listing 5-10.

LISTING 5-10   Initialization Via `initcalls`

```
extern initcall_t __initcall_start[], __initcall_end[], __early_initcall_end[];

static void __init do_initcalls(void)
{
    initcall_t *fn;

    for (fn = __early_initcall_end; fn < __initcall_end; fn++)
        do_one_initcall(*fn);

    /* Make sure there is no pending stuff from the initcall sequence */
    flush_scheduled_work();
}
```

Note that two similar blocks of code exist. Earlier in the initialization process, a similar function called `do_pre_smp_initcalls()` processes part of the list, from `__initcall_start` to `__early_initcall_end`. This code is self-explanatory, except for the two labels marking the loop boundaries: `__initcall_start` and `__initcall_end`. These labels are not found in any C source or header file. They are defined in the linker script file used during the link stage of `vmlinux`. These labels mark the beginning and end of the list of initialization functions populated using the `*_initcall` family of macros. You can see each of the labels by looking at the `System.map` file in the top-level kernel directory. They all begin with the string `__initcall`, as shown in Listing 5-8.

5.5.2 `initcall_debug`

A very interesting kernel command-line parameter allows you to watch these calls being executed during bootup. It is enabled by setting the kernel command-line parameter `initcall_debug`. Simply start your kernel with the kernel command-line parameter `initcall_debug` to enable this diagnostic output.[12]

Here is an example of what you will see when you enable these debug statements:

```
. . .
calling  uhci_hcd_init+0x0/0x100 @ 1
uhci_hcd: USB Universal Host Controller Interface driver
initcall uhci_hcd_init+0x0/0x100 returned 0 after 5639 usecs
. . .
```

Here you see the USB Universal Host Controller Interface driver being called. The first line announces the intention to call the function `uhci_hcd_init`, which is a device driver initialization call from the USB driver. After this announcement is made, the call to the function is executed. The second line is printed by the driver itself. The trace information on the third line includes the return result and the call's duration.

This is a useful way to see the details of kernel initialization, especially the order in which various subsystems and modules get called. More interesting is the call's duration. If you are concerned with system boot time, this is an excellent way to isolate where time is being consumed on boot.

Even on a modestly configured embedded system, dozens of these initialization functions are invoked in this manner. This example is taken from an ARM XScale embedded target, compiled with a default configuration. The default configuration results in 206 such calls to various kernel initialization routines.

5.5.3 Final Boot Steps

Having spawned the `kernel_init()` thread, and after all the various initialization calls have completed, the kernel performs its final steps in the boot sequence. These include freeing the memory used by the initialization functions and data, opening a system console device, and starting the first user space process. Listing 5-11 reproduces the last steps in the kernel's `init` process from `main.c`.

---

[12] You might have to lower the default loglevel on your system to see these debug messages. This is described in many references about Linux system administration. In any case, you should see them in the kernel log file.

LISTING 5-11   Final Kernel Boot Steps from `main.c`

```
static noinline int init_post(void)
    __releases(kernel_lock)
{
<... lines trimmed for clarity ...>
...
if (execute_command) {
     run_init_process(execute_command);
     printk(KERN_WARNING "Failed to execute %s.  Attempting "
                    "defaults...\n", execute_command);
}

run_init_process("/sbin/init");
run_init_process("/etc/init");
run_init_process("/bin/init");
run_init_process("/bin/sh");

panic("No init found.  Try passing init= option to kernel.");
```

Notice that if the code proceeds to the end of this function (`init_post()`), a kernel panic results. If you've spent any time experimenting with embedded systems or custom root file systems, you've undoubtedly encountered this very common error message as the last line of output on your console. It is one of the most frequently asked questions (FAQs) on a variety of public forums related to Linux and embedded systems.

One way or another, one of these `run_init_process()` commands must proceed without error. The `run_init_process()` function does not return on successful invocation. It overwrites the calling process with the new one, effectively replacing the current process with the new one. It uses the familiar `execve()` system call for this functionality. The most common system configurations spawn `/sbin/init` as the userland[13] initialization process. We'll study this functionality in depth in the next chapter.

One option available to the embedded system developer is to use a custom userland initialization program. That is the purpose of the conditional statement in the preceding code snippet. If `execute_command` is non-null, it points to a string containing a custom user-supplied command to be executed in user space. The developer specifies this command on the kernel command line, and it is set via the `__setup` macro we examined earlier in this chapter. A sample kernel command line incorporating several concepts discussed in this chapter might look like this:

```
initcall_debug init=/sbin/myinit console=ttyS1,115200 root=/dev/hda1
```

---

[13] Userland is an often-used term for any program, library, script, or anything else in user space.

This kernel command line instructs the kernel to display all the initialization routines as they are invoked, configures the initial console device as /dev/ttyS1 at 115Kbps, and executes a custom user space initialization process called myinit, which is located in the /sbin directory on the root file system. It directs the kernel to mount its root file system from the device /dev/hda1, which is the first IDE hard drive. Note that, in general, the order of parameters given on the kernel command line is irrelevant. The next chapter covers the details of user space system initialization.

5.6 Summary

- The Linux kernel project is large and complex. Understanding the structure and composition of the final image is key to learning how to customize your own embedded project.

- Many architectures concatenate an architecture-specific bootstrap loader onto the kernel binary image to set up the proper execution environment required by the Linux kernel. We presented the bootstrap loader build steps to differentiate this functionality from the kernel proper.

- Understanding the initialization flow of control will help deepen your knowledge of the Linux kernel and provide insight into how to customize it for your particular requirements.

- We found the kernel entry point in head.o and followed the flow of control into the primary kernel initialization logic, main.c. We looked at a booting system and the messages it produced, along with an overview of many of the important initialization concepts.

- The kernel command-line processing and the mechanisms used to declare and process kernel command-line parameters were presented. This included a detailed look at some advanced coding techniques for calling arbitrary unknown setup routines using linker-produced tables.

- The final kernel boot steps produce the first user space processes. Understanding this mechanism and its options will enable you to customize and troubleshoot embedded Linux startup issues.

5.6.1   Suggestions for Additional Reading

GNU Compiler Collection documentation
http://gcc.gnu.org/onlinedocs/gcc[14]

Using LD, the GNU linker
http://sourceware.org/binutils/docs/ld/index.html

Kernel documentation

```
.../Documentation/kernel-parameters.txt
```

---

[14] Especially the sections on function attributes, type attributes, and variable attributes.

Chapter 6

User Space Initialization

In This Chapter

■ 6.1   Root File System   132

■ 6.2   Kernel's Last Boot Steps   137

■ 6.3   The init Process   140

■ 6.4   Initial RAM Disk   146

■ 6.5   Using initramfs   153

■ 6.6   Shutdown   156

■ 6.7   Summary   156

In Chapter 2, "The Big Picture," we pointed out that the Linux kernel itself is but a small part of any embedded Linux system. After the kernel has initialized itself, it must mount a root file system and execute a set of developer-defined initialization routines. In this chapter, we examine the details of post-kernel system initialization.

We begin by looking at the root file system and its layout. Next we develop and study a minimal system configuration. Later in this chapter, we add functionality to the minimal system configuration to produce useful sample embedded system configurations. We complete the coverage of system initialization by introducing the initial ramdisk, `initrd` and `initramfs`, and its operation and use. The chapter concludes with a brief look at Linux shutdown logic.

6.1 Root File System

In Chapter 5, "Kernel Initialization," we examined the Linux kernel's behavior during the initialization process. We made several references to mounting a root file system. Linux, like many other advanced operating systems, requires a root file system to realize the benefits of its services. Although it is certainly possible to use Linux in an environment without a file system, doing so makes little sense, because most of the features and value of Linux would be lost. It would be similar to putting your entire system application into a bloated device driver or kernel thread. And can you imagine running your Windows PC without a file system?

The root file system refers to the file system mounted at the base of the file system hierarchy, designated simply as `/`. As you will discover in Chapter 9, "File Systems," even a small embedded Linux system typically mounts several file systems on different locations within the file system hierarchy. These include both real and virtual file systems such as `/proc` and `/sys`. The `proc` file system, introduced in Chapter 9, is an example. It is a special-purpose file system mounted at `/proc` under the root file system. The root file system is simply the first file system mounted at the top of the file system hierarchy.

As you will see shortly, the root file system has special requirements for a Linux system. Linux expects the root file system to contain programs and utilities to boot the system, initialize services such as networking and a system console, load device drivers, and mount additional file systems.

6.1.1   FHS: File System Hierarchy Standard

Several kernel developers authored a standard governing the organization and layout of a UNIX file system. The File System Hierarchy Standard (FHS) establishes a minimum baseline of compatibility between Linux distributions and application programs. You'll find a reference to this standard in the last section of this chapter. You are encouraged to review the FHS for a better background of the layout and rationale of UNIX file system organization.

Many Linux distributions have directory layouts closely matching that described in the FHS standard. The standard exists to provide one element of a common base between different UNIX and Linux distributions. The FHS standard allows your application software (and developers) to predict where certain system elements, including files and directories, can be found in the file system.

6.1.2   File System Layout

Where space is a concern, many embedded systems developers create a very small root file system on a bootable device (such as Flash memory). Later, a larger file system is mounted from another device, perhaps a hard disk or network file system (NFS) server. In fact, it is not uncommon to mount a larger root file system on top of the original small one. You'll see an example of that when we examine the initial ramdisk (`initrd` and `initramfs`) later in this chapter.

A simple Linux root file system might contain the following top-level directory entries:

```
        .
    |
    |--bin
    |--dev
    |--etc
    |--home
    |--lib
    |--sbin
    |--usr
    |--var
    |--tmp
```

Table 6-1 lists the most common contents of each of these root directory entries.

TABLE 6-1   Top-Level Directories

Directory	Contents
bin	Binary executables, usable by all users on the system[1]
dev	Device nodes (see Chapter 8, "Device Driver Basics")
etc	Local system configuration files
home	User account files
lib	System libraries, such as the standard C library and many others
sbin	Binary executables usually reserved for superuser accounts on the system
tmp	Temporary files
usr	A secondary file system hierarchy for application programs, usually read-only
var	Contains variable files, such as system logs and temporary configuration files

The very top of the Linux file system hierarchy is referenced by the slash character (/) by itself. For example, to list the contents of the root directory, you would type this:

```
$ ls /
```

This produces a listing similar to the following:

```
root@coyote:/# ls /
bin  dev  etc  home  lib  mnt  opt  proc  root  sbin  tmp  usr  var
root@coyote:/#
```

This directory listing contains directory entries for additional functionality, including /mnt and /proc. As previously noted, /proc is a special file system containing system information, and /mnt is a placeholder for user-mounted devices and file systems. Notice that we reference these directory entries preceded by a slash, indicating that the path to these top-level directories starts from the root directory.

6.1.3   Minimal File System

To illustrate the requirements of the root file system, we have created a minimal root file system. This example was produced on the ADI Engineering Coyote Reference board using an XScale processor. Listing 6-1 is the output from the tree command on this minimal root file system.

---

[1] Often embedded systems do not have user accounts other than a single root user.

LISTING 6-1   Contents of a Minimal Root File System

```
.
|-- bin
|    |-- busybox
|    `-- sh -> busybox
|-- dev
|    `-- console
|-- etc
|    `-- init.d
|        `-- rcS
`-- lib
    |-- ld-2.3.2.so
    |-- ld-linux.so.2 -> ld-2.3.2.so
    |-- libc-2.3.2.so
    `-- libc.so.6 -> libc-2.3.2.so

5 directories, 8 files
```

This root configuration makes use of busybox, a popular and aptly named toolkit for embedded systems. In short, busybox is a stand-alone binary that supports many common Linux command-line utilities. busybox is so pertinent for embedded systems that we devote Chapter 11, "BusyBox," to this flexible utility.

Notice that our sample minimum file system in Listing 6-1 has only eight files in five directories. This tiny root file system boots and provides the user with a fully functional command prompt on the serial console. Any commands that have been enabled in busybox are available to the user.

Starting from /bin, we have the busybox executable and a soft link called sh pointing back to busybox. You will see shortly why this is necessary. The file in /dev is a device node[2] required to open a console device for input and output. Although it is not strictly necessary, the rcS file in the /etc/init.d directory is the default initialization script processed by busybox on startup. Including rcS silences the warning message issued by busybox whenever rcS is missing.

The final directory entry and set of files required are the two libraries, glibc (libc-2.3.2.so) and the Linux dynamic loader (ld-2.3.2.so). glibc contains the standard C library functions, such as printf() and many others that most application programs depend on. The Linux dynamic loader is responsible for loading the binary executable into memory and performing the dynamic linking required by the application's reference to shared library functions. Two additional soft links are included—ld-linux.

---

[2] Device nodes are explained in detail in Chapter 8.

so.2, pointing back to 1d-2.3.2.so, and libc.so.6, referencing libc-2.3.2.so. These links provide version immunity and backward compatibility for the libraries themselves and are found on all Linux systems.

This simple root file system produces a fully functional system. On the ARM/ XScale board on which this was tested, the size of this small root file system was about 1.7MB. It is interesting to note that more than 80 percent of that size is contained within the C library itself. If you need to reduce its size for your embedded system, you might want to investigate the Library Optimizer Tool at http://libraryopt.sourceforge. net/.

6.1.4   The Embedded Root FS Challenge

The challenge of a root file system for an embedded device is simple to explain but not so simple to overcome. Unless you are lucky enough to be developing an embedded system with a reasonably large hard drive or large Flash storage on board, you might find it difficult to fit your applications and utilities onto a single Flash memory device. Although costs continue to come down for Flash storage, there will always be competitive pressure to reduce costs and decrease time to market. One of the single largest reasons Linux continues to grow in popularity as an embedded OS is the huge and growing body of Linux application software.

Trimming a root file system to fit into a given storage space requirement can be daunting. Many packages and subsystems consist of dozens or even hundreds of files. In addition to the application itself, many packages include configuration files, libraries, configuration utilities, icons, documentation files, locale files related to internationalization, database files, and more. The Apache web server from the Apache Software Foundation is an example of a well-known application often found in embedded systems. The base Apache package from one popular embedded Linux distribution contains 254 different files. Furthermore, they aren't all simply copied into a single directory on your file system. They need to be populated in several different locations on the file system for the Apache application to function without modification.

These concepts are some of the fundamental aspects of distribution engineering, and they can be quite tedious. Linux distribution companies such as Red Hat (in the desktop and enterprise market segments) and Mentor Graphics (in the embedded market segment) spend considerable engineering resources on just this: packaging a collection of programs, libraries, tools, utilities, and applications that together make up a Linux distribution. By necessity, building a root file system employs elements of distribution engineering on a smaller scale.

6.1.5   Trial-and-Error Method

Until recently, the only way to populate the contents of your root file system was to use the trial-and-error method. Perhaps the process could be automated by creating a set of scripts for this purpose, but the knowledge of which files are required for a given functionality still must come from the developer. Tools such as Red Hat Package Manager (rpm) can be used to install packages on your root file system. rpm has reasonable dependency resolution within given packages, but it is complex and involves a significant learning curve. Furthermore, using rpm does not lend itself easily to building small root file systems. It has limited capabilities for stripping unnecessary files from the installation, such as documentation and unused utilities for a given package.

6.1.6   Automated File System Build Tools

The leading vendors of embedded Linux distributions ship very capable tools designed to automate the task of building root file systems in Flash or other devices. These tools usually are graphical in nature, enabling the developer to select files by application or functionality. They have features to strip unnecessary files such as documentation from a package. Many let you select at the individual file level. These tools can produce a variety of file system formats for later installation on your choice of device. Contact your favorite embedded Linux distribution vendor for details on these powerful tools.

Some open source build tools automate the task of building a working root file system. Some of the more notable include bitbake from the OpenEmbedded project (www.openembedded.org/) and buildroot (http://buildroot.uclibc.org/.) Chapter 16, "Open Source Build Systems," presents details of some popular build systems.

6.2   Kernel's Last Boot Steps

The preceding chapter introduced the steps the kernel takes in the final phases of system boot. The final snippet of code from .../init/main.c is reproduced in Listing 6-2 for your convenience.

LISTING 6-2   Final Boot Steps from main.c

```
    ...
    if (execute_command) {
            run_init_process(execute_command);
            printk(KERN_WARNING "Failed to execute %s.  Attempting "
                                "defaults...\n", execute_command);
```

LISTING 6-2   Continued

```
    }

    run_init_process("/sbin/init");
    run_init_process("/etc/init");
    run_init_process("/bin/init");
    run_init_process("/bin/sh");

    panic("No init found.  Try passing init= option to kernel.");
```

This is the final sequence of events for the kernel thread called `kernel_init` spawned by the kernel during the final stages of boot. The `run_init_process()` is a small wrapper around the `execve()` function, which is a kernel system call with rather interesting behavior. The `execve()` function never returns if no error conditions are encountered in the call. The memory space in which the calling thread executes is overwritten by the called program's memory image. In effect, the called program directly replaces the calling thread, including inheriting its Process ID (PID).

The basic structure of this initialization sequence has been unchanged for a long time in the development of the Linux kernel. In fact, Linux version 1.0 contained similar constructs. Essentially, this is the start of user space[3] processing. As you can see from Listing 6-2, unless the Linux kernel is successful in executing one of these processes, the kernel will halt, displaying the message passed in the `panic()` system call. If you have been working with embedded systems for any length of time, and especially if you have experience working on root file systems, you are more than familiar with this kernel `panic()` and its message. If you do an Internet search for this `panic()` error message, you will find page after page of hits. When you complete this chapter, you will be an expert at troubleshooting this common failure.

Notice a key ingredient of these processes: They are all programs that are expected to reside on a root file system that has a structure similar to that presented in Listing 6-1. Therefore, we know that we must at least satisfy the kernel's requirement for an `init` process that can execute within its own environment.

In looking at Listing 6-2, this means that at least one of the `run_init_process()` function calls must succeed. You can see that the kernel tries to execute one of four programs in the order in which they are encountered. As you also can see that if none of these four programs succeeds, the booting kernel issues the dreaded `panic()` function call and dies right there. Remember, this snippet of code from `.../init/main.c`

---

[3] In actuality, modern Linux kernels create a userspace-like environment earlier in the boot sequence for specialized activities, which are beyond the scope of this book.

is executed only once on bootup. If it does not succeed, the kernel can do little but complain and halt, which it does through the `panic()` function call.

6.2.1 First User Space Program

On most Linux systems, `/sbin/init` is spawned by the kernel on boot. This is why it is attempted first from Listing 6-2. Effectively, this becomes the first user space program to run. To review, this is the sequence:

1. Mount the root file system.
2. Spawn the first user space program, which, in this discussion, becomes `/sbin/init`.

In our sample minimal root file system from Listing 6-1, the first three attempts at spawning a user space process would fail, because we did not provide an executable file called `init` anywhere on the file system. Recall from Listing 6-1 that we had a soft link called `sh` that pointed back to `busybox`. You should now realize the purpose of that soft link: It causes `busybox` to be executed by the kernel as the initial process while also satisfying the common requirement for a shell executable from user space.[4]

6.2.2 Resolving Dependencies

It is not sufficient to simply include an executable such as `init` on your file system and expect it to boot. For every process you place on your root file system, you must also satisfy its dependencies. Most processes have two categories of dependencies: those that are needed to satisfy unresolved references within a dynamically linked executable, and external configuration or data files that an application might need. We have a tool to find the former, but the latter can be supplied only by at least a cursory understanding of the application in question.

An example will help make this clear. The `init` process is a dynamically linked executable. To run `init`, we need to satisfy its library dependencies. A tool has been developed for this purpose: `ldd`. To understand what libraries a given application requires, simply run your cross-version of `ldd` on the binary:

```
$ ppc_4xx-ldd init
        libc.so.6 => /opt/eldk/ppc_4xxFP/lib/libc.so.6
        ld.so.1 => /opt/eldk/ppc_4xxFP/lib/ld.so.1
$
```

---

[4] When busybox is invoked via the `sh` symbolic link, it spawns a shell. We cover this in detail in Chapter 11.

From this `ldd` output, we can see that the Power Architecture `init` executable in this example is dependent on two libraries—the standard C library (`libc.so.6`) and the Linux dynamic loader (`ld.so.1`).

To satisfy the second category of dependencies for an executable, the configuration and data files that it might need, there is little substitute for some knowledge about how the subsystem works. For example, `init` expects to read its operational configuration from a data file called `inittab` located on `/etc`. Unless you are using a tool that has this knowledge built in, such as those described in Chapter 16, you must supply that knowledge.

6.2.3   Customized Initial Process

It is worth noting that the system user can control which initial process is executed at startup. This is done by a kernel command-line parameter. It is hinted at in Listing 6-2 by the text contained within the `panic()` function call. Building on our kernel command line from Chapter 5, here is how it might look with a user-specified `init` process:

```
console=ttyS0,115200 ip=bootp root=/dev/nfs init=/sbin/myinit
```

Specifying `init=` in the kernel command line in this way, you must provide a binary executable on your root file system in the `/sbin` directory called `myinit`. This would be the first process to gain control at the completion of the kernel's boot process.

6.3   The `init` Process

Unless you are doing something highly unusual, you will never need to provide a customized initial process, because the capabilities of the standard `init` process are very flexible. The `init` program, together with a family of startup scripts that we will examine shortly, implement what is commonly called System V Init, from the original UNIX System V that used this schema. We will now examine this powerful system configuration and control utility.

You saw in the preceding section that `init` is the first user space process spawned by the kernel after completion of the boot process. As you will learn, every process in a running Linux system has a child-parent relationship with another process running in the system. `init` is the ultimate parent of all user space processes in a Linux system. Furthermore, `init` provides the default set of environment parameters for all other processes to inherit, such as the initial system PATH.

Its primary role is to spawn additional processes under the direction of a special configuration file. This configuration file is usually stored as /etc/inittab. init has the concept of a runlevel. A runlevel can be thought of as a system state. Each runlevel is defined by the services that are enabled and programs that are spawned upon entry to that runlevel.

init can exist in a single runlevel at any given time. Runlevels used by init include runlevels from 0 to 6 and a special runlevel called s. Runlevel 0 instructs init to halt the system, and runlevel 6 results in a system reboot. For each runlevel, a set of startup and shutdown scripts is usually provided that define the action a system should take for each runlevel. Actions to perform for a given runlevel are determined by the /etc/inittab configuration file, described shortly.

Several of the runlevels have been reserved for specific purposes in many distributions. Table 6-2 describes the runlevels and their purposes in common use in many Linux distributions.

TABLE 6-2   Runlevels

Runlevel	Purpose
0	System shutdown (halt)
1	Single-user system configuration for maintenance
2	User-defined
3	General-purpose multiuser configuration
4	User-defined
5	Multiuser with graphical user interface on startup
6	System restart (reboot)

The runlevel scripts are commonly found under a directory called /etc/rc.d/init.d. Here you will find most of the scripts that enable and disable individual services. Services can be configured manually by invoking the script and passing one of the appropriate arguments to the script, such as start, stop, or restart. Listing 6-3 displays an example of restarting the NFS service.

LISTING 6-3   NFS Restart

```
$ /etc/init.d/nfs-kernel-server
Shutting down NFS mountd:                        [  OK  ]
Shutting down NFS daemon:                        [  OK  ]
Shutting down NFS quotas:                        [  OK  ]
Shutting down NFS services:                      [  OK  ]
```

LISTING 6-3   Continued
```
Starting NFS services:                              [  OK  ]
Starting NFS quotas:                                [  OK  ]
Starting NFS daemon:                                [  OK  ]
Starting NFS mountd:                                [  OK  ]
```

If you have spent any time with a desktop Linux distribution such as Red Hat or Fedora, you have undoubtedly seen lines like this during system startup.

A runlevel is defined by the services that are enabled at that runlevel. Most Linux distributions contain a directory structure under /etc that contains symbolic links to the service scripts in /etc/rc.d/init.d. These runlevel directories typically are rooted at /etc/rc.d. Under this directory, you will find a series of runlevel directories that contain startup and shutdown specifications for each runlevel. init simply executes these scripts upon entry and exit from a runlevel. The scripts define the system state, and inittab instructs init which scripts to associate with a given runlevel. Listing 6-4 contains the directory structure beneath /etc/rc.d that drives the runlevel startup and shutdown behavior upon entry to or exit from the specified runlevel, respectively.

LISTING 6-4   Runlevel Directory Structure
```
$ ls -l /etc/rc.d
total 96
drwxr-xr-x  2 root root  4096 Oct 20 10:19 init.d
-rwxr-xr-x  1 root root  2352 Mar 16  2009 rc
drwxr-xr-x  2 root root  4096 Mar 22  2009 rc0.d
drwxr-xr-x  2 root root  4096 Mar 22  2009 rc1.d
drwxr-xr-x  2 root root  4096 Mar 22  2009 rc2.d
drwxr-xr-x  2 root root  4096 Mar 22  2009 rc3.d
drwxr-xr-x  2 root root  4096 Mar 22  2009 rc4.d
drwxr-xr-x  2 root root  4096 Mar 22  2009 rc5.d
drwxr-xr-x  2 root root  4096 Mar 22  2009 rc6.d
-rwxr-xr-x  1 root root   943 Dec 31 16:36 rc.local
-rwxr-xr-x  1 root root 25509 Jan 11  2009 rc.sysinit
```

Each of the runlevels is defined by the scripts contained in rcN.d, where N is the runlevel. Inside each rcN.d directory, you will find numerous symlinks arranged in a specific order. These symbolic links start with either a K or an S. Those beginning with S point to service scripts, which are invoked with startup instructions. Those starting with K point to service scripts that are invoked with shutdown instructions. An example with a very small number of services might look like Listing 6-5.

LISTING 6-5   Sample Runlevel Directory

```
lrwxrwxrwx  1 root root 17 Nov 25  2009 S10network -> ../init.d/network
lrwxrwxrwx  1 root root 16 Nov 25  2009 S12syslog  -> ../init.d/syslog
lrwxrwxrwx  1 root root 16 Nov 25  2009 S56xinetd  -> ../init.d/xinetd
lrwxrwxrwx  1 root root 16 Nov 25  2009 K50xinetd  -> ../init.d/xinetd
lrwxrwxrwx  1 root root 16 Nov 25  2009 K88syslog  -> ../init.d/syslog
lrwxrwxrwx  1 root root 17 Nov 25  2009 K90network -> ../init.d/network
```

This code instructs the startup scripts to start three services upon entry to this ficti-
tious runlevel: network, syslog, and xinetd. Because the s* scripts are ordered with a
numeric tag, they will be started in this order. In a similar fashion, when exiting this
runlevel, three services will be terminated: xinetd, syslog, and network. In a similar
fashion, these services will be terminated in the order presented by the two-digit number following the K in the symlink filename. In an actual system, there would undoubtedly be many more entries. You can include your own entries for your own custom
applications as well.

The top-level script that executes these service startup and shutdown scripts is defined in the init configuration file, which we now examine.

6.3.1 inittab

When init is started, it reads the system configuration file /etc/inittab. This file
contains directives for each runlevel, as well as directives that apply to all runlevels.
This file and init's behavior are well documented in man pages on most Linux workstations, as well as by several books covering system administration. We do not attempt
to duplicate those works; we focus on how a developer might configure inittab for an
embedded system. For a detailed explanation of how inittab and init work together,
view the man page on most Linux workstations by typing man init and man inittab.

Let's look at a typical inittab for a simple embedded system. Listing 6-6 contains
a simple inittab example for a system that supports a single runlevel as well as shutdown and reboot.

LISTING 6-6   Simple inittab

```
# /etc/inittab

# The default runlevel (2 in this example)
id:2:initdefault:
```

LISTING 6-6   Continued

```
# This is the first process (actually a script) to be run.
si::sysinit:/etc/rc.sysinit

# Execute our shutdown script on entry to runlevel 0
l0:0:wait:/etc/init.d/sys.shutdown

# Execute our normal startup script on entering runlevel 2
l2:2:wait:/etc/init.d/runlvl2.startup

# This line executes a reboot script (runlevel 6)
l6:6:wait:/etc/init.d/sys.reboot

# This entry spawns a login shell on the console
# Respawn means it will be restarted each time it is killed
con:2:respawn:/bin/sh
```

This very simple[5] inittab script describes three individual runlevels. Each runlevel is associated with a script, which must be created by the developer for the desired actions in each runlevel. When this file is read by init, the first script to be executed is /etc/rc.sysinit. This is denoted by the sysinit tag. Then init enters runlevel 2 and executes the script defined for runlevel 2. From this example, this would be /etc/init.d/runlvl2.startup. As you might guess from the :wait: tag shown in Listing 6-6, init waits until the script completes before continuing. When the runlevel 2 script completes, init spawns a shell on the console (through the /bin/sh symbolic link), as shown in the last line of Listing 6-6. The respawn keyword instructs init to restart the shell each time it detects that it has exited. Listing 6-7 shows what it looks like during boot.

LISTING 6-7   Sample Startup Messages

```
...
VFS: Mounted root (nfs filesystem).
Freeing init memory: 304K
INIT: version 2.78 booting
This is rc.sysinit
INIT: Entering runlevel: 2
This is runlvl2.startup

#
```

---

[5] This inittab is a nice example of a small, purpose-built embedded system.

The startup scripts in this example do nothing except announce themselves for illustrative purposes. Of course, in an actual system, these scripts enable features and services that do useful work! Given the simple configuration in this example, you would enable the services and applications for your particular widget in the /etc/init.d/ runlvl2.startup script. You would do the reverse—disable your applications, services, and devices—in your shutdown and/or reboot scripts. The next section looks at some typical system configurations and the required entries in the startup scripts to enable these configurations.

6.3.2 Sample Web Server Startup Script

Although simple, this sample startup script is designed to illustrate the mechanism and guide you in designing your own system startup and shutdown behavior. This example is based on busybox, which has a slightly different initialization behavior than init. These differences are covered in detail in Chapter 11.

In a typical embedded appliance that contains a web server, you might want several servers available for maintenance and remote access. In this example, we enable servers for HTTP and Telnet access (via inetd). Listing 6-8 contains a simple rc.sysinit script for our hypothetical web server appliance.

LISTING 6-8   Web Server rc.sysinit

```
#!/bin/sh

echo "This is rc.sysinit"

busybox mount -t proc none /proc

# Load the system loggers
/sbin/syslogd
/sbin/klogd

# Enable legacy PTY support for telnetd
busybox mkdir /dev/pts
busybox mknod /dev/ptmx c 5 2
busybox mount -t devpts devpts /dev/pts
```

In this simple initialization script, we first enable the proc file system. The details of this useful subsystem are covered in Chapter 9. Next we enable the system loggers so that we can capture system information during operation. This is especially useful when things go wrong. The last entries enable support for the UNIX PTY subsystem, which is required for the implementation of the Telnet server used for this example.

Listing 6-9 contains the commands in the runlevel 2 startup script. This script contains the commands to enable any services we want to have operational for our appliance.

LISTING 6-9   Sample Runlevel 2 Startup Script

```
#!/bin/sh

echo "This is runlvl2.startup"

echo "Starting Internet Superserver"
inetd

echo "Starting web server"
webs &
```

Notice how simple this runlevel 2 startup script is. First we enable the so-called Internet superserver `inetd`, which intercepts and spawns services for common TCP/IP requests. In our example, we enabled Telnet services through a configuration file called `/etc/inetd.conf`. Then we execute the web server, here called `webs`. That's all there is to it. Although minimal, this is a working configuration for Telnet and web services.

To complete this configuration, you might supply a shutdown script (refer to Listing 6-6), which, in this case, would terminate the web server and the Internet superserver before system shutdown. In our sample scenario, that is sufficient for a clean shutdown.

6.4   Initial RAM Disk

The Linux kernel contains two mechanisms to mount an early root file system to perform certain startup-related system initialization and configuration. First we will discuss the legacy method, the initial ramdisk, or `initrd`. The next section covers the newer method called `initramfs`.

The legacy method for enabling early user space processing is known as the initial RAM disk, or simply `initrd`. Support for this functionality must be compiled into the kernel. This kernel configuration option is found under General Setup, RAM disk support in the kernel configuration utility. Figure 6-1 shows an example of the configuration for `initrd` and `initramfs`.

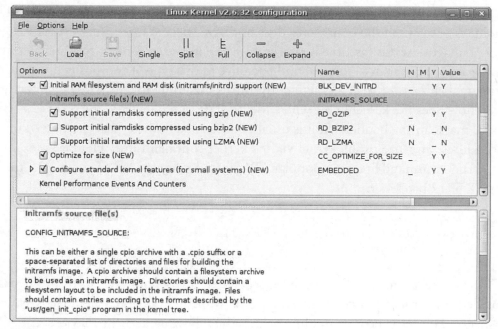

FIGURE 6-1   Linux kernel configuration utility

The initial RAM disk is a small, self-contained root file system that usually contains directives to load specific device drivers before the completion of the boot cycle. In Linux workstation distributions such as Red Hat and Ubuntu, an initial RAM disk is used to load the device drivers for the EXT3 file system before mounting the real root file system. An initrd is frequently used to load a device driver that is required in order to access the real root file system.

6.4.1   Booting with initrd

To use the initrd functionality, the bootloader gets involved on most architectures to pass the initrd image to the kernel. A common scenario is that the bootloader loads a compressed kernel image into memory and then loads an initrd image into another section of available memory. In doing so, it becomes the bootloader's responsibility to pass the load address of the initrd image to the kernel before passing control to it. The exact mechanism differs depending on the architecture, bootloader, and platform implementation. However, the kernel must know where the initrd image is located so it can load it.

Some architectures and platforms construct a single composite binary image. This scheme is used when the bootloader does not have specific Linux support for loading `initrd` images. In this case, the kernel and `initrd` image are simply concatenated into a single composite image. You will find reference to this type of composite image in the kernel makefiles as `bootpImage`. Presently, this is used only for the ARM architecture.[6]

So how does the kernel know where to find the `initrd` image? Unless there is some special magic in the bootloader, it is usually sufficient simply to pass the `initrd` image start address and size to the kernel via the kernel command line. Here is an example of a kernel command line for a popular ARM-based reference board containing the TI OMAP 5912 processor:

```
console=ttyS0,115200 root=/dev/nfs                          \
   nfsroot=192.168.1.9:/home/chris/sandbox/omap-target      \
   initrd=0x10800000,0x14af47
```

This kernel command line has been separated into several lines to fit in the space provided. In actual practice, it is a single line, with the individual elements separated by spaces. This kernel command line defines the following kernel behavior:

- Specify a single console on device `ttyS0` at 115 kilobaud.
- Mount a root file system via NFS, the network file system.
- Find the NFS root file system on host 192.168.1.9 (from directory `/home/chris/sandbox/omap-target`).
- Load and mount an initial ramdisk from physical memory location `0x10800000`, which has a size of `0x14AF47` (1,355,591 bytes).

One additional note regarding this example: Almost universally, the `initrd` image is compressed. The size specified on the kernel command line is the size of the compressed image.

6.4.2   Bootloader Support for `initrd`

Let's look at a simple example based on the popular U-Boot bootloader running on an ARM processor. This bootloader was designed with support for directly booting the Linux kernel. Using U-Boot, it is easy to include an `initrd` image with the kernel image. Listing 6-10 shows a typical boot sequence containing an initial ramdisk image.

---

[6] This technique has largely been deprecated in favor of using `initramfs`, as explained next.

LISTING 6-10   Booting the Kernel with Ramdisk Support

```
[uboot]> tftp 0x10000000 kernel-uImage
...
Load address: 0x10000000
Loading: ########################## done
Bytes transferred = 1069092 (105024 hex)

[uboot]> tftp 0x10800000 initrd-uboot
...
Load address: 0x10800000
Loading: ######################################## done
Bytes transferred = 282575 (44fcf hex)

[uboot]> bootm 0x10000000 0x10800040
Uncompressing kernel.................done.
...
RAMDISK driver initialized: 16 RAM disks of 16384K size 1024 blocksize
...
RAMDISK: Compressed image found at block 0
VFS: Mounted root (ext2 filesystem).
Greetings: this is linuxrc from Initial RAMDisk
Mounting /proc filesystem

BusyBox v1.00 (2005.03.14-16:37+0000) Built-in shell (ash)
Enter 'help' for a list of built-in commands.

# (<<<< Busybox command prompt)
```

Here we get a glimpse of the U-Boot bootloader, which we'll examine in more detail in the next chapter. The tftp command causes U-Boot to download the kernel image from a TFTP server. The kernel image is downloaded and placed into the base of this target system's memory at the 256MB address (0x10000000 hex[7]). Then a second image, the initial ramdisk image, is downloaded from a TFTP server into memory at a higher memory address (256MB + 8MB in this example). Finally, we issue the U-Boot bootm command, which is the "boot from memory" command. The bootm command takes two arguments: the address of the Linux kernel image, optionally followed by an address representing the location of the initial ramdisk image.

---

[7] It just so happens that on this particular board, our physical SDRAM starts at 256MB.

Take special note of one feature of the U-Boot bootloader: It fully supports loading kernel and ramdisk images over an Ethernet connection. This is a very useful development configuration. You can get a kernel and ramdisk image onto your board in other ways as well. You can flash them into your Flash memory using a hardware-based Flash programming tool, or you can use a serial port and download the kernel and file system images via RS-232. However, because these images typically are large (a kernel can be about a megabyte, and a ramdisk can be tens of megabytes), you will save a significant amount of engineering time if you invest in this Ethernet-based TFTP download method. Whatever bootloader you choose, make sure it supports network download of development images.

6.4.3   initrd Magic: linuxrc

When the kernel boots, first it detects the presence of the initrd image. Then it copies the compressed binary file from the specified physical location in RAM into a proper kernel ramdisk and mounts it as the root file system. The magic of initrd comes from the contents of a special file within the initrd image. When the kernel mounts the initial ramdisk, it looks for a specific file called linuxrc. It treats this file as a script file and proceeds to execute the commands contained therein. This mechanism enables the system designer to specify the behavior of initrd. Listing 6-11 shows a sample linuxrc file.

LISTING 6-11   Sample linuxrc File

```
#!/bin/sh

echo 'Greetings: this is 'linuxrc' from Initial Ramdisk'
echo 'Mounting /proc filesystem'
mount -t proc /proc /proc

busybox sh
```

In practice, this file would contain directives required before we mount the real root file system. One example might be to load CompactFlash drivers to obtain a real root file system from a CompactFlash device. For the purposes of this example, we simply spawn a busybox shell and halt the boot process for examination. You can see the # command prompt from Listing 6-10 resulting from this busybox shell. If you were to type the exit command here, the kernel would continue its boot process until complete.

After the kernel copies the ramdisk from physical memory into a kernel ramdisk, it returns this physical memory to the available memory pool. You can think of this as transferring the initrd image from physical memory at the hard-coded address into the kernel's own virtual memory (in the form of a kernel ramdisk device).

One last comment about Listing 6-11: The mount command in which the /proc file system is mounted seems redundant in its use of the word proc. This command would also work:

```
mount -t proc none /proc
```

Notice that the device field of the mount command has been changed to none. The mount command ignores the device field because no physical device is associated with the proc file system. The -t proc is enough to instruct mount to mount the /proc file system on the /proc mount point. I use the former invocation as a mental reminder that we are actually mounting the kernel pseudo device (the /proc file system) on /proc. The mount command ignores this argument. Use the method you prefer. Later, when you type mount at the command line, the device field will show proc instead of none, reminding you that this is a virtual file system.

6.4.4   The initrd Plumbing

As part of the Linux boot process, the kernel must locate and mount a root file system. Late in the boot process, the kernel decides what and where to mount in a function called prepare_namespace(), which is found in .../init/do mounts.c. If initrd support is enabled in the kernel, as illustrated in Figure 6-1, and the kernel command line is so configured, the kernel decompresses the compressed initrd image from physical memory and eventually copies the contents of this file into a ramdisk device (/dev/ram). At this point, we have a proper file system on a kernel ramdisk. After the file system has been read into the ramdisk, the kernel effectively mounts this ramdisk device as its root file system. Finally, the kernel spawns a kernel thread to execute the linuxrc file on the initrd image.[8]

When the linuxrc script has completed execution, the kernel unmounts the initrd and proceeds with the final stages of system boot. If the real root device has a directory called /initrd, Linux mounts the initrd file system on this path (in this context, called

---

[8] Out of necessity (space), this is a very simplified description of the sequence of events. The actual mechanism is similar in concept, but several significant details are omitted for clarity. You are encouraged to consult the kernel source code for more details. See .../init/main.c and .../init/do_mounts*.c.

a mount point). If this directory does not exist in the final root file system, the `initrd` image is simply discarded.

If the kernel command line contains a `root=` parameter specifying a ramdisk (`root=/dev/ram0`, for example), the previously described `initrd` behavior changes in two important ways. First, the processing of the `linuxrc` executable is skipped. Second, no attempt is made to mount another file system as root. This means that you can have a Linux system with `initrd` as the only root file system. This is useful for minimal system configurations in which the only root file system is the ramdisk. Placing `/dev/ram0` on the kernel command line allows the full system initialization to complete with `initrd` as the final root file system.

6.4.5   Building an `initrd` Image

Constructing a suitable root file system image is one of the more challenging aspects of embedded systems. Creating a proper `initrd` image is even more challenging, because it needs to be small and specialized. This section examines `initrd` requirements and file system contents.

Listing 6-12 was produced by running the `tree` utility on our sample `initrd` image from this chapter.

LISTING 6-12   Contents of a Sample `initrd`

```
.
|-- bin
|   |-- busybox
|   |-- echo -> busybox
|   |-- mount -> busybox
|   '-- sh -> busybox
|-- dev
|   |-- console
|   |-- ram0
|   '-- ttyS0
|-- etc
|-- linuxrc
'-- proc

4 directories, 8 files
```

As you can see, it is very small indeed; it takes up a little more than 500KB in uncompressed form. Since it is based on `busybox`, it has many capabilities. Because `busybox` is statically linked for this exercise, it has no dependencies on any system libraries. You will learn more about busybox in Chapter 11.

6.5   Using initramfs

initramfs is the preferred mechanism for executing early user space programs. It is conceptually similar to initrd, as described in the preceding section. It is enabled using the same configuration selections as shown in Figure 6-1. Its purpose is also similar: to enable loading of drivers that might be required before mounting the real (final) root file system. However, it differs in significant ways from the initrd mechanism.

The technical implementation details differ significantly between initrd and initramfs. For example, initramfs is loaded before the call to do_basic_setup(),[9] which provides a mechanism for loading firmware for devices before its driver has been loaded. For more details, see the Linux kernel documentation for this subsystem at .../Documentation/filesystems/ramfs-rootfs-initramfs.txt.

From a practical perspective, initramfs is much easier to use. initramfs is a cpio archive, whereas initrd is a gzipped file system image. This simple difference contributes to the ease of use of initramfs and removes the requirement that you must be root to create it. It is integrated into the Linux kernel source tree, and a small default (nearly empty) image is built automatically when you build the kernel image. Making changes to it is far easier than building and loading a new initrd image.

Listing 6-13 shows the contents of the Linux kernel .../usr directory, where the initramfs image is built. The contents of Listing 6-13 are shown after a kernel has been built.

LISTING 6-13   Kernel initramfs Build Directory

```
$ ls -l usr
total 72
-rw-r--r-- 1 chris chris  1146 2009-12-16 12:36 built-in.o
-rwxr-xr-x 1 chris chris 15567 2009-12-16 12:36 gen_init_cpio
-rw-r--r-- 1 chris chris 12543 2009-12-16 12:35 gen_init_cpio.c
-rw-r--r-- 1 chris chris  1024 2009-06-24 10:57 initramfs_data.bz2.S
-rw-r--r-- 1 chris chris   512 2009-12-16 12:36 initramfs_data.cpio
-rw-r--r-- 1 chris chris  1023 2009-06-24 10:57 initramfs_data.gz.S
-rw-r--r-- 1 chris chris  1025 2009-06-24 10:57 initramfs_data.lzma.S
```

---

[9] do_basic_setup is called from .../init/main.c and calls do_initcalls(). This causes driver module initialization routines to be called. This was described in detail in Chapter 5 and shown in Listing 5-10.

LISTING 6-13   Continued

```
-rw-r--r-- 1 chris chris  1158 2009-12-16 12:36 initramfs_data.o
-rw-r--r-- 1 chris chris  1021 2009-06-24 10:57 initramfs_data.S
-rw-r--r-- 1 chris chris  4514 2009-06-24 10:57 Kconfig
-rw-r--r-- 1 chris chris  2154 2009-12-16 12:35 Makefile
```

A build script in .../scripts called gen_initramfs_list.sh defines a default list of files that will be included in the initramfs archive. The default for recent Linux kernels looks like Listing 6-14.

LISTING 6-14   Sample initramfs File Specification

```
dir /dev 0755 0 0
nod /dev/console 0600 0 0 c 5 1
dir /root 0700 0 0
```

This produces a small default directory structure containing the /root and /dev top-level directories, as well as a single device node representing the console. The details of how to specify items for initramfs file systems are described in the kernel documentation at .../Documentation/filesystems/ramfs-rootfs-initramfs.txt. In summary, the preceding listing produces a directory entry (dir) called /dev, with 0755 file permissions and a user-id and group-id of 0 (root.) The second line defines a device node (nod) called /dev/console, with file permissions of 0600, user and group IDs of 0 (root), being a *character device* (c) with major number 5 and minor number 1.[10] The third line creates another directory called /root similar to the /dev specifier.

6.5.1   Customizing initramfs

There are two ways to customize the initramfs for your particular requirements. Either create a cpio archive with your required files, or specify a list of directories and files whose contents are merged with the default created by gen_initramfs_list.sh. You specify a source for your initramfs files via the kernel-configuration facility. Enable INITRAMFS_SOURCE in your kernel configuration, and point it to a location on your development workstation. This configuration parameter is highlighted in Figure 6-1. The kernel build system will use those files as the source for your initramfs image. Let's see what this looks like using a minimal file system similar to the one built in Listing 6-1.

---

[10] If you are unfamiliar with device nodes and the concept of major numbers and minor numbers, these topics are covered in Chapter 8.

First, we will build a file collection containing the files we want for a minimal system. Because initramfs is supposed to be small and lean, we'll build it around a statically compiled busybox. Compiling busybox statically means it is not dependent on any system libraries. We need very little beyond busybox: a device node for the console in a directory called /dev and a symlink pointing back to busybox called init. Finally, we'll include a busybox startup script to spawn a shell for us to interact with after booting into this initramfs. Listing 6-15 details this minimal file system.

LISTING 6-15   Minimal initramfs Contents

```
$ tree ./usr/myinitramfs_root/
.
|-- bin
|    |-- busybox
|    '-- sh -> busybox
|-- dev
|    '-- console
|-- etc
|    '-- init.d
|         '-- rcS
'-- init -> /bin/sh

4 directories, 5 files
```

When we point the kernel configuration parameter INITRAMFS_SOURCE to the directory where this file structure lives, it automatically builds the initramfs compressed cpio archive and links it into the kernel image.

The reason for the init symlink should be noted. When the kernel is configured for initramfs, it searches for an executable file called /init on the root of the initramfs image. If it finds it, it executes it as the init process with PID (process ID) set to 1. If it does not find it, it skips initramfs and proceeds with normal root file system processing. This logic is found in .../init/main.c. A character pointer called ramdisk_execute_command contains a pointer to this initialization command. By default it is set to the string "/init".

A kernel command-line parameter called rdinit=, when set, overrides this init specifier much the same way that init= does. To use it, simply add it to your kernel command line. For example, we could have set rdinit=/bin/sh on our kernel command line to directly call the busybox shell applet.

6.6   Shutdown

Orderly shutdown of an embedded system is often overlooked in a design. Improper shutdown can affect startup times and can even corrupt certain file system types. One of the more common complaints about using the EXT2 file system (the default in many desktop Linux distributions for several years) is the time it takes for an `fsck` (file system check) on startup after unplanned power loss. Servers with large disk systems can take many hours to properly `fsck` through a collection of large EXT2 partitions.

Each embedded project will likely have its own shutdown strategy. What works for one might or might not work for another. The scale of shutdown can range from a full System V shutdown scheme, to a simple script, to halt or reboot. Several Linux utilities are available to assist in the shutdown process, including the `shutdown`, `halt`, and `reboot` commands. Of course, these must be available for your chosen architecture.

A shutdown script should terminate all user space processes, which results in closing any open files used by those processes. If `init` is being used, issuing the command `init 0` halts the system. In general, the shutdown process first sends all processes the `SIGTERM` signal to notify them that the system is shutting down. A short delay ensures that all processes have the opportunity to perform their shutdown actions, such as closing files, saving state, and so on. Then all processes are sent the `SIGKILL` signal, which results in their termination. The shutdown process should attempt to unmount any mounted file systems and call the architecture-specific halt or reboot routines. The Linux `shutdown` command in conjunction with `init` exhibits this behavior.

6.7   Summary

This chapter presented an in-depth overview of user space initialization on a Linux kernel system. With this knowledge, you should be able to customize your own embedded system startup behavior.

- A root file system is required for all Linux systems. They can be difficult to build from scratch because of complex dependencies by each application.

- The File System Hierarchy standard provides guidance to developers for laying out a file system for maximum compatibility and flexibility.

- We presented a minimal file system as an example of how root file systems are created.

- The Linux kernel's final boot steps define and control a Linux system's startup behavior. Several mechanisms are available, depending on your embedded Linux system's requirements.

- The `init` process is a powerful system configuration and control utility that can serve as the basis for your own embedded Linux system. System initialization based on `init` was presented, along with sample startup script configurations.

- Initial ramdisk (`initrd`) is a Linux kernel feature to allow further startup behavior customization before mounting a final root file system and spawning `init`. We presented the mechanism and a sample configuration for using this powerful feature.

- `initramfs` simplifies the initial ramdisk mechanism while providing similar early startup facilities. It is easier to use, does not require loading a separate image, and is built automatically during each kernel build.

6.7.1 Suggestions for Additional Reading

File System Hierarchy Standard
Maintained by freestandards.org
www.pathname.com/fhs/

Boot process, init, and shutdown
Linux Documentation Project
http://tldp.org/LDP/intro-linux/html/sect_04_02.html

Init man page
Linux Documentation Project
http://tldp.org/LDP/sag/html/init-intro.html

A brief description of System V `init`
http://docs.kde.org/en/3.3/kdeadmin/ksysv/what-is-sysv-init.html

"Booting Linux: The History and the Future"
Werner Almesberger
www.almesberger.net/cv/papers/ols2k-9.ps

Chapter 7

Bootloaders

In This Chapter

■ 7.1 Role of a Bootloader   160

■ 7.2 Bootloader Challenges   161

■ 7.3 A Universal Bootloader: Das U-Boot   166

■ 7.4 Porting U-Boot   174

■ 7.5 Device Tree Blob (Flat Device Tree)   187

■ 7.6 Other Bootloaders   194

■ 7.7 Summary   197

Previous chapters have referred to and even provided examples of bootloader operations. A critical component of an embedded system, the bootloader provides the foundation from which the primary system software is spawned. This chapter starts by examining the bootloader's role in a system. We follow this with an introduction to some common features of bootloaders. Armed with this background, we take a detailed look at a popular bootloader used for embedded systems. We conclude this chapter by introducing a few of the more popular bootloaders.

Numerous bootloaders are in use today. It would be impractical to go into much detail on even the most popular ones. Therefore, we have chosen to explain concepts and use examples based on one of the more popular bootloaders in the open source community for Power Architecture, MIPS, ARM, and other architectures: the U-Boot bootloader.

7.1   Role of a Bootloader

When power is first applied to a processor board, many elements of hardware must be initialized before even the simplest program can run. Each architecture and processor has a set of predefined actions and configurations upon release of reset, which includes fetching initialization code from an onboard storage device (usually Flash memory). This early initialization code is part of the bootloader and is responsible for breathing life into the processor and related hardware components.

Most processors have a default address from which the first bytes of code are fetched upon application of power and release of reset. Hardware designers use this information to arrange the layout of Flash memory on the board and to select which address range(s) the Flash memory responds to. This way, when power is first applied, code is fetched from a well-known and predictable address, and software control can be established.

The bootloader provides this early initialization code and is responsible for initializing the board so that other programs can run. This early initialization code is almost always written in the processor's native assembly language. This fact alone presents many challenges, some of which we examine here.

Of course, after the bootloader has performed this basic processor and platform initialization, its primary role is fetching and booting a full-blown operating system. It is responsible for locating, loading, and passing control to the primary operating system. In addition, the bootloader might have advanced features, such as the capability to validate an OS image, upgrade itself or an OS image, or choose from among several OS images based on a developer-defined policy. Unlike the traditional PC-BIOS model, when the OS takes control, the bootloader is overwritten and ceases to exist.[1]

7.2 Bootloader Challenges

Even a simple "Hello World" program written in C requires significant hardware and software resources. The application developer does not need to know or care much about these details. This is because the C runtime environment transparently provides this infrastructure. A bootloader developer enjoys no such luxury. Every resource that a bootloader requires must be carefully initialized and allocated before it is used. One of the most visible examples of this is Dynamic Random Access Memory (DRAM).

7.2.1 DRAM Controller

DRAM chips cannot be directly read from or written to like other microprocessor bus resources. They require specialized hardware controllers to enable read and write cycles. To further complicate matters, DRAM must be constantly refreshed, or the data contained within will be lost. Refresh is accomplished by sequentially reading each location in DRAM in a systematic manner within the timing specifications set forth by the DRAM manufacturer. Modern DRAM chips support many modes of operation, such as burst mode and dual data rate for high-performance applications. It is the DRAM controller's responsibility to configure DRAM, keep it refreshed within the manufacturer's timing specifications, and respond to the various read and write commands from the processor.

Setting up a DRAM controller is the source of much frustration for the newcomer to embedded development. It requires detailed knowledge of DRAM architecture, the controller itself, the specific DRAM chips being used, and the overall hardware design. This topic is beyond the scope of this book, but you can learn more about this important concept by consulting the references at the end of this chapter. Appendix D,

---

[1] Some embedded designs protect the bootloader and provide callbacks to bootloader routines, but this is almost never a good design approach. Linux is far more capable than bootloaders, so there is often little point in doing so.

"SDRAM Interface Considerations," provides more background on this important topic.

Very little can happen in an embedded system until the DRAM controller and DRAM itself have been properly initialized. One of the first things a bootloader must do is enable the memory subsystem. After it is initialized, memory can be used as a resource. In fact, one of the first actions many bootloaders perform after memory initialization is to copy themselves into DRAM for faster execution.

7.2.2   Flash Versus RAM

Another complexity inherent in bootloaders is that they are required to be stored in nonvolatile storage but usually are loaded into RAM for execution. Again, the complexity arises from the level of resources available for the bootloader to rely on. In a fully operational computer system running an operating system such as Linux, it is relatively easy to compile a program and invoke it from nonvolatile storage. The runtime libraries, operating system, and compiler work together to create the infrastructure necessary to load a program from nonvolatile storage into memory and pass control to it. The aforementioned "Hello World" program is a perfect example. When compiled, it can be loaded into memory and executed simply by typing the name of the executable (`hello`) on the command line (assuming, of course, that the executable exists somewhere on your PATH).

This infrastructure does not exist when a bootloader gains control upon power-on. Instead, the bootloader must create its own operational context and move itself, if required, to a suitable location in RAM. Furthermore, additional complexity is introduced by the requirement to execute from a read-only medium.

7.2.3   Image Complexity

As application developers, we do not need to concern ourselves with the layout of a binary executable file when we develop applications for our favorite platform. The compiler and binary utilities are preconfigured to build a binary executable image containing the proper components needed for a given architecture. The linker places startup (prologue) and shutdown (epilogue) code into the image. These objects set up the proper execution context for your application, which typically starts at `main()`.

This is absolutely not the case with a typical bootloader. When the bootloader gets control, there is no context or prior execution environment. A typical system might not have any DRAM until the bootloader initializes the processor and related hardware. Consider what this means. In a typical C function, any local variables are stored on the stack, so a simple function like the one shown in Listing 7-1 is unusable.

LISTING 7-1 Simple C Function with a Local Variable

```
int setup_memory_controller(board_info_t *p)
  {
    unsigned int *dram_controller_register = p->dc_reg;
...
```

When a bootloader gains control on power-on, there is no stack and no stack pointer. Therefore, a simple C function similar to Listing 7-1 will likely crash the processor, because the compiler will generate code to create and initialize the pointer `dram_controller_register` on the stack, which does not yet exist. The bootloader must create this execution context before any C functions are called.

When the bootloader is compiled and linked, the developer must exercise complete control over how the image is constructed and linked. This is especially true if the bootloader is to relocate itself from Flash to RAM. The compiler and linker must be passed a handful of parameters defining the characteristics and layout of the final executable image. Two primary characteristics conspire to add complexity to the final binary executable image: code organization compatible with the processor's boot requirements, and the execution context, described shortly.

The first characteristic that presents complexity is the need to organize the startup code in a format compatible with the processor's boot sequence. The first executable instructions must be at a predefined location in Flash, depending on the processor and hardware architecture. For example, the AMCC Power Architecture 405GP processor seeks its first machine instructions from a hard-coded address of `0xFFFF_FFFC`. Other processors use similar methods with different details. Some processors can be configured at power-on to seek code from one of several predefined locations, depending on hardware configuration signals.

How does a developer specify the layout of a binary image? The linker is passed a linker description file, also called a linker command script. This special file can be thought of as a recipe for constructing a binary executable image. Listing 7-2 is a snippet from an existing linker description file in use in the U-Boot bootloader, which we'll discuss shortly.

LISTING 7-2   Linker Command Script: Reset Vector Placement

```
SECTIONS
{
  .resetvec 0xFFFFFFFC :
  {
    *(.resetvec)
  } = 0xffff
...
```

A complete description of linker command scripts syntax is beyond the scope of this book. Consult the GNU LD manual referenced at the end of this chapter. Looking at Listing 7-2, we see the beginning of the definition for the output section of the binary ELF image. It directs the linker to place the section of code called .resetvec at a fixed address in the output image, starting at location 0xFFFF_FFFC. Furthermore, it specifies that the rest of this section shall be filled with all 1s (0xffff.) This is because an erased Flash memory array contains all 1s. This technique not only saves wear and tear on the Flash memory, but it also significantly speeds up programming of that sector.

Listing 7-3 is the complete assembly language file from a recent U-Boot distribution that defines the .resetvec code section. It is contained in an assembly language file called .../cpu/ppc4xx/resetvec.s. Notice that this code section cannot exceed 4 bytes in length in a machine with only 32 address bits. This is because only a single instruction is defined in this section, no matter what configuration options are present.

LISTING 7-3   Source Definition of .resetvec

```
/* Copyright MontaVista Software Incorporated, 2000 */
#include <config.h>
      .section .resetvec,"ax"
#if defined(CONFIG_440)
      b _start_440
#else
#if defined(CONFIG_BOOT_PCI) && defined(CONFIG_MIP405)
      b _start_pci
#else
      b _start
#endif
#endif
```

This assembly language file is easy to understand, even if you have no assembly language programming experience. Depending on the particular configuration (as specified by the CONFIG_* macros), an unconditional branch instruction (b in Power Architecture assembler syntax) is generated to the appropriate start location in the main body of code. This branch location is a 4-byte Power Architecture instruction. As we saw in the snippet from the linker command script shown in Listing 7-2, this simple branch instruction is placed in the absolute Flash address of 0xFFFF_FFFC in the output image. As mentioned earlier, the 405GP processor fetches its first instruction from this hard-coded address. This is how the first sequence of code is defined and provided by the developer for this particular architecture and processor combination.

7.2.4   Execution Context

The other primary reason for bootloader image complexity is the lack of execution context. When the sequence of instructions from Listing 7-3 starts executing (recall that these are the first machine instructions after power-on), the resources available to the running program are nearly zero. Default values designed into the hardware ensure that fetches from Flash memory work properly. This also ensures that the system clock has some default values, but little else can be assumed.[2] The reset state of each processor is usually well defined by the manufacturer, but the reset state of a board is defined by the hardware designers.

Indeed, most processors have no DRAM available at startup for temporary storage of variables or, worse, for a stack that is required to use C program calling conventions. If you were forced to write a "Hello World" program with no DRAM and, therefore, no stack, it would be quite different from the traditional "Hello World" example.

This limitation places significant challenges on the initial body of code designed to initialize the hardware. As a result, one of the first tasks the bootloader performs on startup is to configure enough of the hardware to enable at least some minimal amount of RAM. Some processors designed for embedded use have small amounts of on-chip static RAM available. This is the case with the 405GP we've been discussing. When RAM is available, a stack can be allocated using part of that RAM, and a proper context can be constructed to run higher-level languages such as C. This allows the rest of the processor and platform initialization to be written in something other than assembly language.

---

[2] The details differ, depending on architecture, processor, and details of the hardware design.

7.3   A Universal Bootloader: Das U-Boot

Many open source and commercial bootloaders are available, and many more one-of-a-kind homegrown designs are in widespread use today. Most of these have some level of commonality of features. For example, all of them have some capability to load and execute other programs, particularly an operating system. Most interact with the user through a serial port. Support for various networking subsystems (such as Ethernet) is a very powerful but less common feature.

Many bootloaders are specific to a particular architecture. The capability of a bootloader to support a wide variety of architectures and processors can be an important feature to larger development organizations. It is not uncommon for a single development organization to have multiple processors spanning more than one architecture. Investing in a single bootloader across multiple platforms ultimately results in lower development costs.

This section studies an existing bootloader that has become very popular in the embedded Linux community. The official name of this bootloader is Das U-Boot. It is maintained by Wolfgang Denx and hosted at www.denx.de/wiki/U-Boot. U-Boot supports multiple architectures and has a large following of embedded developers and hardware manufacturers who have adopted it for use in their projects and who have contributed to its development.

7.3.1   Obtaining U-Boot

The simplest way to get the U-Boot source code is via `git`. If you have `git` installed on your desktop or laptop, simply issue this command:

```
$ git clone git://git.denx.de/u-boot.git
```

This creates a directory called `u-boot` in the directory in which you executed this command.

If you don't have `git`, or you prefer to download a snapshot instead, you can do so through the `git` server at denx.de. Point your browser to http://git.denx.de/ and click the "summary" link on the first project, `u-boot.git`. This takes you to a summary screen and provides a "snapshot" link, which generates and downloads a tarball that you can install on your system. Select the most recent snapshot, which is at the top of the "shortlog" list.

7.3.2 Configuring U-Boot

For a bootloader to be useful across many processors and architectures, some method of configuring the bootloader is necessary. As with the Linux kernel itself, a bootloader is configured at compile time. This method significantly reduces the complexity of the binary bootloader image, which in itself is an important characteristic.

In the case of U-Boot, board-specific configuration is driven by a single header file specific to the target platform, together with a few soft links in the source tree that select the correct subdirectories based on target board, architecture, and CPU. When configuring U-Boot for one of its supported platforms, issue this command:

```
$ make <platform>_config
```

Here, `platform` is one of the many platforms supported by U-Boot. These platform configuration targets are listed in the top-level U-Boot makefile. For example, to configure for the Spectrum Digital OSK, which contains a TI OMAP 5912 processor, issue this command:

```
$ make omap5912osk_config
```

This configures the U-Boot source tree with the appropriate soft links to select ARM as the target architecture, the ARM926 core, and the 5912 OSK as the target platform.

The next step in configuring U-Boot for this platform is to edit the configuration file specific to this board. This file is found in the U-Boot `../include/configs` subdirectory and is called `omap5912osk.h`. The README file that comes with the U-Boot source code describes the details of configuration and is the best source of this information. (For existing boards that are already supported by U-Boot, it may not be necessary to edit this board-specific configuration file. The defaults may be sufficient for your needs. Sometimes minor edits are needed to update memory size or flash size, because many reference boards can be purchased with varying configurations.)

U-Boot is configured using configuration variables defined in a board-specific header file. Configuration variables have two forms. Configuration options are selected using macros in the form of CONFIG_*XXXX*. Configuration settings are selected using macros in the form of CONFIG_SYS_*XXXX*. In general, configuration *options* (CONFIG_*XXX*) are user-configurable and enable specific U-Boot operational features. Configuration *settings* (CONFIG_SYS_*XXX*) usually are hardware-specific and require detailed knowledge of the underlying processor and/or hardware platform. Board-specific U-Boot configuration is driven by a header file dedicated to that specific platform that contains configuration options and settings appropriate for the underlying platform. The U-Boot source tree includes a directory where these board-specific configuration header files reside. They can be found in .../include/configs from the top-level U-Boot source directory.

You can select numerous features and modes of operation by adding definitions to the board-configuration file. Listing 7-4 is a partial configuration header file for the Yosemite board based on the AMCC 440EP processor.

LISTING 7-4   Portions of the U-Boot Board-Configuration Header File

```
/*-------------------------------------------------------------
 * High Level Configuration Options
 *-------------------------------------------------------------*/
/* This config file is used for Yosemite (440EP) and Yellowstone (440GR)*/
#ifndef CONFIG_YELLOWSTONE
#define CONFIG_440EP        1   /* Specific PPC440EP support    */
#define CONFIG_HOSTNAME     yosemite
#else
#define CONFIG_440GR        1   /* Specific PPC440GR support    */
#define CONFIG_HOSTNAME     yellowstone
#endif
#define CONFIG_440       1   /* ... PPC440 family       */
#define CONFIG_4xx       1   /* ... PPC4xx family       */
#define CONFIG_SYS_CLK_FREQ 66666666   /* external freq to pll */
<...>
/*-----------------------------------------------------------------------
 * Base addresses -- Note these are effective addresses where the
 * actual resources get mapped (not physical addresses)
 *-----------------------------------------------------------------------*/
#define CONFIG_SYS_FLASH_BASE      0xfc000000   /* start of FLASH   */
#define CONFIG_SYS_PCI_MEMBASE     0xa0000000   /* mapped pci memory*/
#define CONFIG_SYS_PCI_MEMBASE1    CONFIG_SYS_PCI_MEMBASE  + 0x10000000
#define CONFIG_SYS_PCI_MEMBASE2    CONFIG_SYS_PCI_MEMBASE1 + 0x10000000
#define CONFIG_SYS_PCI_MEMBASE3    CONFIG_SYS_PCI_MEMBASE2 + 0x10000000
<...>
#ifdef CONFIG_440EP
    #define CONFIG_CMD_USB
    #define CONFIG_CMD_FAT
    #define CONFIG_CMD_EXT2
#endif
<...>
/*-----------------------------------------------------
```

LISTING 7-4   Continued

```
 * External Bus Controller (EBC) Setup
 *----------------------------------------------------*/
#define CONFIG_SYS_FLASH        CONFIG_SYS_FLASH_BASE
#define CONFIG_SYS_CPLD      0x80000000


/* Memory Bank 0 (NOR-FLASH) initialization            */
#define CONFIG_SYS_EBC_PB0AP        0x03017300
#define CONFIG_SYS_EBC_PB0CR        (CONFIG_SYS_FLASH | 0xda000)


/* Memory Bank 2 (CPLD) initialization                 */
#define CONFIG_SYS_EBC_PB2AP        0x04814500
#define CONFIG_SYS_EBC_PB2CR        (CONFIG_SYS_CPLD | 0x18000)
<...>
```

Listing 7-4 gives you an idea of how U-Boot itself is configured for a given board. An actual board-configuration file can contain hundreds of lines similar to those found here. In this example, you can see the definitions for the CPU (CONFIG_440EP), board name (CONFIG_HOSTNAME), clock frequency, and Flash and PCI base memory addresses. We have included examples of configuration variables (CONFIG_XXX) and configuration settings (CONFIG_SYS_XXX). The last few lines are actual processor register values required to initialize the external bus controller for memory banks 0 and 1. You can see that these values can come only from detailed knowledge of the board and processor.

Many aspects of U-Boot can be configured using these mechanisms, including what functionality will be compiled into U-Boot (support for DHCP, memory tests, debugging support, and so on). This mechanism can be used to tell U-Boot how much and what kind of memory is on a given board, and where that memory is mapped. You can learn much more by looking at the U-Boot code directly, especially the excellent README file.

7.3.3   U-Boot Monitor Commands

U-Boot supports more than 70 standard command sets that enable more than 150 unique commands using CONFIG_CMD_* macros. A command set is enabled in U-Boot through the use of configuration setting (CONFIG_*) macros. For a complete list from a recent U-Boot snapshot, consult Appendix B, "U-Boot Configurable Commands." Table 7-1 shows just a few, to give you an idea of the capabilities available.

TABLE 7-1   Some U-Boot Configurable Commands

Command Set	Description Commands
CONFIG_CMD_FLASH	Flash memory commands
CONFIG_CMD_MEMORY	Memory dump, fill, copy, compare, and so on
CONFIG_CMD_DHCP	DHCP support
CONFIG_CMD_PING	Ping support
CONFIG_CMD_EXT2	EXT2 file system support

To enable a specific command, define the macro corresponding to the command you want. These macros are defined in your board-specific configuration file. Listing 7-4 shows several commands being enabled in the board-specific configuration file. There you see CONFIG_CMD_ USB, CONFIG_CMD_FAT, and CONFIG_CMD_EXT2 being defined conditionally if the board is a 440EP.

Instead of specifying each individual CONFIG_CMD_* macro in your own board-specific configuration header, you can start from the full set of commands defined in .../include/config_cmd_all.h. This header file defines every command available. A second header file, .../include/config_cmd_default.h, defines a list of useful default U-Boot command sets such as tftpboot (boot an image from a tftpserver), bootm (boot an image from memory), memory utilities such as md (display memory), and so on. To enable your specific combination of commands, you can start with the default and add and subtract as necessary. Listing 7-4 adds the USB, FAT, and EXT2 command sets to the default. You can subtract in a similar fashion, starting from config_cmd_all.h:

```
#include "condif_cmd_all.h"
#undef CONFIG_CMD_DHCP
#undef CONFIG_CMD_FAT
#undef CONFIG_CMD_FDOS
<...>
```

Take a look at any board-configuration header file in .../include/configs/ for examples.

7.3.4   Network Operations

Many bootloaders include support for Ethernet interfaces. In a development environment, this is a huge time saver. Loading even a modest kernel image over a serial port can take minutes versus a few seconds over an Ethernet link, especially if your board supports Fast or Gigabit Ethernet. Furthermore, serial links are more prone to errors from poorly behaved serial terminals, line noise, and so on.

Some of the more important features to look for in a bootloader include support for the BOOTP, DHCP, and TFTP protocols. If you're unfamiliar with these, BOOTP (Bootstrap Protocol) and DHCP (Dynamic Host Configuration Protocol) enable a target device with an Ethernet port to obtain an IP address and other network-related configuration information from a central server. TFTP (Trivial File Transfer Protocol) allows the target device to download files (such as a Linux kernel image) from a TFTP server. References to these protocol specifications are listed at the end of this chapter. Servers for these services are described in Chapter 12, "Embedded Development Environment."

Figure 7-1 illustrates the flow of information between the target device and a BOOTP server. The client (U-Boot, in this case) initiates the exchange by sending a broadcast packet searching for a BOOTP server. The server responds with a reply packet that includes the client's IP address and other information. The most useful data includes a filename used to download a kernel image.

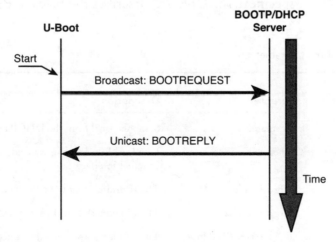

FIGURE 7-1   BOOTP client/server handshake

In practice, dedicated BOOTP servers no longer exist as stand-alone servers. DHCP servers included with your favorite Linux distribution also support BOOTP protocol packets and are almost universally used for BOOTP operations.

The DHCP protocol builds on BOOTP. It can supply the target with a wide variety of configuration information. In practice, the information exchange is often limited by the target/bootloader DHCP client implementation. Listing 7-5 shows a DHCP server configuration block identifying a single target device. This is a snippet from a DHCP configuration file from the Fedora Core 2 DHCP implementation.

LISTING 7-5   DHCP Target Specification

```
host coyote {
      hardware ethernet 00:0e:0c:00:82:f8;
      netmask 255.255.255.0;
      fixed-address 192.168.1.21;
      server-name 192.168.1.9;
      filename "coyote-zImage";
      option root-path "/home/sandbox/targets/coyote-target";
}
...
```

When this DHCP server receives a packet from a device matching the hardware Ethernet address contained in Listing 7-5, it responds by sending that device the parameters in this target specification. Table 7-2 describes the fields in the target specification.

TABLE 7-2   DHCP Target Parameters

DHCP Target Parameter	Purpose	Description
host	Hostname	Symbolic label from the DHCP configuration file
hardware ethernet	Ethernet hardware address	Low-level Ethernet hardware address of the target's Ethernet interface
fixed-address	Target IP address	The IP address that the target will assume
netmask	Target netmask	The IP netmask that the target will assume
server-name	TFTP server IP address	The IP address to which the target will direct requests for file transfers, the root file system, and so on
filename	TFTP filename	The filename that the bootloader can use to boot a secondary image (usually a Linux kernel)
root-path	NFS root path	Defines the network path for the remote NFS root mount

When the bootloader on the target board has completed the BOOTP or DHCP exchange, these parameters are used for further configuration. For example, the bootloader uses the target IP address (fixed-address) to bind its Ethernet port to this IP address. The bootloader then uses the server-name field as a destination IP address to request the file contained in the filename field, which, in most cases, represents a Linux kernel image. Although this is the most common use, this same scenario could be used to download and execute manufacturing test and diagnostics firmware.

It should be noted that the DHCP protocol supports many more parameters than those detailed in Table 7-2. These are simply the more common parameters you might encounter for embedded systems. See the DHCP specification referenced at the end of this chapter for complete details.

7.3.5 Storage Subsystems

Many bootloaders support the capability of booting images from a variety of nonvolatile storage devices in addition to the usual Flash memory. The difficulty in supporting these types of devices is the relative complexity in both hardware and software. To access data on a hard drive, for example, the bootloader must have device driver code for the IDE controller interface, as well as knowledge of the underlying partition scheme and file system. This is not trivial and is one of the tasks more suited to full-blown operating systems.

Even with the underlying complexity, methods exist for loading images from this class of device. The simplest method is to support the hardware only. In this scheme, no knowledge of the file system is assumed. The bootloader simply raw-loads from absolute sectors on the device. This scheme can be used by dedicating an unformatted partition from sector 0 on an IDE-compatible device (such as CompactFlash) and loading the data found there without any structure imposed on the data. This is a simple configuration for loading a kernel image or other binary image from a block storage device. Additional partitions on the device can be formatted for a given file system and can contain complete file systems. After the kernel boots, Linux device drivers can be used to access the additional partitions.

U-Boot can load an image from a specified raw partition or from a partition with a file system structure. Of course, the board must have a supported hardware device (an IDE subsystem), and U-Boot must be so configured. Adding CONFIG_CMD_IDE to the board-specific configuration file enables support for an IDE interface, and adding CONFIG_CMD_BOOTD enables support for booting from a raw partition. If you are porting

U-Boot to a custom board, you will likely have to modify U-Boot to understand your particular hardware.

7.3.6   Booting from Disk

As just described, U-Boot supports several methods for booting a kernel image from a disk subsystem. This simple command illustrates one of the supported methods:

```
=> diskboot 0x400000 0:0
```

To understand this syntax, you must first understand how U-Boot numbers disk devices. The 0:0 in this example specifies the device and partition. In this simple example, U-Boot performs a raw binary load of the image found on the first IDE device (IDE device 0) from the first partition (partition 0) found on this device. The image is loaded into system memory at physical address 0x400000.

After the kernel image has been loaded into memory, the U-Boot bootm command (boot from memory) is used to boot the kernel:

```
=> bootm 0x400000
```

7.4   Porting U-Boot

One of the reasons U-Boot has become so popular is the ease with which new platforms can be supported. Each board port must supply a subordinate makefile that supplies board-specific definitions to the build process. These files are all given the name config.mk. They exist in the .../board/vendor/boardname subdirectory under the U-Boot top-level source directory, where *boardname* specifies a particular board.

As of a recent U-Boot snapshot, more than 460 different board configuration files are named config.mk under the .../boards subdirectory. In this same U-Boot version, 49 different CPU configurations are supported (counted in the same manner). Note that, in some cases, the CPU configuration covers a family of chips, such as ppc4xx, that supports several processors in the Power Architecture 4*xx* family. U-Boot supports a large variety of popular CPUs and CPU families in use today, and a much larger collection of reference boards based on these processors.

If your board contains one of the supported CPUs, porting U-Boot is straightforward. If you must add a new CPU, plan on substantially more effort. The good news is that someone before you has probably done the bulk of the work. Whether you are porting to a new CPU or a new board based on an existing CPU, study the existing source code for specific guidance. Determine what CPU is closest to yours, and clone the functionality found in that CPU-specific directory. Finally, modify the resulting sources to add the specific support for your new CPU's requirements.

7.4.1 EP405 U-Boot Port

The same logic used in porting to a different CPU applies to porting U-Boot to a new board. Let's look at an example. We will use the Embedded Planet EP405 board, which contains the AMCC Power Architecture 405GP processor. The particular board used for this example was provided courtesy of Embedded Planet and came with 64MB of SDRAM and 16MB of on-board Flash. Numerous other devices complete the design.

The first step is to see how close we can come to an existing board. Many boards in the U-Boot source tree support the 405GP processor. A quick grep of the board-configuration header files narrows the choices to those that support the 405GP processor:

```
$ cd .../u-boot/include/configs
$ grep -l CONFIG_405GP *
```

In a recent U-Boot snapshot, 28 board configuration files are configured for the 405GP. After examining a few, we choose the AR405.h configuration as a baseline. It supports the LXT971 Ethernet transceiver, which is also on the EP405. The goal is to minimize any development work by borrowing from similar architectures in the spirit of open source.

We'll tackle the easy steps first. We need a custom board configuration header file for our EP405 board. Copy the board configuration file to a new file with a name appropriate for your board. We'll call ours EP405.h. These commands are issued from the top-level U-Boot source tree:

```
$ cp .../include/configs/AR405.h .../include/configs/EP405.h
```

After you have copied the configuration header file, you must create the board-specific directory and make a copy of the AR405 board files. We don't know yet if we need all of them. That step will come later. After copying the files to your new board directory, edit the filenames appropriately for your board name:

```
$ cd board     <<< from top-level U-Boot source directory
$ mkdir ep405
$ cp esd/ar405/* ep405
```

Now comes the hard part. Jerry Van Baren, a developer and U-Boot contributor, detailed a humorous but realistic process for porting U-Boot in an e-mail posting to the U-Boot mailing list. His complete process, documented in pseudo-C, can be found in the U-Boot README file. The following summarizes the hard part of the porting process in Jerry's style and spirit:

```
while (!running) {
     do {
          Add / modify source code
     } until (compiles);
     Debug;
...
}
```

Jerry's process, as summarized here, is the simple truth. When you have selected a baseline from which to port, you must add, delete, and modify source code until it compiles, and then debug it until it is running without error! There is no magic formula. Porting any bootloader to a new board requires knowledge of many areas of hardware and software. Some of these disciplines, such as setting up SDRAM controllers, are rather specialized and complex. Virtually all of this work involves detailed knowledge of the underlying hardware. Therefore, be prepared to spend many entertaining hours poring over your processor's hardware reference manual, along with the data sheets of numerous other components that reside on your board.

7.4.2   U-Boot Makefile Configuration Target

Now that we have a code base to start from, we must make some modifications to the top-level U-Boot makefile to add the configuration steps for our new board. Upon examining this makefile, we find a section for configuring the U-Boot source tree for the various supported boards. This section can be found starting with the `unconfig` target in the top-level makefile. We now add support for our new board to allow us to configure it. Because we derived our board from the ESD AR405, we will use that rule as the template for building our own. If you follow along in the U-Boot source code, you will see that these rules are placed in the makefile in alphabetical order according to their configuration names. We will be good open-source citizens and follow that lead. We call our configuration target `EP405_config`, again in concert with the U-Boot conventions. Listing 7-6 details the edits you will need to make in your top-level makefile.

LISTING 7-6   Makefile Edits

```
ebony_config:      unconfig
      @$(MKCONFIG) $(@:_config=) ppc ppc4xx ebony amcc

+EP405_config:     unconfig
+      @$(MKCONFIG) $(@:_config=) ppc ppc4xx ep405 ep
+
ERIC_config:       unconfig
      @./mkconfig $(@:_config=) ppc ppc4xx eric
```

Our new configuration rule has been inserted as shown in the three lines preceded by the + character (unified diff format). Edit the top-level makefile using your favorite editor.

Upon completing the steps just described, we have a U-Boot source tree that represents a starting point. It probably will not compile cleanly, so that should be our first step. At least the compiler can give us some guidance on where to start.

7.4.3   EP405 First Build

We now have a U-Boot source tree with our candidate files. Our first step is to configure the build tree for our newly installed EP405 board. Using the configuration target we just added to the top-level makefile, we configure the tree. Listing 7-7 gives you a starting point for where you need to focus your efforts.

LISTING 7-7   Configure and Build for EP405

```
$ make ARCH=ppc CROSS_COMPILE=ppc_405- EP405_config
Configuring for EP405 board...
$ # Now do the build
$ make ARCH=ppc CROSS_COMPILE=ppc_405-
<...lots of build steps...>
make[1]: Entering directory '/home/chris/sandbox/u-boot/board/ep/ep405'
ppc_440ep-gcc  -g  -Os   -mrelocatable -fPIC -ffixed-r14 -meabi -D__KERNEL__
-DTEXT_BASE=0xFFFC0000 -I/home/chris/sandbox/u-boot/include -fno-builtin -ffree-
standing -nostdinc -isystem /opt/pro5/montavista/pro/devkit/ppc/440ep/bin/../lib/
gcc/powerpc-montavista-linux-gnu/4.2.0/include -pipe  -DCONFIG_PPC -D__powerpc__
-DCONFIG_4xx -ffixed-r2 -mstring -msoft-float -Wa,-m405 -mcpu=405 -Wall -Wstrict-
prototypes -fno-stack-protector   -o ep405.o ep405.c -c
ep405.c:25:19: error: ar405.h: No such file or directory
ep405.c:44:22: error: fpgadata.c: No such file or directory
ep405.c:48:27: error: fpgadata_xl30.c: No such file or directory
ep405.c:54:28: error: ../common/fpga.c: No such file or directory
ep405.c: In function 'board_early_init_f':
```

LISTING 7-7   Continued

```
ep405.c:75: warning: implicit declaration of function 'fpga_boot'
ep405.c:91: error: 'ERROR_FPGA_PRG_INIT_LOW' undeclared (first use in this func-
tion)
ep405.c:91: error: (Each undeclared identifier is reported only once
ep405.c:91: error: for each function it appears in.)
ep405.c:94: error: 'ERROR_FPGA_PRG_INIT_HIGH' undeclared (first use in this func-
tion)
ep405.c:97: error: 'ERROR_FPGA_PRG_DONE' undeclared (first use in this function)
make[1]: *** [ep405.o] Error 1
make[1]: Leaving directory '/home/chris/sandbox/u-boot/board/ep/ep405'
make: *** [board/ep/ep405/libep405.a] Error 2
```

At first glance, we notice we need to edit our cloned `ep405.c` file and fix up a few references. These include the board header file and references to the FPGA. We can eliminate these, because the EP405 board doesn't contain an FPGA like the AR405 we derived from. These edits should be straightforward, so we'll leave them as an exercise for the reader. Again, there is no formula better than Jerry's: edit-compile-repeat until the file compiles cleanly. Then comes the hard part—actually making it work. It was not difficult. Less than an hour of editing had the file compiling without errors.

7.4.4   EP405 Processor Initialization

The first task that your new U-Boot port must do correctly is initialize the processor and the memory (DRAM) subsystems. After reset, the 405GP processor core is designed to fetch instructions starting from `0xFFFF_FFFC`. The core attempts to execute the instructions found here. Because this is the top of the memory range, the instruction found here must be an unconditional branch instruction.

This processor core is also hard-coded to configure the upper 2MB memory region so that it is accessible without programming the external bus controller, to which Flash memory is usually attached. This forces the requirement to branch to a location within this address space, because the processor is incapable of addressing memory anywhere else until our bootloader code initializes additional memory regions. We must branch to somewhere at or above `0xFFE0_0000`. How do we know all this? Because we read the 405GP user manual!

The behavior of the 405GP processor core, as just described, places requirements on the hardware designer to ensure that, on power-up, nonvolatile memory (Flash) is mapped to the required upper 2MB memory region. Certain attributes of this initial memory region assume default values on reset. For example, this upper 2MB region will be configured for 256 wait states, three cycles of address to chip select delay, three cycles of chip select to output enable delay, and seven cycles of hold time.[3] This allows maximum freedom for the hardware designer to select appropriate devices or methods of getting instruction code to the processor directly after reset.

We've already seen how the reset vector is installed to the top of Flash in Listing 7-2. When configured for the 405GP, our first lines of code will be found in the file `.../cpu/ppc4xx/start.s`. The U-Boot developers intended this code to be processor-generic. In theory, there should be no need for board-specific code in this file. You will see how this is accomplished.

You don't need to understand Power Architecture assembly language in any depth to understand the logical flow in `start.s`. Many frequently asked questions (FAQs) have been posted to the U-Boot mailing list about modifying low-level assembly code. In nearly all cases, it is not necessary to modify this code if you are porting to one of the many supported processors. It is mature code, with many successful ports running on it. You need to modify the board-specific code (at a bare minimum) for your port. If you find yourself troubleshooting or modifying the early startup assembler code for a processor that has been around for a while, you are most likely heading down the wrong road.

Listing 7-8 reproduces a portion of `start.s` for the 4*xx* architecture.

LISTING 7-8   U-Boot 4xx Startup Code

```
...
#if defined(CONFIG_405GP) || defined(CONFIG_405CR) ||
 defined(CONFIG_405) || defined(CONFIG_405EP)
    /*-------------------------------- */
    /* Clear and set up some registers. */
    /*-------------------------------- */
    addi    r4,r0,0x0000
    mtspr   sgr,r4
    mtspr   dcwr,r4
    mtesr   r4              /* clear Exception Syndrome Reg */
    mttcr   r4              /* clear Timer Control Reg */
    mtxer   r4              /* clear Fixed-Point Exception Reg */
    mtevpr  r4            /* clear Exception Vector Prefix Reg */
    addi    r4,r0,0x1000   /* set ME bit (Machine Exceptions) */
    oris    r4,r4,0x0002         /* set CE bit (Critical Exceptions) */
    mtmsr   r4                   /* change MSR */
```

---

[3] This data was taken directly from the 405GP user's manual, referenced at the end of this chapter.

LISTING 7-8   Continued

```
addi    r4,r0,(0xFFFF-0x10000)  /* set r4 to 0xFFFFFFFF (status in the */
                                /* dbsr is cleared by setting bits to 1) */
mtdbsr  r4                      /* clear/reset the dbsr */


/*--------------------------------- */
/* Invalidate I and D caches. Enable I cache for defined memory regions */
/* to speed things up. Leave the D cache disabled for now. It will be */
/* enabled/left disabled later based on user-selected menu options. */
/* Be aware that the I cache may be disabled later based on the menu */
/* options as well. See miscLib/main.c. */
/*---------------------------------- */
bl      invalidate_icache
bl      invalidate_dcache


/*--------------------------------- */
/* Enable two 128MB cachable regions.    */
/*--------------------------------- */
addis   r4,r0,0x8000
addi    r4,r4,0x0001
mticcr  r4                      /* instruction cache */
isync


addis   r4,r0,0x0000
addi    r4,r4,0x0000
mtdccr  r4                      /* data cache */
```

The first code to execute in `start.s` for the 405GP processor starts about a third of the way into the source file, where a handful of processor registers are cleared or set to sane initial values. The instruction and data caches are then invalidated, and the instruction cache is enabled to speed up the initial load. Two 128MB cacheable regions are set up—one at the high end of memory (the Flash region), and the other at the bottom (normally the start of system DRAM). U-Boot eventually is copied to RAM in this region and executed from there. The reason for this is performance: raw reads from RAM are an order of magnitude (or more) faster than reads from Flash. However, for the 4xx CPU, there is another subtle reason for enabling the instruction cache, as you shall soon discover.

7.4.5 Board-Specific Initialization

The first opportunity for any board-specific initialization comes in `.../cpu/ppc4xx/start.s` just after the cacheable regions have been initialized. Here we find a call to an external assembler language routine called `ext_bus_cntlr_init`:

```
bl ext_bus_cntlr_init    /* Board-specific bus cntrl init */
```

This routine is defined in `.../board/ep405/init.s`, in the new board-specific directory for our board. It provides a hook for very early hardware-based initialization. This is one of the files that has been customized for our EP405 platform. This file contains the board-specific code to initialize the 405GP's external bus controller for our application. Listing 7-9 contains the meat of the functionality from this file. This is the code that initializes the 405GP's external bus controller.

LISTING 7-9   External Bus Controller Initialization

```
    .globl  ext_bus_cntlr_init
ext_bus_cntlr_init:
    mflr    r4              /* save link register         */
    bl      ..getAddr
..getAddr:
    mflr    r3              /* get _this_ address         */
    mtlr    r4              /* restore link register      */
    addi    r4,0,14         /* prefetch 14 cache lines... */
    mtctr   r4              /* ...to fit this function    */
                            /* cache (8x14=112 instr)     */
..ebcloop:
    icbt    r0,r3           /* prefetch cache line for [r3] */
    addi    r3,r3,32        /* move to next cache line    */
    bdnz    ..ebcloop       /* continue for 14 cache lines */

    /*------------------------------------------------- */
    /* Delay to ensure all accesses to ROM are complete */
    /* before changing  bank 0 timings                  */
    /* 200usec should be enough.                        */
    /* 200,000,000 (cycles/sec) X .000200 (sec) =       */
    /* 0x9C40 cycles                                    */
    /*------------------------------------------------- */

    addis   r3,0,0x0
    ori     r3,r3,0xA000 /* ensure 200usec have passed t */
```

LISTING 7-9   Continued

```
    mtctr    r3

..spinlp:
    bdnz     ..spinlp     /* spin loop                      */


    /*------------------------------------------------*/
    /* Now do the real work of this function          */
    /* Memory Bank 0 (Flash and SRAM) initialization  */
    /*------------------------------------------------*/

    addi     r4,0,pb0ap           /* *ebccfga = pb0ap;        */
    mtdcr    ebccfga,r4
    addis    r4,0,EBC0_B0AP@h      /* *ebccfgd = EBC0_B0AP;    */
    ori      r4,r4,EBC0_B0AP@l
    mtdcr    ebccfgd,r4

    addi     r4,0,pb0cr           /* *ebccfga = pb0cr;        */
    mtdcr    ebccfga,r4
    addis    r4,0,EBC0_B0CR@h      /* *ebccfgd = EBC0_B0CR;    */
    ori      r4,r4,EBC0_B0CR@l
    mtdcr    ebccfgd,r4


    /*------------------------------------------------*/
    /* Memory Bank 4 (NVRAM & BCSR) initialization    */
    /*------------------------------------------------*/

    addi     r4,0,pb4ap           /* *ebccfga = pb4ap;        */
    mtdcr    ebccfga,r4
    addis    r4,0,EBC0_B4AP@h      /* *ebccfgd = EBC0_B4AP;    */
    ori      r4,r4,EBC0_B4AP@l
    mtdcr    ebccfgd,r4

    addi     r4,0,pb4cr           /* *ebccfga = pb4cr;        */
    mtdcr    ebccfga,r4
    addis    r4,0,EBC0_B4CR@h      /* *ebccfgd = EBC0_B4CR;    */
    ori      r4,r4,EBC0_B4CR@l
    mtdcr    ebccfgd,r4

    blr                           /* return                   */
```

Listing 7-9 was chosen because it is typical of the subtle complexities involved in low-level processor initialization. It is important to realize the context in which this code is running. It is executing from Flash, before any DRAM is available. There is no stack. This code is preparing to make fundamental changes to the controller that governs access to the very Flash it is executing from. It is well documented for this particular processor that executing code from Flash while modifying the external bus controller to which the Flash is attached can lead to errant reads and a resulting processor crash.

The solution is shown in this assembly language routine. Starting at the label ..getAddr, and for the next seven assembly language instructions, the code essentially prefetches itself into the instruction cache, using the icbt instruction. When the entire subroutine has been successfully read into the instruction cache, it can proceed to make the required changes to the external bus controller without fear of a crash, because it is executing directly from the internal instruction cache. Subtle, but clever! This is followed by a short delay to make sure that all the requested i-cache reads have completed.

When the prefetch and delay have completed, the code proceeds to configure Memory Bank 0 and Memory Bank 4 appropriately for our board. The values come from detailed knowledge of the underlying components and their interconnection on the board. Consult the last section in this chapter for all the details of the Power Architecture assembler and the 405GP processor from which this example was derived.

Consider making a change to this code without a complete understanding of what is happening here. Perhaps you added a few lines and increased its size beyond the range that was prefetched into the cache. It would likely crash (worse, it might crash only sometimes), but stepping through this code with a debugger would not yield a single clue as to why.

The next opportunity for board-specific initialization comes after a temporary stack has been allocated from the processor's data cache. This is the branch to initialize the SDRAM controller around line 727 of . . ./cpu/ppc4xx/start.S:

```
bl sdram_init
```

The execution context now includes a stack pointer and some temporary memory for local data storage—that is, a partial C context, allowing the developer to use C for the relatively complex task of setting up the system SDRAM controller and other initialization tasks. In our EP405 port, the sdram_init() code resides in . . ./board/ep405/ep405.c and is customized for this particular board and DRAM configuration. Because this board does not use a commercially available memory SIMM, it is not possible to determine the configuration of the DRAM dynamically, as with so many other boards supported by U-Boot. It is hard-coded in sdram_init.

Many off-the-shelf memory DDR modules have an SPD (Serial Presence Detect) PROM containing parameters that identify the memory module and its architecture and organization. These parameters can be read under program control via I2C and can be used as input to determine proper parameters for the memory controller. U-Boot has support for this technique but may need modifications to work with your specific board. Many examples of its use can be found in the U-Boot source code. The configuration option CONFIG_SPD_EEPROM enables this feature. You can grep for this option to find examples of its use.

7.4.6   Porting Summary

By now, you can appreciate some of the difficulties of porting a bootloader to a hardware platform. There is simply no substitute for detailed knowledge of the underlying hardware. Of course, we'd like to minimize our investment in time required for this task. After all, we usually are not paid based on how well we understand every hardware detail of a given processor, but rather on our ability to deliver a working solution in a timely manner. Indeed, this is one of the primary reasons open source has flourished. You just saw how easy it is to port U-Boot to a new hardware platform—not because you're an expert on the processor, but because many before us have done the bulk of the hard work already.

Listing 7-10 is the complete list of new or modified files that complete the basic EP405 port for U-Boot. Of course, if there had been new hardware devices for which no support exists in U-Boot, or if we were porting to a new CPU that is not yet supported in U-Boot, this would have been a much more significant effort. The point to be made here, at the risk of sounding redundant, is that there is simply no substitute for detailed knowledge of both the hardware (CPU and subsystems) and the underlying software (U-Boot) to complete a port successfully in a reasonable time frame. If you start the project from that frame of mind, you will have a successful outcome.

LISTING 7-10   New or Changed Files for U-Boot EP405 Port

```
$ git diff HEAD --stat
 Makefile                   |    3 +
 board/ep/ep405/Makefile    |   53 ++++
 board/ep/ep405/config.mk   |   30 ++
 board/ep/ep405/ep405.c     |  329 ++++++++++++++++++++++
 board/ep/ep405/ep405.h     |   44 +++
 board/ep/ep405/flash.c     |  749 ++++++++++++++++++++++++++++++++++++++++++++
 include/configs/EP405.h    |  272 +++++++++++++++
 7 files changed, 1480 insertions(+), 0 deletions(-)
```

Recall that we derived all the files in the .../board/ep405 directory from another directory. Indeed, we didn't create any files from scratch for this port. We borrowed from the work of others and customized where necessary to achieve our goals.

7.4.7 U-Boot Image Format

Now that we have a working bootloader for our EP405 board, we can load and run programs on it. Ideally, we want to run an operating system such as Linux. To do this, we need to understand the image format that U-Boot requires. U-Boot expects a small header on the image file that identifies several attributes of the image. U-Boot provides the mkimage tool (part of the U-Boot source code) to build this image header.

Recent Linux kernel distributions have built-in support for building images directly bootable by U-Boot. Both the arm and powerpc branches of the kernel source tree support a target called uImage. Let's look at the Power Architecture case.

Browsing through the makefile .../arch/powerpc/boot/Makefile, we see the uImage target defining a call to an external wrapper script called, you guessed it, wrapper. Without delving into the syntactical tedium, the wrapper script sets up some default variable values and eventually calls mkimage. Listing 7-11 reproduces this processing from the wrapper script.

LISTING 7-11   mkimage from Wrapper Script

```
case "$platform" in
uboot)
    rm  f "$ofile"
    mkimage -A ppc -O linux -T kernel -C gzip -a $membase -e $membase \
    $uboot_version -d "$vmz" "$ofile"
    if [ -z "$cacheit" ]; then
    rm -f "$vmz"
    fi
    exit 0
    ;;
esac
```

The mkimage utility creates the U-Boot header and prepends it to the supplied kernel image. It writes the resulting image to the final parameter passed to mkimage—in this case, the value of the $ofile variable, which in this example will be called uImage. The parameters are as follows:

- -A specifies the target image architecture.
- -O species the target image OS—in this case, Linux.

- -T specifies the target image type—in this case, a kernel.
- -c specifies the target image compression type—in this case, gzip.
- -a sets the U-Boot loadaddress to the value specified.
- -e sets the U-Boot image entry point to the supplied value.
- -n is a text field used to identify the image to the human user (supplied in the uboot_version variable).
- -d is the executable image file to which the header is prepended.

Several U-Boot commands use this header data both to verify the integrity of the image (U-Boot also puts a CRC signature in the header) and to identify the image type. U-Boot has a command called iminfo that reads the image header and displays the image attributes from the target image. Listing 7-12 contains the results of loading a uImage (bootable Linux kernel image formatted for U-Boot) to the EP405 board via U-Boot's tftp command and executing the iminfo command on the image.[4]

LISTING 7-12   U-Boot iminfo Command

```
=> tftp 400000 uImage-ep405
ENET Speed is 100 Mbps - FULL duplex connection
TFTP from server 192.168.1.9; our IP address is 192.168.1.33
Filename 'uImage-ep405'.
Load address: 0x400000
Loading: #########  done
Bytes transferred = 891228 (d995c hex)
=> iminfo

## Checking Image at 00400000 ...
   Image Name:    Linux-2.6.11.6
   Image Type:    PowerPC Linux Kernel Image (gzip compressed)
   Data Size:     891164 Bytes = 870.3 kB
   Load Address: 00000000
   Entry Point:  00000000
   Verifying Checksum ... OK
=>
```

---

[4] We changed the name of the uImage to reflect the target it corresponds to. In this example, we appended -ep405 to indicate it is a kernel for that target.

7.5   Device Tree Blob (Flat Device Tree)

One of the more challenging aspects of porting Linux (and U-Boot) to your new board is the recent requirement for a device tree blob (DTB). It is also referred to as a flat device tree, device tree binary, or simply device tree. Throughout this discussion, these terms are used interchangeably. The DTB is a database that represents the hardware components on a given board. It is derived from the IBM OpenFirmware specifications and has been chosen as the default mechanism to pass low-level hardware information from the bootloader to the kernel.

Prior to the requirement for a DTB, U-Boot would pass a board information structure to the kernel, which was derived from a header file in U-Boot that had to exactly match the contents of a similar header file in the kernel. It was very difficult to keep them in sync, and it didn't scale well. This was, in part, the motivation for incorporating the flat device tree as a method to communicate low-level hardware details from the bootloader to the kernel.

Similar to U-Boot or other low-level firmware, mastering the DTB requires complete knowledge of the underlying hardware. You can do an Internet search to find some introductory documents that describe the device tree. A great starting point is the Denx Software Engineering wiki page. References are provided at the end of this chapter.

To begin, let's see how the DTB is used during a typical boot sequence. Listing 7-13 shows a boot sequence on a Power Architecture target using U-Boot. The Freescale MPC8548CDS system was used for this example.

LISTING 7-13   Booting Linux with the Device Tree Blob from U-Boot

```
=> tftp $loadaddr 8548/uImage
Speed: 1000, full duplex
Using eTSEC0 device
TFTP from server 192.168.11.103; our IP address is 192.168.11.18
Filename '8548/uImage'.
Load address: 0x600000
Loading:  #################################################
          #################################################
done
Bytes transferred = 1838553 (1c0dd9 hex)
=> tftp $fdtaddr 8548/dtb
Speed: 1000, full duplex
Using eTSEC0 device
TFTP from server 192.168.11.103; our IP address is 192.168.11.18
```

LISTING 7-13   Continued

```
Filename '8548/dtb'.
Load address: 0xc00000
Loading: ##
done
Bytes transferred = 16384 (4000 hex)
=> bootm $loadaddr - $fdtaddr
## Booting kernel from Legacy Image at 00600000 ...
   Image Name:   MontaVista Linux 6/2.6.27/freesc
   Image Type:   PowerPC Linux Kernel Image (gzip compressed)
   Data Size:    1838489 Bytes =  1.8 MB
   Load Address: 00000000
   Entry Point:  00000000
   Verifying Checksum ... OK
## Flattened Device Tree blob at 00c00000
   Booting using the fdt blob at 0xc00000
   Uncompressing Kernel Image ... OK
   Loading Device Tree to 007f9000, end 007fffff ... OK
   <... Linux begins booting here...>
...and away we go!!
```

The primary difference here is that we loaded two images. The large image (1.8MB) is the kernel image. The smaller image (16KB) is the flat device tree. Notice that we placed the kernel and DTB at addresses 0x600000 and 0xc00000, respectively. All the messages from Listing 7-13 are produced by U-Boot. When we use the bootm command to boot the kernel, we add a third parameter, which tells U-Boot where we loaded the DTB.

By now, you are probably wondering where the DTB came from. The easy answer is that it was provided as a courtesy by the board/architecture developers as part of the Linux kernel source tree. If you look at the powerpc branch of any recent Linux kernel tree, you will see a directory called .../arch/powerpc/boot/dts. This is where the "source code" for the DTB resides.

The hard answer is that you must provide a DTB for your custom board. Start with something close to your platform, and modify from there. At the risk of sounding redundant, there is no easy path. You must dive in and learn the details of your hardware platform and become proficient at writing device nodes and their respective properties. Hopefully, this section will start you on your way toward that proficiency.

7.5.1 Device Tree Source

The device tree blob is "compiled" by a special compiler that produces the binary in the proper form for U-Boot and Linux to understand. The dtc compiler usually is provided with your embedded Linux distribution, or it can be found at http://jdl.com/software. Listing 7-14 shows a snippet of the device tree source (DTS) from a recent kernel source tree.

LISTING 7-14   Partial Device Tree Source Listing

```
/*
 * MPC8548 CDS Device Tree Source
 *
 * Copyright 2006, 2008 Freescale Semiconductor Inc.
 *
 * This program is free software; you can redistribute it and/or modify it
 * under  the terms of  the GNU General Public License as published by the
 * Free Software Foundation;  either version 2 of the License, or (at your
 * option) any later version.
 */

/dts-v1/;

/ {
    model = "MPC8548CDS";
    compatible = "MPC8548CDS", "MPC85xxCDS";
    #address-cells = <1>;
    #size-cells = <1>;

    aliases {
        ethernet0 = &enet0;
        ethernet1 = &enet1;
        ethernet2 = &enet2;
        ethernet3 = &enet3;
        serial0 = &serial0;
        serial1 = &serial1;
        pci0 = &pci0;
        pci1 = &pci1;
        pci2 = &pci2;
        rapidio0 = &rio0;
    };

    cpus {
```

LISTING 7-14   Continued

```
        #address-cells = <1>;
        #size-cells = <0>;

        PowerPC,8548@0 {
            device_type = "cpu";
            reg = <0x0>;
            d-cache-line-size = <32>;    // 32 bytes
            i-cache-line-size = <32>;    // 32 bytes
            d-cache-size = <0x8000>;          // L1, 32K
            i-cache-size = <0x8000>;          // L1, 32K
            timebase-frequency = <0>;    //  33 MHz, from uboot
            bus-frequency = <0>;     // 166 MHz
            clock-frequency = <0>;   // 825 MHz, from uboot
            next-level-cache = <&L2>;
        };
    };

    memory {
        device_type = "memory";
        reg = <0x0 0x8000000>;   // 128M at 0x0
    };

    localbus@e0000000 {
        #address-cells = <2>;
        #size-cells = <1>;
        compatible = "simple-bus";
        reg = <0xe0000000 0x5000>;
        interrupt-parent = <&mpic>;

        ranges = <0x0 0x0 0xff000000 0x01000000>;   /*16MB Flash*/

        flash@0,0 {
            #address-cells = <1>;
            #size-cells = <1>;
            compatible = "cfi-flash";
            reg = <0x0 0x0 0x1000000>;
            bank-width = <2>;
            device-width = <2>;
            partition@0x0 {
                label = "free space";
                reg = <0x00000000 0x00f80000>;
            };
```

LISTING 7-14   Continued

```
        partition@0x100000 {
            label = "bootloader";
            reg = <0x00f80000 0x00080000>;
            read-only;
        };
    };
};
<...truncated here...>
```

This is a long listing, but it is well worth the time spent studying it. Although it may seem obvious, it is worth noting that this device tree source is specific to the Freescale MPC8548CDS Configurable Development System. Part of your job as a custom embedded Linux developer is to adopt this DTS to your own MPC8548-based system.

Some of the data shown in Listing 7-14 is self-explanatory. The flat device tree is made up of device nodes. A device node is an entry in the device tree, usually describing a single device or bus. Each node contains a set of properties that describe it. It is, in fact, a tree structure. It can easily be represented by a familiar tree view, as shown in Listing 7-15.

LISTING 7-15   Tree View of DTS

```
|-/ Model: model = "MPC8548CDS", etc.
|
|---- cpus: #address-cells = <1>, etc.
|   |
|   |----  PowerPC,8548@0, etc.
|
|--- Memory: device_type = "memory", etc.
|
|----  localbus@e0000000: #address-cells = <2>, etc.
|   |
|   |---- flash@0,0: #address-cells = <1>, etc.
|
<...>
```

In the first few lines of Listing 7-14, we see the processor model and a property indicating compatibility with other processors in the same family. The first child node describes the CPU. Many of the CPU device node properties are self-explanatory. For example, we can see that the 8548 CPU has data and instruction cache line sizes of

32 bytes and that these caches are both 32KB in size (`0x8000` bytes.) We see a couple properties that show clock frequencies, such as `timebase-frequency` and `clock-frequency`, both of which indicate that they are set by U-Boot. That would be natural, because U-Boot configures the hardware clocks.

The properties called `address-cells` and `size-cells` are worth explaining. A "cell" in this context is simply a 32-bit quantity. `address-cells` and `size-cells` simply indicate the number of cells (32-bit fields) required to specify an address (or size) in the child node.

The `memory` device node offers no mysteries. From this node, it is obvious that this platform contains a single bank of memory starting at address 0, which is 128MB in size.

For complete details of flat device tree syntax, consult the references at the end of this chapter. One of the most useful is the document produced by Power.org, found at www.power.org/resources/downloads/Power_ePAPR_APPROVED_v1.0.pdf.

7.5.2   Device Tree Compiler

Introduced earlier, the device tree compiler (`dtc`) converts the human-readable device tree source into the machine-readable binary that both U-Boot and the Linux kernel understand. Although a `git` tree is hosted on kernel.org for `dtc`, the device tree source has been merged into the kernel source tree and is built along with any Power Architecture kernel from the `.../arch/powerpc` branch.

It is quite straightforward to use the device tree compiler. A typical command to convert source to binary looks like this:

```
$ dtc -O dtb -o myboard.dtb -b 0 myboard.dts
```

In this command, `myboard.dts` is the device tree human-readable source, and `myboard.dtb` is the binary created by this command invocation. The `-o` flag specifies the output format—in this case, the device tree blob binary. The `-o` flag names the output file, and the `-b 0` parameter specifies the physical boot CPU in the multicore case.

Note that the `dtc` compiler allows you to go in both directions. The command example just shown performs a compile from source to device tree binary, whereas a command like this produces source from the binary:

```
$ dtc -I dtb -O dts mpc8548.dtb >mpc8548.dts
```

You can also build the DTB for many well-known reference boards directly from the kernel source. The command looks similar to the following:

```
$ make ARCH=powerpc mpc8548cds.dtb
```

This produces a binary device tree blob from a source file with the same base name (mpc8548cds) and the dts extension. These are found in .../arch/powerpc/boot/dts. A recent kernel source tree had 120 such device tree source files for a range of Power Architecture boards.

7.5.3   Alternative Kernel Images Using DTB

Entering make ARCH=powerpc help at the top-level Linux kernel source tree outputs many lines of useful help, describing the many build targets available. Several architecture-specific targets combine the device tree blob with the kernel image. One good reason to do this is if you are trying to boot a newer kernel on a target that has an older version of U-Boot that does not support the device tree blob. On a recent Linux kernel, Listing 7-16 reproduces the powerpc targets defined for the powerpc architecture.

LISTING 7-16   Architecture-Specific Targets for Powerpc

```
* zImage           - Build default images selected by kernel config
  zImage.*         - Compressed kernel image (arch/powerpc/boot/zImage.*)
  uImage           - U-Boot native image format
  cuImage.<dt>     - Backwards compatible U-Boot image for older
                     versions which do not support device trees
  dtbImage.<dt>    - zImage with an embedded device tree blob
  simpleImage.<dt> - Firmware independent image.
  treeImage.<dt>   - Support for older IBM 4xx firmware (not U-Boot)
  install          - Install kernel using
                     (your) ~/bin/installkernel or
                     (distribution) /sbin/installkernel or
                     install to $(INSTALL_PATH) and run lilo
  *_defconfig      - Select default config from arch/powerpc/configs
```

The zImage is the default, but many targets use uImage. Notice that some of these targets have the device tree binary included in the composite kernel image. You need to decide which is most appropriate for your particular platform and application.

7.6   Other Bootloaders

Here we introduce the more popular bootloaders, describe where they might be used, and summarize their features. This is not intended to be a thorough tutorial; doing so would require a book of its own. Consult the last section of this chapter for further study.

7.6.1   Lilo

The Linux Loader, or Lilo, was widely used in commercial Linux distributions for desktop PC platforms; as such, it has its roots in the Intel x86/IA32 architecture. Lilo has several components. It has a primary bootstrap program that lives on the first sector of a bootable disk drive.[5] The primary loader is limited to a disk sector size, usually 512 bytes. Therefore, its primary purpose is simply to load and pass control to a secondary loader. The secondary loader can span multiple sectors and does most of the bootloader's work.

Lilo is driven by a configuration file and utility that is part of the Lilo executable. This configuration file can be read or written to only under control of the host operating system. That is, the configuration file is not referenced by the early boot code in either the primary or secondary loaders. Entries in the configuration file are read and processed by the Lilo configuration utility during system installation or administration. Listing 7-17 shows a simple `lilo.conf` configuration file describing a typical dual-boot Linux and Windows installation.

LISTING 7-17   Sample Lilo Configuration: `lilo.conf`

```
# This is the global lilo configuration section
# These settings apply to all the "image" sections

boot = /dev/hda
timeout=50
default=linux


# This  describes the primary kernel boot image
# Lilo will display it with the label 'linux'
image=/boot/myLinux-2.6.11.1
        label=linux
        initrd=/boot/myInitrd-2.6.11.1.img
```

---

[5] This is mostly for historical reasons. From the early days of PCs, BIOS programs loaded only the first sector of a disk drive and passed control to it.

LISTING 7-17   Continued

```
        read-only
        append="root=LABEL=/"

# This is the second OS in a dual-boot configuration
# This entry will boot a secondary image from /dev/hda1
other=/dev/hda1
        optional
        label=that_other_os
```

This configuration file instructs the Lilo configuration utility to use the master boot record of the first hard drive (/dev/hda). It contains a delay instruction to wait for the user to press a key before the timeout (5 seconds, in this case). This allows the system operator to select from a list of OS images to boot. If the system operator presses the Tab key before the timeout, Lilo presents a list to choose from. Lilo uses the label tag as the text to display for each image.

The images are defined with the image tag in the configuration file. In Listing 7-17, the primary (default) image is a Linux kernel image with a filename of myLinux-2.6.11.1. Lilo loads this image from the hard drive. It then loads a second file to be used as an initial ramdisk. This is the file myInitrd-2.6.11.1.img. Lilo constructs a kernel command line containing the string "root=LABEL=/" and passes this to the Linux kernel upon execution. This instructs Linux where to get its root file system after boot.

7.6.2 GRUB

Many current commercial Linux distributions now ship with the GRUB bootloader. GRUB, or GRand Unified Bootloader, is a GNU project. It has many enhanced features not found in Lilo. The biggest difference between GRUB and Lilo is GRUB's capability to understand file systems and kernel image formats. Furthermore, GRUB can read and modify its configuration at boot time. GRUB also supports booting across a network, which can be a tremendous asset in an embedded environment. GRUB offers a command-line interface at boot time to modify the boot configuration.

Like Lilo, GRUB is driven by a configuration file. Unlike Lilo's static configuration, however, the GRUB bootloader reads this configuration at boot time. This means that the configured behavior can be modified at boot time for different system configurations.

Listing 7-18 is a sample GRUB configuration file. This is the configuration file from the PC on which this book was written. The GRUB configuration file is called `grub.conf`[6] and usually is placed in a small partition dedicated to storing boot images. On the machine from which this example was taken, that directory is called `/boot`.

LISTING 7-18   Sample GRUB Configuration File: `grub.conf`

```
default=0
timeout=3
splashimage=(hd0,1)/grub/splash.xpm.gz

title Fedora Core 2 (2.6.9)
        root (hd0,1)
        kernel /bzImage-2.6.9 ro root=LABEL=/ rhgb proto=imps quiet
        initrd /initrd-2.6.9.img

title Fedora Core (2.6.5-1.358)
        root (hd0,1)
        kernel /vmlinuz-2.6.5-1.358 ro root=LABEL=/ rhgb quiet

title That Other OS
        rootnoverify (hd0,0)
        chainloader +1
```

GRUB first presents the user with a list of images that are available to boot. The title entries from Listing 7-18 are the image names presented to the user. The default tag specifies which image to boot if no keys have been pressed in the timeout period, which is 3 seconds in this example. Images are counted starting from 0.

Unlike Lilo, GRUB can actually read a file system on a given partition to load an image from. The `root` tag specifies the root partition from which all filenames in the `grub.conf` configuration file are rooted. In this sample configuration, the root is partition number 1 on the first hard disk drive, specified as `root(hd0,1)`. Partitions are numbered from 0; this is the second partition on the first hard disk.

The images are specified as filenames relative to the specified root. In Listing 7-18, the default boot image is a Linux 2.6.9 kernel with a matching initial ramdisk image called `initrd-2.6.9.img`. Notice that the GRUB syntax has the kernel command-line parameters on the same line as the kernel file specification.

---

[6] Some newer distributions call this file `menu.1st`.

7.6.3   Still More Bootloaders

Numerous other bootloaders have found their way into specific niches. For example, Redboot is another open source bootloader that Intel and the XScale community have adopted for use on various evaluation boards based on the Intel IXP and Marvel PXA processor families. Micromonitor is in use by board vendors such as Cogent and others. YAMON[7] has found popularity in MIPs circles. LinuxBIOS is used primarily in X86 environments. In general, when you consider a boot loader, you should consider some important factors up front:

- Does it support my chosen processor?
- Has it been ported to a board similar to my own?
- Does it support the features I need?
- Does it support the hardware devices I intend to use?
- Is there a large community of users where I might get support?
- Are there any commercial vendors from which I can purchase support?

These are some of the questions you must answer when considering what bootloader to use in your embedded project. Unless you are doing something on the "bleeding edge" of technology using a brand-new processor, you are likely to find that someone has already done the bulk of the hard work in porting a bootloader to your chosen platform. Use the resources listed at the end of this chapter to help make your final decisions.

7.7   Summary

This chapter examined the role of the bootloader and discovered the limited execution context in which a bootloader must exist. We covered one of the most popular bootloaders, U-Boot, in some detail. We walked through the steps of a typical port to a board with similar support in U-Boot. We briefly introduced additional bootloaders in use today so that you can make an informed choice for your particular requirements.

- The bootloader's role in an embedded system cannot be overstated. It is the first piece of software that takes control upon applying power.

---

[7] In an acknowledgment of the number of bootloaders in existence, the YAMON user's guide bills itself as Yet Another MONitor.

- Das U-Boot has become a popular universal bootloader for many processor architectures. It supports a large number of processors, reference hardware platforms, and custom boards.

- U-Boot is configured using a series of configuration variables in a board-specific header file. Appendix B contains a list of all the standard U-Boot command sets supported in a recent U-Boot release.

- Porting U-Boot to a new board based on a supported processor is relatively straightforward.

- There is no substitute for detailed knowledge of your processor and hardware platform when bootloader modification or porting must be accomplished.

- You may need a device tree binary for your board, especially if it is Power Architecture and soon perhaps ARM.

7.7.1   Suggestions for Additional Reading

Application Note: Introduction to Synchronous DRAM
Maxwell Technologies
www.maxwell.com/pdf/me/app_notes/Intro_to_SDRAM.pdf

Using LD, the GNU linker
Free Software Foundation
http://sourceware.org/binutils/docs/ld/index.html

The DENX U-Boot and Linux Guide (DLUG) for TQM8xxL
Wolfgang Denx, et al., Denx Software Engineering
www.denx.de/twiki/bin/view/DULG/Manual

RFC 793, "Trivial File Transfer Protocol"
The Internet Engineering Task Force
www.ietf.org/rfc/rfc783.txt

RFC 951, "Bootstrap Protocol"
The Internet Engineering Task Force
www.ietf.org/rfc/rfc951.txt

RFC 1531, "Dynamic Host Control Protocol"
The Internet Engineering Task Force
www.ietf.org/rfc/rfc1531.txt

PowerPC 405GP Embedded Processor user manual
International Business Machines, Inc.

Programming Environments Manual for 32-bit Implementations of the PowerPC
Architecture
Freescale Semiconductor, Inc.

Lilo Bootloader
www.tldp.org/HOWTO/LILO.html

GRUB Bootloader
www.gnu.org/software/grub/

Device tree documentation
Linux Kernel Source Tree
`.../Documentation/powerpc/booting-without-of.txt`

Device trees everywhere
David Gibson, Benjamin Herrenschmidt
http://ozlabs.org/people/dgibson/papers/dtc-paper.pdf

Excellent list of flat device tree references
www.denx.de/wiki/U-Boot/UBootFdtInfo#Background_Information_on_Flatte

Chapter 8

Device Driver Basics

In This Chapter

- 8.1 Device Driver Concepts   202
- 8.2 Module Utilities   212
- 8.3 Driver Methods   217
- 8.4 Bringing It All Together   222
- 8.5 Building Out-of-Tree Drivers   223
- 8.6 Device Drivers and the GPL   224
- 8.7 Summary   225

One of the more challenging aspects of system design is partitioning functionality in a rational manner. The familiar device driver model found in UNIX and Linux provides a natural partitioning of functionality between your application code and hardware or kernel devices. This chapter helps you understand this model and the basics of Linux device driver architecture. After reading this chapter, you will have a solid foundation for continuing your study of device drivers using one of the references listed at the end of this chapter.

This chapter begins by presenting Linux device driver concepts and describing the build system for drivers within the kernel source tree. We examine the Linux device driver architecture and present an example of a simple working driver. We introduce the user space utilities for loading and unloading kernel modules.[1] We present a simple application to illustrate the interface between applications and device drivers. We conclude this chapter with a discussion of the relationship between device drivers and the GNU Public License.

8.1   Device Driver Concepts

Many experienced embedded developers struggle initially with the concept of device drivers in a virtual memory operating system. This is because many popular legacy real-time operating systems do not have a similar architecture. The idea of virtual memory and kernel space versus user space frequently introduces complexity that is unfamiliar to experienced embedded developers.

One of the fundamental purposes of a device driver is to isolate the user programs from ready access to critical kernel data structures and hardware devices. Furthermore, a well-written device driver hides from the user the complexity and variability of the hardware device. For example, a program that wants to write data to the hard disk doesn't need to know if the disk drive uses 512-byte or 1024-byte sectors. The user simply opens a file and issues a `write` command. The device driver handles the details and isolates the user from the complexities and perils of hardware device

---

[1] The terms *module* and *device driver* are used here interchangeably.

programming. The device driver provides a consistent user interface to a large variety of hardware devices. It provides the basis for the familiar UNIX/Linux convention that everything must be represented as a file.

8.1.1 Loadable Modules

Unlike some other operating systems, Linux lets you add and remove kernel components at runtime. Linux is structured as a monolithic kernel with a well-defined interface for adding and removing device driver modules dynamically after boot time. This feature not only provides flexibility for the user, but it also has proven invaluable to the device driver developer. Assuming that your device driver is reasonably well behaved, you can insert and remove the device driver from a running kernel at will during the development cycle instead of rebooting the kernel every time you want to test a change.

Loadable modules have particular importance to embedded systems. Loadable modules enhance field upgrade capabilities. For example, the module itself can be updated in a live system without the need for a reboot. Modules can be stored on media other than the root (boot) device, which can be space-constrained.

Of course, device drivers can also be statically compiled into the kernel, and, for many drivers, this is completely appropriate. Consider, for example, a kernel configured to mount a root file system from a network-attached NFS server. In this scenario, you configure the network-related drivers (TCP/IP and the network interface card driver) to be compiled into the main kernel image so that they are available during boot for mounting the remote root file system. You can use the initial ramdisk functionality as described in Chapter 6, "User Space Initialization," as an alternative to having these drivers compiled statically as part of the kernel proper. In this case, the necessary modules and a script to load them would be included in the initial ramdisk image.

Loadable modules are installed after the kernel has booted. Startup scripts can load device driver modules, and modules can also be "demand loaded" when needed. Linux can request a module when a service is requested that requires a particular module.[2]

Terminology has never been standardized when discussing kernel modules. Many terms have been and continue to be used interchangeably when discussing Linux device drivers. Throughout this and later chapters, the terms device driver, loadable kernel module (LKM), loadable module, and module are all used to describe a kernel device driver module.

---

[2] This mechanism is described in great detail in Chapter 19, "udev."

8.1.2   Device Driver Architecture

The basic Linux device driver model is familiar to UNIX/Linux system developers. Although the device driver model continues to evolve, some fundamental constructs have remained nearly constant over the course of UNIX/Linux evolution. Device drivers are broadly classified into two basic categories: character devices and block devices. Character devices can be thought of as serial streams of sequential data. Examples of character devices include serial ports and keyboards. Block devices are characterized by the capability to read and write blocks of data to and from random locations on an addressable medium. Examples of block devices include hard drives and USB Flash drives.

8.1.3   Minimal Device Driver Example

Because Linux supports loadable device drivers, it is relatively easy to demonstrate a simple device driver skeleton. Listing 8-1 shows a loadable device driver module that contains the bare minimum structure to be loaded and unloaded by a running kernel.

LISTING 8-1   Minimal Device Driver

```
/* Example Minimal Character Device Driver */
#include <linux/module.h>

static int __init hello_init(void)
{
    printk(KERN_INFO "Hello Example Init\n");

    return 0;
}

static void __exit hello_exit(void)
{
    printk("Hello Example Exit\n");
}

module_init(hello_init);
module_exit(hello_exit);

MODULE_AUTHOR("Chris Hallinan");
MODULE_DESCRIPTION("Hello World Example");
MODULE_LICENSE("GPL");
```

The skeletal driver shown in Listing 8-1 contains enough structure for the kernel to load and unload the driver and to invoke the initialization and exit routines. Let's look at how this is done, because it illustrates some important high-level concepts that are useful for device driver development.

A device driver is a special kind of binary module. Unlike a stand-alone binary executable application, a device driver cannot simply be executed from a command prompt. The 2.6 kernel series requires that the binary be in a special "kernel object" format. When properly built, the device driver binary module contains a `.ko` suffix. The build steps and compiler options required to create the `.ko` module object can be complex. Here we outline a set of steps to harness the power of the Linux kernel build system without requiring you to become an expert in it, which is beyond the scope of this book.

8.1.4 Module Build Infrastructure

A device driver must be compiled against the kernel on which it will execute. Although it is possible to load and execute kernel modules built against a different kernel version, it is risky to do so unless you are certain that the module does not rely on any features of your new kernel. The easiest way to do this is to build the module within the kernel's own source tree. This ensures that as the developer changes the kernel configuration, his custom driver is automatically rebuilt with the correct kernel configuration. It is certainly possible to build your drivers outside the kernel source tree. However, in this case, you are responsible for making sure that your device driver build configuration stays in sync with the kernel you want to run your driver on. This typically includes compiler switches, the location of kernel header files, and kernel configuration options.

For the sample driver introduced in Listing 8-1, the following changes were made to the stock Linux kernel source tree to enable building this sample driver. We'll explain each step in detail:

1. Starting from the top-level Linux source directory, create a directory under `.../drivers/char` called `examples`.

2. Add a menu item to the kernel configuration to enable building `examples` and to specify a built-in or loadable kernel module.

3. Add the new `examples` subdirectory to the `.../drivers/char/Makefile` conditional on the menu item created in step 2.

4. Create a makefile for the new `examples` directory, and add the `hello1.o` module object to be compiled conditional on the menu item created in step 2.

5. Create the driver `hello1.c` source file from Listing 8-1.

Adding the `examples` directory under the `.../drivers/char` subdirectory is self-explanatory. After this directory is created, two files are created in this directory: the module source file itself from Listing 8-1, and the makefile for the `examples` directory. The makefile for `examples` is quite trivial. It contains this single line:

```
obj-$(CONFIG_EXAMPLES) += hello1.o
```

Adding the menu item to the kernel configuration utility is a little more involved. Listing 8-2 contains a patch that, when applied to the `.../drivers/char/Kconfig` file from a recent Linux release, adds the configuration menu item to enable our `examples` configuration option. In case you're unfamiliar with the unified diff format, each line in Listing 8-2 preceded by a single plus character (+) is inserted in the file between the indicated lines (those without the leading +).

LISTING 8-2   *Kconfig* Patch for *examples*

```
diff --git a/drivers/char/Kconfig b/drivers/char/Kconfig
index 6f31c94..0805290 100644
--- a/drivers/char/Kconfig
+++ b/drivers/char/Kconfig
@@ -4,6 +4,13 @@

 menu "Character devices"

+config EXAMPLES
+       tristate "Enable Examples"
+       default M
+       ---help---
+         Enable compilation option for Embedded Linux Primer
+         driver examples
+
 config VT
        bool "Virtual terminal" if EMBEDDED
        depends on !S390
```

When applied to `Kconfig` in the `.../drivers/char` subdirectory of a recent Linux kernel, this patch results in a new kernel configuration option called `CONFIG_EXAMPLES`.

As a reminder from our discussion on building the Linux kernel in Chapter 4, "The Linux Kernel: A Different Perspective," the configuration utility is invoked as follows (this example assumes the ARM architecture):

```
$ make ARCH=arm CROSS_COMPILE=xscale_be- gconfig
```

After the configuration utility is invoked using a command similar to this one, our new `Enable Examples` configuration option appears under the Character devices menu, as indicated in the patch. Because it is defined as type `tristate`, the kernel developer has three choices:

(N) No. Do not compile `examples`.

(Y) Yes. Compile `examples` and link with the final kernel image.

(M) Module. Compile `examples` as a dynamically loadable module.

Figure 8-1 shows the resulting gconfig screen with the new configuration option added. A dash (-) in the check box selects module, as indicated in the M column on the right. A check mark in the check box selects yes, indicating that the driver module should be compiled as part of the kernel proper. An empty check box indicates that the option is not selected.

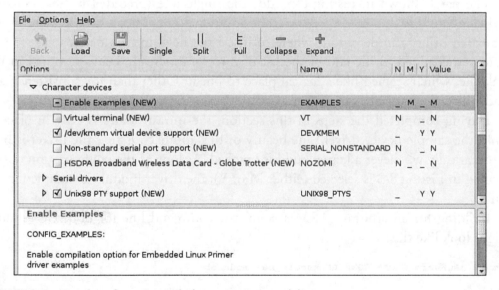

FIGURE 8-1 Kernel configuration with the *examples* module

Now that we have added the configuration option to enable compiling our `examples` device driver module, we need to modify the makefile in `.../drivers/char` to instruct the build system to descend into our new `examples` subdirectory if the configuration option `CONFIG_EXAMPLES` is present in our configuration. Listing 8-3 contains the patch for this against the makefile in a recent Linux release.

LISTING 8-3   Makefile Patch for *examples*

```
diff --git a/drivers/char/Makefile b/drivers/char/Makefile
index f957edf..f1b373d 100644
--- a/drivers/char/Makefile
+++ b/drivers/char/Makefile
@@ -102,6 +102,7 @@
 obj-$(CONFIG_MWAVE)             += mwave/
 obj-$(CONFIG_AGP)              += agp/
 obj-$(CONFIG_PCMCIA)           += pcmcia/
 obj-$(CONFIG_IPMI_HANDLER)     += ipmi/
+obj-$(CONFIG_EXAMPLES)         += examples/

 obj-$(CONFIG_HANGCHECK_TIMER)  += hangcheck-timer.o
 obj-$(CONFIG_TCG_TPM)          += tpm/
```

The patch shown in Listing 8-3 adds the single line (preceded by the +) to the makefile found in `.../drivers/char`. The additional lines of context are there so that the patch utility can determine where to insert the new line. Our new `examples` directory was added to the end of the list of directories already being searched in this makefile, which seemed like a logical place to put it. Other than for consistency and readability, the location is irrelevant.

Having completed the steps in this section, the infrastructure is now in place to build the sample device driver. The beauty of this approach is that the driver is built automatically whenever a kernel build is invoked. As long as the configuration option defined in Listing 8-3 is selected (either M or Y), the driver module is included in the build.

Building for an arbitrary ARM system, the command line for building modules might look like this:

```
$ make ARCH=arm CROSS_COMPILE=xscale_be- modules
```

Listing 8-4 shows the build after a typical editing session on the module (all other modules have already been built in this kernel source tree).

LISTING 8-4   Module Build Output

```
$ make ARCH=arm CROSS_COMPILE=xscale_be- modules
  CHK     include/linux/version.h
make[1]: 'include/asm-arm/mach-types.h' is up to date.
  CHK     include/linux/utsrelease.h
  SYMLINK include/asm -> include/asm-arm
  CALL    scripts/checksyscalls.sh
  CC [M]  drivers/char/examples/hello1.o
  Building modules, stage 2.
  MODPOST 76 modules
  LD [M]  drivers/char/examples/hello1.ko
```

8.1.5   Installing a Device Driver

Now that this driver is built, we can load and unload it on a running kernel to observe its behavior. Before we can load the module, we need to copy it to an appropriate location on our target system. Although we could put it anywhere we want, a convention is in place for kernel modules and where they are populated on a running Linux system. As with module compilation, it is easiest to let the kernel build system do that for us. The makefile target `modules_install` automatically places modules in the system in a logical layout. You simply need to supply the desired location as a prefix to the default path.

In a standard Linux workstation installation, you might already know that the device driver modules live in `/lib/modules/<kernel-version>/...` ordered in a manner similar to the device driver directory hierarchy in the Linux kernel tree.[3] The `<kernel-version>` string is produced by executing the command `uname -r` on your target Linux system. If you do not provide an installation prefix to the kernel build system, by default your modules are installed in your own workstation's `/lib/modules/...` directory. Since we are embedded developers, and we are cross-compiling, this is probably not what you intended. You can point to a temporary location in your home directory and manually copy the modules to your target's file system. Alternatively, if your target embedded system uses NFS root mount to a directory on your local development workstation, you can install the modules directly to the target file system. The following example assumes the latter:

```
$ make ARCH=arm CROSS_COMPILE=xscale_be-              \
    INSTALL_MOD_PATH=/home/chris/sandbox/coyote-target \
    modules_install
```

---

[3] This path is used by Red Hat and Fedora distributions and is also required by the File System Hierarchy Standard. referenced at the end of this chapter. Other distributions might use different locations in the file system for kernel modules.

This places all your modules in the directory `coyote-target`, which on this sample system is exported via NFS and mounted as root on the target system.[4]

8.1.6   Loading a Module

Having completed all the necessary steps, we are now in a position to load and test the device driver module. Listing 8-5 shows the output resulting from loading and subsequently unloading the device driver on the embedded system.

LISTING 8-5   Loading and Unloading a Module

```
# modprobe hello1              <<< Load the driver, must be root
Hello Example Init
# modprobe -r hello1           <<< Unload the driver, must be root
Hello Example Exit
#
```

You should be able to correlate the output with our device driver source code found in Listing 8-1. The module does no work other than printing messages to the kernel log system via `printk()`, which we see on our console.[5] When the module is loaded, the module-initialization function is called. We specify the initialization function that will be executed on module insertion using the `module_init()` macro. We declare it as follows:

```
module_init(hello_init);
```

In our initialization function, we simply print the obligatory hello message and return. In a real device driver, this is where you would perform any initial resource allocation for our module. In a similar fashion, when we unload the module (using the `modprobe -r` command), our module exit routine is called. As shown in Listing 8-1, the exit routine is specified using the `module_exit()` macro. In a real driver, this is where you undo everything that was done on entry, such as freeing any memory or returning the device to a known, harmless state.

That's all there is to a skeletal device driver capable of live insertion in an actual kernel. The following sections introduce additional functionality to our loadable device driver module that illustrates how a user space program would interact with a device driver module.

---

[4] Hosting a target board and NFS root mount are covered in detail in Chapter 12, "Embedded Development Environment."

[5] If you don't see the messages on the console, either disable your syslogd logger or lower the console loglevel. We describe how to do this in Chapter 14, "Kernel Debugging Techniques."

8.1.7 Module Parameters

Many device driver modules can accept parameters to modify their behavior. Examples include enabling debug mode, setting verbose reporting, and specifying module-specific options. The `insmod` utility (and the `modprobe` utility, introduced later) accepts module parameters (also called options in some contexts) by specifying them after the module name. Listing 8-6 shows our modified `hello1.c` example, adding a single module parameter to enable debug mode.

LISTING 8-6   Sample Driver with a Parameter

```
/* Example Minimal Character Device Driver */
#include <linux/module.h>

static int debug_enable = 0;        /* Added driver parameter */
module_param(debug_enable, int, 0);  /* and these 2 lines */
MODULE_PARM_DESC(debug_enable, "Enable module debug mode.");

static int __init hello_init(void)
{
    /* Now print value of new module parameter */
    printk("Hello Example Init - debug mode is %s\n",
           debug_enable ? "enabled" : "disabled");

    return 0;
}

static void __exit hello_exit(void)
{
    printk("Hello Example Exit\n");
}

module_init(hello_init);
module_exit(hello_exit);

MODULE_AUTHOR("Chris Hallinan");
MODULE_DESCRIPTION("Hello World Example");
MODULE_LICENSE("GPL");
```

Three lines have been added to our sample device driver module. The first declares a static integer to hold our debug flag. The second line is a macro defined in `.../include/linux/moduleparam.h` (included by `modules.h`) that registers the module parameter with the kernel module subsystem. The third new line is a macro that registers a string description associated with the parameter with the kernel module subsystem. The purpose of this will become clear when we examine the `modinfo` command later in this chapter.

If we now use `insmod` to insert our sample module, and add the `debug_enable` option, we should see the resulting output, based on our modified `hello1.c` module from Listing 8-6.

```
$ insmod /lib/modules/.../examples/hello1.ko debug_enable=1
Hello Example Init - debug mode is enabled
```

Or, if we omit the optional module parameter:

```
$ insmod /lib/modules/.../examples/hello1.ko
Hello Example Init - debug mode is disabled
```

8.2   Module Utilities

Listing 8-5 briefly introduced module utilities. There we used the module utility `modprobe` to insert and remove a device driver module from a running Linux kernel. A number of small utilities are used to manage device driver modules. This section introduces them. You are encouraged to refer to the man page for each utility for complete details. If you want to know more about how loadable modules and the Linux kernel interact,, consult the source code for these utilities. The section at the end of this chapter tells you where they can be found.

8.2.1   `insmod`

The `insmod` utility is the simplest way to insert a module into a running kernel. You supply a complete pathname, and `insmod` does the work. For example:

```
$ insmod /lib/modules/'uname -r'/kernel/drivers/char/examples/hello1.ko
```

This loads the module `hello1.ko` into the kernel. The output would be the same as shown in Listing 8-5—namely, the Hello message. The `insmod` utility is a simple program that does not require or accept any command-line options. It requires a full pathname because it has no logic for searching for the module. Most often, you will use `modprobe`, described shortly, because it has many more features and capabilities, including the capability to determine and load any dependencies that may be required for a given module.

8.2.2   `lsmod`

The `lsmod` utility is also trivial. It simply displays a formatted list of the modules that are inserted into the kernel. Recent versions take no parameters and simply format the output of `/proc/modules`.[6] Listing 8-7 is an example of the output from `lsmod`.

LISTING 8-7   *lsmod* Output Format

```
$ lsmod
Module              Size  Used by
ext3              121096  0
jbd               49656   1 ext3
loop              12712   0
hello1            1412    0
$
```

Notice the rightmost column, "Used by." It indicates that the device driver module is in use and shows the dependency chain. In this example, the `jbd` module (journaling routines for journaling file systems) is being used by the `ext3` module, the default journaling file system for many popular Linux desktop distributions. This means that the `ext3` device driver depends on the presence of `jbd`.

8.2.3   `modprobe`

This is where the cleverness of `modprobe` comes into play. Listing 8-7 shows the relationship between the `ext3` and `jbd` modules. The `ext3` module depends on the `jbd` module. The `modprobe` utility can discover this relationship and load the dependent modules in the proper order. The following command loads both the `jbd.ko` and `ext3.ko` driver modules:

`$ modprobe ext3`

The `modprobe` utility has several command-line options that control its behavior. As we saw earlier, `modprobe` can be used to remove modules, including the modules on

---

[6] `/proc/modules` is part of the `/proc` file system, which is introduced in Chapter 9, "File Systems."

which a given module depends. Here is an example of module removal that removes both `jbd.ko` and `ext3.ko`:

```
$ modprobe -r ext3
```

The `modprobe` utility is driven by a configuration file called `modprobe.conf`. This enables a system developer to associate devices with device drivers. For a simple embedded system, `modprobe.conf` might be empty or might contain very few lines. The `modprobe` utility is compiled with a set of default rules that establish the defaults in the absence of a valid `modprobe.conf`. Invoking `modprobe` with only the `-c` option displays the set of default rules that `modprobe` uses.

Listing 8-8 shows a typical `modprobe.conf`, which might be found on a system containing two Ethernet interfaces. One is a wireless adapter based on the Prism2 chipset, and the other is a typical PCI Ethernet card. This system also contains a sound subsystem based on an integrated Intel sound chipset.

LISTING 8-8   Typical *modprobe.conf* File

```
$ cat /etc/modprobe.conf
alias eth1 orinoci_pci
options eth1 orinoco_debug=9
alias eth0 e100
alias snd-card-0 snd-intel8x0
options snd-card-0 index=0
$
```

When the kernel boots and discovers the wireless chipset, this configuration file instructs `modprobe` to load the orinoco_pci device driver, bound to kernel device eth1. It then passes the optional module parameter orinoco_debug=9 to the device driver. The same action is taken upon discovery of the sound card hardware. Notice the optional parameters associated with the sound driver snd-intel8x0.

Note that the `modprobe.conf` functionality has largely been displaced by the functionality of `udev`. This is covered in Chapter 19. However, you might find `modprobe.conf` on older embedded systems, so knowing how to configure it may prove helpful.

8.2.4 depmod

How does `modprobe` know about the dependencies of a given module? The `depmod` utility plays a key role in this process. When `modprobe` is executed, it searches for a file called `modules.dep` in the same directory where the modules are installed. The `depmod` utility creates this module-dependency file.

This file contains a list of all the modules that the kernel build system is configured for, along with dependency information for each. It is a simple file format, in which each device driver module occupies one line in the file. If the module has dependencies, they are listed in order following the module name. For example, in Listing 8-7, we saw that the `ext3` module had a dependency on the `jbd` module. The dependency line in `modules.dep` would look like this:

```
ext3.ko: jbd.ko
```

In actual practice, each module name is preceded by its absolute path in the file system to avoid ambiguity. We have omitted the path information for readability. A more complicated dependency chain, such as sound drivers, might look like this:

```
snd-intel8x0.ko: snd-ac97-codec.ko snd-pcm.ko snd-timer.ko \
snd.ko soundcore.ko snd-page-alloc.ko
```

Again, we have removed the leading path components for readability. Each module filename in the `modules.dep` file is an absolute filename, with complete path information, and it exists on a single line. The preceding example was placed on two lines to fit the page width.

Normally, `depmod` is run automatically during a kernel build. However, in a cross-development environment, you must have a cross version of `depmod` that knows how to read the modules that are compiled in the native format of your target architecture. Alternatively, most embedded distributions have a method and init script entries to run `depmod` on each boot, to guarantee that the module dependencies are kept up to date.

8.2.5 rmmod

The `rmmod` utility is also trivial. It simply removes a module from a running kernel. Pass it the module name as a parameter. There is no need to include a pathname or file extension. For example:

```
# rmmod hello1        <<< Must be root
Hello Example Exit
```

The only interesting point to understand here is that when you use `rmmod`, it executes the module's `*_exit()` function, as shown here, from our `hello1.c` example of Listings 8-1 and 8-6.

It should be noted that, unlike `modprobe`, `rmmod` does not remove dependent modules. Use `modprobe -r` for this.

8.2.6 `modinfo`

You might have noticed the last three lines of the skeletal driver in Listing 8-1, and later in Listing 8-6. These macros are there to place tags in the binary module to facilitate their administration and management. Listing 8-9 is the result of `modinfo` executed on our `hello1.ko` module.

LISTING 8-9   *modinfo* Output

```
$ modinfo hello1
filename:      /lib/modules/../kernel/drivers/char/examples/hello1.ko
license:       GPL
description:   Hello World Example
author:        Chris Hallinan
depends:
vermagic:      2.6.32-07500-g8bea867 mod_unload modversions ARMv5
parm:          debug_enable:Enable module debug mode. (int)
```

The first field is obvious: It is the full filename of the device driver module. For readability, we have truncated the path again. The following lines are a direct result of the descriptive macros found at the end of Listing 8-6—namely, the filename, author, and license information. These are simply tags for use by the module utilities; they do not affect the behavior of the device driver itself. You can learn more about `modinfo` from its man page and the `modinfo` source.

One very useful feature of `modinfo` is learning what parameters the module supports. From Listing 8-9, you can see that this module supports just one parameter. This was the one we added in Listing 8-6, `debug_enable`. The listing gives the name, type (in this case, an int), and the descriptive text field we entered with the MODULE_PARM_DESC() macro. This can be very handy, especially for modules in which you might not have easy access to the source code.

8.3 Driver Methods

We've covered much ground in our short treatment of module utilities. The remaining sections describe the basic mechanism for communicating with a device driver from a user space program (your application code).

We have introduced the two fundamental methods responsible for the module's one-time initialization and exit processing. Recall from Listing 8-1 that your module init and exit routines are identified by `module_init()` and `module_exit()`. We discovered that these routines are invoked when the module is inserted into or removed from a running kernel. Now we need some methods to interface with our device driver from our application program. After all, two of the more important reasons we use device drivers are to isolate the user from the perils of writing code in kernel space and to present a unified method to communicate with hardware or kernel-level devices.

8.3.1 Driver File System Operations

After the device driver is loaded into a live kernel, the first action we must take is to prepare the driver for subsequent operations. The `open()` method is used for this purpose. After the driver has been opened, we need routines for reading and writing to the driver. A `release()` routine is provided to clean up after operations are complete (basically, a `close()` call). Finally, a special system call is provided for nonstandard communication with the driver. This is called `ioctl()`. Listing 8-10 adds this infrastructure to our sample device driver.

LISTING 8-10   Adding File System Ops to *hello.c*

```
#include <linux/module.h>
#include <linux/fs.h>

#define HELLO_MAJOR 234

static int debug_enable = 0;
module_param(debug_enable, int, 0);
MODULE_PARM_DESC(debug_enable, "Enable module debug mode.");

struct file_operations hello_fops;

static int hello_open(struct inode *inode, struct file *file)
{
    printk("hello_open: successful\n");
```

LISTING 8-10   Continued

```
    return 0;
}

static int hello_release(struct inode *inode, struct file *file)
{
    printk("hello_release: successful\n");
    return 0;
}

static ssize_t hello_read(struct file *file, char *buf, size_t count,
            loff_t *ptr)
{
    printk("hello_read: returning zero bytes\n");
    return 0;
}

static ssize_t hello_write(struct file *file, const char *buf,
            size_t count, loff_t * ppos)
{
    printk("hello_write: accepting zero bytes\n");
    return 0;
}

static int hello_ioctl(struct inode *inode, struct file *file,
            unsigned int cmd, unsigned long arg)
{
    printk("hello_ioctl: cmd=%ld, arg=%ld\n", cmd, arg);
    return 0;
}

static int __init hello_init(void)
{
    int ret;
    printk("Hello Example Init - debug mode is %s\n",
            debug_enable ? "enabled" : "disabled");
    ret = register_chrdev(HELLO_MAJOR, "hello1", &hello_fops);
        if (ret < 0) {
            printk("Error registering hello device\n");
            goto hello_fail1;
        }
    printk("Hello: registered module successfully!\n");
```

LISTING 8-10 Continued

```
    /* Init processing here... */

    return 0;

hello_fail1:
    return ret;
}

static void __exit hello_exit(void)
{
    printk("Hello Example Exit\n");
}

struct file_operations hello_fops = {
    owner:   THIS_MODULE,
    read:    hello_read,
    write:   hello_write,
    ioctl:   hello_ioctl,
    open:    hello_open,
    release: hello_release,
};

module_init(hello_init);
module_exit(hello_exit);

MODULE_AUTHOR("Chris Hallinan");
MODULE_DESCRIPTION("Hello World Example");
MODULE_LICENSE("GPL");
```

This expanded device driver example includes many new lines. From the top, we had to add a new kernel header file to get the definitions for the file system operations. We also defined a major number for our device driver. (Note to device driver authors: This is not the proper way to allocate a device driver major number. Refer to the Linux kernel documentation [.../Documentation/devices.txt] or to one of the excellent texts on device drivers for guidance on the allocation of major device numbers. For this simple example, we simply chose one that we know isn't in use on our system.)

Next we see definitions for four new functions—our open, close, read, and write methods. In keeping with good coding practices, we've adopted a consistent naming scheme that will help our code's readability and maintainability. Our new methods are called `hello_open()`, `hello_release()`, `hello_read()`, and `hello_write()`, re-spectively. For the purposes of this simple exercise, they are do-nothing functions that simply print a message to the kernel log subsystem.

Notice that we've also added a new function call to our `hello_init()` routine. This line registers our device driver with the kernel. With that registration call, we pass a structure containing pointers to the required methods. The kernel uses this structure, of type `struct file_operations`, to bind our specific device functions with the appro-priate requests from the file system. When an application opens a device represented by our device driver and requests a `read()` operation, the file system associates that generic `read()` request with our module's `hello_read()` function. The following sec-tions examine this process in detail.

8.3.2   Allocation of Device Numbers

It must be noted that the examples in this book are designed to give you an overall idea of the architecture of device drivers and how they fit into the big picture. It is not meant to be a tutorial on device driver development. This topic is covered in the two excellent texts listed at the end of this chapter.

With that caveat, it should be noted that the method by which we allocate a *major* device number in Listing 8-10 has been superseded by a much more robust method. Usually you will not specify a device number in your driver. You will use methods that allow the kernel to specify a device number for you. This avoids collisions with device numbers and scales much better than manually assigning your own device number. This process is described fully in Chapter 3 of *Linux Device Drivers*, 3rd Edition, ref-erenced at the end of this chapter.

8.3.3   Device Nodes and `mknod`

To understand how an application binds its requests to a specific device represented by our device driver, we must understand the concept of a device node. A device node is a special file type in Linux that represents a device. Virtually all Linux distributions keep device nodes in a common location (specified by the Filesystem Hierarchy Standard[7]), in a directory called `/dev`. A dedicated utility is used to create a device node on a file system. This utility is called `mknod`.

---

[7] This standard is referred to at the end of this chapter.

An example of node creation is the best way to illustrate its functionality and the information it conveys. In keeping with our simple device driver example, let's create the proper device node to exercise it:

```
$ mknod /dev/hello1 c 234 0
```

After executing this command on our target embedded system, we end up with a new file called /dev/hello1 that represents our device driver module. If we list this file, it looks like this:

```
$ ls -l /dev/hello1
crw-r--r--   1 root  root  234, 0 Jul 14 2005 /dev/hello1
```

The parameters we passed to mknod include the name, type, and major and minor numbers for our device driver. The name we chose was hello1. Because we are demonstrating the use of a character driver, we use c to indicate that. The major number is 234, the number we chose for this example, and the minor number is 0.

By itself, the device node is just another file on our file system. However, because of its special status as a device node, we use it to bind to an installed device driver. If an application process issues an open() system call with our device node as the path parameter, the kernel searches for a valid device driver registered with a major number that matches the device node—in this case, 234. This is the mechanism by which the kernel associates our particular device to the device node.

As most C programmers know, the open() system call, or any of its variants, returns a reference (file descriptor) that our applications use to issue subsequent file system operations, such as read, write, and close. This reference is then passed to the various file system operations, such as read and write, or their variants.

If you're curious about the purpose of the minor number, it is a mechanism for handling multiple devices or subdevices with a single device driver. It is not used by the operating system; it is simply passed to the device driver. The device driver can use the minor number in any way it sees fit. For example, with a multiport serial card, the major number would specify the driver. The minor number might specify one of the multiple ports handled by the same driver on the multiport card. Consult one of the excellent texts on device drivers for further details.

One final note is worthy of mention. The preceding discussion about device nodes is meant for instructional purposes. On most modern Linux systems, you will never actually create a device node. Device node creation is handled automatically by udev. This functionality is explained fully in Chapter 19.

8.4   Bringing It All Together

Now that we have a skeletal device driver, we can load and exercise it. Listing 8-11 is a simple user space application that exercises our device driver. We've already seen how to load the driver. Simply compile it and issue the `make modules_install` command to place it on your file system, as described earlier.

LISTING 8-11   Exercising Our Device Driver

```
#include <stdio.h>
#include <stdlib.h>
#include <sys/types.h>
#include <sys/stat.h>
#include <fcntl.h>
#include <unistd.h>

int main(int argc, char **argv)
{
    /* Our file descriptor */
    int fd;
    int rc = 0;
    char *rd_buf[16];

    printf("%s: entered\n", argv[0]);

    /* Open the device */
    fd = open("/dev/hello1", O_RDWR);
    if ( fd == -1 ) {
        perror("open failed");
        rc = fd;
        exit(-1);
    }
    printf("%s: open: successful\n", argv[0]);

    /* Issue a read */
    rc = read(fd, rd_buf, 0);
    if ( rc == -1 ) {
        perror("read failed");
        close(fd);
        exit(-1);
    }
    printf("%s: read: returning %d bytes!\n", argv[0], rc);

    close(fd);
    return 0;
}
```

This simple file, compiled on an ARM XScale system, demonstrates the binding of application to device driver through the device node. Like the device driver, it doesn't do any useful work, but it does demonstrate the concepts as it exercises some of the methods we introduced in the device driver of Listing 8-10.

First we issue an open() system call[8] on our device node created earlier. If the open succeeds, we indicate that with a message to the console. Next we issue a read() command and again print a message to the console on success. Notice that a read of 0 bytes is perfectly acceptable as far as the kernel is concerned. In actual practice, this indicates an end-of-file or out-of-data condition. Your device driver defines that special condition. When complete, we simply close the file and exit. Listing 8-12 captures the output of running this sample application on an ARM XScale target.

LISTING 8-12   Using the Sample Driver

```
$ modprobe hello1
Hello Example Init - debug mode is disabled
Hello: registered module successfully!
$ ./use-hello
./use-hello: entered
./use-hello: open: successful
./use-hello: read: returning zero bytes!
$
```

8.5 Building Out-of-Tree Drivers

It is often convenient to build device drivers outside of the kernel source tree. Using a simple makefile patterned after one of the many in the kernel source tree makes this job easy. Driver makefiles in the Linux kernel source tree usually are quite simple. Over half of the more than 450 driver makefiles contain fewer than ten lines. Five percent contain just a single line!

If we build a makefile for our hello1 example to build it outside the kernel tree, it might look like this:

```
obj-$(CONFIG_EXAMPLES)            += hello1.o
```

Create a makefile in a directory of your choice, and place the hello1.c source code there. Next, create a new file named Makefile in the same directory. The makefile

---

[8] Actually, the open() call is a C library wrapper function around the Linux sys_open() system call.

should contain the single line just shown. Then execute the following build command from this directory (which you just created):

```
$ make ARCH=arm CROSS_COMPILE=xscale_be- -C \
    <path/to/your/linux-2.6> SUBDIRS=$PWD modules
```

Of course, you replace `<path/to/your/linux-2.6>` with the path to your own Linux source tree. This `make` command, when invoked, switches to your kernel source tree via the `-c` parameter, and instructs the build to build those targets defined in SUBDIRS. It's that simple.

As soon as you understand the concepts, you can build your makefile to have a bit more intelligence. For example, it can define SUBDIRS and the path to your kernel if you like. It is important to realize that your kernel configuration must have CONFIG_ EXAMPLES defined to either =m or =y. You can check this in your `.config` file. As expected, if CONFIG_EXAMPLES is not defined, your `hello1.c` module will not be compiled.

8.6   Device Drivers and the GPL

Disclaimer   You may have seen the Internet acronym IANAL. This acronym applies here: I am not a lawyer. The most sound advice you could be given is to consult an attorney who is well versed in intellectual property and copyright law, preferably one who has some professional experience with open source licenses.

Much discussion and debate surround the issue of device drivers and how the terms of the GNU Public License apply to device drivers. The first test is well understood: If your device driver (or any software, for that matter) is based, even in part, on existing GPL software, it is considered a derived work. For example, if you start with a current Linux device driver and modify it to suit your needs, this is certainly considered a derived work. Therefore, you are obligated to license this modified device driver under the terms of the work it was derived from, presumably the GPL, observing all its requirements.

This is where the debate comes in. Some of these concepts have not yet been tested in court. The prevailing opinion of the legal and open source communities is that if a work can be proven to be independently derived,[9] and a given device driver does not assume "intimate knowledge" of the Linux kernel, the developers are free to license it in any way they see fit. If modifications are made to the kernel to accommodate a special need of the driver, it is considered a derived work and therefore is subject to the GPL.

---

[9] This practice is not unique to open source. Copyright and patent infringement are ongoing concerns for all developers.

A large and growing body of information exists in the open source community regarding these issues. It seems likely that, at some point in the future, these concepts will be tested in a court of law, and a precedent will be established. How long that might take is anyone's guess. If you are interested in gaining a better understanding of the legal issues surrounding Linux and open source, you might enjoy www.open-bar.org.

8.7 Summary

This chapter presented a high-level overview of device driver basics and how they fit into the architecture of a Linux system. Now that you're armed with the basics, if you're new to device drivers, you can jump into one of the excellent texts devoted to device driver writers, as listed in the last section. This chapter concluded by introducing the relationship between kernel device drivers and the Open Source GNU Public License.

- Device drivers enforce a rational separation between unprivileged user applications and critical kernel resources such as hardware and other devices. They present a well-known unified interface to applications.

- The minimum infrastructure to load a device driver is only a few lines of code. We presented this minimum infrastructure and built on the concepts to a simple shell of a driver module.

- Device drivers configured as loadable modules can be inserted into and removed from a running kernel after kernel boot.

- Module utilities are used to manage the insertion, removal, and listing of device driver modules. We covered the details of the module utilities used for these functions.

- Device nodes on your file system provide the glue between your user space application and the device driver.

- Driver methods implement the familiar open, read, write, and close functionality commonly found in UNIX/Linux device drivers. This mechanism was explained by example, including a simple user application to exercise these driver methods.

8.7.1   Suggestions for Additional Reading

Linux Device Drivers, 3rd Edition
Alessandro Rubini and Jonathan Corbet
O'Reilly Publishing, 2005

Essential Linux Device Drivers
Sreekrishnan Venkateswaran
Prentice Hall, 2008

Filesystem Hierarchy Standard
http://en.wikipedia.org/wiki/Filesystem_Hierarchy_Standard

Rusty's Linux Kernel Page
Module Utilities for 2.6
Rusty Russell
http://kernel.org/pub/linux/kernel/people/rusty/

Chapter 9

File Systems

In This Chapter

■ 9.1 Linux File System Concepts   228

■ 9.2 ext2   230

■ 9.3 ext3   235

■ 9.4 ext4   237

■ 9.5 ReiserFS   238

■ 9.6 JFFS2   239

■ 9.7 *cramfs*   242

■ 9.8 Network File System   244

■ 9.9 Pseudo File Systems   248

■ 9.10 Other File Systems   255

■ 9.11 Building a Simple File System   256

■ 9.12 Summary   258

Perhaps one of the most important decisions an embedded developer makes is which file system(s) to deploy. Some file systems optimize for performance, whereas others optimize for size. Still others optimize for data recovery after device or power failure. This chapter introduces the major file systems in use on Linux systems and examines the characteristics of each as they apply to embedded designs. It is not the intent of this chapter to examine the internal technical details of each file system. Instead, this chapter examines the operational characteristics and development issues related to each file system presented.

Starting with the most popular file system in use on earlier Linux desktop distributions, we introduce concepts from the Second Extended File System (ext2) to lay a foundation for further discussion. Next we look at its successor, the Third Extended File System (ext3), which has enjoyed much popularity as the default file system for many Linux desktop and server distributions. We then describe the improvements that led to ext4.

After introducing some fundamentals, we examine a variety of specialized file systems, including those optimized for data recovery and storage space, and those designed for use on Flash memory devices. The Network File System (NFS) is presented, followed by a discussion of the more important pseudo file systems, including the */proc* file system and `sysfs`.

9.1 Linux File System Concepts

Before delving into the details of the individual file systems, let's look at the big picture of how data is stored on a Linux system. In our study of device drivers in Chapter 8, "Device Driver Basics," we looked at the structure of a character device. In general, character devices store and retrieve data in serial streams. The most basic example of a character device is a serial port or mouse. In contrast, block devices store and retrieve data in equal-sized chunks of data at a time, in random locations on an addressable medium. For example, a typical IDE hard disk controller can transfer 512 bytes of data at a time to and from a specific, addressable location on the physical medium.

9.1.1   Partitions

Before we begin our discussion of file systems, we start by introducing partitions, the logical division of a physical device on which a file system exists. At the highest level, data is stored on physical devices in partitions. A partition is a logical division of the physical medium (hard disk, Flash memory) whose data is organized following the specifications of a given partition type. A physical device can have a single partition covering all its available space, or it can be divided into multiple partitions to suit a particular task. A partition can be thought of as a logical disk onto which a complete file system can be written.

Figure 9-1 shows the relationship between partitions and file systems.

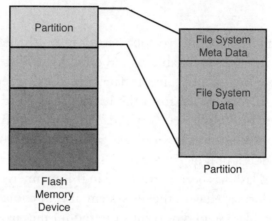

FIGURE 9-1   Partitions and file systems

Linux uses a utility called `fdisk` to manipulate partitions on block devices. A recent `fdisk` utility found on many Linux distributions has knowledge of more than 90 different partition types. In practice, only a few are commonly used on Linux systems. Some common partition types are Linux, FAT32, and Linux Swap.

Listing 9-1 displays the output of the `fdisk` utility targeting a CompactFlash device connected to a USB port. On this particular target system, the physical CompactFlash device was assigned to the device node `/dev/sdb`.[1]

---

[1] You will learn how this is done in Chapter 19, "udev."

LISTING 9-1   Displaying Partition Information Using *fdisk*

```
# fdisk /dev/sdb

Command (m for help): p

Disk /dev/sdb: 49 MB, 49349120 bytes
4 heads, 32 sectors/track, 753 cylinders
Units = cylinders of 128 * 512 = 65536 bytes

   Device Boot      Start         End      Blocks   Id  System
/dev/sdb1    *          1         180       11504   83  Linux
/dev/sdb2             181         360       11520   83  Linux
/dev/sdb3             361         540       11520   83  Linux
/dev/sdb4             541         753       13632   83  Linux
```

For this discussion, we have created four partitions on the device using the fdisk utility. One of them is marked bootable, as indicated by the asterisk in the Boot column. This reflects a *boot indicator* flag in the data structure that represents the partition table on the device. As you can see from the listing, the logical unit of storage used by fdisk is a cylinder.[2] On this device, a cylinder contains 64KB. On the other hand, Linux represents the smallest unit of storage as a logical block. You can deduce from this listing that a block is a unit of 1024 bytes.

After the CompactFlash has been partitioned in this manner, each device representing a partition can be formatted with the file system of your choice. When a partition is formatted with a given file system type, Linux can mount the corresponding file system from that partition.

9.2   ext2

Building on Listing 9-1, we need to format the partitions created with fdisk. To do so, we use the Linux mkfs.ext2 utility. mkfs.ext2 is similar to the familiar DOS format command. This utility makes a file system of type ext2 on the specified partition. mkfs. ext2 is specific to the ext2 file system; other file systems have their own versions of these utilities. Listing 9-2 captures the output of this process.

---

[2] The term *cylinder* was borrowed from the unit of storage on a rotational medium. It consists of the data under a group of heads on a given sector of a disk device. Here it is used for compatibility purposes with existing file system utilities.

LISTING 9-2   Formatting a Partition Using *mkfs.ext2*

```
# mkfs.ext2 /dev/sdb1 -L CFlash_Boot_Vol
mke2fs 1.40.8 (13-Mar-2008)
Filesystem label=CFlash_Boot_Vol
OS type: Linux
Block size=1024 (log=0)
Fragment size=1024 (log=0)
2880 inodes, 11504 blocks
575 blocks (5.00%) reserved for the super user
First data block=1
Maximum filesystem blocks=11796480
2 block groups
8192 blocks per group, 8192 fragments per group
1440 inodes per group
Superblock backups stored on blocks:
     8193

Writing inode tables: done
Writing superblocks and filesystem accounting information: done

This filesystem will be automatically checked every 33 mounts or 180
days, whichever comes first.  Use tune2fs -c or -i to override.
```

Listing 9-2 contains much detail relating to the ext2 file system. It's an excellent way to begin understanding the operational characteristics of ext2. This partition was formatted as type ext2 (we know this because we used the ext2 `mkfs` utility) with a volume label of `CFlash_Boot_Vol`. It was created on a Linux partition (OS Type:) with a block size of 1024 bytes. Space was allocated for 2,880 inodes, occupying 11,504 blocks. An *inode* is the fundamental data structure representing a single file. For more detailed information about the internal structure of the ext2 file system, see the last section of this chapter.

Looking at the output of `mkfs.ext2` in Listing 9-2, we can ascertain certain characteristics of how the storage device is organized. We already know that the block size is 1024 bytes. If necessary for your particular application, `mkfs.ext2` can be instructed to format an ext2 file system with different block sizes. Current implementations allow block sizes of 1,024, 2,048, and 4,096 blocks.

Block size is always a compromise for best performance. On one hand, large block sizes waste more space on disks with many small files, because each file must fit into an integral number of blocks. Any leftover fragment above `block_size` * *n* must occupy another full block, even if only 1 byte. On the other hand, very small block sizes increase the file system overhead of managing the metadata that describes the block-to-file mapping. Benchmark testing on your particular hardware implementation and data formats is the only way to be sure you have selected an optimum block size.

9.2.1   Mounting a File System

After a file system has been created, we can mount it on a running Linux system. The kernel must be compiled with support for our particular file system type, either as a compiled-in module or as a dynamically loadable module. The following command mounts the previously created ext2 file system on a mount point that we specify:

```
# mount /dev/sdb1 /mnt/flash
```

This example assumes that we have a directory created on our target Linux machine called /mnt/flash. This is called the mount point because we are installing (mounting) the file system rooted at this point in our file system hierarchy. We are mounting the Flash device described earlier that was assigned to the device /dev/sdb1. On a typical Linux desktop (development) machine, we need to have root privileges to execute this command.[3] The mount point is any directory path on your file system that you decide, which becomes the top level (root) of your newly mounted device. In the preceding example, to reference any files on your Flash device, you must prefix the path with /mnt/flash.

The mount command has many options. Several options that mount accepts depend on the target file system type. Most of the time, mount can determine the type of file system on a properly formatted file system known to the kernel. We'll provide additional usage examples for the mount command as we proceed through this chapter.

Listing 9-3 displays the directory contents of a Flash device configured for an arbitrary embedded system.

LISTING 9-3   Flash Device Listing

```
$ ls -l /mnt/flash
total 24
drwxr-xr-x  2 root root  1024 Jul 18 20:18 bin
drwxr-xr-x  2 root root  1024 Jul 18 20:18 boot
drwxr-xr-x  2 root root  1024 Jul 18 20:18 dev
drwxr-xr-x  2 root root  1024 Jul 18 20:18 etc
drwxr-xr-x  2 root root  1024 Jul 18 20:18 home
```

---

[3] File systems can be made mountable by nonroot users, as with cdrom, using appropriate entries in /etc/fstab.

LISTING 9-3   Continued

```
drwxr-xr-x  2 root root  1024 Jul 18 20:18 lib
drwx------  2 root root 12288 Jul 17 13:02 lost+found
drwxr-xr-x  2 root root  1024 Jul 18 20:18 proc
drwxr-xr-x  2 root root  1024 Jul 18 20:18 root
drwxr-xr-x  2 root root  1024 Jul 18 20:18 sbin
drwxr-xr-x  2 root root  1024 Jul 18 20:18 tmp
drwxr-xr-x  2 root root  1024 Jul 18 20:18 usr
drwxr-xr-x  2 root root  1024 Jul 18 20:18 var
$
```

Listing 9-3 is an example of what an embedded system's root file system might look like at the top (root) level. Chapter 6, "User Space Initialization," provides guidance on and examples of how to determine the contents of the root file system.

9.2.2   Checking File System Integrity

The e2fsck command is used to check the integrity of an ext2 file system. A file system can become corrupted for several reasons. By far the most common reason is an unexpected power failure. Linux distributions close all open files and unmount file systems during the shutdown sequence (assuming an orderly shutdown of the system). However, when we are dealing with embedded systems, unexpected power-downs are common, so we need to provide some defensive measures against these cases. e2fsck is our first line of defense.

Listing 9-4 shows the output of e2fsck run on our CompactFlash from the previous examples. It has been formatted and properly unmounted, so no errors should occur.

LISTING 9-4   Clean File System Check

```
# e2fsck /dev/sdb1
e2fsck 1.40.8 (13-Mar-2008)
CFlash_Boot_Vol: clean, 11/2880 files, 471/11504 blocks
#
```

The e2fsck utility checks several aspects of the file system for consistency. If no issues are found, e2fsck issues a message similar to that shown in Listing 9-4. Note that e2fsck should be run only on an unmounted file system. Although it is possible to run it on a mounted file system, doing so can cause significant damage to internal file system structures on the disk or Flash device.

To offer a more interesting example, Listing 9-5 was created by pulling the CompactFlash device out of its socket while it was still mounted. We intentionally created a file and started an editing session on that file before removing it from the system. This can result in corruption of the data structures describing the file, as well as the actual data blocks containing the file's data.

LISTING 9-5   Corrupted File System Check

```
# e2fsck -y /dev/sdb1
e2fsck 1.40.8 (13-Mar-2008)
/dev/sdb1 was not cleanly unmounted, check forced.
Pass 1: Checking inodes, blocks, and sizes
Inode 13, i_blocks is 16, should be 8.  Fix? yes

Pass 2: Checking directory structure
Pass 3: Checking directory connectivity
Pass 4: Checking reference counts
Pass 5: Checking group summary information

/dev/sdb1: ***** FILE SYSTEM WAS MODIFIED *****
/dev/sdb1: 25/2880 files (4.0% non-contiguous), 488/11504 blocks
#
```

From Listing 9-5, you can see that e2fsck detected that the CompactFlash was not cleanly unmounted. Furthermore, you can see the processing on the file system during e2fsck checking. The e2fsck utility makes five passes over the file system, checking various elements of the internal file system's data structures. An error associated with a file, identified by inode[4] 13, was automatically fixed because the -y flag was included on the e2fsck command line.

Of course, in a real system, you might not be this lucky. Some types of file system errors cannot be repaired using e2fsck. Moreover, the embedded system designer should understand that if power has been removed without proper shutdown, the boot cycle can be delayed by the length of time it takes to scan your boot device and repair any errors. Indeed, if these errors are not repairable, the system boot is halted, and manual intervention is indicated. Furthermore, it should be noted that if your file system is large, the file system check (fsck) can take minutes or even hours for large multigigabyte file systems.

Another defense against file system corruption is to ensure that writes are committed to disk immediately when written. The sync utility can be used to force all queued

---

[4] A file on a file system is represented by an internal ext2 data structure called an inode.

I/O requests to be committed to their respective devices. One strategy to minimize the window of vulnerability for data corruption from unexpected power loss or drive failure is to issue the `sync` command after every file write or strategically as needed by your application requirements. The trade-off is, of course, a performance penalty. Deferring disk writes is a performance optimization used in all modern operating systems. Using `sync` effectively defeats this optimization.

The ext2 file system has matured as a fast, efficient, and robust file system for Linux systems. However, if you need the additional reliability of a journaling file system, or if boot time after unclean shutdown is an issue in your design, you should consider the ext3 file system.

9.3 ext3

The ext3 file system has become a powerful, high-performance, and robust journaling file system. It is currently the default file system for many popular desktop Linux distributions.

The ext3 file system is basically an extension of the ext2 file system with added journaling capability. Journaling is a technique in which each change to the file system is logged in a special file so that recovery is possible from known journaling points. One of the primary advantages of the ext3 file system is its ability to be mounted directly after an unclean shutdown. As stated in the preceding section, when a system shuts down unexpectedly, such as during a power failure, the system forces a file system consistency check, which can be a lengthy operation. With ext3 file systems, a consistency check is unneeded, because the journal can simply be played back to ensure the file system's consistency.

Without going into design details that are beyond the scope of this book, we will quickly explain how a journaling file system works. A journaling file system contains a special file, often hidden from the user, that is used to store file system metadata[5] and file data itself. This special file is referred to as the journal. Whenever the file system is subject to a change (such as a write operation), the changes are first written to the journal. The file system drivers make sure that this write is committed to the journal before the actual changes are posted and committed to the storage medium (disk or Flash, for example). After the changes have been logged in the journal, the driver posts

---

[5] Metadata is data about the file, as opposed to the file's data itself. Examples include a file's date, time, size, blocks used, and so on.

the changes to the actual file and metadata on the medium. If a power failure occurs during the media write and a reboot occurs, all that is necessary to restore consistency to the file system is to replay the changes in the journal.

One of the most significant design goals for the ext3 file system was that it be both backward- and forward-compatible with the ext2 file system. It is possible to convert an ext2 file system to an ext3 file system and back again without reformatting or rewriting all the data on the disk. Let's see how this is done.[6] Listing 9-6 details the procedure.

LISTING 9-6   Converting an ext2 File System to an ext3 File System

```
# mount /dev/sdb1 /mnt/flash        <<< Mount the ext2 file system
# tune2fs -j /dev/sdb1              <<< Create the journal
tune2fs 1.37 (21-Mar-2005)
Creating journal inode: done
This filesystem will be automatically checked every 23 mounts or 180
days, whichever comes first.  Use tune2fs -c or -i to override.
#
```

Notice that first we mounted the file system on /mnt/flash for illustrative purposes only. Normally, we would execute this command on an unmounted ext2 partition. The design behavior for tune2fs when the file system is mounted is to create the journal file called .journal, a hidden file. A file in Linux preceded by a period (.) is considered a hidden file; most Linux command-line file utilities silently ignore files of this type. In Listing 9-7, we can see that the ls command is invoked with the -a flag, which tells the ls utility to list all files.

LISTING 9-7   ext3 Journal File

```
$ ls -al /mnt/flash
total 1063
drwxr-xr-x  15 root root    1024 Aug 25 19:25 .
drwxrwxrwx   5 root root    4096 Jul 18 19:49 ..
drwxr-xr-x   2 root root    1024 Aug 14 11:27 bin
drwxr-xr-x   2 root root    1024 Aug 14 11:27 boot
drwxr-xr-x   2 root root    1024 Aug 14 11:27 dev
drwxr-xr-x   2 root root    1024 Aug 14 11:27 etc
drwxr-xr-x   2 root root    1024 Aug 14 11:27 home
-rw-------   1 root root 1048576 Aug 25 19:25 .journal
drwxr-xr-x   2 root root    1024 Aug 14 11:27 lib
drwx------   2 root root   12288 Aug 14 11:27 lost+found
```

---

[6] Converting a file system in this manner should be considered a development activity only.

LISTING 9-7 Continued

```
drwxr-xr-x   2 root root    1024 Aug 14 11:27 proc
drwxr-xr-x   2 root root    1024 Aug 14 11:27 root
drwxr-xr-x   2 root root    1024 Aug 14 11:27 sbin
drwxr-xr-x   2 root root    1024 Aug 14 11:27 tmp
drwxr-xr-x   2 root root    1024 Aug 14 11:27 usr
drwxr-xr-x   2 root root    1024 Aug 14 11:27 var
```

Now that we have created the journal file on our Flash module, it is effectively formatted as an ext3 file system. The next time the system is rebooted or the e2fsck utility is run on the partition containing the newly created ext3 file system, the journal file is automatically made invisible. Its metadata is stored in a reserved inode set aside for this purpose. As long as the .journal file is visible in the directory listing, it is dangerous to modify or delete this file.

It is possible and sometimes advantageous to create the journal file on a different device. For example, if your system has more than one physical device, you can place your ext3 journaling file system on the first drive and have the journal file on the second drive. This method works regardless of whether your physical storage is based on Flash or rotational media. To create the journaling file system from an existing ext2 file system with the journal file in a separate partition, invoke tune2fs in the following manner:

```
# tune2fs -J device=/dev/sda1 -j /dev/sdb1
```

For this to work, you must have already formatted the device where the journal is to reside with a journal file—it must be an ext3 file system.

9.4 ext4

The ext4 file system builds on the success of the ext3 file system. Like its predecessor, it is a journaling file system. It was developed as a series of patches designed to remove some of the limitations of the ext3 file system. It is likely that ext4 will become the default file system for a number of popular Linux distributions.

The ext4 file system removed the 16-terabyte limit for file systems, increasing the size to 1 exbibyte (2^{60} bytes, if you can count that high!) and supports individual file sizes up to 1024 gigabytes. (I can't pronounce exbibyte, much less comprehend that quantity!) Several other improvements have been made to increase performance for the types of loads expected on large server and database systems, where ext4 is expected to be the default.

If your embedded system requirements include support for large, high-performance journaling file systems, you might consider investigating ext4.

9.5   ReiserFS

The ReiserFS file system has enjoyed popularity among some desktop distributions such as SuSE and Gentoo. Reiser4 is the current incarnation of this journaling file system. Like the ext3 file system, ReiserFS guarantees that either a given file system operation completes in its entirety, or none of it completes. Unlike ext3, Reiser4 has introduced an API for system programmers to guarantee the atomicity of a file system transaction. Consider the following example:

A database program is busy updating records in the database. Several writes are issued to the file system. Power is lost after the first write but before the last one has completed. A journaling file system guarantees that the metadata changes have been stored to the journal file so that when power is again applied to the system, the kernel can at least establish a consistent state of the file system. That is, if file A was reported as having 16KB before the power failure, it will be reported as having 16KB afterward, and the directory entry representing this file (actually, the inode) properly records the file's size. This does not mean, however, that the file data was properly written to the file; it indicates only that there are no errors on the file system. Indeed, it is likely that data was lost by the database program in the previous scenario, and it would be up to the database logic to recover the lost if, in fact, recovery is even possible.

Reiser4 implements high-performance "atomic" file system operations designed to protect both the state of the file system (its consistency) and the data involved in a file system operation. Reiser4 provides a user-level API to enable programs such as database managers to issue a file system write command that is guaranteed to either succeed in its entirety or fail in a similar manner. This guarantees not only that file system consistency is maintained, but also that no partial data or garbage data remains in files after a system crash.

For more details and the actual software for ReiserFS, consult the references at the end of this chapter.

9.6   JFFS2

Flash memory has been used extensively in embedded products. Because of the nature of Flash memory technology, it is inherently less efficient and more prone to data corruption caused by power loss. This is due to much larger write times. The inefficiency stems from the block size. Block sizes of Flash memory devices are often measured in the tens or hundreds of kilobytes. Flash memory can be erased only a block at a time, although writes usually can be executed 1 byte or word at a time. To update a single file, an entire block must be erased and rewritten.

It is well known that the distribution of file sizes on any given Linux machine (or other OS) contains many more smaller files than larger files. The histogram shown in Figure 9-2, generated with `gnuplot`, illustrates the distribution of file sizes on a typical Linux development system.

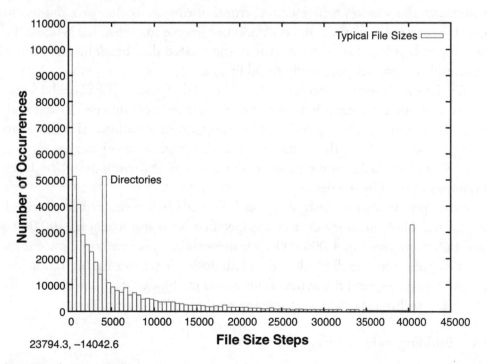

FIGURE 9-2   File sizes in bytes

Figure 9-2 shows that the majority of file sizes are well below approximately 5KB. The spike at 4096 represents directories. Directory entries (also files themselves) are exactly 4096 bytes in length, and there are many of them. The spike above 40,000 bytes is an artifact of the measurement. It is a count of the number of files greater than approximately 40KB, the end of the measurement quantum. It is interesting to note that the vast majority of files are very small.

Small file sizes present a unique challenge to the Flash file system designer. Because Flash memory must be erased an entire block at a time, and the size of a Flash block is often many multiples of the smaller file sizes, Flash is subject to time-consuming block rewriting operations. For example, assume that a 128KB block of Flash is being used to hold a couple dozen files of 4096 bytes or less. Now assume that one of those files needs to be modified. This causes the Flash file system to invalidate the entire 128KB block and rewrite every file in the block to a newly erased block. This can be a time-consuming process.

Because Flash writes can be time-consuming (much slower than hard disk writes), this increases the window where data corruption can occur due to a sudden loss of power. Unexpected power loss is a common occurrence in embedded systems. For instance, if power is lost during the rewrite of the 128KB data block just mentioned, all of the couple dozen files potentially could be lost.

Enter the second-generation Journaling Flash File System (JFFS2). The issues just discussed and other problems have been largely reduced or eliminated by the design of JFFS2. The original JFFS was designed by Axis Communications AB of Sweden and was targeted specifically at the commonly available Flash memory devices of the time. The JFFS had knowledge of the Flash architecture and, more important, architectural limitations imposed by the devices.

Another problem with Flash file systems is that Flash memory has a limited lifetime. Typical Flash memory devices are specified for a minimum of 100,000 write cycles, and, more recently, 1,000,000-cycle devices have become common. This specification is applicable to each block of the Flash device. This unusual limitation imposes the requirement to spread the writes evenly across the blocks of a Flash memory device. JFFS2 uses a technique called wear leveling to accomplish this function.

9.6.1   Building a JFFS2 Image

Building a JFFS2 image is relatively straightforward. Although you can build a JFFS2 image on your workstation without kernel support, you cannot mount it. Before proceeding, ensure that your kernel has support for JFFS2 and that your development workstation contains a compatible version of the mkfs.jffs2 utility. These utilities can be downloaded and built from source code, ftp://ftp.infradead.org/pub/mtd-utils/.

Preferably, they should be available from your desktop Linux package maintainer. For example, on Ubuntu, they can be installed by executing this command:

```
$ sudo apt-get install mtd-tools
```

Your distribution may call them something different, such as mtd-utils. Consult the documentation that came with your desktop Linux distribution.

JFFS2 images are built from a directory that contains the desired files on the file system image. Listing 9-8 shows a typical directory structure for a Flash device designed to be used as a root file system.

LISTING 9-8   Directory Layout for a JFFS2 File System

```
$ ls -l
total 44
drwxr-xr-x  2 root root 4096 Aug 14 11:27 bin
drwxr-xr-x  2 root root 4096 Aug 14 11:27 dev
drwxr-xr-x  2 root root 4096 Aug 14 11:27 etc
drwxr-xr-x  2 root root 4096 Aug 14 11:27 home
drwxr-xr-x  2 root root 4096 Aug 14 11:27 lib
drwxr-xr-x  2 root root 4096 Aug 14 11:27 proc
drwxr-xr-x  2 root root 4096 Aug 14 11:27 root
drwxr-xr-x  2 root root 4096 Aug 14 11:27 sbin
drwxr-xr-x  2 root root 4096 Aug 14 11:27 tmp
drwxr-xr-x  2 root root 4096 Aug 14 11:27 usr
drwxr-xr-x  2 root root 4096 Aug 14 11:27 var
$
```

When suitably populated with runtime files, this directory layout can be used as a template for the mkfs.jffs2 command. The mkfs.jffs2 command produces a properly formatted JFFS2 file system image from a directory tree such as that shown in Listing 9-8. Command-line parameters are used to pass mkfs.jffs2 the directory location as well as the name of the output file to receive the JFFS2 image. The default is to create the JFFS2 image from the current directory. Listing 9-9 shows the command for building the JFFS2 image.

LISTING 9-9   *mkfs.jffs2* Command Example

```
# mkfs.jffs2 -d ./jffs2-image-dir -o jffs2.bin
# ls -l
total 4772
-rw-r--r--   1 root  root   1098640 Sep 17 22:03 jffs2.bin
drwxr-xr-x  13 root  root      4096 Sep 17 22:02 jffs2-image-dir
#
```

The directory structure and files from Listing 9-8 are in the jffs2-image-dir directory in our example. We arbitrarily execute the mkfs.jffs2 command from the directory above our file system image. Using the -d flag, we tell the mkfs.jffs2 command where the file system template is located. We use the -o flag to name the output file to which the resulting JFFS2 image is written. The resulting image, jffs2.bin, is used in Chapter 10, "MTD Subsystem," when we examine the JFFS2 file together with the MTD subsystem.

It should be pointed out that any Flash-based file system that supports write operations is subject to conditions that can lead to premature failure of the underlying Flash device. For example, enabling system loggers (syslogd and klogd) configured to write their data to Flash-based file systems can easily overwhelm a Flash device with continuous writes. Some categories of program errors can also lead to continuous writes. Care must be taken to limit Flash writes to values within the lifetime of Flash devices.

9.7   *cramfs*

From the README file in the cramfs project, the goal of cramfs is to "cram a file system into a small ROM." The cramfs file system is very useful for embedded systems that contain a small ROM or FLASH memory that holds static data and programs. Borrowing again from the cramfs README file, "cramfs is designed to be simple and small, and compress things well."

The cramfs file system is read-only. It is created with a command-line utility called mkcramfs. If you don't have it on your development workstation, you can download it from the URL provided at the end of this chapter. As with JFFS2, mkcramfs builds a file system image from a directory specified on the command line. Listing 9-10 details the procedure for building a cramfs image. We use the same file system structure from Listing 9-8 that we used to build the JFFS2 image.

LISTING 9-10   **mkcramfs** Command Example

```
# mkcramfs
usage: mkcramfs [-h] [-v] [-b blksize] [-e edition] [-i file] [-n name]
dirname outfile
 -h         print this help
 -E         make all warnings errors (non-zero exit status)
 -b blksize use this blocksize, must equal page size
 -e edition set edition number (part of fsid)
 -i file    insert a file image into the filesystem (requires >= 2.4.0)
```

LISTING 9-10 Continued

```
-n name      set name of cramfs filesystem
-p           pad by 512 bytes for boot code
-s           sort directory entries (old option, ignored)
-v           be more verbose
-z           make explicit holes (requires >= 2.3.39)
dirname      root of the directory tree to be compressed
outfile      output file


# mkcramfs . ../cramfs.image
warning: gids truncated to 8 bits (this may be a security concern)
# ls -l ../cramfs.image
-rw-rw-r--  1 chris chris 1019904 Sep 19 18:06 ../cramfs.image
```

The mkcramfs command was initially issued without any command-line parameters to reproduce the usage message. Because this utility has no man page, this is the best way to understand its usage. We subsequently issued the command specifying the current directory (.) as the source of the files for the cramfs file system, and a file called cramfs.image as the destination. Finally, we listed the file just created, and we see a new file called cramfs.image.

Note that if your kernel is configured with cramfs support, you can mount this file system image on your Linux development workstation and examine its contents. Of course, because it is a read-only file system, you cannot modify it. Listing 9-11 demonstrates mounting the cramfs file system on a mount point called /mnt/flash.

LISTING 9-11   Examining the *cramfs* File System

```
# mount -o loop cramfs.image /mnt/flash
# ls -l /mnt/flash
total 6
drwxr-xr-x  1 root   root 704 Dec 31  1969 bin
drwxr-xr-x  1 root   root   0 Dec 31  1969 dev
drwxr-xr-x  1 root   root 416 Dec 31  1969 etc
drwxr-xr-x  1 root   root   0 Dec 31  1969 home
drwxr-xr-x  1 root   root 172 Dec 31  1969 lib
drwxr-xr-x  1 root   root   0 Dec 31  1969 proc
drws------  1 root   root   0 Dec 31  1969 root
drwxr-xr-x  1 root   root 272 Dec 31  1969 sbin
drwxrwxrwt  1 root   root   0 Dec 31  1969 tmp
drwxr-xr-x  1 root   root 124 Dec 31  1969 usr
drwxr-xr-x  1 root   root 212 Dec 31  1969 var
#
```

You might have noticed the warning message regarding group ID (GID) in Listing 9-10 when the `mkcramfs` command was executed. The `cramfs` file system uses very terse metadata to reduce file system size and increase the speed of execution. One of the "features" of the `cramfs` file system is that it truncates the group ID field to 8 bits. Linux uses the 16-bit group ID field. The result is that files created with group IDs greater than 255 are truncated with the warning issued in Listing 9-10.

Although somewhat limited in terms of maximum file sizes, maximum number of files, and so on, the `cramfs` file system is ideal for boot ROMs, in which read-only operation and fast compression are desirable features.

9.8   Network File System

If you have developed in the UNIX environment, you undoubtedly are familiar with the Network File System (NFS). Properly configured, NFS enables you to export a directory on an NFS server and mount that directory on a remote client machine as if it were a local file system. This is useful in general for large networks of UNIX/Linux machines, and it can be a panacea to the embedded developer. Using NFS on your target board, an embedded developer can have access to a huge number of files, libraries, tools, and utilities during development and debugging, even if the target embedded system is resource-constrained.

As with the other file systems, your kernel must be configured with NFS support, for both the server-side functionality and the client side. NFS server and client functionality is independently configured in the kernel configuration.

Detailed instructions for configuring and tuning NFS are beyond the scope of this book, but a short introduction will help illustrate how useful NFS can be during development in the embedded environment. See the section at the end of this chapter for a pointer to detailed information about NFS, including the complete NFS Howto.

On your development workstation with NFS enabled, a configuration file contains a list specifying each directory that you want to export via the Network File System. On Red Hat, Ubuntu, and most other distributions, this file is located in the `/etc` directory and is named `exports`. Listing 9-12 is a sample `/etc/exports`, such as might be found on a development workstation used for embedded development.

LISTING 9-12   Contents of **/etc/exports**

```
$ cat /etc/exports
# /etc/exports
/coyote-target  *(rw,sync,no_root_squash,no_all_squash,no_subtree_check)
/home/chris/workspace  *(rw,sync,no_root_squash,no_all_squash,no_subtree_check)
$
```

This file contains the names of two directories on a Linux development workstation. The first directory contains a target file system for an ADI Engineering Coyote reference board. The second directory is a general workspace that contains projects targeted for an embedded system. This is arbitrary; you can configure NFS any way you choose.

On an embedded system with NFS enabled, the following command mounts the ... /workspace directory exported by the NFS server on a mount point of our choosing:

```
# mount -t nfs pluto:/home/chris/workspace /workspace
```

Notice some important points about this command. We are instructing the mount command to mount a remote directory (on a machine named pluto, our development workstation in this example) onto a local mount point called /workspace. For the command semantics to work, two requirements must be met on the embedded target. First, for the target to recognize the symbolic machine name pluto, it must be able to resolve the symbolic name. The easiest way to do this is to place an entry in the /etc/hosts file on the target. This allows the networking subsystem to resolve the symbolic name to its corresponding IP address. The entry in the target's /etc/hosts file would look like this:

```
192.168.11.9          pluto
```

The second requirement is that the embedded target must have a directory in its root directory called /workspace. (You may choose any pathname you wish. For example, you could mount it on /mnt/mywork.) This is called a mount point. The requirement is that the target must have a directory created with the same name as given on the mount command.

The mount command in the preceding example causes the contents of the NFS server's /home/chris/workspace directory to be available on the embedded system's /workspace path.

This is quite useful, especially in a cross-development environment. Let's say that you are working on a large project for your embedded device. Each time you make changes to the project, you need to move that application to your target so that you can test and debug it. Using NFS in the manner just described, assuming that you are working in the NFS exported directory on your host, the changes are immediately available on your target embedded system without the need to upload the newly compiled project files. This can speed development considerably.

9.8.1   Root File System on NFS

Mounting your project workspace on your target embedded system is very useful for development and debugging because it facilitates rapid access to changes and source code for source-level debugging. This is especially useful when the target system is severely resource-constrained. NFS really shines as a development tool when you mount your embedded system's root file system entirely from an NFS server. In Listing 9-12, notice the `coyote-target` entry. This directory on your development workstation could contain hundreds or thousands of files compatible with your target architecture.

The leading embedded Linux distributions targeted at embedded systems ship tens of thousands of files compiled and tested for the chosen target architecture. To illustrate this, Listing 9-13 contains a directory listing of the `coyote-target` directory referenced in Listing 9-12.

LISTING 9-13   Target File System Example Summary

```
$ du -h --max-depth=1
724M     ./usr
4.0K     ./opt
39M      ./lib
12K      ./dev
27M      ./var
4.0K     ./tmp
3.6M     ./boot
4.0K     ./workspace
1.8M     ./etc
4.0K     ./home
4.0K     ./mnt
8.0K     ./root
29M      ./bin
32M      ./sbin
4.0K     ./proc
```

LISTING 9-13 Continued

```
64K      ./share
855M     .
$
$ find -type f | wc -l
29430
```

This target file system contains just shy of a gigabyte worth of binary files targeted at the ARM architecture. As you can see from the listing, this is more than 29,000 binary, configuration, and documentation files. This would hardly fit on the average Flash device found on an embedded system!

This is the power of an NFS root mount. For development purposes, it can only increase productivity if your embedded system is loaded with all the tools and utilities you are familiar with on a Linux workstation. Indeed, likely dozens of command-line tools and development utilities that you have never seen can help you shave time off your development schedule. You will learn more about some of these useful tools in Chapter 13, "Development Tools."

Configuring your embedded system to mount its root file system via NFS at boot time is relatively straightforward. First, you must configure your target's kernel for NFS support. There is also a configuration option to enable root mounting of an NFS remote directory. This is illustrated in Figure 9-3.

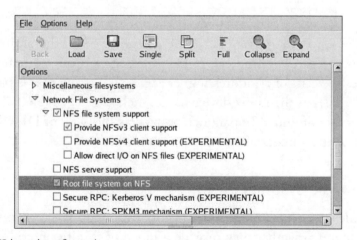

FIGURE 9-3   NFS kernel configuration

Notice that NFS file system support has been selected, along with support for "Root file system on NFS." After these kernel-configuration parameters have been selected, all that remains is to somehow feed information to the kernel so that it knows where to look for the NFS server. Several methods can be used to do this; some depend on the chosen target architecture and choice of bootloader. At a minimum, the kernel can be passed the proper parameters on the kernel command line to configure its IP port and server information on power-up. A typical kernel command line might look like this:

```
console=ttyS0,115200 ip=bootp root=/dev/nfs
```

This tells the kernel to expect a root file system via NFS and to obtain the relevant parameters (server name, server IP address, and root directory to mount) from a BOOTP server. This is a common and tremendously useful configuration during the development phase of a project. If you are statically configuring your target's IP address, your kernel command line might look like this:

```
console=ttyS0,115200                                          \
ip=192.168.11.139:192.168.11.1:192.168.11.1:255.255.255.0:coyote1:eth0:off  \
nfsroot=192.168.11.1:/coyote-target  \
root=/dev/nfs
```

Of course, this would all be on one line. The `ip=` parameter is defined in . . . /`Documentation/`
`filesystems/nfsroot.txt` and has the following syntax, all on one line:

```
ip=<client-ip>:<server-ip>:<gw-ip>
:<netmask>:<hostname>:<device>:<autoconf>
```

Here, `client-ip` is the target's IP address; `server-ip` is the address of the NFS server; `gw-ip` is the gateway (router), in case the server is on a different subnet; and `netmask` defines the class of IP addressing. `hostname` is a string that is passed as the target hostname; `device` is the Linux device name, such as `eth0`; and `autoconf` defines the protocol used to obtain initial IP parameters, such as BOOTP or DHCP. It can also be set to `off` for no autoconfiguration.

9.9   Pseudo File Systems

A number of file systems fall under the category of Pseudo File Systems in the kernel-configuration menu. Together they provide a range of facilities useful in a wide range of applications. For additional information, especially on the `/proc` file system, spend an afternoon poking around this useful system facility. References to additional reading material can be found in the last section of this chapter.

9.9.1 /proc File System

The /proc file system takes its name from its original purpose: an interface that allows the kernel to communicate information about each running process on a Linux system. Over the course of time, it has grown and matured to provide much more than process information. We introduce the highlights here; a complete tour of the /proc file system is left as an exercise for you.

The /proc file system has become a virtual necessity for all but the simplest of Linux systems, even embedded ones. Many user-level functions rely on the contents of the /proc file system to do their job. For example, the mount command, issued without any parameters, lists all the currently active mount points on a running system, from the information delivered by /proc/mounts. If the /proc file system is unavailable, the mount command silently returns. Listing 9-14 illustrates this on the ADI Engineering Coyote board.

LISTING 9-14   Mount Dependency on **/proc**

```
# mount
rootfs on / type rootfs (rw)
/dev/root on / type nfs
(rw,v2,rsize=4096,wsize=4096,hard,udp,nolock,addr=192.168.11.19)
tmpfs on /dev/shm type tmpfs (rw)
/proc on /proc type proc (rw,nodiratime)

< Now unmount proc and try again ...>

# umount /proc
# mount
#
```

Notice in Listing 9-14 that /proc itself is listed as a mounted file system, as type proc mounted on /proc. This is not doublespeak; your system must have a mount point called /proc at the top-level directory tree as a destination for the /proc file system to be mounted on.[7] To mount the /proc file system, use the mount command, as with any other file system:

```
$ mount -t proc /proc /proc
```

---

[7] It is certainly possible to mount /proc anywhere you like on your file system, but all the utilities (including mount) that require proc expect to find it mounted on /proc.

The general form of the `mount` command, from the man page, is:

```
mount [-t fstype] something somewhere
```

In the preceding invocation, we could have substituted `none` for `/proc`, as follows:

```
$ mount -t proc none /proc
```

This looks somewhat less like doublespeak. The `something` parameter is not strictly necessary, because `/proc` is a pseudo file system, not a real physical device. However, specifying `/proc` as in the earlier example helps remind us that we are mounting the `/proc` file system on the `/proc` directory (or, more appropriately, on the `/proc` mount point).

Of course, by this time, it might be obvious that to get `/proc` file system functionality, it must be enabled in the kernel configuration. This kernel-configuration option can be found on the File Systems submenu under the category Pseudo File Systems.

Each user process running in the kernel is represented by an entry in the `/proc` file system. For example, the `init` process introduced in Chapter 6 is always assigned the process ID (PID) of 1. Processes in the `/proc` file system are represented by a directory that is given the PID number as its name. For example, the `init` process with a PID of 1 would be represented by a `/proc/1` directory. Listing 9-15 shows the contents of this directory on our embedded Coyote board.

LISTING 9-15 *init* Process */proc* Entries

```
# ls -l /proc/1
total 0
-r--------   1 root   root    0 Jan  1 00:25 auxv
-r--r--r--   1 root   root    0 Jan  1 00:21 cmdline
lrwxrwxrwx   1 root   root    0 Jan  1 00:25 cwd -> /
-r--------   1 root   root    0 Jan  1 00:25 environ
lrwxrwxrwx   1 root   root    0 Jan  1 00:25 exe -> /sbin/init
dr-x------   2 root   root    0 Jan  1 00:25 fd
-r--r--r--   1 root   root    0 Jan  1 00:25 maps
-rw-------   1 root   root    0 Jan  1 00:25 mem
-r--r--r--   1 root   root    0 Jan  1 00:25 mounts
-rw-r--r--   1 root   root    0 Jan  1 00:25 oom_adj
-r--r--r--   1 root   root    0 Jan  1 00:25 oom_score
lrwxrwxrwx   1 root   root    0 Jan  1 00:25 root -> /
-r--r--r--   1 root   root    0 Jan  1 00:21 stat
-r--r--r--   1 root   root    0 Jan  1 00:25 statm
-r--r--r--   1 root   root    0 Jan  1 00:21 status
dr-xr-xr-x   3 root   root    0 Jan  1 00:25 task
-r--r--r--   1 root   root    0 Jan  1 00:25 wchan
```

These entries, which are present in the /proc file system for each running process, contain much useful information, especially for analyzing and debugging a process. For example, the cmdline entry contains the complete command line used to invoke the process, including any arguments. The cwd and root directories contain the processes' view of the current working directory and current root directory.

One of the more useful entries for system debugging is the maps entry. This contains a list of each virtual memory segment assigned to the program, along with attributes for each. Listing 9-16 is the output from /proc/1/maps in our example of the init process.

LISTING 9-16 *init* Process Memory Segments from */proc*

```
# cat /proc/1/maps
00008000-0000f000 r-xp 00000000 00:0a 9537567    /sbin/init
00016000-00017000 rw-p 00006000 00:0a 9537567    /sbin/init
00017000-0001b000 rwxp 00017000 00:00 0
40000000-40017000 r-xp 00000000 00:0a 9537183    /lib/ld-2.3.2.so
40017000-40018000 rw-p 40017000 00:00 0
4001f000-40020000 rw-p 00017000 00:0a 9537183    /lib/ld-2.3.2.so
40020000-40141000 r-xp 00000000 00:0a 9537518    /lib/libc-2.3.2.so
40141000-40148000 ---p 00121000 00:0a 9537518    /lib/libc-2.3.2.so
40148000-4014d000 rw-p 00120000 00:0a 9537518    /lib/libc-2.3.2.so
4014d000-4014f000 rw-p 4014d000 00:00 0
befeb000-bf000000 rwxp befeb000 00:00 0
#
```

The usefulness of this information is readily apparent. You can see the program segments of the init process itself in the first two entries. You can also see the memory segments used by the shared library objects being used by the init process. The format is as follows:

```
vmstart-vmend  attr  pgoffset  devname inode filename
```

Here, vmstart and vmend are the starting and ending virtual memory addresses, respectively. attr indicates memory region attributes, such as read, write, and execute, and tells whether this region is shareable. pgoffset is the page offset of the region (a kernel virtual memory parameter). devname, displayed as *xx:xx*, is a kernel representation of the device ID associated with this memory region. The memory regions that are not associated with a file are also not associated with a device—thus the 00:00. The final two entries are the inode and file associated with the given memory region. Of course, if a memory segment is not accociated with a file, the inode field will contain 0. These are usually data segments.

Other useful entries are listed for each process. The status entry contains information about the running process, including items such as the parent PID, user and group IDs, virtual memory usage, signals, and capabilities. More details can be obtained from the references at the end of this chapter.

Some frequently used /proc entries are cpuinfo, meminfo, and version. The cpuinfo entry lists attributes that the kernel discovers about the processor(s) running on the system. The meminfo entry provides statistics on the total system memory. The version entry mirrors the Linux kernel version string, together with information on what compiler and machine were used to build the kernel.

The kernel generates many more useful /proc entries; we have only scratched the surface of this useful subsystem. Many utilities have been designed for extracting and reporting information contained in the /proc file system. Two popular examples are top and ps, which every embedded Linux developer should be intimately familiar with. These are introduced in Chapter 13. Other utilities useful for interfacing with the /proc file system include free, pkill, pmap, and uptime. See the procps package for more details.

9.9.2   sysfs

Like the /proc file system, sysfs is not representative of an actual physical device. Instead, sysfs models specific kernel objects such as physical devices and provides a way to associate devices with device drivers. Some agents in a typical Linux distribution depend on the information on sysfs.

We can get some idea of what kinds of objects are exported by looking directly at the directory structure exported by sysfs. Listing 9-17 shows the top-level /sys directory on our Coyote board.

LISTING 9-17   Top-Level **/sys** Directory Contents

```
# ls -l /sys
drwxr-xr-x  2 root root 0 Jan  1 00:00 block
drwxr-xr-x 10 root root 0 Jan  1 00:00 bus
drwxr-xr-x 23 root root 0 Jan  1 00:00 class
drwxr-xr-x  4 root root 0 Jan  1 00:00 dev
drwxr-xr-x  6 root root 0 Jan  1 00:00 devices
drwxr-xr-x  2 root root 0 Jan  1 00:00 firmware
drwxr-xr-x  2 root root 0 Jan  1 00:00 fs
```

LISTING 9-17 Continued

```
drwxr-xr-x  4 root root 0 Jan  1 00:00 kernel
drwxr-xr-x 20 root root 0 Jan  1 00:00 module
#
```

sysfs provides a top-level subdirectory for several system elements, including the system buses. For example, under the `block` subdirectory, each block device is represented by a subdirectory entry. The same holds true for the other directories at the top level.

Most of the information stored by sysfs is in a format more suitable for machines rather than humans to read. For example, to discover the devices on the PCI bus, you could look directly at the `/sys/bus/pci` subdirectory. On our Coyote board, which has a single PCI device attached (an Ethernet card), the directory looks like this:

```
# ls -l /sys/bus/pci/devices/
0000:00:0f.0 -> ../../../devices/pci0000:00/0000:00:0f.0
```

Parts of the output were trimmed for clarity. This entry is actually a symbolic link pointing to another node in the sysfs directory tree. The name of the symbolic link is the kernel's representation of the PCI bus, and it points to a devices subdirectory called `pci0000:00` (the PCI bus representation). This subdirectory contains a number of subdirectories and files representing attributes of this specific PCI device. As you can see, the data is rather difficult to discover and parse.

A useful utility can help you browse the sysfs file system directory structure. Called `systool`, it comes from the sysfsutils package found on sourceforge.net. Here is how `systool` would display the PCI bus from the previous discussion:

```
$ systool -b pci
"Bus = "pci"
  0000:00:0f.0 8086:1229
```

Again we see the kernel's representation of the bus and device (0f), but this tool displays the vendor ID (8086 = Intel) and device ID (1229 = eepro100 Ethernet card) obtained from the `/sys/devices/pci0000:00` branch of `/sys`, where these attributes are kept. Executed with no parameters, `systool` displays the top-level system hierarchy. Listing 9-18 is an example from our Coyote board.

LISTING 9-18   Output from *systool*

```
$ systool
Supported sysfs buses:
        hid
        i2c
        ide
        mdio_bus
        pci
        platform
        scsi
        usb
Supported sysfs classes:
        atm
        bdi
        block
        firmware
        hwmon
        i2c-adapter
        i2c-dev
        ide_port
        input
        leds
        mdio_bus
        mem
        misc
        mtd
        net
        pci_bus
        rtc
        scsi_device
        scsi_disk
        scsi_host
        tty
Supported sysfs devices:
        pci0000:00
        platform
        system
        virtual
Supported sysfs modules:
        8250
        ehci_hcd
        hid
        ide_gd_mod
```

LISTING 9-18   Continued

```
    kernel
    libata
    lockd
    mousedev
    nfs
    printk
    scsi_mod
    spurious
    sunrpc
    tcp_cubic
    uhci_hcd
    usb_storage
    usbcore
    usbhid
```

You can see from this listing the variety of system information available from sysfs. Many utilities use this information to determine the characteristics of system devices or to enforce system policies, such as power management and hot-plug capability.

You can learn more about sysfs from http://en.wikipedia.org/wiki/Sysfs and the references found there.

9.10   Other File Systems

Linux supports numerous file systems. Space does not permit us to cover all of them. However, you should be aware of some important file systems frequently found in embedded systems.

The ramfs file system is best considered from the context of the Linux source code module that implements it. Listing 9-19 reproduces the first several lines of that file.

LISTING 9-19   Linux ramfs Source Module Comments

```
/*
 * Resizable simple ram filesystem for Linux.
 *
 * Copyright (C) 2000 Linus Torvalds.
 *               2000 Transmeta Corp.
 *
 * Usage limits added by David Gibson, Linuxcare Australia.
 * This file is released under the GPL.
 */
```

LISTING 9-19   Continued

```
/*
 * NOTE! This filesystem is probably most useful not as a real
 * filesystem, but as an example of how virtual filesystems can be
 * written.
 *
 * It doesn't get much simpler than this. Consider that this file
 * implements the full semantics of a POSIX-compliant read-write
 * filesystem.
```

This module was written primarily as an example of how virtual file systems can be written. One of the primary differences between this file system and the ramdisk facility found in modern Linux kernels is its capability to shrink and grow according to its use. A ramdisk does not have this property. This source module is compact and well written. It is presented here for its educational value. You are encouraged to study this example if you want to learn more about Linux file systems.

The tmpfs file system is similar to and related to ramfs. Like ramfs, everything in tmpfs is stored in kernel virtual memory, and the contents of tmpfs are lost on power-down or reboot. The tmpfs file system is useful for fast temporary file storage. A good example of tmpfs use is to mount your /tmp directory on a tmpfs. It improves performance for applications that use many small temporary files. This is also a great way to keep your /tmp directory clean, because its contents are lost on every reboot. Mounting tmpfs is similar to any other virtual file system:

```
# mount -t tmpfs /tmpfs /tmp
```

As with other virtual file systems such as /proc, the first tmpfs parameter in this mount command is a "no-op." In other words, it could be the word none and still function. However, it is a good reminder that you are mounting a virtual file system called tmpfs.

9.11   Building a Simple File System

It is straightforward to build a simple file system image. Here we demonstrate the use of the Linux kernel's loopback device. The loopback device enables the use of a regular file as a block device. In short, we build a file system image in a regular file and use the Linux loopback device to mount that file in the same way any other block device is mounted.

To build a simple root file system, start with a fixed-sized file containing all 0s:

```
# dd if=/dev/zero of=./my-new-fs-image bs=1k count=512
```

This command creates a file of 512KB containing nothing but 0s. We fill the file with 0s to aid in compression later and to have a consistent data pattern for uninitialized data blocks within the file system. Exercise caution when using the dd command. Executing dd with no boundary (count=) or with an improper boundary can fill up your hard drive and possibly crash your system. dd is a powerful tool; use it with the respect it deserves. Simple typos in commands such as dd, executed as root, have destroyed countless file systems.

When we have the new image file, we actually format the file to contain the data structures defined by a given file system. In this example, we build an ext2 file system. Listing 9-20 details the procedure.

LISTING 9-20   Creating an ext2 File System Image

```
# /sbin/mkfs.ext2 ./my-new-fs-image
mke2fs 1.40.8 (13-Mar-2008)
./my-new-fs-image is not a block special device.
Proceed anyway? (y,n) y
Filesystem label=
OS type: Linux
Block size=1024 (log=0)
Fragment size=1024 (log=0)
64 inodes, 512 blocks
25 blocks (4.88%) reserved for the super user
First data block=1
Maximum filesystem blocks=524288
1 block group
8192 blocks per group, 8192 fragments per group
64 inodes per group

Writing inode tables: done
Writing superblocks and filesystem accounting information: done

This filesystem will be automatically checked every 21 mounts or 180
days, whichever comes first.  Use tune2fs -c or -i to override.
```

Like dd, the mkfs.ext2 command can destroy your system, so use it with care. In this example, we asked mkfs.ext2 to format a file rather than a hard drive partition (block device) for which it was intended. As such, mkfs.ext2 detected that fact and asked us to confirm the operation. After confirming, mkfs.ext2 proceeded to write an ext2 superblock and file system data structures into the file. We can then mount this file like any block device, using the Linux loopback device:

```
# mount -o loop ./my-new-fs-image /mnt/flash
```

This command mounts the file `my-new-fs-image` as a file system on the mount point named `/mnt/flash`. The mount point name is unimportant; you can mount it wherever you want, as long as the mount point exists. Use `mkdir` to create your mount point.

After the newly created image file is mounted as a file system, we are free to make changes to it. We can add and delete directories, make device nodes, and so on. We can use tar to copy files into or out of it. When the changes are complete, they are saved in the file, assuming that you didn't exceed the size of the device. Remember, using this method, the size is fixed at creation time and cannot be changed.

9.12   Summary

This chapter introduced a variety of file systems in use on both desktop/server Linux systems and embedded systems. File systems specific to embedded use and especially Flash file systems were described. The important pseudo file systems also were covered.

- Partitions are the logical division of a physical device. Numerous partition types are supported under Linux.

- A file system is mounted on a mount point in Linux. The root file system is mounted at the root of the file system hierarchy and is referred to as `/`.

- The popular ext2 file system is mature and fast. It is often found on embedded and other Linux systems such as Red Hat and the Fedora Core series.

- The ext3 file system adds journaling on top of the ext2 file system for better data integrity and system reliability.

- ReiserFS is another popular and high-performance journaling file system found on many embedded and other Linux systems.

- JFFS2 is a journaling file system optimized for use with Flash memory. It contains Flash-friendly features such as wear leveling for longer Flash memory lifetime.

- cramfs is a read-only file system perfect for small-system boot ROMs and other read-only programs and data.

- NFS is one of the most powerful development tools for the embedded developer. It can bring the power of a workstation to your target device. Learn how to use NFS as your embedded target's root file system. The convenience and time savings will be worth the effort.

- Many pseudo file systems are available on Linux. A few of the more important ones were presented here, including the `/proc` file system and sysfs.

- The RAM-based tmpfs file system has many uses for embedded systems. Its most significant improvement over traditional ramdisks is the capability to resize itself dynamically to meet operational requirements.

9.12.1 Suggestions for Additional Reading

"Design and Implementation of the Second Extended Filesystem"
Rémy Card, Theodore Ts'o, and Stephen Tweedie
First published in the Proceedings of the First Dutch International Symposium on Linux
http://e2fsprogs.sourceforge.net/ext2intro.html

"A Non-Technical Look Inside the EXT2 File System"
Randy Appleton
www.linuxjournal.com/article/2151

Red Hat's New Journaling File System: ext3
Michael K. Johnson
www.redhat.com/support/wpapers/redhat/ext3/

Reiser4 File System
http://en.wikipedia.org/wiki/Reiser4

JFFS: The Journaling Flash File System
David Woodhouse
http://sources.redhat.com/jffs2/jffs2.pdf

README file from the cramfs project
Unsigned (assumed to be the project author)
http://sourceforge.net/projects/cramfs/

NFS home page
http://nfs.sourceforge.net

The /proc file system documentation
www.tldp.org/LDP/lkmpg/2.6/html/c712.htm

"File System Performance: The Solaris OS, UFS, Linux ext3, and ReiserFS"
A technical whitepaper
Dominic Kay
www.sun.com/software/whitepapers/solaris10/fs_performance.pdf

## Chapter 10

MTD Subsystem

In This Chapter

- 10.1   MTD Overview   262
- 10.2   MTD Partitions   267
- 10.3   MTD Utilities   279
- 10.4   UBI File System   284
- 10.5   Summary   287

The Memory Technology Device (MTD) subsystem grew out of the need to support a wide variety of memory-like devices such as Flash memory chips. Many different types of Flash chips are available, along with numerous methods to program them, partly because of the many specialized and high-performance modes that are supported. The MTD layer architecture enables the separation of the low-level device complexities from the higher-layer data organization and storage formats that use memory and flash devices.

This chapter introduces the MTD subsystem and provides some simple examples of its use. First we look at what is required of the kernel to support MTD services. We show some simple operations on a development workstation with MTD enabled to help you understand the basics of this subsystem. This chapter also integrates MTD and the JFFS2 file system.

Then this chapter discusses the concept of partitions as they relate to the MTD layer. We examine the details of building partitions from a bootloader and how the Linux kernel detects them. The chapter continues with a brief introduction to the MTD utilities. We conclude by putting it all together and booting a target board using an in-Flash JFFS2 file system image.

10.1 MTD Overview

Simply stated, MTD is a device driver layer that provides a uniform API for interfacing with raw Flash devices. MTD supports a wide variety of Flash devices. However, MTD is *not* a block device. MTD deals with devices in units of erase blocks that are not always a uniform size, whereas block devices operate on fixed-size read/write blocks called sectors. Block devices have two primary operations—read and write to a sector—and MTDs have three: read, write, and erase. MTD devices have a limited write life cycle, and MTD has logic to spread the write operations over the device's life span to increase the device's life span. This is called *wear leveling*.

Contrary to popular belief, SD/MMC cards, CompactFlash cards, USB Flash drives, and other popular devices are not MTD devices. These devices all contain internal Flash translation layers that handle MTD-like functions such as block erasure and wear leveling. Therefore, these devices appear to the system as traditional block devices and do not require the specialized handling of MTD.

Most device drivers in Linux are either character or block devices. MTD is neither. Although translation mechanisms can make MTD look like a character or block device, MTD is unique in Linux driver architecture. This is because MTD drivers must perform Flash-specific operations such as the *erase block* and *wear leveling* operations, which have no parallel in traditional block drivers.

10.1.1   Enabling MTD Services

To use MTD services, your kernel must be configured with MTD enabled. This applies equally to your development workstation and your embedded system. For simplicity, we'll demonstrate MTD operations on your development workstation. To follow along, you must have MTD enabled on your workstation as described here. In a similar fashion, you must also have MTD enabled on your embedded target to use MTD capabilities there.

MTD has many configuration options, some of which can be confusing. The best way to understand the myriad choices is simply to begin working with them. To illustrate the mechanics of the MTD subsystem and how it fits in with the system, we'll begin with some simplethat you can perform on your Linux development workstation. Figure 10-1 shows the kernel configuration (invoked per the usual make ARCH=<arch> gconfig) necessary to enable the bare-minimum MTD functionality. Listing 10-1 displays the .config file entries resulting from the selections shown in Figure 10-1. These configuration options are found under Device drivers in the kernel configuration utility.

LISTING 10-1   Basic MTD Configuration from *. config*

```
CONFIG_MTD=y
CONFIG_MTD_CHAR=y
CONFIG_MTD_BLOCK=y
CONFIG_MTD_MTDRAM=m
CONFIG_MTDRAM_TOTAL_SIZE=8192
CONFIG_MTDRAM_ERASE_SIZE=128
```

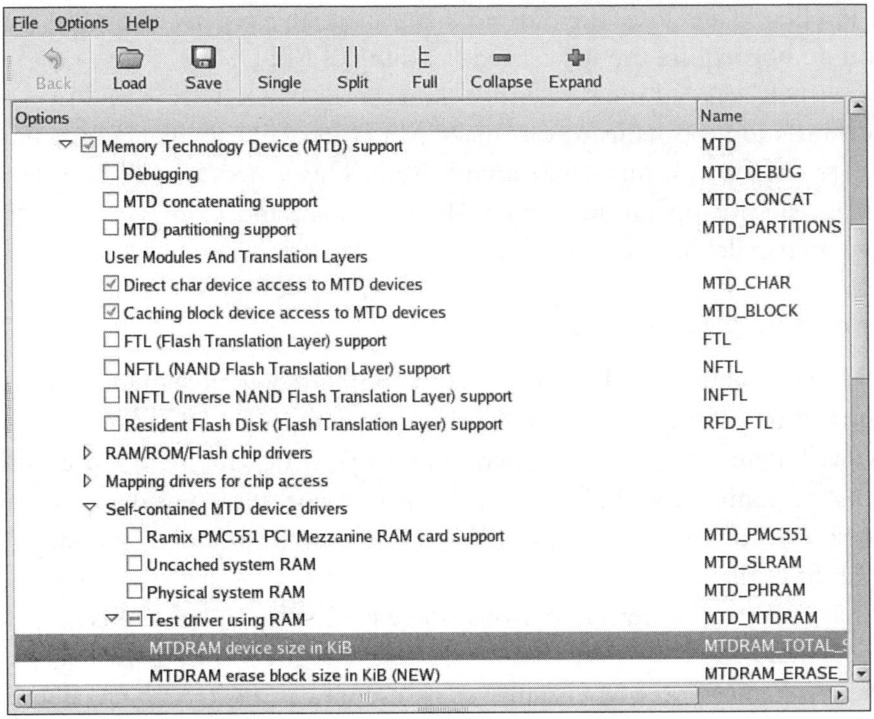

FIGURE 10-1   MTD configuration

The MTD subsystem is enabled through the first configuration option, which you select by checking the first box shown in Figure 10-1, Memory Technology Device (MTD) Support. The next two entries from the configuration shown in Figure 10-1 enable special device-level access to the MTD devices, such as Flash memory, from user space. The first one (CONFIG_MTD_CHAR) enables character device mode access, essentially a sequential access characterized by byte-at-a-time sequential read and write access. The second (CONFIG_MTD_BLOCK) enables access to the MTD device in block device mode, the access method used for disk drives, in which blocks of multiple bytes of data are read or written at one time. These access modes allow the use of familiar Linux commands to read and write data to Flash memory, as you will see shortly.

The CONFIG_MTD_MTDRAM element enables a special test driver that allows us to examine the MTD subsystem on our development host even if no MTD devices (such as Flash memory) are available. Remember, we are working with MTD on our development workstation in these examples as a convenient way to get familiar with the MTD subsystem. You would rarely if ever do this on an embedded target.

Coupled with this configuration selection are two parameters associated with the RAM-based test driver: the device size and the erase size. For this example, we have specified 8192KB total size and 128KB erase size. The objective of this test driver is to emulate a Flash device, primarily to facilitate MTD subsystem testing and development. Because Flash memory is architected using fixed-size erase blocks, the test driver also contains the concept of erase blocks. You will see how these parameters are used shortly.

10.1.2 MTD Basics

Recent Linux kernel releases have MTD integrated, so you don't need to apply MTD patches to enable it. If you feel the need to be on the leading edge of MTD development, you can download the latest source code from the MTD home page, listed in the last section of this chapter. Of course, in either case, MTD must be enabled in your kernel configuration, as shown in Figure 10-1.

After MTD is enabled, we can examine how this subsystem works on our Linux development workstation. Using the test RAM driver we just configured, we can mount a JFFS2 image using an MTD device. Assuming that you created a JFFS2 image as detailed in Chapter 9, "File Systems," you might want to mount it and examine it. The image we built in Chapter 9 was called jffs2.bin.[1] Recall from Chapter 9 that we built the jffs2.bin image using this command:

```
# mkfs.jffs2 -d ./jffs2-image-dir -o jffs2.bin
```

The Linux kernel does not support mounting a JFFS2 file system image directly on a loopback device, such as is possible with ext2 and other file system images. So we must use a different method. This can be achieved using the MTD RAM test driver on our development Linux workstation. Listing 10-2 illustrates the steps.

LISTING 10-2 Mounting JFFS2 on an MTD RAM Device
```
# modprobe jffs2
# modprobe mtdblock
# modprobe mtdram
# dd if=jffs2.bin of=/dev/mtdblock0
 4690+1 records in
 4690+1 records out
# mkdir /mnt/flash
```

[1] You can easily re-create a minimal file system for this exercise by using the example from Listing 6-1.

LISTING 10-2   Continued

```
# mount -t jffs2 /dev/mtdblock0 /mnt/flash
# ls -l /mnt/flash
total 0
drwxr-xr-x    2 root root 0 Sep 17 22:02 bin
drwxr-xr-x    2 root root 0 Sep 17 21:59 dev
drwxr-xr-x    7 root root 0 Sep 17 15:31 etc
drwxr-xr-x    2 root root 0 Sep 17 22:02 lib
drwxr-xr-x    2 root root 0 Sep 17 15:31 proc
drwxr-xr-x    2 root root 0 Sep 17 22:02 sbin
drwxrwxrwt    2 root root 0 Sep 17 15:31 tmp
drwxr-xr-x    9 root root 0 Sep 17 15:31 usr
drwxr-xr-x   14 root root 0 Sep 17 15:31 var
#
```

In Listing 10-2, we first install the loadable modules that the Linux kernel requires to support JFFS2 and the MTD subsystem. We load the `jffs2` module followed by the `mtdblock` and `mtdram` modules. After the necessary device drivers are loaded, we use the Linux `dd` command to copy our JFFS2 file system image into the MTD RAM test driver using the `mtdblock` device. In essence, we are using system RAM as a backing device to emulate an MTD block device.

After we have copied our JFFS2 file system image into the MTD block device, we can mount it using the `mount` command, in the manner shown in Listing 10-2. After the MTD pseudo-device has been mounted, we can work with the JFFS2 file system image in any way we choose. The only limitation using this method is that we cannot change the size of the image. Its size is limited by two factors. First, when we configured the MTD RAM test device in the Linux kernel configuration user interface, we gave it a maximum size of 8MB. Second, when we created the JFFS2 image, we fixed the size of the image using the `mkfs.jffs2` utility. The image size was determined by the contents of the directory we specified when we created it. Refer to Listing 9-9 in Chapter 9 to recall how our `jffs2.bin` image was built.

It is important to realize the limitations of using this method to examine the contents of a JFFS2 file system. Consider what we did: We copied the contents of a file (the JFFS2 file system binary image) into a kernel block device (`/dev/mtdblock0`). We then mounted the kernel block device (`/dev/mtdblock0`) as a JFFS2 file system. After we did this, we could then use all the traditional file system utilities to examine and even modify the file system. Tools such as `ls`, `df`, `dh`, `mv`, `rm`, and `cp` can all be used to examine and modify the file system. However, unlike the loopback device, there is no connection between the file we copied and the mounted JFFS2 file system image. Therefore, if we unmount the file system after making changes, the changes will be lost. If you want to save the changes, you must copy them back into a file. One such method is the following:

```
# dd if=/dev/mtdblock0 of=./your-modified-fs-image.bin
```

This command creates a file called `your-modified-fs-image.bin` that is the same size as the `mtdblock0` device that was specified during configuration. In our example, it would be 8MB. Lacking suitable JFFS2 editing facilities, this is a perfectly valid way to examine and modify a JFFS2 file system. More important, it illustrates the basics of the MTD subsystem on our development system without real Flash memory. Now let's look at some hardware that contains physical Flash devices.

10.1.3 Configuring MTD on Your Target

To use MTD with the Flash memory on your board, you must have MTD configured correctly. You must do the following to configure MTD for your board, Flash, and Flash layout:

- Specify the partitioning on your Flash device.
- Specify the type of Flash and location.
- Configure the proper Flash driver for your chosen chip.
- Configure the kernel with the appropriate driver(s).

Each of these steps is explored in the following sections.

10.2 MTD Partitions

Most Flash devices on a given hardware platform are divided into several sections, called partitions, similar to the partitions found on a typical desktop workstation hard drive. The MTD subsystem supports such Flash partitions. The MTD subsystem must be configured for MTD partitioning support. Figure 10-2 shows the configuration options for MTD partitioning support from a recent Linux kernel snapshot.

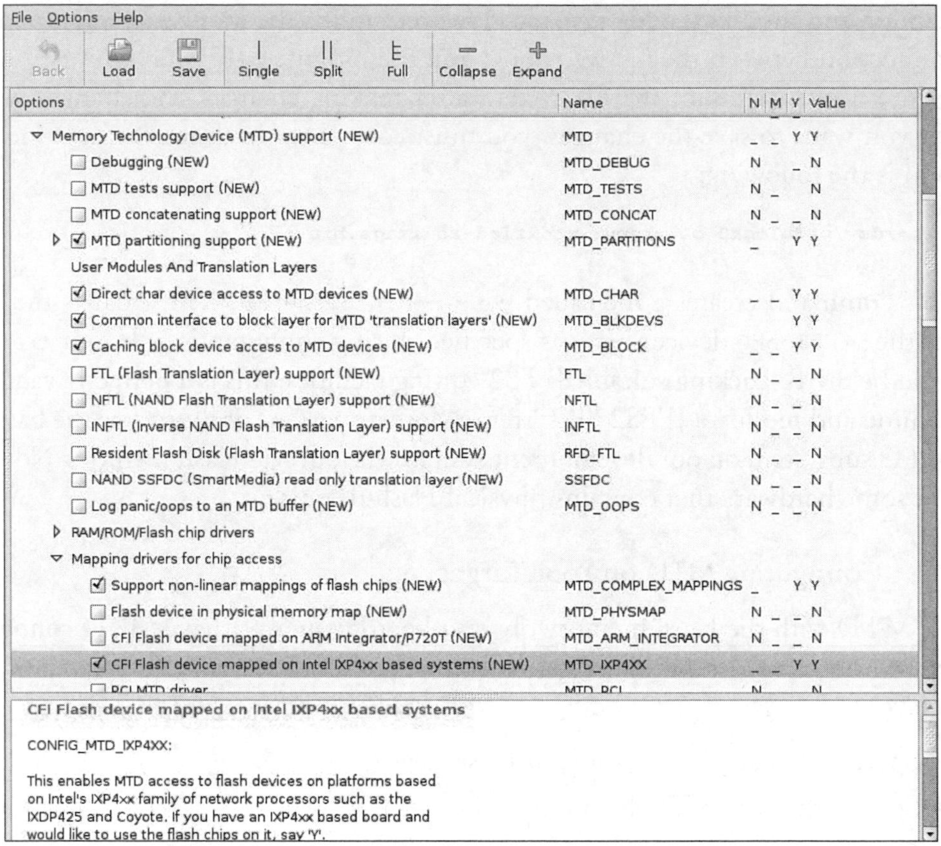

FIGURE 10-2   Kernel configuration for MTD partitioning support

You can communicate the partition data to the Linux kernel in several ways. You can see the configuration options for each in Figure 10-2 under "MTD partitioning support." The following methods currently are supported:

- Redboot partition table parsing
- Kernel command-line partition table definition
- Board-specific mapping drivers
- TI AR7 partitioning support

MTD also allows configurations without partition data. In this case, MTD simply treats the entire Flash memory as a single device.

10.2.1 Redboot Partition Table Partitioning

One of the more common methods of defining and detecting MTD partitions stems from one of the original implementations: Redboot partitions. Redboot is a bootloader found on many embedded boards, especially ARM XScale boards such as the ADI Engineering Coyote Reference Platform.

The MTD subsystem defines a method for storing partition information on the Flash device itself, similar in concept to a partition table on a hard disk. In the case of the Redboot partitions, the developer reserves and specifies a Flash erase block that holds the partition definitions. A mapping driver is selected that calls the partition parsing functions during boot to detect the partitions on the Flash device. Figure 10-2 shows the mapping driver for our sample board; it is the final highlighted entry defining CONFIG_MTD_IXP4XX.

As usual, taking a detailed look at an example helps illustrate these concepts. We start by looking at the information provided by the Redboot bootloader for the Coyote platform. Listing 10-3 captures some of the output from the Redboot bootloader upon power-up.

LISTING 10-3   Redboot Messages on Power-Up

```
Platform: ADI Coyote (XScale)
IDE/Parallel Port CPLD Version: 1.0
Copyright (C) 2000, 2001, 2002, Red Hat, Inc.

RAM: 0x00000000-0x04000000, 0x0001f960-0x03fd1000 available
FLASH: 0x50000000 - 0x51000000, 128 blocks of 0x00020000 bytes each.
...
```

This console output tells us that RAM on this board is physically mapped starting at address 0x00000000 and that Flash is mapped at physical address 0x50000000 through 0x51000000. We can also see that Flash has 128 blocks of 0x00020000 (128KB) each.

Redboot contains a command to create and display partition information stored on Flash. Listing 10-4 is the output of the fis list command, part of the Flash Image System family of commands available in the Redboot bootloader.

LISTING 10-4   Redboot Flash Partition List

```
RedBoot> fis list
Name            FLASH addr   Mem addr     Length       Entry point
RedBoot         0x50000000   0x50000000   0x00060000   0x00000000
```

LISTING 10-4   Continued

```
RedBoot config    0x50FC0000  0x50FC0000  0x00001000  0x00000000
FIS directory     0x50FE0000  0x50FE0000  0x00020000  0x00000000
RedBoot>
```

From Listing 10-4, we see that the Coyote board has three partitions defined on the Flash. The partition named RedBoot contains the executable Redboot bootloader image. The partition named RedBoot config contains the configuration parameters maintained by the bootloader. The final partition named FIS directory holds information about the partition table itself.

When properly configured, the Linux kernel can detect and parse this partition table and create MTD partitions representing the physical partitions on Flash. Listing 10-5 reproduces a portion of the boot messages that are output from the aforementioned ADI Engineering Coyote board, booting a Linux kernel configured with support for detecting Redboot partitions.

LISTING 10-5   Detecting Redboot Partitions on Linux Boot

```
...
IXP4XX-Flash.0: Found 1 x16 devices at 0x0 in 16-bit bank
 Intel/Sharp Extended Query Table at 0x0031
Using buffer write method
Searching for RedBoot partition table in IXP4XX-Flash.0 at offset 0xfe0000
3 RedBoot partitions found on MTD device IXP4XX-Flash0
Creating 3 MTD partitions on "IXP4XX-Flash.0":
0x00000000-0x00060000 : "RedBoot"
0x00fc0000-0x00fc1000 : "RedBoot config"
0x00fe0000-0x01000000 : "FIS directory"
...
```

The first message in Listing 10-5 is printed when the Flash chip is detected, via the Common Flash Interface (CFI) driver, enabled through CONFIG_MTD_CFI. CFI is an industry-standard method for determining the Flash chip's characteristics, such as manufacturer, device type, total size, and erase block size. See the last section for a link to the CFI specification.

CFI is enabled through the kernel-configuration utility under the Memory Technology Device (MTD) top-level menu. Select "Detect flash chips by Common Flash Interface (CFI) probe" under "RAM/ROM/Flash chip drivers," as shown in Figure 10-3.

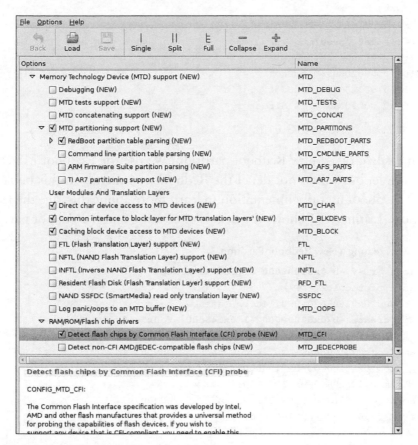

FIGURE 10 3 Kernel configuration for MTD CFI support

Because we also enabled `CONFIG_MTD_REDBOOT_PARTS` (see Figure 10-3), MTD scans for the Redboot partition table on the Flash chip. Notice also that the chip has been enumerated with the device name `IXP4XX-Flash.0`. You can see from Listing 10-5 that the Linux kernel has detected three partitions on the Flash chip, as enumerated previously using the `fis list` command in Redboot.

When the infrastructure is in place as described here, the Linux kernel automatically detects and creates kernel data structures representing the three Flash partitions. Evidence of these can be found in the `/proc` file system when the kernel has completed initialization, as shown in Listing 10-6.

LISTING 10-6   Kernel MTD Flash Partitions

```
root@coyote:~# cat /proc/mtd
dev:    size     erasesize  name
mtd0: 00060000 00020000 "RedBoot"
mtd1: 00001000 00020000 "RedBoot config"
mtd2: 00020000 00020000 "FIS directory"
#
```

We can easily create a new Redboot partition. We use the Redboot FIS commands for this example, but we do not detail the Redboot commands in this book. You can consult the Redboot user documentation to learn more about this. See the last section for references. Listing 10-7 shows the details of creating a new Redboot partition.

LISTING 10-7   Creating a New Redboot Partition

```
RedBoot> load -r -v -b 0x01008000 coyote-40-zImage
Using default protocol (TFTP)
Raw file loaded 0x01008000-0x0114dccb, assumed entry at 0x01008000
RedBoot> fis create -b 0x01008000 -l 0x145cd0 -f 0x50100000 MyKernel
... Erase from 0x50100000-0x50260000: ...........
... Program from 0x01008000-0x0114dcd0 at 0x50100000: ....
... Unlock from 0x50fe0000-0x51000000: .
... Erase from 0x50fe0000-0x51000000: .
... Program from 0x03fdf000-0x03fff000 at 0x50fe0000: .
... Lock from 0x50fe0000-0x51000000: .
```

First, we load the image to be used to create the new partition. We use our kernel image for the example and load it to memory address 0x01008000. We then create the new partition using the Redboot fis create command. We instruct Redboot to create the new partition in an area of Flash starting at 0x50100000. You can see the action as Redboot first erases this area of Flash and then programs the kernel image. In the final sequence, Redboot unlocks its directory area and updates the FIS Directory with the new partition information. Listing 10-8 shows the output of fis list with the new partition. Compare this with the output shown in Listing 10-4.

LISTING 10-8   New Redboot Partition List

```
RedBoot> fis list
```

Name	FLASH addr	Mem addr	Length	Entry point
RedBoot	0x50000000	0x50000000	0x00060000	0x00000000
RedBoot config	0x50FC0000	0x50FC0000	0x00001000	0x00000000
FIS directory	0x50FE0000	0x50FE0000	0x00020000	0x00000000
MyKernel	0x50100000	0x50100000	0x00160000	0x01008000

Of course, when we boot the Linux kernel, it discovers the new partition, and we can operate on it as we see fit. You might have realized the other benefit of this new partition: We can now boot the kernel from Flash instead of having to load it using TFTP every time. The Redboot command for accomplishing this is shown next. Simply pass the Redboot `exec` command the Flash starting address of the partition and the length of the image to transfer into RAM:

```
RedBoot> exec -b 0x50100000 -l 0x145cd0
   Uncompressing Linux.......... done, booting the kernel.
   ...
```

10.2.2   Kernel Command-Line Partitioning

As detailed in Section 10.2, "MTD Partitions," the raw Flash partition information can be communicated to the kernel using other methods. Indeed, possibly the most straightforward way, though perhaps not the simplest, is to manually pass the partition information directly on the kernel command line. Of course, as you have learned, some bootloaders make that easy (such as U-Boot), whereas others do not have a facility to pass a kernel command line to the kernel upon boot. In these cases, the kernel command line must be configured at compile time and therefore is more difficult to change, requiring a recompile of the kernel itself each time the partitions are modified.

To enable command-line partitioning in the MTD subsystem, your kernel must be configured for this support. You can see this configuration option in Figure 10-2 under "MTD partitioning support." Select the option for command-line partition table parsing, which defines the CONFIG_MTD_CMDLINE_PARTS option.

Listing 10-9 shows the format for defining a partition on the kernel command line (taken from .../drivers/mtd/cmdlinepart.c).

LISTING 10-9   Kernel Command-Line MTD Partition Format

```
mtdparts=<mtddef>[;<mtddef]
 * <mtddef>   := <mtd-id>:<partdef>[,<partdef>]
 * <partdef>  := <size>[@offset][<name>][ro]
 * <mtd-id>   := unique name used in mapping driver/device (mtd->name)
 * <size>     := std linux memsize OR "-" to denote all remaining space
 * <name>     := '(' NAME ')'
```

Each `mtddef` parameter passed on the kernel command line defines a separate partition. As shown in Listing 10-9, each `mtddef` definition has several parts. You can specify a unique ID, partition size, and offset from the start of the Flash. You can also pass the partition a name and, optionally, the read-only attribute. Referring to our Redboot partition definitions shown in Listing 10-4, we could statically define these on the kernel command line as follows:

```
mtdparts=MainFlash:384K(Redboot),4K(config),128K(FIS),-(unused)
```

With this definition, the kernel would instantiate four MTD partitions, with an MTD ID of MainFlash, containing the sizes and layout matching those found in Listing 10-4.

10.2.3 Mapping Driver

The final method for defining your board-specific Flash layout is to use a dedicated board-specific mapping driver. The Linux kernel source tree contains many examples of mapping drivers, located in .../drivers/mtd/maps. Any one of these will provide a good example of how to create your own. The implementation details vary by architecture.

The mapping driver is a proper kernel module, complete with `module_init()` and `module_exit()` calls, as described in Chapter 8, "Device Driver Basics." A typical mapping driver is small and easy to navigate, often containing fewer than a couple dozen lines of C.

Listing 10-10 reproduces a section of .../drivers/mtd/maps/pq2fads.c. This mapping driver defines the Flash device on a Freescale PQ2FADS evaluation board that supports the MPC8272 and other processors.

LISTING 10-10   PQ2FADS Flash Mapping Driver

```
...
static struct mtd_partition pq2fads_partitions[] = {
        {
#ifdef CONFIG_ADS8272
                .name        = "HRCW",
                .size        = 0x40000,
                .offset      = 0,
                .mask_flags = MTD_WRITEABLE,    /* force read-only */
        }, {
                .name        = "User FS",
                .size        = 0x5c0000,
                .offset      = 0x40000,
#else
```

LISTING 10-10   Continued

```
                .name        = "User FS",
                .size        = 0x600000,
                .offset         = 0,
#endif
        }, {
                .name        = "uImage",
                .size        = 0x100000,
                .offset        = 0x600000,
                .mask_flags  = MTD_WRITEABLE,   /* force read-only */
        }, {
                .name        = "bootloader",
                .size        = 0x40000,
                .offset        = 0x700000,
                .mask_flags  = MTD_WRITEABLE,   /* force read-only */
        }, {
                .name        = "bootloader env",
                .size        = 0x40000,
                .offset          = 0x740000,
                .mask_flags  = MTD_WRITEABLE,   /* force read-only */
        }
};

/* pointer to MPC885ADS board info data */
extern unsigned char __res[];

static int __init init_pq2fads_mtd(void)
{
        bd_t *bd = (bd_t *)__res;
        physmap_configure(bd->bi_flashstart, bd->bi_flashsize,
                        PQ2FADS_BANK_WIDTH, NULL);

        physmap_set_partitions(pq2fads_partitions,
                        sizeof (pq2fads_partitions) /
                        sizeof (pq2fads_partitions[0]));
        return 0;
}

static void __exit cleanup_pq2fads_mtd(void)
{
}

module_init(init_pq2fads_mtd);
module_exit(cleanup_pq2fads_mtd);
...
```

This simple but complete Linux device driver communicates the PQ2FADS Flash mapping to the MTD subsystem. Recall from Chapter 8 that when a function in a device driver is declared with the `module_init()` macro, it is automatically invoked during Linux kernel boot. In this PQ2FADS mapping driver, the module initialization function `init_pq2fads_mtd()` performs just two simple calls:

- `physmap_configure()` passes to the MTD subsystem the Flash chip's physical address, size, and bank width, along with any special setup function required to access the Flash.

- `physmap_set_partitions()` passes the board's unique partition information to the MTD subsystem from the partition table defined in the `pq2fads_partitions[]` array found at the start of this mapping driver.

Following this simple example, you can derive a mapping driver for your own board.

10.2.4   Flash Chip Drivers

MTD supports a wide variety of Flash chips and devices. Chances are very good that your chosen chip is also supported. The most common Flash chips support the Common Flash Interface (CFI) mentioned earlier. Older Flash chips might have JEDEC support, which is an older Flash compatibility standard. Figure 10-4 shows the kernel configuration from a recent Linux kernel snapshot. This version supports many Flash types.

If your Flash chip is not supported, you must provide a device file yourself. Using one of the many examples in `.../drivers/mtd/chips` as a starting point, customize or create your own Flash device driver. Better yet, unless the chip was just introduced with some newfangled interface, someone probably has already produced a driver.

10.2.5   Board-Specific Initialization

Along with a mapping driver, your board-specific (platform) setup must provide the underlying definitions for proper MTD Flash system operation. Listing 10-11 reproduces the relevant portions of `.../arch/arm/mach-ixp4xx/coyote-setup.c`.

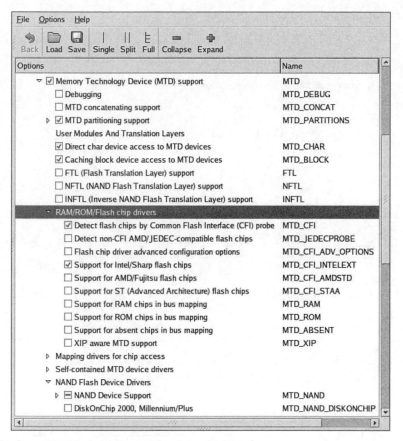

FIGURE 10-4   Flash device support

LISTING 10-11   Coyote-Specific Board Setup

```
static struct flash_platform_data coyote_flash_data = {
    .map_name   = "cfi_probe",
    .width      = 2,
};

static struct resource coyote_flash_resource = {
    .flags          = IORESOURCE_MEM,
};

static struct platform_device coyote_flash = {
```

LISTING 10-11   Continued

```
        .name        = "IXP4XX-Flash",
        .id          = 0,
        .dev         = {
                .platform_data = &coyote_flash_data,
        },
        .num_resources      = 1,
        .resource    = &coyote_flash_resource,
};


...


static struct platform_device *coyote_devices[] __initdata = {
        &coyote_flash,
        &coyote_uart
};


static void __init coyote_init(void)
{

        ...


        platform_add_devices(coyote_devices,
                                ARRAY_SIZE(coyote_devices));

}


...
```

Starting from the bottom of Listing 10-11, the `coyote_init()` function calls `platform_add_devices()`, specifying the Coyote-specific devices defined earlier in this file. You'll notice that two devices are defined just above the `coyote_init()` routine. The one we're interested in for this discussion is `coyote_flash`. This structure of type `struct platform_device` contains all the important details needed by the Linux kernel and MTD subsystem.

The `.name` member of the `coyote_flash` structure binds our platform-specific Flash resource to a mapping driver with the same name. You can see this in the mapping driver file `.../drivers/mtd/maps/ixp4xx.c`. The `.resource` member communicates the base address of the Flash on the board. The `.dev` member, which contains a `.platform_data` member, ties our Flash setup to a chip driver. In this case, we have specified that our board will use the CFI probe method, specified in the kernel configuration as `CONFIG_MTD_CFI`. You can see this configuration selection in Figure 10-4.

Depending on your own architecture and board, you can use a method similar to this to define the Flash support for your own board.

10.3 MTD Utilities

The MTD package contains a number of system utilities useful for setting up and managing your MTD subsystem. The utilities are built separately from the primary MTD subsystem, which should be built from within your Linux kernel source tree. These utilities can be built in a manner similar to any other cross-compiled user space code.

You must exercise caution when using these utilities, because Linux provides no protection from mistakes. A single-digit typo can wipe out the bootloader on your hardware platform. This can ruin your day unless you've backed it up and know how to reprogram it using a JTAG Flash programmer.

In keeping with a common practice throughout this book, we cannot devote sufficient space to cover every MTD utility. We highlight the most common and useful ones and leave it as an exercise for you to explore the rest. A recent MTD snapshot contained more than 20 binary utilities.

The flash_* family of utilities is useful for raw device operations on an MTD partition. These include flashcp, flash_erase, flash_info, flash_lock, flash_unlock, and others. Hopefully their names are descriptive enough to give you some idea of their function. After partitions are defined and enumerated as kernel devices, any of these user space utilities can be run on a partition. We repeat the warning we issued earlier: If you execute flash_erase on the partition containing your bootloader, you'll be the proud owner of a silicon paperweight. If you intend to experiment like this, it's a good idea to have a backup of your bootloader image and to know how to re-Flash it using a hardware JTAG emulator or another Flash programming tool.

Our new partition created in Listing 10-7 (MyKernel) shows up in the kernel running on the Coyote board, as detailed in Listing 10-12. Here you can see the new partition we created instantiated as the kernel device mtd1.

LISTING 10-12   Kernel MTD Partition List

```
root@coyote:~# cat /proc/mtd
dev:    size    erasesize  name
mtd0: 00060000 00020000  "RedBoot"
mtd1: 00160000 00020000  "MyKernel"
mtd2: 00001000 00020000  "RedBoot config"
mtd3: 00020000 00020000  "FIS directory"
```

Using the MTD utilities, we can perform a number of operations on the newly created partition. The following is the result of a flash_erase command on the partition:

```
# flash_erase /dev/mtd1
Erase Total 1 Units
Performing Flash Erase of length 131072 at offset 0x0 done
```

To copy a new kernel image to this partition, use the flashcp command:

```
root@coyote:~# flashcp /workspace/coyote-40-zImage /dev/mtd1
```

It gets a bit more interesting working with a root file system partition. We have the option of using the bootloader or the Linux kernel to place the initial image on the Redboot Flash partition. First, we use Redboot to create the new partition that will hold our root file system. The following command creates a new partition on the Flash device called RootFS starting at physical memory address 0x50300000, with a length of 30 blocks. Remember, a block, generically called an erase unit, is 128KB on this Flash chip.

```
RedBoot> fis create -f 0x50300000 -l 0x600000 -n RootFS
```

Next, we boot the kernel and copy the root file system image into the new partition we have named RootFS. This is accomplished with the following command from a Linux command prompt on your target board. Note that this assumes you have already placed your file system image in a directory accessible to your board. As mentioned many times throughout this book, NFS root mount is your best friend during development.

```
root@coyote:~# flashcp /rootfs.ext2 /dev/mtd2
```

The file system can be anywhere from a couple megabytes up to the largest size we have allowed on this partition, so this can take some time. Remember, this operation involves programming (sometimes called flashing) the image into the Flash memory. After copying, we can mount the partition as a file system. Listing 10-13 displays the sequence.

LISTING 10-13   Mounting the MTD Flash Partition as an ext2 File System

```
root@coyote:~# mount -t ext2 /dev/mtdblock2 /mnt/remote ro
root@coyote:~# ls -l /mnt/remote/
total 16
```

LISTING 10-13 Continued

```
drwxr-xr-x  2 root  root  1024 Nov 19  2005 bin
drwxr-xr-x  2 root  root  1024 Oct 26  2005 boot
drwxr-xr-x  2 root  root  1024 Nov 19  2005 dev
drwxr-xr-x  5 root  root  1024 Nov 19  2005 etc
drwxr-xr-x  2 root  root  1024 Oct 26  2005 home
drwxr-xr-x  3 root  root  1024 Nov 19  2005 lib
drwxr-xr-x  3 root  root  1024 Nov 19  2005 mnt
drwxr-xr-x  2 root  root  1024 Oct 26  2005 opt
drwxr-xr-x  2 root  root  1024 Oct 26  2005 proc
drwxr-xr-x  2 root  root  1024 Oct 26  2005 root
drwxr-xr-x  2 root  root  1024 Nov 19  2005 sbin
drwxr-xr-x  2 root  root  1024 Oct 26  2005 srv
drwxr-xr-x  2 root  root  1024 Oct 26  2005 sys
drwxr-xr-x  2 root  root  1024 Oct 26  2005 tmp
drwxr-xr-x  6 root  root  1024 Oct 26  2005 usr
drwxr-xr-x  2 root  root  1024 Nov 19  2005 var
root@coyote:~#
```

Listing 10-13 has two important subtleties. Notice that we have specified `/dev/mtdblock2` on the `mount` command line. This is the MTD block driver that enables us to access the MTD partition as a block device. Specifying `/dev/mtd2` instructs the kernel to use the MTD character driver. Both `mtdchar` and `mtdblock` are pseudo drivers used to provide either character-based or block-oriented access to the underlying Flash partition. Because `mount` expects a block device, you must use the block-device specifier. Figure 10-1 shows the kernel configuration that enables these access methods. The respective kernel configuration macros are `CONFIG_MTD_CHAR` and `CONFIG_MTD_BLOCK`.

The second subtlety is the use of the read-only (`ro`) command-line switch on the `mount` command. It is perfectly acceptable to mount an ext2 image from Flash using the MTD block emulation driver for read-only purposes. However, there is no support for writing to an ext2 device using the `mtdblock` driver. This is because ext2 has no knowledge of Flash erase blocks. For write access to a Flash-based file system, we need to use a file system with Flash knowledge, such as JFFS2.

10.3.1 JFFS2 Root File System

Creating a JFFS2 root file system is a straightforward process. In addition to compression, JFFS2 supports *wear leveling*, a feature designed to increase Flash lifetime by fairly distributing the write cycles across the blocks of the device. As pointed out in

Chapter 9, Flash memory is subject to a limited number of write cycles. Wear leveling should be considered a mandatory feature in any Flash-based file system you employ. As mentioned elsewhere in this book, you should consider Flash memory as a write-occasional medium. Specifically, you should avoid allowing any processes that require frequent writes to target the Flash file system. Be especially aware of any logging programs, such as `syslogd`.

We can build a JFFS2 image on our development workstation using the ext2 image we used on our Redboot `RootFS` partition. The compression benefits will be immediately obvious. The image we used in the previous `RootFS` example was an ext2 file system image. Here is the listing in long (`-l`) format:

```
# ls -l rootfs.ext2
-rw-r--r--  1 root root 6291456 Nov 19 16:21 rootfs.ext2
```

Now let's convert this file system image to JFFS2 using the `mkfs.jffs2` utility found in the MTD package. Listing 10-14 shows the command and results.

LISTING 10-14   Converting RootFS to JFFS2

```
# mount -o loop rootfs.ext2 /mnt/flash/
# mkfs.jffs2 -r /mnt/flash -e 128 -b -o rootfs.jffs2
# ls -l rootfs.jffs2
-rw-r--r--  1 root root 2401512 Nov 20 10:08 rootfs.jffs2
#
```

First we mount the ext2 file system image on a loopback device on an arbitrary mount point on our development workstation. Next we invoke the MTD utility `mkfs.jffs2` to create the JFFS2 file system image. The `-r` flag tells `mkfs.jffs2` where the root file system image is located. The `-e` instructs `mkfs.jffs2` to build the image while assuming a 128KB block size. The default block size is 64KB. JFFS2 does not exhibit its most efficient behavior if the Flash device contains a different block size than the block size of the image. Finally, we display a long listing and discover that the resulting JFFS2 root file system image has been reduced in size by more than 60 percent. When you are working with limited Flash memory, this is a substantial reduction in precious Flash resource usage.

Take note of an important command-line flag passed to `mkfs.jffs2` in Listing 10-14. The `-b` flag is the `-big-endian` flag. It instructs the `mkfs.jffs2` utility to create a JFFS2 Flash image suitable for use on a big-endian target. Because we are targeting the ADI Engineering Coyote board, which contains an Intel IXP425 processor running in big-endian mode, this step is crucial for proper operation. If you fail to specify big-endian, you will get several screens full of complaints from the kernel as it tries to negotiate the superblock of a JFFS2 file system that is essentially gibberish.[2] Would you like to guess how I remembered this important detail?

In a manner similar to the previous example, we can copy this image to our Redboot RootFS Flash partition using the flashcp utility. Then we can boot the Linux kernel using a JFFS2 root file system. Listing 10-15 provides the details, running the MTD utilities on our target hardware.

LISTING 10-15   Copying JFFS2 to the *RootFS* Partition

```
root@coyote:~# cat /proc/mtd
dev:    size    erasesize  name
mtd0: 00060000 00020000 "RedBoot"
mtd1: 00160000 00020000 "MyKernel"
mtd2: 00600000 00020000 "RootFS"
mtd3: 00001000 00020000 "RedBoot config"
mtd4: 00020000 00020000 "FIS directory"
root@coyote:~# flash_erase /dev/mtd2
Erase Total 1 Units
Performing Flash Erase of length 131072 at offset 0x0 done
root@coyote:~# flashcp /rootfs.jffs2 /dev/mtd2
root@coyote:~#
```

It is important to note that you must have the JFFS2 file system enabled in your kernel configuration. Execute make ARCH=<arch> gconfig and select JFFS2 under File Systems, Miscellaneous File Systems. Another useful hint is to use the -v (verbose) flag on the MTD utilities. This provides progress updates and other useful information during the Flash operations.

We have already seen how to boot a kernel with the Redboot exec command. Listing 10-16 details the sequence of commands to load and boot the Linux kernel with our new JFFS2 file system as root.

LISTING 10-16   Booting with JFFS2 as the Root File System

```
RedBoot> load -r -v -b 0x01008000 coyote-zImage
Using default protocol (TFTP)
Raw file loaded 0x01008000-0x0114decb, assumed entry at 0x01008000
RedBoot> exec -c "console=ttyS0,115200 rootfstype=jffs2 root=/dev/mtdblock2"
Using base address 0x01008000 and length 0x00145ecc
Uncompressing Linux...... done, booting the kernel.
...
```

---

[2] The kernel can be configured to operate with a wrong-endian MTD file system, at the cost of reduced performance. In some configurations (such as multiprocessor designs), this can be a useful feature.

10.4   UBI File System

The Unsorted Block Image (UBI) File System was designed to overcome some of the limitations of the JFFS2 file system. It can be considered the successor to JFFS2, although JFFS2 remains in widespread use on embedded Linux devices containing Flash memory. The UBI File System (UBIFS) is layered on top of UBI devices, which in turn depends on MTD devices.

UBIFS improves on one of the more significant limitations of the JFFS2 file system: mount time. JFFS2 maintains its indexing metadata in system memory and must read this index to build a complete directory tree each time the system boots. This can require reading a significant portion of the Flash device. In contrast, UBIFS maintains its indexing metadata on the Flash device itself, negating the need to scan and rebuild this data on each mount. Therefore, UBIFS mounts many times faster than JFFS2.

UBIFS also supports write caching, which can be a significant performance enhancement. You can read more about the advantages of UBIFS at www.linux-mtd. infradead.org/doc/ubifs.html.

10.4.1   Configuring for UBIFS

To use UBIFS, your kernel needs to have UBI support enabled. Two different kernel configuration menu items must be enabled in your kernel configuration to enable UBIFS. First, enable support for MTD_UBI. This option can be found in your kernel configuration under Device Drivers --> Memory Technology Device (MTD) support --> UBI - Unsorted block images --> Enable UBI. After this item is chosen, it enables the file system support configuration options found under File Systems --> Miscellaneous filesystems --> UBIFS file system support.

10.4.2   Building a UBIFS Image

Building a UBIFS image is a little more tricky than building a JFFS2 image. The additional complexity comes from the NAND Flash technology. Building a UBIFS image requires that you have knowledge of the NAND Flash architecture on your target system. This will become clear in a moment. You will also need a fairly recent version of MTD Utils installed on your development workstation. MTD Utils can be found at git://git.infradead.org/mtd-utils.git.

Listing 10-17 details the process for creating the UBIFS image on your development workstation. Assume for this exercise that you have the desired contents of your file system in a directory called rootfs.

LISTING 10-17   Building the UBIFS Image

```
$ mkfs.ubifs -m 2048 -e 129024 -c 1996 -o ubifs.img -r ./rootfs
$ ubinize -m 2048 -p 128KiB -s 512 -o ubi.img ubinize.cfg
$ ls -l
total 200880
drwxr-xr-x 17 chris chris      4096 2010-03-01 11:33 rootfs
-rw-r--r--  1 chris chris 101799936 2010-03-01 11:55 ubifs.img
-rw-r--r--  1 chris chris 103677952 2010-03-01 11:58 ubi.img
-rw-r--r--  1 chris chris       112 2010-03-01 11:54 ubinize.cfg
```

The raw UBIFS image is built using the `mkfs.ubifs` utility, from the mtd-utils package. This produces the target file `ubifs.img`. It is critical that the correct parameters are passed to `mkfs.ubifs`. These parameters come from your hardware design and NAND Flash architecture. The `-m` specifies the minimum I/O unit size—in this case, 2KB. The `-e` specifies the logical erase block (LEB) size for the image. The maximum number of LEBs for the image is specified by `-c`. The name of the output image is specified using `-o`. For this example, we have named it `ubifs.img`.

Now that we have the UBIFS image, we must generate the UBI volume image. We use the `ubinize` tool (part of the mtd-utils package) for this. Once again, we must use the correct parameters for our target environment. In addition, you will notice that `ubinize` requires a configuration file. The `ubinize.cfg` file contains the volume name, among other things, as we will see shortly.

Listing 10-17 specifies the minimum I/O size, as in `mkfs.ubifs`, as 2KB. Here we specify the physical erase block size, given by the `-p` parameter. In our case, we are using NAND Flash with a 128KiB physical erase block size. The `-s` parameter specifies a subpage size, which is the minimum I/O unit. We name the target output file using `-o ubi.img`. We will flash this image into our device.

The configuration file used by `ubinize` specifies the volumes to be generated by the `ubinize` tool. Listing 10-18 details the simple configuration we used for Listing 10-17.

LISTING 10-18   *ubinize* Configuration File

```
$ cat ubinize.cfg
[ubifs]
mode=ubi
image=ubifs.img
vol_id=0
vol_size=200MiB
vol_type=dynamic
vol_name=rootfs
```

Here you can see that we named the volume rootfs and that the raw image comes from the file called `ubifs.img`. Recall from Listing 10-17 that this was the image produced by the `mkfs.ubifs` utility. You can read more about the `ubinize` configuration file from the man page for that utility.

Once we have the final image, we can flash it to our device. We will use the `ubiformat` command for that. You cannot simply flash the raw image to the device. This is because NAND Flash as used by the UBI layer contains special headers that record the erase count, among other things, for each physical erase block. This is used for wear leveling. Using `ubiformat` preserves these error count headers. Listing 10-19 shows the details.

LISTING 10-19   Using the UBIFS Image

```
root@beagleboard:~# flash_eraseall /dev/mtd4
Erasing 128 Kibyte @ f980000 -- 100 % complete.
root@beagleboard:~# ubiformat /dev/mtd4 -s 512 -f /ubi.img
ubiformat: mtd4 (NAND), size 261619712 bytes (249.5 MiB), 131072 eraseblocks of
131072 bytes (128.0 KiB), min. I/O size 2048 bytes
<...>
root@beagleboard:~# ubiattach /dev/ubi_ctrl -m 4
UBI device number 0, total 1996 LEBs (257531904 bytes, 245.6 MiB), available 0
LEBs (0 bytes), LEB size 129024 bytes (126.0 KiB)
root@beagleboard:~# mount -t ubifs  ubi0:rootfs /mnt/ubifs
root@beagleboard:~# ls /mnt/ubifs
bin     dev     home    linuxrc  mnt      sbin     sys     usr
boot    etc     lib     media    proc     srv      tmp     var
```

Here you can see the sequence of events leading to mounting of the UBIFS file system. First, we erase the Flash device, using `flash_eraseall`, one of the utilities from mtd-utils. Consider your need to use this erase utility, because it does not preserve error counters. This would be a first-time-use scenario.

The `ubiformat` command places the image on the NAND Flash in our example. The `-s` specifies the subpage size, which must agree with the image, and the `-f` is used to select the image file. After this operation completes, we can *attach* the UBI device, which is required before the UBI device is mounted. `ubiattach` requires the UBI control device (`/dev/ubi_ctrl`) and a specifier to select which MTD device to attach. Because we wrote the image to MTD partition 4 (`/dev/mtd4`), we specify this to `ubiattach` using the `-m 4` parameter.

With all of this in place, we can now mount the UBIFS image. Notice in Listing 10-19 that we pass the volume name specified in the `ubinize.cfg` configuration file to the `mount` command.

10.4.3 Using UBIFS as the Root File System

Now that we have an image in place on `/dev/mtd4`, we can instruct the kernel to mount this file system as its root file system. To do so, pass the following kernel command-line parameters to the kernel:

```
ubi.mtd=4 root=ubi0:rootfs rw rootfstype=ubifs
```

This set of kernel command-line parameters instructs the kernel to attach the mtd4 device to ubi0 and to mount the resulting UBI device as the root file system. If you run into difficulties, make sure you include an appropriate `rootdelay` option on your kernel command line. For this exercise, `rootdelay=1` was required to allow time for the UBI and UBIFS layers to be ready when it came time to mount the UBIFS as the root file system.

10.5 Summary

This chapter presented one of the more important and difficult-to-master topics of interest to the embedded developer. MTD is present in some form on many embedded systems.

- The Memory Technology Device (MTD) subsystem provides support for memory devices such as Flash memory in the Linux kernel.
- MTD must be enabled in your Linux kernel configuration. Several figures in this chapter detailed the configuration options.
- As part of the MTD kernel configuration, the proper Flash driver(s) for your Flash chips must be selected. Figure 10-4 showed the chip drivers supported in a recent Linux kernel snapshot.
- Your Flash memory device can be managed as a single large device or can be divided into multiple partitions.
- Several methods are available for communicating the partition information to the Linux kernel. These include Redboot partition information, kernel command-line parameters, and mapping drivers.

- A mapping driver, together with definitions supplied by your architecture-specific board support, defines your Flash configuration to the kernel.

- MTD comes with a number of user space utilities to manage the images on your Flash devices.

- The Journaling Flash File System 2 (JFFS2) is a good companion to the MTD subsystem for small, efficient Flash-based file systems. In this chapter, we built a JFFS2 image and mounted it as root on our target device.

- UBIFS improves on JFFS2 and is rapidly gaining popularity in embedded systems.

10.5.1 Suggestions for Additional Reading

MTD Linux home page
www.linux-mtd.infradead.org/

Redboot user documentation
http://ecos.sourceware.org/ecos/docs-latest/redboot/redboot-guide.html

Common Flash Memory Interface Specification
AMD Corporation
www.amd.com/us-en/assets/content_type/DownloadableAssets/cfi_r20.pdf

Chapter 11

BusyBox

In This Chapter

- 11.1   Introduction to BusyBox   290
- 11.2   BusyBox Configuration   291
- 11.3   BusyBox Operation   293
- 11.4   Summary   303

The man page for BusyBox declares that BusyBox is "The Swiss Army Knife of Embedded Linux." This is a fitting description, for BusyBox is a small and efficient replacement for a large collection of standard Linux command-line utilities. It often serves as the foundation for a resource-limited embedded platform. This chapter introduces BusyBox and provides an excellent starting point for customizing your own BusyBox installation.

Previous chapters referred to BusyBox. This chapter presents the details of this useful package. After a brief introduction to BusyBox, we explore the BusyBox configuration utility. This is used to tailor BusyBox to your particular requirements. We then discuss the requirements for cross-compiling the BusyBox package.

BusyBox operational issues are considered, including how it is used in an embedded system. We examine the BusyBox initialization sequence and explain how it departs from the standard System V initialization. This chapter also presents a sample initialization script. After seeing the steps for installing BusyBox on a target system, you will learn about some of the BusyBox commands and their limitations.

11.1   Introduction to BusyBox

BusyBox has gained tremendous popularity in the embedded Linux community. It is remarkably easy to configure, compile, and use. In addition, it has the potential to significantly reduce the overall system resources required to support a wide collection of common Linux utilities. BusyBox provides compact replacements for many traditional full-blown utilities found on most desktop and embedded Linux distributions. Examples include the file utilities such as `ls`, `cat`, `cp`, `dir`, `head`, and `tail`; general utilities such as `dmesg`, `kill`, `halt`, `fdisk`, `mount`, and `umount`; and many more. BusyBox also provides support for more-complex operations, such as `ifconfig`, `netstat`, `route`, and other network utilities.

BusyBox is modular and highly configurable and can be tailored to suit your particular requirements. The package includes a configuration utility similar to the one used to configure the Linux kernel and therefore will seem quite familiar.

The commands in BusyBox generally are simpler implementations than their full-blown counterparts. In some cases, only a subset of the usual command-line options are supported. In practice, however, you will find that the BusyBox subset of command functionality is more than sufficient for most general embedded requirements.

11.1.1   BusyBox Is Easy

If you can configure and build the Linux kernel, you will find BusyBox quite straight-forward to configure, build, and install. The steps are similar:

1. Execute a configuration utility and enable your choice of features.
2. Run `make` to build the package.
3. Install the binary and a series of *symbolic links*[1] on your target system.

You can build and install BusyBox on your development workstation or your target embedded system. BusyBox works equally well in both environments. However, you must take care when installing on your development workstation that you keep it isolated in a working directory, to avoid overwriting your system's startup files or primary utilities.

11.2   BusyBox Configuration

To initiate the BusyBox configuration, the command is the same as that used with the Linux kernel for the `ncurses` library-based configuration utility. Note that, in a similar fashion to the Linux kernel, `make help` produces much useful information on available make targets. The command to configure is:

```
$ make menuconfig
```

Figure 11-1 shows the top-level BusyBox configuration.

Space does not permit coverage of each configuration option. However, some of the options deserve mention. Some of the more important BusyBox configuration options appear under Busybox Settings ---> Build Options. Here you will find configuration options necessary to cross-compile the BusyBox application. Listing 11-1 details the options found under Build Options in a recent BusyBox snapshot. Select Build Options from the top-level BusyBox configuration utility to navigate to this screen.

---

[1] We cover the details of symbolic links shortly.

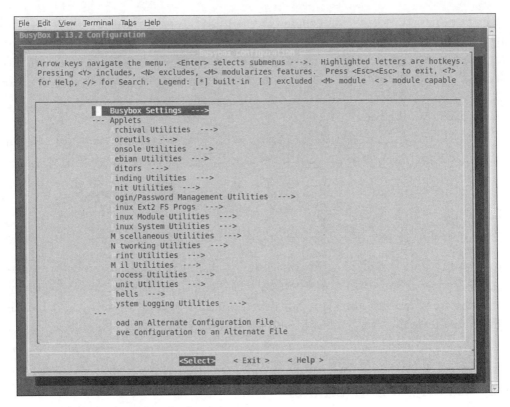

FIGURE 11-1   Top-level BusyBox Configuration menu

LISTING 11-1   BusyBox Build Options

```
[ ] Build BusyBox as a static binary (no shared libs)
[ ]    Build BusyBox as a position independent executable
[ ] Force NOMMU build
[ ] Build shared libbusybox
[*] Build with Large File Support (for accessing files > 2 GB)
()   Cross Compiler prefix
```

The first option is useful for building very minimal embedded systems. It allows BusyBox to be compiled and linked statically so that no dynamically loaded libraries (libc-*, for example) are required at runtime on the target system. Without this option, BusyBox requires various libraries so that it can run. We can easily determine what libraries BusyBox (or any other binary) requires on our target system by using the ldd command. Listing 11-2 is the output of ldd cross-compiled for ARM xscale.

LISTING 11-2   BusyBox Library Dependencies

```
$ xscale_be-ldd busybox
    linux-gate.so.1 =>  (0xb8087000)
    libm.so.6 => /lib/tls/i686/cmov/libm.so.6 (0xb804d000)
    libc.so.6 => /lib/tls/i686/cmov/libc.so.6 (0xb7efe000)
    /lib/ld-linux.so.2 (0xb8088000)
```

Notice that the BusyBox utility, as compiled using the default configuration, requires the four shared libraries shown in Listing 11-2. Had we elected to build BusyBox as a static binary, ldd would simply issue a message telling us that the BusyBox binary is not a dynamic executable. In other words, it requires no shared libraries to resolve any unresolved dependencies in the executable. Static linking yields a smaller overall footprint on a root file system because no shared libraries are required. However, building an embedded application without shared libraries means that none of the familiar C library functions are available to your applications. To give you an idea of the relative size difference between a statically linked BusyBox and the same configuration compiled against shared libraries, a statically linked busybox is about 1.5MB versus 778KB for a dynamically linked image for a recent version of BusyBox.

11.2.1   Cross-Compiling BusyBox

As mentioned at the beginning of the chapter, the authors of BusyBox intended the package to be used in a cross-development environment, so building BusyBox in such an environment is quite easy. In earlier versions of BusyBox the only requirement was to specify the prefix to the cross-compiler by selecting the option to build BusyBox with a cross-compiler. This has been superseded by the more standard method of specifying an environment variable similar to building other packages such as the Linux kernel. To cross-compile with a specific cross-compiler on your development workstation, simply define CROSS_COMPILE in your environment. Some examples of CROSS_COMPILE values are arm5vt_le-, xscale_be-, and ppc_linux-. Note that you can also specify the cross-compiler prefix in the configuration utility just described. We cover compiler prefixes related to cross-compiling in more detail in the next chapter when we examine the embedded development environment.

11.3   BusyBox Operation

When you build BusyBox, you end up with a binary called—you guessed it—BusyBox. BusyBox can be invoked from the binary name itself, but it is usually launched via a *symlink*. When BusyBox is invoked without command-line parameters, it produces a list of the functions that were enabled via the configuration. Listing 11-3 shows such an output (it has been formatted to fit the page width).

LISTING 11-3   BusyBox Usage

```
root@coyote # busybox
BusyBox v1.13.2 (2010-02-24 16:04:14 EST) multi-call binary
Copyright (C) 1998-2008 Erik Andersen, Rob Landley, Denys Vlasenko and
others. Licensed under GPLv2.
See source distribution for full notice.

Usage: busybox [function] [arguments]...
   or: function [arguments]...

   BusyBox is a multi-call binary that combines many common Unix
   utilities into a single executable.  Most people will create a link
   to busybox for each function they wish to use and BusyBox will act
   like whatever it was invoked as!

Currently defined functions:
   [, [[, addgroup, adduser, ar, ash, awk, basename, blkid, bunzip2,
   bzcat, cat, chattr, chgrp, chmod, chown, chpasswd, chroot, chvt,
   clear, cmp, cp, cpio, cryptpw, cut, date, dc, dd, deallocvt,
   delgroup, deluser, df, dhcprelay, diff, dirname, dmesg, du,
   dumpkmap, dumpleases, echo, egrep, env, expr, false, fbset,
   fbsplash, fdisk, fgrep, find, free, freeramdisk, fsck, fsck.minix,
   fuser, getopt, getty, grep, gunzip, gzip, halt, head, hexdump,
   hostname, httpd, hwclock, id, ifconfig, ifdown, ifup, init, insmod,
   ip, kill, killall, klogd, last, less, linuxrc, ln, loadfont,
   loadkmap, logger, login, logname, logread, losetup, ls, lsmod,
   makedevs, md5sum, mdev, microcom, mkdir, mkfifo, mkfs.minix, mknod,
   mkswap, mktemp, modprobe, more, mount, mv, nc, netstat, nice,
   nohup, nslookup, od, openvt, passwd, patch, pidof, ping, ping6,
   pivot_root, poweroff, printf, ps, pwd, rdate, rdev, readahead,
   readlink, readprofile, realpath, reboot, renice, reset, rm, rmdir,
   rmmod, route, rtcwake, run-parts, sed, seq, setconsole, setfont,
   sh, showkey, sleep, sort, start-stop-daemon, strings, stty, su,
   sulogin, swapoff, swapon, switch_root, sync, sysctl, syslogd, tail,
   tar, tee, telnet, telnetd, test, tftp, time, top, touch, tr,
   traceroute, true, tty, udhcpc, udhcpd, umount, uname, uniq, unzip,
   uptime, usleep, vi, vlock, watch, wc, wget, which, who, whoami,
   xargs, yes, zcat
```

From Listing 11-3, you can see the list of functions that are enabled in this BusyBox build. They are listed in alphabetical order (ignoring the shell scripting [and [[operators) from `addgroup` to `zcat`, a utility used to decompress the contents of a compressed file. This list represents the set of utilities enabled in this particular BusyBox build.

To invoke a particular function, execute `busybox` with one of the defined functions passed on the command line. For example, to display a listing of files in the root directory, execute this command:

```
[root@coyote]# busybox ls /
```

Another important message from the BusyBox usage message shown in Listing 11-3 is the short description of the program. It describes BusyBox as a multicall binary, combining many common utilities into a single executable. This is the purpose of the symlinks mentioned earlier. BusyBox was intended to be invoked by a symlink named for the function it will perform. This removes the burden of having to type a two-word command to invoke a given function, and it presents the user with a set of familiar commands for the similarly named utilities. Listings 11-4 and 11-5 should make this clear.

Listing 11-4 shows the target directory structure as built by the BusyBox package via the `make install` command in the `busybox` source tree.

LISTING 11-4   BusyBox Symlink Structure from *make install*

```
[root@coyote]$ ls -l /
total 12
drwxrwxr-x  2 root    root 4096 Dec  3 13:38 bin
lrwxrwxrwx  1 root    root   11 Dec  3 13:38 linuxrc -> bin/busybox
drwxrwxr-x  2 root    root 4096 Dec  3 13:38 sbin
drwxrwxr-x  4 root    root 4096 Dec  3 13:38 usr
```

The executable `busybox` file is found in the /bin directory, and symlinks have been populated throughout the rest of the structure pointing back to /bin/busybox. Listing 11-5 expands on the directory structure of Listing 11-4.

LISTING 11-5   BusyBox Symlink Structure: Tree Detail

```
[root@coyote]$ tree
.
|-- bin
|   |-- addgroup -> busybox
|   |-- busybox
```

LISTING 11-5   Continued

```
|    |-- cat -> busybox
|    |-- cp -> busybox
<...>
|    `-- zcat -> busybox
|-- linuxrc -> bin/busybox
|-- sbin
|    |-- halt -> ../bin/busybox
|    |-- ifconfig -> ../bin/busybox
|    |-- init -> ../bin/busybox
|    |-- klogd -> ../bin/busybox
<...>
|    `-- syslogd -> ../bin/busybox
`-- usr
    |-- bin
    |    |-- [ -> ../../bin/busybox
    |    |-- basename -> ../../bin/busybox
<...>
    |    |-- xargs -> ../../bin/busybox
    |    `-- yes -> ../../bin/busybox
    `-- sbin
        `-- chroot -> ../../bin/busybox
```

The output shown in Listing 11-5 has been significantly truncated for readability and to avoid a three-page listing. Each line containing an ellipsis (...) indicates where this listing has been pruned to show only the first few and last few entries of that given directory. In actuality, more than 100 symlinks can be populated in these directories, depending on what functionality you have enabled using the BusyBox configuration utility.

Notice the BusyBox executable itself, the second entry from the /bin directory. Also in the /bin directory are symlinks pointing back to busybox for addgroup, cat, cp, and so on, all the way to zcat. Again, the entries between cp and zcat have been omitted from this listing for readability. With this symlink structure, the user simply enters the actual name of the utility to invoke its functionality. For example, to configure a network interface using the BusyBox ifconfig utility, the user might enter a command similar to this:

```
$ ifconfig eth1 192.168.1.14
```

This would invoke the BusyBox executable through the `ifconfig` symlink. BusyBox examines how it was called. In other words, it reads `argv[0]` to determine what functionality is being requested.

11.3.1 BusyBox `init`

Notice the symlink in Listing 11-5 called `init`. In Chapter 6, "User Space Initialization," you learned about the `init` program and its role in system initialization. Recall that the kernel attempts to execute a program called `/sbin/init` as the last step in kernel initialization. There is no reason why BusyBox can't emulate the `init` functionality, and that's exactly how the system illustrated in Listing 11-5 is configured. BusyBox handles the `init` functionality.

BusyBox handles system initialization differently from standard System V `init`. A Linux system using the System V (SysV) initialization as described in Chapter 6 requires an `inittab` file accessible in the `/etc` directory. BusyBox also reads an `inittab` file, but the syntax of the `inittab` file is different. In general, you should not need to use an `inittab` if you are using BusyBox. Consider the advice in the BusyBox man page: If you need runlevels, use System V initialization.[2]

Let's see what this looks like on an embedded system. We have created a small root file system based on BusyBox. We configured BusyBox for static linking, eliminating the need for any shared libraries. Listing 11-6 is a `tree` listing of this root file system. We built this small file system using the steps outlined in Chapter 9, "File Systems," in Section 9.11, "Building a Simple File System." We do not detail the procedure again here. The files in our simple file system are shown in Listing 11-6.

LISTING 11-6   Minimal BusyBox Root File System

```
$ tree
.
|-- bin
|    |-- busybox
|    |-- cat -> busybox
|    |-- dmesg -> busybox
|    |-- echo -> busybox
|    |-- hostname -> busybox
|    |-- ls -> busybox
|    |-- ps -> busybox
|    |-- pwd -> busybox
```

---

[2] We covered the details of System V initialization in Chapter 6.

LISTING 11-6   Continued

```
|    '-- sh -> busybox
|-- dev
|    '-- console
|-- etc
'-- proc
4 directories, 10 files
```

This BusyBox-based root file system occupies little more than the size needed for busybox itself. In this configuration, using static linking and supporting nearly 100 utilities, the BusyBox executable comes in at less than 2MB:

```
# ls -l /bin/busybox
-rwxr-xr-x 1 chris chris 1531600 2010-01-28 15:49 /bin/busybox
```

Now let's see how this system behaves. Listing 11-7 captures the console output at power-up on this BusyBox-based embedded system.

LISTING 11-7   BusyBox Default Startup

```
...
Looking up port of RPC 100003/2 on 192.168.1.9
Looking up port of RPC 100005/1 on 192.168.1.9
VFS: Mounted root (nfs filesystem).
Freeing init memory: 96K
Bummer, could not run '/etc/init.d/rcS': No such file or directory

Please press Enter to activate this console.


BusyBox v1.01 (2005.12.03-19:09+0000) Built-in shell (ash)
Enter 'help' for a list of built-in commands.

-sh: can't access tty; job control turned off
/ #
```

Listing 11-7 was run on an embedded board configured for NFS root mount. We export a directory on our workstation that contains the simple file system image detailed in Listing 11-6. As one of the final steps in the boot process, the Linux kernel on our target board mounts a root file system via NFS. When the kernel attempts to execute /sbin/init, it fails (by design) because there is no /sbin/init on our file system. However, as we have seen, the kernel also attempts to execute /bin/sh. In our

BusyBox-configured target, this succeeds, and `busybox` is launched via the symlink `/bin/sh` on our root file system.

The first thing BusyBox does is complain that it can't find `/etc/init.d/rcS`. This is the default initialization script that BusyBox searches for. Instead of using `inittab`, this is the preferred method to initialize an embedded system based on BusyBox.

When it has completed initialization, BusyBox displays a prompt asking the user to press Enter to activate a console. When BusyBox detects the Enter key, it executes an `ash` shell session waiting for user input. The final message about job control is a result of the fact that, in this particular example (and on most typical embedded systems), we are creating the system console on a serial terminal. The Linux kernel contains code to disable job control if it detects the console on a serial terminal.

This example produced a working system, with nearly 100 Linux utilities available, including core utilities, file utilities, network support, and a reasonably capable shell. You can see that this simple package provides a powerful platform upon which to build your own system applications. Of course, it should be noted that without any support for libc and other system libraries, you would face a formidable task implementing your applications. You would have to provide support for all the usual standard C library calls and other library functions that a typical C program relies on. Alternatively, you could statically link your applications against the libraries they depend on, but if you have more than a couple applications using this method, your applications will likely exceed the combined size of linking dynamically and having the shared libraries on your target.

11.3.2 Sample `rcS` Initialization Script

Before BusyBox spawns an interactive shell, it tries to execute commands from a script called `/etc/init.d/rcS`, as shown in Listing 11-7. It is here where your applications come to life in a BusyBox system. A simple `rcS` initialization script is provided in Listing 11-8.

LISTING 11-8 Simple *rcS* BusyBox Startup Script

```
#!/bin/sh

echo "Mounting proc"
mount -t proc /proc /proc

echo "Starting system loggers"
syslogd
```

LISTING 11-8   Continued

```
klogd

echo "Configuring loopback interface"
ifconfig lo 127.0.0.1

echo "Starting inetd"
xinetd

# start a shell
busybox sh
```

This simple script is mostly self-explanatory. First, it is important to mount the
/proc file system on its reserved mount point, /proc. This is because many utilities get
their information from the /proc file system. This is explained more fully in Chapter 9.
Next we launch the system loggers as early as possible, to capture any startup problems.
Following the system log daemons, we configure the local loopback interface for the
system. Again, a number of traditional Linux facilities assume that a loopback interface
is present, and if your system has support for sockets configured, you should enable
this interface. The last thing we do before starting a shell is launch the Internet superserver xinetd. This program sits in the background, listening for network requests
on any configured network interfaces. For example, to initiate a telnet session to the
board, xinetd intercepts the request for telnet connection and spawns a telnet server
to handle the session.

Instead of starting a shell, your own applications can be launched from this rcs
initialization script. Listing 11-8 is a simple example of a telnet-enabled target board
running basic services such as system and kernel loggers.

11.3.3   BusyBox Target Installation

The discussion of BusyBox installation can proceed only when you understand the use
and purpose of symlinks. The BusyBox makefile contains a target called install. Executing make install creates a directory structure containing the BusyBox executable and
a symlink tree. This environment needs to be migrated to your target embedded system's root directory, complete with the symlink tree. As explained earlier, the symlink
tree eliminates the need to type busybox command for each command. Instead, to see a
listing of files in a given directory, the user simply types ls. The symlink executes Busy-
Box as described previously and invokes the ls functionality. Review Listings 11-4 and

11-5 to see the symlink tree. Note that the BusyBox build system creates links only for the functionality that you have enabled via the configuration utility.

The easiest way to populate your root file system with the necessary symlink farm is to let the BusyBox build system do it for you. Simply mount your root file system on your development workstation and pass CONFIG_PREFIX to the BusyBox makefile. Listing 11-9 shows the procedure.

LISTING 11-9   Installing BusyBox on the Root File System

```
$ mount -o loop bbrootfs.ext2 /mnt/remote
$ make CONFIG_PREFIX=/mnt/remote install
  /mnt/remote/bin/ash -> busybox
  /mnt/remote/bin/cat -> busybox
  /mnt/remote/bin/chgrp -> busybox
  /mnt/remote/bin/chmod -> busybox
  /mnt/remote/bin/chown -> busybox
...
  /mnt/remote/usr/bin/xargs -> ../../bin/busybox
  /mnt/remote/usr/bin/yes -> ../../bin/busybox
  /mnt/remote/usr/sbin/chroot -> ../../bin/busybox


--------------------------------------------------
You will probably need to make your busybox binary
setuid root to ensure all configured applets will
work properly.
--------------------------------------------------

$ chmod +s /mnt/remote/bin/busybox
$ ls -l /mnt/remote/bin/busybox
-rwsr-sr-x  1 root root 552132  ... /mnt/remote/bin/busybox
```

First we mount the root file system binary image on our desired mount point—in this case, /mnt/remote, a favorite of mine. Then we invoke the BusyBox make install command, passing it CONFIG_PREFIX, specifying where we want the symlink tree and BusyBox executable file to be placed. Although it isn't obvious from the listing, the makefile invokes a script called applets/install.sh to do the bulk of the work. The script walks through a file containing all the enabled BusyBox applets and creates a symlink for each one on the path we have specified using the CONFIG_PREFIX. The script is very chatty; it outputs a line for each symlink created. For brevity, only the first few and last few symlink announcements are displayed in Listing 11-9. The ellipsis in the listing represents those that have been eliminated.

The message about setuid is also displayed by the install script to remind you that it might be necessary to make your BusyBox executable setuid root. This allows BusyBox functions that require root access to function properly even when invoked by a non-root user. This is not strictly necessary, especially in an embedded Linux environment, where it is common to have only a root account on a system. If this is necessary for your installation, the required command (chmod +s) is shown in Listing 11-9.

The result of this installation step is that the BusyBox binary and symlink tree are installed on our target root file system. The end result looks very similar to Listing 11-4.

It is useful to note that BusyBox also has an option to enable creation of this symlink tree on the target system at runtime. This option is enabled in the BusyBox configuration and is invoked at runtime by executing BusyBox with the -install option. You must have the /proc file system mounted on your target system for this support to work.

11.3.4 BusyBox Applets

In a recent BusyBox snapshot, 282 commands (also called applets) were documented in the man page. Sufficient support exists for reasonably complex shell scripts, including support for Bash shell scripting. BusyBox supports awk and sed, frequently found in Bash scripts. BusyBox supports network utilities such as ping, ifconfig, traceroute, and netstat. Some commands are specifically included for scripting support, including true, false, and yes.

Spend a few moments perusing Appendix C, "BusyBox Commands," where you can find a summary of each BusyBox command. After you have done so, you will have a better appreciation of the capabilities of BusyBox and how it might be applicable to your own embedded Linux project.

As mentioned at the beginning of this chapter, many of the BusyBox commands contain a limited subset of features and options compared to their full-featured counterparts. In general, you can get help on any given BusyBox command at runtime by invoking the command with the --help option. This produces a usage message with a brief description of each supported command option. The BusyBox gzip applet is a useful example of a BusyBox command that supports a limited set of options. Listing 11-10 displays the output from gzip -help on a BusyBox target.

LISTING 11-10   BusyBox *gzip* Applet Usage

```
/ # gzip --help
BusyBox v1.13.2 (2010-02-24 16:04:14 EST) multi-call binary

Usage: gzip [OPTION]... [FILE]...

Compress FILEs (or standard input)

Options:
        -c      Write to standard output
        -d      Decompress
        -f      Force
```

The BusyBox version of gzip supports just three command-line options. Its full-featured counterpart supports more than 15 different command-line options. For example, the full-featured gzip utility supports a --list option that produces compression statistics for each file on the command line. No such support exists for BusyBox gzip. This is usually not a significant limitation for embedded systems. We present this information so that you can make an informed choice when deciding on BusyBox. When the full capabilities of a utility are needed, the solution is simple: Delete support for that particular utility in the BusyBox configuration, and add the standard Linux utility to your target system. In this way you can mix BusyBox utilities and the standard Linux utilities on the same embedded system.

11.4   Summary

This chapter described BusyBox, one of the most popular utilities in the embedded Linux landscape. BusyBox has also found a place in desktop and server distributions, as part of a rescue image as well as the initial ramdisk typically found in these distributions. This chapter covered how to configure, build, and install this important utility. We also examined the differences in system initialization when using BusyBox-based systems.

- BusyBox is a powerful tool for embedded systems that replaces many common Linux utilities in a single multicall binary.
- BusyBox can significantly reduce the size of your root file system image.
- BusyBox is easy to use and has many useful features.

- Configuring BusyBox is straightforward, using an interface similar to that used for Linux configuration.

- BusyBox can be configured as a statically or dynamically linked application, depending on your particular requirements.

- System initialization is somewhat different with BusyBox; those differences were covered in this chapter.

- BusyBox has support for many commands. Appendix C itemizes all the available BusyBox commands from a recent release.

11.4.1   Suggestions for Additional Reading

BusyBox Project home
www.busybox.net/

BusyBox man page
www.busybox.net/downloads/BusyBox.html

Chapter 12

Embedded Development Environment

In This Chapter

- 12.1 Cross-Development Environment 306
- 12.2 Host System Requirements 311
- 12.3 Hosting Target Boards 312
- 12.4 Summary 322

The configuration and services available on your host development system can have a huge impact on your success as an embedded developer. This chapter examines the unique requirements of a cross-development environment and some of the tools and techniques that an embedded developer needs to know to be productive.

We begin by examining a typical cross-development environment. Using the familiar "Hello World" example, we detail the important differences between host-based applications and those targeted for embedded systems. We also look at differences in the toolchains for native versus embedded application development. We then present host system requirements and detail the use of some important elements of your host system. We conclude this chapter with an example of a target board being hosted by a network-based host.

12.1 Cross-Development Environment

Developers new to embedded development often struggle with the concepts of and differences between native and cross-development environments. Indeed, a system often has three compilers and three (or more) versions of standard header files (such as `stdlib.h`). Debugging an application on your target embedded system can be difficult without the right tools and host-based utilities. You must manage and keep separate the files and utilities designed to run on your host system from those you intend to use on your target.

When we use the term *host* in this context, we are referring to the development workstation that is sitting on your desktop and running your favorite Linux desktop distribution.[1] Conversely, when we use the term *target*, we are referring to your embedded hardware platform. Therefore, native development denotes the compilation and building of applications on and for your host system. Cross-development denotes the compilation and building of applications on the host system that will be run on the embedded system. Keeping these definitions in mind will help you stay on track throughout this chapter.

---

[1] Webster's defines nonsense as "an idea that is absurd or contrary to good sense." It is the author's opinion that developing embedded Linux platforms on a non-Linux/UNIX host is nonsensical.

Figure 12-1 shows the layout of a typical cross-development environment. A host PC is connected to a target board through one or more physical connections. It is most convenient if both serial and Ethernet ports are available on the target. Later, when we discuss kernel debugging, you will realize that a second serial port can be a valuable asset.

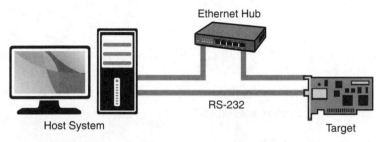

FIGURE 12-1   Cross-development setup

In the most common scenario, the developer has a serial terminal on the host connected to the RS-232 serial port, possibly one or more telnet or SSH terminal sessions to the target board, and potentially one or more debug sessions using Ethernet as the connection medium. This cross-development setup provides a great deal of flexibility. The basic idea is that the host system provides the horsepower to run the compilers, debuggers, editors, and other utilities, and the target executes only the applications designed for it. You can certainly run compilers and debuggers on the target system, but we assume that your host system has more resources available, including processor horsepower, RAM, disk storage, and Internet connectivity. In fact, it is not uncommon for a target embedded board to have no human-input devices or output displays.

12.1.1 "Hello World" Embedded

A properly configured cross-development system hides a great deal of complexity from the average application developer. Looking at a simple example will help uncover and explain some of the mystery. When we compile a simple "Hello World" program, the toolchain (compiler, linker, and associated utilities) makes many assumptions about the host system we are building on and the program we are compiling. Actually, they are not assumptions, but a collection of rules that the compiler references to build a proper binary.

Listing 12-1 reproduces a simple "Hello World" program.

LISTING 12-1   Hello World Again

```c
#include <stdio.h>

int main(int argc, char **argv)
{
    printf("Hello World\n");
    return 0;
}
```

Even the casual application developer will realize some important points about this C source file. First, the function `printf()` is referenced but not defined in this file. If we omit the `#include` directive containing the prototype for the `printf()` function, the compiler emits this familiar message:

```
hello.c:5: warning: implicit declaration of function 'printf'
```

This introduces some interesting questions:

- Where is the file `stdio.h` located, and how is it found?
- Where is the `printf()` function object code stored on your system, and how is this reference resolved in the binary executable?

Somehow it seems that the compiler just knows how to put together a proper binary file that can be executed from the command line. To further complicate matters, the final executable contains startup and shutdown prologue code that we never see but that the linker automatically includes. This prologue deals with details such as the environment and arguments passed to your program, startup and shutdown housekeeping, exit handling, and more.

To build the "Hello World" application, we can use a simple command-line invocation of the compiler, similar to this:

```
$ gcc -o hello hello.c
```

This produces the binary executable file called `hello`, which we can execute directly from the command line. Defaults referenced by the compiler provide guidance on where include files will be found. In a similar fashion, the linker knows how to resolve the reference to the `printf()` function by including a reference to the library where it is defined. This, of course, is the standard C library.

We can query the toolchain to see some of the defaults that were used. Listing 12-2 is a partial listing of the output from cpp when passed the -v flag. You might already know that cpp is the C preprocessor component of the GNU gcc toolchain. We have added some formatting (white space only) to improve readability.

LISTING 12-2   Default Native *cpp* Search Directories

```
$ cpp -v /dev/null
Reading specs from /usr/lib/gcc-lib/i386-redhat-linux/3.3.3/specs
Configured with: ../configure --prefix=/usr
--mandir=/usr/share/man --infodir=/usr/share/info
--enable-shared --enable-threads=posix --disable-checking
--disable-libunwind-exceptions --with-system-zlib
--enable-__cxa_atexit -host=i386-redhat-linux

Thread model: posix
gcc version 3.3.3 20040412 (Red Hat Linux 3.3.3-7)
 /usr/lib/gcc-lib/i386-redhat-linux/3.3.3/cc1 -E -quiet -v -
ignoring nonexistent directory "/usr/i386-redhat-linux/include"

#include "..." search starts here:
#include <...> search starts here:
 /usr/local/include
 /usr/lib/gcc-lib/i386-redhat-linux/3.3.3/include
 /usr/include
End of search list.
/usr/lib/
```

This simple query produces some useful information. First, we can see how the compiler was configured using the familiar ./configure utility. The default thread model is posix, which determines the thread library your application gets linked against if you employ threading functions. Finally, you see the default search directories for #include directives.

But what if we want to build hello.c for a different architecture, such as Power Architecture? When we compile an application program for a Power Architecture target using a cross-compiler on our host machine, we must make sure that the compiler does not use the default host include directories or library paths. Using a properly configured cross-compiler is the first step, and having a well-designed cross-development environment is the second.

Listing 12-3 is the output from a popular open-source cross-development tool-chain known as the Embedded Linux Development Kit (ELDK), assembled and maintained by Denx Software Engineering. This particular installation was configured for the Power Architecture 82xx toolchain. Again, we have added some white space to the output for readability.

LISTING 12-3   Default Cross-Search Directories

```
$ ppc_82xx-cpp -v /dev/null
Reading specs from /opt/eldk/usr/bin/..
/lib/gcc-lib/ppc-linux/3.3.3/specs

Configured with: ../configure --prefix=/usr
--mandir=/usr/share/man --infodir=/usr/share/info
--enable-shared --enable-threads=posix --disable-checking
--with-system-zlib --enable-__cxa_atexit --with-newlib
--enable-languages=c,c++ --disable-libgcj
--host=i386-redhat-linux -target=ppc-linux

Thread model: posix

gcc version 3.3.3 (DENX ELDK 3.1.1 3.3.3-10)
 /opt/eldk/usr/bin/../lib/gcc-lib/ppc-linux/3.3.3/cc1
-E -quiet -v -iprefix /opt/eldk/usr/bin/..
/lib/gcc-lib/ppc-linux/3.3.3/ -D__unix__ -D__gnu_linux__
-D__linux__ -Dunix -D__unix -Dlinux -D__linux -Asystem=unix
-Asystem=posix - -mcpu=603

ignoring nonexistent directory "/opt/eldk/usr/ppc-linux/sys-include"
ignoring nonexistent directory "/opt/eldk/usr/ppc-linux/include"
#include "..." search starts here:

#include <...> search starts here:
 /opt/eldk/usr/lib/gcc-lib/ppc-linux/3.3.3/include
 /opt/eldk/ppc_82xx/usr/include

End of search list.
```

Here you can see that the default search paths for include directories are now adjusted to point to your cross versions instead of the native include directories. This seemingly obscure detail is critical to being able to develop applications and compile open source packages for your embedded system. It is one of the most confusing topics to even experienced application developers who are new to embedded systems.

12.2 Host System Requirements

Your development workstation must include several important components and systems. First, you need a properly configured cross toolchain. You can download and compile one yourself or obtain one of the many commercial toolchains available. Building one yourself is beyond the scope of this book; however, several good references are available. See the last section of this chapter for recommendations.

The next major item you need is a Linux distribution targeted for your embedded system architecture. This includes hundreds to potentially thousands of files that will populate your embedded system's file system(s). Again, the choices are to build your own or to obtain one of the commercial ones. One of the more popular open source embedded system distributions is the aforementioned ELDK. The ELDK is available for many Power Architecture, ARM, and other embedded targets. The topic of building an embedded Linux distribution from scratch would require a book of this size in itself; therefore, it's beyond the scope of our discussion. We introduce open source build systems in Chapter 16, "Open Source Build Systems."

In summary, your development host requires four separate and distinct capabilities:

- Cross toolchain and libraries
- Target system packages, including programs, utilities, and libraries
- Host tools such as editors, debuggers, and utilities
- Servers for hosting your target board, as covered in the next section

If you install a ready-built embedded Linux development environment on your workstation, either a commercial variety or one freely available in the open source community, the toolchain and components have already been preconfigured to work together. For example, the toolchain has been configured with default directory search paths that match the location of the target header files and system libraries on your development workstation. The situation becomes much more complex if your requirements include support for multiple architectures and processors on your development workstation. This is the reason that commercial embedded Linux distributions exist.

12.2.1 Hardware Debug Probe

In addition to the components just listed, you should consider some type of hardware-assisted debugging. This consists of a hardware probe connected to your host (often via Ethernet) and connected to your target via a debug connector on the board. Many solutions are available. The de facto standard in the Linux community remains the Abatron BDI-3000. This topic is covered in detail in Chapter 14, "Kernel Debugging Techniques."

12.3   Hosting Target Boards

Referring to Figure 12-1, you will notice an Ethernet connection from the target-embedded board to the host-development system. This is not strictly necessary; indeed, some smaller embedded devices do not have an Ethernet interface. However, this is the exception rather than the rule. Having an Ethernet connection available on your target board is worth its cost in silicon! This enables the NFS root mount configuration, which can save you days or weeks of development time.

While developing your embedded Linux kernel, you will compile and download kernels and root file systems to your embedded board many times. Many embedded development systems and bootloaders support TFTP and assume that the developer will use it. TFTP is a lightweight protocol for moving files between a TFTP server and TFTP client over Ethernet, similar to FTP.

Using TFTP from your bootloader to load the kernel will save you countless hours waiting for serial downloads, even at higher serial baud rates. And loading your root file system or ramdisk image can take much longer, because these images can grow to many tens of megabytes or more, depending on your requirements. The investment in your time to configure and use TFTP will definitely pay off and is highly recommended. Very few designs can't afford the real estate to include an Ethernet port during development, even if it is depopulated for production.

12.3.1   TFTP Server

Configuring TFTP on your Linux development host is not difficult. Of course, the details might vary, depending on which Linux distribution you choose for your development workstation. The guidelines presented here are based on popular desktop Linux distributions.

TFTP is a TCP/IP service that must be enabled on your workstation. To enable the TFTP service, you must instruct your workstation to respond to incoming TFTP packets. The easiest way to do this is to run a TFTP server daemon. Most modern desktop Linux distributions have multiple packages available to provide this service. HPA's TFTP server will be used as the basis for the examples here. It can be obtained from ftp://ftp.kernel.org/pub/software/network/tftp.

On modern Ubuntu and other Debian-based systems, the HPA TFTP server can be installed as follows:[2]

```
$ sudo apt-get install tftpd-hpa
```

Configuring this TFTP server is easy. There is a single configuration file on Ubuntu and other distributions called /etc/default/tftpd-hpa. This file needs to be customized to your particular requirements. Listing 12-4 shows a typical example of this configuration file.

LISTING 12-4   TFTP Configuration

```
#Defaults for tftpd-hpa
RUN_DAEMON="yes"
OPTIONS="-l -c -s /tftpboot"
```

The first thing you must do is enable the service. When you first install the tftpd-hpa package, RUN_DAEMON defaults to "no". To enable the service, you must change the default "no" to "yes", as shown in Listing 12-4.

The second line defines the command-line options to the daemon itself, usually /usr/sbin/in.tftpd. The -s switch tells in.tftpd to switch to the specified directory (/tftpboot) upon startup, which causes this directory to be the root of your TFTP server. The -c flag allows the creation of new files. This is useful to write files to the server from the target. The BDI-3000 (covered later in this book) has such a capability, and it will not work without the -c. The -l argument instructs the TFTP daemon to run in the background and listen on the TFTP port for incoming TFTP packets.

Once the changes are made to this configuration file, you must restart the TFTP server so that they take effect:

```
$ sudo /etc/init.d/tftpd-hpa restart
```

In any case, consult the documentation that came with your distribution for options on how to enable the TFTP server on your specific distribution.

12.3.2 BOOTP/DHCP Server

Having a DHCP server on your development host simplifies the configuration management for your embedded target. We have already established the reasons why an

---

[2] Do not confuse this with the TFTP client package, which is named tftp-hpa.

Ethernet interface on your target hardware is a good idea. When Linux boots on your target board, it needs to configure the Ethernet interface before the interface will be useful. Moreover, if you are using an NFS root mount configuration on your target board, Linux needs to configure your target's Ethernet interface before the boot process can complete. We covered NFS in detail in Chapter 9, "File Systems."

In general, Linux can use two methods to initialize its Ethernet/IP interface during boot:

- Hard-code the Ethernet interface parameters either on the Linux kernel command line or in the default configuration, such as a static IP configuration.

- Configure the kernel to automatically detect the network settings at boot time.

For obvious reasons, the second choice is more flexible. DHCP or BOOTP is the protocol your target and server use to accomplish the automatic detection of network settings. For details on the DHCP and BOOTP protocols, see the last section of this chapter.

A DHCP server controls the IP address assignments for IP subnets for which it has been configured, and for DHCP or BOOTP clients that have been configured to participate. A DHCP server listens for requests from a DHCP client (such as your target board) and assigns addresses and other pertinent information to the client as part of the boot process. A typical DHCP exchange (see Listing 12-5) can be examined by starting your DHCP server with the -d debug switch and observing the output when a target machine requests configuration.

LISTING 12-5   Typical DHCP Exchange

```
tgt> DHCPDISCOVER from 00:09:5b:65:1d:d5 via eth0
svr> DHCPOFFER on 192.168.0.9 to 00:09:5b:65:1d:d5 via eth0
tgt> DHCPREQUEST for 192.168.0.9 (192.168.0.1) from \
       00:09:5b:65:1d:d5 via eth0
svr> DHCPACK on 192.168.0.9 to 00:09:5b:65:1d:d5 via eth0
```

The sequence starts with the client (target) transmitting a broadcast frame attempting to discover a DHCP server. This is shown by the DHCPDISCOVER message. The server responds (if it has been so configured and enabled) by offering an IP address for the client. This is evidenced by the DHCPOFFER message. The client then responds by testing this IP address locally. The testing includes sending the DHCPREQUEST packet to the DHCP server, as shown. Finally, the server responds by acknowledging the IP address assignment to the client, thus completing the automatic target configuration.

It is interesting to note that a properly configured client will remember the last address it was assigned by a DHCP server. The next time it boots, it will skip the DHCP-DISCOVER stage and proceed directly to the DHCPREQUEST stage, assuming that it can reuse the same IP address that the server previously assigned. A booting Linux kernel does not have this capability and emits the same sequence every time it boots.

Configuring your host's DHCP server is not difficult. As usual, our advice is to consult the documentation that came with your desktop Linux distribution. On a Red Hat or Fedora distribution, the configuration entry for a single target might look like Listing 12-6.

LISTING 12-6   Sample DHCP Server Configuration

```
# Example DHCP Server configuration
allow bootp;

subnet 192.168.1.0 netmask 255.255.255.0 {
 default-lease-time 1209600;      # two weeks
  option routers 192.168.1.1;
  option domain-name-servers 1.2.3.4;
  group {
    host pdna1 {
      hardware ethernet 00:30:bd:2a:26:1f;
      fixed-address 192.168.1.68;
      filename "uImage-pdna";
      option root-path "/home/chris/sandbox/pdna-target";
    }
  }
}
```

This is a simple example, meant only to show the kind of information you can pass to your target system. A one-to-one mapping of the target MAC address to its assigned IP address is defined by this host definition. In addition to its fixed IP address, you can pass other information to your target. In this example, the default router and DNS server addresses are passed to your target, along with the filename of a file of your choice, and a root path for your kernel to mount an NFS root file system from. The filename might be used by your bootloader to load a kernel image from your TFTP server. You can also configure your DHCP server to hand out IP addresses from a predefined range, but it is very convenient to use a fixed address such as that shown in Listing 12-6.

You must first enable the DHCP server on your Linux development workstation. This is typically done through your main menu or at the command line. Consult the documentation for your Linux distribution for details suitable for your environment. For example, to enable the DHCP server on a Fedora Core Linux distribution, simply type the following command from a root command prompt:

```
$ /etc/init.d/dhcpd start
```

  or

```
$ /etc/init.d/dhcpd restart
```

You must do this each time you start your development workstation, unless you configure it to start automatically. Consult the documentation associated with your distribution for instructions on how to do this. You will usually find a reference to enabling services or something similar. In this example, dhcpd is considered a system *service*.

Many nuances are involved with installing a DHCP server, so unless your server is on a private network, it is advisable to check with your system administrator before going live with your own. If you coexist with a corporate LAN, it is very possible that you will interfere with its own DHCP service.

12.3.3   NFS Server

Using an NFS root mount for your target board is a very powerful development tool. Here are some of the advantages of this configuration for development:

- Your root file system is not size-restricted by your board's own limited resources, such as Flash memory.
- Changes made to your application files during development are immediately available to your target system.
- You can debug and boot your kernel before developing and debugging your root file system.

The steps for setting up an NFS server vary depending on which desktop Linux distribution you are using. As with the other services described in this chapter, you must consult the documentation for your Linux distribution for the details appropriate to your configuration. The NFS service must be started from either your startup scripts, a graphical menu, or the command line. For example, the command to start NFS services from a root command prompt for a Fedora Core Linux desktop is as follows:

```
$ /etc/init.d/nfs start
```

  or

```
$ /etc/init.d/nfs restart
```

Note that on later Ubuntu and other distributions this command has been changed to `/etc/init.d/nfs-kernel-server`.

You must do this each time you start your desktop Linux workstation. (This and other services can be started automatically on booting. Consult the documentation for your desktop Linux distribution.) In addition to enabling the service, your kernel must be compiled with support for NFS. Although DHCP and TFTP are both user space utilities, NFS requires kernel support. This is true on both your development workstation and your target board. Figure 12-2 shows the configuration options for NFS in the kernel. Notice that there are configuration options for both NFS server and client support. Note also the option "Root file system on NFS." Your target kernel must have this option configured for NFS root mount operation.

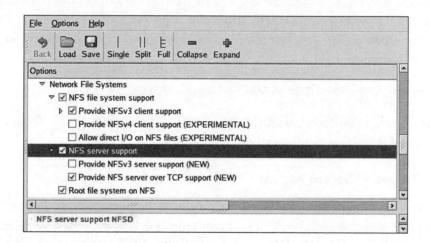

FIGURE 12-2 NFS kernel configuration

The NFS server gets its instructions from an exports file located on your development workstation. It is commonly found in `/etc/exports`. Listing 12-7 is an example of a simple exports entry.

LISTING 12-7 Simple NFS *exports* File

```
$ cat /etc/exports
# /etc/exports
/home/chris/sandbox/coyote-target \ *(rw,sync,no_root_squash,no_all_squash,no_sub-
tree_check)
/home/chris/sandbox/pdna-target \ *(rw,sync,no_root_squash,no_all_squash,no_sub-
tree_check)
/home/chris/workspace \ *(rw,sync,no_root_squash,no_all_squash,no_subtree_check)
```

These entries allow a client to remotely mount any of the three directories shown. The attributes following the directory specification instruct the NFS server to allow connections from any IP address (*) and to mount the respective directories with the given attributes (read/write with `no_root_squash`). The latter attribute enables a client with root privileges to exercise those privileges on the given directory. It is usually required when working with embedded systems because they often have only root accounts.

The `no_all_squash` attribute ensures that the uid and gid of an incoming NFS request are honored, instead of being mapped to a default anonymous account. The `no_subtree_check` attribute disables subtree checking on your server. This can improve performance and reliability in some circumstances. Consult your NFS server documentation and the man page describing the exports file for more details.

You can test your NFS configuration right from your workstation. Assuming that you have NFS services enabled (which requires that both the NFS server and client components are enabled), you can mount a local NFS export as you would mount any other file system:

```
# mount -t nfs localhost:/home/chris/workspace /mnt/remote
```

If this command succeeds and the files in `.../workspace` are available on `/mnt/remote`, your NFS server configuration is working.

12.3.4 Target NFS Root Mount

Mounting your target through NFS root mount is not difficult, and, as mentioned elsewhere, it is a very useful development configuration. However, a set of details must be correct before it will work. The steps required are as follows:

1. Configure your NFS server, and export a proper target file system for your architecture.
2. Configure your target kernel with NFS client services and root file system on NFS.
3. Enable kernel-level autoconfiguration of your target's Ethernet interface.
4. Provide your target Ethernet IP configuration using the kernel command line or static kernel configuration option.
5. Provide a kernel command line enabled for NFS.

We presented the kernel configuration in Figure 12-2 when we explained the NFS server configuration. You must make sure that your target kernel configuration has NFS client services enabled, and, in particular, you must enable the option for Root file system on NFS. Specifically, make sure that your kernel has CONFIG_NFS_FS=y and CONFIG_ROOT_NFS=y. Obviously, you cannot configure NFS as loadable modules if you intend to boot via NFS root mount.

Kernel-level autoconfiguration is a TCP/IP configuration option found under the Networking tab in the kernel configuration utility. Enable CONFIG_IP_PNP on your target kernel. When this is selected, you are presented with several options for automatic configuration. Select either BOOTP or DHCP, as described earlier. Figure 12-3 illustrates the kernel configuration for kernel-level autoconfiguration.

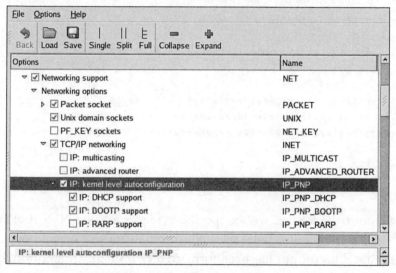

FIGURE 12-3   Kernel-level autoconfiguration

When your server and target kernel are configured, you need to provide your target Ethernet configuration using one of the methods described earlier. If your bootloader supports a kernel command line, that is the easiest method. Here is what a kernel command line to support NFS root mount might look like:

```
console=ttyS0,115200 root=/dev/nfs rw ip=dhcp \
    nfsroot=192.168.1.9:/home/chris/sandbox/pdna-target
```

12.3.5   U-Boot NFS Root Mount Example

U-Boot is a good example of a bootloader that supports a configurable kernel command line. Using U-Boot's nonvolatile environment feature, we can store our kernel command line in a parameter specially named for this purpose. To enable the NFS command line in U-Boot, we do the following (all on one line in our serial terminal):

```
setenv bootargs console=ttyS0,115200 root=/dev/nfs rw \
    ip=dhcp nfsroot=192.168.1.9:/home/chris/sandbox/pdna-target
```

Then we load a kernel using our TFTP server. Listing 12-8 shows what this might look like on a Power Architecture embedded target.

LISTING 12-8   Loading a Kernel Using the TFTP Server

```
=> tftpboot 200000 uImage-pdna        <<< Entered at U-Boot prompt
Using FEC ETHERNET device
TFTP from server 192.168.1.9; our IP address is 192.168.1.68
Filename 'uImage-pdna'.
Load address: 0x200000
Loading: #################################################
         #################################################
         ######################################
done
Bytes transferred = 911984 (dea70 hex)
=>
```

When we boot the kernel, we see specific evidence of our NFS root mount configuration. Listing 12-9 reproduces selected output from the kernel boot messages to demonstrate this. This output has been formatted (with many lines omitted and white space added) for readability.

LISTING 12-9   Booting with NFS Root Mount

```
Uncompressing Kernel Image ... OK
Linux version 2.6.14 (chris@pluto) (gcc version 3.3.3
(DENX ELDK 3.1.1 3.3.3-10)) #1 Mon Jan 2 11:58:48 EST 2006
.

.
Kernel command line: console=ttyS0,115200 root=/dev/nfs rw
nfsroot=192.168.1.9:/home/chris/sandbox/pdna-target ip=dhcp
.

.
```

LISTING 12-9   Continued

```
Sending DHCP requests ... OK
IP-Config: Got DHCP answer from 192.168.1.9, my address is 192.168.1.68
IP-Config: Complete:
     device=eth0, addr=192.168.1.68, mask=255.255.255.0,
     gw=255.255.255.255, host=192.168.1.68, domain=,
     nis-domain=(none), bootserver=192.168.1.9,
     rootserver=192.168.1.9,
     rootpath=/home/chris/sandbox/pdna-target
.
.
Looking up port of RPC 100003/2 on 192.168.1.9
Looking up port of RPC 100005/1 on 192.168.1.9
VFS: Mounted root (nfs filesystem).
.
.
.


BusyBox v0.60.5 (2005.06.07-07:03+0000) Built-in shell (msh)
Enter 'help' for a list of built-in commands.


#
```

In Listing 12-9, first we see the kernel banner, followed by the kernel command line. We specified four items in this kernel command line:

- Console device (/dev/console)
- Root device (/dev/nfs)
- NFS root path (/home/chris/sandbox/pdna-target)
- IP kernel-level autoconfiguration method (dhcp)

Shortly thereafter, we see the kernel attempting kernel-level autoconfiguration via DHCP. This begins with the "Sending DHCP requests" console message. When the server responds and the DHCP exchange completes, the kernel displays the detected configuration in the following lines. You can see from this listing that the DHCP server has assigned the target the IP address 192.168.1.68. Compare the settings obtained via autoconfiguration with the DHCP server configuration in Listing 12-6. You can use a similar server configuration to assign the IP address and NFS root path to your target.

When the kernel has completed the IP autoconfiguration, it can mount the root file system using the supplied parameters. You can see this from the three lines ending with the VFS (virtual file subsystem) message announcing that it has mounted the NFS root file system. After the NFS root file system has been mounted, initialization completes as described in Chapter 5, "Kernel Initialization."

It is also possible to pass target IP settings to the kernel in a static fashion instead of having the kernel obtain IP settings from a DHCP or BOOTP server. IP settings can be passed using the kernel command line directly. In this case, the kernel command line might look similar to this:

```
console=console=ttyS0,115200 \
    ip=192.168.1.68:192.168.1.9::255.255.255.0:pdna:eth0:off \
    root=/dev/nfs rw nfsroot=192.168.1.9:/home/chris/pdna-target
```

12.4   Summary

This chapter provided the background to build and configure a development workstation suitable for embedded development work. Several key servers were introduced, along with information on how to install and configure them. We concluded this chapter by looking at one of the most powerful tools available to the embedded developer: the NFS server.

- Many features of a development environment greatly facilitate efficiency for embedded cross-development. Most of these fall under the category of tools and utilities. We cover this aspect in detail in the next chapter, where we describe development tools.

- A properly configured development host is a critical asset for the embedded developer.

- Toolchains employed for cross-development must be properly configured to match your host system's target Linux environment.

- Your development host must have target components installed that your toolchain and binary utilities can reference. These components include target header files, libraries, target binaries, and their associated configuration files. In short, you need to assemble or obtain an embedded Linux distribution.

- Configuring target servers such as TFTP, DHCP, and NFS will greatly increase your productivity as an embedded Linux developer. This chapter introduced configuration examples for each.

12.4.1 Suggestions for Additional Reading

GCC online documentation
http://gcc.gnu.org/onlinedocs/

Building and testing gcc/glibc cross toolchains
http://kegel.com/crosstool/

"The TFTP Protocol, Version 2"
RFC 1350
www.ietf.org/rfc/rfc1350.txt?number=1350

"Bootstrap Protocol (BOOTP)"
RFC 951
www.ietf.org/rfc/rfc0951.txt?number=951

"Dynamic Host Configuration Protocol"
RFC 2131
www.ietf.org/rfc/rfc2131.txt?number=2131

## Chapter 13

Development Tools

In This Chapter

- 13.1   GNU Debugger (GDB)   326
- 13.2   Data Display Debugger   333
- 13.3   `cbrowser/cscope`   335
- 13.4   Tracing and Profiling Tools   337
- 13.5   Binary Utilities   355
- 13.6   Miscellaneous Binary Utilities   361
- 13.7   Summary   364

A typical embedded Linux development environment includes many useful tools. Some are complex and require a great deal of proficiency to master. Others are simple and have been all but ignored by developers of embedded systems. Some tools might require customization for a particular environment. Many run "right out of the box" and provide the developer with useful information without much effort. This chapter presents a cross-section of the most important (and frequently neglected) tools available to the embedded Linux engineer.

It is impossible to provide complete details on the tools and utilities presented in this chapter. That would take an entire book by itself! Rather than provide a complete reference, our goal is to introduce the basic usage of each one. You are encouraged to pursue additional study on these and other important development tools. The man page (or other documentation) for each tool is a great place to start.

The GNU Debugger (GDB) is introduced first, followed by a brief look at the Data Display Debugger, a graphical front end for GDB. Next we cover a series of utilities designed to give the developer a look at the behavior of programs and the system as a whole. These include *strace*, *ltrace*, *top*, and *ps*, often overlooked by inexperienced Linux developers. We then present some crash dump and memory-analysis tools. The chapter concludes by introducing some of the more useful binary utilities.

13.1   GNU Debugger (GDB)

If you spend much time developing Linux applications, you will undoubtedly spend many hours getting to know the GNU Debugger. GDB is arguably the most important tool in the developer's toolbox. It has a long history, and its capabilities have blossomed to include low-level hardware-specific debugging support for a wide variety of architectures and microprocessors. It should be noted that the GDB user manual is nearly as large as this book. Our intention here is to introduce GDB to get you started. You are encouraged to study the user manual referenced in the last section.

Because this is a book about embedded Linux development, we use a version of GDB that has been compiled as a cross-debugger. That is, the debugger itself runs on your development host, but it understands only binary executables in the architecture for which it was configured at compile time. The next few examples use GDB compiled for a Linux development host and an XScale (ARM) target processor. Although we use the short name gdb, we present examples based on the XScale-enabled cross-gdb from the Monta Vista embedded Linux distribution for ARM XScale. The binary is called xscale_be-gdb. It is still GDB, but it is configured for a cross-development environment.

The GDB debugger is a complex program that offers many configuration options during the build process. It is not our intention to provide guidance on building gdb; that has been covered in other literature. For the purposes of this chapter, we assume that you have obtained a working GDB configured for the architecture and host development environment you will be using.

13.1.1 Debugging a Core Dump

One of the most common reasons to drag GDB out of the toolbox is to evaluate a core dump. This process is quick and easy and often leads to immediate identification of the offending code. A core dump is a file generated by the kernel when an application program generates a fault, such as accessing a memory location it does not own. Many conditions can trigger a core dump,[1] but SIGSEGV (segmentation fault) is by far the most common. A SIGSEGV is a Linux kernel signal that is generated on illegal memory accesses by a user process. When this signal is generated, the kernel terminates the process. The kernel then dumps a core image if it is so enabled.

To enable generation of a core dump, your process must have the authority to enable a core dump. This is achieved by setting the process's resource limits using the setrlimit() C function call, or from a BASH or BusyBox shell command prompt using ulimit. It is not uncommon to find the following line in the initialization scripts of an embedded system to enable the generation of core dumps on process errors:

```
ulimit -c unlimited
```

---

[1] See SIG_KERNEL_COREDUMP_MASK in .../include/linux/signal.h for a definition of which signals generate a core dump.

This BASH built-in command is used to set the size limit of a core dump. In the preceding instance, the size is set to `unlimited`. You can issue this command from the shell to show the current setting:

```
$ ulimit
unlimited
```

When an application program generates a segmentation fault (for example, by writing to a memory address outside its permissible range), Linux terminates the process and generates a core dump, if so enabled. The core dump is a snapshot of the running process at the time the segmentation fault occurred.

It helps to have debugging symbols enabled in your binary. GDB produces much more useful output with debugging symbols (`gcc -g`) enabled during the build. However, it is still possible to determine the sequence of events leading to the segmentation fault, even if the binary was compiled without debugging symbols. You might need to do a bit more investigative work without the aid of debugging symbols. In this case, you must manually correlate virtual addresses to locations within your program.

Listing 13-1 shows the results of a core dump analysis session using GDB. The output has been reformatted slightly to fit the page. We have used some demonstration software to intentionally produce a segmentation fault. Here is the output of the process (called webs) that generated the segmentation fault:

```
root@coyote:# ./webs
Segmentation fault (core dumped)
```

LISTING 13-1   Core Dump Analysis Using GDB

```
$ xscale_be-gdb webs core
GNU gdb 6.3 (MontaVista 6.3-20.0.22.0501131 2005-07-23)
Copyright 2004 Free Software Foundation, Inc.
GDB is free software, covered by the GNU General Public
License, and you are welcome to change it and/or distribute copies of it under
certain conditions.
Type "show copying" to see the conditions.
There is absolutely no warranty for GDB.  Type "show warranty" for details.
This GDB was configured as "--host=i686-pc-linux-gnu
-target=armv5teb-montavista-linuxeabi"...

Core was generated by './webs'.
Program terminated with signal 11, Segmentation fault.
```

LISTING 13-1   Continued

```
Reading symbols from /opt/montavista/pro/.../libc.so.6...done.
Loaded symbols for /opt/montavista/pro/.../libc.so.6
Reading symbols from /opt/montavista/pro/.../ld-linux.so.3...done.
Loaded symbols for /opt/montavista/pro/.../ld-linux.so.3
#0  0x00012ac4 in ClearBlock (RealBigBlockPtr=0x0, l=100000000) at led.c:43
43                    *ptr = 0;

(gdb) l
38
39     static int ClearBlock(char * BlockPtr, int l)
40     {
41         char * ptr;
42         for (ptr = BlockPtr; (ptr - BlockPtr) < l; ptr++)
43             *ptr = 0;
44         return 0;
45     }
46     static int InitBlock(char * ptr, int n)
47     {
(gdb) p ptr
$1 = 0x0
(gdb)
```

13.1.2   Invoking GDB

The first line of Listing 13-1 shows how GDB was invoked from the command line. Because we are doing cross-debugging, we need the cross-version of GDB that has been compiled for our host and target system. We invoke our version of cross-gdb as shown and pass xscale_be-gdb the name of the binary followed by the name of the core dump file—in this case, simply core. After GDB prints several banner lines describing its configuration and other information, it displays the reason for the termination: signal 11, which indicates a segmentation fault.[2]

Several lines follow as GDB loads the binary, the libraries it depends on, and the core file. The last line printed upon GDB startup is the current location of the program when the fault occurred. The line preceded by the #0 string indicates the stack frame (stack frame zero in a function called ClearBlock() at virtual address 0x00012ac4).

---

[2] Signals and their associated numbers are defined in .../arch/<arch>/include/asm/signal.h in your Linux kernel source tree.

The following line starting with 43 is the line number of the offending source line from a file called led.c. From there, GDB displays its command prompt and waits for input.

To provide some context, we enter the gdb list command, using its abbreviated form, l. GDB recognizes command abbreviations where no ambiguity exists. Here the program error begins to present itself. Here is the offending line, according to GDB's analysis of the core dump:

```
43              *ptr = 0;
```

Next we issue the gdb print command on the ptr variable, abbreviated as p. As you can see from Listing 13-1, the value of the pointer ptr is 0. So we conclude that the reason for the segmentation fault is the classic null pointer dereference, a common programming error in many programming languages. From here, we can elect to use the backtrace command to see the call chain leading to this error, which might take us back to the source of the error. Listing 13-2 displays these results.

LISTING 13-2   Backtrace Command

```
(gdb) bt
#0   0x00012ac4 in ClearBlock (RealBigBlockPtr=0x0, l=100000000) at led.c:43
#1   0x00012b08 in InitBlock (ptr=0x0, n=100000000) at led.c:48
#2   0x00012b50 in ErrorInHandler (wp=0x325c8, urlPrefix=0x2f648 "/Error",
     webDir=0x2f660 "", arg=0, url=0x34f30 "/Error", path=0x34d68 "/Error",
     query=0x321d8 "") at led.c:61
#3   0x000126cc in websUrlHandlerRequest (wp=0x325c8) at handler.c:273
#4   0x0001f518 in websGetInput (wp=0x325c8, ptext=0xbefffc40,
     pnbytes=0xbefffc38) at webs.c:664
#5   0x0001ede0 in websReadEvent (wp=0x325c8) at webs.c:362
#6   0x0001ed34 in websSocketEvent (sid=1, mask=2, iwp=206280) at webs.c:319
#7   0x00019740 in socketDoEvent (sp=0x34fc8) at sockGen.c:903
#8   0x00019598 in socketProcess (sid=1) at sockGen.c:845
#9   0x00012be8 in main (argc=1, argv=0xbefffe14) at main.c:99
(gdb)
```

The backtrace displays the call chain all the way back to main(), the start of the user's program. A stack frame number precedes each line of the backtrace. You can switch to any given stack frame using the gdb frame command. Listing 13-3 is an example of this. Here we switch to stack frame 2 and display the source code in that frame. As in the previous examples, the lines preceded by the (gdb) command prompt are the commands we issue to GDB, and the other lines are the GDB output.

LISTING 13-3   Moving Around Stack Frames in GDB

```
(gdb) frame 2
#2  0x00012b50 in ErrorInHandler (wp=0x325c8, urlPrefix=0x2f648 "/Error",
    webDir=0x2f660 "", arg=0, url=0x34f30 "/Error", path=0x34d68 "/Error",
    query=0x321d8 "") at led.c:61
61              return InitBlock(p, siz);
(gdb) l
56
57              siz = 10000 * sizeof(BigBlock);
58
59              p = malloc(siz);
60      /*  if (p) */
61              return InitBlock(p, siz);
62      /*  else return (0);  */
63      }
64
65
(gdb)
```

As you can see, with a little help from the source code available using the list command, it would be a simple process to trace the code back to the source of the errant null pointer. In fact, notice the source of the segmentation fault we have produced for this example. In Listing 13-3, we see that the check of the return value in the call to malloc() has been commented out. In this example, the malloc() call failed, leading to the operation on a null pointer two frames later in the call chain. Although this example is both contrived and trivial, many crashes of this type are remarkably easy to track down using a similar method with GDB and core dumps. You can also see the null pointer by looking at the parameter values in the function call. This often leads you directly to the stack frame where the null pointer originated.

13.1.3   Debug Session in GDB

We conclude this introduction to GDB by showing a typical debug session. In the previous demonstration of a program crash, we could have elected to step through the code to narrow down the cause of the failure. Of course, if you get a core dump, you should always start there. However, in other situations, you might want to set breakpoints and step through running code. Listing 13-4 details how we start GDB in preparation for a debug session. Note that the program must have been compiled with the debug flag enabled in the gcc command line for GDB to be useful in this context.

Refer to Figure 12-1 in Chapter 12, "Embedded Development Environment"; this is a cross-debug session with GDB running on your development host, debugging a program running on your target. We cover the complete details of remote application debugging in Chapter 15, "Debugging Embedded Linux Applications."

LISTING 13-4   Initiating a GDB Debug Session

```
$ xscale_be-gdb -silent webs

(gdb) target remote 192.168.1.21:2001
0x40000790 in ?? ()
(gdb) b main
Breakpoint 1 at 0x12b74: file main.c, line 78.
(gdb) c
Continuing.

Breakpoint 1, main (argc=1, argv=0xbefffe04) at main.c:78
78              bopen(NULL, (60 * 1024), B_USE_MALLOC);
(gdb) b ErrorInHandler
Breakpoint 2 at 0x12b30: file led.c, line 57.
(gdb) c
Continuing.

Breakpoint 2, ErrorInHandler (wp=0x311a0, urlPrefix=0x2f648 "/Error",
    webDir=0x2f660 "", arg=0, url=0x31e88 "/Error", path=0x31918 "/Error",
    query=0x318e8 "") at led.c:57
57              siz = 10000 * sizeof(BigBlock);
(gdb) next
59              p = malloc(siz);
(gdb) next
61              return InitBlock(p, siz);
(gdb) p p
$1 =(unsigned char *) 0x0
(gdb) p siz
$2 =   100000000
(gdb)
```

Examining this simple debug session, first we connect to our target board using the gdb `target` command. (We cover remote debugging in more detail in Chapter 15.) When we are connected to our target hardware, we set a breakpoint at `main()` using the gdb break (abbreviated b) command. Then we issue the gdb `continue` (abbreviated c) command to resume program execution. If we had any program arguments, we could have issued them on the command line when we invoked GDB.

We hit the breakpoint set at `main()`, and then set another one at `ErrorInHandler()`, followed by the continue command, again abbreviated. When this new breakpoint is hit, we begin to step through the code using the `next` command. There we encounter the call to `malloc()`. Following the `malloc()` call, we examine the return value and discover the failure, as indicated by the null return value. Finally, we print the value of the parameter in the `malloc()` call and see that a very large memory region (100 million bytes) is being requested, which fails.

Although trivial, the GDB examples in this section should enable the newcomer to become immediately productive with GDB. Few people have really mastered GDB—it is complex and has many capabilities. Section 13.2, "Data Display Debugger," introduces a graphical front end to GDB that can ease the transition if you're unfamiliar with GDB.

One final note about GDB: No doubt you have noticed the many banner lines GDB displays on the console when it is first invoked, as in Listing 13-1. In these examples, as stated earlier, we used a cross-gdb from the Monta Vista embedded Linux distribution. The banner lines contain a vital piece of information that the embedded developer must be aware of: GDB's host and target specifications. In Listing 13-1, we saw the following output when GDB was invoked:

```
This GDB was configured as "--host=i686-pc-linux-gnu -
target=armv5teb-montavista-linuxeabi"
```

In this instance, we invoked a version of GDB that was compiled to execute from a Linux PC—specifically, an i686 running the GNU/Linux operating system. Equally critical, this instance of GDB was compiled to debug ARM binary code generated from the armv5teb big endian toolchain.

One of the most common mistakes made by newcomers to embedded development is to use the wrong GDB while trying to debug target executables. If something isn't working right, you should immediately check your GDB configuration to make sure that it makes sense for your environment. You cannot use your native GDB to debug target code!

13.2 Data Display Debugger

The Data Display Debugger (DDD), shown in Figure 13-1, is a graphical front end to GDB and other command-line debuggers. DDD has many advanced features beyond simply viewing source code and stepping through a debug session.

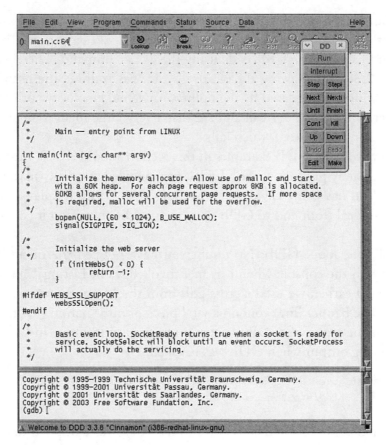

FIGURE 13-1   Data Display Debugger

DDD is invoked as follows:

```
$ ddd --debugger xscale_be-gdb webs
```

Without the `--debugger` flag, DDD would attempt to invoke the native GDB on your development host. This is not what you want if you are planning to debug an application on your target system. The second argument on the DDD command line is the program you will be debugging. See the DDD man page for additional details.

Using the command tool as shown in Figure 13-1, you can step through your program. You can set breakpoints either graphically or via the GDB console window at the bottom of the DDD screen. For target debugging, you must first connect your debugger to the target system as we did in Listing 13-4, using the `target` command. This command is issued in the GDB window of the DDD main screen.

When you are connected to the target, you can execute commands similar to the sequence just shown to isolate the program failure. Figure 13-2 shows the DDD display during the later phase of this debugging session.

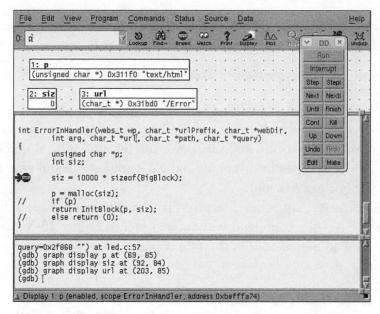

FIGURE 13-2   Debug session in DDD

Notice that in Figure 13-2, we have initiated the display of some important program variables that can help us narrow the cause of the segmentation fault. We can watch these variables as we step through the program using the command tool shown in the figure.

DDD is a powerful graphical front end for GDB. It is relatively easy to use and widely supported for many development hosts. Consult the last section of this chapter for a link to the GNU DDD documentation.

It should be noted that over the course of time, Eclipse has eclipsed (pun intended!) DDD as the debugger of choice. Space does not permit detailed coverage of Eclipse. References to Eclipse are included at the end of this chapter in case you would like more information.

13.3 cbrowser/cscope

We introduce cbrowser because support for this handy tool has found its way into the Linux kernel source tree. cbrowser is a simple source-code browsing tool that makes it easy to navigate around a large source tree following symbols. Some distributions, such as Ubuntu, have `cbrowser` in their repository, but others, such as the recent Fedora, do not. On Ubuntu, simply type the following:

```
$ sudo apt-get install cbrowser
```

The Linux kernel makefile supports building the database that `cbrowser` uses. Here is a sample invocation from a recent Linux kernel snapshot:

```
$ make ARCH=powerpc CROSS_COMPILE=ppc_82xx- cscope
```

This produces the `cscope` symbol database that `cbrowser` uses. `cscope` is the engine; `cbrowser` is the graphical user interface. You can use `cscope` on its own if you want. It is command-line-driven and very powerful, but not quite as quick or easy for navigating a large source tree in this point-and-click era. If `vi` is still your favorite editor, `cscope` might be just for you!

To invoke `cbrowser`, enter the directory that contains your `cscope` database, and simply type the `cbrowser` command without arguments. Figure 13-3 shows a sample session. You can read more about both of these useful tools in the references listed in the last section.

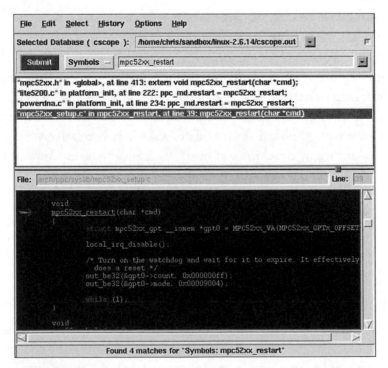

FIGURE 13-3   cbrowser in action

13.4 Tracing and Profiling Tools

Many useful tools can provide you with various views of the system. Some tools offer a high-level perspective. You can discover what processes are running on your system and which processes are consuming the most CPU bandwidth. Other tools can provide detailed analysis, such as where memory is being allocated or, even more useful, where it is being leaked. The next few sections introduce the most important tools and utilities in this category. We have space for only a cursory introduction to these tools; references are provided where appropriate for additional details.

13.4.1 `strace`

`strace` is a useful trace utility found in virtually all Linux distributions. `strace` captures and displays information for every kernel system call executed by a Linux application program. `strace` is especially handy because it can be run on programs for which no source code is available. It is not necessary to compile the program with debug symbols as it is with GDB. Furthermore, `strace` can be a very insightful educational tool. As the man page states, "Students, hackers, and the overly-curious will find that a great deal can be learned about a system and its system calls by tracing even ordinary programs."

While preparing the sample software for the GDB section earlier in this chapter, I decided to use a software project unfamiliar to me—an early version of the GoAhead embedded web server. The first attempt at compiling and linking the project led to an interesting example for `strace`. Starting the application from the command line silently returned control to the console. No error messages were produced, and a look into the system logs also produced no clues. It simply would not run.

`strace` quickly identified the problem. Listing 13-5 shows the output from invoking `strace` on this application. Many lines from this output have been deleted due to space considerations. The unedited output is over one hundred lines long.

LISTING 13-5 *strace* Output: GoAhead Web Demo

```
01 root@coyote:$ strace ./websdemo
02 execve("./websdemo", ["./websdemo"], [/* 14 vars */]) = 0
03 uname({sys="Linux", node="coyote", ...}) = 0
04 brk(0)                            = 0x10031050
05 open("/etc/ld.so.preload", O_RDONLY) = -1 ENOENT (No such file or
   directory)
06 open("/etc/ld.so.cache", O_RDONLY)  = -1 ENOENT (No such file or
   directory)
```

LISTING 13-5   Continued

```
07 open("/lib/libc.so.6", O_RDONLY)          = 3
08 read(3, "\177ELF\1\2\1\0\0\0\0\0\0\0\0\0\3\0\24\0\0\0\1\0\1\322"..., 1024) =
1024
09 fstat64(0x3, 0x7fffefc8)                  = 0
10 mmap(0xfe9f000, 1379388, PROT_READ|PROT_EXEC, MAP_PRIVATE, 3, 0) = 0xfe9f000
11 mprotect(0xffd8000, 97340, PROT_NONE)     = 0
12 mmap(0xffdf000, 61440, PROT_READ|PROT_WRITE|PROT_EXEC,MAP_PRIVATE|MAP_FIXED, 3,
0x130000) = 0xffdf000
13 mmap(0xffee000, 7228, PROT_READ|PROT_WRITE|PROT_EXEC,
MAP_PRIVATE|MAP_FIXED| MAP_ANONYMOUS, -1, 0) = 0xffee000
14 close(3)                                  = 0
15 brk(0)                                    = 0x10031050
16 brk(0x10032050)                           = 0x10032050
17 brk(0x10033000)                           = 0x10033000
18 brk(0x10041000)                           = 0x10041000
19 rt_sigaction(SIGPIPE, {SIG_IGN}, {SIG_DFL}, 8) = 0
20 stat("./umconfig.txt", 0x7ffff9b8)        = -1 ENOENT (No such file or
directory)
21 uname({sys="Linux", node="coyote", ...}) = 0
22 gettimeofday({3301, 178955}, NULL)        = 0
23 getpid()                                  = 156
24 open("/etc/resolv.conf", O_RDONLY)        = 3
25 fstat64(0x3, 0x7fffd7f8)                  = 0
26 mmap(NULL, 4096, PROT_READ|PROT_WRITE, MAP_PRIVATE|MAP_ANONYMOUS, -1, 0) =
0x30017000
27 read(3, "#\n# resolv.conf  This file is th"..., 4096) = 83
28 read(3, "", 4096)                         = 0
29 close(3)                                  = 0
...   <<< Lines 30-81 removed for brevity
82 socket(PF_INET, SOCK_DGRAM, IPPROTO_IP) = 3
83 connect(3, {sa_family=AF_INET, sin_port=htons(53),
sin_addr=inet_addr("0.0.0.0")}, 28) = 0
84 send(3, "\267s\1\0\0\1\0\0\0\0\0\0\6coyotea\0\0\1\0\1", 24, 0) = 24
85 gettimeofday({3301, 549664}, NULL)        = 0
86 poll([{fd=3, events=POLLIN, revents=POLLERR}], 1, 5000) = 1
87 ioctl(3, 0x4004667f, 0x7fffe6a8)          = 0
88 recvfrom(3, 0x7fffff1f0, 1024, 0, 0x7fffe668, 0x7fffe6ac) = -1
ECONNREFUSED (Connection refused)
89 close(3)                                  = 0
90 socket(PF_INET, SOCK_DGRAM, IPPROTO_IP) = 3
91 connect(3, {sa_family=AF_INET, sin_port=htons(53),
sin_addr=inet_addr("0.0.0.0")}, 28) = 0
```

LISTING 13-5   Continued

```
92 send(3, "\267s\1\0\0\1\0\0\0\0\0\0\6coyote\0\0\1\0\1", 24, 0) = 24
93 gettimeofday({3301, 552839}, NULL)      = 0
494 poll([{fd=3, events=POLLIN, revents=POLLERR}], 1, 5000) = 1
95 ioctl(3, 0x4004667f, 0x7fffe6a8)        = 0
96 recvfrom(3, 0x7ffff1f0, 1024, 0, 0x7fffe668, 0x7fffe6ac) = -1
ECONNREFUSED (Connection refused)
97 close(3)                                = 0
98 exit(-1)                                = ?
99 root@coyote:/home/websdemo#
```

Line numbers have been added to the output produced by strace to make this listing more readable. The application is spawned under strace on line 01. In its simplest form, simply put the strace command directly in front of the name of the program you want to examine. This is how the output in Listing 13-5 was produced.

Each line of this trace represents a discrete kernel system call that the websdemo application makes into the kernel. We don't need to analyze and understand each line of the trace, although it is quite instructive to do so. We are looking for any anomalies that might help pinpoint why the program won't run. In the first several lines, the environment in which the program will execute is prepared. We see several open() system calls to /etc/ld.so.*, which is the Linux dynamic linker-loader (ld.so) doing its job. In fact, line 06 is a clue that this sample embedded board had not been properly configured. A linker cache file should be produced by running ldconfig. (The linker cache substantially speeds up searching for shared library references.) This was subsequently resolved by running ldconfig on the target.[3]

Down through line 19 is more basic housekeeping, mostly by the loader and libc initializing. Notice in line 20 that the program looks for a configuration file but does not find one. That could be an important issue when we get the software running. Starting with line 24, the program begins to set up and configure the appropriate networking resources it needs. Lines 24 through 29 open and read a Linux system file containing instructions for the DNS service to resolve hostnames. Local network configuration activity continues through line 81. Most of this activity consists of network setup and configuration necessary to build the networking infrastructure for the program itself. This portion of the listing has been removed for brevity and clarity.

---

[3] See man ldconfig for details on creating a linker cache for your target system.

Notice especially the network activity starting on line 82. Here the program tries to establish a TCP/IP connection to an IP address of all 0s. Line 82 is reproduced here for convenience:

```
socket(PF_INET, SOCK_DGRAM, IPPROTO_IP) = 3
```

A couple points about Listing 13-5 are worth noting. We might not know all the details of every system call, but we can get a general idea of what is happening. The `socket()` system call is similar to a file system `open()` call. The return value, indicated by the = sign in this case, represents a Linux file descriptor. Knowing this, we can associate the activity from line 82 through the `close()` system call in line 89 with file descriptor 3.

We are interested in this group of related system calls because we see an error message in line 88: `Connection refused`. At this point, we still don't know why the program won't run, but this appears abnormal. Let's investigate. Line 82, the system call to `socket()`, establishes an endpoint for IP communication. Line 83 is curious, because it tries to establish a connection to a remote endpoint (socket) containing an IP address of all 0s. We don't have to be network experts to suspect that this might be causing trouble.[4] Line 83 provides another important clue: The port parameter is set to 53. A quick Internet search for TCP/IP port numbers reveals that port 53 is the Domain Name Service (DNS).

Line 84 provides yet another clue. Our board has a hostname of coyote. This can be seen as part of the command prompt in line 01 of Listing 13-5. It appears that this activity is a DNS lookup for our board's hostname, which is failing. As an experiment, we add an entry to our target system's `/etc/hosts`[5] file to associate our locally defined hostname with the board's locally assigned IP address, as follows:

```
coyote  192.168.1.21      #The IP address we assigned
```

Voilà. Our program begins to function normally. Although we might not know exactly why this would lead to a program failure (TCP/IP networking experts might), our `strace` output led us to the fact that a DNS lookup for our board name was failing. When we corrected that, the program started happily and began serving web pages. To recap, this was a program for which we had no source code to reference, and it had no symbols compiled into its binary image. Using `strace`, we were able to determine the cause of the program failure and implement a solution.

---

[4] Sometimes an all-0s address is appropriate in this context. However, we are investigating why the program terminated abnormally, so we should consider this suspect.

[5] See `man hosts` for details of this system administration file.

13.4.2   **strace** Variations

The strace utility has many command-line options. One of the more useful is the ability to select a subset of system calls for tracing. For example, if you want to see only the network-related activity of a given process, issue the command as follows:

```
$ strace -e trace=network process_name
```

This produces a trace of all the network-related system calls, such as socket(), connect(), recvfrom(), and send(). This is a powerful way to view the network activity of a given program. Several other subsets are available. For example, you can view only a program's file-related activities, with open(), close(), read(), write(), and so on. Additional subsets include process-related system calls, signal-related system calls, and IPC-related system calls.

It is worth noting that strace can deal with tracing programs that spawn additional processes. Invoking strace with the -f option instructs strace to follow child processes that are created using the fork() system call. The strace command has numerous possibilities. The best way to become proficient with this powerful utility is to use it. Make it a point to seek out and read the latest open source documentation with this and the other tools we present. In this case, man strace on most Linux hosts will produce enough material to keep you experimenting for an afternoon!

One very useful way to employ strace is to use the -c option. This option produces a high-level profiling of your application. Using the -c option, strace accumulates statistics on each system call, how many times it was encountered, how many times errors were returned, and the time spent in each system call. Listing 13-6 is an example of running strace -c on the webs demo from the previous example.

LISTING 13-6   Profiling Using *strace*

```
root@coyote$ strace -c ./webs
% time     seconds  usecs/call     calls    errors syscall
------ ----------- ----------- --------- --------- --------
 29.80    0.034262         189       181           send
 18.46    0.021226        1011        21        10 open
 14.11    0.016221         130       125           read
 11.87    0.013651         506        27         8 stat64
  5.88    0.006762         193        35           select
  5.28    0.006072          76        80           fcntl64
  3.47    0.003994          65        61           time
  2.79    0.003205        3205         1           execve
```

LISTING 13-6 Continued

1.71	0.001970	90	22	3	recv
1.62	0.001868	85	22		close
1.61	0.001856	169	11		shutdown
1.38	0.001586	144	11		accept
0.41	0.000470	94	5		mmap2
0.26	0.000301	100	3		mprotect
0.24	0.000281	94	3		brk
0.17	0.000194	194	1	1	access
0.13	0.000150	150	1		lseek
0.12	0.000141	47	3		uname
0.11	0.000132	132	1		listen
0.11	0.000128	128	1		socket
0.09	0.000105	53	2		fstat64
0.08	0.000097	97	1		munmap
0.06	0.000064	64	1		getcwd
0.05	0.000063	63	1		bind
0.05	0.000054	54	1		setsockopt
0.04	0.000048	48	1		rt_sigaction
0.04	0.000046	46	1		gettimeofday
0.03	0.000038	38	1		getpid
------	-----------	-----------	---------	---------	-----------
100.00	0.114985		624	22	total

This is a very useful way to get a high-level view of where your application is consuming time and where errors are occurring. Some errors might be a normal part of your application's operation, but others might be consuming time in ways that you did not anticipate. From Listing 13-6, we can see that the syscall with the longest duration was the execve(), which is the call that the shell used to spawn the application. As you can see, it was called only once. Another interesting observation is that the send() system call was the most frequently used syscall. This makes sense, because the application is a small web server.

Bear in mind that, like the other tools we have been discussing here, strace must be compiled for your target architecture. strace is executed on your target board, not your development host. You must use a version that is compatible with your architecture. If you purchase a commercial embedded Linux distribution, you should make sure that this utility is included for your chosen architecture.

13.4.3 `ltrace`

The `ltrace` and `strace` utilities are closely related. The `ltrace` utility does for library calls what `strace` does for system calls. It is invoked in a similar fashion. You precede the program to be traced by the tracer utility, as follows:

```
$ ltrace ./example
```

Listing 13-7 reproduces the output of `ltrace` on a small sample program that executes a handful of standard C library calls.

LISTING 13-7   Sample *ltrace* Output

```
$ ltrace ./example
__libc_start_main(0x8048594, 1, 0xbfffff944, 0x80486b4, 0x80486fc <unfinished ...>
malloc(256)                                = 0x804a008
getenv("HOME")                             = "/home/chris"
strncpy(0x804a008, "/home", 5)             = 0x804a008
fopen("foo.txt", "w")                      = 0x804a110
printf("$HOME = %s\n", "/home/chris"$HOME = /home/chris
)              = 20
fprintf(0x804a110, "$HOME = %s\n", "/home/chris") = 20
fclose(0x804a110)                          = 0
remove("foo.txt")                          = 0
free(0x804a008)                            = <void>
+++ exited (status 0) +++
$
```

For each library call, the name of the call is displayed, along with varying portions of the parameters to the call. Similar to `strace`, the return value of the library call is then displayed. As with `strace`, this tool can be used on programs for which source code is unavailable.

Similar to `strace`, a variety of switches affect the behavior of `ltrace`. You can display the value of the program counter at each library call, which can be helpful in understanding your application's program flow. As with `strace`, you can use `-c` to accumulate and report count, error, and time statistics, making a useful, simple profiling tool. Listing 13-8 displays the results of our simple sample program using the `-c` option.

LISTING 13-8   Profiling Using *ltrace*

```
$ ltrace -c ./example
$HOME = /home/chris
% time     seconds  usecs/call     calls      function
------ ----------- ----------- --------- ----------------
 24.16    0.000231         231         1 printf
 16.53    0.000158         158         1 fclose
 16.00    0.000153         153         1 fopen
 13.70    0.000131         131         1 malloc
 10.67    0.000102         102         1 remove
  9.31    0.000089          89         1 fprintf
  3.35    0.000032          32         1 getenv
  3.14    0.000030          30         1 free
  3.14    0.000030          30         1 strncpy
------ ----------- ----------- --------- ----------------
100.00    0.000956                     9 total
```

The ltrace tool is available only for programs that have been compiled to use dynamically linked shared library objects. This is the usual default, so unless you explicitly specify -static when compiling, you can use ltrace on the resulting binary. Also similar to strace, you must use an ltrace binary that has been compiled for your target architecture. These utilities are run on the target, not the host development system.

13.4.4 ps

With the possible exception of strace and ltrace, no tools are neglected by the embedded systems developer more often than top and ps. Given the myriad options available for each utility, we could easily devote an entire chapter to these useful system-profiling tools. They are almost universally available on your favorite target in embedded Linux distributions.

Both of these utilities make use of the /proc file system, as described in Chapter 9, "File Systems." Much of the information they convey can be learned from the /proc file system if you know what to look for and how to parse the resulting information. These tools present that information in a convenient human-readable form.

The ps utility lists all the running processes on a machine. However, it is quite flexible and can be tailored to provide much useful data on the state of a machine and the processes running on it. For example, ps can display the scheduling policy of each process. This is particularly useful for systems that employ real-time processes.

Without any options, ps displays all processes that have the same user ID as the user who invoked the command, and only those processes associated with the terminal on which the command was issued. This is useful when many jobs have been spawned by that user and terminal.

Passing options to ps can be confusing, because ps supports a wide variety of standards (as in POSIX versus UNIX) and three distinct options styles: BSD, UNIX, and GNU. In general, BSD options are single or multiple letters, with no dash. UNIX options are the familiar dash-letter combinations, and GNU uses long argument formats preceded by double dashes. Refer to the man page for details of your ps implementation.

Everyone who uses ps likely has a favorite invocation. One particularly useful general-purpose invocation is ps aux. This displays every process on the system. Listing 13-9 is an example from a running embedded target board.

LISTING 13-9   Process Listing

```
$ ps aux
USER      PID %CPU %MEM    VSZ   RSS TTY     STAT START   TIME COMMAND
root        1  0.0  0.8   1416   508 ?       S    00:00   0:00 init [3]
root        2  0.0  0.0      0     0 ?       S<   00:00   0:00 [ksoftirqd/0]
root        3  0.0  0.0      0     0 ?       S<   00:00   0:00 [desched/0]
root        4  0.0  0.0      0     0 ?       S<   00:00   0:00 [events/0]
root        5  0.0  0.0      0     0 ?       S<   00:00   0:00 [khelper]
root       10  0.0  0.0      0     0 ?       S<   00:00   0:00 [kthread]
root       21  0.0  0.0      0     0 ?       S<   00:00   0:00 [kblockd/0]
root       62  0.0  0.0      0     0 ?       S    00:00   0:00 [pdflush]
root       63  0.0  0.0      0     0 ?       S    00:00   0:00 [pdflush]
root       65  0.0  0.0      0     0 ?       S<   00:00   0:00 [aio/0]
root       36  0.0  0.0      0     0 ?       S    00:00   0:00 [kapmd]
root       64  0.0  0.0      0     0 ?       S    00:00   0:00 [kswapd0]
root      617  0.0  0.0      0     0 ?       S    00:00   0:00 [mtdblockd]
root      638  0.0  0.0      0     0 ?       S    00:00   0:00 [rpciod]
bin       834  0.0  0.7   1568   444 ?       Ss   00:00   0:00 /sbin/portmap
root      861  0.0  0.0      0     0 ?       S    00:00   0:00 [lockd]
root      868  0.0  0.9   1488   596 ?       Ss   00:00   0:00 /sbin/syslogd -r
root      876  0.0  0.7   1416   456 ?       Ss   00:00   0:00 /sbin/klogd -x
root      884  0.0  1.1   1660   700 ?       Ss   00:00   0:00 /usr/sbin/rpc.statd
root      896  0.0  0.9   1668   584 ?       Ss   00:00   0:00 /usr/sbin/inetd
root      909  0.0  2.2   2412  1372 ?       Ss+  00:00   0:00 -bash
telnetd   953  0.3  1.1   1736   732 ?       S    05:58   0:00 in.telnetd
root      954  0.2  2.1   2384  1348 pts/0   Ss   05:58   0:00 -bash
root      960  0.0  1.2   2312   772 pts/0   R+   05:59   0:00 ps aux
```

This is but one of the many ways to view output data using ps. The columns are as follows:

- The USER and process ID (PID) fields are self-explanatory.
- The %CPU field expresses the percentage of CPU utilization since the beginning of the process's lifetime; thus, CPU usage will almost never add up to 100 percent.
- The %MEM field indicates the ratio of the process's resident memory footprint to the total available physical memory.
- The VSZ field is the virtual memory size of the process in kilobytes.
- RSS is the resident set size. It indicates the nonswapped physical memory that a process has used, also in kilobytes.
- TTY is the process's controlling terminal.

Most of the processes in this example are not associated with a controlling terminal. The ps command that generated Listing 13-9 was issued from a telnet session, as indicated by the pts/0 terminal device.

The STAT field describes the state of the process at the time this snapshot was produced. S means that the process is sleeping, waiting on an event of some type, often I/O. R means that the process is in a runnable state (that is, the scheduler is free to give it control of the CPU if nothing of a higher priority is waiting). The angle bracket next to the state letter indicates that this process has a higher priority.

The final column is the command name. Those listed in brackets are kernel threads. Many more symbols and options are available; refer to the man page for ps for complete details.

13.4.5 top

Whereas ps is a one-time snapshot of the current system, top takes periodic snapshots of the state of the system and its processes. Similar to ps, top has numerous command-line and configuration options. It is interactive and can be reconfigured while running to customize the display to your particular needs.

Entered without options, top displays all running processes in a fashion very similar to the ps aux command presented in Listing 13-9, updated every 3 seconds. Of course, this and many other aspects of top are user-configurable. The first few lines of the top screen display system information, also updated every 3 seconds. This includes the system uptime, the number of users, information on the number of processes and their state, and much more.

Listing 13-10 shows top in its default configuration, resulting from executing top from the command line without parameters.

LISTING 13-10 Default *top* Display

```
top - 06:23:14 up  6:23,  2 users,  load average: 0.00, 0.00, 0.00
Tasks:  24 total,   1 running,  23 sleeping,   0 stopped,   0 zombie
Cpu(s):  0.0% us,  0.3% sy,  0.0% ni, 99.7% id,  0.0% wa,  0.0% hi,  0.0% si
Mem:     62060k total,    17292k used,    44768k free,       0k buffers
Swap:        0k total,        0k used,       0k free,   11840k cached

  PID USER      PR  NI  VIRT  RES  SHR S %CPU %MEM   TIME+  COMMAND
  978 root      16   0  1924  952  780 R  0.3  1.5  0:01.22 top
    1 root      16   0  1416  508  452 S  0.0  0.8  0:00.47 init
    2 root       5 -10     0    0    0 S  0.0  0.0  0:00.00 ksoftirqd/0
    3 root       5 -10     0    0    0 S  0.0  0.0  0:00.00 desched/0
    4 root      -2  -5     0    0    0 S  0.0  0.0  0:00.00 events/0
    5 root      10  -5     0    0    0 S  0.0  0.0  0:00.09 khelper
   10 root      18  -5     0    0    0 S  0.0  0.0  0:00.00 kthread
   21 root      20  -5     0    0    0 S  0.0  0.0  0:00.00 kblockd/0
   62 root      20   0     0    0    0 S  0.0  0.0  0:00.00 pdflush
   63 root      15   0     0    0    0 S  0.0  0.0  0:00.00 pdflush
   65 root      19  -5     0    0    0 S  0.0  0.0  0:00.00 aio/0
   36 root      25   0     0    0    0 S  0.0  0.0  0:00.00 kapmd
   64 root      25   0     0    0    0 S  0.0  0.0  0:00.00 kswapd0
  617 root      25   0     0    0    0 S  0.0  0.0  0:00.00 mtdblockd
  638 root      15   0     0    0    0 S  0.0  0.0  0:00.34 rpciod
  834 bin       15   0  1568  444  364 S  0.0  0.7  0:00.00 portmap
  861 root      20   0     0    0    0 S  0.0  0.0  0:00.00 lockd
  868 root      16   0  1488  596  504 S  0.0  1.0  0:00.11 syslogd
  876 root      19   0  1416  456  396 S  0.0  0.7  0:00.00 klogd
  884 root      18   0  1660  700  612 S  0.0  1.1  0:00.02 rpc.statd
  896 root      16   0  1668  584  504 S  0.0  0.9  0:00.00 inetd
  909 root      15   0  2412 1372 1092 S  0.0  2.2  0:00.34 bash
  953 telnetd   16   0  1736  736  616 S  0.0  1.2  0:00.27 in.telnetd
  954 root      15   0  2384 1348 1096 S  0.0  2.2  0:00.16 bash
```

The default columns from Listing 13-10 are the PID, the user, the process priority, the process nice value, the virtual memory used by the process, the resident memory footprint, the amount of shared memory used by the task, and other fields that are identical to those described in the previous ps example.

Space permits only a cursory introduction to these useful utilities. You are encouraged to spend an afternoon with the man pages for `top` and `ps` to explore the richness of their capabilities.

13.4.6 `mtrace`

`mtrace` is a simple utility that analyzes and reports on calls to `malloc()`, `realloc()`, and `free()` in your application. It is easy to use and can potentially help spot trouble in your application. As with other userland tools we have described in this chapter, `mtrace` must be configured and compiled for your target architecture. `mtrace` is a `malloc` replacement library that is installed on your target. Your application enables it with a special function call. Your embedded Linux distribution should contain the `mtrace` package.

To demonstrate this utility, we created a simple program that creates dynamic data on a simple linked list. Each list item was dynamically generated, as was each data item we placed on the list. Listing 13-11 shows the simple list structure.

LISTING 13-11   Simple Linear Linked List

```
struct blist_s {
  struct blist_s *next;
  char *data_item;
  int item_size;
  int index;
};
```

Each list item was dynamically created using `malloc()` as follows and subsequently was placed at the end of the linked list:

```
struct blist_s *p = malloc( sizeof(struct blist_s) );
```

Each variable-sized data item in the list was also dynamically generated and added to the list item before being placed at the end of the list. This way, every list item was created using two calls to `malloc()`—one for the list item itself, represented by `struct blist_s`, just shown, and one for the variable data item. We then generated 10,000 records on the list containing variable string data, resulting in 20,000 calls to `malloc()`.

For you to use `mtrace`, three conditions must be satisfied:

- A header file, `mcheck.h`, must be included in the source file.
- The application must call `mtrace()` to install the handlers.

- The environment variable MALLOC_TRACE must specify the name of a writeable file to which the trace data is written.

When these conditions are satisfied, each call to one of the traced functions generates a line in the raw trace file defined by MALLOC_TRACE. The trace data looks like this:

```
@ ./mt_ex:[0x80486ec] + 0x804a5f8 0x10
```

The @ sign signals that the trace line contains an address or function name. The program is executing at the address in square brackets, 0x80486ec. Using binary utilities or a debugger, we could easily associate this address with a function. The plus sign (+) indicates that this is a call to allocate memory. A call to free() would be indicated by a minus sign. The next field indicates the virtual address of the memory location being allocated or freed. The last field is the size, which is included in every call to allocate memory.

This data format is not very user-friendly. For this reason, the mtrace utility includes a utility that analyzes the raw trace data and reports on any inconsistencies. The analysis utility is a Perl script supplied with the mtrace package. In the simplest case, the Perl script prints a single line with the message No memory leaks. Listing 13-12 shows the output that results when memory leaks are detected.

LISTING 13-12 *mtrace* Error Report

```
$ mtrace ./mt_ex mtrace.log

Memory not freed.
-----------------
   Address     Size     Caller
0x0804aa70    0x0a   at /home/chris/temp/mt_ex.c:64
0x0804abc0    0x10   at /home/chris/temp/mt_ex.c:26
0x0804ac60    0x10   at /home/chris/temp/mt_ex.c:26
0x0804acc8    0x0a   at /home/chris/temp/mt_ex.c:64
```

As you can see, this simple tool can help you spot trouble before it happens, as well as find trouble when it occurs. Notice that the Perl script displays the filename and line number of each call to malloc() that does not have a corresponding call to free() for the given memory location. This requires debugging information in the executable file generated by passing the -g flag to the compiler. If no debugging information is found, the script simply reports the address of the function calling malloc().

13.4.7 `dmalloc`

`dmalloc` picks up where `mtrace` leaves off. The `mtrace` package is a simple, relatively nonintrusive package most useful for simple detection of `malloc`/free unbalance conditions. The `dmalloc` package lets you detect a much wider range of dynamic memory-management errors. Compared to `mtrace`, `dmalloc` is highly intrusive. Depending on the configuration, `dmalloc` can slow your application to a crawl. It is definitely not the right tool if you suspect memory errors due to race conditions or other timing issues. `dmalloc` (and `mtrace`, to a lesser extent) will definitely change the timing of your application.

`dmalloc` is a very powerful dynamic memory-analysis tool. It is highly configurable and, therefore, somewhat complex. It takes some time to learn and master this tool. However, from QA testing to bug squashing, it could become one of your favorite development tools.

`dmalloc` is a debug `malloc` library replacement. These conditions must be satisfied for you to use `dmalloc`:

- Application code must include the `dmalloc.h` header file.
- The application must be linked against the `dmalloc` library.
- The `dmalloc` library and utility must be installed on your embedded target.
- Certain environment variables that the `dmalloc` library references must be defined before you run your application on the target.

Although it is not strictly necessary, you should include `dmalloc.h` in your application program. This allows `dmalloc` to include file and line number information in the output.

Link your application against the `dmalloc` library of your choice. The `dmalloc` package can be configured to generate several different libraries, depending on your selections during package configuration. The following examples use the `libdmalloc.so` shared library object. Place the library (or a symlink to it) in a path where your compiler can find it. The command to compile your application might look something like this:

```
$ ppc_82xx-gcc -g -Wall -o mtest_ex -L../dmalloc-5.4.2/ -ldmalloc mtest_ex.c
```

This command line assumes that you've placed the `dmalloc` library (`libdmalloc.so`) in a location searched by the `-L` switch on the command line—namely, the `../dmalloc-5.4.2` directly above the current directory.

To install the `dmalloc` library on your target, place it in your favorite location (perhaps `/usr/local/lib`). You might need to configure your system to find this library. On our sample Power Architecture system, we added the path `/usr/local/lib` to the `/etc/ld.so.conf` file and invoked the `ldconfig` utility to update the library search cache.

The last step in preparation is to set an environment variable that the `dmalloc` library uses to determine the level of debugging that will be enabled. The environment variable contains a debug bit mask that concatenates a number of features into a single convenient variable. Yours might look something like this:

```
DMALLOC_OPTIONS=debug=0x4f4ed03,inter=100,log=dmalloc.log
```

Here, `debug` is the debug-level bit mask, and `inter` sets an interval count at which the `dmalloc` library performs extensive checks on itself and the heap. The `dmalloc` library writes its log output to the file indicated by the `log` variable.

The `dmalloc` package comes with a utility to generate the `DMALLOC_OPTIONS` environment variable based on flags passed to it. The documentation in the `dmalloc` package details this quite thoroughly, so we will not reproduce it here. The example just shown was generated with the following `dmalloc` invocation:

```
$ dmalloc -p check-fence -l dmalloc.log -i 100 high
```

When these steps are complete, you should be able to run your application against the `dmalloc` debug library.

`dmalloc` produces quite a detailed output log. Listing 13-13 shows sample `dmalloc` log output for a sample program that intentionally generates some memory leaks.

LISTING 13-13   *dmalloc* Log Output

```
2592: 4002: Dmalloc version '5.4.2' from 'http://dmalloc.com/'
2592: 4002: flags = 0x4f4e503, logfile 'dmalloc.log'
2592: 4002: interval = 100, addr = 0, seen # = 0, limit = 0
2592: 4002: starting time = 2592
2592: 4002: process pid = 442
2592: 4002: Dumping Chunk Statistics:
2592: 4002: basic-block 4096 bytes, alignment 8 bytes
2592: 4002: heap address range: 0x30015000 to 0x3004f000, 237568 bytes
2592: 4002:    user blocks: 18 blocks, 73652  bytes (38%)
2592: 4002:    admin blocks: 29 blocks, 118784 bytes (61%)
2592: 4002:    total blocks: 47 blocks, 192512 bytes
2592: 4002: heap checked 41
```

LISTING 13-13 Continued

```
2592: 4002: alloc calls: malloc 2003, calloc 0, realloc 0, free 1999
2592: 4002: alloc calls: recalloc 0, memalign 0, valloc 0
2592: 4002: alloc calls: new 0, delete 0
2592: 4002:   current memory in use: 52 bytes (4 pnts)
2592: 4002:   total memory allocated: 27546 bytes (2003 pnts)
2592: 4002:   max in use at one time: 27546 bytes (2003 pnts)
2592: 4002: max alloced with 1 call: 376 bytes
2592: 4002: max unused memory space: 37542 bytes (57%)
2592: 4002: top 10 allocations:
2592: 4002:  total-size count in-use-size  count  source
2592: 4002:      16000  1000          32      2  mtest_ex.c:36
2592: 4002:      10890  1000          20      2  mtest_ex.c:74
2592: 4002:        256     1           0      0  mtest_ex.c:154
2592: 4002:      27146  2001          52      4  Total of 3
2592: 4002: Dumping Not-Freed Pointers Changed Since Start:
2592: 4002:  not freed: '0x300204e8|s1' (10 bytes) from 'mtest_ex.c:74'
2592: 4002:  not freed: '0x30020588|s1' (16 bytes) from 'mtest_ex.c:36'
2592: 4002:  not freed: '0x30020688|s1' (16 bytes) from 'mtest_ex.c:36'
2592: 4002:  not freed: '0x300208a8|s1' (10 bytes) from 'mtest_ex.c:74'
2592: 4002:  total-size  count  source
2592: 4002:         32      2  mtest_ex.c:36
2592: 4002:         20      2  mtest_ex.c:74
2592: 4002:         52      4  Total of 2
2592: 4002: ending time = 2592, elapsed since start = 0:00:00
```

It is important to note that this log is generated upon program exit. (dmalloc has many options and modes of operation; it is possible to configure dmalloc to print output lines when errors are detected.)

The first half of the output log reports high-level statistics about the heap and the application's overall memory usage. Totals are produced for each of the malloc library calls, such as malloc(), free(), and realloc(). Interestingly, this default log reports on the top ten allocations and the source location where they occurred. This can be very useful for overall system-level profiling.

Toward the end of the log, we see evidence of memory leaks in our application. You can see that the dmalloc library detected four instances of memory that was allocated but apparently never freed. Because we included dmalloc.h and compiled with debug symbols, dmalloc placed the source location where the memory was allocated into the log.

As with the other tools we've covered in this chapter, space permits only a brief introduction to this very powerful debug tool. `dmalloc` can detect many other conditions and limits. For example, `dmalloc` can detect when a freed pointer has been written. It can tell whether a pointer was used to access data outside its bounds but within the application's permissible address range. In fact, `dmalloc` can be configured to log almost any memory transaction through the `malloc` family of calls. `dmalloc` is a tool that is sure to pay back many times the effort taken to become proficient with it.

13.4.8 Kernel Oops

Although not strictly a tool, a kernel oops contains much useful information to help you troubleshoot the cause. A kernel oops results from a variety of kernel errors, from simple memory errors produced by a process (fully recoverable, in most cases) to a hard kernel panic. Recent Linux kernels support display of symbolic information in addition to the raw hexadecimal address values. Listing 13-14 shows a kernel oops from a Power Architecture target.

LISTING 13-14 Kernel Oops Display

```
$ modprobe loop
Oops: kernel access of bad area, sig: 11 [#1]
NIP: C000D058 LR: C0085650 SP: C7787E80 REGS: c7787dd0 TRAP: 0300  Not tainted
MSR: 00009032 EE: 1 PR: 0 FP: 0 ME: 1 IR/DR: 11
DAR: 00000000, DSISR: 22000000
TASK = c7d187b0[323] 'modprobe' THREAD: c7786000
Last syscall: 128
GPR00: 0000006C C7787E80 C7D187B0 00000000 C7CD25CC FFFFFFFF 00000000 80808081
GPR08: 00000001 C034AD80 C036D41C C034AD80 C0335AB0 1001E3C0 00000000 00000000
GPR16: 00000000 00000000 00000000 100170D8 100013E0 C9040000 C903DFD8 C9040000
GPR24: 00000000 C9040000 C9040000 00000940 C778A000 C7CD25C0 C7CD25C0 C7CD25CC
NIP [c000d058] strcpy+0x10/0x1c
LR [c0085650] register_disk+0xec/0xf0
Call trace:
 [c00e170c] add_disk+0x58/0x74
 [c90061e0] loop_init+0x1e0/0x430 [loop]
 [c002fc90] sys_init_module+0x1f4/0x2e0
 [c00040a0] ret_from_syscall+0x0/0x44
Segmentation fault
```

Notice that the register dump includes symbolic information where appropriate. Your kernel must have KALLSYMS enabled for this symbolic information to be available.

Figure 13-4 shows the configuration options under the General Setup main menu.

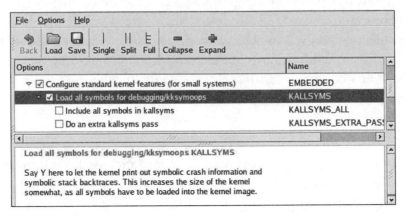

FIGURE 13-4   Symbol support for oops

Much of the information in a kernel oops message is directly related to the processor. Having some knowledge of the underlying architecture is necessary to fully understand the oops message.

Analyzing the oops shown in Listing 13-14, we see right away that the oops was generated due to a "kernel access of bad area, sig: 11." We already know from previous examples in this chapter that signal 11 is a segmentation fault.

The first section is a summary showing the reason for the oops, a few important pointers, and the offending task. In Listing 13-14, NIP is the next instruction pointer, which is decoded later in the oops message. This points to the offending code that led to the oops. LR is a Power Architecture register and usually indicates the return address for the currently executing subroutine. SP is the stack pointer. REGS indicates the kernel address for the data structure containing the register dump data. TRAP indicates the type of exception that this oops message relates to. Referring to the PowerPC architecture user manual referenced at the end of Chapter 7, "Bootloaders," we see that a TRAP 0300 is a Data Storage Interrupt, which is triggered by a data memory access error.

On the third line of the oops message, we see additional Power Architecture machine registers, such as MSR (machine state register) and a decode of some of its bits. On the next line, we see the DAR (data access register), which often contains the offending memory address. The DSISR register contents can be used in conjunction with the PowerPC architecture reference to discover much detail about the specific reason for the exception.

An oops message also contains the task pointer and the decoded task name to help you quickly determine what task or thread was running at the time of the oops. We also see a detailed processor register dump, which can be used for additional clues. Again, we need knowledge of the architecture and compiler register usage to make sense of the clues from the register values. For example, the PowerPC architecture uses the r3 register for return values from C functions.

The last part of the oops message provides a stack backtrace with symbol decode if symbols are enabled in the kernel. Using this information, we can construct a sequence of events that led to the offending condition.

In this simple example, we have learned a great deal of information from this oops message. We know that it is a Power Architecture Data Storage Exception, caused by an error in a data memory access (as opposed to an instruction fetch memory access). The DAR register tells us that the data address that generated this exception was 0x0000_0000. We know that the `modprobe` process produced the error. From the backtrace and NIP (next instruction pointer), we know that it was in a call to `strcpy()` that can be traced directly back to the `loop_init()` function in the `loop.ko` module, which `modprobe` was trying to insert at the time of the exception. Given this information, tracking down the source of this errant null pointer dereference should be easy.

13.5 Binary Utilities

Binary utilities, or binutils, are a critical component of any toolchain. Indeed, to build a compiler, you must first have successfully built binutils. This section briefly introduces the more useful tools that the embedded developer needs to know about. As with most of the other tools in this chapter, these are cross-utilities and must be built to execute on your development host while operating on binary files targeted to your chosen architecture. Alternatively, you could compile or obtain versions of these to run on your target, but we assume a cross-development environment for these examples.

13.5.1 `readelf`

The `readelf` utility examines the composition of your target ELF binary file. This is particularly useful for building images targeted for ROM or Flash memory where explicit control of the image layout is required. It is also a great tool for learning how your toolchain builds images and for understanding the ELF file format.

For example, to display the symbol table in an ELF image, use this command:

```
$ readelf -s <elf-image>
```

To discover and display all the sections in your ELF image, use this command:

```
$ readelf -e <elf-image>
```

Use the -s flag to list the section headers in your ELF image. You might be surprised to learn that even a simple seven-line "Hello World" program contains 38 separate sections. Some of them will be familiar to you, such as the .text and .data sections. Listing 13-15 contains a partial listing of sections from our "Hello World" example. For simplicity, we have listed only those sections that are likely to be familiar or relevant to the embedded developer.

LISTING 13-15   *readelf* Section Headers

```
$ ppc_82xx-readelf -S  hello-ex
There are 38 section headers, starting at offset 0x32f4:

Section Headers:
[ Nr] Name            Type       Addr     Off    Size   ES Flg Lk Inf Al
...
[11] .text            PROGBITS   100002f0 0002f0 000568 00  AX  0   0  4
...
[13] .rodata          PROGBITS   10000878 000878 000068 00   A  0   0  4
...
[15] .data            PROGBITS   100108e0 0008e0 00000c 00  WA  0   0  4
...
[22] .sdata           PROGBITS   100109e0 0009e0 00001c 00  WA  0   0  4
[23] .sbss            NOBITS     100109fc 0009fc 000000 00  WA  0   0  1
...
[25] .bss             NOBITS     10010a74 0009fc 00001c 00  WA  0   0  4
...
```

The .text section contains the executable program code. The .rodata section contains constant data in your program. The .data section generally contains initialized global data used by the C library prologue code and can contain large initialized data items from your application. The .sdata section is used for smaller initialized global data items and exists on only some architectures. Some processor architectures can make use of optimized data access when the attributes of the memory area are known. The .sdata and .sbss sections enable these optimizations. The .bss and .sbss sections contain uninitialized data in your program. These sections occupy no space in the program image. Their memory space is allocated and initialized to 0 on program startup by C library prologue code.

We can dump any of these sections and display the contents. Given this line in your C program declared outside of any function, we can examine how it is placed in the .rodata section:

```
char *hello_rodata = "This is a read-only data string\n";
```

Issue the readelf command specifying the section number we want to dump from Listing 13-15:

```
$ ppc_82xx-readelf -x 13 hello-ex
Hex dump of section '.rodata':
  0x10000878 100189e0 10000488 1000050c 1000058c ...............
  0x10000888 00020001 54686973 20697320 61207265 ....This is a read-
  0x10000898 61642d6f 6e6c7920 64617461 20737472 only data string
  0x100008a8 696e670a 00000000 54686973 20697320 .....This is
  0x100008b8 73746174 69632064 6174610a 00000000 static data.....
  0x100008c8 48656c6c 6f20456d 62656464 65640a00 Hello Embedded..
  0x100008d8 25730a00 25780a00                   %s..%x..
```

We see that the initialized global variable that we declared is represented in the .rodata section, together with all the constant strings defined in the program.

13.5.2   Examining Debug Information Using readelf

One of the more useful features of readelf is to display the debug information contained in an ELF file. When the -g compiler flag is issued during a compilation, the compiler generates debug information in a series of sections within the resulting ELF file. We can use readelf to display these ELF section headers within the ELF file:

```
$ ppc-linux-readelf -S ex_sync | grep debug
  [28] .debug_aranges    PROGBITS    00000000 000c38 0000b8 00    0   0   8
  [29] .debug_pubnames   PROGBITS    00000000 000cf0 00007a 00    0   0   1
  [30] .debug_info       PROGBITS    00000000 000d6a 00079b 00    0   0   1
  [31] .debug_abbrev     PROGBITS    00000000 001505 000207 00    0   0   1
  [32] .debug_line       PROGBITS    00000000 00170c 000354 00    0   0   1
  [33] .debug_frame      PROGBITS    00000000 001a60 000080 00    0   0   4
  [34] .debug_str        PROGBITS    00000000 001ae0 00014d 00    0   0   1
```

Using readelf with the --debug-dump option, we can display the contents of any one of these .debug_* sections. You will see how this information can be useful in Chapter 14, "Kernel Debugging Techniques," when we discuss the challenge of debugging optimized kernel code.

Debug information can be very large. Displaying all the debug information in the Linux kernel ELF file vmlinux produces more than six million lines of output. However daunting it might appear, having at least a familiarity with debug information will make you a better embedded engineer.

Listing 13-16 is a partial listing of the contents of the .debug_info section from a small sample application. For space considerations, it shows only a few records.

LISTING 13-16 Partial Debug Info Dump

```
$ ppc-linux-readelf -debug-dump=info ex_sync
1 The section .debug_info contains:
2
3   Compilation Unit @ 0:
4    Length:        109
5    Version:       2
6    Abbrev Offset: 0
7    Pointer Size:  4
8  <0><b>: Abbrev Number: 1 (DW_TAG_compile_unit)
9      DW_AT_stmt_list   : 0
10     DW_AT_low_pc      : 0x10000368
11     DW_AT_high_pc     : 0x1000038c
12     DW_AT_name        :
../sysdeps/powerpc/powerpc32/elf/start.S
13     DW_AT_comp_dir    : /var/tmp/BUILD/glibc-2.3.3/csu
14     DW_AT_producer    : GNU AS 2.15.94
15     DW_AT_language    : 32769   (MIPS assembler)
...
394  <1><5a1>: Abbrev Number: 14 (DW_TAG_subprogram)
395     DW_AT_sibling     : <5fa>
396     DW_AT_external    : 1
397     DW_AT_name        : main
398     DW_AT_decl_file   : 1
399     DW_AT_decl_line   : 9
400     DW_AT_prototyped  : 1
401     DW_AT_type        : <248>
402     DW_AT_low_pc      : 0x100004b8
403     DW_AT_high_pc     : 0x10000570
404     DW_AT_frame_base  : 1 byte block: 6f       (DW_OP_reg31)
...
423  <2><5e9>: Abbrev Number: 16 (DW_TAG_variable)
424     DW_AT_name        : mybuf
425     DW_AT_decl_file   : 1
426     DW_AT_decl_line   : 11
```

LISTING 13-16   Continued

```
427        DW_AT_type        : <600>
428        DW_AT_location    : 2 byte block: 91 20    (DW_OP_fbreg: 32)
...
```

The first record identified by the Dwarf2[6] tag `DW_TAG_compile_unit` identifies the first compilation unit of this Power Architecture executable. It is a file called `start.S`, which provides startup prologue for a C program. The next record identified by `DW_TAG_subprogram` identifies the start of the user program, the familiar function `main()`. This Dwarf2 debug record contains a reference to the file and line number where `main()` is found. The final record in Listing 13-16 identifies a local variable in the `main()` routine called `mybuf`. Again, the line number and file are provided by this record. You can deduce from this information that `main()` is at line 9, and `mybuf` is at line 11 of the source file. Other debug records in the ELF file correlate the filename via the Dwarf2 `DW_AT_decl_file` attribute.

You can discover all the details of the Dwarf2 debug information format via the reference given in the last section of this chapter.

13.5.3   `objdump`

The `objdump` utility has considerable overlap with the `readelf` tool. However, one of the more useful features of `objdump` is its capability to display disassembled object code. Listing 13-17 provides an example of disassembly of the `.text` section of the simple "Hello World" Power Architecture version. We include only the `main()` routine to save space. The entire dump, including C library prologue and epilogue, would consume many pages.

LISTING 13-17   Disassembly Using *objdump*

```
$ ppc_82xx-objdump -S -m powerpc:common -j .text hello
...
10000488 <main>:
10000488:      94 21 ff e0      stwu     r1,-32(r1)
1000048c:      7c 08 02 a6      mflr     r0
10000490:      93 e1 00 1c      stw      r31,28(r1)
10000494:      90 01 00 24      stw      r0,36(r1)
10000498:      7c 3f 0b 78      mr       r31,r1
1000049c:      90 7f 00 08      stw      r3,8(r31)
```

---

[6] A reference to the Dwarf2 Debug Information Specification is provided at the end of this chapter.

LISTING 13-17 Continued

```
100004a0:          90 9f 00 0c      stw      r4,12(r31)
100004a4:          3d 20 10 00      lis      r9,4096
100004a8:          38 69 08 54      addi     r3,r9,2132
100004ac:          4c c6 31 82      crclr    4*cr1+eq
100004b0:          48 01 05 11      bl       100109c0
<__bss_start+0x60>
100004b4:          38 00 00 00      li       r0,0
100004b8:          7c 03 03 78      mr       r3,r0
100004bc:          81 61 00 00      lwz      r11,0(r1)
100004c0:          80 0b 00 04      lwz      r0,4(r11)
100004c4:          7c 08 03 a6      mtlr     r0
100004c8:          83 eb ff fc      lwz      r31,-4(r11)
100004cc:          7d 61 5b 78      mr       r1,r11
100004d0:          4e 80 00 20      blr
...
```

Much of the code from the simple `main()` routine is stack frame creation and destruction. The actual call to `printf()` is represented by the branch link (`bl`) instruction near the center of the listing at address `0x100004b0`. This is a Power Architecture function call. Because this program was compiled as a dynamically linked object, we will not have an address for the `printf()` function until runtime, when it is linked with the shared library `printf()` routine. Had we compiled this as a statically linked object, we would see the symbol and corresponding address for the call to `printf()`.

13.5.4 `objcopy`

`objcopy` formats and, optionally, converts the format of a binary object file. This utility is quite useful for generating code for ROM or Flash resident images. The U-Boot bootloader introduced in Chapter 7 makes use of `objcopy` to produce binary and s-record[7] output formats from the final ELF file. This sample usage illustrates the capabilities of `objcopy` and its use to build Flash images:

```
$ ppc_82xx-objcopy --gap-fill=0xff -O binary u-boot u-boot.bin
```

This `objcopy` invocation shows how an image might be prepared for Flash memory. The input file—u-boot, in this example—is the complete ELF U-Boot image, including symbols and relocation information. The `objcopy` utility takes only the relevant

---

[7] S-record files are an ASCII representation of a binary file, used by many device programmers and software binary utilities.

sections containing program code and data and places the image in the output file, specified here as `u-boot.bin`.

Flash memory contains all 1s in its erased state. Therefore, filling gaps in a binary image with all 1s improves programming efficiency and prolongs the life of the Flash memory, which has limited write cycles. This is done with the `--gap-fill` parameter to `objcopy`.

This is but one simple example usage of `objcopy`. This utility can be used to generate s-records and convert from one format to another. See the man page for complete details.

13.6 Miscellaneous Binary Utilities

Your toolchain contains several additional useful utilities. Learning to use these utilities is straightforward. You will find many uses for these helpful tools.

13.6.1 `strip`

The `strip` utility can be used to remove symbols and debug information from a binary. This is frequently used to save space on an embedded device. In the cross-development model, it is convenient to place stripped binaries on the target system and leave the unstripped version on your development host. Using this method, symbols are available for cross-debugging on your development host while saving space on the target. `strip` has many options, which are described in the man page.

13.6.2 `addr2line`

When we highlighted `mtrace` in Listing 13-12, you saw that the output from the `mtrace` analysis script contained file and line number information. The `mtrace` Perl script used the `addr2line` utility to read the debug information contained in the executable ELF file and display a line number corresponding to the address. Using the same `mtrace` sample executable, we can find a filename and line number for a virtual address:

```
$ addr2line -f -e mt_ex 0x80487c6
    put_data
    /home/chris/examples/mt_ex.c:64
```

Notice that the function `put_data()` is also listed together with the file and line number. This says that the address `0x80487c6` is on line 64 of the `mt_ex.c` file, in the put_data() function. This is even more useful in larger binaries consisting of multiple filenames, such as the Linux kernel:

```
$ ppc_82xx-addr2line -f -e vmlinux c000d95c
    mpc52xx_restart
    arch/ppc/syslib/mpc52xx_setup.c:41
```

This particular example highlights one of the points repeated throughout this chapter: This is an architecture-specific tool. You must use a tool configured and compiled to match the architecture of the target binary you are using. As with the cross-compiler, addr2line is a cross tool and part of the binary utilities package.

13.6.3 strings

The strings utility examines ASCII string data in binary files. This is especially useful for examining memory dumps when source code or debug symbols might not be available. You might often discover that you can narrow the cause of a crash by tracing the strings back to the offending binary. Although strings does have a few command-line options, it is easy to learn and use. See the man page for further details.

13.6.4 ldd

Although not strictly a binary utility, the ldd script is another useful tool for the embedded developer. It is part of the C library package and exists on virtually every Linux distribution. ldd lists the shared object library dependencies for a given object file or files. We introduced ldd in Chapter 11, "BusyBox." See Listing 11-2 for a sample usage. The ldd script is particularly useful during development of ramdisk images. One of the most common failures asked about on the various embedded Linux mailing lists is a kernel panic after mounting root:

```
VFS: Mounted root (nfs filesystem).
Freeing unused kernel memory: 96k init
Kernel panic - not syncing: No init found.  Try passing init=option to kernel.
```

One of the most common causes is that the root file system image (be it ramdisk, Flash, or NFS root file system) does not have the supporting libraries for the binaries that the kernel is trying to execute. Using ldd, you can determine which libraries each of your binaries requires and make sure that you include them in your ramdisk or other root file system image. In the previous sample kernel panic, init was indeed on the file system, but the Linux dynamic loader, `ld.so.1`, was missing. Using `ldd` is quite straightforward:

```
$ xscale_be-ldd init
    libc.so.6 => /opt/mvl/.../lib/libc.so.6 (0xdead1000)
    ld-linux.so.3 => /opt/mvl/.../lib/ld-linux.so.3 (0xdead2000)
```

This simple example demonstrates that the `init` binary requires two dynamic library objects: libc and ld-linux. Both must be on your target and must be accessible to your init binary—that is, they must be readable and executable.

13.6.5 nm

The `nm` utility displays symbols from an object file. This can be useful for a variety of tasks. For example, suppose that, when cross-compiling a large application, you encounter unresolved symbols. You can use `nm` to find which object module contains those symbols and then modify your build environment to include it.

The `nm` utility provides attributes for each symbol. For example, you can discover whether this symbol is local or global, and whether it is defined or referenced in only a particular object module. Listing 13-18 reproduces several lines from the output of `nm` run on the U-Boot ELF image `u-boot`.

LISTING 13-18   Displaying Symbols Using *nm*

```
$ ppc_85xx-nm u-boot
...
fff23140 b base_address
fff24c98 B BootFile
fff06d64 T BootpRequest
fff00118 t boot_warm
fff21010 d border
fff23000 A __bss_start
...
```

Notice the link addresses of these U-Boot symbols. They were linked for a Flash device that lives in the highest portion of the memory map on this particular board. This listing contains only a few sample symbols, for discussion purposes. The middle column is the symbol type. A capital letter indicates a global symbol, and lowercase indicates a local symbol. B indicates that the symbol is located in the `.bss` section. T indicates that the symbol is located in the `.text` section. D indicates that the symbol is located in the `.data` section. A indicates that this address is absolute and is not subject to modification by an additional link stage. This absolute symbol indicates the start of the `.bss` section and is used by the code that clears the `.bss` on startup, as required for a C execution environment.

13.6.6 `prelink`

The `prelink` utility is often used in systems in which startup time is important. A dynamically linked ELF executable must be linked at runtime when the program is first loaded. This can take significant time in a large application. `prelink` prepares the shared libraries and the object files that depend on them to provide a priori knowledge of the unresolved library references. In effect, this can reduce the startup time of a given application. The man page has complete details on the use of this handy utility.

13.7 Summary

This chapter examined some of the more important tools available to the embedded Linux developer. We showed how ordinary utilities can be used in powerful ways to analyze system behavior. We presented many of the utilities found in binutils, including `readelf`, `objdump`, `objcopy`, and several others.

- The GNU Debugger (GDB) is a complex and powerful debugger with many capabilities. We presented the basics to get you started.
- The DDD graphical front end for GDB integrates source code and data display with the power of GDB command-line interface capabilities.
- `cbrowser` is a useful aid for understanding large projects. It uses the `cscope` database to rapidly find and display symbols and other elements of C source code.
- Linux is supported by many profiling and trace tools. We presented several, including `strace`, `ltrace`, `top`, and `ps`, and the memory profilers `mtrace` and `dmalloc`.
- Embedded developers often need to build custom images such as those required for bootloaders and firmware images. For these tasks, knowledge of binutils is indispensable.

13.7.1 Suggestions for Additional Reading

GDB: The GNU Project Debugger
www.gnu.org/software/gdb/gdb.html

GDB Pocket Reference
Arnold Robbins
O'Reilly Media, 2005

Data Display Debugger
www.gnu.org/software/ddd/

cbrowser home page
www.ziplink.net/~felaco/cbrowser/

cscope home page
http://cscope.sourceforge.net/index.html

dmalloc: Debug Malloc Library
http://dmalloc.com/

Tool Interface Standard (TIS) Executable and Linking Format (ELF) Specification
Version 1.2
TIS Committee, May 1995

Tool interface standards
DWARF Debugging Information Format Specification
Version 2.0
TIS Committee, May 1995

The Eclipse Project
www.eclipse.org/

## Chapter 14

Kernel Debugging Techniques

In This Chapter

- 14.1   Challenges to Kernel Debugging   368
- 14.2   Using KGDB for Kernel Debugging   369
- 14.3   Kernel Debugging Techniques   381
- 14.4   Hardware-Assisted Debugging   410
- 14.5   When It Doesn't Boot   417
- 14.6   Summary   421

Often the pivotal factor in achieving development timetables comes down to your efficiency in finding and fixing bugs. Debugging inside the Linux kernel can be quite challenging. No matter how you approach it, kernel debugging will always be complex. This chapter examines some of the complexities and presents ideas and methods to improve your debugging skills inside the kernel and device drivers.

14.1   Challenges to Kernel Debugging

Debugging a modern operating system involves many challenges. Virtual memory operating systems present their own unique challenges. Gone are the days when we could replace a processor with an in-circuit emulator. Processors have become far too fast and complex. Moreover, pipeline architectures hide important code-execution details. This is because memory accesses on the bus can be ordered differently from code execution, and particularly because of internal caching of instruction streams. It is not always possible to correlate external bus activity to internal processor instruction execution, except at a rather coarse level.

Here are some of the challenges you will encounter while debugging Linux kernel code:

- Linux kernel code is highly optimized for speed of execution in many areas.

- Compilers use optimization techniques that complicate the correlation of C source to actual machine instruction flow. Inline functions are a good example of this.

- Single-stepping through compiler optimized code often produces unusual and unexpected results.

- Virtual memory isolates user space memory from kernel memory and can make various debugging scenarios especially difficult.

- Some code cannot be stepped through with traditional debuggers.

- Startup code can be especially difficult because of its proximity to the hardware and the limited resources available (for example, no console, limited memory mapping, and so on).

The Linux kernel has matured into a very high-performance operating system that can compete with the best commercial operating systems. Many areas within the kernel do not lend themselves to easy analysis by simply reading the source code. Knowledge of the architecture and detailed design are often necessary to understand the code flow in a particular area. Several good books are available that describe the kernel design in detail. Refer to the last section of this chapter for recommendations.

GCC is an optimizing compiler. By default, the Linux kernel is compiled with the -O2 compiler flag. This enables many optimization algorithms that can change the fundamental structure and order of your code.[1] For example, the Linux kernel makes heavy use of inline functions. Inline functions are small functions declared with the inline keyword, which results in the function's being included directly in the execution thread instead of generating a function call with the associated overhead.[2] Inline functions require a minimum of -O1 optimization level. Therefore, you cannot turn off optimization, which would be desirable to facilitate debugging.

In many areas within the Linux kernel, single-stepping through code is difficult or impossible. The most obvious examples are code paths that modify the virtual memory settings. When your application makes a system call that results in entry into the kernel, this results in a change in address space as seen by the process. In fact, any transition that involves a processor exception changes the operational context and can be difficult or impossible to single-step through.

14.2   Using KGDB for Kernel Debugging

Two popular methods enable symbolic source-level debugging within the Linux kernel:

- Using KGDB as a remote GDB agent
- Using a hardware JTAG probe to control the processor

JTAG debugging is covered in Section 14.4, "Hardware-Assisted Debugging."

KGDB (Kernel GDB) is a set of Linux kernel patches that provide an interface to GDB through its remote serial protocol.[3] KGDB implements a GDB stub that communicates with a cross-gdb running on your host development workstation. Until recently, KGDB on the target required a serial connection to the development host.

---

[1] See the GCC manual referenced at the end of this chapter for details on the optimization levels.

[2] Inline functions are like macros, but with the advantage of compile-time type checking.

[3] A simplified version of KGDB was merged into Linux 2.6.26 mainline, but without support for some features, including KGDB over Ethernet and other features.

Some targets support KGDB connection via Ethernet and even USB. Complete support for KGDB is still not in the mainline kernel.org kernel. You need to port KGDB to your chosen target or obtain an embedded Linux distribution for your chosen architecture and platform that contains KGDB support. Most commercial embedded Linux distributions available today support KGDB.

It is worth noting that you will find some differences between architectures and platforms when it comes to KGDB support. Unless the platform developer specifically enabled KGDB, it may not work for your particular platform. You will notice differences in the kernel configuration options for KGDB across various architectures and platforms. The only way to guarantee that KGDB is supported for your platform is to either port it yourself or obtain your Linux kernel and distribution for a commercial vendor that supports KGDB on your platform. For reference documentation, see the last section of this chapter.

Figure 14-1 shows the KGDB debug setup. Up to three connections to the target board are used. Ethernet is used to enable NFS root mount and telnet sessions from the host. If your board has a ramdisk image in Flash that it mounts as a root file system, you can eliminate the Ethernet connection.

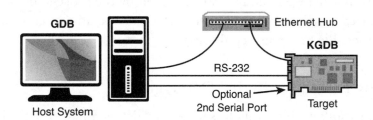

FIGURE 14-1   KGDB debug setup

A serial port is dedicated for the connection between KGDB and GDB running on the development host system, and an optional second serial port serves as a console. Systems that have only one serial port make KGDB somewhat more cumbersome to use.

As shown in Figure 14-1, the debugger (your cross-version of GDB) runs on your development host system. KGDB is part of the kernel running on your target system. KGDB implements the hooks required to interface GDB with your target board to enable features such as setting breakpoints, examining memory, and enabling single-step program execution.

14.2.1 KGDB Kernel Configuration

As mentioned, there are differences between architectures and platforms with respect to KGDB support. The following example is based on the Power Architecture MPC8548 CPU on the CDS platform from Freescale Semiconductor, using the commercial MontaVista Linux distribution, which added this KGDB support. Some of the features in this example are unavailable from mainline kernel source code, because including KGDB support in the kernel has been discouraged for a long time and is only recently (Linux 2.6.26) starting to appear in generic form.

KGDB is a kernel feature and must be enabled in your kernel. KGDB is selected from the Kernel hacking menu, as shown in Figure 14-2. (Many items have been removed from the Kernel hacking menu for this figure to fit on the page. Yours will have many more entries before the KGDB options.) As part of the configuration, you must select the I/O driver for KGDB to use. In this example, we chose the serial port via KGDB_8250. Notice also in Figure 14-2 that we enable the option to compile the kernel with debug information. This adds the -g compiler flag to the build process to enable symbolic debugging.

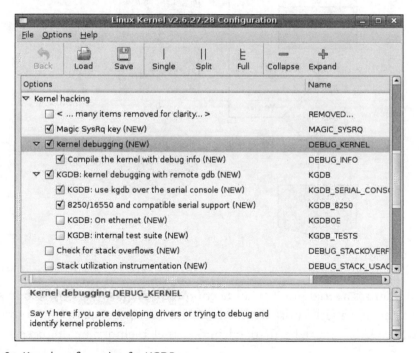

FIGURE 14-2   Kernel configuration for KGDB

14.2.2   Target Boot with KGDB Support

After your kernel is built with KGDB support, it must be enabled at runtime. In general, KGDB is enabled by passing a command-line switch to the kernel using the kernel command line. If KGDB support is compiled into the kernel but not enabled using a command-line switch, it does nothing. When KGDB is enabled, you can instruct the kernel to stop at a KGDB-enabled breakpoint very early in the boot cycle to allow you to connect to the target using GDB. Figure 14-3 shows the logic for generating an initial breakpoint when KGDB is enabled.

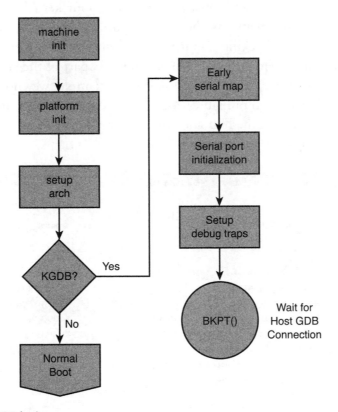

FIGURE 14-3   KGDB logic

KGDB requires a serial port for connection to the host.[4] The first step in setting up KGDB is to enable a serial port very early in the boot process. In many architectures, the hardware UART must be mapped into kernel memory before access. After the

---

[4] You can configure KGDB to use Ethernet and even USB on some architectures and platforms.

address range is mapped, the serial port is initialized. Debug trap handlers are then installed to allow processor exceptions to trap into the debugger.

Listing 14-1 displays the terminal output when booting with KGDB enabled. This example is based on the Freescale MPC8548CDS reference board, which ships with the U-Boot bootloader.

LISTING 14-1   Booting with KGDB Enabled Using U-Boot

```
=> setenv bootargs console=ttyS1,115200 root=/dev/nfs rw ip=dhcp kgdbwait
kgdb8250=ttyS1,115200
=> tftp 600000 mpc8548.uImage
Speed: 1000, full duplex
Using eTSEC0 device
TFTP from server 192.168.0.9; our IP address is 192.168.0.18
Filename '8548/uImage'.
Load address: 0x600000
Loading: #################################################################
        #############################################################
done
Bytes transferred = 1854347 (1c4b8b hex)
=> tftp c00000 mpc8548.dtb
Speed: 1000, full duplex
Using eTSEC0 device
TFTP from server 192.168.0.9; our IP address is 192.168.0.18
Filename '8548/dtb'.
Load address: 0xc00000
Loading: ##
done
Bytes transferred = 16384 (4000 hex)
=> bootm 600000 - c00000
## Booting kernel from Legacy Image at 00600000 ...
   Image Name:   MontaVista Linux 6/2.6.27/freesc
   Image Type:   PowerPC Linux Kernel Image (gzip compressed)
   Data Size:    1854283 Bytes =  1.8 MB
   Load Address: 00000000
   Entry Point:  00000000
   Verifying Checksum ... OK
## Flattened Device Tree blob at 00c00000
   Booting using the fdt blob at 0xc00000
   Uncompressing Kernel Image ... OK
   Loading Device Tree to 007f9000, end 007fffff ... OK
kgdb8250: ttyS1 init delayed, use io/mmio/mbase syntax for early init.
Using MPC85xx CDS machine description
```

LISTING 14-1   Continued

```
Memory CAM mapping: CAM0=256Mb, CAM1=0Mb, CAM2=0Mb residual: 0Mb
Linux version 2.6.27.28.freescale-8548cds.0908010910 (chris@pluto) (gcc version
4.3.3 (MontaVista Linux Sourcery G++ 4.3-217) ) #1 PREEMPT Mon Mar 29 11:09:48 EDT
2010
console [udbg0] enabled
setup_arch: bootmem
mpc85xx_cds_setup_arch()
<... many messages deleted ...>
Serial: 8250/16550 driver4 ports, IRQ sharing enabled
serial8250.0: ttyS0 at MMIO 0xe0004500 (irq = 42) is a 16550A
serial8250.0: ttyS1 at MMIO 0xe0004600 (irq = 42) is a 16550A
console handover: boot [udbg0] -> real [ttyS1]
kgdb: Registered I/O driver kgdb8250.
kgdb: Waiting for connection from remote gdb...
```

Most of the boot sequence is familiar from our coverage of U-Boot in Chapter 7, "Bootloaders." Recall from Chapter 7 that the kernel command line is defined by the U-Boot `bootargs` environment variable. Notice that we have added the `kgdbwait` parameter, which instructs the kernel to force an early breakpoint and wait for the host debugger (your cross-gdb) to connect.

Notice that the boot sequence did not complete. Because we placed `kgdbwait` on the command line, the kernel completed initialization up until the serial port drivers were loaded and then hit a predefined breakpoint. At this point, it waits indefinitely for an external debugger to connect.

You should also notice the second new kernel command-line parameter. This particular architecture (Power) and platform (8548CDS) use the 8250 serial driver and a special 8250-based KGDB driver implemented by `.../drivers/serial/8250_kgdb.c`. You must tell KGDB which serial port to use for debugging, using a syntax similar to that used for describing a console device.

Now that the kernel is set up and waiting for the host debugger, we can begin our debugging session. We invoke cross-gdb from our host development workstation and connect to the target through GDB's remote protocol. In this example, we are sharing the serial port with the console, so we must disconnect the terminal emulator from the target before trying to connect with GDB. Listing 14-2 highlights the GDB connection process. This assumes that we have already exited our terminal emulator and freed the serial port for GDB to use.

LISTING 14-2   Connecting to KGDB

```
$ ppc_85xx-gdb -q vmlinux
(gdb) target remote /dev/ttyS0
Remote debugging using /dev/ttyS0
0xc0058360 in kgdb_register_io_module (new_kgdb_io_ops=0x1)
   at kernel/kgdb.c:1802
1802         wmb(); /* Sync point before breakpoint */
(gdb) l
1797   * the debugger.
1798   */
1799   void kgdb_breakpoint(void)
1800   {
1801         atomic_set(&kgdb_setting_breakpoint, 1);
1802         wmb(); /* Sync point before breakpoint */
1803         arch_kgdb_breakpoint();
1804         wmb(); /* Sync point after breakpoint */
1805         atomic_set(&kgdb_setting_breakpoint, 0);
1806   }
(gdb)
```

Here we have performed three actions:

- Invoked our cross-gdb, passing it the kernel ELF file vmlinux
- Connected to the target using the target remote command
- Issued the list command, using its abbreviated form l to display our location in the source code

At the risk of pointing out the obvious, the vmlinux image that we pass to GDB must be from the same kernel build that produced the kernel binary running on your target board. It also must have been compiled with the -g compiler flag to contain debug information. Recall from Chapter 13, "Development Tools," Section 13.5.2, that you can use your cross-readelf tool to verify that your vmlinux image was compiled with debug symbols. Use a command similar to this to verify that you have debug sections in your ELF file:

```
$ ppc_85xx-readelf -S vmlinux | grep debug
```

When we issued the target remote command, GDB responded by displaying the location of the program counter (PC). In this example, the kernel is stopped in the `kgdb_breakpoint()` function at line 1802 in file `.../kernel/kgdb.c`. When we issue the `continue` (c) command, execution resumes from this point.

14.2.3   Useful Kernel Breakpoints

We have now established a debug connection with the kernel on our target board. When we issue the GDB continue (c) command, the kernel proceeds to boot, and if no problems occur, the boot process completes. At this stage, you may want to place some breakpoints to establish your particular debug session. Two of the most common are highlighted in Listing 14-3.

LISTING 14-3   Common Kernel Breakpoints

```
(gdb) b panic
Breakpoint 1 at 0xc02d1a84: file arch/powerpc/include/asm/thread_info.h, line 87.
(gdb) b sys_sync
Breakpoint 2 at 0xc00baae4: file fs/sync.c, line 41.
(gdb) c
Continuing.
```

Using the GDB `breakpoint` command, again using its abbreviated version, we enter two breakpoints. One is at `panic()`, and the other is at the sync system call entry `sys_sync()`. The former allows the debugger to be invoked if a later event generates a panic. This enables examination of the system state at the time of the panic. The second is a useful way to halt the kernel and trap into the debugger from user space by entering the `sync` command from a terminal running on your target hardware.

We are now ready to proceed with our debugging session. We have a KGDB-enabled kernel running on our target, paused at a KGDB-defined breakpoint. We established a connection to the target with our host-based cross debugger—in this case, invoked as `ppc_85xx-gdb`—and we have entered a pair of useful system breakpoints. Now we can direct our debugging activities to the task at hand.

One caveat: By definition, we cannot use KGDB for stepping through code before the `breakpoint()` used to establish the connection between a KGDB-enabled kernel and cross-gdb on our host. Figure 14-3 is a rough approximation of the code that executes before KGDB gains control. Debugging this early code requires the use of a hardware-assisted debug probe. We cover this topic in Section 14.4, "Hardware-Assisted Debugging."

Once your initial breakpoints have been set up, and you issue the `continue` command, you can stop execution at any time simply by issuing Ctrl-C to your cross-gdb. Listing 14-4 shows how this might look.

LISTING 14-4   Kernel Debug Session in Progress

```
(gdb) c
Continuing.


<<<<<<< User types Ctl-C here >>>>>>>>>

Program received signal SIGTRAP, Trace/breakpoint trap.
0xc0058048 in kgdb_breakpoint () at kernel/kgdb.c:1802
1802          wmb(); /* Sync point before breakpoint */
(gdb) bt
#0  0xc0058048 in kgdb_breakpoint () at kernel/kgdb.c:1802
#1  0xc019bcdc in kgdb8250_interrupt (irq=<value optimized out>,
     dev_id=<value optimized out>) at drivers/serial/8250_kgdb.c:145
#2  0xc005a4f0 in handle_IRQ_event (irq=42, action=0xcf80af20)
     at kernel/irq/handle.c:140
#3  0xc005c19c in handle_fasteoi_irq (irq=42, desc=0xc039a950)
     at kernel/irq/chip.c:424
#4  0xc0004b04 in do_IRQ (regs=<value optimized out>)
     at include/linux/irq.h:289
#5  0xc000f310 in ret_from_except_full ()
#6  0xc0008144 in cpu_idle () at arch/powerpc/kernel/idle.c:59
#7  0xc02d022c in rest_init () at init/main.c:481
#0  0xc036e75c in start_kernel () at init/main.c:691
#9  0xc00003d0 in skpinv ()
(gdb)
```

You can see the effects of compiler optimization in Listing 14-4. This is discussed further in Section 14.3.2.

14.2.4   Sharing a Console Serial Port with KGDB

Although it is possible to use a single serial port for your system console as well as for KGDB over serial, it is certainly not ideal. KGDB exists in various states of completeness, depending on your architecture and platform. Once you depart from x86 architectures, things become less certain. KGDB has many connection options, including using serial ports, Ethernet ports, and even USB on some platforms. It is a sure bet that not all of these combinations are tested on any given platform.

It has been stated elsewhere in this book: If you believe you will need to engage in kernel debugging using KGDB, the cost of an extra serial port is easily justifiable, especially if it can be depopulated for production if necessary to meet cost goals. The aggravation saved (read developer's time) will more than pay back the incremental development costs.

To share the serial port between the console and KGDB, you need two command-line parameters. Use the kernel command-line parameter `kgdboc` to specify which serial port to use, and use `kgdbcon` to specify that you will share this port with the console. Specify the `kgdboc` parameter with a serial console, in a manner similar to that for describing the console device on the kernel command line:

```
kgdbcon kgdboc=ttyS1,115200
```

When you boot the kernel and connect with KGDB, any console messages are displayed by your cross-gdb. Listing 14-5 shows what this looks like. First we boot the target using the extra kernel command-line parameters just mentioned. The target boots to a login prompt. Now we must enable KGDB using the SysRequest function. The easiest way to do this from a serial port on the console is to use the /proc interface:

```
root@8548:~# echo g >/proc/sysrq-trigger
SysRq : GDB
Entering KGDB
```

Now we disconnect our serial terminal from the console to free it for use by KGDB. We then launch our cross-gdb, and the session continues as shown in Listing 14-5.

LISTING 14-5   Sharing the Serial Console with KGDB

```
$ ppc_85xx-gdb -q vmlinux
(gdb) target remote /dev/ttyS0
Remote debugging using /dev/ttyS0
0xc0058098 in sysrq_handle_gdb (key=0x11, tty=0x8ddf) at kernel/kgdb.c:1802
1802        wmb(); /* Sync point before breakpoint */
(gdb) b sys_sync
Breakpoint 1 at 0xc00baae4: file fs/sync.c, line 41.
(gdb) b panic
Breakpoint 2 at 0xc02d1a84: file arch/powerpc/include/asm/thread_info.h, line 87.
(gdb) c
Continuing.
<<<< After logging in via SSH on another terminal
<<<< we execute `modprobe ipv6' at this point in time
```

LISTING 14-5   Continued

```
[New Thread 1665]
NET: Registered protocol family 10
lo: Disabled Privacy Extensions
ADDRCONF(NETDEV_UP): eth1: link is not ready
tun10: Disabled Privacy Extensions
```

As shown in Listing 14-5, we set breakpoints and continue, allowing the kernel to run again, with our breakpoints set. On a separate terminal window on our host, we ssh into the target and load a module. In this case, it is `ipv6.ko`. It doesn't really matter what module we use. Our goal is to generate some kernel `printk` messages to verify that they actually arrive on the GDB terminal window. You can see these messages starting with the `[New Thread 1665]` line. These are kernel `printk` messages routed to the system console and routed from KGDB via GDB remote protocol to the GDB console. Very cool indeed.

14.2.5   Debugging Very Early Kernel Code

The techniques just described do not allow for the debugging of very early kernel code during kernel initialization. In fact, the best you can do is to debug initialization code after the serial driver has been called and registered. On some architectures and platforms, this capability is provided by two kernel command-line parameters: `kgdbwait` and `kgdb8250`.[5]

Support for early kernel debug requires a KGDB I/O driver that supports early kernel debug. The most common (and least intrusive) I/O method for early kernel debug using KGDB is the serial driver. An example of this is the `kgdb8250` driver referenced earlier. It should be obvious that this driver will need to be compiled into the kernel to be available for early kernel debug.

As we saw in Listing 14-1, `kgdb8250` is used to tell KGDB which serial port to use. However, using an alternative syntax, we can invoke an early serial initialization routine that will allow very early kernel debugging. Using `kgdbwait` we can instruct the kernel to halt very early in the initialization sequence to wait for commands from the user. Add these variables to the kernel command line to enable early kernel debugging using KGDB:

```
kgdb8250=ttyS1,115200 kgdbwait
```

---

[5] This early debug support was provided by MontaVista in its commercial embedded Linux offering for the MPC8548 platform. Currently it is unavailable in mainstream kernel sources. Your kernel would need to be patched with these early serial drivers in order to duplicate this functionality.

It is important to realize that the order of these kernel command-line parameters is critical. You must supply the KGDB I/O driver first (in our example it is `kgdb8250`) so that it can be initialized before `kgdbwait` is encountered. Since `kgdbwait` basically causes a debug breakpoint, infrastructure must be in place to communicate to a debugger prior to issuing the breakpoint.

Another point to remember is that this support typically is platform-specific. That is, your kernel and platform must support some type of early kernel debug I/O driver for this functionality to be available. Your platform might have different hardware available for this purpose, so it is up to you (or your embedded Linux vendor) to supply the early kernel debug I/O driver.

For the `kgdb8250` I/O driver, you can also supply a complete specification that passes the driver detailed information for your specific board. This can include what type of I/O is required to access this driver, its base address, and optionally a register shift value and IRQ along with baud rate. In this form, it looks like this:

```
kgdb8250=<io|mmio|mbase>,<address>[/<regshift>],<baud rate>,<irq>
```

14.2.6   KGDB Support in the Mainline Kernel

As of Linux 2.6.26, generic KGDB support has been incorporated into the Linux kernel available from kernel.org. Once the kernel has been compiled with KGDB support as described earlier, two kernel command-line parameters are used to configure KGDB at runtime. `kgdboc` is used to specify the serial port to use, and `kgdbwait` is used to cause the kernel to execute a breakpoint on boot to allow the debugger (`gdb`) to gain control. The syntax for `kgdboc` is the same as that for `kgdb8250`, as just described in Section 14.2.5, specifying the serial port and baud rate. `kgdbwait` is used stand-alone without parameters. Similar to the example in Section 14.2.5, the kernel command-line parameters for enabling KGDB in Linux 2.6.26 and above are as follows. Note that the order of these parameters is important. The serial port must be specified before you can instruct the kernel to perform the breakpoint:

```
kgdboc=ttyS1,115200 kgdbwait
```

On boot, the kernel performs most of the system initialization and then waits for the debugger to connect. Listing 14-6 illustrates this sequence.

LISTING 14-6   Booting with Generic KGDB from Kernel.org

```
<... boot kernel using kgdboc=ttyS0,115200 kgdbwait ...>
... (many boot messages)
Serial: 8250/16550 driver, 2 ports, IRQ sharing enabled
serial8250.0: ttyS0 at MMIO 0xffe04500 (irq = 42) is a 16550A
console handover: boot [udbg0] -> real [ttyS0]
serial8250.0: ttyS1 at MMIO 0xffe04600 (irq = 42) is a 16550A
kgdb: Registered I/O driver kgdboc.
kgdb: Waiting for connection from remote gdb...
```

At this point, the kernel is waiting for connection from a remote GDB session, and debugging can begin. Notice that this is fairly late in the kernel boot sequence. To debug a generic Linux kernel any earlier in the boot sequence, you must use hardware-assisted debugging using a JTAG probe. This is described shortly.

14.3 Kernel Debugging Techniques

One of the more common reasons you might find yourself stepping through kernel code is to modify or customize the platform-specific code for your custom board. Let's see how this might be done using the AMCC Yosemite board. We place a breakpoint at the platform-specific architecture setup functionv and then continue until that breakpoint is encountered. Listing 14-7 shows the sequence.

LISTING 14-7   Debugging Architecture Setup Code

```
(gdb) b yosemite_setup_arch
    Breakpoint 3 at 0xc021a488:
        file arch/ppc/platforms/4xx/yosemite.c, line 308.
(gdb) c
Continuing.
Can't send signals to this remote system.  SIGILL not sent.

Breakpoint 3, yosemite_setup_arch () at arch/ppc/platforms/4xx/yosemite.c:308
308                 yosemite_set_emacdata();
(gdb) l
303     }
304
305     static void __init
306     yosemite_setup_arch(void)
307     {
308                 yosemite_set_emacdata();
```

LISTING 14-7   Debugging Architecture Setup Code

```
309
310             ibm440gx_get_clocks(&clocks, YOSEMITE_SYSCLK, 6 * 1843200);
311             ocp_sys_info.opb_bus_freq = clocks.opb;
312
(gdb)
```

When the breakpoint at `yosemite_setup_arch()` is encountered, control passes to GDB at line 308 of `yosemite.c`. The `list` (`l`) command displays the source listing centered on the breakpoint at line 308. The warning message about SIGILL displayed by GDB after the continue (c) command can be safely ignored. It is part of GDB's way of testing the capabilities of the remote system. It first sends a remote `continue_with_signal` command to the target. The KGDB implementation for this target board does not support this command; therefore, it is NAKed by the target. GDB responds by displaying this informational message and issuing the standard remote continue command instead.

14.3.1   gdb Remote Serial Protocol

GDB includes a debug switch that enables us to observe the remote protocol being used between GDB on your development host and the target. This can be very useful for understanding the underlying protocol, as well as for troubleshooting targets that exhibit unusual or errant behavior. To enable this debug mode, issue the following command:

```
(gdb) set debug remote 1
```

With remote debugging enabled, it is instructive to observe the continue command in action and the steps taken by GDB. Listing 14-8 illustrates the use of the continue command with remote debugging enabled.

LISTING 14-8   Remote Protocol Example: continue Command

```
(gdb) c
Continuing.
Sending packet: $mc0000000,4#80...Ack
Packet received: c022d200
Sending packet: $Mc0000000,4:7d821008#68...Ack
Packet received: OK
Sending packet: $mc0016de8,4#f8...Ack
```

LISTING 14-8 Remote Protocol Example: continue Command

```
Packet received: 38600001
Sending packet: $Mc0016de8,4:7d821008#e0...Ack
Packet received: OK
Sending packet: $mc005bd5c,4#23...Ack
Packet received: 38600001
Sending packet: $Mc005bd5c,4:7d821008#0b...Ack
Packet received: OK
Sending packet: $mc021a488,4#c8...Ack
Packet received: 4bfffbad
Sending packet: $Mc021a488,4:7d821008#b0...Ack
Packet received: OK
Sending packet: $c#63...Ack
    <<< program running, gdb waiting for event
```

Although it might look daunting at first, what is happening here is easily understood. In summary, GDB is restoring all its breakpoints on the target. Recall from Listing 14-3 that we entered two breakpoints—one at panic() and one at sys_sync(). Later, in Listing 14-7, we added a third breakpoint at yosemite_setup_arch(). Thus, there are three active user-specified breakpoints. These can be displayed by issuing the GDB info breakpoints command. As usual, we use the abbreviated version:

```
(gdb) i b
Num Type           Disp Enb Address    What
1   breakpoint     keep y   0xc0016de8 in panic at kernel/panic.c:74
2   breakpoint     keep y   0xc005bd5c in sys_sync at fs/buffer.c:296
3   breakpoint     keep y   0xc021a488 in yosemite_setup_arch at
arch/ppc/platforms/4xx/yosemite.c:308
        breakpoint already hit 1 time
(gdb)
```

Now compare the previous breakpoint addresses with the addresses in the GDB remote $m packet in Listing 14-8. The $m packet is a "read target memory" command, and the $M packet is a "write target memory" command. Once for each breakpoint, the address of the breakpoint is read from target memory, stored locally on the host by GDB (so that it can be restored later), and replaced with the Power Architecture trap instruction twge r2, r2 (0x7d821008). This results in control passing back to the debugger. Figure 14-4 illustrates this action.

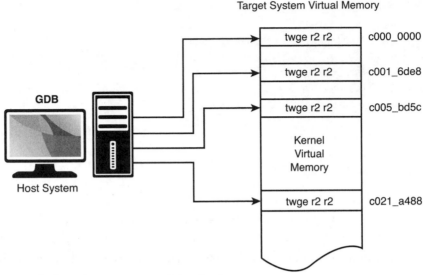

FIGURE 14-4   GDB inserting target memory breakpoints

You might have noticed that GDB is updating four breakpoints, whereas we entered only three. The first one, at target memory location 0xc000_0000, is put there by GDB automatically upon startup. This location is the base address of the linked kernel image from the ELF file—essentially, _start. It is equivalent to a breakpoint at main() for user space debugging and is done by GDB automatically. The other three breakpoints are the ones we entered earlier.

The same thing happens in reverse when an event occurs that returns control to GDB. Listing 14-9 details the action when our breakpoint at yosemite_setup_arch() is encountered.

LISTING 14-9   Remote Protocol: Breakpoint Hit

```
Packet received: T0440:c021a488;01:c020ff90;
Sending packet: $mc0000000,4#80...Ack  <<< Read memory @c0000000
Packet received: 7d821008
Sending packet: $Mc0000000,4:c022d200#87...Ack  <<< Write memory
Packet received: OK
Sending packet: $mc0016de8,4#f8...Ack
Packet received: 7d821008
Sending packet: $Mc0016de8,4:38600001#a4...Ack
Packet received: OK
Sending packet: $mc005bd5c,4#23...Ack
```

LISTING 14-9   Continued

```
Packet received: 7d821008
Sending packet: $Mc005bd5c,4:38600001#cf...Ack
Packet received: OK
Sending packet: $mc021a488,4#c8...Ack
Packet received: 7d821008
Sending packet: $Mc021a488,4:4bfffbad#d1...Ack
Packet received: OK

Sending packet: $mc021a484,c#f3...Ack
Packet received: 900100244bfffbad3fa0c022
Breakpoint 3, yosemite_setup_arch () at arch/ppc/platforms/4xx/yosemite.c:308
308                 yosemite_set_emacdata();
(gdb)
```

The $T packet is a GDB Stop Reply packet. It is sent by the target to GDB when a breakpoint is encountered. In our example, the $T packet returns the value of the program counter and register r1.[6] The rest of the activity is the reverse of that shown in Listing 14-8. The Power Architecture trap breakpoint instructions are removed, and GDB restores the original instructions to their respective memory locations.

14.3.2   Debugging Optimized Kernel Code

At the start of this chapter, we said that one of the challenges of debugging kernel code results from compiler optimization. We noted that the Linux kernel is compiled by default with optimization level -O2. Here we illustrate one of the many ways optimization can complicate the debugging process.

The related Internet mail lists are strewn with questions about what appear to be broken tools. Sometimes the poster reports that his debugger is single-stepping backward or that his line numbers do not line up with his source code. Here we present an example to illustrate the complexities that optimizing compilers bring to source-level debugging. In this example, the line numbers that GDB reports when a breakpoint is hit do not match up with the line numbers in our source file due to function inlining.

For this demonstration, we use the same debug code snippet as shown in Listing 14-7. Listing 14-10 shows the results of this debugging session.

---

[6] As pointed out earlier, the GDB remote protocol is detailed in the GDB manual cited at the end of this chapter.

LISTING 14-10   Optimized Architecture-Setup Code

```
$ ppc_44x-gdb --silent vmlinux
(gdb) target remote /dev/ttyS0
Remote debugging using /dev/ttyS0
breakinst () at arch/ppc/kernel/ppc-stub.c:825
825          }
(gdb) b panic
Breakpoint 1 at 0xc0016b18: file kernel/panic.c, line 74.
(gdb) b sys_sync
Breakpoint 2 at 0xc005a8c8: file fs/buffer.c, line 296.
(gdb) b yosemite_setup_arch
Breakpoint 3 at 0xc020f438: file arch/ppc/platforms/4xx/yosemite.c, line 116.
(gdb) c
Continuing.

Breakpoint 3, yosemite_setup_arch ()
    at arch/ppc/platforms/4xx/yosemite.c:116
116             def = ocp_get_one_device(OCP_VENDOR_IBM, OCP_FUNC_EMAC, 0);
(gdb) l
111             struct ocp_def *def;
112             struct ocp_func_emac_data *emacdata;
113
114             /* Set mac_addr and phy mode for each EMAC */
115
116             def = ocp_get_one_device(OCP_VENDOR_IBM, OCP_FUNC_EMAC, 0);
117             emacdata = def->additions;
118             memcpy(emacdata->mac_addr, __res.bi_enetaddr, 6);
119             emacdata->phy_mode = PHY_MODE_RMII;
120
(gdb) p yosemite_setup_arch
$1 = {void (void)} 0xc020f41c <yosemite_setup_arch>
```

Referring to Listing 14-7, notice that the function yosemite_setup_arch() actually falls on line 306 of the file yosemite.c. Compare that with Listing 14-10. We hit the breakpoint, but GDB reports the breakpoint at file yosemite.c line 116. It appears at first glance to be a mismatch of line numbers between the debugger and the corresponding source code. Is this a GDB bug? First, let's confirm what the compiler produced for debug information. Using the `readelf` tool[7] described in Chapter 13, we can examine the debug information for this function produced by the compiler:

```
$ ppc_44x-readelf --debug-dump=info vmlinux | grep -u6 \
  yosemite_setup_arch | tail -n 7
   DW_AT_name          : (indirect string, offset: 0x9c04): yosemite_setup_arch
   DW_AT_decl_file     : 1
   DW_AT_decl_line     : 307
   DW_AT_prototyped    : 1
   DW_AT_low_pc        : 0xc020f41c
   DW_AT_high_pc       : 0xc020f794
   DW_AT_frame_base    : 1 byte block: 51      (DW_OP_reg1)
```

We don't have to be experts at reading DWARF2 debug records[8] to recognize that the function in question is reported at line 307 in our source file. We can confirm this using the `addr2line` utility, also introduced in Chapter 13. We can use the address derived from GDB in Listing 14-10:

```
$ ppc_44x-addr2line  -e vmlinux 0xc020f41c
  arch/ppc/platforms/4xx/yosemite.c:307
```

At this point, GDB is reporting our breakpoint at line 116 of the `yosemite.c` file. To understand what is happening, we need to look at the assembler output of the function as reported by GDB. Listing 14-11 is the output from GDB after the `disassemble` command is issued on the `yosemite_setup_arch()` function.

LISTING 14-11   Disassemble Function *yosemite_setup_arch*

```
(gdb) disassemble yosemite_setup_arch
0xc020f41c <yosemite_setup_arch+0>:      mflr    r0
0xc020f420 <yosemite_setup_arch+4>:      stwu    r1,-48(r1)
0xc020f424 <yosemite_setup_arch+8>:      li      r4,512
0xc020f428 <yosemite_setup_arch+12>:     li      r5,0
0xc020f42c <yosemite_setup_arch+16>:     li      r3,4116
0xc020f430 <yosemite_setup_arch+20>:     stmw    r25,20(r1)
0xc020f434 <yosemite_setup_arch+24>:     stw     r0,52(r1)
0xc020f438 <yosemite_setup_arch+28>:     bl      0xc000d344 <ocp_get_one_device>
0xc020f43c <yosemite_setup_arch+32>:     lwz     r31,32(r3)
0xc020f440 <yosemite_setup_arch+36>:     lis     r4,-16350
0xc020f444 <yosemite_setup_arch+40>:     li      r28,2
0xc020f448 <yosemite_setup_arch+44>:     addi    r4,r4,21460
```

---

[7] Remember to use your cross-version of readelf, such as ppc_44x-readelf for the PowerPC 44x architecture.

[8] A reference to the DWARF debug specification appears at the end of this chapter.

LISTING 14-11   Continued

```
0xc020f44c <yosemite_setup_arch+48>:     li      r5,6
0xc020f450 <yosemite_setup_arch+52>:     lis     r29,-16350
0xc020f454 <yosemite_setup_arch+56>:     addi    r3,r31,48
0xc020f458 <yosemite_setup_arch+60>:     lis     r25,-16350
0xc020f45c <yosemite_setup_arch+64>:     bl      0xc000c708 <memcpy>
0xc020f460 <yosemite_setup_arch+68>:     stw     r28,44(r31)
0xc020f464 <yosemite_setup_arch+72>:     li      r4,512
0xc020f468 <yosemite_setup_arch+76>:     li      r5,1
0xc020f46c <yosemite_setup_arch+80>:     li      r3,4116
0xc020f470 <yosemite_setup_arch+84>:     addi    r26,r25,15104
0xc020f474 <yosemite_setup_arch+88>:     bl      0xc000d344 <ocp_get_one_device>
0xc020f478 <yosemite_setup_arch+92>:     lis     r4,-16350
0xc020f47c <yosemite_setup_arch+96>:     lwz     r31,32(r3)
0xc020f480 <yosemite_setup_arch+100>:    addi    r4,r4,21534
0xc020f484 <yosemite_setup_arch+104>:    li      r5,6
0xc020f488 <yosemite_setup_arch+108>:    addi    r3,r31,48
0xc020f48c <yosemite_setup_arch+112>:    bl      0xc000c708 <memcpy>
0xc020f490 <yosemite_setup_arch+116>:    lis     r4,1017
0xc020f494 <yosemite_setup_arch+120>:    lis     r5,168
0xc020f498 <yosemite_setup_arch+124>:    stw     r28,44(r31)
0xc020f49c <yosemite_setup_arch+128>:    ori     r4,r4,16554
0xc020f4a0 <yosemite_setup_arch+132>:    ori     r5,r5,49152
0xc020f4a4 <yosemite_setup_arch+136>:    addi    r3,r29,-15380
0xc020f4a8 <yosemite_setup_arch+140>:    addi    r29,r29,-15380
0xc020f4ac <yosemite_setup_arch+144>:    bl      0xc020e338 <ibm440gx_get_clocks>
0xc020f4b0 <yosemite_setup_arch+148>:    li      r0,0
0xc020f4b4 <yosemite_setup_arch+152>:    lis     r11,-16352
0xc020f4b8 <yosemite_setup_arch+156>:    ori     r0,r0,50000
0xc020f4bc <yosemite_setup_arch+160>:    lwz     r10,12(r29)
0xc020f4c0 <yosemite_setup_arch+164>:    lis     r9,-16352
0xc020f4c4 <yosemite_setup_arch+168>:    stw     r0,8068(r11)
0xc020f4c8 <yosemite_setup_arch+172>:    lwz     r0,84(r26)
0xc020f4cc <yosemite_setup_arch+176>:    stw     r10,8136(r9)
0xc020f4d0 <yosemite_setup_arch+180>:    mtctr   r0
0xc020f4d4 <yosemite_setup_arch+184>:    bctrl
0xc020f4d8 <yosemite_setup_arch+188>:    li      r5,64
0xc020f4dc <yosemite_setup_arch+192>:    mr      r31,r3
0xc020f4e0 <yosemite_setup_arch+196>:    lis     r4,-4288
0xc020f4e4 <yosemite_setup_arch+200>:    li      r3,0
0xc020f4e8 <yosemite_setup_arch+204>:    bl      0xc000c0f8 <ioremap64>
End of assembler dump.
(gdb)
```

Again, we need not be Power Architecture assembly language experts to understand what is happening here. Notice the labels associated with the Power Architecture `bl` instruction. This is a function call in Power Architecture mnemonics. The symbolic function labels are the important data points. After a cursory analysis, we see several function calls near the start of this assembler listing:

```
Address      Function
0xc020f438   ocp_get_one_device()
0xc020f45c   memcpy()
0xc020f474   ocp_get_one_device()
0xc020f48c   memcpy()
0xc020f4ac   ibm440gx_get_clocks()
```

Listing 14-12 reproduces portions of the source file `yosemite.c`. Correlating the functions we found in the GDB disassemble output, we see those labels occurring in the function `yosemite_set_emacdata()`, around the line numbers reported by GDB when the breakpoint at `yosemite_setup_arch()` was encountered. The key to understanding this anomaly is to notice the subroutine call at the very start of `yosemite_setup_arch()`. The compiler has inlined the call to `yosemite_set_emacdata()` instead of generating a function call, as would be expected by simple inspection of the source code. This inlining produced the mismatch in the line numbers when GDB hit the breakpoint. Even though the `yosemite_set_emacdata()` function was not declared using the `inline` keyword, GCC inlined the function as a performance optimization.

LISTING 14-12 Portions of Source File **yosemite.c**

```
109 static void __init yosemite_set_emacdata(void)
110 {
111         struct ocp_def *def;
112         struct ocp_func_emac_data *emacdata;
113
114         /* Set mac_addr and phy mode for each EMAC */
115
116         def = ocp_get_one_device(OCP_VENDOR_IBM, OCP_FUNC_EMAC, 0);
117         emacdata = def->additions;
118         memcpy(emacdata->mac_addr, __res.bi_enetaddr, 6);
119         emacdata->phy_mode = PHY_MODE_RMII;
120
121         def = ocp_get_one_device(OCP_VENDOR_IBM, OCP_FUNC_EMAC, 1);
122         emacdata = def->additions;
123         memcpy(emacdata->mac_addr, __res.bi_enet1addr, 6);
```

LISTING 14-12   Continued

```
124             emacdata->phy_mode = PHY_MODE_RMII;
125 }
126

...

304
305 static void __init
306 yosemite_setup_arch(void)
307 {
308         yosemite_set_emacdata();
309
310         ibm440gx_get_clocks(&clocks, YOSEMITE_SYSCLK, 6 * 1843200);
311         ocp_sys_info.opb_bus_freq = clocks.opb;
312
313         /* init to some ~sane value until calibrate_delay() runs */
314         loops_per_jiffy = 50000000/HZ;
315
316         /* Setup PCI host bridge */
317         yosemite_setup_hose();
318
319 #ifdef CONFIG_BLK_DEV_INITRD
320     if (initrd_start)
321             ROOT_DEV = Root_RAM0;
322     else
323 #endif
324 #ifdef CONFIG_ROOT_NFS
325                 ROOT_DEV = Root_NFS;
326 #else
327                 ROOT_DEV = Root_HDA1;
328 #endif
329
330         yosemite_early_serial_map();
331
332         /* Identify the system */
333         printk( "AMCC PowerPC " BOARDNAME " Platform\n" );
334 }
335
```

To summarize the previous discussion:

- We entered a breakpoint in GDB at yosemite_setup_arch().
- When the breakpoint was hit, we found ourselves at line 116 of the source file, which was far removed from the function where we defined the breakpoint.

- We produced a disassembly listing of the code at `yosemite_setup_arch()` and discovered the labels to which this sequence of code was branching.

- Comparing the labels to our source code, we discovered that the compiler placed the `yosemite_set_emacdata()` subroutine inline with the function where we entered a breakpoint, causing potential confusion.

This explains the line numbers reported by GDB when the original breakpoint in `yosemite_setup_arch()` was hit.

Recall that Listing 14-4 contained several examples of another type of optimization, with the debugger reporting `value optimized out` on certain variables. These are examples of where a local variable has been replaced by a processor register for the duration of the function. Therefore, the local variable has been optimized out by the compiler. This is easily illustrated using a snippet of U-Boot code from the `cmd_bootm.c` file. Listing 14-13 shows a few lines from the `do_bootm()` function.

LISTING 14-13   Example of Local Variable Optimized Out

```
584 int do_bootm (cmd_tbl_t *cmdtp, int flag, int argc, char *argv[])
 585 {
586          ulong          iflag;
587          ulong          load_end = 0;
588          int            ret;

<...many lines omitted>

 652          ret = bootm_load_os(images.os, &load_end, 1);
 653
 654          if (ret < 0) {
 655                  if (ret == BOOTM_ERR_RESET)
 656                          do_reset (cmdtp, flag, argc, argv);
 ...
```

Stepping through this code using a BDI-2000/3000 using your cross-gdb would look something like this:

```
(gdb) l 654
649          dcache_disable();
650     #endif
651
652          ret = bootm_load_os(images.os, &load_end, 1);
653
```

```
654            if (ret < 0) {
655                    if (ret == BOOTM_ERR_RESET)
656                            do_reset (cmdtp, flag, argc, argv);
657                    if (ret == BOOTM_ERR_OVERLAP) {
658                            if (images.legacy_hdr_valid) {
(gdb) p ret
$2 = <value optimized out>
```

Notice after the call to `bootm_load_os()`, we read the value returned by the function, which, according to the source code on line 652, is stored in a local variable called `ret`. Attempting to display the value of `ret` results in the now-familiar `<value optimized out>` message. Because we know that Power Architecture returns its function call results in register R3, we can display the return code by displaying R3 immediately after this call returns:

```
(gdb) mon rd
GPR00: 0ff7c9ec 0ff4db40 0ff4df64 00000000
GPR04: 00000002 00000000 0ff50ac8 00002538
GPR08: 00001000 00000020 00003538 00000001
GPR12: 24044022 1001a5b8 00000000 00000000
GPR16: 0ff88af4 00000000 00000000 00000000
GPR20: 00000000 00000000 0fff10f4 00000000
GPR24: 00000001 00000000 0ffab9d0 00000004
GPR28: 0ff50a40 0fff0b34 0ffaf0f0 00000000
CR   : 42044048     MSR: 00021200
(gdb)
```

This command issues the BDI-2000/3000 `rd` command (display general-purpose registers) directly and returns the results. GPR03 (R3) contains 0s, indicating that the function call was successful.

Compilers employ many different kinds of optimization algorithms. This example presented just one: function inlining. Each can confuse a debugger (the human and the machine) in a different way. The challenge is to understand what is happening at the machine level and translate that into what we as developers intended. You can see now the benefits of using the minimum possible optimization level for debugging.

14.3.3   GDB User-Defined Commands

You might already know that GDB looks for an initialization file on startup, called `.gdbinit`. When first invoked, GDB loads this initialization file (usually found in the user's home directory) and acts on the commands within it. One of my favorite combinations is to connect to the target system and set initial breakpoints. In this case, the contents of .gdbinit would look like Listing 14-14.

LISTING 14-14   Simple GDB Initialization File

```
$ cat ~/.gdbinit
set history save on
set history filename ~/.gdb_history
set output-radix 16

define connect
#    target remote bdi:2001
     target remote /dev/ttyS0
     b panic
     b sys_sync
end
```

This simple .gdbinit file enables the storing of command history in a user-specified file and sets the default output radix for printing of values. Then it defines a GDB user-defined command called connect. (User-defined commands are also often called macros.) When this command is issued at the GDB command prompt, GDB connects to the target system using the desired method (the serial port in this example) and sets the system breakpoints at panic() and sys_sync(). The network method (*host:port*) is commented out; we discuss this method in Section 14.4.

There is no end to the creative uses of GDB user-defined commands. When debugging in the kernel, it is often useful to examine global data structures such as task lists and memory maps. Here we present several useful GDB user-defined commands that can display specific kernel data that you might need to access during your kernel debugging.

14.3.4   Useful Kernel GDB Macros

During kernel debugging, it is often useful to view the processes that are running on the system, as well as some common attributes of those processes. The kernel maintains a linked list of tasks described by struct task_struct. The address of the first task in the list is contained in the kernel global variable init_task, which represents the initial task spawned by the kernel during startup. Each task contains a struct list_head, which links the tasks in a circular linked list. These two ubiquitous kernel structures are described in the following header files:

```
struct task_struct              .../include/linux/sched.h
struct list_head                .../include/linux/list.h
```

Using GDB macros, we can traverse the task list and display useful information about the tasks. It is easy to modify the macros to extract the data you might be interested in. It is also a very useful tool for learning the details of kernel internals.

The first macro we examine in Listing 14-15 (find_task) is a simple one that searches the kernel's linked list of task_struct structures until it finds the given task. If the task is found, the macro displays the name of the task.

LISTING 14-15   GDB *find_task* Macro

```
 1 # Helper function to find a task given a PID or the
 2 # address of a task_struct.
 3 # The result is set into $t
 4 define find_task
 5   # Addresses greater than _end: kernel data...
 6   # ...user passed in an address
 7   if ((unsigned)$arg0 > (unsigned)&_end)
 8     set $t=(struct task_struct *)$arg0
 9   else
10     # User entered a numeric PID
11     # Walk the task list to find it
12     set $t=&init_task
13     if (init_task.pid != (unsigned)$arg0)
14       find_next_task $t
15       while (&init_task!=$t && $t->pid != (unsigned)$arg0)
16         find_next_task $t
17       end
18       if ($t == &init_task)
19         printf "Couldn't find task; using init_task\n"
20       end
21     end
22   end
23   printf "Task \"%s\":\n", $t->comm
24 end
```

Place this text in your .gdbinit file and restart GDB, or source it[9] using GDB's source command. (We explain the find_next_task macro later, in Listing 14-19.) Invoke it as follows:

```
(gdb) find_task 910
    Task "syslogd":
```

Note that you can also pass an address to the find_task macro as follows:

```
(gdb) find_task 0xCFFDE470
    Task "bash":
```

Of course, you will have to supply valid parameters based on your own particular debug scenario.

Line 4 of Listing 14-15 defines the macro name. Line 7 decides whether the input argument is a PID (a numeric entry starting at 0 and limited to a few million) or a task_struct address that must be greater than the end of the Linux kernel image itself, defined by the symbol _end.[10] If it's an address, the only action required is to cast it to the proper type to enable dereferencing the associated task_struct. This is done at line 8. As the comment in line 3 states, this macro returns a GDB convenience variable typecast to a pointer to a struct task_struct.

If the input argument is a numeric PID, the list is traversed to find the matching task_struct. Lines 12 and 13 initialize the loop variables (GDB does not have a for statement in its macro command language), and lines 15 through 17 define the search loop. The find_next_task macro is used to extract the pointer to the next task_struct in the linked list. Finally, if the search fails, a sane return value is set (the address of init_task) so that it can be safely used in other macros.

Building on the find_task macro in Listing 14-15, we can easily create a simple ps command that displays useful information about each process running on the system.

Listing 14-16 defines a GDB macro called ps that displays interesting information from a running process, extracted from the struct task_struct for the given process. It is invoked like any other GDB command, by typing its name followed by any required input parameters. Notice that this user-defined command requires a single argument, either a PID or the address of a task_struct.

---

[9] A helpful shortcut for macro development is the GDB source command. This command opens and reads a source file containing macro definitions.

[10] The symbol _end is defined in the linker script file during the final link.

LISTING 14-16   GDB Print Process Information Macro

```
1 define ps
2    # Print column headers
3    task_struct_header
4    set $t=&init_task
5    task_struct_show $t
6    find_next_task $t
7    # Walk the list
8    while &init_task!=$t
9      # Display useful info about each task
10     task_struct_show $t
11     find_next_task $t
12   end
13 end
14
15 document ps
16 Print points of interest for all tasks
17 end
```

This ps macro is similar to the find_task macro, except that it requires no input arguments and it adds a macro (task_struct_show) to display the useful information from each task_struct. Line 3 prints a banner line with column headings. Lines 4 through 6 set up the loop and display the first task. Lines 8 through 11 loop through each task, calling the task_struct_show macro for each.

Notice also the inclusion of the GDB document command. This allows the GDB user to get help by issuing the help ps command from the GDB command prompt as follows:

```
(gdb) help ps
    Print points of interest for all tasks
```

Listing 14-17 displays the output of this macro on a target board running only minimal services.

LISTING 14-17   GDB *ps* Macro Output

```
(gdb) ps
Address      PID State      User_NIP    Kernel-SP  device comm
0xC01D3750     0 Running                0xC0205E90 (none) swapper
0xC04ACB10     1 Sleeping   0x0FF6E85C  0xC04FFCE0 (none) init
0xC04AC770     2 Sleeping               0xC0501E90 (none) ksoftirqd/0
0xC04AC3D0     3 Sleeping               0xC0531E30 (none) events/0
```

LISTING 14-17   Continued

```
0xC04AC030      4 Sleeping                       0xC0533E30  (none)  khelper
0xC04CDB30      5 Sleeping                       0xC0535E30  (none)  kthread
0xC04CD790     23 Sleeping                       0xC06FBE30  (none)  kblockd/0
0xC04CD3F0     45 Sleeping                       0xC06FDE50  (none)  pdflush
0xC04CD050     46 Sleeping                       0xC06FFE50  (none)  pdflush
0xC054B7B0     48 Sleeping                       0xC0703E30  (none)  aio/0
0xC054BB50     47 Sleeping                       0xC0701E20  (none)  kswapd0
0xC054B410    629 Sleeping                       0xC0781E60  (none)  kseriod
0xC054B070    663 Sleeping                       0xCFC59E30  (none)  rpciod/0
0xCFFDE0D0    675 Sleeping  0x0FF6E85C  0xCF86DCE0  (none)  udevd
0xCF95B110    879 Sleeping  0x0FF0BE58  0xCF517D80  (none)  portmap
0xCFC24090    910 Sleeping  0x0FF6E85C  0xCF61BCE0  (none)  syslogd
0xCF804490    918 Sleeping  0x0FF66C7C  0xCF65DD70  (none)  klogd
0xCFE350B0    948 Sleeping  0x0FF0E85C  0xCF67DCE0  (none)  rpc.statd
0xCFFDE810    960 Sleeping  0x0FF6E85C  0xCF5C7CE0  (none)  inetd
0xCFC24B70    964 Sleeping  0x0FEEBEAC  0xCF64FD80  (none)  mvltd
0xCFE35B90    973 Sleeping  0x0FF66C7C  0xCFEF7CE0  ttyS1   getty
0xCFE357F0    974 Sleeping  0x0FF4B85C  0xCF6EBCE0  (none)  in.telnetd
0xCFFDE470    979 Sleeping  0x0FEB6950  0xCF675DB0  ttyp0   bash
0xCFFDEBB0    982<Running   0x0FF6EB6C  0xCF7C3870  ttyp0   sync
(gdb)
```

The bulk of the work done by this `ps` macro is performed by the `task_struct_show` macro. As shown in Listing 14-17, the `task_struct_show` macro displays the following fields from each `task_struct`:

- **Address**—Address of the `task_struct` for the process
- **PID**—Process ID
- **State**—Current state of the process
- **User_NIP**—User space next instruction pointer
- **Kernel_SP**—Kernel stack pointer
- **device**—Device associated with this process
- **comm**—Name of the process (or command)

It is relatively easy to modify the macro to show the items of interest for your particular kernel debugging task. The only complexity is in the simplicity of the macro language. Because function equivalents such as `strlen` do not exist in GDB's user-defined command language, screen formatting must be done by hand.

Listing 14-18 shows the `task_struct_show` macro that produced the preceding listing.

LISTING 14-18   GDB *task_struct_show* Macro

```
1  define task_struct_show
2    # task_struct addr and PID
3    printf "0x%08X %5d", $arg0, $arg0->pid
4
5    # Place a '<' marker on the current task
6    #  if ($arg0 == current)
7    # For PowerPC, register r2 points to the "current" task
8    if ($arg0 == $r2)
9      printf "<"
10   else
11     printf " "
12   end
13
14   # State
15   if ($arg0->state == 0)
16     printf "Running    "
17   else
18     if ($arg0->state == 1)
19       printf "Sleeping  "
20     else
21       if ($arg0->state == 2)
22         printf "Disksleep "
23       else
24         if ($arg0->state == 4)
25           printf "Zombie    "
26         else
27           if ($arg0->state == 8)
28             printf "sTopped   "
29           else
30             if ($arg0->state == 16)
31               printf "Wpaging   "
32             else
33               printf "%2d        ", $arg0->state
34             end
35           end
36         end
37       end
38     end
```

LISTING 14-18   Continued

```
39    end
40
41    # User NIP
42    if ($arg0->thread.regs)
43      printf "0x%08X ", $arg0->thread.regs->nip
44    else
45      printf "              "
46    end
47
48    # Display the kernel stack pointer
49    printf "0x%08X ", $arg0->thread.ksp
50
51    # device
52    if ($arg0->signal->tty)
53      printf "%s   ", $arg0->signal->tty->name
54    else
55      printf "(none) "
56    end
57
58    # comm
59    printf "%s\n", $arg0->comm
60 end
```

Line 3 displays the address of the `task_struct`. Lines 8 through 12 display the process ID. If this is the current process (the process that was currently running on this CPU when the breakpoint was hit), it is marked with a < character.

Lines 14 through 39 decode and display the state of the process. This is followed by displaying the user process next instruction pointer (NIP) and the kernel stack pointer (SP). Finally, the device associated with the process is displayed, followed by the name of the process (stored in the `->comm` element of the `task_struct`).

It is important to note that this macro is architecture-dependent, as shown in lines 7 and 8. In general, macros such as these are highly architecture- and version-dependent. Anytime a change in the underlying structure is made, macros such as these must be updated. However, if you spend a lot of time debugging the kernel using GDB, the payback is often worth the effort.

For completeness, we present the find_next_task macro. Its implementation is less than obvious and deserves explanation. (It is assumed that you can easily deduce the task_struct_header that completes the series necessary for the ps macro presented in this section. It is nothing more than a single line arranging the column headers with the correct amount of white space.) Listing 14-19 presents the find_next_task macro used in our ps and find_task macros.

LISTING 14-19   GDB *find_next_task* Macro

```
define find_next_task
  # Given a task address, find the next task in the linked list
  set $t = (struct task_struct *)$arg0
  set $offset=( (char *)&$t->tasks - (char *)$t)
  set $t=(struct task_struct *)( (char *)$t->tasks.next- (char *)$offset)
end
```

The function performed by this macro is simple. The implementation is slightly less than straightforward. The goal is to return the ->next pointer, which points to the next task_struct in the linked list. However, the task_struct structures are linked by the address of the struct list_head member called tasks, as opposed to the common practice of being linked by the starting address of the task_struct itself. Because the ->next pointer points to the address of the task structure element in the next task_struct on the list, we must subtract to get the address of the top of the task_struct itself. The value we subtract from the ->next pointer is the offset from that pointer's address to the top of task_struct. First we calculate the offset, and then we use that offset to adjust the ->next pointer to point to the top of task_struct. Figure 14-5 should make this clear.

Now we present a final macro called lsmod that will be useful in the next section when we discuss debugging loadable modules. Listing 14-20 is a simple macro that displays the kernel's list of currently installed loadable modules.

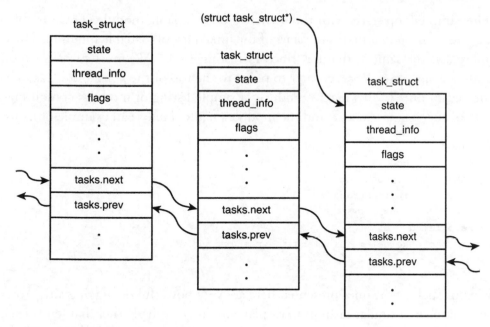

FIGURE 14-5   Task structure list linking

LISTING 14-20   GDB List Modules Macro

```
1 define lsmod
2   printf "Address\t\tModule\n"
3   set $m=(struct list_head *)&modules
4   set $done=0
5   while ( !$done )
6     # list_head is 4-bytes into struct module
7     set $mp=(struct module *)((char *)$m->next - (char *)4)
8     printf "0x%08X\t%s\n", $mp, $mp->name
9     if ( $mp->list->next == &modules)
10       set $done=1
11     end
12     set $m=$m->next
13   end
14 end
15
16 document lsmod
17 List the loaded kernel modules and their start addresses
18 end
```

This simple loop starts with the kernel's global variable module. This variable is a struct list_head that marks the start of the linked list of loadable modules. The only complexity is the same as that described in Listing 14-19. We must subtract an offset from the struct list_head pointer to point to the top of the struct module. This is performed in line 7. This macro produces a simple listing of modules containing the address of the struct module and the module's name. Here is an example of its use:

```
(gdb) lsmod
Address         Module
0xD1012A80      ip_conntrack_tftp
0xD10105A0      ip_conntrack
0xD102F9A0      loop
(gdb) help lsmod
List the loaded kernel modules and their start addresses
(gdb)
```

Macros such as the ones presented here are very powerful debugging aids. You can create macros in a similar fashion to display anything in the kernel that lends itself to easy access, especially the major data structures maintained as linked lists. Examples include process memory map information, module information, file system information, timer lists, and so on. The information presented here should get you started.

14.3.5 Debugging Loadable Modules

One of the typical reasons for using KGDB is to debug loadable kernel modules—that is, device drivers. One of the more convenient features of loadable modules is that under most circumstances, it is not necessary to reboot the kernel for each new debugging session. You can start a debugging session, make some changes, recompile, and reload the module without the hassle and delay of a complete kernel reboot.

The complication associated with debugging loadable modules is in gaining access to the symbolic debug information contained in the module's object file. Because loadable modules are dynamically linked when they are loaded into the kernel, the symbolic information contained in the object file is useless until the symbol table is adjusted.

Recall from our earlier examples how we invoke GDB for a kernel debugging session:

```
$ ppc_4xx-gdb vmlinux
```

This launches a GDB debugging session on your host and reads the symbol information from the Linux kernel ELF file vmlinux. Of course, you will not find symbols for any loadable modules in this file. Loadable modules are separate compilation units and are linked as individual stand-alone ELF objects. Therefore, if we intend to perform any source-level debugging on a loadable module, we need to load its debug symbols from the ELF file. GDB provides this capability in its add-symbol-file command.

The add-symbol-file command loads symbols from the specified object file, assuming that the module itself has already been loaded. However, we are faced with chicken-and-egg syndrome. We don't have any symbol information until the loadable module has been loaded into the kernel, and the add-symbol-file command is issued to read in the module's symbol information. However, after the module has been loaded, it is too late to set breakpoints and debug the module's *_init and related functions because they have already executed.

The solution to this dilemma is to place a breakpoint in the kernel code that is responsible for loading the module, after it has been linked but before its initialization function has been called. This work is done by .../kernel/module.c. Listing 14-21 shows the relevant portions of module.c.

LISTING 14-21 **module.c**: Module Initialization

```
. . .
2292            /* Drop lock so they can recurse */
2293            mutex_unlock(&module_mutex);
2294
2295            blocking_notifier_call_chain(&module_notify_list,
2296                        MODULE_STATE_COMING, mod);
2297
2298            /* Start the module */
2299            if (mod->init != NULL)
2300                    ret = do_one_initcall(mod->init);
2301            if (ret < 0) {
2302                    /* Init routine failed: abort.  Try to protect us from
2303                        buggy refcounters. */
2304                    mod->state = MODULE_STATE_GOING;
. . .
```

We load the module using the modprobe utility, which was demonstrated in Listing 8-5 in Chapter 8, "Device Driver Basics." It looks like this:

```
$ modprobe loop
```

This command issues a special system call that directs the kernel to load the module. The module loading begins at `load_module()` in `module.c`. After the module has been loaded into kernel memory and dynamically linked, control is passed to the module's `*_init` function. This is shown in lines 2299 and 2300 from a recent copy of `module.c`, as shown in Listing 14-21. We place our breakpoint here. This enables us to add the symbol file to GDB and subsequently set breakpoints in the module. We demonstrate this process using the Linux kernel's loopback driver, called `loop.ko`. This module has no dependencies on other modules and is reasonably easy to demonstrate.

Listing 14-22 shows the GDB commands to initiate this debugging session on `loop.ko`.

LISTING 14-22   Initiate Module Debug Session: *loop.ko*

```
 1 $ ppc-linux-gdb --silent vmlinux
 2 (gdb) connect   <<< remember, this is a user-defined func
 3 breakinst () at arch/ppc/kernel/ppc-stub.c:825
 4 825     }
 5 Breakpoint 1 at 0xc0016b18: file kernel/panic.c, line 74.
 6 Breakpoint 2 at 0xc005a8c8: file fs/buffer.c, line 296.
 7 (gdb) b kernelmodule.c:2299
 8 Breakpoint 3 at 0xc0055b28: file kernel/module.c, line 2299.
 9 (gdb) c
10 Continuing.
11 >>>> Here we let the kernel finish booting
12     and then load the loop.ko module on the target
13
14 Breakpoint 3, sys_init_module (umod=0x48030000, len=<optimized out>,
15   . uargs=<value optimized out>) at kernel/module.c:2299
16 2299                    ret = mod->init();
17 (gdb) lsmod
18 Address       Module
19 0xD1069A60    loop
20 (gdb) set $m=(struct module *)0xD1069a60
21 (gdb) p $m->module_core
22 $1 = (void *) 0xd1066000
23 (gdb) add-symbol-file ./drivers/block/loop.ko 0xd1066000
24 add symbol table from file "./drivers/block/loop.ko" at
25         .text_addr = 0xd1066000
26 (y or n) y
27 Reading symbols from /home/chris/sandbox/linux-2.6.27/
drivers/block       /loop.ko...done.
28 (gdb)
```

Starting with line 2, we use the GDB user-defined macro connect created in Listing 14-14 to connect to the target board and set our initial breakpoints. We then add the breakpoint in `module.c`, as shown in line 7, and we issue the continue (c) command. Now the kernel completes the boot process, and we establish a telnet session into the target and load the `loop.ko` module (not shown). When the loop module is loaded, we immediately hit breakpoint 3. GDB then displays the information shown in lines 14 through 16.

At this point, we need to discover the address where the Linux kernel linked our module's `.text` section. Linux stores this address in the module information structure `struct module` in the `module_core` element. Using the `lsmod` macro we defined in Listing 14-20, we obtain the address of the `struct module` associated with our `loop.ko` module. This is shown in lines 17 through 19. Now we use this structure address to obtain the module's `.text` address from the `module_core` structure member. We pass this address to the GDB `add-symbol-file` command, and GDB uses this address to adjust its internal symbol table to match the actual addresses where the module was linked into the kernel. From there, we can proceed in the usual manner to set breakpoints in the module, step through code, examine data, and so on.

We conclude this section with a demonstration of placing a breakpoint in the loop-back module's initialization function so that we can step through the module's initialization code. The complication here is that the kernel loads the module's initialization code into a separately allocated portion of memory so that it can be freed after use. Recall from Chapter 5, "Kernel Initialization," our discussion of the `__init` macro. This macro expands into a compiler attribute that directs the linker to place the marked portion of code into a specially named ELF section. In essence, any function defined with this attribute is placed in a separate ELF section named `.init.text`. Its use is similar to the following:

```
static int __init loop_init(void){...}
```

This invocation would place the compiled `loop_init()` function into the `.init. text` section of the `loop.ko` object module. When the module is loaded, the kernel allocates a chunk of memory for the main body of the module, which is pointed to by the `struct module` member named `module_core`. It then allocates a separate chunk of memory to hold the `.init.text` section. After the initialization function is called, the kernel frees the memory that contained the initialization function. Because the object module is split like this, we need to inform GDB of this addressing scheme to be able to use symbolic data for debugging the initialization function. Listing 14-23 demonstrates these steps.

LISTING 14-23   Debugging Module *init* Code

```
$ ppc-linux-gdb -q vmlinux
(gdb) target remote /dev/ttyS0
Remote debugging using /dev/ttyS0
breakinst () at arch/ppc/kernel/ppc-stub.c:825
825        }

<< Place a breakpoint before calling module init >>
(gdb) b kernel/module.c:2299
Breakpoint 1 at 0xc0036418: file kernel/module.c, line 2299.
(gdb) c
Continuing.
[New Thread 1468]
[Switching to Thread 1468]

Breakpoint 3, sys_init_module (umod=0x48030000, len=<optimized out>,
    uargs=<value optimized out>) at kernel/module.c:2299
2299          if (mod->init != NULL)

<< Discover init addressing from struct module >>

(gdb) lsmod
Address         Module
0xD1069A60      loop
(gdb) set $m=(struct module *)0xD1069A60
(gdb) p $m->module_core
$1 = (void *) 0xd1066000
(gdb) p $m->module_init
$2 = (void *) 0xd101e000

<< Now load a symbol file using the core and init addrs >>

(gdb) add-symbol-file ./drivers/block/loop.ko 0xd1066000 -s .init.text 0xd101e000
add symbol table from file "./drivers/block/loop.ko" at
      .text_addr = 0xd1066000
      .init.text_addr = 0xd101e000
(y or n) y
Reading symbols from /home/chris/sandbox/linux-2.6.27/drivers/block/
loop.ko...done.
```

LISTING 14-23   Continued

```
(gdb) b loop_init
Breakpoint 4 at 0xd101e008: file drivers/block/loop.c, line 1517.
(gdb) c
Continuing.

<< Breakpoint hit, proceed to debug module init function >>

Breakpoint 4, loop_init () at drivers/block/loop.c:1517
1517            part_shift = 0;
(gdb) l
1512              *      load, user can further extend loop device by create dev node
1513              *      themselves and have kernel automatically instantiate actual
1514              *      device on-demand.
1515              */
1516
1517            part_shift = 0;
1518            if (max_part > 0)
1519                    part_shift = fls(max_part);
1520
1521            if (max_loop > 1UL << (MINORBITS - part_shift))
(gdb)
```

14.3.6   `printk` Debugging

Debugging kernel and device driver code using `printk()` is a popular technique, most-ly because `printk` has evolved into a very robust method. You can call `printk` from almost any context, including from interrupt handlers. `printk` is the kernel's version of the familiar `printf()` C library function. `printk` is defined in `.../kernel/printk.c`.

It is important to understand the limitations of using `printk` for debugging. First, `printk` requires a console device. Moreover, although the console device is configured as early as possible during kernel initialization, many calls to `printk` occur before the console device has been initialized. We present a method to cope with this limitation later, in Section 14.5, "When It Doesn't Boot."

The `printk` function allows the addition of a string marker that identifies the level of severity of a given message. The header file `.../include/linux/kernel.h` defines eight levels:

```
#define     KERN_EMERG      "<0>" /* system is unusable */
#define     KERN_ALERT      "<1>" /* action must be taken immediately */
```

```
#define     KERN_CRIT      "<2>" /* critical conditions */
#define     KERN_ERR       "<3>" /* error conditions */
#define     KERN_WARNING   "<4>" /* warning conditions */
#define     KERN_NOTICE    "<5>" /* normal but significant condition */
#define     KERN_INFO      "<6>" /* informational */
#define     KERN_DEBUG     "<7>" /* debug-level messages */
```

A simple `printk` message might look like this:

```
printk("foo() entered w/ %s\n", arg);
```

If the severity string is omitted, as shown here, the kernel assigns a default severity level, which is defined in `printk.c`. In recent kernels, this is set at severity level 4, KERN_WARNING. Specifying `printk` with a severity level (the preferred method) might look something like this:

```
printk(KERN_CRIT "vmalloc failed in foo()\n");
```

No, this unusual C syntax is not a typo. KERN_CRIT is a text string itself, so a comma is not needed to separate parameters. In fact, if a comma were included, the function would not produce the expected results. The compiler automatically concatenates the strings into a single string. By default, all `printk` messages below a predefined loglevel are displayed on the system console device. The default console loglevel is defined in `printk.c`. In recent Linux kernels, it has the value 7. This means that any `printk` message that is greater in importance than KERN_DEBUG (found in `.../include/linux/kernel.h`) is displayed on the console.

You can set the default kernel loglevel in a variety of ways. At boot time, you can specify the default loglevel on your target board by passing the appropriate kernel command-line parameters to the kernel at boot time. Three kernel command-line options defined in `main.c` affect the default loglevel:

- `debug` sets the console loglevel to 10.
- `quiet` sets the console loglevel to 4.
- `loglevel=` sets the console loglevel to your choice of value.

Using the `debug` log level effectively displays every `printk` message. Using `quiet` displays all `printk` messages of severity KERN_ERR or higher.

printk messages can be logged to files on your target or via the network. Use klogd (kernel log daemon) and syslogd (system log daemon) to control the logging behavior of printk messages. These popular utilities are described in man pages and many Linux references and therefore are not described here.

14.3.7 Magic SysReq Key

The Magic SysReq key is a useful debugging aid that is invoked through a series of special predefined key sequences that send messages directly to the kernel. For many target architectures and boards, you use a simple terminal emulator on a serial port as a system console. For these architectures, the Magic SysReq key is defined as a break character followed by a command character. Consult the documentation on the terminal emulator you use to find out how to send a break character. Many Linux developers use the minicom terminal emulator. For minicom, you send the break character by pressing Ctrl-A F. If you use screen, pressing Ctrl-A Ctrl-B sends a break. After sending the break in this manner, you have 5 seconds to enter the command character before the command sequence times out.

This useful kernel tool can be very helpful for development and debugging, but it can also cause data loss and system corruption. Indeed, the b command immediately reboots your system without any notification or preparation. Open files are not closed, disks are not synced, and file systems are not unmounted. When the reboot (b) command is issued, control is immediately passed to your architecture's reset vector in a most abrupt and stunning manner. Use this powerful tool at your own peril!

This feature is well documented in the Linux kernel documentation subdirectory in a file called sysrq.txt. There you find the details of many architectures and descriptions of available commands.

Another way to set the kernel loglevel just discussed is to use the Magic SysReq key. The command is a number from 0 through 9, which results in the default loglevel being set to the number passed in. From minicom, press Ctrl-A F followed by a number, such as 9. Here is how it looks on the terminal after you sending the break sequence:

```
$ SysRq : Changing Loglevel
  Loglevel set to 9
```

Commands can be used to dump registers, shut down your system, reboot your system, dump a list of processes, dump current memory information to your console, and more. See the documentation file in any recent Linux kernel for details.

This feature is most commonly used when something causes your system to lock up. Often the Magic SysReq key provides a way to learn something from an otherwise dead system.

14.4   Hardware-Assisted Debugging

By now you've probably realized that you cannot debug very early kernel startup code with KGDB. This is because KGDB is not initialized until after most of the low-level hardware initialization code has executed. Furthermore, if you are assigned the task of bringing up a brand-new board design and porting a bootloader and the Linux kernel, having a hardware-debug probe is without a doubt the most efficient means of debugging problems in these early stages of board porting.

You can choose from a wide variety of hardware-debug probes. For the examples in this section, we use a unit manufactured by Abatron called the BDI-2000 (see www. abatron.ch). These units are often called JTAG probes because they use a low-level communications method that was first employed for boundary scan testing of integrated circuits defined by the Joint Test Action Group (JTAG). Abatron has since released its newer BDI-3000, which features a faster (100MB) Ethernet interface.

A JTAG probe contains a small connector designed for connection to your target board. It is often a simple square-pin header and ribbon cable arrangement. Most modern high-performance CPUs contain a JTAG interface that is designed to provide this software debugging capability. The JTAG probe connects to this CPU JTAG interface. The other side of the JTAG probe connects to your host development system, usually through Ethernet, USB, or a parallel port. Figure 14-6 details the setup for the Abatron unit.

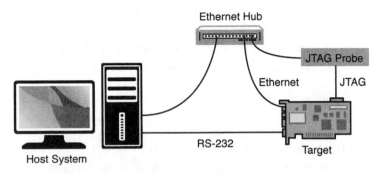

FIGURE 14-6   Hardware JTAG probe debugging

JTAG probes can be complicated to set up. This is a direct result of the complexity of the CPU to which they are connected. When power is applied to a target board and its CPU comes out of reset, almost nothing is initialized. In fact, many processors need at least a small amount of initialization before they can do anything. Many methods are available for getting this initial configuration into the CPU. Some CPUs read a hardware-configuration word or initial values of specific pins to learn their power-on configuration. Others rely on reading a default location in a simple nonvolatile storage device such as Flash. When using a JTAG probe, especially to bring up a new board design, a minimum level of CPU and board initialization must be performed before anything else can be done. Many JTAG probes rely on a configuration file for this initialization.

The Abatron unit uses a configuration file to initialize the target hardware it is connected to, as well as to define other operational parameters of the debugger. This configuration file contains directives that initialize the CPU, memory system, and other necessary board-level hardware. It is the developer's responsibility to customize this configuration file with the proper directives for his own board. The details of the configuration command syntax can be found in the JTAG probe's documentation. However, only the embedded developer can create the unique configuration file required for a given board design. This requires detailed knowledge of the CPU and board-level design features. Much like creating a custom Linux port for a new board, there is no shortcut or substitute for this task.

Appendix F, "Sample BDI-2000 Configuration File," contains a sample Abatron configuration file for a custom board based on the Freescale Semiconductor MPC5200 embedded controller. In that appendix, you can see the necessary setup for a custom board. Notice the liberal use of comments describing various registers and initialization details. This makes it easier to update and maintain over time, and it can help you get the configuration right the first time.

Hardware probes generally are used in two ways. Most have a user interface of some type that enables the developer to use features of the probe. Examples of this are to program Flash or download binary images. The second usage is as a front end to GDB or other source-level debuggers. We'll demonstrate both usage scenarios.

14.4.1 Programming Flash Using a JTAG Probe

Many hardware probes include the capability to program a wide variety of Flash memory chips. The Abatron BDI-3000 is no exception. The BDI-3000 configuration file includes a [FLASH] section to define the characteristics of the target Flash. Refer to Appendix F for a sample. The [FLASH] section defines attributes of the Flash chip as used in a particular design, such as the chip type, the size of the device, and its data bus width. Also defined are the location in memory and a description of the chip's storage organization.

When updating one portion of the Flash, you often want to preserve the contents of other portions of the same Flash. In this case, your hardware probe must have some way to limit the sectors that are being erased. In the case of the Abatron unit, this is done by adding a line starting with the keyword ERASE for each sector to be erased. When the `erase` command is issued to the Abatron unit using its telnet user interface, all sectors defined with an ERASE specification are erased. Listing 14-24 demonstrates erasing a portion of Flash on a target board and subsequently programming a new U-Boot bootloader image.

LISTING 14-24   Erase and Program Flash

```
$ telnet bdi
Trying 192.168.1.129...
Connected to bdi (192.168.1.129).
Escape character is '^]'.
BDI Debugger for Embedded PowerPC
==================================
...  (large volume of help text)

uei> erase
Erasing flash at 0xfff00000
Erasing flash at 0xfff10000
Erasing flash at 0xfff20000
Erasing flash at 0xfff30000
Erasing flash at 0xfff40000
Erasing flash passed
uei> prog 0xfff00000 u-boot.bin BIN
Programming u-boot.bin , please wait ....
Programming flash passed
uei>
```

First we establish a telnet session to the Abatron BDI-2000. After some initialization, we are presented with a command prompt. When the `erase` command is issued, the Abatron displays a line of output for each section defined in the configuration file. With the configuration shown in Appendix F, we define five erase sectors. This reserves up to 256KB of space for the U-Boot bootloader binary.

The `prog` command is shown with all three of its optional parameters. These specify the location in memory where the new image is to be loaded, the name of the image file, and the format of the file—in this case, a binary file. You can specify these parameters in the BDI-2000 configuration file. In this case, the command reduces to simply `prog` without parameters.

This example only scratches the surface of these two BDI-2000 commands. Many more combinations of usage and capabilities are supported. Each hardware JTAG probe has its own way to specify Flash erasure and programming capabilities. Consult the documentation for your particular device for the specifics.

14.4.2   Debugging with a JTAG Probe

Instead of interfacing directly with a JTAG probe through its user interface, many JTAG probes can interface with your source-level debugger. By far the most popular debugger supported by hardware probes for Linux is the GDB debugger. In this usage scenario, GDB is instructed to begin a debug session with the target using an external connection, usually an Ethernet connection. Rather than communicate directly with the JTAG probe through a user interface, the debugger passes commands back and forth between itself and the JTAG probe. In this model, the JTAG probe uses the GDB remote protocol to control the hardware on behalf of the debugger. Refer to Figure 14-6 for connection details.

JTAG probes are especially useful for source-level debugging of bootloader and early startup code. In this example, we demonstrate the use of GDB and an Abatron BDI-2000 for debugging portions of the U-Boot bootloader on a Power Architecture target board.

Many processors contain debugging registers that include the capability to set traditional address breakpoints (stop when the program reaches a specific address) as well as data breakpoints (stop on conditional access of a specified memory address). When debugging code resident in read-only memory such as Flash, this is the only way to set a breakpoint. However, these registers typically are limited. Many processors contain only one or two such registers. You must understand this limitation before using hardware breakpoints. The following example demonstrates this.

Using a setup such as that shown in Figure 14-6, assume that our target board has U-Boot stored in Flash. When we presented bootloaders in Chapter 7, you learned that U-Boot and other bootloaders typically copy themselves into RAM as soon as possible after startup. This is because hardware read (and write) cycles from RAM are orders of magnitude faster than typical read-only memory devices such as Flash. This presents two specific debugging challenges. First, we cannot modify the contents of read-only memory (to insert a software breakpoint), so we must rely on processor-supported breakpoint registers for this purpose.

The second challenge comes from the fact that only one of the execution contexts (Flash or RAM) can be represented by the ELF executable file from which GDB reads its symbolic debugging information. In the case of U-Boot, it is linked for the Flash environment where it is initially stored. The early code relocates itself and performs any necessary address adjustments. This means that we need to work with GDB within both of these execution contexts. Listing 14-25 shows an example of such a debug session.

LISTING 14-25   U-Boot Debugging Using a JTAG Probe

```
$ ppc-linux-gdb -q u-boot
(gdb) target remote bdi:2001
Remote debugging using bdi:2001
_start () at /home/chris/sandbox/u-boot-1.1.4/cpu/mpc5xxx/start.S:91
91         li     r21, BOOTFLAG_COLD    /* Normal Power-On */
Current language:  auto; currently asm

<< Debug a flash resident code snippet >>
(gdb) mon break hard
(gdb) b board_init_f
Breakpoint 1 at 0xfff0457c: file board.c, line 366.
(gdb) c
Continuing.

Breakpoint 1, board_init_f (bootflag=0x7fc3afc) at board.c:366
366               gd = (gd_t *) (CFG_INIT_RAM_ADDR + CFG_GBL_DATA_OFFSET);
Current language:  auto; currently c
(gdb) bt
#0  board_init_f (bootflag=0x1) at board.c:366
#1  0xfff0456c in board_init_f (bootflag=0x1) at board.c:353
(gdb) i frame
Stack level 0, frame at 0xf000bf50:
 pc = 0xfff0457c in board_init_f (board.c:366); saved pc 0xfff0456c
 called by frame at 0xf000bf78
 source language c.
 Arglist at 0xf000bf50, args: bootflag=0x1
 Locals at 0xf000bf50, Previous frame's sp is 0x0
```

LISTING 14-25   Continued

```
<< Now debug a memory resident code snippet after relocation >>
(gdb) del 1
(gdb) symbol-file
Discard symbol table from '/home/chris/sandbox/u-boot-1.1.4-powerdna/u-boot'?
(y or n) y
No symbol file now.
(gdb) add-symbol-file u-boot 0x7fa8000
add symbol table from file "u-boot" at
        .text_addr = 0x7fa8000
(y or n) y
Reading symbols from u-boot...done.
(gdb) b board_init_r
Breakpoint 2 at 0x7fac6c0: file board.c, line 608.
(gdb) c
Continuing.


Breakpoint 2, board_init_r (id=0x7f85f84, dest_addr=0x7f85f84) at board.c:608
608              gd = id;      /* initialize RAM version of global data */
(gdb) i frame
Stack level 0, frame at 0x7f85f38:
 pc = 0x7fac6c0 in board_init_r (board.c:608); saved pc 0x7fac6b0
 called by frame at 0x7f85f68
 source language c.
 Arglist at 0x7f85f38, args: id=0x7f85f84, dest_addr=0x7f85f84
 Locals at 0x7f85f38, Previous frame's sp is 0x0
(gdb) mon break soft
(gdb)
```

Study this example carefully. Some subtleties are definitely worth taking the time to understand. First, we connect to the Abatron BDI-2000 using the `target remote` command. The IP address in this case is that of the Abatron unit, represented by the symbolic name bdi.[11] By default, the Abatron BDI-2000 uses port 2001 for its remote GDB protocol connection.

Next we issue a command to the BDI-2000 using the GDB `mon` command. The `mon` command tells GDB to pass the rest of the command directly to the remote hardware device. Therefore, `mon break hard` sets the BDI-2000 into hardware breakpoint mode.

We then set a hardware breakpoint at `board_init_f`. This is a routine that executes while still running out of Flash memory at address `0xfff0457c`. After the breakpoint

---

[11] An entry in the host system's `/etc/hosts` file enables the symbolic IP address reference.

is defined, we issue the continue (c) command to resume execution. Immediately, the breakpoint at `board_init_f` is encountered, and we are free to do the usual debugging activities, including stepping through code and examining data. You can see that we have issued the `bt` command to examine the stack backtrace and the `i frame` command to examine the details of the current stack frame.

Now we continue execution again, but this time we know that U-Boot copies itself to RAM and resumes execution from its copy in RAM. So we need to change the debugging context while keeping the debugging session alive. To accomplish this, we discard the current symbol table (using the `symbol-file` command with no arguments) and load in the same symbol file again using the `add-symbol-file` command. This time, we instruct GDB to offset the symbol table to match where U-Boot has relocated itself to memory. This ensures that our source code and symbolic debugging information match the actual memory-resident image.

After the new symbol table is loaded, we can add a breakpoint to a location that we know will reside in RAM when it is executed. This is where one of the subtle complications is exposed. Because we know that U-Boot is currently running in Flash but is about to move itself to RAM and jump to its RAM-based copy, we must still use a hardware breakpoint. Consider what happens at this point if we use a software breakpoint. GDB dutifully writes the breakpoint opcode into the specified memory location, but U-Boot overwrites it when it copies itself to RAM. The net result is that the breakpoint is never hit, and we begin to suspect that our tools are broken. After U-Boot has entered the RAM copy and our symbol table has been updated to reflect the RAM-based addresses, we are free to use RAM-based breakpoints. This is reflected by the last command in Listing 14-25, which sets the Abatron BDI-2000 back to soft breakpoint mode.

Why do we care about using hardware versus software breakpoints? If we had unlimited hardware breakpoint registers, we wouldn't. But this is never the case. Here is what it looks like when you run out of processor-supported hardware breakpoint registers during a debug session on a 4xx processor:

```
(gdb) b flash_init
Breakpoint 3 at 0x7fbebe0: file flash.c, line 70.
(gdb) c
Continuing.
warning: Cannot insert breakpoint 3:
Error accessing memory address 0x7fbebe0: Unknown error 4294967295.
```

Because we are debugging remotely, we aren't told about the resource constraint until we try to resume after entering additional breakpoints. This is because of how GDB handles breakpoints. When a breakpoint is hit, GDB restores all the breakpoints with the original opcodes for that particular memory location. When it resumes execution, it restores the breakpoint opcodes at the specified locations. You can observe this behavior by enabling GDB's remote debug mode, as we saw earlier:

```
(gdb) set debug remote 1
```

14.5   When It Doesn't Boot

One of the most frequently asked questions on the various mailing lists that serve embedded Linux goes something like this:

```
I am trying to boot Linux on my board, and I get stuck after this message
prints to my console:
"Uncompressing Kernel Image . . . OK."
```

Thus starts the long and sometimes frustrating learning curve of embedded Linux! Many things that can go wrong could lead to this common failure. With some knowledge and a JTAG debugger, there are ways to determine what went awry.

14.5.1   Early Serial Debug Output

CONFIG_SERIAL_TEXT_DEBUG, which we covered in the first edition of this book, has been deprecated in recent Linux kernels. Reference to this configuration parameter has been removed from the kernel sources.

However, CONFIG_EARLY_PRINTK is available on most architectures. This feature is on by default in most kernel configurations. When on, it enables serial console output much sooner than the registration of the serial driver. On most Linux ports, there is nothing to do to enable this; it is on by default.

14.5.2   Dumping the `printk` Log Buffer

When we discussed `printk` debugging in Section 14.3.6, we pointed out some of the limitations of this method. `printk` itself is a very robust implementation. One of its shortcomings is that you can't see any `printk` messages until later in the boot sequence, when the console device has been initialized. Very often, when your board hangs on boot, quite a few messages are stuck in the `printk` buffer. If you know where to find them, you can often pinpoint the exact problem that is causing the boot to hang. Indeed, many times you will discover that the kernel has encountered an error that led to a call to `panic()`. The output from `panic()` has likely been dumped into the `printk` buffer, and you can often pinpoint the exact line of offending code.

This is best accomplished with a JTAG debugger, but it is still possible to use a bootloader and its memory dump capability to display the contents of the `printk` buffer after a reset. Some corruption of memory contents might occur as a result of the reset, but log buffer text is usually very readable.

The actual buffer where `printk` stores its message text is declared in the `printk` source file `.../kernel/printk.c`:

```
static char __log_buf[__LOG_BUF_LEN];
```

We can easily determine the linked location of this buffer from the Linux kernel map file `System.map`:

```
$ grep __log_buf System.map
  c022e5a4 b __log_buf
```

If the system happens to hang upon booting, right after the `Uncompressing Kernel Image . . . OK` message appears, reboot and use the bootloader to examine the buffer. Because the relationship between kernel virtual memory and physical memory is fixed and constant on a given architecture, we can do a simple conversion. The address of `__log_buf` shown earlier is a kernel virtual address; we must convert it into a physical address. On this particular Power Architecture processor, that conversion is a simple subtraction of the constant `KERNELBASE` address, `0xc0000000`. This is where we probe in memory to read the contents, if any, of the `printk` log buffer.

Listing 14-26 is an example of the listing as displayed by the U-Boot memory dump command.

LISTING 14-26   Dump of Raw *printk* Log Buffer

```
=> md 22e5a4
0022e5a4: 3c353e4c 696e7578 20766572 73696f6e    <5>Linux version
0022e5b4: 20322e36 2e313320 28636872 6973406a     2.6.13 (chris@
0022e5c4: 756e696f 72292028 67636320 76657273    junior) (gcc
0022e5d4: 696f6e20 332e342e 3320284d 6f6e7461    version 3.4.3 (Monta
0022e5e4: 56697374 6120332e 342e332d 32352e30    Vista 3.4.3-25.0
0022e5f4: 2e37302e 30353031 39363120 32303035    .70.0501961 2005
0022e604: 2d31322d 31382929 20233131 20547565    -12-18)) #11 Tue
```

LISTING 14-26   Continued

```
0022e614:  20466562  20313420  32313a30  353a3036      Feb 14 21:05:06
0022e624:  20455354  20323030  360a3c34  3e414d43       EST 2006.<4>AMC
0022e634:  4320506f  77657250  43203434  30455020      C PowerPC 440EP
0022e644:  596f7365  6d697465  20506c61  74666f72      Yosemite Platform.
0022e654:  6d0a3c37  3e4f6e20  6e6f6465  20302074      <7>On node 0
0022e664:  6f74616c  70616765  733a2036  35353336      totalpages: 65536
0022e674:  0a3c373e  2020444d  41207a6f  6e653a20      .<7>   DMA zone:
0022e684:  36353533  36207061  6765732c  204c4946      65536 pages, LIF
0022e694:  4f206261  7463683a  33310a3c  373e2020      O batch:31.<7>
=>
0022e6a4:  4e6f726d  616c207a  6f6e653a  20302070      Normal zone: 0
0022e6b4:  61676573  2c204c49  464f2062  61746368      pages, LIFO batch
0022e6c4:  3a310a3c  373e2020  48696768  4d656d20      :1.<7>   HighMemzone:
0022e6d4:  7a6f6e65  3a203020  70616765  732c204c      0 pages,
0022e6e4:  49464f20  62617463  683a310a  3c343e42      LIFO batch:1.<4>
0022e6f4:  75696c74  2031207a  6f6e656c  69737473      Built 1 zonelists
0022e704:  0a3c353e  4b65726e  656c2063  6f6d6d61      .<5>Kernel command
0022e714:  6e64206c  696e653a  20636f6e  736f6c65      line: console
0022e724:  3d747479  53302c31  31353230  3020726f      =ttyS0,115200
0022e734:  6f743d2f  6465762f  6e667320  72772069      root=/dev/nfs rw
0022e744:  703d6468  63700a3c  343e5049  44206861      ip=dhcp.<4>PID
0022e754:  73682074  61626c65  20656e74  72696573      hash table entries
0022e764:  3a203230  34382028  6f726465  723a2031      : 2048 (order:
0022e774:  312c2033  32373638  20627974  6573290a      11, 32768 bytes).
0022e784:  00000000  00000000  00000000  00000000      ................
0022e794:  00000000  00000000  00000000  00000000      ................
=>
```

It is not very pretty to read, but the data is there. We can see in this particular example that the kernel crashed someplace after initializing the PID hash table entries. With some additional use of `printk` messages, we can begin to close in on the actual source of the crash.

As shown in this example, this is a technique that can be used with no additional tools. You can see the importance of some kind of early serial port output during boot if you are working on a new board port.

It's worth noting that the bootloader on some platforms performs initialization on memory contents before completing initialization. On these platforms, the kernel log buffer contents are destroyed, and this technique cannot be used without modifying the bootloader code.

14.5.3   KGDB on Panic

If KGDB is enabled, the kernel attempts to pass control back to KGDB upon error exceptions. In some cases, the error itself is readily apparent. To use this feature, a connection must already be established between KGDB and GDB. When the exception condition occurs, KGDB emits a Stop Reply packet to GDB, indicating the reason for the trap into the debug handler, as well as the address where the trap condition occurred. Listing 14-27 illustrates the sequence.

LISTING 14-27   Trapping Crash on Panic Using KGDB

```
$ ppc-_4xx-gdb -q vmlinux
(gdb) target remote /dev/ttyS0
Remote debugging using /dev/ttyS0

(gdb) c
Continuing.

<< KGDB gains control from panic() on crash >>
Program received signal SIGSEGV, Segmentation fault.
0xc0215d6c in pcibios_init () at arch/ppc/kernel/pci.c:1263
1263            *(int *)-1 = 0;
(gdb) bt
#0  0xc0215d6c in pcibios_init () at arch/ppc/kernel/pci.c:1263
#1  0xc020e728 in do_initcalls () at init/main.c:563
#2  0xc020e7c4 in do_basic_setup () at init/main.c:605
#3  0xc0001374 in init (unused=0x20) at init/main.c:677
#4  0xc00049d0 in kernel_thread ()
Previous frame inner to this frame (corrupt stack?)
(gdb)
```

The crash in this example was contrived by a simple write to an invalid memory location (all 1s). We first establish a connection from GDB to KGDB and allow the kernel to continue to boot. Notice that we didn't even bother to set breakpoints. When the crash occurs, we see the line of offending code and get a nice backtrace to help us determine its cause.

14.6 Summary

- Linux kernel debugging presents many complexities, especially in a cross-development environment. Understanding how to navigate these complexities is the key to successful kernel debugging.
- KGDB is a very useful kernel-level GDB stub that enables direct symbolic source-level debugging inside the Linux kernel and device drivers. It uses the GDB remote protocol to communicate with your host-based cross-gdb.
- Understanding (and minimizing) compiler optimizations helps you make sense of seemingly strange debugger behavior when stepping through compiler-optimized code.
- GDB supports user-defined commands, which can be very useful for automating tedious debugging tasks such as iterating kernel linked lists and accessing complex variables.
- Kernel-loadable modules present their own challenges to source-level debugging. You can debug the module's initialization routine by placing a breakpoint in `module.c` at the call to `mod->init()`.
- `printk` and the Magic SysReq key provide additional tools to help isolate problems during kernel development and debugging.
- Hardware-assisted debugging using a JTAG probe lets you debug Flash or ROM resident code where other debugging methods can be cumbersome or otherwise impossible.
- Enabling `CONFIG_EARLY_PRINTK` on architectures where this feature is supported is a powerful tool for debugging a new kernel port.
- Examining `printk log_buf` often leads to the cause of a silent kernel crash on boot on architectures that support it.
- KGDB passes control to GDB on a kernel panic, enabling you to examine a backtrace and isolate the cause of the kernel panic.

14.6.1   Suggestions for Additional Reading

Linux Kernel Development, 3rd Edition
Robert Love
Addison-Wesley, 2010

The Linux Kernel Primer
Claudia Salzberg Rodriguez et al.
Prentice Hall, 2005

"Using the GNU Compiler Collection"
Richard M. Stallman and the GCC Developer Community
GNU Press, a division of Free Software Foundation
http://gcc.gnu.org/onlinedocs/

Debugging with GDB
Richard Stallman, Roland Pesch, Stan Shebs, et al.
Free Software Foundation
www.gnu.org/software/gdb/documentation/

Using kgdb and the kgdb Internals
www.kernel.org/doc/htmldocs/kgdb.html

Tool Interface Standards
DWARF Debugging Information Format Specification
Version 2.0
TIS Committee, May 1995

Chapter 15

Debugging Embedded
Linux Applications

In This Chapter

- 15.1   Target Debugging   424

- 15.2   Remote (Cross) Debugging   424

- 15.3   Debugging with Shared Libraries   429

- 15.4   Debugging Multiple Tasks   435

- 15.5   Additional Remote Debug Options   442

- 15.6   Summary   443

The preceding chapter explored the use of GDB for debugging kernel code and code resident in Flash, such as bootloader code. This chapter continues our coverage of GDB for debugging application code in user space. We extend our coverage of remote debugging and the tools and techniques used for this particular debugging environment.

15.1 Target Debugging

We explored several important debugging tools in Chapter 13, "Development Tools." strace and ltrace can be used to observe and characterize a process's behavior and often isolate problems. dmalloc can help isolate memory leaks and profile memory usage. ps and top are useful for examining the state of processes. These relatively small tools are designed to run directly on the target hardware.

Debugging Linux application code on an embedded system has its own unique challenges. Resources on your embedded target are often limited. RAM and nonvolatile storage limitations might prevent you from running target-based development tools. You might not have an Ethernet port or other high-speed connection. Your target embedded system might not have a graphical display, keyboard, or mouse.

This is where your cross-development tools and an NFS root mount environment can yield large dividends. Many tools, especially GDB, have been architected to execute on your development host while actually debugging code on a remote target. GDB can be used to interactively debug your target code or to perform a postmortem analysis of a core file generated by an application crash. We covered the details of application core dump analysis in Chapter 13.

15.2 Remote (Cross) Debugging

Cross-development tools were developed primarily to overcome the resource limitations of embedded platforms. A modest-size application compiled with symbolic debug information can easily exceed several megabytes. With cross debugging, the heavy lifting can be done on your development host. When you invoke your cross version of GDB on your development host, you pass it an ELF file compiled with symbolic debug information. On your target, you can strip[1] the ELF file of all unnecessary debugging information to keep the resulting image to its minimum size.

We introduced the `readelf` utility in Chapter 13. In Chapter 14, "Kernel Debugging Techniques," we used it to examine the debug information in an ELF file compiled with symbolic debugging information. Listing 15-1 contains the output of `readelf` for a relatively small web server application compiled for the ARM architecture.

LISTING 15-1   ELF File Debug Information for the Sample Program

```
$ xscale_be-readelf -S websdemo
There are 39 section headers, starting at offset 0x3dfd0:

Section Headers:
[Nr] Name            Type       Addr     Off    Size   ES Flg Lk Inf Al
[ 0]                 NULL       00000000 000000 000000 00      0  0  0
[ 1] .interp         PROGBITS   00008154 000154 000013 00  A   0  0  1
[ 2] .note.ABI-tag   NOTE       00008168 000168 000020 00  A   0  0  4
[ 3] .note.numapolicy NOTE      00008188 000188 000074 00  A   0  0  4
[ 4] .hash           HASH       000081fc 0001fc 00022c 04  A   5  0  4
[ 5] .dynsym         DYNSYM     00008428 000428 000460 10  A   6  1  4
[ 6] .dynstr         STRTAB     00008888 000888 000211 00  A   0  0  1
[ 7] .gnu.version    VERSYM     00008a9a 000a9a 00008c 02  A   5  0  2
[ 8] .gnu.version_r  VERNEED    00008b28 000b28 000020 00  A   6  1  4
[ 9] .rel.plt        REL        00008b48 000b48 000218 08  A   5 11  4
[10] .init           PROGBITS   00008d60 000d60 000018 00  AX  0  0  4
[11] .plt            PROGBITS   00008d78 000d78 000338 04  AX  0  0  4
[12] .text           PROGBITS   000090b0 0010b0 019fe4 00  AX  0  0  4
[13] .fini           PROGBITS   00023094 01b094 000018 00  AX  0  0  4
[14] .rodata         PROGBITS   000230b0 01b0b0 0023d0 00  A   0  0  8
[15] .ARM.extab      PROGBITS   00025480 01d480 000000 00  A   0  0  1
[16] .ARM.exidx      ARM_EXIDX  00025480 01d480 000008 00  AL 12  0  4
[17] .eh_frame_hdr   PROGBITS   00025488 01d488 00002c 00  A   0  0  4
[18] .eh_frame       PROGBITS   000254b4 01d4b4 00007c 00  A   0  0  4
[19] .init_array     INIT_ARRAY 0002d530 01d530 000004 00  WA  0  0  4
[20] .fini_array     FINI_ARRAY 0002d534 01d534 000004 00  WA  0  0  4
[21] .jcr            PROGBITS   0002d538 01d538 000004 00  WA  0  0  4
```

---

[1]   Remember to use your cross version of `strip`, such as `ppc_82xx-strip`.

LISTING 15-1   Continued

```
[22] .dynamic           DYNAMIC      0002d53c 01d53c 0000d0 08   WA   6   0   4
[23] .got               PROGBITS     0002d60c 01d60c 000118 04   WA   0   0   4
[24] .data              PROGBITS     0002d728 01d728 0003c0 00   WA   0   0   8
[25] .bss               NOBITS       0002dae8 01dae8 0001c8 00   WA   0   0   4
[26] .comment           PROGBITS     00000000 01dae8 000940 00        0   0   1
[27] .debug_aranges     PROGBITS     00000000 01e428 0004a0 00        0   0   8
[28] .debug_pubnames    PROGBITS     00000000 01e8c8 001aae 00        0   0   1
[29] .debug_info        PROGBITS     00000000 020376 013d27 00        0   0   1
[30] .debug_abbrev      PROGBITS     00000000 03409d 002ede 00        0   0   1
[31] .debug_line        PROGBITS     00000000 036f7b 0034a2 00        0   0   1
[32] .debug_frame       PROGBITS     00000000 03a420 003380 00        0   0   4
[33] .debug_str         PROGBITS     00000000 03d7a0 000679 00        0   0   1
[34] .note.gnu.arm.ide  NOTE         00000000 03de19 00001c 00        0   0   1
[35] .debug_ranges      PROGBITS     00000000 03de35 000018 00        0   0   1
[36] .shstrtab          STRTAB       00000000 03de4d 000183 00        0   0   1
[37] .symtab            SYMTAB       00000000 03e5e8 004bd0 10       38 773   4
[38] .strtab            STRTAB       00000000 0431b8 0021bf 00        0   0   1
Key to Flags:
W (write), A (alloc), X (execute), M (merge), S (strings)
I (info), L (link order), G (group), x (unknown)
O (extra OS processing required) o (OS specific), p (processor specific)
$
```

You can see from Listing 15-1 that many sections contain debug information. A section with the name .comment contains more than 2KB (0x940) of information that is not necessary for the application to function. The size of this sample file, including debug information, is more than 275KB, as shown here:

```
$ ls -l websdemo
-rwxrwxr-x  1 chris chris 283511 Nov 8 18:48 websdemo
```

If we strip this file using our cross-strip utility, we can minimize its size to preserve resources on our target system. Listing 15-2 shows the results.

LISTING 15-2   Strip Target Application

```
$ xscale_be-strip -s -R .comment -o websdemo-stripped websdemo
$ ls -l websdemo*
-rwxrwxr-x 1 chris chris 283491 Apr  9 09:19 websdemo
-rwxrwxr-x 1 chris chris 123156 Apr  9 09:21 websdemo-stripped
$
```

Here we strip both the symbolic debug information and the `.comment` section from the executable file. We specify the name of the stripped binary using the `-o` command-line switch. You can see that the stripped binary is less than half its original size. Of course, for larger applications, this space savings can be even more significant. A recent Linux kernel compiled with debug information was larger than 18MB. After stripping, as in Listing 15-2, the resulting binary was slightly larger than 2MB!

For debugging in this fashion, you place the stripped version of the binary on your target system and keep a local unstripped copy on your development workstation containing symbolic information needed for debugging. You use `gdbserver` on your target board to provide an interface back to your development host, where you run the full-blown version of GDB (your cross-gdb, of course) on your unstripped binary.

15.2.1 `gdbserver`

Using `gdbserver` allows you to run GDB from a development workstation rather than on the target embedded Linux platform. This configuration has obvious benefits. For starters, it is common for your development workstation to have far more CPU power, memory, and hard-drive storage than your embedded platform. In addition, it is common for the source code for your application under debug to exist on the development workstation and not on the embedded platform.

`gdbserver` is a small program that runs on the target board and allows remote debugging of a process on the board. It is invoked on the target board specifying the program to be debugged, as well as an IP address and port number on which it will listen for connection requests from GDB. Listing 15-3 shows the startup sequence for initiating a debug session on your target board.

LISTING 15-3   Starting `gdbserver` on Your Target Board

```
$ gdbserver localhost:2001 websdemo-stripped
Process websdemo-stripped created; pid = 197
Listening on port 2001
```

This example starts `gdbserver` configured to listen for an Ethernet TCP/IP connection on port 2001, ready to debug our stripped binary program called `websdemo-stripped`.

From our development workstation, we launch GDB, passing it the name of the binary executable containing symbolic debug information that we want to debug as an argument. After GDB initializes, we issue a command to connect to the remote target board. Listing 15-4 shows this sequence.

LISTING 15-4   Starting a Remote GDB Session

```
$ xscale_be-gdb -q websdemo
(gdb) target remote 192.168.1.141:2001
Remote debugging using 192.168.1.141:2001
0x40000790 in ?? ()
(gdb) p main        <<<< Display address of main function
$1 = {int (int, char **)} 0x12b68 <main>
(gdb) b main        <<<< Place breakpoint at main()
Breakpoint 1 at 0x12b80: file main.c, line 72.
(gdb)
```

Listing 15-4 invokes cross-gdb on your development host. When GDB is running, we issue the GDB `target remote` command. This command causes GDB to initiate a TCP/IP connection from your development workstation to your target board, with the indicated IP address on port 2001. When `gdbserver` accepts the connection request, it prints a line similar to this:

```
Remote debugging from host 192.168.0.10
```

Now GDB is connected to the target board's `gdbserver` process, ready to accept commands from GDB. The rest of the session is exactly the same as if you were debugging an application locally. This is a powerful tool. It lets you use the power of your development workstation for the debug session, leaving only a small, relatively unobtrusive GDB stub and your program being debugged on the target board. In case you were wondering, `gdbserver` for this particular ARM target is only 54KB, as shown here:

```
root@coyote:~# ls -l /usr/bin/gdbserver
-rwxr-xr-x  1 root root 54344 Jun 26  2009 /usr/bin/gdbserver
```

The one caveat is often the subject of the frequently asked questions (FAQ) on mailing lists. You must be using a GDB on your development host that was configured as a cross debugger. It is a binary program that runs on your development workstation (usually x86) and that understands binary executable images compiled for another architecture. This is an important and frequently overlooked fact. You cannot debug a Power Architecture target with a native GDB such as that found in a typical Ubuntu desktop Linux installation. You must have a GDB configured for your host and target combination.

When GDB is invoked, it displays a banner consisting of several lines of information, and then it displays its compiled configuration. Listing 15-5 is an example of the GDB used for some examples in this book. It is part of an embedded Linux distribution provided by MontaVista Software configured for Power Architecture cross-development.

LISTING 15-5   Invocation of cross-gdb

```
$ ppc_82xx-gdb
GNU gdb 6.0 (MontaVista 6.0-8.0.4.0300532 2003-12-24)
Copyright 2003 Free Software Foundation, Inc.
GDB is free software, covered by the GNU General Public License, and
you are welcome to change it and/or distribute copies of it under
certain conditions.  Type "show copying" to see the conditions.
There is absolutely no warranty for GDB. Type "show warranty" for
details.
This GDB was configured as "--host=i686-pc-linux-gnu
--target=powerpc-hardhat-linux".
(gdb)
```

Notice the last lines of this GDB startup message. This is the configuration compiled into this version of GDB. It was compiled to execute on an x86 (i686) PC host running GNU/Linux and to debug binary programs compiled for a Power Architecture processor running GNU/Linux. This is specified by the --host and --target variables displayed by the banner text. It is also a part of the configuration string passed to ./configure when building GDB.

15.3   Debugging with Shared Libraries

Now that you understand how to invoke a remote debug session using GDB on the host and gdbserver on the target, we turn our attention to the complexities of shared libraries and debug symbols. Unless your application is a statically linked executable (linked with the -static linker command-line switch), many symbols in your application will reference code outside your application. Obvious examples include the use of standard C library routines such as fopen, printf, malloc, and memcpy. Less obvious examples might include calls to application-specific functions such as jack_transport_locate() (a routine from the JACK low-latency audio server), which calls a library function outside the standard C libraries.

To have symbols from these routines available, you must satisfy two requirements for GDB:

- You must have debug versions of the libraries available.
- GDB must know where to find them.

If you don't have debug versions of the libraries available, you can still debug your application; you just won't have any debug information available for library routines called by your application. Often this is perfectly acceptable—unless, of course, you are developing a shared library object as part of your embedded project.

Look back at Listing 15-4, where we invoked GDB on a remote target. After GDB connected using the `target remote` command, GDB issued a two-line response:

```
Remote debugging using 192.168.1.141:2001
0x40000790 in ?? ()
```

This confirms that GDB connected to our target at the indicated IP address and port. GDB then reports the location of the program counter as `0x40000790`. Why do we get question marks instead of a symbolic location? Because this is the Linux dynamic loader (`ld-x.y.z.so`), and this particular platform does not have debug symbols available for this shared library. How do we know this?

Recall the discussion of the `/proc` file system in Chapter 9, "File Systems." One of the more useful entries was the maps entry (see Listing 9-16 in Chapter 9) in the per-process directory structure. We know the process ID (PID) of our target application from the `gdbserver` output shown in Listing 15-3. Our process was assigned PID 197. Given that, we can see the memory segments in use right after process startup, as shown in Listing 15-6.

LISTING 15-6   Initial Target Memory Segment Mapping

```
root@coyote:~# cat /proc/197/maps
00008000-00026000 r-xp 00000000 00:0e 4852444    ./websdemo-stripped
0002d000-0002e000 rw-p 0001d000 00:0e 4852444    ./websdemo-stripped
40000000-40017000 r-xp 00000000 00:0a 4982583    /lib/ld-2.3.3.so
4001e000-40020000 rw-p 00016000 00:0a 4982583    /lib/ld-2.3.3.so
bedf9000-bee0e000 rwxp bedf9000 00:00 0          [stack]
root@coyote:~#
```

Here we see the target `websdemo-stripped` application occupying two memory segments. The first is the read-only executable segment at `0x8000`, and the second is a read-write data segment at 0x2d000. The third memory segment is the one of interest. It is the Linux dynamic linker's executable code segment. Notice that it starts at address 0x40000000. If we investigate further, we can confirm that GDB is actually sitting at the first line of code for the dynamic linker, before any code from our own application has been executed. Using our cross version of readelf, we can confirm the linker's starting address as follows:

```
# xscale_be-readelf -S ld-2.3.3.so | grep \.text
[ 9] .text     PROGBITS     00000790 000790 012c6c 00  AX  0   0 16
```

From this data, we conclude that the address that GDB reports on startup is the first instruction from ld-2.3.3.so, the Linux dynamic linker/loader. You can use this technique to get a rough idea of where your code is if you don't have symbolic debug information for a process or shared library.

Remember that we are executing this cross readelf command on our development host. Therefore, the ld-2.3.3.so file, itself an XScale binary object, must be accessible to your development host. Most typically, this file resides on your development host and is a component of your embedded Linux distribution installed on your host.

15.3.1 Shared Library Events in GDB

GDB can alert you to shared library events. This can be useful for understanding your application's behavior or the behavior of the Linux loader, or for setting breakpoints in shared library routines you want to debug or step through. Listing 15-7 illustrates this technique. Normally, the complete path to the library is displayed. This listing has been edited for better readability.

LISTING 15-7   Stopping GDB on Shared Library Events

```
$ xscale_be-gdb -q websdemo
(gdb) target remote 192.168.1.141:2001
Remote debugging using 192.168.1.141:2001
0x40000790 in ?? ()
(gdb) i shared      <<< Display loaded shared libs
No shared libraries loaded at this time.
(gdb) b main        <<< Break at main
Breakpoint 1 at 0x12b80: file main.c, line 72.
(gdb) c
Continuing.
```

LISTING 15-7   Continued

```
Breakpoint 1, main (argc=0x1, argv=0xbec7fdc4) at main.c:72
72              int localvar = 9;
(gdb) i shared
From        To          Syms Read   Shared Object Library
0x40033300  0x4010260c  Yes         /opt/mvl/.../lib/tls/libc.so.6
0x40000790  0x400133fc  Yes         /opt/mvl/.../lib/ld-linux.so.3
(gdb) set stop-on-solib-events 1
(gdb) c
Continuing.
Stopped due to shared library event
(gdb) i shared
From        To          Syms Read   Shared Object Library
0x40033300  0x4010260c  Yes         /opt/mvl/.../lib/tls/libc.so.6
0x40000790  0x400133fc  Yes         /opt/mvl/.../lib/ld-linux.so.3
0x4012bad8  0x40132104  Yes         /opt/mvl/.../libnss_files.so.2
(gdb)
```

When the debug session is first started, no shared libraries are loaded. You can see this with the first i shared command. This command displays the shared libraries that are currently loaded. Setting a breakpoint at our application's main() function, we see that two shared libraries are now loaded. These are the Linux dynamic linker/loader and the standard C library component libc.

From here, we issue the set stop-on-solib-event command and continue program execution. When the application tries to execute a function from another shared library, that library is loaded. In case you are wondering, the gethostbyname() function is encountered and causes the next shared object to load.

This example illustrates an important cross-development concept. The binary application (ELF image) running on the target contains information on the libraries it needs to resolve its external references. We can view this information easily using the ldd command, introduced in Chapter 11, "BusyBox," and detailed in Chapter 13. Listing 15-8 shows the output of ldd invoked from the target board.

LISTING 15-8   ldd Executed on the Target Board

```
root@coyote:/workspace# ldd websdemo
        libc.so.6 => /lib/tls/libc.so.6 (0x40020000)
        /lib/ld-linux.so.3 (0x40000000)
root@coyote:/workspace#
```

Notice that the paths to the shared libraries on the target are absolute paths starting at /lib on the root file system. But GDB running on your host development workstation cannot use these paths to find the libraries. You should realize that doing so would result in your host GDB loading libraries from the wrong architecture. Your host is likely x86, whereas in this example, the target is ARM XScale.

If you invoke your cross version of ldd, you will see the paths that were preconfigured into your toolchain. Your toolchain must know where these files exist on your host development system.[2] Listing 15-9 illustrates this. Again, we have edited the listing for readability; long paths have been abbreviated.

LISTING 15-9   ldd Executed on the Development Host

```
$ xscale_be-ldd websdemo
    libc.so.6 => /opt/mvl/.../xscale_be/target/lib/libc.so.6 (0xdead1000)
    ld-linux.so.3 => /opt/mvl/.../xscale_be/target/lib/ld-linux.so.3 (0xdead2000)
$
```

Your cross toolchain should be preconfigured with these library locations. Not only does your host GDB need to know where they are located, but, of course, your compiler and linker also need to know.[3] GDB can tell you where it is configured to look for these libraries using the show solib-absolute-prefix command:

```
(gdb) show solib-absolute-prefix
Prefix for loading absolute shared library symbol files is
"/opt/mvl/pro/devkit/arm/xscale_be/target".
(gdb)
```

You can set or change where GDB searches for shared libraries using the GDB commands set solib-absolute-prefix and set solib-search-path. If you are developing your own shared library modules or have custom library locations on your system, you can use solib-search-path to instruct GDB where to look for your libraries. For more details about these and other GDB commands, consult the online GDB manual referenced at the end of this chapter.

One final note about ldd. You might have noticed the addresses from Listing 15-8 and Listing 15-9 associated with the libraries. ldd displays the load address for the start

---

[2] It is certainly possible to pass these locations to your compiler, linker, and debugger for every invocation, but any good embedded Linux distribution will configure these defaults into the toolchain as a convenience to the developer.

[3] Of course, your compiler also needs to know the location of target files such as architecture-specific system and library header files.

of these code segments as they would be if the program were loaded by the Linux dynamic linker/loader. Executed on the target, the addresses shown in Listing 15-5 make perfect sense, and we can correlate these with the /proc/<pid>/maps listing of the running process on the target. Listing 15-10 displays the memory segments for this target process after it is completely loaded and running.

LISTING 15-10   Memory Segments from /proc/<pid>/maps on Target

```
root@coyote:~# cat /proc/197/maps
00008000-00026000 r-xp 00000000 00:0e 4852444     /workspace/websdemo-stripped
0002d000-0002e000 rw-p 0001d000 00:0e 4852444     /workspace/websdemo-stripped
0002e000-0005e000 rwxp 0002e000 00:00 0           [heap]
40000000-40017000 r-xp 00000000 00:0a 4982583     /lib/ld-2.3.3.so
40017000-40019000 rw-p 40017000 00:00 0
4001e000-4001f000 r--p 00016000 00:0a 4982583     /lib/ld-2.3.3.so
4001f000-40020000 rw-p 00017000 00:0a 4982583     /lib/ld-2.3.3.so
40020000-4011d000 r-xp 00000000 00:0a 4982651     /lib/tls/libc-2.3.3.so
4011d000-40120000 ---p 000fd000 00:0a 4982651     /lib/tls/libc-2.3.3.so
40120000-40124000 rw-p 000f8000 00:0a 4982651     /lib/tls/libc-2.3.3.so
40124000-40126000 r--p 000fc000 00:0a 4982651     /lib/tls/libc-2.3.3.so
40126000-40128000 rw-p 000fe000 00:0a 4982651     /lib/tls/libc-2.3.3.so
40128000-4012a000 rw-p 40128000 00:00 0
4012a000-40133000 r-xp 00000000 00:0a 4982652     /lib/tls/libnss_files-2.3.3.so
40133000-4013a000 ---p 00009000 00:0a 4982652     /lib/tls/libnss_files-2.3.3.so
4013a000-4013b000 r--p 00008000 00:0a 4982652     /lib/tls/libnss_files-2.3.3.so
4013b000-4013c000 rw-p 00009000 00:0a 4982652     /lib/tls/libnss_files-2.3.3.so
becaa000-becbf000 rwxp becaa000 00:00 0           [stack]
root@coyote:~#
```

Notice the correlation of the target ldd output from Listing 15-8 to the memory segments displayed in the /proc file system for this process. The start of the Linux loader (the beginning of the .text segment) is 0x40000000, and the start of libc is at 0x40020000. These are the virtual addresses where these portions of the application have been loaded; they are reported by the target invocation of ldd. However, the load addresses reported by the cross version of ldd in Listing 15-9 (0xdead1000 and 0xdead2000) are there to remind you that these libraries cannot be loaded on your host system (they are ARM architecture binaries). These load addresses are simply placeholders.

15.4   Debugging Multiple Tasks

Generally the developer is presented with two different debugging scenarios when dealing with multiple threads of execution. Processes can exist in their own address space or can share an address space (and other system resources) with other threads of execution. The first scenario (independent processes not sharing common address space) must be debugged using separate independent debug sessions. Nothing prevents you from using gdbserver on multiple processes on your target system and using a separate invocation of GDB on your development host to coordinate a debug session for multiple cooperating but independent processes.

15.4.1   Debugging Multiple Processes

When a process being debugged under GDB uses the fork() system call[4] to spawn a new process, GDB can take one of two courses of action. It can continue to control and debug the parent process, or it can stop debugging the parent process and attach to the newly formed child process. You can control this behavior using the set follow-fork-mode command. The two modes are follow parent and follow child. The default behavior is for GDB to follow the parent. In this case, the child process executes immediately upon a successful fork.

Listing 15-11 reproduces a snippet of a simple program that forks multiple processes from its main() routine.

LISTING 15-11   Using fork() to Spawn a Child Process

```
. . .
  for( i=0; i<MAX_PROCESSES; i++ ) {
    /* Creating child process */
    pid[i] = fork();            /* Parent gets non-zero PID */
    if ( pid[i] == -1 ) {
      perror("fork failed");
      exit(1);
    }

    if ( pid[i] == 0 ) {        /* Indicates child's code path */
      worker_process();         /* The forked process calls this */
    }
```

---

[4] We will use the term system call, but fork() in this context is actually the C library function, which in turn calls the Linux sys_fork() system call.

LISTING 15-11   Continued

```
}

/* Parent's main control loop */
while ( 1 ) {
...
}
```

This simple loop creates MAX_PROCESSES new processes using the `fork()` system call. Each newly spawned process executes a body of code defined by the function `worker_process()`. When this code is run under GDB in default mode, GDB detects the creation of the new threads of execution (processes) but remains attached to the parent's thread of execution. Listing 15-12 illustrates this GDB session.

LISTING 15-12   GDB in `follow-fork-mode = parent`

```
(gdb) target remote 192.168.1.141:2001
0x40000790 in ?? ()
(gdb) b main
Breakpoint 1 at 0x8888: file forker.c, line 104.
(gdb) c
Continuing.
[New Thread 356]
[Switching to Thread 356]

Breakpoint 1, main (argc=0x1, argv=0xbe807dd4) at forker.c:104
104         time(&start_time);
(gdb) b worker_process
Breakpoint 2 at 0x8784: file forker.c, line 45.
(gdb) c
Continuing.
Detaching after fork from child process 357.
Detaching after fork from child process 358.
Detaching after fork from child process 359.
Detaching after fork from child process 360.
Detaching after fork from child process 361.
Detaching after fork from child process 362.
Detaching after fork from child process 363.
Detaching after fork from child process 364.
```

Notice that eight child processes were spawned, with PID values from 357 to 364. The parent process was instantiated with PID 356. When the breakpoint in `main()`

was hit, we entered a breakpoint at the `worker_process()` routine, which each child process executes upon `fork()`. Letting the program continue from `main`, we see each of the new processes spawned and detached by the debugger. They never hit the breakpoint because GDB is attached to the main process, which never executes the `worker_process()` routine.

If you need to debug each process, you must execute a separate independent GDB session and attach to the child process after it is `forked()`. The GDB documentation referenced at the end of this chapter outlines a useful technique to place a call to `sleep()` in the child process, giving you time to attach a debugger to the new process. Attaching to a new process is explained in Section 15.5.2, "Attaching to a Running Process."

If you simply need to follow the child process, set `follow-fork-mode` to follow `child` before your parent reaches the `fork()` system call, as shown in Listing 15-13.

LISTING 15-13 GDB in `follow-fork-mode = child`

```
(gdb) target remote 192.168.1.141:2001
0x40000790 in ?? ()
(gdb) set follow-fork-mode child
(gdb) b worker_process
Breakpoint 1 at 0x8784: file forker.c, line 45.
(gdb) c
Continuing.
[New Thread 401]
Attaching after fork to child process 402.
[New Thread 402]
[Switching to Thread 402]

Breakpoint 1, worker_process () at forker.c:45
45          int my_pid = getpid();
(gdb) c
Continuing.
```

Here we see the parent process being instantiated as PID 401. When the first child is spawned by the `fork()` system call, GDB detaches silently from the parent thread of execution and attaches to the newly spawned child process having PID 402. GDB is now in control of the first child process and honors the breakpoint set at `worker_process()`. Notice, however, that the other child processes spawned by the code snippet from Listing 15-11 are not debugged and continue to run to their own completion.

In summary, using GDB in this fashion, you are limited to debugging a single process at a time. You can debug through the `fork()` system call, but you have to decide which thread of execution to follow through the `fork()` call—the parent or the child. As mentioned in the introduction to this section, you can use multiple independent GDB sessions if you must debug more than one cooperating process at a time.

15.4.2   Debugging Multithreaded Applications

If your application uses the POSIX thread library for its threading functions, GDB has additional capabilities to handle concurrent debugging of a multithreaded application. The Native POSIX Thread Library (NPTL) has become the de facto standard thread library in use on Linux systems, including embedded Linux systems. The rest of this discussion assumes that you are using this thread library.

For this section, we use a demonstration program that spawns a number of threads using the `pthread_create()` library function in a simple loop. After the threads are spawned, the `main()` routine simply waits for keyboard input to terminate the application. Each thread displays a short message on the screen and sleeps for a predetermined time. Listing 15-14 shows the startup sequence on the target board.

LISTING 15-14   Target Threads Demo Startup

```
root@coyote:/apps # gdbserver localhost:2001 ./tdemo
Process ./tdemo created; pid = 671
Listening on port 2001
Remote debugging from host 192.168.1.10
    ^^^^^  Previous three lines displayed by gdbserver

tdemo main() entered: My pid is 671
Starting worker thread 0
Starting worker thread 1
Starting worker thread 2
Starting worker thread 3
```

As in our previous examples, `gdbserver` prepares the application for running and waits for a connection from our host-based cross-gdb. When GDB connects, `gdbserver` reports the connection with the `Remote debugging...` message. Now we start GDB on the host and connect. Listing 15-15 reproduces this half of the session.

LISTING 15-15   Host GDB Connecting to Target Threads Demo

```
$ xscale_be-gdb -q tdemo
(gdb) target remote 192.168.1.141:2001
0x40000790 in ?? ()
(gdb) b tdemo.c:97
Breakpoint 1 at 0x88ec: file tdemo.c, line 97.
(gdb) c
Continuing.
[New Thread 1059]
[New Thread 1060]
[New Thread 1061]
[New Thread 1062]
[New Thread 1063]
[Switching to Thread 1059]

Breakpoint 1, main (argc=0x1, argv=0xbefffdd4) at tdemo.c:98
98                 int c = getchar();
(gdb)
```

Here we connect to the target (resulting in the Remote debugging...message shown in Listing 15-14), set a breakpoint just past the loop where we spawned the new threads, and continue. When the new thread is created, GDB displays a notice along with the thread ID. Thread 1059 is the tdemo application, doing its work directly from the main() function. Threads 1060 through 1063 are the new threads created from the call to pthread_create().

When GDB hits the breakpoint, it displays the message [Switching to Thread 1059], indicating that this was the thread of execution that encountered the breakpoint. It is the active thread for the debugging session, referred to as the current thread in the GDB documentation.

GDB enables us to switch between threads and perform the usual debugging operations such as setting additional breakpoints, examining data, displaying a backtrace, and working with the individual stack frames within the current thread. Listing 15-16 provides examples of these operations, continuing with our debugging session started in Listing 15-15.

LISTING 15-16   GDB Operations on Threads

```
...
(gdb) c
Continuing.
                  <<< Ctl-C to interrupt program execution
Program received signal SIGINT, Interrupt.
0x400db9c0 in read () from /opt/mvl/.../lib/tls/libc.so.6
(gdb) i threads
  5 Thread 1063  0x400bc714 in nanosleep ()
   from /opt/mvl/.../lib/tls/libc.so.6
  4 Thread 1062  0x400bc714 in nanosleep ()
   from /opt/mvl/.../lib/tls/libc.so.6
  3 Thread 1061  0x400bc714 in nanosleep ()
   from /opt/mvl/.../lib/tls/libc.so.6
  2 Thread 1060  0x400bc714 in nanosleep ()
   from /opt/mvl/.../lib/tls/libc.so.6
* 1 Thread 1059  0x400db9c0 in read ()
   from /opt/mvl/.../lib/tls/libc.so.6
(gdb) thread 4              <<< Make Thread 4 the current thread
[Switching to thread 4 (Thread 1062)]
#0  0x400bc714 in nanosleep ()
   from /opt/mvl/.../lib/tls/libc.so.6
(gdb) bt
#0  0x400bc714 in nanosleep ()
   from /opt/mvl/.../lib/tls/libc.so.6
#1  0x400bc4a4 in __sleep (seconds=0x0) at sleep.c:137
#2  0x00008678 in go_to_sleep (duration=0x5) at tdemo.c:18
#3  0x00008710 in worker_2_job (random=0x5) at tdemo.c:36
#4  0x00008814 in worker_thread (threadargs=0x2) at tdemo.c:67
#5  0x40025244 in start_thread (arg=0xffffffdfc) at pthread_create.c:261
#6  0x400e8fa0 in clone () at../sysdeps/unix/sysv/linux/arm/clone.S:82
#7  0x400e8fa0 in clone () at../sysdeps/unix/sysv/linux/arm/clone.S:82
(gdb) frame 3
#3  0x00008710 in worker_2_job (random=0x5) at tdemo.c:36
36           go_to_sleep(random);
(gdb) l                     <<< Generate listing of where we are
31      }
32
33      static void worker_2_job(int random)
34      {
35          printf("t2 sleeping for %d\n", random);
36          go_to_sleep(random);
37      }
```

LISTING 15-16   Contiued

```
38
39        static void worker_3_job(int random)
40        {
(gdb)
```

A few points are worth mentioning. GDB assigns its own integer value to each thread and uses these values to reference the individual threads. When a breakpoint is hit in a thread, all threads within the process are halted for examination. GDB marks the current thread with an asterisk (*). You can set unique breakpoints within each thread—assuming, of course, that they exist in a unique context. If you set a breakpoint in a common portion of code where all threads execute, the thread that hits the breakpoint first is arbitrary.

The GDB user documentation referenced at the end of this chapter contains more useful information related to debugging in a multithreaded environment.

15.4.3 Debugging Bootloader/Flash Code

Debugging Flash resident code presents its own unique challenges. The most obvious limitation is the way in which GDB and `gdbserver` cooperate in setting target breakpoints. When we discussed the GDB remote serial protocol in Chapter 14, you learned how breakpoints are inserted into an application.[5] GDB replaces the opcode at the breakpoint location with an architecture-specific opcode that passes control to the debugger. However, in ROM or Flash, GDB cannot overwrite the opcode, so this method of setting breakpoints is useless.

Most modern processors contain some number of debug registers that can be used to get around this limitation. These capabilities must be supported by architecture- and processor-specific hardware probes or stubs. The most common technique for debugging Flash and ROM resident code is to use JTAG hardware probes. These probes support the setting of processor-specific hardware breakpoints. This topic was covered in detail in Chapter 14. Refer to Section 14.4.2, "Debugging with a JTAG Probe," for details.

---

[5] Refer to Listing 14-7.

15.5   Additional Remote Debug Options

Sometimes you might want to use a serial port for remote debugging. For other tasks, you might find it useful to attach the debugger to a process that is already running. These simple but useful operations are detailed here.

15.5.1   Debugging Using a Serial Port

Debugging using a serial port is quite straightforward. Of course, you must have a serial port available on your target that is not being used by another process, such as a serial console. The same limitation applies to your host. A serial port must be available. If both of these conditions can be met, simply replace the *IP address:port number* specification passed to `gdbserver` with a serial port specification. Use the same technique when connecting to your target from your host-based GDB.

On your target:

```
root@coyote:/apps # gdbserver /dev/ttyS0 ./tdemo
Process ./tdemo created; pid = 698
Remote debugging using /dev/ttyS0
```

From your host:

```
$ xscale_be-gdb -q tdemo
(gdb) target remote /dev/ttyS1
Remote debugging using /dev/ttyS1
0x40000790 in ?? ()
```

15.5.2   Attaching to a Running Process

It is often advantageous to connect to a process to examine its state while it is running instead of killing the process and starting it again. With `gdbserver`, this task is trivial:

```
root@coyote:/apps # ps ax | grep tdemo
 1030 pts/0     S1+    0:00 ./tdemo
root@coyote:/apps # gdbserver localhost:2001 --attach 1030
Attached; pid = 1030
Listening on port 2001
```

When you are finished examining the process under debug, you can issue the GDB `detach` command. This detaches the `gdbserver` from the application on the target and terminates the debug session. The application continues where it left off. This is a very useful technique for examining a running program. Be aware, though, that when you attach to the process, it halts, waiting for instructions from you. It does not resume execution until instructed to do so, using either the `continue` or `detach` command. Also note that you can use the `detach` command at almost any time to end the debug session and leave the application running on the target.

15.6 Summary

- Remote (cross) debugging enables symbolic debugging using host development workstation resources for the heavy lifting, preserving often-scarce target resources.

- `gdbserver` runs on the target system and acts as the glue between the cross-gdb running on a development host and the process being debugged on the target.

- GDB on the host typically uses IP connections via Ethernet to send commands to and receive commands from `gdbserver` running on the target. The GDB remote protocol is used between GDB and `gdbserver`.

- GDB can halt on shared library events and can automatically load shared library symbols when available. Your toolchain should be configured for the default paths on your cross-development system. Alternatively, you can use GDB commands to set the search paths for shared library objects.

- GDB can be used to debug multiple independent processes using multiple concurrent GDB sessions.

- GDB can be configured to follow a forked process on a `fork()` system call. Its default mode is to continue debugging the parent—the caller of `fork()`.

- GDB has features to facilitate debugging multithreaded applications written to POSIX thread APIs. The current default Linux thread library is the Native POSIX Thread Library (NPTL).

- GDB supports attaching to and detaching from a running process.

15.6.1   Suggestions for Additional Reading

GDB: The GNU Project Debugger
Online documentation
http://sourceware.org/gdb/onlinedocs/

GDB Pocket Reference
Arnold Robbins
O'Reilly Media, 2005

Chapter 16

Open Source Build Systems

In This Chapter

- 16.1 Why Use a Build System?   446
- 16.2 Scratchbox   447
- 16.3 Buildroot   451
- 16.4 OpenEmbedded   454
- 16.5 Summary   464

Software build systems have been around for a long time. Historically, they have taken many forms, from simple script-driven or make-based systems to complex and often proprietary software programs designed to build a particular project. Several open source build systems have come and gone, while a few have survived the test of time.

This chapter presents some of the more popular build systems and takes a detailed look at one build system that has emerged as a leading contender for building embedded Linux systems: OpenEmbedded.

16.1   Why Use a Build System?

There are many sources of complete, embedded Linux distributions. Embedded Linux distributions can be found online, obtained through free download, or purchased from commercial embedded Linux suppliers. Often these embedded Linux distributions are fixed in their functionality and difficult to change. They often come with binary-only solutions, such as important toolchains and critical packages, without instructions for actually generating these elements from source.

A capable embedded Linux build system helps you create an embedded Linux distribution tailored to your unique requirements. This must include a cross-toolchain and all the packages required for your project. Your build system should be able to generate root file systems in your choice of binary formats, your embedded Linux kernel image with your configuration, a bootloader image, and any other necessary files and utilities so that these can be properly deployed.

It is absolutely nontrivial to build an embedded Linux distribution—or, for that matter, any Linux distribution—from scratch. Just imagine trying to assemble all the components that make up your desktop Linux distribution. Don't forget to include the toolchain, because for embedded applications, contrary to popular belief, obtaining commercial-quality toolchains for non-x86 architectures is quite difficult without dedicated knowledge of and experience in cross-toolchain development and testing for your chosen architecture.

Compiling the list of components you need can be your first challenge. Where will your toolchain come from? What about required system libraries and bootloaders? Where will you get these? What packages will you need to support the various hardware devices and software applications you are planning for your product? What are the dependencies for each of the packages you plan to use? Which file systems will you use, and how do you build them? How will you track package versions and their dependencies? How can you determine which versions of packages and tools are compatible with one another? How will you manage updates and upgrades to your embedded Linux distribution and resulting embedded product? How are patches integrated after the fact?

These and other questions face the embedded systems developer as the project plans take shape. A well-designed and easily supported embedded Linux build system is a perfect tool to help answer these questions and lead to a rapid project deployment that is readily maintainable.

The next few sections introduce several of the more popular build systems. We will spend considerable time describing one of the most promising and popular embedded Linux build systems—OpenEmbedded.

16.2 Scratchbox

Scratchbox is a cross-compilation toolkit that became popular during its use in the Maemo project targeting the Nokia N770 handheld computer. The Maemo project has since been merged with Moblin to become MeeGo (www.meego.com).

According to the Scratchbox website, ARM and X86 targets are supported, with experimental support for PowerPC and MIPS. The latest installation manual claims support for PowerPC targets.

16.2.1 Installing Scratchbox

Installation is straightforward following the instructions on the Scratchbox website. For Debian-based systems such as Ubuntu, add this line to the `/etc/apt/sources.list` file:

```
deb http://scratchbox.org/debian stable main
```

Then perform an update, install the required packages, and add your username[1] to Scratchbox. This sequence is shown in Listing 16-1.

LISTING 16-1   Scratchbox Installation

```
$ sudo apt-get update
$ sudo apt-get install scratchbox-core
$ sudo sb-adduser <your username>
```

Note that this sequence of instructions requires root access. This is not a huge problem so long as you have root access to your build machine. Many developers at larger enterprises do not, according to IT policy. You should consider whether this is an issue for your application.

Also note that after you use `sb-adduser` to add your username to the Scratchbox infrastructure, you must log out and then log in again with a new shell to pick up the changes in group membership. This is described fully in the Scratchbox documentation.

16.2.2   Creating a Cross-Compilation Target

After you have installed Scratchbox, you must follow several steps before a build can begin. First, you must install a toolchain and qemu (a popular processor emulator) for target emulation. Then you must log into Scratchbox and perform an initial setup using a Scratchbox menu-driven utility. Scratchbox toolchain installation is not difficult if you are using a Debian-based distribution such as Ubuntu. Several toolchains are available from Scratchbox. Check its website, under the Download tab, for current versions. For this example, we chose an ARM compiler:

```
$ sudo apt-get install scratchbox-toolchain-arm-linux-cs2010q1-202
$ sudo apt-get install scratchbox-devkit-qemu
```

Next, log in as a Scratchbox user and create a target for cross-compilation. Use the Scratchbox `login` program to log in:

```
$ /scratchbox/login
```

After you are logged in as a Scratchbox user, invoke the configuration utility. You do this using a menu-based utility called `sb-menu`. Invoke the configuration menu as follows:

```
$ [sbox-NO-TARGET: ~] > sb-menu
```

---

[1] This must be your current Linux home user account name.

Figure 16-1 shows the main configuration screen that results from this command.

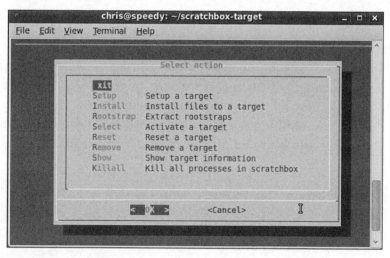

FIGURE 16-1   Scratchbox menuconfig

Using the installation documentation found on the Scratchbox website (`installdoc.pdf`) as your guide (www.scratchbox.org/documentation/docbook/installdoc.html), set up your Scratchbox environment by following these steps:

1. Create a new target under Setup called `mytarget`.
2. Select a cross-compiler when prompted after target selection.
3. Select devkits, and then select qemu.
4. Select CPU transparency, and then select qemu-arm-sb.

With these steps completed, exit the `sb-menu` utility. Now you are ready to explore the Scratchbox environment.

For our brief demo, we will use a simple Hello World program. Using your favorite editor from within the Scratchbox shell, create a simple Hello World program similar to Listing 16-2.

LISTING 16-2   Simple Hello World Example

```
#include <stdio.h>

int main(int argc, char **argv)
{
    printf("Hello world\n");
        return 0;
}
```

Now compile the program within the Scratchbox environment:

```
[sbox-mytarget: ~] > gcc -o hello-arm hello.c
```

This uses the Scratchbox ARM toolchain you just installed to compile the `hello.c` file. This command invokes the ARM toolchain through a Scratchbox wrapper. You can see the toolchain wrappers in `/scratchbox/compilers/bin`. The wrapper determines which compiler to call based on the target specifications you just created. Then you can verify that the resulting file is an ARM binary, and you can run it in the Scratchbox shell using the qemu emulation technology provided by the Scratchbox environment:

```
[sbox-mytarget: ~] > file hello-arm
hello-arm: ELF 32-bit LSB executable, ARM, version 1 (SYSV), for GNU/Linux 2.6.16,
dynamically linked (uses shared libs), not stripped
[sbox-mytarget: ~] > ./hello-arm
Hello
```

While this is a trivial example, it illustrates the Scratchbox environment and methodology. The Scratchbox model is to provide the developer with a development environment that looks like the target. The advantage of this approach is that many open source packages that are difficult to cross-compile are made easier by the use of target emulation.

Of course, the actual use cases for Scratchbox are much more complex than this example, but the architecture and approach are apparent. In actual practice, you would have numerous packages and other software programs that are compiled under the Scratchbox environment, perhaps by a series of makefiles or a custom build script that you generate particular to your requirements.

Scratchbox includes a remote shell feature that allows the developer to perform certain actions (both interactive and noninteractive) directly on real target hardware. It works similar to the familiar remote shell (`rsh`). It is called `sbrsh` and is available as part of the Scratchbox installation. More details about `sbrsh` can be found in the Scratchbox documentation.

Scratchbox has good documentation. If you want to learn more about Scratchbox, install it on your system and follow the documentation found on its website (www.scratchbox.org).

16.3 Buildroot

Buildroot is a set of makefiles and patches in a system designed to build a complete embedded Linux distribution. According to the Buildroot website, its major features include the following:

- It can build all the required components for your embedded Linux product, including cross-compiler, root file system, kernel image, and bootloader.
- It allows for simple configuration using the familiar Linux kernel menuconfig and related utilities.
- It supports several hundred packages for user space applications and libraries, including GTK2, Qt, GStreamer, and many network utilities.
- It supports uClibc or glibc, among other target libraries.
- It has a simple structure based on the makefile language that is well understood.

16.3.1 Buildroot Installation

The first thing you need to do is locate and download a Buildroot snapshot. The easiest way to do this is using git. Of course, using git without specifying a tag means that you are getting the latest top of tree, which, in any open source project, has its risks of instability. For the less bold, stable snapshots are available for download. They are listed on the downloads page at the Buildroot website at http://buildroot.uclibc.org/downloads/buildroot.html. For these examples, we will use git:

```
$ git clone git://git.buildroot.net/buildroot
```

16.3.2 Buildroot Configuration

After the snapshot (or git repository) is installed, you can begin the configuration. Enter the directory where you installed Buildroot, and issue the familiar configuration command:

```
$ make menuconfig
```

This brings up a configuration utility that by now should be very familiar. You saw a similar configuration menu with Linux kernel configuration, as well as with Scratch-box. Figure 16-2 shows what this looks like.

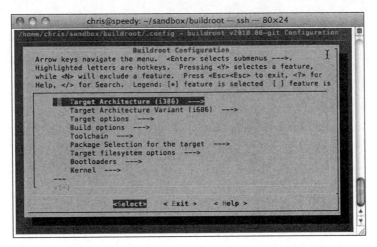

FIGURE 16-2   Buildroot configuration

Buildroot's configuration is extensive. You have many options to choose from to configure the properties of your embedded Linux distribution that Buildroot creates. Here are some of the more important attributes you must select:

- Target architecture
- Architecture variant, such as PowerPC 603e or ARM 920t
- Target options, such as board devices and serial ports
- Build options, which define build-related options such as the location of build and download directories, parallelism (the number of simultaneous jobs), and other build attributes
- Toolchain options, including library type (uClibc or glibc) and compiler version.
- Package selection, such as what software packages will be on your target

16.3.3   Buildroot Build

After you have performed a simple configuration, you kick off the build simply by typing make. If your configuration is good and you are lucky,[2] you will end up with a

---

[2] There are many reasons why builds of this type can fail, which we will describe shortly.

complete embedded Linux distribution. The build is likely to take some time, because it is downloading and building many software components and performing a number of steps to achieve that goal. A lot of output will stream up your serial terminal while the build is under way. Buildroot is performing the following general steps:

- Download source files for all the configured packages and toolchains
- Build the cross-compilation toolchain
- Using the cross-toolchain, configuring and compiling all the requested packages
- Building a kernel image if configured to do so
- Creating a root file system in the format of your choosing

When the build has finished, the results can be seen in the . . ./output directory. This is shown in Listing 16-3.

LISTING 16-3   Buildroot Output Directory Structure

```
chris@speedy:~/sandbox/buildroot$ ls -l output
total 28
drwxr-xr-x   7 chris chris 4096 2010-07-31 16:45 build
drwxr-xr-x   3 chris chris 4096 2010-07-31 16:45 host
drwxr-xr-x   2 chris chris 4096 2010-07-31 16:45 images
drwxr-xr-x   5 chris chris 4096 2010-07-31 16:34 staging
drwxr-xr-x   2 chris chris 4096 2010-07-31 16:44 stamps
drwxr-xr-x  16 chris chris 4096 2010-07-31 16:45 target
drwxr xr x  18 chris chris 4096 2010 07 31 16:41 toolchain
```

The proper root file system is found in . . ./output/images. Because we specified the ext2 file system when we configured the build, we find a rootfs.ext2 image in the images subdirectory:

```
chris@speedy:~/sandbox/buildroot$ ls -l ./output/images/
total 3728
-rw-r--r-- 1 chris chris 3817472 2010-07-31 16:45 rootfs.ext2
-rwxr-xr-x 1 chris chris   65656 2010-07-31 17:31 u-boot.bin
```

Buildroot is quite flexible and has many configuration options. Buildroot can build U-Boot for a specific board, simply by specifying the board name from the U-Boot makefile (without the _config suffix) during Buildroot configuration. For this example, ap920t was specified, and a U-Boot image (u-boot.bin) was also generated. The Buildroot documentation has more details on this.

The other directories in Buildroot's output subdirectories, as shown in Listing 16-3, include directories to hold intermediate build targets. The `staging` subdirectory is used to hold the build targets of packages that are themselves dependencies of other packages. The `toolchain` directory contains components necessary for cross-toolchain compilation. The `host` directory contains host-specific tools that were built to support Buildroot's operation. These include programs such as `fakeroot` (used to build the root file system without root privileges) and programs for image generation. The `target` directory is a near-replica of the root file system image, but it cannot be used directly as the root file system. The user, group, permissions, and device nodes are incorrect. Fakeroot uses this target directory to build the final image. Finally, the `build` directory is where all the components (except for the cross-toolchain) are built.

Buildroot is a powerful build system that can build a complete embedded Linux distribution. Consult the Buildroot documentation at http://buildroot.uclibc.org/docs.html for full details.

16.4   OpenEmbedded

There is much debate about evolution, but when it comes to OpenEmbedded, it becomes quickly obvious that OpenEmbedded evolved from several technologies that came before it. OpenEmbedded shares some of its conceptual origins with the Portage build system from Gentoo, but it also builds on some concepts from other build systems, including Buildroot.

The OpenEmbedded home page (www.openembedded.org) claims that OpenEmbedded "...offers a best-in-class cross-compile environment." Given the limitations of other open source build systems, and the flexibility of OpenEmbedded, this might just be accurate. The website also lists the following as OpenEmbedded advantages:

- It supports many hardware architectures.
- It supports multiple releases for those architectures.
- It contains tools for speeding up the process of re-creating the base after changes have been made.
- It's easy to customize.
- It runs on any Linux distribution.
- It cross-compiles thousands of packages, including GTK+, Qt, X Windows, Mono, and Java.

OpenEmbedded has gained significant traction in both commercial and open source projects. Many commercial development organizations have adopted OpenEmbedded as their preferred build system. Indeed, some commercial suppliers of Embedded Linux, including Mentor Graphics and MontaVista Software, have adopted OpenEmbedded as the basis for their commercial embedded Linux offerings.

16.4.1   OpenEmbedded Composition

OpenEmbedded is composed of two primary elements, as shown in Figure 16-3. BitBake is the build engine, which is a powerful and flexible build tool. Metadata is the set of instructions that tell BitBake what to build.

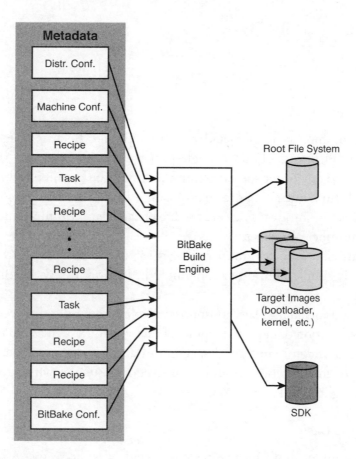

FIGURE 16-3   BitBake and metadata

BitBake processes the metadata, which provides instructions that describe what to build. At the end of the build process, BitBake produces all the requested images, including the root file system, kernel, bootloader, and intermediate images such as device tree binary (in the case of Power Architecture). One of the more powerful features of OpenEmbedded is its ability to create software development kits (SDKs). These SDKs can contain toolchains, libraries, and header files for application developers to use in a self-contained development environment.

16.4.2   BitBake Metadata

Metadata can be roughly grouped into four categories, each of which fulfills a specific role:

- Recipes
- Classes
- Tasks
- Configuration

The most common type of metadata is a recipe file. Recipes usually contain the instructions for BitBake to build a single package. Recipes describe the package, its dependencies, and any other special action that might be required to build a package.

Classes perform a role similar to that of classes in an object-oriented programming language such as C++ or Java. They are used to encapsulate common functionality used across a large number of recipes.

Tasks are usually used to group packages for use in building a root file system. They are usually simple files, often containing little more than a few lines of package dependencies.

Configuration metadata plays an important role in defining the overall behavior of BitBake. Configuration data provides global build variables such as build paths, default image construction commands, and specifics of a particular machine. It also defines characteristics of the distribution under construction, such as which toolchain and C library (uClibc, glibc, and so on) to use.

16.4.3   Recipe Basics

The most common unit of OpenEmbedded metadata is the recipe. A recipe is usually a single file or small collection of files that build a single package. Examining a simple recipe is a good way to begin understanding the OpenEmbedded metadata language.

Listing 16-4 is the OpenEmbedded version of Hello World. This recipe builds a simple Hello World application and prepares it for inclusion in the final root file system. It is called `hello_1.0.0.bb` on the file system.

LISTING 16-4   Simple OpenEmbedded Recipe: **hello_1.0.0.bb**

```
DESCRIPTION = "Hello demo project"
PR = "r0"
LICENSE = "GPL"

SRC_URI = "http://localhost/sources/hello-1.0.0.tar.gz"

SRC_URI[md5sum] = "90a8ffd73e4b467b6d4852fb95e493b9"
SRC_URI[sha256sum] = "fd626b829cf1df265abfceac37c2b5629f2ba8fbc3897add29f-
9661caa40fe12"

do_install() {
        install -m 0755 -d ${D}${bindir}
        install -m 0755 ${S}/hello ${D}${bindir}/hello
}
```

The first few fields are little more than administrative:

- DESCRIPTION—Descriptive information about the package itself
- PR—Package (recipe) version number
- LICENSE—The package license

SRC_URI must be present in every recipe. It defines the method (http in this example) and location (localhost/sources/hello-1.1.0.tar.gz) that BitBake will use to locate and obtain the files that make up the package. Source code can be *fetched*[3] in many forms using a variety of methods. For example, source can be fetched from a git, svn, or cvs repository, either local or remote. Source can be fetched from a file or tarball either locally or on an Internet server.

SRC_URI[md5sum] is one method of specifying a checksum that can be used to validate proper fetching of a source archive. If a remote md5 or sha256 signature file is available, it is tested against these values to ensure correct download.

The do_install method is a function override of BitBake's default install method. In this sample recipe, the do_install method defines two steps using the Linux install command: It creates an output directory in which to place the build artifact

---

[3] One of the BitBake modules is called the "fetcher."

(our `hello` binary), and it places that binary in the directory just created. The directories are specified using a syntax commonly found in autotools configuration scripts and build files. `{bindir}` refers to `/bin` on the target. The S and D are OpenEmbedded metadata convenience variables that refer to the source and destination directories, respectively. You can read more about the `install` command on your favorite Linux desktop on its man page, `man install`.

Recipes in OpenEmbedded can contain directives in either Python language or bash shell script language. Our example in Listing 16-4 contains only bash shell script language. Discussion of Python is beyond the scope of this section.

You may be wondering how this simple recipe can result in building the Hello World application. We saw an install step defined in the recipe, but there was little else in the way of build instructions. BitBake processes each recipe using a default set of steps, defined in OpenEmbedded *classes*. BitBake classes are files ending in `.bbclass`. Most of the default processing steps come from a special base class called `base.bbclass`. It is here that the default commands to fetch, unpack, configure, compile, and install are defined.

Listing 16-5 shows the BitBake output while building the hello package. BitBake can accept any recipe or *task*[4] as a target for building.

LISTING 16-5   BitBake Hello Recipe Processing

```
chris@speedy:~/sandbox/build01$ bitbake hello
<...>
NOTE: Executing runqueue
NOTE: Running task 10 of 38 (ID: 5, NOTE: Running task 10 of 38 (ID: 5,
/hello_1.0.0.bb, do_fetch)
NOTE: Running task 11 of 38 (ID: 0, /hello_1.0.0.bb, do_unpack)
NOTE: Running task 15 of 38 (ID: 1, /hello_1.0.0.bb, do_patch)
NOTE: Running task 16 of 38 (ID: 7, /hello_1.0.0.bb, do_configure)
NOTE: Running task 17 of 38 (ID: 8, /hello_1.0.0.bb, do_compile)
NOTE: Running task 18 of 38 (ID: 2, /hello_1.0.0.bb, do_install)
NOTE: Running task 19 of 38 (ID: 10, /hello_1.0.0.bb, do_package)
NOTE: Running task 25 of 38 (ID: 13, /hello_1.0.0.bb, do_package_write_ipk)
NOTE: Running task 26 of 38 (ID: 9, /hello_1.0.0.bb, do_package_write)
NOTE: Running task 29 of 38 (ID: 3, /hello_1.0.0.bb, do_populate_sysroot)
NOTE: Running task 30 of 38 (ID: 12, /hello_1.0.0.bb, do_package_stage)
NOTE: Running task 37 of 38 (ID: 11, /hello_1.0.0.bb, do_package_stage_all)
NOTE: Running task 38 of 38 (ID: 4, /hello_1.0.0.bb, do_build)
NOTE: Tasks Summary: Attempted 38 tasks of which 25 didn't need to be rerun and 0
failed.
```

---

[4] Recall that a "task" is a special kind of OpenEmbedded metadata (recipe) that is often used to group packages for inclusion in a root file system.

Note that this listing has been reformatted for easier reading. Each line has been truncated to remove the full path to the `hello_1.0.0.bb` recipe file, and several lines not relevant to the discussion have been removed.

From Listing 16-5, we can see the individual steps that BitBake uses to build the package defined by the `hello_1.0.0.bb` recipe. The first step (fetch) downloads the hello tarball from the server. Unpack untars the tarball into a working directory defined by the configuration metadata. We saw in Listing 16-4 that this working directory can be referenced by a metadata variable called S. The `do_patch` step applies any required patches that are present in the metadata.

Configure follows patch. In this simple recipe, it is a null method. It does nothing, because there is nothing to configure. The next task is the compile step. Here is where a generic make command is issued in the hello source working directory, expecting a package makefile to do the work of building the package. Following this is the install step. Notice from Listing 16-5 that we have overridden the default install stage with our own definition for install. Our version of install takes precedence. It installs the `hello` binary as described in the discussion of Listing 16-4.

The next few steps related to packaging result in building a binary package containing the files we populated with our install method. A detailed discussion of packaging is beyond the scope of this section, but realize that every recipe creates a binary package, of the form specified by the metadata. Usually this is the `.ipk` package format—a compact, lightweight packaging technology designed especially for embedded Linux applications. The resulting package is placed in a special output directory that BitBake created for the purpose.

The populate and staging steps move any required files to a special staging location so that if other subsequent packages depend on artifacts from this build, they will be available. Also, the root file system is ultimately compiled from the contents of special recipe-specific directories where the build artifacts are collected. This is the work of the `do_build` method.

After BitBake has completed processing this recipe successfully, the package is built. Then the build artifacts (usually a binary or library or a set of these) are placed in a special recipe-specific directory so that other programs can refer to them during the build. Subsequent image-building recipes can gather the build artifacts from these recipe-specific directories for inclusion in a final root file system.

The next few sections discuss the other major categories of metadata—tasks, classes, and configuration.

16.4.4   Metadata Tasks

A task is a recipe that is used to group packages together, usually for the purpose of building root file systems. Tasks do not produce output packages with artifacts in them, because they would be empty. They may or may not have "task" in their name.

Note that the term *task* in OpenEmbedded terminology is overloaded. We speak of BitBake tasks, which are the steps that BitBake performs, such as `do_compile`, or we refer to tasks as these special recipes. Beware of the terminology!

Listing 16-6 shows a simple task from a recent snapshot of OpenEmbedded. This task specifies the required packages for generic Java support. When the root file system is finally assembled, it will contain the packages specified in task-java.bb.

LISTING 16-6   `task-java.bb`

```
DESCRIPTION = "Base task package for Java"
PR = "r2"
LICENSE = "MIT"

inherit task

RDEPENDS_${PN} = "\
    cacao \
    classpath-awt \
    java2-runtime \
    librxtx-java \
"
```

Some tasks can be complex, but this task is relatively simple and illustrates the basic idea behind a task. The obligatory header fields are present, including DESCRIPTION, PR, and LICENSE. The `inherit` keyword illustrates the use of the next metadata type we will discuss—classes and their role in inheritance. You can think of this directive as similar to `#include` in C. It specifies that the variables and methods defined in task.bbclass should be incorporated into this recipe as it is processed by BitBake.

The RDEPENDS_${PN} variable in Listing 16-6 is the syntax used to define runtime dependencies. PN evaluates to the package name, basically just the basename of the recipe filename—in this example, `task-java`. When this `task-java.bb` recipe is included in an image build, the runtime dependencies listed under its RDEPENDS cause these packages to be built and included in the final image. If you have followed along with these examples and downloaded an OpenEmbedded snapshot, you can see this task in action in the image recipe `x11-gpe-java-image.bb`.

16.4.5 Metadata Classes

A class in OpenEmbedded is similar to classes in object-oriented languages such as C++ and Java. It is used to encapsulate common functionality that can be shared by many other recipes. Classes are used in OpenEmbedded for many common functions.

We saw an example of the use of a class in the `task-java.bb` recipe in Listing 16-6. This task class can be found in a file called `task.bbclass` in a subdirectory of the `openembedded` repository called `classes`. It performs some housekeeping for functions required by all tasks. Among them are directives to tell BitBake that this recipe does not itself produce any build artifacts that require packaging or incorporation into the final root file system. It also includes logic that produces `-dbg` and `-dev` versions of the packages that are incorporated by the task itself.

One of the more commonly used classes is `autotools.bbclass`. This class provides the familiar autotools functionality around which many common Linux packages are built. You are probably familiar with autotools-based packages. If you have ever downloaded source code and unpacked and compiled it on a Linux desktop using the familiar sequence of `./configure`, `make`, and `make install`, you have built an autotools-based project.

The `autotools.bbclass` class provides this functionality. If you have a source package that uses autotools, the recipe can be quite simple, even if the package itself is not.

Listing 16-7 displays a simple autotools-based recipe. It has been slightly reformatted for readability with no loss of functionality.

LISTING 16-7 Simple Autotools-Based Recipe: **rdesktop_1.5.0.bb**

```
DESCRIPTION = "Rdesktop rdp client for X"
HOMEPAGE = "http://www.rdesktop.org"
DEPENDS = "virtual/libx11 openssl"
SECTION = "x11/network"
LICENSE = "GPL"
PR = "r2"

inherit autotools

SRC_URI = "${SOURCEFORGE_MIRROR}/rdesktop/rdesktop-${PV}.tar.gz"

EXTRA_OECONF = "--with-openssl=${STAGING_EXECPREFIXDIR} "
```

It hardly gets any simpler than this. This recipe provides build instructions for rdesktop, an rdp client for X. The standard header is present, including DESCRIPTION, LICENSE, PR, and so on. Next comes the autotools functionality from autotools. bbclass, incorporated via the inherit keyword. The SRC_URI tells BitBake where and how to obtain the source code.

The last item illustrates one of the key features of autotools-based projects. If you've ever passed commands to ./configure while building an autotools-based project, you will find this familiar. The EXTRA_OECONF variable is simply passed to rdesktop's ./configure when the configure step is executed. This particular example passes the --with-openssl flag to the rdesktop ./configure script. This causes rdesktop to be configured with openssl functionality and tells it where to find the openssl support files needed to compile with this feature enabled.

Classes are used in OpenEmbedded for a wide variety of purposes. You can see all the current classes defined in the .../openembedded/classes directory.

16.4.6   Configuring OpenEmbedded

One of the most difficult aspects of using OpenEmbedded is to get a working configuration. Many things need to be defined in order to build an embedded Linux distribution. Here are some of the more obvious attributes that must be defined:

- Target architecture
- Processor type
- Machine features such as serial port and baud rate and Flash organization
- Choice of C library, such as glibc or one of the several embedded-optimized alternatives
- Toolchain and binutils version and source (external or built by BitBake)
- Root file system image type
- Kernel version

Of course, there is much more to the configuration than what is listed here. Configuration metadata can be generalized in four broad categories: BitBake, machine, distribution, and local. BitBake configuration (bitbake.conf) is in many ways like BitBake's plumbing. It defines system-wide variables such as system paths, target file system layout, and many architecture-dependent build variables. Unless you are doing something peculiar, you should not have to edit this file.

Machine configuration is placed in a configuration file named for the machine it describes. Recent OpenEmbedded snapshots contain configuration files describing more than 250 machines.[5] This is the proper place to define machine-specific features such as serial port configuration and any specific requirements for image format, kernel version, and bootloader version. Target architecture is usually specified in the machine file.

Distribution configuration defines aspects of the entire embedded Linux distribution that you are building. Current versions of OpenEmbedded have distribution configuration files for over 35 different named distributions. Angstrom and OpenMoko are two examples that have received a lot of attention from OpenEmbedded developers.

Attributes of the distribution that are defined in a distribution configuration file include toolchain type, C library type, and distribution version. You will often place a minimum specification for your base root file system within this configuration file. See the many examples in the OpenEmbedded metadata for more details.

The last category of configuration is `local.conf`. This is where you tune and customize a distribution to your liking. Your `local.conf` can be simple or complex, depending on your needs. At a minimum, your `local.conf` must define your machine type and distribution choice, which ties together the machine and distribution configurations for your custom embedded Linux distribution. OpenEmbedded metadata contains a sample `local.conf` with many comments that makes a good starting point. There are also specific examples of `local.conf` online. OpenEmbedded instructions can be found for the BeagleBoard on the BeagleBoard wiki at http://elinux.org/BeagleBoard#OpenEmbedded.

16.4.7   Building Images

The most powerful recipes in OpenEmbedded are image recipes. You can build an entire embedded Linux distribution using a properly constructed image recipe. The OpenEmbedded collection of metadata contains nearly one hundred image recipes. You can either use them as is or modify them to suit your particular requirements.

Some of the more common image recipes include `console-image` and `x11-image`. The former builds a basic bootable image that boots to a command prompt. The latter produces an image designed to drive a graphics display, including the required graphics libraries for X11 support.

---

[5] The term "machine" is used to refer to a specific hardware platform.

It is easy to build these images using BitBake:

```
$ bitbake console-image
```

This simple command builds a root file system that contains a collection of packages sufficient to boot your embedded device to a command prompt. There is nothing to prevent you from adding other outputs to your image recipe. For example, you could construct a recipe that will produce your root file system, kernel image, bootloader image, and any other files required for your target board.

We could devote an entire book to the subject of OpenEmbedded. Hopefully this short introduction will help you get started with this powerful build system. There is no substitute for diving in and getting your hands dirty with the technology.

16.5   Summary

Several open source build systems are available. We have provided introductory coverage of three of the most popular. OpenEmbedded is the latest build system to gain wide adoption and significant numbers of developers working on the project. Any one of these build systems can help you with the significant challenge of building a custom embedded Linux system for your product:

- Scratchbox is an environment that emulates the target architecture to ease the process of cross-compilation.
- Buildroot has enjoyed popularity in a number of projects and has a good following of developers and users in its development community.
- OpenEmbedded builds on the state of the art and represents the latest technology in embedded Linux build systems.

16.5.1   Suggestions for Additional Reading

Scratchbox website and documentation
www.scratchbox.org/

Buildroot home page
www.buildroot.org

OpenEmbedded home page
www.openembedded.org

Chapter 17

Linux and Real Time

In This Chapter

■ 17.1 What Is Real Time?   466

■ 17.2 Kernel Preemption   469

■ 17.3 Real-Time Kernel Patch   473

■ 17.4 Real-Time Kernel Performance Analysis   478

■ 17.5 Summary   485

When Linux began life on an Intel i386 processor, no one expected the success that Linux would enjoy in server applications. That success has led to Linux's being ported to many different architectures and being used by developers for embedded systems from cellular handsets to telecommunications switches. Not long ago, if your application had real-time requirements, you might not have included Linux among the choices for your operating system. That has all changed with the developments in real-time Linux driven, in large part, by audio and multimedia applications.

This chapter starts with a brief look at the historical development of real-time Linux features. Then we look at the facilities available to the real-time programmer and how these facilities are used.

17.1 What Is Real Time?

Ask five people what "real time" means, and chances are, you will get five different answers. Some might even cite numbers. For the purposes of this discussion, we will cover various scenarios and then propose a definition. Many requirements can be said to be *soft* real time, and others are called *hard* real time.

17.1.1 Soft Real Time

Most agree that soft real time means that the operation has a deadline. If the deadline is missed, the quality of the experience could be diminished but not fatal. Your desktop workstation is a perfect example of soft real-time requirements. When you are editing a document, you expect to see the results of your keystrokes on the screen immediately. When playing your favorite mp3 file, you expect to have high-quality audio without any clicks, pops, or gaps in the music.

In general terms, humans cannot see or hear delays of less than a few tens of milliseconds. Of course, musicians will tell you that music can be colored by delays smaller than that. If a deadline is missed by these so-called soft real-time events, the results may be undesirable, leading to a lower level of "quality" for the experience, but not catastrophic.

17.1.2 Hard Real Time

Hard real time is characterized by the results of a missed deadline. In a hard real-time system, if a deadline is missed, the results are often catastrophic. Of course, catastrophic is a relative term. If your embedded device is controlling the fuel flow to a jet aircraft engine, missing a deadline to respond to pilot input or a change in operational characteristics can lead to disastrous results.

Note that the deadline's duration has no bearing on the real-time characteristic. Servicing the tick on an atomic clock is such an example. As long as the tick is processed within the 1-second window before the next tick, the data remains valid. Missing the processing on a tick might throw off our global positioning systems by feet or even miles!

With this in mind, we draw on a commonly used set of definitions for soft and hard real time. With soft real-time systems, the value of a computation or result is diminished if a deadline is missed. With hard real-time systems, if a single deadline is missed, the system is considered to have failed by definition, and this may have catastrophic consequences.

17.1.3 Linux Scheduling

UNIX and Linux were both designed for fairness in their process scheduling. That is, the scheduler tries its best to allocate available resources across all processes that need the CPU and guarantee each process that it can make progress. This very design objective is counter to the requirement for a real-time process. A real-time process must be given absolute priority to run when it becomes ready to run. Real time means having predictable and repeatable latency.

17.1.4 Latency

Real-time processes are often associated with a physical event, such as an interrupt arriving from a peripheral device. Figure 17-1 illustrates the latency components in a Linux system. Latency measurement begins upon receipt of the interrupt we want to process. This is indicated by time t0 in Figure 17-1. Sometime later, the interrupt occurs, and control is passed to the interrupt service routine (ISR), as indicated by time t1. This interrupt latency is almost entirely dictated by the maximum interrupt off time[1]—the time spent in a thread of execution that has hardware interrupts disabled.

---

[1] We neglect the context switching time for interrupt processing because it is often negligible compared to interrupt off time.

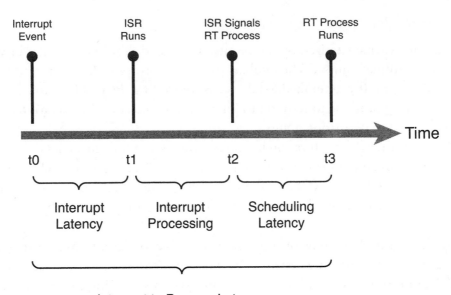

FIGURE 17-1   Latency components

It is considered good design practice to minimize the processing done in the actual ISR. Indeed, this execution context is limited in capability (for example, an ISR cannot call a blocking function, one that might sleep). Therefore, it is desirable to simply service the hardware device and leave the data processing to a Linux bottom half, also called softirqs. There are several types of bottom-half processing; they are best described in Robert Love's book *Linux Kernel Development*. See the section at the end of this chapter for the reference.

When the ISR/bottom half has finished its processing, the usual case is to wake up a user space process that is waiting for the data. This is indicated by time t2 in Figure 17-1. Some time later, the scheduler selects the real-time process to run, and the process is given the CPU. This is indicated by time t3 in Figure 17-1. Scheduling latency is affected primarily by the number of processes waiting for the CPU and the priorities among them. Setting the Real Time attribute on a process (SCHED_FIFO or SCHED_RR) gives it higher priority over normal Linux processes and allows it to be the next process selected to run, assuming that it is the highest-priority real-time process waiting for the CPU. The highest-priority real-time process that is ready to run (not blocked on I/O) will always run. You'll see how to set this attribute shortly.

17.2 Kernel Preemption

In the early Linux days of Linux 1.x, kernel preemption did not exist. This meant that when a user space process requested kernel services, no other task could be scheduled to run until that process blocked (went to sleep) waiting on something (usually I/O) or until the kernel request completed. Making the kernel preemptable[2] meant that while one process was running in the kernel, another process could preempt the first and be allowed to run even though the first process had not completed its in-kernel processing. Figure 17-2 illustrates this sequence of events.

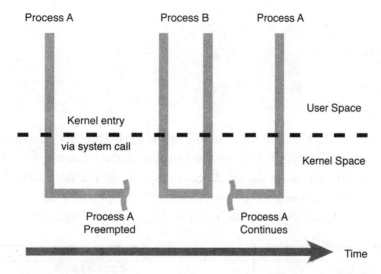

FIGURE 17-2   Kernel preemption

In this figure, Process A has entered the kernel via a system call. Perhaps it was a call to `write()` to a device such as the console or a file. While executing in the kernel on behalf of Process A, Process B with higher priority is woken up by an interrupt. The kernel preempts Process A and assigns the CPU to Process B, even though Process A had neither blocked nor completed its kernel processing.

17.2.1 Impediments to Preemption

The challenge in making the kernel fully preemptable is to identify all the places in the kernel that must be protected from preemption. These are the critical sections within

---

[2] Interestingly, there is much debate over the correct spelling of preemptable! I defer to the survey done by Rick Lehrbaum at www.linuxdevices.com/articles/AT5136316996.html.

the kernel where preemption cannot be allowed to occur. For example, assume that Process A in Figure 17-2 is executing in the kernel performing a file system operation. At some point, the code might need to write to an in-kernel data structure representing a file on the file system. To protect that data structure from corruption, the process must lock out all other processes from accessing the shared data structure. Listing 17-1 illustrates this concept using C syntax.

LISTING 17-1   Locking Critical Sections

```
...
  preempt_disable();
  ...
  /* Critical section */
  update_shared_data();
  ...
  preempt_enable();
...
```

If we did not protect shared data in this fashion, the process updating the shared data structure could be preempted in the middle of the update. If another process attempted to update the same shared data, corruption of the data would be virtually certain. The classic example is when two processes are operating directly on common variables and making decisions on their values. Figure 17-3 illustrates such a case.

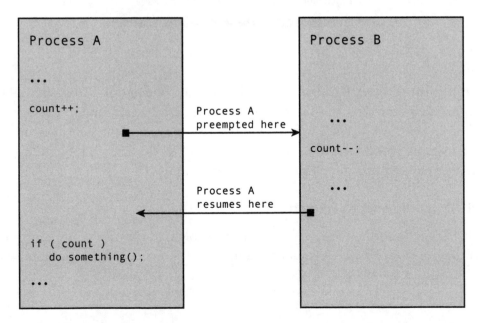

FIGURE 17-3   Shared data concurrency error

In Figure 17-3, Process A is interrupted after updating the shared data but before it makes a decision based on it. By design, Process A cannot detect that it has been preempted. Process B changes the value of the shared data before Process A gets to run again. As you can see, Process A will be making a decision based on a value determined by Process B. If this is not the behavior you seek, you must disable preemption in Process A around the shared data—in this case, the operation and decision on the variable count.

17.2.2 Preemption Models

The first solution to kernel preemption was to place checks at strategic locations within the kernel code where it was known to be safe to preempt the current thread of execution. These locations included entry and exit to system calls, release of certain kernel locks, and return from interrupt processing. At each of these points, code similar to Listing 17-2 was used to perform preemption.

LISTING 17-2   Check for Preemption a la the Linux 2.4+ Preempt Patch

```
...
  /*
   * This code is executed at strategic locations within
   * the Linux kernel where it is known to be safe to
   * preempt the current thread of execution
   */
  if (kernel_is_preemptable() && current->need_resched)
    preempt_schedule();
...

  /*
   * This code is in .../kernel/sched.c and is invoked from
   * those strategic locations as above
   */
  #ifdef CONFIG_PREEMPT
  asmlinkage void preempt_schedule(void)
  {
    while (current->need_resched) {
        ctx_sw_off();
        current->state |= TASK_PREEMPTED;
        schedule();
        current->state &= ~TASK_PREEMPTED;
        ctx_sw_on_no_preempt();
    }
  }
  #endif
...
```

The first snippet of code in Listing 17-2 (simplified from the actual code) is invoked at the strategic locations described earlier, where it is known that the kernel is safe to preempt. The second snippet of code in Listing 17-2 is the actual code from an early Linux 2.4 kernel with the preempt patch applied. This interesting `while` loop causes a context switch via the call to `schedule()` until all requests for preemption have been satisfied.

Although this approach led to reduced latencies in the Linux system, it was not ideal. The developers working on low latency soon realized the need to "flip the logic." With earlier preemption models, we had this:

- The Linux kernel was fundamentally nonpreemptable.
- Preemption checks were sprinkled around the kernel at strategic locations known to be safe for preemption.
- Preemption was enabled only at these known-safe points.

To achieve a further significant reduction in latency, we want the following in a preemptable kernel:

- The Linux kernel is fully preemptable everywhere.
- Preemption is disabled only around critical sections.

This is where the kernel developers have been heading since the original preemptable kernel patch series. However, this is no easy task. It involves poring over the entire kernel source code base, analyzing exactly what data must be protected from concurrency, and disabling preemption at only those locations. The method used for this has been to instrument the kernel for latency measurements, find the longest latency code paths, and fix them. The more recent Linux 2.6 kernels can be configured for very low-latency applications because of the effort that has gone into this "lock-breaking" methodology.

17.2.3   SMP Kernel

It is interesting to note that much of the work involved in creating an efficient multiprocessor architecture also benefits real time. Symmetric multiprocessing (SMP) is a multiprocessing architecture in which multiple CPUs, usually residing on one board, share the same memory and other resources. The SMP challenge is more complex than the uniprocessor challenge because there is an additional element of concurrency to protect against. In the uniprocessor model, only a single task can execute in the kernel at a time. Protection from concurrency involves only protection from interrupt or exception processing. In the SMP model, multiple threads of execution in the kernel are possible in addition to the threat from interrupt and exception processing.

SMP has been supported from as far back as early Linux 2.x kernels. A big kernel lock (BKL) was used to protect against concurrency in the transition from uniprocessor to SMP operation. The BKL is a global spinlock, which prevents any other tasks from executing in the kernel. In his excellent book *Linux Kernel Development*, Robert Love characterized the BKL as the "redheaded stepchild of the kernel." In describing the characteristics of the BKL, Robert jokingly added "evil" to its list of attributes!

Early implementations of the SMP kernel based on the BKL led to significant inefficiencies in scheduling. It was found that one of the CPUs could be kept idle for long periods of time. Much of the work that led to an efficient SMP kernel also directly benefited real-time applications—primarily lowered latency. Replacing the BKL with smaller-grained locking surrounding only the actual shared data to be protected led to significantly reduced preemption latency.

17.2.4 Sources of Preemption Latency

A real-time system must be able to service its real-time tasks within a specified upper boundary of time. Achieving consistently low preemption latency is critical to a real-time system. The two single largest contributors to preemption latency are interrupt-context processing and critical section processing where interrupts are disabled. You have already learned that a great deal of effort has been targeted at reducing the size (and thus the duration) of the critical sections. This leaves interrupt-context processing as the next challenge. This was answered with the Linux 2.6 real-time patch.

17.3 Real-Time Kernel Patch

Support for hard real time is still not in the mainline kernel.org source tree. To enable hard real time, a patch must be applied. The real-time kernel patch is the cumulative result of several initiatives to reduce Linux kernel latency. The patch had many contributors, and it is currently maintained by Ingo Molnar; you can find it at www.kernel.org/pub/linux/kernel/projects/rt/. The soft real-time performance of the 2.6 Linux kernel has improved significantly since the early 2.6 kernel releases. When 2.6 was first released, the 2.4 Linux kernel was substantially better in soft real-time performance. Since about Linux 2.6.12, soft real-time performance in the single-digit milliseconds on a reasonably fast x86 processor is readily achieved. Getting repeatable latencies in the microsecond range requires the real-time patch.

The real-time patch adds several important features to the Linux kernel. Figure 17-4 displays the configuration options for Preemption mode when the real-time patch has been applied.

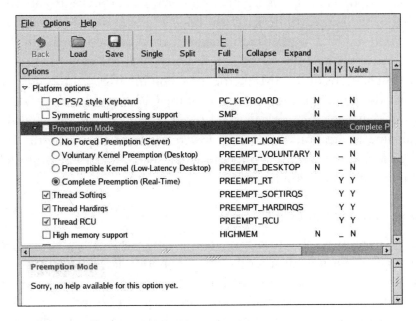

FIGURE 17-4   Preemption modes with real-time patch

The real-time patch adds a fourth preemption mode called PREEMPT_RT, or Preempt Real Time. The four preemption modes are as follows:

- PREEMPT_NONE—No forced preemption. Overall latency is good on average, but some occasional long delays can occur. Best suited for applications for which overall throughput is the top design criterion.

- PREEMPT_VOLUNTARY—First stage of latency reduction. Additional explicit preemption points are placed at strategic locations in the kernel to reduce latency. Some loss of overall throughput is traded for lower latency.

- PREEMPT_DESKTOP—This mode enables preemption everywhere in the kernel except when processing within critical sections. This mode is useful for soft real-time applications such as audio and multimedia. Overall throughput is traded for further reductions in latency.

- PREEMPT_RT—Features from the real-time patch are added, including replacing spinlocks with preemptable mutexes. This enables involuntary preemption everywhere within the kernel except for areas protected by `preempt_disable()`. This mode significantly smoothes out the variation in latency (jitter) and allows a low and predictable latency for time-critical real-time applications.

If kernel preemption is enabled in your kernel configuration, you can disable it at boot time by adding the following kernel parameter to the kernel command line:

```
preempt=0
```

17.3.1   Real-Time Features

Several new Linux kernel features are enabled with CONFIG_PREEMPT_RT. Figure 17-4 shows several new configuration settings. These and other features of the real-time Linux kernel patch are described here.

The real-time patch converts most spinlocks in the system to priority-inheritance mutexes. This reduces overall latency at the cost of additional overhead in spinlock (mutex) processing, resulting in reduced overall system throughput. The benefit of converting spinlocks to mutexes is that they can be preempted. If Process A is holding a lock, and Process B at a higher priority needs the same lock, Process A can preempt Process B in the case where it is holding a mutex.

With CONFIG_PREEMPT_HARDIRQS selected, interrupt service routines (ISRs) are forced to run in process context. This gives the developer control over the priority of ISRs, because they become schedulable entities. As such, they also become preemptable to allow higher-priority hardware interrupts to be handled first. Because they can be scheduled, you can assign them a priority in a similar fashion to other tasks based on your system's requirements.

This is a powerful feature. Some hardware architectures do not enforce interrupt priorities. Those that do might not enforce the priorities consistent with your specified real-time design goals. Using CONFIG_PREEMPT_HARDIRQS, you are free to define the priorities at which each IRQ will run.

CONFIG_PREEMPT_SOFTIRQS reduces latency by running softirqs within the context of the kernel's softirq daemon (ksoftirqd). ksoftirqd is a proper Linux task (process). As such, it can be prioritized and scheduled along with other tasks. If your kernel is configured for real time, and `CONFIG_PREEMPT_SOFTIRQS` is enabled, the ksoftirqd kernel task is elevated to real-time priority to handle the softirq processing.[3] Listing 17-3 shows the code responsible for this from a recent Linux kernel, found in ... `/kernel/softirq.c`.

LISTING 17-3   Promoting ksoftirqd to Real-Time Status

```
static int ksoftirqd(void * __data)
{
    /* Priority needs to be below hardirqs */
    struct sched_param param = { .sched_priority = MAX_USER_RT_PRIO/2 - 1};
    struct softirqdata *data = __data;
    u32 softirq_mask = (1 << data->nr);
    struct softirq_action *h;
    int cpu = data->cpu;

    sys_sched_setscheduler(current->pid, SCHED_FIFO, &param);
    current->flags |= PF_SOFTIRQ;
...
```

Here we see that the `ksoftirqd` kernel task is promoted to a real-time task (`SCHED_FIFO`) using the `sys_sched_setscheduler()` kernel function.

17.3.2   O(1) Scheduler

The O(1) scheduler has been around since the days of Linux 2.5. It is mentioned here because it is a critical component of a real-time solution. The O(1) scheduler is a significant improvement over the previous Linux scheduler. It scales better for systems with many processes and helps produce lower overall latency.

In case you are wondering, O(1) is a mathematical designation for a system of the first order. In this context, it means that the time it takes to make a scheduling decision is not dependent on the number of processes on a given runqueue. The old Linux scheduler did not have this characteristic, and its performance degraded with the number of processes.[4]

---

[3] See *Linux Kernel Development*, referenced at the end of this chapter, to learn more about softirqs.

[4] We refer you again to Robert Love's book for an excellent discussion of the O(1) scheduler and a delightful diatribe on algorithmic complexity, from which the notation O(1) is derived.

17.3.3   Creating a Real-Time Process

You can designate a process as real time by setting a process attribute that the scheduler uses as part of its scheduling algorithm. Listing 17-4 shows the general method.

LISTING 17-4   Creating a Real-Time Process

```
#include <sched.h>

#define MY_RT_PRIORITY MAX_USER_RT_PRIO /* Highest possible */

int main(int argc, char **argv)
{
      ...
      int rc, old_scheduler_policy;
      struct sched_param my_params;
      ...

      /* Passing zero specifies caller's (our) policy */
      old_scheduler_policy = sched_getscheduler(0);

      my_params.sched_priority = MY_RT_PRIORITY;
      /* Passing zero specifies callers (our) pid */
      rc = sched_setscheduler(0, SCHED_RR, &my_params);
      if ( rc == -1 )
            handle_error();
      ...
}
```

This code snippet does two things in the call to `sched_setscheduler()`. It changes the scheduling policy to SCHED_RR and raises its priority to the maximum possible on the system. Linux supports three scheduling policies:

- SCHED_OTHER—Normal Linux process, fairness scheduling.

- SCHED_RR—Real-time process with a time slice. In other words, if it does not block, it is allowed to run for a given period of time determined by the scheduler.

- SCHED_FIFO—Real-time process that runs until it either blocks or explicitly yields the processor, or until another higher-priority SCHED_FIFO process becomes runnable.

The man page for `sched_setscheduler()` provides more detail on the three different scheduling policies.

17.4   Real-Time Kernel Performance Analysis

The instrumentation for examining real-time kernel performance was once somewhat ad hoc. Those days are over. Ftrace has replaced the older tracing mechanisms that existed when the first edition of this book was published. Ftrace is a powerful set of tracing tools that can give the developer a detailed look at what is going on inside the kernel. Complete documentation on the Ftrace system can be found in the kernel source tree at `.../Documentation/trace/ftrace.txt`.

17.4.1   Using Ftrace for Tracing

Ftrace must be enabled in your kernel configuration before it can be used. Figure 17-5 shows the relevant kernel configuration parameters from a recent kernel release.

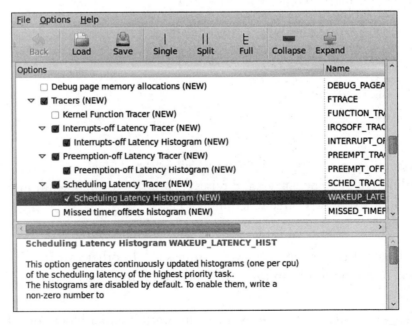

FIGURE 17-5   Kernel configuration for Ftrace

Ftrace has many available modules. It is prudent to select only those you might need for a particular test session, because each one adds some level of overhead to the kernel.

The general framework for enabling tracing is through its interface exported to the debugfs file system. Assuming that you have properly enabled Ftrace in your kernel configuration, you must then mount the debugfs. This is done as follows:

```
# mount -t debugfs debug /sys/kernel/debug
```

When this is complete, you should find a directory under /sys/kernel/debug called tracing. This tracing directory contains all the controls and output sources for Ftrace data. This will become more clear as we interact with this system in the following sections. As suggested in the kernel documentation, we will use a symlink called /tracing to simplify reporting and interacting with the Ftrace subsystems:

```
# ln -s /sys/kernel/debug/tracing /tracing
```

From here on, we will reference /tracing instead of the longer /sys/kernel/debug/ tracing.

17.4.2 Preemption Off Latency Measurement

The kernel uses calls to disable preemption during processing in critical shared data structures. When preemption is disabled, interrupts can still occur, but a higher-priority process cannot run. You can profile the preempt off times using the preemptoff functionality of Ftrace.

To enable measurement of preemption off latency, enable PREEMPT_TRACER and PREEMPT_OFF_HIST in the Kernel hacking submenu of your kernel configuration. This trace mode enables the detection of the longest latency paths with preemption disabled.

The general method for arming Ftrace for a preemptoff measurement is as follows:

```
# echo preemptoff >/tracing/current_tracer
# echo latency-format > /tracing/trace_options
# echo 0 >/tracing/tracing_max_latency
# echo 1 > /tracing/tracing_enabled
 <do some processing>
# echo 0 > /tracing/tracing_enable
```

Listing 17-5 shows the trace output resulting from this sequence of commands. Notice that the maximum latency of 221 microseconds is displayed in the header.

LISTING 17-5   Preemptoff Trace

```
# cat /tracing/trace
# tracer: preemptoff
#
# preemptoff latency trace v1.1.5 on 2.6.33.4-rt20
# --------------------------------------------------------------------
# latency: 221 us, #239/239, CPU#0 | (M:preempt VP:0, KP:0, SP:0 HP:0 #P:8)
#    -----------------
#    | task: -0 (uid:0 nice:0 policy:0 rt_prio:0)
#    -----------------
#  => started at: acpi_idle_enter_bm
#  => ended at:   rest_init
#
#
#                    _------=> CPU#
#                   / _-----=> irqs-off
#                  | / _----=> need-resched
#                  || / _---=> hardirq/softirq
#                  ||| / _--=> preempt-depth
#                  |||| /_--=> lock-depth
#                  |||||/      delay
#  cmd     pid    |||||| time  |  caller
#     \    /      ||||||   \   |  /
  <idle>-0       0d..1.   0us : acpi_idle_do_entry <-acpi_idle_enter_bm
  <idle>-0       0d..1.   1us : ktime_get_real <-acpi_idle_enter_bm
  <idle>-0       0d..1.   1us : getnstimeofday <-ktime_get_real
  <idle>-0       0d..1.   1us : ns_to_timeval <-acpi_idle_enter_bm
  <idle>-0       0d..1.   1us : ns_to_timespec <-ns_to_timeval
<... many lines omitted for brievity...>
  <idle>-0       0d..3.   220us : native_apic_mem_write <-lapic_next_event
  <idle>-0       0d..3.   220us : _raw_spin_unlock_irqrestore
<-tick_broadcast_oneshot_control
  <idle>-0       0d..2.   220us : _raw_spin_unlock_irqrestore <-clockevents_notify
  <idle>-0       0d..1.   220us : enter_idle <-cpu_idle
  <idle>-0       0d..1.   221us : __rcu_read_lock <-__atomic_notifier_call_chain
  <idle>-0       0d..1.   221us : __rcu_read_unlock
<-__atomic_notifier_call_chain
  <idle>-0       0d..1.   221us : cpu_idle <-rest_init
  <idle>-0       0d..1.   221us : stop_critical_timings <-rest_init

# cat /tracing/tracing_max_latency
221
```

Notice the last two lines of Listing 17-5. Here we have displayed the maximum latency value captured by Ftrace by displaying the contents of `tracing_max_latency`. This value will always be updated with the maximum latency recorded and the output of the trace file (the entire contents of Listing 17-5) that corresponds to the path through the system associated with this longest latency.

17.4.3   Wakeup Latency Measurement

One of the most critical measurements of interest to real-time developers is how long it takes to get the high-priority task running after it has been signaled to do so. When a real-time process (one with the `SCHED_FIFO` or `SCHED_RR` scheduling attribute) is running in your system, it is by definition sharing the processor with other tasks. When an event needs servicing, the real-time task is woken up. In other words, the scheduler is informed that it needs to run. Wakeup timing is the time from the wakeup event until the task actually gets the CPU and begins to run.

Ftrace has a wakeup and wakeup_rt trace facility. This facility records and traces the longest latency from wakeup to running while the tracer is enabled.

Listing 17-6 was generated from a simple C test program that creates and writes to a file. Prior to the file I/O, the test program elevates itself to `SCHED_RR` with priority 99 and sets up the tracing system using writes to stdio, similar to issuing the following commands from the shell:

```
# echo 0 > /tracing/tracing_enabled
# echo 0 > /tracing/tracing_max_latency (resets the max record back to zero)
# echo wakeup > /tracing/current_tracer
# echo 1 > /tracing/tracing_enabled
```

After our test program issues these commands, tracing has completed. Listing 17-6 shows the results. Notice in this case that the maximum wakeup latency is reported as 7 microseconds.

LISTING 17-6   Wakeup Timing Trace

```
root@speedy:~# cat /tracing/trace
# tracer: wakeup
#
# wakeup latency trace v1.1.5 on 2.6.33.4-rt20
# --------------------------------------------------------------------
# latency: 7 us, #35/35, CPU#4 | (M:preempt VP:0, KP:0, SP:0 HP:0 #P:8)
#    -----------------
#    | task: -6006 (uid:0 nice:0 policy:2 rt_prio:99)
#    -----------------
#
#                  _------=> CPU#
#                 / _-----=> irqs-off
#                | / _----=> need-resched
#                || / _---=> hardirq/softirq
#                ||| / _--=> preempt-depth
#                |||| /_--=> lock-depth
#                |||||/     delay
#  cmd     pid   |||||| time  |  caller
#    \    /      ||||||  \    |  /
    sshd-1789    4d.h3.  0us :   1789:120:R   + [004]  6006:  0:S rt
    sshd-1789    4d.h3.  1us : wake_up_process <-hrtimer_wakeup
    sshd-1789    4d.h2.  1us : check_preempt_wakeup <-try_to_wake_up
    sshd-1789    4d.h2.  1us : resched_task <-check_preempt_wakeup
    sshd-1789    4dNh2.  2us : task_woken_rt <-try_to_wake_up .
    sshd-1789    4dNh2.  2us : _raw_spin_unlock_irqrestore <-try_to_wake_up
    sshd-1789    4dNh1.  2us : preempt_schedule <-_raw_spin_unlock_irqrestore
    sshd-1789    4dNh..  2us : preempt_schedule <-try_to_wake_up
    sshd-1789    4dNh..  2us : _raw_spin_lock <-__run_hrtimer
    sshd-1789    4dNh1.  3us : _raw_spin_unlock <-hrtimer_interrupt
    sshd-1789    4dNh..  3us : preempt_schedule <-_raw_spin_unlock
    sshd-1789    4dNh..  3us : tick_program_event <-hrtimer_interrupt
    sshd-1789    4dNh..  3us : tick_dev_program_event <-tick_program_event
    sshd-1789    4dNh..  4us : ktime_get <-tick_dev_program_event
    sshd-1789    4dNh..  4us : clockevents_program_event
<-tick_dev_program_event
    sshd-1789    4dNh..  4us : lapic_next_event <-clockevents_program_event
    sshd-1789    4dNh..  4us : native_apic_mem_write <-lapic_next_event
    sshd-1789    4dNh..  4us : irq_exit <-smp_apic_timer_interrupt
    sshd-1789    4dN.1.  4us : rcu_irq_exit <-irq_exit
    sshd-1789    4dN.1.  5us : idle_cpu <-irq_exit
    sshd-1789    4dN...  5us : preempt_schedule_irq <-retint_kernel
    sshd-1789    4dN...  5us : __schedule <-preempt_schedule_irq
```

LISTING 17-6   Continued

```
sshd-1789    4dN...    5us : rcu_sched_qs <-__schedule
sshd-1789    4dN.1.    6us : _raw_spin_lock_irq <-__schedule
sshd-1789    4d..2.    6us : put_prev_task_fair <-__schedule
sshd-1789    4d..2.    6us : update_curr <-put_prev_task_fair
sshd-1789    4d..2.    6us : task_of <-update_curr
sshd-1789    4d..2.    6us : cpuacct_charge <-update_curr
sshd-1789    4d..2.    6us : __rcu_read_lock <-cpuacct_charge
sshd-1789    4d..2.    7us : __rcu_read_unlock <-cpuacct_charge
sshd-1789    4d..2.    7us : __enqueue_entity <-put_prev_task_fair
sshd-1789    4d..2.    7us : pick_next_task_rt <-__schedule
sshd-1789    4d..2.    7us : dequeue_pushable_task <-pick_next_task_rt
sshd-1789    4d..3.    8us : __schedule <-preempt_schedule_irq
sshd-1789    4d..3.    8us :   1789:120:R ==> [004]  6006:  0:R rt
```

When the test program runs, it performs the file I/O and then sleeps. This guarantees that it will yield the processor even if it did not block on I/O. The trace shown in Listing 17-6 is quite interesting. From the header, you see that the test program ran as PID 6006 with priority 99. You also see that the maximum latency reported was 7 microseconds—certainly a very acceptable value.

The first line of the trace output is the wakeup event. A process with PID 1789 was running (ssh daemon) at the time. The last trace is the actual context switch from sshd to the test program running as PID 6006 with RT priority. The lines between the wakeup and context switch are the kernel path taken, along with the relative times.

Refer to the a.../Documentation subdirectory of the Linux kernel source tree for trace/ftrace.txt for additional details.

The maximum latency is provided separately in another trace file. To display the maximum wakeup latency during a particular tracing run, simply issue this command:

```
root@speedy:~# cat /tracing/tracing_max_latency
7
```

17.4.4   Interrupt Off Timing

To enable measurement of maximum interrupt off timing, make sure your kernel has IRQSOFF_TRACER enabled in your kernel configuration. This option measures time spent in critical sections with IRQs disabled. This feature works the same as wakeup latency timing. To enable the measurement, do the following as root:

```
# echo irqsoff >/tracing/current_tracer
# echo latency-format > /tracing/trace_options
# echo 0 > /tracing/tracing_max_latency
# echo 1 > /tracing/tracing_enabled
< ... some processing ...>
# echo 0 > /tracing/tracing_enabled
```

To read the current maximum, simply display the contents of /tracing/tracing_max_latency:

```
# cat /tracing/tracing_max_latency
97
```

You will notice that the latency measurements for both wakeup latency and interrupt off latency are enabled and displayed using the same file. This means, of course, that only one measurement can be configured at a time, or the results might be invalid. Because these measurements add significant runtime overhead, it would be unwise to enable them all at once anyway.

17.4.5   Soft Lockup Detection

To enable soft lockup detection, enable DETECT_SOFTLOCKUP in the kernel configuration. This feature enables the detection of long periods of running in kernel mode without a context switch. This feature exists in non-real-time kernels but is useful for detecting very-high-latency paths or soft deadlock conditions. To use soft lockup detection, simply enable the feature and watch for any reports on the console or system log. Reports similar to this will be emitted:

```
BUG: soft lockup detected on CPU0
```

When the kernel emits this message, it is usually accompanied by a backtrace and other information such as the process name and PID. It will look similar to a kernel oops message, complete with processor registers. See .../kernel/softlockup.c for details. This information can be used to help track down the source of the lockup condition.

17.5   Summary

Linux is increasingly being used in systems where real-time performance is required. Examples include multimedia applications and robot, industrial, and automotive controllers. This chapter presented fundamental concepts and analysis techniques to help you develop and debug real-time applications.

- Real-time systems are characterized by deadlines. When a missed deadline results in inconvenience or a diminished customer experience, this is called soft real time. In contrast, hard real-time systems are considered failed when a deadline is missed.

- Kernel preemption was the first significant feature in the Linux kernel that addressed system-wide latency.

- Recent Linux kernels support several preemption modes, ranging from no preemption to full real-time preemption.

- The real-time patch adds several key features to the Linux kernel, resulting in reliable low latencies.

- The real-time patch includes several important measurement tools to aid in debugging and characterizing a real-time Linux implementation.

17.5.1   Suggestion for Additional Reading

Linux Kernel Development, 3rd Edition
Robert Love
Addison-Wesley, 2010

Chapter 18

Universal Serial Bus

In This Chapter

- 18.1 USB Overview   488
- 18.2 Configuring USB   495
- 18.3 sysfs and USB Device Naming   500
- 18.4 Useful USB Tools   502
- 18.5 Common USB Subsystems   508
- 18.6 USB Debug   516
- 18.7 Summary   519

By anyone's measure, Universal Serial Bus (USB) has been wildly successful. USB was originally designed to overcome the shortcomings of the various I/O interfaces found on the PC architecture. Today it is difficult to find an electronic device at your local electronics superstore that does not have a USB port. Digital cameras, printers, cell phones, IP telephones, and, of course, keyboards and mice are typical examples of devices that have USB interfaces. However, the list is much longer than the average reader would guess. Even some of my guitar pedals have USB interfaces!

Gone are the days when you needed special-purpose input/output hardware for common devices. The promise of USB has actually been realized, unlike a host of other technologies that have come and gone. Indeed, as this second edition was being prepared, the first experimental Linux drivers for USB 3.0 had just been released. And it is notable that Linux was the first OS to have such support!

18.1   USB Overview

USB can seem complex at first. It has a plethora of devices and a fairly large variety of embedded host controllers. It has several modes of operation, and a given controller on a processor (or external to it) may have multiple modes of operation. If you've looked at the full list of USB configuration options in a recent Linux kernel, you quickly realize that it can be confusing to configure. We can eliminate some of that confusion by understanding some basic USB concepts.

18.1.1   USB Physical Topology

USB is a master/slave bus topology. Each USB bus can have only one master, which is called a *host controller*. Figure 18-1 illustrates the basic topology.

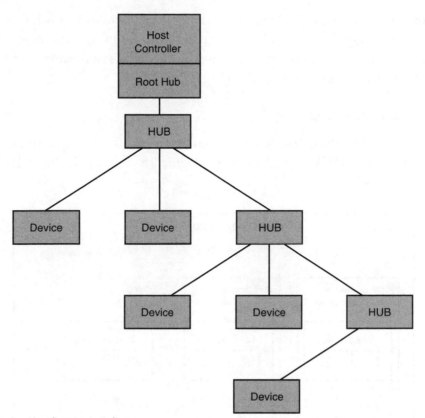

FIGURE 18-1   Simple USB topology

The host controller is always associated with a *root hub*. The root hub provides an attachment point to the host controller and provides the hub functions at the top of the USB hierarchy. The most common arrangement is that a host controller and root hub combination are brought out directly to a connector (through a transceiver chip) on the edge of the board. It is this connector that end users see.

The devices shown in Figure 18-1 are *endpoints*—physical USB appliances that plug into a USB hub. A device may support several *functions*, such as an audio interface that provides input and output functionality. The important concept here is that every USB device plugs into one and only one hub upstream of its location in the topology.

Devices on the USB bus are operated in a polled manner, controlled by the host controller. Only one device at a time can communicate on the bus, as directed by the host controller. Mechanisms exist in the specification to allocate a specified portion of bandwidth to a given function within a device.

One of USB's most successful features is that it is dynamic and truly hot-swappable. Devices can be plugged into the USB bus at any time. Software running on the computer (Linux, of course) that contains the host controller is responsible for configuring the USB devices when they appear in the topology.

18.1.2   USB Logical Topology

To better understand the software components and data flow in a USB system, it is useful to understand USB's logical topology. Figure 18-2 shows the logical makeup of a hypothetical USB device.

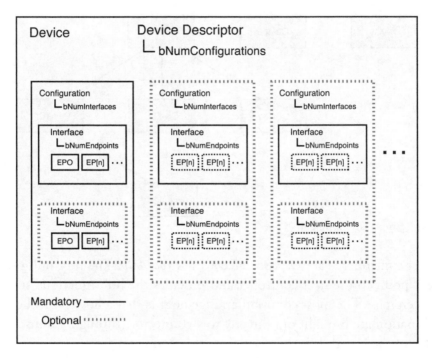

FIGURE 18-2   USB device functional block diagram

Each USB device has a number of descriptors[1] that allow software to discover capabilities and configure functionality. Every device must have a single device descriptor, which contains information such as manufacturer (idVendor), product (idProduct), serial

---

[1] These descriptors are described in Chapter 9, "File Systems," of the USB 2.0 specification, referenced at the end of this chapter.

number (iSerialNumber), and the number of configurations (bNumConfigurations). The identifiers in parentheses are the actual field names referenced in the USB 2.0 specification.

Every configuration identified in the device descriptor has a configuration descriptor. The configuration descriptor contains the number of interfaces (bNumInterfaces) available for each configuration and also indicates the maximum power required when operated in this configuration (bMaxPower). Most often, a USB device contains only a single configuration. However, some devices may have high and low power modes, or even different functions available in a single device. These types of devices may contain multiple configurations. Plug your iPod into a USB host, and you will see an example of multiple configurations, interfaces, and endpoints!

Each interface described by a configuration descriptor has an interface descriptor. The interface descriptor contains a field specifying how many endpoints a device has (bNumEndpoints). Endpoint 0 is always assumed to exist and is not included in the interface count. The interface descriptor also includes information describing the interface class, subclass, and protocol as defined by the USB specifications.

The USB endpoint is the actual logical element that software communicates with during operation of the USB device. Each endpoint described by an interface descriptor (excluding endpoint 0) contains an endpoint descriptor. The endpoint descriptor defines the endpoint's communication parameters, including the endpoint address and various endpoint attributes describing the characteristics of the data transfer from each endpoint.

Later in this chapter, we introduce the utility lsusb, which allows you to read these descriptors.

More details can be found in the complete Universal Serial Bus specification referenced at the end of this chapter.

18.1.3 USB Revisions

USB 1.0 was introduced well over a decade ago. The current USB 2.0 specification document shows a revision history as early as November 1994, and that was already revision 0.7. The original specification called for a data transfer rate of 12 megabits per second (Mbps), with a low-speed rate defined as 1.5 Mbps. The 2.0 revision of the USB spec was finalized in April 2000.[2] USB 2.0 defined a high-speed data transfer rate of 480 Mbps. There is now a 3.0 revision of the USB specification, specifying

---

[2] According to the revision history in the current USB 2.0 specification.

data transfer rates into gigabits per second and adding yet another speed definition: SuperSpeed.

It can be difficult to remember the difference between full speed and high speed. Here is a summary:

USB 1.0 Low speed   1.5 Mbps

USB 1.0 Full speed   12 Mbps

USB 2.0 High speed   480 Mbps

USB 3.0 Super speed   5 Gbps

18.1.4   USB Connectors

Unless you are a USB expert, the variety of USB connector and cable configurations can be confusing. The most familiar connector type, defined by the original specification, is the USB A connector. This is the familiar rectangular connector most commonly found on laptop and desktop PCs. The plug end of the USB A connector, by definition, always points upstream, toward the host controller/root hub. Figure 18-3 shows a standard USB A plug.

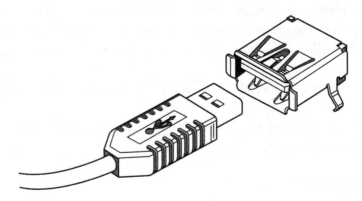

FIGURE 18-3   USB A plug

A peripheral (slave) device such as a printer or scanner often has the USB B receptacle and accepts a USB B plug, also defined by the original USB specification. A common cable suitable for connection between a host (such as a PC) and a peripheral (such as a printer) has an A plug on one end and a B plug on the other. It is more narrow than the A plug and has more of a D shape than rectangular. The USB B connector by definition always points downstream, or away from the host controller/root hub. Figure 18-4 shows a USB B plug.

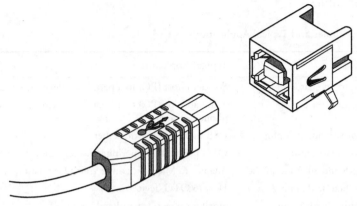

FIGURE 18-4   USB B plug

There are also a couple of miniature plug configurations. Smaller form factor devices such as cell phones and PDAs drove the requirement for even smaller plugs and receptacles. The USB Mini-A connector has been made obsolete by the specifications, although it is still in use. The Mini-B connector is widely used on small peripheral devices.

The Micro-USB specification defines three additional connectors—a Micro-B plug and receptacle, a Micro-AB receptacle, and a Micro-A plug. The Micro-AB receptacle is for use only on USB On-The-Go (OTG) appliances, discussed later.

To summarize the standard A and B connectors, the A receptacle is always on the host side (the A plug always points upstream), and the B connector is always on the peripheral side (the B plug always points downstream.) Table 18-1 summarizes these characteristics.

TABLE 18-1   USB Connector Summary

Connector	Plug	Receptacle
A series	Points toward the host (or hub)	Functions as host (or hub) output
B series	Points toward the peripheral	Functions as peripheral (or hub) input

18.1.5   USB Cable Assemblies

The latest USB specifications define the cable assemblies listed in Table 18-2 as the only compliant cables.

TABLE 18-2   USB Cables and Typical Applications

Cable Type	Typical Application
Standard-A plug to Standard-B plug	Standard host (PC) to a peripheral device such as a printer
Standard-A plug to Mini-B plug	Standard host (PC) to a small form factor peripheral such as a cell phone or camera
Captive cable with Standard-A plug	USB mouse, keyboard tether
Micro-A plug to Micro-B plug	OTG peripheral to peripheral, such as a camera to a printer
Micro-A plug to Standard-A receptacle	Adapter to Micro-A, connecting a keyboard to a PDA, for example
Micro-B plug to Standard-A plug	Host to OTG device
Captive cable with Micro-A plug	Small form factor peripheral tether

It is possible to purchase other types of cable assemblies that are not listed here. These are typically available to resolve special cases, such as obsolete (or misdesigned) hardware. For example, the BeagleBoard requires a special adapter with a Mini-A plug on one end and a USB-A receptacle on the other. The Mini-A plug has pins 4 and 5 shorted, which appears to be required by the transceiver on the BeagleBoard for it to be configured for host mode operation.

18.1.6   USB Modes

One of the more confusing aspects of USB to the uninitiated is the various modes of operation. We hear terms such as USB On-The-Go (OTG), gadget, and peripheral. Hopefully we have taken the confusion out of the different speed ratings and connector types. This section briefly covers the various modes of USB controllers and devices.

The USB controller and receptacle on a standard desktop PC is called a USB host. Because USB is a master-slave bus, by definition one node on a USB bus must provide the master functionality. This is the host. You will hear it referred to as host mode or simply the USB host. The host controller, in association with the root hub, is the low-level piece of hardware that operates the USB master/slave bus protocol. The USB host is always the bus master.

The other end of a simple USB network is the device end. Sometimes this is called a USB gadget.[3] Gadget functionality within the Linux kernel simply refers to the ability to operate as a device in slave mode. Once you enter the embedded world, you no longer assume that the processing device acts as a host. For example, you might have a Linux-powered smart phone with a USB connector and a USB controller designed to operate a device, or the slave end of a USB link.

Many embedded systems need to operate in both master (host) and slave (device) modes from the same controller. A personal digital assistant (PDA) is a good example of this requirement. Your PDA might have a requirement to connect to a USB host, such as your desktop PC in order to synchronize its data to a master database located on your PC, or to get a software update. On the other hand, you might want to connect a USB keyboard to your PDA to facilitate typing. These USB devices must be able to operate in both host and device modes. This is called USB On-The-Go (OTG). As an added benefit, the USB OTG specification allows switching roles on-the-fly, without having to pull out a plug and reconnect it in the opposite mode.

18.2   Configuring USB

Like most functionality not directly related to the core Linux kernel operations, USB functionality is optional and must be enabled in your kernel configuration. As with most other auxiliary functionality, USB can be compiled into the kernel image or can be configured as loadable modules for dynamically loading into a booted kernel. For purposes of this text, we will use loadable modules, because this helps bring visibility to which components are required for specific functionality.

One of the barriers to properly configuring USB is simply the volume of options in a typical kernel config for USB. On a very recent kernel, configured as allmodconfig,[4] almost 300 different device driver modules (*.ko files) were related to USB. Of course, many of those drivers are for particular USB devices, but looking through the configuration options for USB, it is clear that a little know-how will go a long way!

In the following examples, we'll look at the Freescale Semiconductor i.MX31 Applications Processor on the i.MX31 PDK development platform. It makes for an interesting example, because it contains three host controllers that can be configured in a variety of operational modes.

---

[3] The Linux USB developers coined the term "gadget" to avoid confusion with the overused term "device," as in device drivers.

[4] The Linux kernel make target, mostly for build testing, that builds a configuration with all modules where possible.

Figure 18-5 shows a portion of the USB configuration options from a recent Linux kernel configured for the ARM architecture and the Freescale Semiconductor i.MX31 PDK reference board.

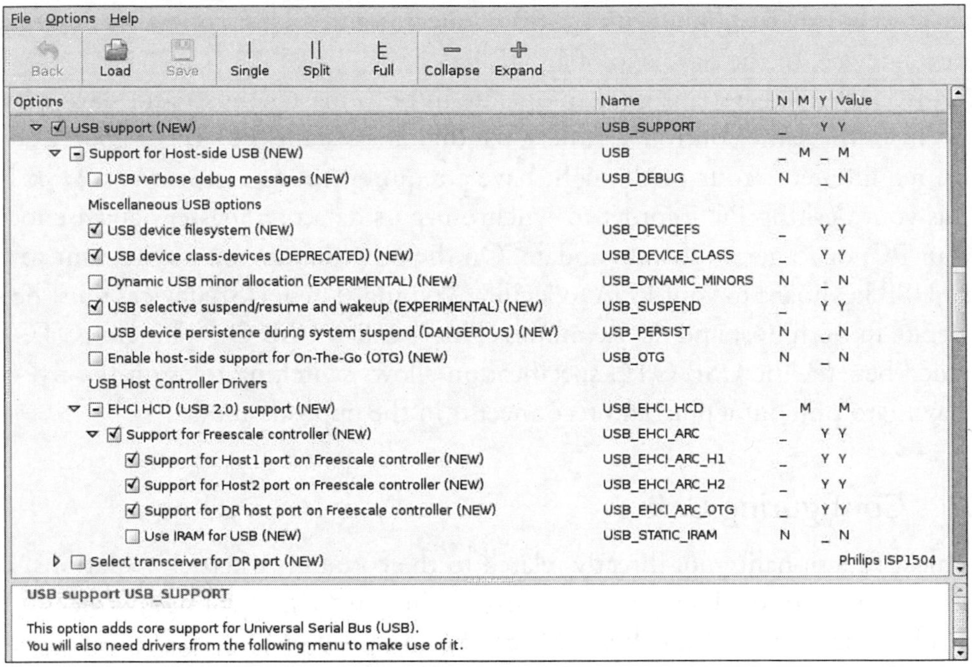

FIGURE 18-5   Part of the USB configuration for i.MX31

There are many more options than can be shown here. These are just the initial ones. You must first select USB_SUPPORT to see any further USB configuration options. Notice that USB is selected as M (module), meaning that the kernel build system will compile the USB drivers as loadable modules.

Let's look at the minimal configuration to get USB operational on the i.MX31. For all USB configurations, the module called usbcore.ko is required. It is selected automatically whenever CONFIG_USB is selected.[5] You can see this easily by looking at the makefile for the core part of the USB driver support, shown in Listing 18-1. This makefile is found at .../drivers/usb/core/Makefile.[6]

---

[5] You may recall from earlier chapters that actual configuration variables always start with CONFIG_, but this is omitted from the GUIs that we use to configure the kernel. For example, USB_SUPPORT in Figure 18-3 actually translates to CONFIG_ USB_SUPPORT in the kernel's configuration file, .config.

[6] Remember that this notation describes the location of the file from your top-level kernel directory.

LISTING 18-1   Makefile for the USB Core

```
#
# Makefile for USB Core files and filesystem
#

usbcore-objs     := usb.o hub.o hcd.o urb.o message.o driver.o \
                    config.o file.o buffer.o sysfs.o endpoint.o \
                    devio.o notify.o generic.o quirks.o

ifeq ($(CONFIG_PCI),y)
        usbcore-objs     += hcd-pci.o
endif

ifeq ($(CONFIG_USB_DEVICEFS),y)
        usbcore-objs     += inode.o devices.o
endif

obj-$(CONFIG_USB)        += usbcore.o

ifeq ($(CONFIG_USB_DEBUG),y)
EXTRA_CFLAGS += -DDEBUG
endif
```

Looking at the various makefiles that drive the kernel's build system is always a great way to figure out what components are required, or the reverse—what configuration options are required for a specific function. For example, in Listing 18-1, you can see that we need to enable CONFIG_USB to get usbcore included in the build. As we learned in Chapter 4, "The Linux Kernel: A Different Perspective," if CONFIG_USB is set to m, this device driver is compiled as a loadable kernel module and provides USB host support.

18.2.1   USB Initialization

Booting the i.MX31 into a minimal configuration, we can load the usbcore module as follows:

```
# modprobe usbcore
```

This loads the USB core module, which handles common functions for the rest of the USB collection of drivers. These functions include housekeeping such as register and deregister functions for various elements and provide an interface to drive USB hardware. This takes much of the complexity out of writing drivers for USB hardware. You can see the public symbols by using your cross-nm utility. You learned about nm in Chapter 13, "Development Tools." Here is an example of using your cross-nm to display USB registration functions:

```
$ arm_v6_vfp_le-nm usbcore.ko  | grep T.*_register
0000adc0 T usb_register_dev
000094b0 T usb_register_device_driver
00009560 T usb_register_driver
0000fcf8 T usb_register_notify
```

usbcore also contains functions for buffer handling; support for usbfs, the hub class driver; and many other functions dealing with communication with the underlying USB controller.

usbcore is not very useful by itself. It does not contain any low-level host controller drivers. These are separate modules, and they can differ depending on the hardware you are using. For example, the BeagleBoard, which contains the TI OMAP3530 Applications Processor, has a built-in dual-role[7] controller. This controller is the Inventra™ USB Hi-Speed Dual-Role Controller. The driver for this host controller is called musb_hdrc.

On many platforms, the USB host controller is designed to conform to the Enhanced Host Controller Interface (EHCI),[8] which describes the register-level interface for an industry-standard USB host controller. In this case, the driver, when compiled as a loadable module, is called ehci-hcd.ko. Let's see what happens when we load that driver on the Freescale i.MX31, as shown in Listing 18-2.

LISTING 18-2   Installing the USB Host Controller Driver on i.MX31

```
root@imx31:~# modprobe ehci-hcd
usbcore: registered new interface driver usbfs
usbcore: registered new interface driver hub
usbcore: registered new device driver usb
fsl-ehci fsl-ehci.0: Freescale On-Chip EHCI Host Controller
fsl-ehci fsl-ehci.0: new USB bus registered, assigned bus number 1
fsl-ehci fsl-ehci.0: irq 35, io mem 0x43f88200
```

---

[7] Dual-role controllers can act as USB hosts or USB peripherals and can switch between the two functions while in operation. As you will quickly learn, this is referred to as USB On-The-Go (OTG).

[8] A reference to this EHCI specification appears at the end of this chapter.

LISTING 18-2   Continued

```
fsl-ehci fsl-ehci.0: USB 2.0 started, EHCI 1.00, driver 10 Dec 2004
usb usb1: configuration #1 chosen from 1 choice
hub 1-0:1.0: USB hub found
hub 1-0:1.0: 1 port detected
fsl-ehci fsl-ehci.1: Freescale On-Chip EHCI Host Controller
fsl-ehci fsl-ehci.1: new USB bus registered, assigned bus number 2
fsl-ehci fsl-ehci.1: irq 36, io mem 0x43f88400
fsl-ehci fsl-ehci.1: USB 2.0 started, EHCI 1.00, driver 10 Dec 2004
usb usb2: configuration #1 chosen from 1 choice
hub 2-0:1.0: USB hub found
hub 2-0:1.0: 1 port detected
fsl-ehci fsl-ehci.2: Freescale On-Chip EHCI Host Controller
fsl-ehci fsl-ehci.2: new USB bus registered, assigned bus number 3
fsl-ehci fsl-ehci.2: irq 37, io mem 0x43f88000
fsl-ehci fsl-ehci.2: USB 2.0 started, EHCI 1.00, driver 10 Dec 2004
usb usb3: configuration #1 chosen from 1 choice
hub 3-0:1.0: USB hub found
hub 3-0:1.0: 1 port detected
```

There is much useful information here. Note that we had the console log level set so that these messages appear on the console. First we see usbcore registration functions in action. We see registration messages for the usbfs interface driver, the hub interface driver, and the EHCI (usb host mode) driver itself. You will learn about usbfs shortly.

Next we see the three host controllers being initialized. Recall that the Freescale i.MX31 Application Processor contains three separate USB controllers. We see these controllers being enumerated as fsl-ehci.0, fsl-ehci.1, and fsl-ehci.2. You can see the interrupt (IRQ) assignment and the base address of the register file that is associated with each USB controller. Notice that in each case the root hub is enumerated. The root hub is a fundamental component of the USB architecture and always is associated with the host controller. It is required in order to connect peripheral devices (hubs or other USB devices) to the host controller.

It is worth noting that we did not need to separately install usbcore, as we did at the start of this section. modprobe understands how to determine required dependencies for a given module. Simply issue the following command:

```
# modprobe ehci-hcd
```

This loads its dependency, usbcore, before loading the ehci-hcd driver. This mechanism is explained in Chapter 8, "Device Driver Basics." In fact, on many platforms that use the udev system, these steps are automated by udev. This is covered in Chapter 19.

18.3   sysfs and USB Device Naming

As described in Chapter 9, "File Systems," the sysfs file system is basically a view of kernel objects, or *kobjects*. Each USB device is represented in sysfs. Look at /sys/bus/usb/devices on any USB-enabled system. Listing 18-3 shows how it looks on my Freescale i.MX31 PDK board. Note that I have truncated the ls -l format to fit the page width by removing all the columns except the filename.

LISTING 18-3   Output of /sys/bus/usb/devices on i.MX31

```
root@imx31:~# ls -l /sys/bus/usb/devices/
total 0
1-0:1.0 -> ../../../devices/platform/fsl-ehci.0/usb1/1-0:1.0
2-0:1.0 -> ../../../devices/platform/fsl-ehci.1/usb2/2-0:1.0
2-1 -> ../../../devices/platform/fsl-ehci.1/usb2/2-1
2-1.1 -> ../../../devices/platform/fsl-ehci.1/usb2/2-1/2-1.1
2-1.1:1.0 -> ../../../devices/platform/fsl-ehci.1/usb2/2-1/2-1.1/2-1.1:1.0
2-1:1.0 -> ../../../devices/platform/fsl-ehci.1/usb2/2-1/2-1:1.0
3-0:1.0 -> ../../../devices/platform/fsl-ehci.2/usb3/3-0:1.0
usb1 -> ../../../devices/platform/fsl-ehci.0/usb1
usb2 -> ../../../devices/platform/fsl-ehci.1/usb2
usb3 -> ../../../devices/platform/fsl-ehci.2/usb3
```

All the entries in /sys/bus/usb/devices are links to other portions of the sysfs hierarchy. Notice the numeric names, such as 1-0:1.0. In this naming scheme, the first numeral is the root hub, or the top level of the USB hierarchy for this particular bus. The second number is the port number that a given device is connected to. The third number (the one after the colon) is the configuration number of the USB device, followed by the device's interface number. The configuration and interface elements are logical components of all USB devices, as described in Section 18.1.2.

To summarize:

```
1-0:1.0
| | | |----- interface number
| | |------- configuration number
| |--------- hub port
|----------- root_hub
```

If additional hubs are added to the topology, they are added to the device name by adding a dot (.) followed by the hub port number, chained to the upstream port. For example, if we add a hub to the topology just shown, we might end up with `1-0.2:1.0`. This assumes we have a downstream hub with at least two ports, with the device plugged into port number 2.

If you examine the content of each directory linked, you can determine what component is being referenced. For example, the first entry in Listing 18-3 represents a logical USB interface. You can tell this by looking at the files (also called sysfs attributes) pointed to by the symbolic link `1-0:1.0`. It contains entries from the interface descriptor, such as `bInterfaceNumber` and `bNumEndpoints`, both elements of the USB 2.0 interface descriptor. The first two entries in Listing 18-3 represent the single interface associated with two of the internal USB controllers/root hubs in the Freescale i.MX31.

The third entry in Listing 18-3 (`2-1`) represents an external hub connected to the second USB bus. In particular, it is a representation of the `struct usb_device` for this hub.

The three entries in Listing 18-3 starting with `usb` represent the buses themselves. You can see that this system has three buses, because the Freescale i.MX31 processor has three USB controllers. The bus number is the final digit in the `usb` name. The USB buses are numbered starting with 1.

In summary, here are some examples:

- `3-0:1.0` represents an interface (`struct usb_interface`) connected to bus 3. This is the root hub interface for bus 3.

- `2-1` represents a device (`struct usb_device`). In the configuration from this example, this is an external hub connected to the root hub on bus 2.

- `2-1.3` represents a downstream device (`struct usb_device`) from device `2-1`, connected to its port 3.

- usb2 represents a USB bus, number 2 (also a `struct usb_device`).
- 2-1.3.4:1.0 represents an interface (my iPod) running in configuration 1, connected to port 4 of its parent hub, which is connected to port 3 of its parent and then to the root hub on bus 2!

18.4 Useful USB Tools

A number of useful tools and utilities can help you better understand your system, configure drivers, and get detailed information about your USB subsystem. This section introduces them.

18.4.1 USB File System

The USB File System (USBFS) is another type of virtual file system. It is not available until you mount it. Some Linux systems automatically mount USBFS, but many do not. For you to use USBFS, it must also be enabled in your kernel. Select CONFIG_USB_DEVICEFS under USB Support in your kernel configuration. Note that this system is deprecated but is still included in recent kernels and is useful for understanding your USB system configuration. Because several utilities depend on it, it will likely be around for some time.

After your kernel is configured for USB_DEVICEFS (most Linux distributions have this enabled by default), you must mount this virtual file system to use it:

```
# mount -t usbfs usbfs /proc/bus/usb
```

After it is enabled, you should get a listing similar to Listing 18-4.

LISTING 18-4 Directory Listing: /proc/bus/usb

```
root@imx31:~# ls -l /proc/bus/usb
total 0
dr-xr-xr-x 2 root root 0 Jun  7 14:00 001
-r--r--r-- 1 root root 0 Jun  7 14:36 devices
```

After the USBFS is mounted, you can get a human-readable listing of the devices found in the USB topology, as shown in Listing 18-5.

LISTING 18-5 Output of `/proc/bus/usb/devices`

```
root@imx31:~# cat /proc/bus/usb/devices
T:  Bus=03 Lev=00 Prnt=00 Port=00 Cnt=00 Dev#=  1 Spd=480 MxCh= 1
B:  Alloc=  0/800 us ( 0%), #Int=  0, #Iso=  0
D:  Ver= 2.00 Cls=09(hub  ) Sub=00 Prot=01 MxPS=64 #Cfgs=  1
P:  Vendor=0000 ProdID=0000 Rev= 2.06
S:  Manufacturer=Linux 2.6.24-335-g47af517 ehci_hcd
S:  Product=Freescale On-Chip EHCI Host Controller
S:  SerialNumber=fsl-ehci.2
C:* #Ifs= 1 Cfg#= 1 Atr=e0 MxPwr=  0mA
I:* If#= 0 Alt= 0 #EPs= 1 Cls=09(hub  ) Sub=00 Prot=00 Driver=hub
E:  Ad=81(I) Atr=03(Int.) MxPS=    4 Ivl=256ms

T:  Bus=02 Lev=00 Prnt=00 Port=00 Cnt=00 Dev#=  1 Spd=480 MxCh= 1
B:  Alloc=  0/800 us ( 0%), #Int=  1, #Iso=  0
D:  Ver= 2.00 Cls=09(hub  ) Sub=00 Prot=01 MxPS=64 #Cfgs=  1
P:  Vendor=0000 ProdID=0000 Rev= 2.06
S:  Manufacturer=Linux 2.6.24-335-g47af517 ehci_hcd
S:  Product=Freescale On-Chip EHCI Host Controller
S:  SerialNumber=fsl-ehci.1
C:* #Ifs= 1 Cfg#= 1 Atr=e0 MxPwr=  0mA
I:* If#= 0 Alt= 0 #EPs= 1 Cls=09(hub  ) Sub=00 Prot=00 Driver=hub
E:  Ad=81(I) Atr=03(Int.) MxPS=    4 Ivl=256ms

T:  Bus=02 Lev=01 Prnt=01 Port=00 Cnt=01 Dev#=  2 Spd=480 MxCh= 4
D:  Ver= 2.00 Cls=09(hub  ) Sub=00 Prot=01 MxPS=64 #Cfgs=  1
P:  Vendor=05e3 ProdID=0608 Rev= 7.02
S:  Product=USB2.0 Hub
C:* #Ifs= 1 Cfg#= 1 Atr=e0 MxPwr=100mA
I:* If#= 0 Alt= 0 #EPs= 1 Cls=09(hub  ) Sub=00 Prot=00 Driver=hub
E:  Ad=81(I) Atr=03(Int.) MxPS=    1 Ivl=256ms

T:  Bus=01 Lev=00 Prnt=00 Port=00 Cnt=00 Dev#=  1 Spd=480 MxCh= 1
B:  Alloc=  0/800 us ( 0%), #Int=  0, #Iso=  0
D:  Ver= 2.00 Cls=09(hub  ) Sub=00 Prot=01 MxPS=64 #Cfgs=  1
P:  Vendor=0000 ProdID=0000 Rev= 2.06
S:  Manufacturer=Linux 2.6.24-335-g47af517 ehci_hcd
S:  Product=Freescale On-Chip EHCI Host Controller
S:  SerialNumber=fsl-ehci.0
C:* #Ifs= 1 Cfg#= 1 Atr=e0 MxPwr=  0mA
I:* If#= 0 Alt= 0 #EPs= 1 Cls=09(hub  ) Sub=00 Prot=00 Driver=hub
E:  Ad=81(I) Atr=03(Int.) MxPS=    4 Ivl=256ms
```

The format of this printout is documented in . . ./Documentation/usb/proc_usb_ info.txt in the kernel source tree. In summary, each T line documents a new USB device. T stands for topology. The T line contains additional information that can be used to build a topological diagram of the current USB bus. Each T line contains, in order, the bus number (Bus), level in the hierarchy (Lev), parent level (Prnt), port on the parent device (Port), the count of devices at this level (Cnt), device number (Dev#), speed (Spd), and the maximum number of children (MxCh).

Additional lines describe bandwidth requirements (B:), device descriptor (D:), product ID (P:), string descriptors associated with the device (S:), configuration descriptor (C:), interface descriptor (I:), and endpoint descriptor (E:).

18.4.2　Using usbview

The most valuable way to use this information is by using a program that builds the bus topology with this information contained in it. Greg Kroah-Hartman wrote a program called usbview that is still available on many Linux distributions. It uses the GTK library to graphically display the USB topology containing the information retrieved from the usbfs file system. I have taken that program and removed the GTK stuff so that it can be run in text mode on an embedded system without graphics. It is available on this book's companion website. Search for usbview-text.

Listing 18-6 shows how the output looks from usbview-text when run on the Freescale i.MX31. The output is truncated to show only a single device—in this case, my iPod. This device contains multiple configurations and illustrates many of the concepts we've discussed up to now.

LISTING 18-6　Output of usbview-text

```
root@imx31:~# /tmp/usbview-text
Bus 2 Device 3  ******** New Device ********
Device Name: iPod
Manufacturer: Apple Inc.
Serial Number: 00xxxxxxxxxx
Speed: 480Mb/s (high)
USB Version:  2.00
Device Class: 00(>ifc )
Device Subclass: 00
Device Protocol: 00
Maximum Default Endpoint Size: 64
Number of Configurations: 2
```

LISTING 18-6   Continued

```
Vendor Id: 05ac
Product Id: 1261
Revision Number:  0.01

Config Number: 1
    Number of Interfaces: 1
    Attributes: c0
    MaxPower Needed: 500mA

    Interface Number: 0
        Name: usb-storage
        Alternate Number: 0
        Class: 08(stor.)
        Sub Class: 06
        Protocol: 50
        Number of Endpoints: 2

            Endpoint Address: 83
            Direction: in
            Attribute: 2
            Type: Bulk
            Max Packet Size: 512
            Interval: 0ms

            Endpoint Address: 02
            Direction: out
            Attribute: 2
            Type: Bulk
            Max Packet Size: 512
            Interval: 0ms

Config Number: 2
    Number of Interfaces: 3
    Attributes: c0
    MaxPower Needed: 500mA

    Interface Number: 0
        Name:
        Alternate Number: 0
        Class: 01(audio)
        Sub Class: 01
        Protocol: 00
```

LISTING 18-6   Continued

```
        Number of Endpoints: 0

    Interface Number: 1
        Name:
        Alternate Number: 0
        Class: 01(audio)
        Sub Class: 02
        Protocol: 00
        Number of Endpoints: 0

    Interface Number: 1
        Name:
        Alternate Number: 1
        Class: 01(audio)
        Sub Class: 02
        Protocol: 00
        Number of Endpoints: 1

            Endpoint Address: 81
            Direction: in
            Attribute: 1
            Type: Isoc
            Max Packet Size: 192
            Interval: 1ms

    Interface Number: 2
        Name:
        Alternate Number: 0
        Class: 03(HID  )
        Sub Class: 00
        Protocol: 00
        Number of Endpoints: 1

            Endpoint Address: 83
            Direction: in
            Attribute: 3
            Type: Int.
            Max Packet Size: 64
            Interval: 125us
```

This output lists the information from the various descriptors (device, configuration, interface, and endpoint descriptors) for the iPod in question. The first thing to notice is that it contains two configurations—representing a mass storage device and an audio recording and playback device.

Configuration 1 contains a single interface with two endpoints, both designed for bulk data transfer, one in each direction. These endpoints are for reading and storing data on the internal Flash as represented by the USB storage device.

Configuration 2 contains three interfaces. Interface 0 contains no endpoints. Interface 1 contains one endpoint, which is an isochronous interface. This transfer type is for streaming real-time data such as audio or video, which occupies a predetermined amount of bandwidth. Interface 2 contains a single endpoint of type Interrupt. This endpoint transfer type is designed for timely but reliable delivery of data, such as from a mouse or keyboard.

18.4.3   USB Utils (`lsusb`)

A package called usbutils provides a utility called `lsusb`, which provides functionality similar to `lspci`. `lsusb` makes use of `libusb`, which must be on your system before you can use it. Check to make sure that your embedded distribution contains both packages (most do).

`lsusb` allows you to enumerate all the USB buses in your system and display information about each device on those buses. Listing 18-7 displays the physical bus topology by passing the `-t` flag to `lsusb`.

LISTING 18-7   USB Bus Physical Topology

```
root@imx31:~# lsusb -t
/:  Bus 03.Port 1: Dev 1, Class=root_hub, Driver=fsl-ehci/1p, 480M
/:  Bus 02.Port 1: Dev 1, Class=root_hub, Driver=fsl-ehci/1p, 480M
    |__ Port 1: Dev 2, If 0, Class=hub, Driver=hub/4p, 480M
        |__ Port 1: Dev 3, If 0, Class=stor., Driver=usb-storage, 480M
/:  Bus 01.Port 1: Dev 1, Class=root_hub, Driver=fsl-ehci/1p, 480M
```

Here you can see all three buses of the i.MX31 with a hub plugged into the second bus and my iPod plugged into port 1 of that hub. You can also display the descriptors for all devices or target just a single device:

```
root@imx31:~# lsusb -s 2:3
Bus 002 Device 003: ID 05ac:1261 Apple, Inc. iPod Classic
```

This format of the `lsusb` command displays device number 3 from bus number 2. Adding the `-v` flag would dump all the descriptors for the device, which would produce far too much data for a listing here. I leave that as an exercise for you. If you have an iPod, that makes for interesting output, because it has two configurations and multiple interfaces and endpoints.

18.5   Common USB Subsystems

This section introduces the more common USB subsystems that you are likely to encounter. Most are easy to set up and use. Together with udev (covered in Chapter 19) they can be automatically configured and ready to use immediately after you plug in your favorite USB device.

The following sections detail a standard USB class as defined by the USB Class Specification Documents. The intent of a standardized USB class is that one common class driver can be used to support a wide variety of different vendors' devices. When the device manufacturer conforms to the class specifications, you can operate the device without a vendor-specific device driver, using only the class driver for the class.

18.5.1   USB Mass Storage Class

Probably the single most common USB "class" or subsystem used in embedded systems is USB mass storage. It enables external USB Flash drives and other peripherals with internal storage or a high-speed external disk drive such as the Western Digital My Book™. USB storage must be configured in your kernel. One of the more confusing aspects of USB storage is that it requires SCSI subsystem support. In fact, on more recent kernels, when you select kernel support for USB mass storage, CONFIG_SCSI and CONFIG_BLK_DEV_HD are selected automatically.

As usual, these modules can be statically compiled into the kernel or configured as dynamically loadable modules. In these examples, we will use modules because they better illustrate what components and, therefore, configuration are required to get things working properly. Of course, you should know by now that you need `usbcore` and `ehci-hcd` as the base set of USB drivers. (Note that this assumes that we are continuing to use the Freescale i.MX31 Applications Processor in these examples. Other boards may need a different host controller driver, such as BeagleBoard, which uses `musb_hdrc`.)

To recognize the USB storage class of device, we need to include the `usb_storage` driver. However, this driver depends on `scsi_mod`, so we need that also. If your system is properly configured, modprobe should be able to detect the dependency and load scsi_mod for you when you load usb_storage. These dependencies are located in your modules.dep file, which is found in /lib/modules/`uname -r`/modules.dep. Simply search for usb-storage, and you will see its dependencies listed on the same line.

Let's see what this looks like. Listing 18-8 shows the results of inserting the usb-storage module.

LISTING 18-8   Modules for usb-storage

```
root@imx31:~# modprobe usb-storage
SCSI subsystem initialized
Initializing USB Mass Storage driver...
usbcore: registered new interface driver usb-storage
USB Mass Storage support registered.
root@imx31:~# lsmod
Module              Size    Used by
usb_storage         35872   0
scsi_mod            97552   1 usb_storage
ehci_hcd            30836   0
usbcore             129752  3 usb_storage,ehci_hcd
```

Now if we plug a USB storage device into a hub port, it will be detected as a usb_storage device by the usb-storage driver:

```
usb 2-1.2: new high speed USB device using fsl-ehci and address 6
usb 2-1.2: configuration #1 chosen from 2 choices
scsi1 : SCSI emulation for USB Mass Storage devices
scsi 1:0:0:0: Direct-Access     Apple    iPod     1.62 PQ: 0 ANSI: 0
```

However, we need an additional driver in order to access the partitions on the USB storage device. This is where the SCSI emulation layer comes in. The sd-mod driver is responsible for handling SCSI disk devices. After we load this module, the disk device within the USB storage device is enumerated, together with any and all partitions on the device. Listing 18-9 displays the results.

LISTING 18-9   Adding the sd-mod Driver

```
root@imx31:~# modprobe sd_mod
sd 1:0:0:0: [sda] 19488471 4096-byte hardware sectors (79825 MB)
sd 1:0:0:0: [sda] Write Protect is off
sd 1:0:0:0: [sda] Assuming drive cache: write through
```

LISTING 18-9   Continued

```
sd 1:0:0:0: [sda] 19488471 4096-byte hardware sectors (79825 MB)
sd 1:0:0:0: [sda] Write Protect is off
sd 1:0:0:0: [sda] Assuming drive cache: write through
 sda: sda1
sd 1:0:0:0: [sda] Attached SCSI removable disk
root@imx31:~# lsmod
Module                 Size   Used by
sd_mod                20720   0
usb_storage           35872   0
scsi_mod              97552   2 sd_mod,usb_storage
ehci_hcd              30836   0
usbcore              129752   3 usb_storage,ehci_hcd
```

Now we have everything we need to mount the disk partition and access its contents. We can see from Listing 18-9 that the single partition on this USB storage device was enumerated as sda1. Assuming that we have a device node /dev/sda1 and kernel support for the file system type, we can now mount this device:

```
# mount /dev/sda1 /your/favorite/mount/point
```

When udev is installed and properly configured on your embedded device, all the device node creation is done automatically. We cover udev in detail in the next chapter. For completeness, we'll show you how to create this device node on your system if udev is not present. The sysfs file system contains an entry for sda1:

```
root@imx31:~# find /sys -name sda1
/sys/block/sda/sda1
```

This sysfs entry has an attribute called dev. This attribute lists the major and minor number that the kernel assigned to the /dev/sda1 device. On my Freescale i.MX31, it is assigned major=8, minor=1. Using this information, we create a device node, and then we can mount and access the partition. Listing 18-10 contains the final results.

LISTING 18-10   Creating a Device Node and Mounting the SD Device

```
root@imx31~:# cat /sys/block/sda/sda1/dev
8:1
root@imx31:~# mknod /dev/sda1 b 8 1
root@imx31:~# mkdir /media/disk
root@imx31:~# mount /dev/sda1 /media/disk
```

LISTING 18-10   Continued

```
root@imx31:~# dir /media/disk
total 80
drwxr-xr-x 2 root root 16384 Oct 13  2008 Calendars
drwxr-xr-x 2 root root 16384 Oct 13  2008 Contacts
drwxr-xr-x 2 root root 16384 Oct 13  2008 Notes
drwxr-xr-x 2 root root 16384 Oct 13  2008 Recordings
drwxr-xr-x 8 root root 16384 Oct 13  2008 iPod_Control
```

mknod was covered in detail in Chapter 8.

18.5.2   USB HID Class

USB HID (Human Input Devices) is probably the most common USB device found on desktop Linux boxes, and sometimes on embedded systems. HID devices are relatively simple to use. The configuration options for USB HID support are found under Device Drivers --> HID Devices on the kernel configuration menu. You need to enable CONFIG_ HID_SUPPORT, CONFIG_HID, and CONFIG_USB_HID. This is the generic HID driver that implements the USB-defined HID class driver support. Simply insert the usbhid module, and modprobe automatically includes its dependency, the HID core driver (hid):

```
root@imx31:~# modprobe usbhid
usbcore: registered new interface driver usbhid
usbhid: v2.6:USB HID core driver
root@imx31:~# lsmod
Module          Size   Used by
usbhid          18980  0
hid             31428  1 usbhid
ehci_hcd        30836  0
usbcore         129752 3 usbhid,ehci_hcd
```

With this infrastructure in place, most common HID devices, such as mice, keyboards, and joysticks that conform to the HID Class Driver specification, should be recognized and enabled. When I plug in my Kensington USB wireless travel mouse, I see this:

```
usb 2-1.4: new low speed USB device using fsl-ehci and address 4
usb 2-1.4: configuration #1 chosen from 1 choice
input: Kensington USB Mouse as /devices/platform/fsl-ehci.1/usb2/2-1/
2-1.4/2-1.4:1.0/input/input2
input: USB HID v1.10 Mouse [Kensington Kensington USB Mouse] on
usb-fsl-ehci.1-1.4
```

As we did for USB storage, we can find the device numbers that the kernel assigned when it enumerated the mouse in the sysfs file system. Because we already know that the device numbers are contained in the dev attribute, we search for something reasonable:

```
root@imx31:~# find /sys -name dev | grep input
/sys/devices/platform/fsl-ehci.1/usb2/2-1/2-1.4/2-1.4:1.0/input/input2/event2/dev
/sys/devices/virtual/input/input0/event0/dev
/sys/devices/virtual/input/input1/event1/dev
```

Because we plugged the mouse device into port 4 of an external hub, we select the device with physical address 2-1.4:1-0:

```
root@imx31:~# cat /sys/devices/platform/fsl-ehci.1/usb2/2-1/2-1.4/2-1.4:1.0/input
➥/input2/event2/dev
13:66
```

Finally, we create the device node using these device numbers:

```
root@imx31:~# mknod /dev/mouse c 13 66
```

You are now ready to use the device. As with USB storage, if you have a working udev configuration (as described in the next chapter), you don't need to create the device node manually. This is the job of udev.

18.5.3   USB CDC Class Drivers

USB Communications Device Class (CDC) drivers were designed to provide a common driver framework for entire classes of common communications devices. Several standard CDC classes have been defined, including ATM, Ethernet, ISDN PSTN (common telephony), wireless mobile devices, cable modems, and similar devices.

One of the best uses of CDC class drivers is the Ethernet CDC functionality. It can be very handy to have Ethernet connectivity on an embedded device during development that might not have an Ethernet interface. There are many examples of such devices, such as cellular phones and PDAs.

There are two different ways to accomplish this functionality. One is to set up a point-to-point link between a host and a peripheral device directly using a standard

USB cable. The other model uses an Ethernet "dongle," basically an Ethernet interface with a USB plug. We will look at both methods.[9]

Setting up a direct USB link between a host and a peripheral is relatively straightforward. Of course, you must have the proper hardware. For example, you cannot connect a laptop PC to a desktop PC using only a USB cable. This is because one end of every USB link must be an "upstream" device (host or hub), and the other end must be a "downstream" device (peripheral device or "gadget"). Remember, USB is a master-slave protocol.

We will use BeagleBoard as an example of USB-USB direct networking using the CDC class driver. You must enable this functionality in your kernel. Of course, you must have your host controller driver, which, for BeagleBoard, is musb_hdrc.ko. This is enabled by selecting USB_MUSB_HDRC in your beagle kernel config. For BeagleBoard, you must also select TWL4030_USB[10] to enable the USB transceiver. Enable peripheral mode by selecting USB_GADGET_MUSB_HDRC under USB Gadget support. Finally, select Ethernet Gadget (USB_ETH) support under USB Gadget Drivers. This is the driver with CDC Ethernet support for the peripheral (slave) side of the link.

On your desktop or laptop host, you need to load usbnet.ko. On most modern desktop distributions, udev does this automatically after you plug in the USB cable coming from the BeagleBoard. This assumes that you have already enabled your Beagle's g_ether driver and configured the interface. Let's see what that looks like. Listing 18-11 shows the relevant steps.

LISTING 18-11   Beagle g_ether Configuration

```
# modprobe twl4030_usb
twl4030_usb twl4030_usb: Initialized TWL4030 USB module
# modprobe g_ether
musb_hdrc: version 6.0, musb-dma, peripheral, debug=0
musb_hdrc: USB Peripheral mode controller at d80ab000 using DMA, IRQ 92
g_ether gadget: using random self ethernet address
g_ether gadget: using random host ethernet address
usb0: MAC ae:9e:55:32:0a:c9
usb0: HOST MAC c2:de:61:36:21:9c
g_ether gadget: Ethernet Gadget, version: Memorial Day 2008
g_ether gadget: g_ether ready
```

---

[9] Although it may use common elements of CDC, using an Ethernet dongle in the following example is not strictly through a CDC class driver.

[10] It is more convenient to compile TWL4030_USB directly into the kernel (=y) because there is little reason to ever remove it. It is required for all USB modes and takes up very little space.

LISTING 18-11   Continued

```
# lsmod
Module                  Size  Used by
g_ether                23664  0
musb_hdrc              35524  1 g_ether
twl4030_usb             5744  0
# ifconfig usb0 192.168.4.2
```

After we load the two device drivers as shown in Listing 18-11, you notice that a usb0 interface has been created and enumerated. lsmod shows which modules are loaded after these steps. Notice that modprobe automatically loaded the musb_hdrc module.

The final step is to configure the interface with a valid IP address. Now the Ethernet interface over usb0 is ready for showtime. When the USB cable from the BeagleBoard is connected to my Ubuntu 8.04 laptop, here are the resulting log entries:

```
usb 7-3: new high speed USB device using ehci_hcd and address 13
usb 7-3: configuration #1 chosen from 1 choice
usb0: register 'cdc_ether' at usb-0000:00:1d.7-3, CDC Ethernet Device,
32:89:fb:38:00:04
usbcore: registered new interface driver cdc_ether
ADDRCONF(NETDEV_CHANGE): usb0: link becomes ready
```

Notice that the host side of the link has automatically installed cdc_ether.ko and its dependent module, usbnet.ko. On my Ubuntu 8.04 laptop:

```
$ lsmod | head -n 3
Module                  Size  Used by
cdc_ether               7168  0
usbnet                 20232  1 cdc_ether
```

Now we configure the host-side usb0 interface with a valid IP address (easiest if it's on the same subnet), and we are done. We now have a working Ethernet interface from the BeagleBoard to a laptop USB host interface. Note that if your laptop/desktop distribution was not running udev (for some unimaginable reason) or was not properly configured, you would have to manually load usbnet and cdc_ether on the host end of your link. If a properly configured peripheral device such as the BeagleBoard is connected to a USB host port on your desktop/laptop host, loading these modules will create and enumerate a usb0 interface.

18.5.4   USB Network Support

Another method of enabling Ethernet on an embedded device with a USB port is to use an Ethernet "dongle" plugged into a USB host port. These dongles are readily available at many electronics stores and online. The one we will use in this next example was purchased from Radio Shack. It is a nondescript unit manufactured in China, containing an ASIX chipset. When plugged into a USB host port, it becomes a fully operational Ethernet port.

You need to enable support for this functionality in your kernel. For this particular dongle, you must enable USB_USBNET and USB_NET_AX8817X. These options are found under Device Drivers --> Network Devices --> USB Network Support in your kernel configuration utility. After loading the necessary USB low-level drivers, load the ASIX driver and plug in the Ethernet dongle. The ASIX driver is loaded as follows:

```
# modprobe asix
usbcore: registered new interface driver asix
# usb 1-1.3: new high speed USB device using musb_hdrc and address 3
usb 1-1.3: configuration #1 chosen from 1 choice
eth0 (asix): not using net_device_ops yet
eth0: register 'asix' at usb-musb_hdrc-1.3, ASIX AX88772 USB 2.0 Ethernet,
00:50:b6:03:c8:f8
```

First you see the messages from the low-level USB support, enumerating the new USB device (1-1.3). Then the ASIX driver takes over and creates a new Ethernet interface, eth0. Unless you override the choices by passing parameters to the ASIX module while loading, it creates a random Ethernet MAC address for you.

The next step is simply to configure the interface with a valid IP address:

```
# ifconfig eth0 192.168.4.159
eth0: link up, 100Mbps, full-duplex, lpa 0xCDE1
eth0: link up, 100Mbps, full-duplex, lpa 0xCDE1
# ping 192.168.4.1
PING 192.168.4.1 (192.168.0.1) 56(84) bytes of data.
64 bytes from 192.168.4.1: icmp_seq=1 ttl=64 time=1002 ms
64 bytes from 192.168.4.1: icmp_seq=2 ttl=64 time=0.305 ms
64 bytes from 192.168.4.1: icmp_seq=3 ttl=64 time=0.336 ms
```

That's all there is to it!

18.6   USB Debug

Numerous debug options are available when USB support is enabled. Enabling verbose debug messages is a good way to see what is going on in your system. Enable USB_DEBUG in your kernel configuration to see debug messages from usbcore and the hub driver (part of usbcore.) Enabling USB_ANNOUNCE_NEW_DEVICES produces a report for each device inserted, listing vendor, product, manufacturer, and serial number strings from the device's descriptors. Both of these options enable output to syslog and are found under USB Support --> Support for Host-side USB.

Listing 18-12 displays the syslog entries after you plug in the Ethernet dongle from the preceding example with the debug configuration options just mentioned compiled into the kernel.

LISTING 18-12   Debug Output from Ethernet Dongle Insertion

```
user.info  kernel: usb 1-1.3: new high speed USB device using musb_hdrc
and address 3
user.debug kernel: usb 1-1.3: default language 0x0409
user.info  kernel: usb 1-1.3: New USB device found, idVendor=0b95, idProduct=7720
Jan  1 00:02:38 (none) user.info kernel: usb 1-1.3: New USB device strings:
Mfr=1, Product=2, SerialNumber=3
user.info  kernel: usb 1-1.3: Product: AX88772
user.info  kernel: usb 1-1.3: Manufacturer: ASIX Elec. Corp.
user.info  kernel: usb 1-1.3: SerialNumber: 000001
user.debug kernel: usb 1-1.3: uevent
user.debug kernel: usb 1-1.3: usb_probe_device
user.info  kernel: usb 1-1.3: configuration #1 chosen from 1 choice
user.debug kernel: usb 1-1.3: adding 1-1.3:1.0 (config #1, interface 0)
user.debug kernel: usb 1-1.3:1.0: uevent
user.debug kernel: drivers/usb/core/inode.c: creating file '003'
```

Most of the log entries are self-explanatory. You may be wondering about the last log entry, announcing the creation of file '003'. You may especially scratch your head when you can't find this file on your target system. It is part of the usb device file system, usbfs, and it is not visible until you mount usbfs as described earlier:

```
# mount -t usbfs usbfs /proc/bus/usb
```

After usbfs is mounted, you see the file created under /proc/bus/usb/001, which represents the USB interface just instantiated. The 001 is the bus number, and 003 represents the device. The file is not human-readable; it contains data from the descriptors of the USB interface.

Some platforms and drivers may have platform-specific debug options. For example, BeagleBoard kernels using the `musb_hdrc` driver can be compiled with debug functionality. Enable USB_MUSB_DEBUG in your kernel configuration to get this functionality. To make use of it, you must pass a debug level into the `musb_hdrc` driver when it is loaded. This particular option can produce verbose debug information, including information on each USB message sent between devices. You may recall that you pass a module parameter into a module by specifying it on the `modprobe` command line, or in distribution-specific configuration files. This example sets the debug level to 3 in the `musb_hdrc` driver:

```
# modprobe musb_hdrc debug=3
```

18.6.1 `usbmon`

If you are hard-core, you can try `usbmon`. This is a USB packet sniffer much like `tcpdump`. The word "packet" is not really used in USB, but the concept is the same. `usbmon` allows you to capture raw traces of the transfers between devices on a USB bus. If you were developing a USB device from scratch, for example, it might come in handy.

To use `usbmon`, you must first enable DEBUG_FS, which is found in the Kernel Hacking menu in your kernel configuration. You must also enable USB_MON, found under Device Drivers --> USB Support --> Support for host side USB.

After it is enabled, you must mount the debugfs file system as follows:

```
# mount -t debugfs debugfs /sys/kernel/debug
```

Then load the `usbmon.ko` driver:

```
# modprobe usbmon
```

After this is done, tracing is enabled. You see the debug sockets created by the `usbmon` driver in `/sys/kernel/debug/usbmon`. The kernel dumps the packets into these debug sockets. Like `tcpdump`, they are dumped in text format, which makes them (somewhat) human-readable. Simply start `cat` on one of the sockets. Listing 18-13 shows a few lines of trace when a USB Flash drive is inserted into a BeagleBoard with `usbmon` enabled.

LISTING 18-13   usbmon **Trace**

```
# cat /sys/kernel/debug/usbmon/0u
c717ee40 1830790883 C Ii:1:002:1 0:2048 1 D
c717ee40 1830790944 S Ii:1:002:1 -115:2048 1 <
c717e140 1830791005 S Ci:1:002:0 s a3 00 0000 0003 0004 4 <
c717e140 1830791249 C Ci:1:002:0 0 4 = 01010100
c717e140 1830791279 S Co:1:002:0 s 23 01 0010 0003 0000 0
c717e140 1830791524 C Co:1:002:0 0 0
c717e140 1830791554 S Co:1:002:0 s 23 03 0016 0003 0000 0
```

The cat process was started before the USB Flash drive was inserted. Fifty-three lines of output were generated, indicating that 53 USB packets[11] were transmitted. It is beyond the scope of this book to go into the format and details of this output trace. You can refer to the write-up in the kernel source tree at ...`/Documentation/usb/usbmon.txt` for those details. However, more detailed knowledge of internal USB architecture is required to fully understand it. References are given at the end of this chapter if you want to take the next step in your knowledge of USB.

18.6.2   Useful USB Miscellanea

Often, when you plug a USB device into a host, nothing much happens. Many things could be wrong, but the most likely case is that no device driver is available for the device. If, upon insertion of a USB device, you see messages like these in the syslog, this means that the device was recognized, its descriptors were read, and a configuration was chosen, but Linux could not find an appropriate device driver for the device:

```
usb 1-1.1: new high speed USB device using ehci_hcd and address 5
usb 1-1.1: configuration #1 chosen from 1 choice
```

The remedy is to find and enable the correct device driver for your USB widget. Of course, as an embedded developer, you may just have to write one yourself.

Although it may seem obvious, systems that depend on USB devices such as a keyboard or mouse should configure these device drivers as statically linked into the kernel (=y). This prevents the possibility that the console could be lost on removal of a dependent module.

---

[11] The term "packet" is not in the USB vocabulary. However, the details are beyond the scope of this book. See the references at the end of the chapter if you want to dive in deeper.

18.7 Summary

This chapter presented the foundation for understanding the rather complex USB subsystem. It described the topology and concepts and examined how USB is configured and used. The most commonly used USB subsystems were discussed.

- You can better understand USB by examining its physical and logical topology.
- The different types of USB cables and connectors was covered.
- Several examples of USB configuration were presented.
- sysfs was presented in Chapter 9, and its use with USB was covered here.
- Several useful tools for understanding and troubleshooting USB were covered in detail.
- Class drivers including mass storage, HID, and CDC were introduced.
- The chapter concluded with some helpful debug tools and tips.

18.7.1 Suggestions for Additional Reading

Universal Serial Bus System Architecture, 2nd Edition
Don Anderson
Mindshare, Inc., 2001

Enhanced Host Controller Interface Specification for Universal Serial Bus
Version 1.0
Intel Corporation
www.intel.com/technology/usb/download/ehci-r10.pdf

Essential Linux Device Drivers
Chapter 11, "Universal Serial Bus"
Sreekrishnan Venkateswaran
Prentice Hall, 2008

Linux Device Drivers, 3rd Edition
Chapter 13, "USB"
Jonathan Corbet, Alessandro Rubini, Greg Kroah-Hartman
O'Reilly, 2005

Universal Serial Bus Specification
Revision 2.0, April 27, 2000
www.usb.org/developers/docs/usb_20_052709.zip

USB Approved Class Specification Documents
www.usb.org/developers/devclass_docs

Chapter 19

udev

In This Chapter

■ 19.1   What Is udev?   522

■ 19.2   Device Discovery   523

■ 19.3   Default udev Behavior   525

■ 19.4   Understanding udev Rules   527

■ 19.5   Loading Platform Device Drivers   538

■ 19.6   Customizing udev Behavior   540

■ 19.7   Persistent Device Naming   541

■ 19.8   Using udev with busybox   545

■ 19.9   Summary   548

Like many Linux kernel subsystems, udev has evolved over time based on a variety of input from users, developers, and distribution maintainers, as well as historical experience from earlier attempts to solve a similar problem. udev replaces devfs, which was an attempt to solve the problem of the runaway /dev directory and to address the requirement to create the /dev directory dynamically based on discovery of the hardware present in a system.

As with many topics in this book, a thorough treatment of udev would take a small book of its own. This chapter takes a quick look at udev, what it can do for you, and how it works.

19.1 What Is udev?

As a brief review, /dev is the Linux system directory that contains special file system entries called device nodes. Device nodes were introduced in Chapter 8, "Device Driver Basics," Section 8.3.3, "Device Nodes and mknod." These special files can be thought of as "pointers" to actual device drivers that control and give applications access to the device. A device node creates an association between a human-readable name and a kernel device major and minor number pair. A device node also contains an attribute marker that specifies the type of device it references, such as block or character devices.

In the not-so-distant past, Linux systems came with thousands of device nodes, statically created, usually by a script such as MAKEDEV. Chances are, if you have Linux running on your home or work machine, you still can find the MAKEDEV script on your system.

Without some automated method of determining what devices are present on a system, Linux distribution maintainers simply used MAKEDEV to populate /dev with virtually every possible device that could be encountered. It is not difficult to understand that this brute-force approach was not ideal.

udev is the latest and greatest subsystem designed to populate the /dev directory dynamically, based on information provided by the kernel as devices are discovered. It has evolved into a very flexible and powerful way to invoke policy upon the detection of a piece of hardware in the system. Notice that I did not say "load a device driver" or "create a device node" upon the detection of a piece of hardware. Indeed, udev often performs these actions by default, but you can customize the actions that take place when a particular device is discovered. udev's default behavior is to create a device node with the name of the device as supplied by the kernel.

There are many ways a device can suddenly appear in your Linux system long after it has been booted. Some obvious examples are plugging a USB device into a USB port or enabling the wireless interface using a switch found on many laptops. Hot-plugging a hard drive into a fault-tolerant chassis might be another.

19.2   Device Discovery

When the kernel discovers a new device, it creates a *uevent* that is delivered to a listener on a netlink socket[1] in user space. That listener is udev. Listing 19-1 shows a typical uevent as delivered by the kernel. It was captured using the `udevadm` utility as follows and then plugging a USB four-port hub into the USB host port on a BeagleBoard:

```
# udevadm monitor --environment
```

(Note that earlier versions of udev use separate commands, such `udevmonitor` or `udevtrigger`. Newer versions have rolled all these tools into one admin program, `udevadm`, as shown here. Check which version you are running if this command isn't recognized.)

LISTING 19-1   Typical uevent: USB Device

```
KERNEL[1244031028.077331] add   /devices/platform/musb_hdrc/usb1/1-1 (usb)
ACTION=add
DEVPATH=/devices/platform/musb_hdrc/usb1/1-1
SUBSYSTEM=usb
DEVTYPE=usb_device
DEVICE=/proc/bus/usb/001/002
PRODUCT=5e3/608/702
TYPE=9/0/1
BUSNUM=001
DEVNUM=002
SEQNUM=321
MAJOR=189
MINOR=1
```

---

[1] You can learn more about netlink sockets at http://en.wikipedia.org/wiki/Netlink.

Listing 19-1 shows the first kernel uevent that is emitted upon detection of a USB four-port hub when plugged into the USB port on a BeagleBoard. The first line signifies that this uevent is an "add" operation, meaning that the kernel detected the USB device. Its kernel name is

```
/devices/platform/musb_hdrc/usb1/1-1
```

When the kernel detects a new device, one of the default actions it takes is to create an entry in the sysfs file system, nearly always mounted on /sys. The DEVPATH attribute represents its location within the /sys directory hierarchy and is referenced in many places in udev rules and utilities. Other attributes indicate device type, device, product (vendor and/or device ID), and some information on where the device physically exists hierarchically on the USB bus. The DEVICE attribute is the kernel's idea of a device node for this device. This device was detected on USB bus number 001 and has been assigned device number 002 by the kernel.

In Listing 19-1, the product vendor code is 5e3, and the device is 608. Referring to the list maintained at www.linux-usb.org/usb.ids, vendor 05e3 is Genesys Logic, Inc., and product ID 0608 is a USB 2.0 four-port hub.

A uevent sequence number is incremented for every uevent emitted. Finally, the major and minor numbers for a device driver are included in the uevent. The major number of 189 has been assigned in this case, with a minor number of 1.

When udev receives the uevent, it scans its rules database (described in Section 19.4). udev looks for matches with the attributes of the device that prescribe the actions to take based on those attributes. In the absence of any matching rule, udev's default behavior is simply to create the device node with the name supplied by the kernel, having the major and minor numbers specified in the kernel uevent. In this case, the behavior would be to create the following device node, as displayed by ls -1:

```
crw-rw---- 1 root root 189, 0 Jun  4 16:37 usbdev1.1
```

Rules exist in udev to allow the system designer or distribution maintainer to apply custom actions suitable for specific applications. Most often, the default rules specify the creation of an appropriate device node in /dev. They typically also include the creation of a symlink pointing to this newly created device node, which may be a well-known shorthand name that applications use to access the device. We will look at udev rules in detail in a moment.

19.3 Default udev Behavior

You might be surprised to know that the uevent detailed in Listing 19-1 is the first of many kernel uevents to be delivered. Listing 19-2 details every uevent generated by the kernel upon insertion of this four-port hub. This listing was generated with the following udev command:

```
# udevadm monitor --kernel
```

LISTING 19-2 Kernel uevents on a Four-Port Hub Insertion

KERNEL× add	/devices/platform/musb_hdrc/usb1/1-1 (usb)	
KERNEL× add	/devices/platform/musb_hdrc/usb1/1-1/1-1:1.0 (usb)	
KERNEL× add	/class/usb_endpoint/usbdev1.2_ep81 (usb_endpoint)	
KERNEL× add	/class/usb_device/usbdev1.2 (usb_device)	
KERNEL× add	/class/usb_endpoint/usbdev1.2_ep00 (usb_endpoint)	

Note that the timestamp has been removed and replaced with ts to help this listing fit on the page and make it easier to read. Every uevent has a timestamp like the one shown in Listing 19-1. You can see that five events were generated by the insertion of the four-port USB hub. These represent the various components of the USB device hierarchy. USB and its architecture was described in Chapter 18, "Universal Serial Bus."

Listing 19-3 shows the device nodes that udev has created up to this point. These device nodes are created in /dev. These device nodes represent udev's default behavior. For this introductory exercise, no rules have been supplied to udev to customize its behavior.

LISTING 19-3 Initial USB Devices Created by udev

```
crw-rw---- 1 root root 189, 0 Jan  1 02:03 usb1
crw-rw---- 1 root root 189, 0 Jan  1 02:03 usbdev1.1
crw-rw---- 1 root root 253, 1 Jan  1 02:03 usbdev1.1_ep00
crw-rw---- 1 root root 253, 0 Jan  1 02:03 usbdev1.1_ep81
crw-rw---- 1 root root 189, 1 Jan  1 02:04 usbdev1.2
crw-rw---- 1 root root 253, 3 Jan  1 02:04 usbdev1.2_ep00
crw-rw---- 1 root root 253, 2 Jan  1 02:04 usbdev1.2_ep81
```

Figure 19-1 shows the hardware configuration that produced the devices shown in Listing 19-3.

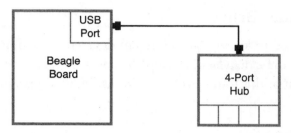

FIGURE 19-1   USB four-port hub setup

The first line in Listing 19-3 represents the host controller on the BeagleBoard. As we learned in Chapter 18, we can see what it is by looking at its attributes in /sys. It is the high-speed dual-rate USB controller (generically referred to as the USB host controller) that is part of the Texas Instruments OMAP3530 chip on the BeagleBoard. This is how we examine the device attributes using /sys:

```
# cd /sys/devices/platform/musb_hdrc/usb1
# cat idVendor idProduct product
1d6b
0002
MUSB HDRC host driver
```

The next three lines in Listing 19-3 represent the internal one-port hub that is always architecturally associated with the USB host controller. This is the root hub, as discussed in Chapter 18. You can think of the physical connector as that one-port hub. As discussed in Chapter 18, the USB device consists of logical entities called interfaces and endpoints. The device named `usbdev1.1` represents the USB interface, and the devices named `usbdev1.1_ep00` and `usbdev1.1_ep81` represent the logical endpoints in the hub—the actual logical entities that communicate across the USB bus.

After we plugged the four-port hub into the BeagleBoard's USB port, the last three device nodes in Listing 19-3 were generated by udev using its default behavior. Notice the numbering of the device nodes, with the `.2` representing the second hub in a connected hierarchy of USB hubs.

You might wonder if different names might better represent devices of this type. If the device were meant directly for use by application programs, such as a USB mouse, a name such as `usbdev1.3_ep00`[2] wouldn't be very user-friendly. This is where udev's rules come in.

---

[2] This is exactly what a device node representing a mouse (or any other device) would be called if you plugged it directly into this four-port hub.

19.4 Understanding udev Rules

The real power of udev comes from its rules engine. System designers and distribution maintainers use udev rules to organize the /dev hierarchy and assign user-friendly names to the device nodes it creates. More often than not, the default device name is created, and a symlink with a user-friendly name is created alongside it, associating the kernel name with a user-friendly name.

udev's rules engine can also be used to load device drivers (modules). In fact, using udev rules, you can perform just about any action you can imagine upon detection of insertion or removal of a device. However, the most common use of udev rules is device renaming—creating symbolic links with human-readable names—and device driver loading.

Let's look at a typical set of rules that udev uses to decide what action(s) to take after receiving a uevent from the kernel. In recent versions of udev, the default location for udev rules is /lib/udev/rules.d. We will use this as the default location throughout the rest of this discussion. Many distributions place udev rules in /etc/udev/rules.d. Rules files typically are customized by distribution maintainers. They often are grouped according to functionality to make them easier to maintain. If you are sitting near a Linux machine while reading this, you might take a moment to browse its rules files.

Although the default directory in which udev looks for rules is /lib/udev/rules.d, udev also looks in /etc/udev/rules.d. Any rules files found there override rules files with the same name in /lib/udev/rules.d, allowing you to override the default rules.

In modern Linux distributions, the rules files taken together form the road map for actions to be taken upon device discovery or removal. My laptop distribution has 31 rules files with almost 1,400 lines and almost 700 individual rules! If you scan through these rules files, you begin to appreciate the flexibility and power of udev.

When udev is first started, it reads all the rules found in /lib/udev/rules.d/ and builds an internal rules table. When a device is discovered, udev matches the actions and attributes passed by the kernel in the uevent against the global table of rules it maintains. When a match is found, the action(s) determined by that rule (or set of rules) are carried out. Let's look at an example.

Continuing with the previous BeagleBoard example, let's see what happens when we plug an ordinary mouse into the USB port. With no rules, udev creates the obligatory device nodes using the raw name supplied by the kernel in the uevent:

```
root@beagle:~# ls -l /dev/usbdev1.2*
crw-rw---- 1 root root 189, 1 Jan  1 00:21 /dev/usbdev1.2
crw-rw---- 1 root root 253, 3 Jan  1 00:21 /dev/usbdev1.2_ep00
crw-rw---- 1 root root 253, 2 Jan  1 00:21 /dev/usbdev1.2_ep81
```

These devices represent the basic USB infrastructure. No other devices were created. If you are at all familiar with input devices in Linux, you might expect to find a device called mouse-something. Many common applications expect to find a mouse with such a device name. Furthermore, no device drivers were loaded to handle the newly inserted mouse. In a properly configured desktop system, assuming a modern and properly functioning Linux distribution, you would find a device with a common name (such as mouse*), and you would expect the input device driver and mouse driver to have been loaded.[3]

Recall from Chapter 8 that we can check which modules are loaded using the lsmod command:

```
root@beagle:~# lsmod
Module                  Size  Used by
musb_hdrc              36352  0
usbcore               143324  2 musb_hdrc
```

Remember, this is a bare-bones system with no udev rules. Only the host controller driver (musb_hdrc) and USB core subsystem (usbcore) are currently loaded, and they were loaded by hand for this example. We'll see later how udev can load these platform drivers automatically. The interesting point here is that no device drivers were loaded to handle a mouse (input) device!

Now let's add a couple of rules for udev to process, as detailed in Listing 19-4.

LISTING 19-4   Simple udev Rules

```
DRIVER!="?*", ENV{MODALIAS}=="?*", RUN{ignore_error}+="/sbin/modprobe -b
$env{MODALIAS}"
KERNEL=="mouse*|mice|event*",       NAME="input/%k", MODE="0640"
```

These two rules are placed in a randomly named file ending in .rules located in /lib/udev/rules.d.[4] The first rule contains the magic that loads the device driver. This rule matches if the kernel uevent attribute DRIVER is not set (indicating that the kernel does not know or supply a driver name). The rule instructs udev to RUN the modprobe program, passing it the contents of the MODALIAS environment variable. We will examine MODALIAS shortly, but for now, assume it is a "clue" that modprobe uses to load the appropriate device driver.

---

[3] This assumes you are dealing with a system configured for dynamically loading device drivers.

[4] Of course, in a production environment, we might impose a more sensible name and organizational structure on our rules files.

After the device driver is loaded, the mouse device is recognized beyond just a generic USB device. The driver recognizes the mouse functions and registers itself as a mouse driver. When the driver is loaded, another series of kernel uevents is generated, which causes further rules processing to begin. This is where the second rule comes in.

The second rule matches for any kernel uevent with the device named `mouse*` or `mice` or `event*`. When a match is found, this rule instructs udev to create a device node in a subdirectory called `input`. udev assumes that `/dev` is the root path of device nodes unless otherwise overridden—but this should almost never be done on a production system. The device node assumes the name of the kernel device, as specified here by the `%k` substitution operator. The device node is created with mode 0640, meaning read/write for user, read-only for group, and no access for other. Listing 19-5 shows the resulting device nodes after the drivers are loaded, and Listing 19-6 displays the modules that are loaded and active after this mouse insert event and udev rules processing. Notice that the usbhid, mousedev, and evdev modules have been loaded and are ready to be used by application devices. You can double-check on your system that the modules have been properly loaded by entering the following command:

```
# cat /dev/input/mouse0
```

If you move the mouse with this command active, you see control characters received on that device. Of course, they are not human-readable characters, and your terminal device might complain! The screen program on ttyUSB0 displays this data quite nicely on my Ubuntu 80.4 host.

LISTING 19-5   `/dev` Entries for the Mouse Device

```
root@beagle:~# ls -l /dev/input/
total 0
crw-r----- 1 root root 13, 64 Jan  3 21:38 event0
crw-r----- 1 root root 13, 63 Jan  3 21:38 mice
crw-r----- 1 root root 13, 32 Jan  3 21:38 mouse0
```

The device named `event0` represents the first event stream, which is a high-level description of an input event. The device named `mice` represents a mixed input from all mouse devices—hence the plural form of mouse! The device named `mouse0` is the low-level mouse device itself.

LISTING 19-6   `lsmod` **After udev Processing**

```
root@beagle:~# lsmod
Module              Size  Used by
evdev               9080  0
mousedev           11692  0
usbhid             16548  0
hid                36944  1 usbhid
musb_hdrc          36352  0
usbcore           143324  3 usbhid,musb_hdrc
```

You might be wondering how all the modules in Listing 19-6 were loaded by the two simple rules presented in Listing 19-4. These device drivers were located and loaded through the magic of a modalias.

19.4.1   Modalias

When a device is detected, such as the USB mouse we have been using here as an example, the kernel sends out a series of uevents reporting the addition of the device. Listing 19-7 details the kernel uevents emitted when the USB mouse is plugged into the USB port on a BeagleBoard. Listing 19-7 was produced using the following command:

```
# udevadm monitor --kernel
```

LISTING 19-7   Kernel uevents on a USB Mouse Insert

```
KERNEL× add      /devices/platform/musb_hdrc/usb1/1-1 (usb)
KERNEL× add      /devices/platform/musb_hdrc/usb1/1-1/1-1:1.0 (usb)
KERNEL× add      /class/usb_endpoint/usbdev1.2_ep81 (usb_endpoint)
KERNEL× add      /class/usb_device/usbdev1.2 (usb_device)
KERNEL× add      /class/usb_endpoint/usbdev1.2_ep00 (usb_endpoint)
KERNEL× add      /module/hid (module)
KERNEL× add      /bus/hid (bus)
KERNEL× add      /module/usbhid (module)
KERNEL× add      /bus/hid/drivers/generic-usb (drivers)
KERNEL× add      /devices/platform/musb_hdrc/usb1/1-1/1-1:1.0/
0003:047D:1035.0001 (hid)
KERNEL× add      /class/input/input0 (input)
KERNEL× add      /bus/usb/drivers/usbhid (drivers)
KERNEL× add      /module/mousedev (module)
KERNEL× add      /class/input/mice (input)
KERNEL× add      /class/input/input0/mouse0 (input)
```

LISTING 19-7 Continued

```
KERNELx add      /class/misc/psaux (misc)
KERNELx add      /module/evdev (module)
KERNELx add      /class/input/input0/event0 (input)
```

Timestamps have been shortened to `ts` for readability. Each kernel event would contain a timestamp similar to the one shown in Listing 19-1. You may be surprised to see 18 events emitted upon insertion of a simple USB mouse. The first five events report the addition of the raw USB devices themselves and represent the architectural components of the USB implementation. These are the USB device, interface, and endpoints. Let's look at the full text of the uevent emitted for USB interface 1-1:1.0.[5] Listing 19-8 contains the full text of that kernel uevent as reported by `udevadm`:

```
# udevadm monitor --environment
```

LISTING 19-8   Kernel uevent for USB Interface 1-1:1.0

```
KERNELx add      /devices/platform/musb_hdrc/usb1/1-1/1-1:1.0 (usb)
ACTION=add
DEVPATH=/devices/platform/musb_hdrc/usb1/1-1/1-1:1.0
SUBSYSTEM=usb
DEVTYPE=usb_interface
DEVICE=/proc/bus/usb/001/002
PRODUCT=47d/1035/100
TYPE=0/0/0
INTERFACE=3/1/2
MODALIAS=usb:v047Dp1035d0100dc00dsc00dp00ic03isc01ip02
SEQNUM=322
```

Notice the MODALIAS field. At first glance, it looks like gibberish. The string can be parsed into individual elements that are attributes that the USB device exposes to the device driver. Some of the fields are obvious:

v047D   Vendor ID (047D stands for Kensington)

p1035   Product ID (1035 is the Kensington product ID for a wireless mouse)

Other fields are device-, class-, and subsystem-specific. They may include attributes such as device, device class, and subclass. These attributes provide low-level hardware details to the driver. It is beyond the scope of this discussion to get into these details.

---

[5] This numbering scheme was covered in Chapter 18.

The important part of this discussion is to realize that the `modprobe` utility can load a module from this MODALIAS. Let's see how this works.

From the command line of a BeagleBoard, the following command causes two device drivers to be loaded. This assumes that you have already loaded the platform USB driver (`musb_hdrc`) and `usbcore` and that `udevd` is not running:

```
# modprobe usb:v047Dp1035d0100dc00dsc00dp00ic03isc01ip02
```

Executing this `modprobe` command causes two new modules to be loaded—`hid` and `usbhid`. You can see this by executing the `lsmod` command again:

```
root@beagle:~# lsmod
Module                  Size  Used by
usbhid                 16548  0
hid                    36944  1 usbhid
musb_hdrc              36352  0
usbcore               143324  3 usbhid,musb_hdrc
```

This `modprobe` invocation causes `modprobe` to attempt to load `usbhid`. Because `hid` is a dependency of `usbhid`, it is loaded first. When `modprobe` is invoked, it consults a file called `modules.alias`, which lives in `/lib/modules/`uname -r``. This file is created by a utility called `depmod`, whose purpose is to create a database of module dependencies. If you look at the contents of `modules.alias`, you will find many lines that look very similar to the MODALIAS string of Listing 19-8. `modprobe` matches the alias passed on the command line with a line in the `modules.alias` file. If a match is found, the module in the alias file is loaded. Here is what the matching line in `modules.alias` contains:

```
alias usb:v*p*d*dc*dsc*dp*ic03isc*ip* usbhid
```

Looking at this line from `modules.alias`, it becomes clear what the `ic` field is. The USB interface class `0x03` defines human input devices (HIDs). This line basically says to accept any values (because of the wildcard, *) for all fields, and if the interface class (ic) field contains a 0x03, load `usbhid`. Voilà!

The modalias entries that are compiled in your `modules.alias` file come from the device drivers themselves. In the example here, you will find the following line in the kernel's `hid.mod.c` source file:

```
MODULE_ALIAS("usb:v*p*d*dc*dsc*dp*ic03isc*ip*");
```

When the modules are compiled and placed on your system, the depmod utility gathers all these strings and builds the modules.alias file for reference by modprobe. Take a look at the modules.alias file on your Linux box, and then look at the drivers subdirectory of any recent Linux kernel, and you can match up the entries. This is how udev causes modules to be automatically loaded—via MODALIAS. In the sample rule shown in Listing 19-4, the second line containing the modprobe directive actually says the following: If the DEVICE environment variable is not set, and there is text in the MODALIAS environment variable as passed in the kernel uevent, pass the MODALIAS to modprobe to load the module. Any module dependencies, such as hid in our example, are also loaded. This is a very powerful feature of udev.

19.4.2   Typical udev Rules Configuration

As mentioned, the set of rules that governs udev behavior on your embedded Linux box is the responsibility of the system designer or embedded Linux distribution provider. In some cases, a package provider adds rules to support its specific functionality. Any recent mainstream Linux distribution provides a good example to follow. Listing 19-9 shows the list of default rules found in a recent snapshot of the Moblin distribution.

LISTING 19-9   Default udev Rules from the Moblin Linux Distribution

```
$ ls -l /Moblin/lib/udev/rules.d/
total 60
-rw-r--r-- 1 root root  652 2009-05-10 04:02 10-moblin.rules
-rw-r--r-- 1 root root  348 2009-05-10 04:02 40-alsa.rules
-rw-r--r-- 1 root root  172 2009-05-10 04:02 50-firmware.rules
-rw-r--r-- 1 root root 4548 2009-05-10 04:02 50-udev-default.rules
-rw-r--r-- 1 root root  141 2009-05-10 04:02 60-cdrom_id.rules
-rw-r--r-- 1 root root  715 2009-05-10 04:02 60-persistent-serial.rules
-rw-r--r-- 1 root root 1518 2009-05-10 04:02 60-persistent-storage-tape.rules
-rw-r--r-- 1 root root  708 2009-05-10 04:02 60-persistent-v4l.rules
-rw-r--r-- 1 root root  525 2009-05-10 04:02 61-persistent-storage-edd.rules
-rw-r--r-- 1 root root  390 2009-05-10 04:02 75-cd-aliases-generator.rules
-rw-r--r-- 1 root root 2403 2009-05-10 04:02 75-persistent-net-generator.rules
-rw-r--r-- 1 root root  137 2009-05-10 04:02 79-fstab_import.rules
-rw-r--r-- 1 root root  779 2009-05-10 04:02 80-drivers.rules
-rw-r--r-- 1 root root  234 2009-05-10 04:02 95-udev-late.rules
```

Notice the grouping of rules files. In a fashion similar to system V initscripts, numbers are used to fix the read order. The rules files are processed in the same order as Listing 19-9. A few of these are worth peeking into.

The rules file `50-udev-default.rules` is part of the udev package (from a current udev snapshot) and is provided by the udev team as an example. As it turns out, the Moblin version is very close to this default version found in the udev package. This rules file establishes a set of defaults for many common Linux devices, including character devices such as ttys, ptys, serial devices, memory devices such as `/dev/null` and `/dev/zero`, and many other devices commonly found on any Linux system.

Other rules files provide distribution-specific attributes and actions for specific classes of devices. In the Moblin rules file collection, these include ALSA rules for sound devices, CD-ROM rules definitions, and several sets of rules designed to provide persistent device names for several categories of devices. You can find much more detail in the udev documentation, which is referenced at the end of this chapter.

Another comment about udev rules is worth mentioning. Unless you use a specific syntax to cause other behavior, udev rules are cumulative. In other words, you may have several rules for a single device, spanning multiple rules files, each matching on different attributes. Each of the actions defined by those rules is applied to the device or subsystem in question. For instance, you can separate rules that give names to devices from rules that apply permissions. Recent Ubuntu distributions have an example of this idea in rules files named `20- names.rules` and `40-basic-permissions.rules`.

Looking at `20-names.rules` and `40-basic-permissions.rules` easily illustrates the "stacking" nature of udev rules. A single device can match multiple rules, and these rules taken together define the actions taken for a specified subsystem or device. For example, consider common sound devices such as `controlC0`, the sound card interface. A rule in `20-names.rules` might look like this:

```
KERNEL=="controlC[0-9]*", NAME="snd/%k"
```

This rule simply matches the kernel devices called `controlC0`, `controlC1`, and so on and assigns the device name `snd/%k`. `%k` refers to the actual name that the kernel passes to udev—in this case, `controlC`. The `snd/` prepended to the device name instructs udev to create that device node under a subdirectory in `/dev` called `snd`. So you end up with `/dev/snd/controlC0` as the device node for the first sound card interface.

The next rule from `40-permissions.rules` might look like this:

```
KERNEL="controlC[0-9]*",  MODE="0666"
```

This rule, when scanned by udev, is basically concatenated to the preceding rule and causes the device node to be created with read/write permissions for all (user, group, and other).

In this way, Linux distributions can create clean rule sets that separate functionality for easy maintenance. In this discussion, you can see that the rules for assigning device names to categories (such as subdirectories under /dev) are maintained in one rules file, and the rules to set permissions for these devices are maintained in a separate file dealing exclusively with permissions. This is very clean and easy to maintain.

To be an expert, you should study the excellent document referenced at the end of this chapter, "Writing udev Rules," by Daniel Drake.

One final note about rules: udev is event-driven. It doesn't do anything unless an event is triggered. For example, even though udev monitors its rules directory using inotify and rescans the rules if you modify a rules file, no action is taken on a recently edited rule until a device that uses that rule is removed and reinstalled.[6]

19.4.3 Initial System Setup for udev

udev is a user space process. As such, it doesn't get to run until the kernel has completed the boot process and mounted a root file system. The vast majority of Linux systems, embedded or not, run init as the very first process, as described in Chapter 6, "User Space Initialization." In a system where udev is in charge of creating device nodes, we must provide some mechanism for init and its child processes to access the most commonly required devices before udev is run. These usually include the console device; input/output devices including stdin, stdout, and stderr; and a few others.

The simplest and most common method for small embedded systems is simply to have a few static device nodes already created on /dev, and then to mount a tmpfs on top of /dev for use by udev before starting udev. Listing 19-10 is an example of a simplified startup script for udev-based systems.

LISTING 19-10   Simple udev Startup Script

```
#!/bin/sh
# Simplified udev init script
# Assumes we've already mounted our virtual file systems, i.e. /proc, /sys, etc.

# mount /dev as a tmpfs
mount -n -t tmpfs -o mode=0755 udev /dev

# Copy default static devices, which were duplicated here
cp -a -f /lib/udev/devices/* /dev

# udev does all the work of hotplug now
```

---

[6] You can cause a manual trigger using udevadm trigger, which would cause your change to be applied.

LISTING 19-10   Continued

```
if [ -e /proc/sys/kernel/hotplug ]; then
    echo "" > /proc/sys/kernel/hotplug
fi

# Now start the udev daemon
/sbin/udevd --daemon

# Process devices already created by the kernel during boot
/sbin/udevadm trigger

# Wait until initial udevd processing (from the trigger event)
# has completed
/sbin/udevadm settle
```

This script is the minimum required functionality to configure your system for dynamically created device nodes using udev. The first thing it does is mount a tmpfs (temporary RAM-based file system utilizing virtual memory) on top of /dev. When the mount command succeeds, any previous contents of /dev are gone, and /dev shows up as an empty directory.

The next action is to copy a small set of static device nodes to replace the collection you need for boot, such as console, standard input/output, and a few others. Listing 19-11 is an example of such a collection, which was placed in /lib/udev/devices during file system creation. The original location is up to you; it is not particularly important.

The last action of the script in Listing 19-10 is to make sure no hotplug agent is specified in /proc. The kernel delivers uevents to this user space agent it specified. However, we want udev to receive these messages over the netlink socket, as described earlier, so we null this entry.

LISTING 19-11   Default Static Device Nodes

```
root@beagle:~# ls -l /lib/udev/devices/
total 8
crw-------  1 root root 5, 1 Jun  8  2009 console
crw-rw-rw-  1 root root 1, 3 Jun  8  2009 null
crw-rw-rw-  1 root root 5, 2 Jun  8  2009 ptmx
drwxrw-r--  2 root root 4096 Jun  8  2009 pts
drwxrw-r--  2 root root 4096 Jun  8  2009 shm
lrwxrwxrwx  1 root root   15 Jun  8  2009 stderr -> /proc/self/fd/2
lrwxrwxrwx  1 root root   15 Jun  8  2009 stdin -> /proc/self/fd/0
lrwxrwxrwx  1 root root   15 Jun  8  2009 stdout -> /proc/self/fd/1
```

Now that we've set up everything, it's time to start the udevd daemon. You can see this in Listing 19-10 on the line calling /sbin/udevd. If you've studied this startup script, you may be wondering what the last actions are all about.

19.4.3.1 Coldplug Processing

During the kernel boot process, various subsystems are initialized, and many devices are discovered and registered, along with their corresponding entries in /sys. On the BeagleBoard used for the examples in this chapter, nearly 200 devices are reported in /sys that ordinarily would be processed by udev for possible device node creation, or device driver load. The problem is that udev is not started until some time after init runs; therefore, those nearly 200 devices remain unprocessed by udev. This is the reason the trigger facility exists in udev.

Take a look at the last two shell commands in the script of Listing 19-10. udevdadm trigger causes udev to process all the entries in /sys by playing back the kernel uevents and processing them in the normal fashion. To illustrate the scope of this processing without taking up the next 12 pages in this book, we'll show the count of devices in /dev before and after the trigger event, using the following command:

```
root@beagle:~# find /dev -type c -o -type b -o -type l | wc -l
6
```

Note that the three device nodes found in this find command match exactly the contents of Listing 19-11. Our initial set of static devices has exactly three character devices, and three symbolic links, for a total of six entries. The final two entries in Listing 19-11 are directories we filtered out with the find command just shown.

After running the udevadm trigger command in our sample startup script of Listing 19-10, which causes udev to *play back* all the kernel uevents, we see that more than 100 new devices and over 400 symbolic links have been created. This is illustrated by the following sequence of commands:

```
root@beagle:~# udevadm trigger
root@beagle:~# udevadm settle
root@beagle:~# find /dev -type c -o -type b | wc -l
135
root@beagle:~# find /dev -type c -o -type b -o -type l | wc -l
410
```

Now that udev has processed all the devices that the kernel found during boot, we find 132 new device nodes, for a total of 135 (including the original three from our static collection). Adding in the symbolic links, we now have a total of 410 files in /dev that can reference a device. This is how udev "post-processes" the devices that the kernel creates during boot. From now on, as long as the udevd daemon remains running, the kernel reports to udev any devices that are added or removed, and udev processes them according to its rules set.

19.5   Loading Platform Device Drivers

Platform device drivers are easy to load dynamically using udev. A default rule found in the udev package can be installed on your embedded system. This rule should look like the first rule in Listing 19-4. It is reproduced here for convenience:

```
DRIVER!="?*", ENV{MODALIAS}=="?*", RUN{ignore_error}+="/sbin/modprobe
-b $env{MODALIAS}"
```

This rule says to run modprobe, passing the value of MODALIAS to modprobe under the following conditions: MODALIAS is set by the driver, and the DRIVER environment variable is not. As long as your driver contains a MODULE_ALIAS macro with the proper format, this is passed to modprobe to be matched with the information collected in the modules.alias file produced by depmod. This is explained in detail in Section 19.4.1.

As an example, let's look at the platform driver for the Inventra dual-role USB controller driver found on the OMAP3530 on the BeagleBoard. Listing 19-12 shows a few lines from this USB host controller driver from a recent Linux kernel. The last line contains the magic that translates to an entry to the modules.alias file, which modprobe uses to select which driver to load.

LISTING 19-12   Portion of musb_hdrc.c

```
#define MUSB_DRIVER_NAME "musb_hdrc"
const char musb_driver_name[] = MUSB_DRIVER_NAME;

MODULE_DESCRIPTION(DRIVER_INFO);
MODULE_AUTHOR(DRIVER_AUTHOR);
MODULE_LICENSE("GPL");
MODULE_ALIAS("platform:" MUSB_DRIVER_NAME);
```

The macro MODULE_ALIAS effectively creates a char string (const char) that is placed in a special section of the device driver (module) object file. This string is similar to an environment variable and exists in the form alias="string". This special section is named .modinfo and contains attributes describing various aspects of the driver. You can see this section header using your cross version of readelf. Recall that we covered the details of readelf in Chapter 13, "Development Tools." The .modinfo section can be seen using the following command:

```
$ arm_v7_vfp_le-readelf -e drivers/usb/musb/musb_hdrc.ko | grep modinfo
  [11] .modinfo          PROGBITS         00000000 0063dc 0001ec 00   A   0   0   4
```

To see the human-readable contents of the .modinfo section, use the modinfo command, which comes from the module-init-tools package:

```
$ modinfo drivers/usb/musb/musb_hdrc.ko
filename:       drivers/usb/musb/musb_hdrc.ko
alias:          platform:musb_hdrc
license:        GPL
author:         Mentor Graphics, Texas Instruments, Nokia
description:    Inventra Dual-Role USB Controller Driver, v6.0
srcversion:     70956E00448DDC456F54F73
depends:        usbcore
vermagic:       2.6.29.1_omap3-omap3530_evm-00003-g1c23d15 mod_unload
modversions ARMv7
parm:           debug:Debug message level. Default = 0 (uint)
parm:           fifo_mode:initial endpoint configuration (ushort)
parm:           use_dma:enable/disable use of DMA (bool)
```

Notice the module alias—platform:musb_hdrc. As soon as you have all the pieces in place, you should be able to manually load your device driver using the modalias string, as it would be passed from udev:

```
# modprobe platform:musb_hdrc
```

Of course, if udev is configured correctly, with a rule similar to the one shown in Listing 19-4, udev loads this module for you using the modalias string. The module is loaded after the call to udevadm trigger found in the sample udev startup script shown in Listing 19-10. That's all there is to it!

19.6   Customizing udev Behavior

Your own imagination might be the limit of what you can do with udev. For one thing, you can run your own programs upon device add or remove. For example, a rule such as the following might be used to kick off a software upgrade process when someone plugs a USB storage device into your embedded Linux appliance:

```
ACTION="add", KERNEL=="sd[a-d][0-9]", RUN+="/bin/myloader"
```

Your program `/bin/myloader` is handed a copy of the udev environment related to this device. Next, your program can validate the contents of the newly installed device and initiate any actions that might be required. This is one way to automate the process of installing a new software image on your embedded Linux box.

If you choose this approach, it might be wise to fork and detach, allowing the udev parent process to complete and return. This action avoids any unpleasant surprises in case udev decides now or in future revisions to kill any child processes it deems to be taking too much time to complete. Also, consider the unique execution environment. When your program runs, it inherits a minimal execution environment provided by udev. This may be insufficient for your needs. You might need to create your own environment for your special handler program to complete its tasks.

19.6.1   udev Customization Example: USB Automounting

Listing 19-13 demonstrates a set of rules that can automatically mount a USB Flash drive inserted into your embedded Linux box.

LISTING 19-13   USB Automounting Rules

```
# Handle all usb storage devices from sda<n> to sdd<n>
ACTION=="add", KERNEL=="sd[a-d][0-9]", SYMLINK+="usbdisk%n", NAME="%k"
ACTION=="add", KERNEL=="sd[a-d][0-9]", RUN+="/bin/mkdir -p /media/usbdisk%n"
ACTION=="add", KERNEL=="sd[a-d][0-9]", RUN+="/bin/mount /dev/%k /media/usbdisk%n"
ACTION=="remove", KERNEL=="sd[a-d][0-9]", RUN+="/bin/umount /media/usbdisk%n"
ACTION=="remove", KERNEL=="sd[a-d][0-9]", RUN+="/bin/rmdir /media/usbdisk%n"
```

Upon device detection, udev creates a symbolic link to the actual device called usbdisk*n*, where *n* is the device number. For example, consider usbdisk0: after udev processing is complete. You would have a symbolic link called /dev/usbdisk0 pointing to the actual device. Next, the RUN directive would create a directory under /media with the same name. Notice that because the -p option is passed to mkdir, all entries along this new path are created if they don't already exist. The final action on `add` is to mount the newly found device on the new mount point created in `/media`. When the device is later removed, `umount` is executed, and the directory is removed.

Inserting the USB Flash drive into a BeagleBoard with the preceding rules located in `/lib/udev/rules/99-usb-automount.rules` results in the following:

```
# ls /media
usbdisk1
# ls /media/usbdisk1/
u-boot.bin          uImage-beagle
```

19.7 Persistent Device Naming

Persistent device naming is implemented in udev by default, using a scheme originally proposed by Hannes Reinecke. The persistent naming rules are in the rules files containing the string "`persistent`". Let's examine how this all works.

If you look at your `/dev` directory in your udev-based system, you can see this in action for disk-based devices.

Listing 19-14 shows the files in the `/dev/disk` directory on my BeagleBoard after two USB Flash drives have been inserted into a hub attached to the BeagleBoard USB port.

LISTING 19-14 Symlink `by-id` in `/dev/disk`

```
# ls -l /dev/disk/by-id/
mmc-SD02G_0x5079cde8 -> ../../mmcblk0
mmc-SD02G_0x5079cde8-part1 -> ../../mmcblk0p1
mmc-SD02G_0x5079cde8-part2 -> ../../mmcblk0p2
usb-Flash_Drive_SM_USB20_AA04012700008398-0:0 -> ../../sdb
usb-Flash_Drive_SM_USB20_AA04012700008398-0:0-part1 -> ../../sdb1
usb-SanDisk_Cruzer_Mini_SNDK8BA6040286306704-0:0 -> ../../sda
usb-SanDisk_Cruzer_Mini_SNDK8BA6040286306704-0:0-part1 -> ../../sda1
```

The output of `ls -l` has been trimmed here to avoid the clutter of uninteresting data. Seven symlinks in this directory are called `by-id`. Each symlink points back to a device node created by udev for the device in question. Here we see, from top to bottom, an SD card, a generic USB Flash drive, and a Cruzer Mini USB Flash drive. In each case, first is the disk device, and then each partition found on the device is enumerated. You can see two partitions on the SD card (the `mmcblk0` is the disk device, and the mmcblk0p1 and mmcblk0p2 are the partitions) and, in similar fashion, one partition each on the USB Flash drives.

The symlink is the persistent name. You can now remove the USB Flash drives and reinsert them into different hub ports. udev, through its helper utility usb_id, assigns the same names (symlinks) to the device pointing to the correct device node, which is not necessarily the same raw device node as the first time you plugged them in.

19.7.1   udev Helper Utilities

The unique ID strings shown in Listing 19-14 were produced either by reading the raw device in question or by querying attribute data in /sys. This is done by a small collection of helper utilities found in the extras directory of the udev git tree. There are several, including scsi_id, cdrom_id, path_id, and volume_id. See the udev git tree under the subdirectory extras for all of them. We will look at the usb_id utility to gain an understanding of how they work.

The rule that generates the persistent name (unique ID) comes from 60-persistent-storage.rules in the udev source tree:

```
KERNEL=="sd*[!0-9]|sr*", ENV{ID_SERIAL}!="?*", SUBSYSTEMS=="usb",
IMPORT{program}="usb_id --export %p"
```

This rule says that for any kernel device with an ACTION of add or change,[7] where the kernel device name is sd* or sr* and does not contain a device number (the base disk device itself, not a partition), call the program usb_id and capture its output from stdout as environment variables. %p is a udev string substitution operator and refers to the DEVPATH—the device path in /sys. Let's see what this looks like if we execute it manually on the console:

```
# /lib/udev/usb_id --export /devices/platform/musb_hdrc/usb1/1-1/1-1.2/1-1.2:1.0
/host1/target1:0:0/1:0:0:0/block/sda/sda1
ID_VENDOR=SanDisk
ID_VENDOR_ENC=SanDisk\x20
ID_VENDOR_ID=0781
ID_MODEL=Cruzer_Mini
ID_MODEL_ENC=Cruzer\x20Mini\x20\x20\x20\x20\x20
ID_MODEL_ID=5150
ID_REVISION=0.1
```

---

[7] Look at the 60-persistent-storage.rules file to see exactly how this is done. The add|change clause is at the top of the rules file in a pseudo if statement, which bypasses the entire rules file if ACTION is not add or change.

```
ID_SERIAL=SanDisk_Cruzer_Mini_SNDK8BA6040286306704-0:0
ID_SERIAL_SHORT=SNDK8BA6040286306704
ID_TYPE=disk
ID_INSTANCE=0:0
ID_BUS=usb
ID_USB_INTERFACES=:080650:
ID_USB_INTERFACE_NUM=00
ID_USB_DRIVER=usb-storage
```

When this `usb_id` command is executed as part of a rule, the output is imported as part of the environment for this particular udev event. Later in the same rules file (`60-persistent-storage.rules`), you find this rule:

```
KERNEL=="sd*|sr*", ENV{DEVTYPE}=="disk", ENV{ID_SERIAL}=="?*",
SYMLINK+="disk/by-id/$env{ID_BUS}-$env{ID_SERIAL}"
```

This rule actually creates the persistent name, which was produced by `usb_id`. This rule says for a kernel uevent where ACTION is either `add` or `change`, and the kernel device name is sd* or sr* (a SCSI-type disk device), and the udev environment variable DEVTYPE is set to `disk`, and the udev environment variable ID_SERIAL is a non-null string, create the symlink with the concatenation of ID_BUS and ID_SERIAL joined by a dash (-). That is the resulting symlink, as shown in Listing 19-14.

These utilities are not necessarily meant to be used by the end user. It is much easier to use the `udevadm info` command to get information you might need to make use of persistent device names. Listing 19-15 has an example of the output of `udevadm info` for the same device we've been discussing here, the Cruzer Mini USB Flash drive. This utility is easier to use and is meant to be used by a system admin or developer. We will pass it the device name from /dev—in this example, the first partition of the sda device.

LISTING 19-15   Device Query Using `udevadm`

```
# udevadm info --query=env --name=/dev/sda1
DEVPATH=/devices/platform/musb_hdrc/usb1/1-1/1-1.2/1-1.2:1.0/host1/
target1:0:0/1:0:0:0/block/sda/sda1
MAJOR=8
MINOR=1
DEVTYPE=partition
DEVNAME=/dev/sda1
ID_VENDOR=SanDisk
ID_VENDOR_ENC=SanDisk\x20
```

LISTING 19-15   Continued

```
ID_VENDOR_ID=0781
ID_MODEL=Cruzer_Mini
ID_MODEL_ENC=Cruzer\x20Mini\x20\x20\x20\x20\x20
ID_MODEL_ID=5150
ID_REVISION=0.1
ID_SERIAL=SanDisk_Cruzer_Mini_SNDK8BA6040286306704-0:0
ID_SERIAL_SHORT=SNDK8BA6040286306704
ID_TYPE=disk
ID_INSTANCE=0:0
ID_BUS=usb
ID_USB_INTERFACES=:080650:
ID_USB_INTERFACE_NUM=00
ID_USB_DRIVER=usb-storage
DEVLINKS=/dev/block/8:1 /dev/disk/by-id/usb-SanDisk_Cruzer_Mini_SNDK-
8BA6040286306704-0:0-part1 /dev/usbdisk1
```

So how can we use this data? We saw earlier a method to mount USB Flash disks using udev rules. We can use the unique identifier as produced here by `udevadm info` to build rules in a udev rules file. Note that we can use any of these attributes if it makes sense to do so.

The most common way to use this infrastructure is to provide human-readable or easily recognizable names for devices in a persistent manner. Consider the following rule, for example:

```
ACTION=="add", ENV{ID_SERIAL}=="SanDisk_Cruzer_Mini_SNDK8BA6040286306704-0:0",
SYMLINK+="cruzer"
```

This would cause a new symlink to be added to your /dev directory, pointing at whatever device name the kernel and udev created for this device:

```
# ls -l /dev/cruzer
lrwxrwxrwx  1 root  root  4 Jan  1 22:12 /dev/cruzer -> sda1
```

Revisiting our USB automounting rules from Listing 19-13, we can create rules that will always mount this particular Cruzer Mini USB Flash disk on a mount point of our choice, regardless of which order it is inserted in or where it ends up in the USB device hierarchy:

```
ACTION=="add", ENV{ID_SERIAL}=="SanDisk_Cruzer_Mini_SNDK8BA6040286306704-0:0",
RUN+="/bin/mkdir -p /media/cruzer"
```

```
ACTION=="add", ENV{ID_SERIAL}=="SanDisk_Cruzer_Mini_SNDK8BA6040286306704-0:0",
RUN+="/bin/mount /dev/%k /media/cruzer"
```

Using these rules, in the sample case installed in a file called `99-usb-automount.rules`, each time you insert your Cruzer Mini USB Flash drive (no matter in what order or on what hub port), it will always be mounted and the contents made available on `/media/cruzer`. That's the magic of udev and persistent device naming!

19.8   Using udev with busybox

Look back at the first rule in Listing 19-4. This rule causes `modprobe` to be invoked with the `-b` flag. This flag is used to check against a modules blacklist, if present. Currently this is incompatible with the busybox implementation of `modprobe`.[8] When `modprobe` is run without modification, you simply don't see any drivers loaded when that is the expected action. The error invoking `modprobe` will not be apparent, because the udev daemon is the recipient of messages on stdout and stderr while executing programs in its context. Therefore, error messages are not displayed on the console.

The simplest way around this is to use the *real* version of `modprobe`—that is, include the module-init-tools package in your embedded system. This package provides the full versions of `modprobe`, `lsmod`, and `insmod`. You need to compile busybox with support for `depmod` disabled or, at a minimum, remove the busybox symbolic links pointing the module-init-tools utilities back to busybox. Depending on how you have configured your busybox, you may have either links or *scriptlets*—simple script wrappers that invoke busybox for each supported function. See Chapter 11, "BusyBox," for more details on these installation options.

19.8.1   busybox mdev

busybox has tiny versions of many popular and useful Linux utilities, so why not a udev implementation? Simply stated, mdev is busybox's answer to udev. mdev exists to dynamically create device nodes in `/dev` upon device discovery. Because it is a simplified implementation, it does not possess the richness and flexibility of the stand-alone udev package.

As with udev, busybox mdev requires sysfs support in the kernel, as well as being hotplug-enabled. It is hard to imagine a modern embedded Linux system without these kernel subsystems enabled![9]

---

[8] Tested on busybox v1.41.1.

[9] OK, I can imagine a very minimal system with hotplug and sysfs disabled, but it would be very specific and limited in functionality.

mdev uses the older hotplug infrastructure to receive kernel uevents. Recall from Listing 19-10 that for udev, we made sure that the /proc file for the hotplug agent name was nulled (disabled), so the kernel would not pass uevents to this agent. busybox mdev requires the hotplug agent to be itself, called through /bin/mdev. So the first order of business in a startup script is to set this /proc file to point to mdev:

```
echo "/bin/mdev" > /proc/sys/kernel/hotplug
```

Of course, this must be done after mounting /proc in your startup script. Not so obvious is the requirement to have /sys mounted as well. When these steps are complete, you start the utility. Listing 19-16 is a sample startup script using busybox mdev.

LISTING 19-16   Sample Startup Script for busybox mdev

```
#!/bin/sh

# mount virtual file systems
mount -t proc /proc /proc
mount -t sysfs /sys /sys
mount -t tmpfs /tmp /tmp
mount -t devpts /pts /dev/pts

# mount /dev as a tmpfs
mount -n -t tmpfs -o mode=0755 udev /dev

# Copy default static devices, which were duplicated here
cp -a -f /lib/udev/devices/* /dev

# Set hotplug agent
echo "/bin/mdev" > /proc/sys/kernel/hotplug

# Start busybox mdev
/bin/mdev -s
```

mdev's default behavior is simply to create a device node in /dev with the same name as the kernel device name passed in the uevent. This is quite useful if you don't need the flexibility of the stand-alone udev. It usually results in a well-known device name for the device in question.

In Listing 19-16, the -s flag passed to mdev upon its invocation is similar to the udevadm trigger action. It causes mdev to scan /sys and create device nodes for devices found there. In this way, device nodes are created for initial devices that have already been discovered by the kernel, before `init` gets to run (or, in the busybox case, `busybox init`).

Booting a busybox configured system, with udev removed and before mdev is started, we have this:

```
# find /dev -type b -o -type c | wc -l
3
```

Executing `/bin/mdev` (which is a busybox link or scriptlet pointing to `/bin/busybox` itself) results in this:

```
# find /dev -type b -o -type c | wc -l
130
```

19.8.2   Configuring mdev

busybox mdev can be customized by an optional configuration file called `/etc/mdev.conf`. It is largely used to customize the permissions of device nodes created by mdev. By default, mdev creates device nodes with *uid:gid* set to root:root, and permissions of 0660. Entries in `/etc/mdev.conf` are simple and take this form:

```
device uid:gid octal permissions
```

device is a simple regex of the device name, similar to udev's device name specification. The rest of the fields are self-explanatory, with the note that *uid* and *gid* are numeric, and not the ASCII user/group name.

Some examples follow. The following mdev rule changes the default permissions to 777, leaving the default *user:group* at root:root. You can use this to change the default user and/or group as well:

```
.* 0:0 777
```

You also can rename (and relocate) device nodes using `/etc/mdev.conf`. This rule moves all mouse devices to a subdirectory called `input` in dev:

```
mouse* 0:0 660 input/
```

You can learn more about busybox mdev in its documentation files contained in the busybox source tree.

19.9   Summary

This chapter presented the details of udev, a Linux utility that adds a great deal of value to any Linux distribution. Correct use of udev helps create a very user-friendly system that can discover and configure devices without human intervention.

- We started this chapter by introducing udev and describing its purpose.
- udev's default behavior was presented as a foundation for understanding how to customize it.
- We examined a typical system setup to demonstrate the complexities of using udev.
- Customizing udev was discussed to allow system designers and distribution maintainers to build systems tailored to specific use cases.
- For busybox users, we examined the busybox mdev utility, a lightweight alternative to udev.
- We concluded by looking at some examples of busybox mdev configuration.

19.9.1   Suggestions for Additional Reading

"Udev: A Userspace Implementation of devfs"
Greg Kroah-Hartman
www.kroah.com/linux/talks/ols_2003_udev_paper/Reprint-Kroah-Hartman-OLS2003.pdf

Linux Allocated Devices
Torben Mathiasen, maintainer
www.lanana.org/docs/device-list/devices.txt

Linux Device Drivers, 3rd Edition
(especially Chapter 14, "The Linux Device Model")
Jonathan Corbet, Alessandro Rubini, and Greg Kroah-Hartman
O'Reilly, 2005

"Writing udev Rules"
Daniel Drake
http://reactivated.net/writing_udev_rules.html

Persistent Device Names in Linux 2.6.x
Hannes Reinecke
July 12, 2004

Appendix A

GNU Public License

In This Appendix

- Preamble   550
- Terms and Conditions for Copying, Distribution, and Modification   551
- No Warranty   555

This is an exact reproduction of the GNU Public License (GPL) as authored and published by the Free Software Foundation. An electronic copy can be obtained at www.fsf.org. This is GPL Version 2. A new GPL Version 3 has been published, but the vast majority of programs released under GPL V2, including the Linux kernel, are still using V2. Therefore, GPL V2 is reproduced here in its entirety for reference.

Version 2, June 1991

Copyright © 1989, 1991 Free Software Foundation, Inc.

51 Franklin Street, Fifth Floor, Boston, MA 02110-1301, USA

Everyone is permitted to copy and distribute verbatim copies of this license document, but changing it is not allowed.

Preamble

The licenses for most software are designed to take away your freedom to share and change it. By contrast, the GNU General Public License is intended to guarantee your freedom to share and change free software—to make sure the software is free for all its users. This General Public License applies to most of the Free Software Foundation's software and to any other program whose authors commit to using it. (Some other Free Software Foundation software is covered by the GNU Lesser General Public License instead.) You can apply it to your programs, too.

When we speak of free software, we are referring to freedom, not price. Our General Public Licenses are designed to make sure that you have the freedom to distribute copies of free software (and charge for this service if you wish), that you receive source code or can get it if you want it, that you can change the software or use pieces of it in new free programs, and that you know you can do these things.

To protect your rights, we need to make restrictions that forbid anyone to deny you these rights or to ask you to surrender the rights. These restrictions translate to certain responsibilities for you if you distribute copies of the software, or if you modify it.

For example, if you distribute copies of such a program, whether gratis or for a fee, you must give the recipients all the rights that you have. You must make sure that they, too, receive or can get the source code. And you must show them these terms so they know their rights.

We protect your rights with two steps: (1) copyright the software, and (2) offer you this license which gives you legal permission to copy, distribute, and/or modify the software.

Also, for each author's protection and ours, we want to make certain that everyone understands that there is no warranty for this free software. If the software is modified by someone else and passed on, we want its recipients to know that what they have is not the original, so that any problems introduced by others will not reflect on the original authors' reputations.

Finally, any free program is threatened constantly by software patents. We wish to avoid the danger that redistributors of a free program will individually obtain patent licenses, in effect making the program proprietary. To prevent this, we have made it clear that any patent must be licensed for everyone's free use or not licensed at all.

The precise terms and conditions for copying, distribution and modification follow.

Terms and Conditions for Copying, Distribution, and Modification

0.   This License applies to any program or other work which contains a notice placed by the copyright holder saying it may be distributed under the terms of this General Public License. The "Program", below, refers to any such program or work, and a "work based on the Program" means either the Program or any derivative work under copyright law: that is to say, a work containing the Program or a portion of it, either verbatim or with modifications and/or translated into another language. (Hereinafter, translation is included without limitation in the term "modification".) Each licensee is addressed as "you".

Activities other than copying, distribution and modification are not covered by this License; they are outside its scope. The act of running the Program is not restricted, and the output from the Program is covered only if its contents constitute a work based on the Program (independent of having been made by running the Program). Whether that is true depends on what the Program does.

1.   You may copy and distribute verbatim copies of the Program's source code as you receive it, in any medium, provided that you conspicuously and appropriately publish on each copy an appropriate copyright notice and disclaimer of warranty; keep intact all the notices that refer to this License and to the absence of any warranty; and give any other recipients of the Program a copy of this License along with the Program.

You may charge a fee for the physical act of transferring a copy, and you may at your option offer warranty protection in exchange for a fee.

2.   You may modify your copy or copies of the Program or any portion of it, thus forming a work based on the Program, and copy and distribute such modifications or work under the terms of Section 1 above, provided that you also meet all of these conditions:

   a. You must cause the modified files to carry prominent notices stating that you changed the files and the date of any change.

   b. You must cause any work that you distribute or publish, that in whole or in part contains or is derived from the Program or any part thereof, to be licensed as a whole at no charge to all third parties under the terms of this License.

   c. If the modified program normally reads commands interactively when run, you must cause it, when started running for such interactive use in the most ordinary way, to print or display an announcement including an appropriate copyright notice and a notice that there is no warranty (or else, saying that you provide a warranty) and that users may redistribute the program under these conditions, and telling the user how to view a copy of this License. (Exception: if the Program itself is interactive but does not normally print such an announcement, your work based on the Program is not required to print an announcement.)

These requirements apply to the modified work as a whole. If identifiable sections of that work are not derived from the Program, and can be reasonably considered independent and separate works in themselves, then this License, and its terms, do not apply to those sections when you distribute them as separate works. But when you distribute the same sections as part of a whole which is a work based on the Program, the distribution of the whole must be on the terms of this License, whose permissions for other licensees extend to the entire whole, and thus to each and every part regardless of who wrote it.

Thus, it is not the intent of this section to claim rights or contest your rights to work written entirely by you; rather, the intent is to exercise the right to control the distribution of derivative or collective works based on the Program.

In addition, mere aggregation of another work not based on the Program with the Program (or with a work based on the Program) on a volume of a storage or distribution medium does not bring the other work under the scope of this License.

3.   You may copy and distribute the Program (or a work based on it, under Section 2) in object code or executable form under the terms of Sections 1 and 2 above provided that you also do one of the following:

a. Accompany it with the complete corresponding machine-readable source code, which must be distributed under the terms of Sections 1 and 2 above on a medium customarily used for software interchange; or,

b. Accompany it with a written offer, valid for at least three years, to give any third party, for a charge no more than your cost of physically performing source distribution, a complete machine-readable copy of the corresponding source code, to be distributed under the terms of Sections 1 and 2 above on a medium customarily used for software interchange; or,

c. Accompany it with the information you received as to the offer to distribute corresponding source code. (This alternative is allowed only for noncommercial distribution and only if you received the program in object code or executable form with such an offer, in accord with Subsection b above.)

The source code for a work means the preferred form of the work for making modifications to it. For an executable work, complete source code means all the source code for all modules it contains, plus any associated interface definition files, plus the scripts used to control compilation and installation of the executable. However, as a special exception, the source code distributed need not include anything that is normally distributed (in either source or binary form) with the major components (compiler, kernel, and so on) of the operating system on which the executable runs, unless that component itself accompanies the executable.

If distribution of executable or object code is made by offering access to copy from a designated place, then offering equivalent access to copy the source code from the same place counts as distribution of the source code, even though third parties are not compelled to copy the source along with the object code.

4.   You may not copy, modify, sublicense, or distribute the Program except as expressly provided under this License. Any attempt otherwise to copy, modify, sublicense, or distribute the Program is void, and will automatically terminate your rights under this License. However, parties who have received copies, or

rights, from you under this License will not have their licenses terminated so long as such parties remain in full compliance.

5.   You are not required to accept this License, since you have not signed it. However, nothing else grants you permission to modify or distribute the Program or its derivative works. These actions are prohibited by law if you do not accept this License. Therefore, by modifying or distributing the Program (or any work based on the Program), you indicate your acceptance of this License to do so, and all its terms and conditions for copying, distributing, or modifying the Program or works based on it.

6.   Each time you redistribute the Program (or any work based on the Program), the recipient automatically receives a license from the original licensor to copy, distribute or modify the Program subject to these terms and conditions. You may not impose any further restrictions on the recipients' exercise of the rights granted herein. You are not responsible for enforcing compliance by third parties to this License.

7.   If, as a consequence of a court judgment or allegation of patent infringement or for any other reason (not limited to patent issues), conditions are imposed on you (whether by court order, agreement or otherwise) that contradict the conditions of this License, they do not excuse you from the conditions of this License. If you cannot distribute so as to satisfy simultaneously your obligations under this License and any other pertinent obligations, then as a consequence you may not distribute the Program at all. For example, if a patent license would not permit royalty-free redistribution of the Program by all those who receive copies directly or indirectly through you, then the only way you could satisfy both it and this License would be to refrain entirely from distribution of the Program.

If any portion of this section is held invalid or unenforceable under any particular circumstance, the balance of the section is intended to apply and the section as a whole is intended to apply in other circumstances.

It is not the purpose of this section to induce you to infringe any patents or other property right claims or to contest validity of any such claims; this section has the sole purpose of protecting the integrity of the free software distribution system, which is implemented by public license practices. Many people have made generous contributions to the wide range of software distributed through that system in reliance on consistent application of that system; it is up to the author/donor to decide if he or she is willing to distribute software through any other system and a licensee cannot impose that choice.

This section is intended to make thoroughly clear what is believed to be a consequence of the rest of this License.

8.   If the distribution and/or use of the Program is restricted in certain countries either by patents or by copyrighted interfaces, the original copyright holder who places the Program under this License may add an explicit geographical distribution limitation excluding those countries, so that distribution is permitted only in or among countries not thus excluded. In such case, this License incorporates the limitation as if written in the body of this License.

9.   The Free Software Foundation may publish revised and/or new versions of the General Public License from time to time. Such new versions will be similar in spirit to the present version, but may differ in detail to address new problems or concerns.

Each version is given a distinguishing version number. If the Program specifies a version number of this License which applies to it and "any later version", you have the option of following the terms and conditions either of that version or of any later version published by the Free Software Foundation. If the Program does not specify a version number of this License, you may choose any version ever published by the Free Software Foundation.

10. If you wish to incorporate parts of the Program into other free programs whose distribution conditions are different, write to the author to ask for permission. For software which is copyrighted by the Free Software Foundation, write to the Free Software Foundation; we sometimes make exceptions for this. Our decision will be guided by the two goals of preserving the free status of all derivatives of our free software and of promoting the sharing and reuse of software generally.

No Warranty

11. BECAUSE THE PROGRAM IS LICENSED FREE OF CHARGE, THERE IS NO WARRANTY FOR THE PROGRAM, TO THE EXTENT PERMITTED BY APPLICABLE LAW. EXCEPT WHEN OTHERWISE STATED IN WRITING THE COPYRIGHT HOLDERS AND/OR OTHER PARTIES

PROVIDE THE PROGRAM "AS IS" WITHOUT WARRANTY OF ANY
KIND, EITHER EXPRESSED OR IMPLIED, INCLUDING, BUT NOT
LIMITED TO, THE IMPLIED WARRANTIES OF MERCHANTABILITY
AND FITNESS FOR A PARTICULAR PURPOSE. THE ENTIRE RISK
AS TO THE QUALITY AND PERFORMANCE OF THE PROGRAM IS
WITH YOU. SHOULD THE PROGRAM PROVE DEFECTIVE, YOU
ASSUME THE COST OF ALL NECESSARY SERVICING, REPAIR, OR
CORRECTION.

12.   IN NO EVENT UNLESS REQUIRED BY APPLICABLE LAW OR
AGREED TO IN WRITING WILL ANY COPYRIGHT HOLDER, OR
ANY OTHER PARTY WHO MAY MODIFY AND/OR REDISTRIBUTE
THE PROGRAM AS PERMITTED ABOVE, BE LIABLE TO YOU FOR
DAMAGES, INCLUDING ANY GENERAL, SPECIAL, INCIDENTAL
OR CONSEQUENTIAL DAMAGES ARISING OUT OF THE USE OR
INABILITY TO USE THE PROGRAM (INCLUDING BUT NOT LIMIT-
ED TO LOSS OF DATA OR DATA BEING RENDERED INACCURATE
OR LOSSES SUSTAINED BY YOU OR THIRD PARTIES OR A FAILURE
OF THE PROGRAM TO OPERATE WITH ANY OTHER PROGRAMS),
EVEN IF SUCH HOLDER OR OTHER PARTY HAS BEEN ADVISED
OF THE POSSIBILITY OF SUCH DAMAGES.

Appendix B

U-Boot Configurable Commands

U-Boot has more than 70 configurable commands. These are summarized in Table B-1 from a recent U-Boot snapshot. In addition to these are a large number of nonstandard commands, some of which depend on specific hardware or are experimental. For the complete and up-to-date listing, consult the source code. The commands listed here are defined in the `.../include/config_cmd_all.h` header file from the top-level U-Boot source directory.

TABLE B-1   U-Boot Configurable Commands

Command Set	Commands
CONFIG_CMD_AMBAPP	Prints a summary of AMBA Bus Plug & Play information
CONFIG_CMD_ASKENV	Prompt for environment variable
CONFIG_CMD_AT91_SPIMUX	Unimplemented in recent U-Boot source
CONFIG_CMD_AUTOSCRIPT	Autoscript support
CONFIG_CMD_BDI	Bdinfo: display board information
CONFIG_CMD_BEDBUG	Includes BedBug debugger
CONFIG_CMD_BMP	BMP support
CONFIG_CMD_BOOTD	Bootd: boot default command
CONFIG_CMD_BSP	Board-specific functions
CONFIG_CMD_CACHE	icache, dcache commands
CONFIG_CMD_CDP	Cisco Discovery Protocol
CONFIG_CMD_CONSOLE	coninfo: display console info
CONFIG_CMD_DATE	Support for RTC, date/time, and so on
CONFIG_CMD_DHCP	DHCP support
CONFIG_CMD_DIAG	Diagnostics
CONFIG_CMD_DISPLAY	Display support
CONFIG_CMD_DOC	Disk-on-chip support
CONFIG_CMD_DTT	Digital therm and thermostat
CONFIG_CMD_ECHO	echo arguments
CONFIG_CMD_EDITENV	Interactively edit an environment variable
CONFIG_CMD_EEPROM	EEPROM read/write support
CONFIG_CMD_ELF	ELF (VxWorks) load/boot command

TABLE B-1   Continued

Command Set	Commands
CONFIG_CMD_EXT2	EXT2 support
CONFIG_CMD_FAT	FAT support
CONFIG_CMD_FDC	Floppy disk support
CONFIG_CMD_FDOS	Floppy DOS support
CONFIG_CMD_FLASH	flinfo, erase, protect
CONFIG_CMD_FPGA	FPGA configuration support
CONFIG_CMD_HWFLOW	RTS/CTS hardware flow control
CONFIG_CMD_I2C	I2C serial bus support
CONFIG_CMD_IDE	IDE hard disk support
CONFIG_CMD_IMI	iminfo
CONFIG_CMD_IMLS	Lists all found images
CONFIG_CMD_IMMAP	IMMR dump support
CONFIG_CMD_IRQ	irqinfo
CONFIG_CMD_ITEST	Integer (and string) test
CONFIG_CMD_JFFS2	JFFS2 support
CONFIG_CMD_KGDB	kgdb
CONFIG_CMD_LICENSE	Print GPL license text
CONFIG_CMD_LOADB	loadb
CONFIG_CMD_LOADS	loads
CONFIG_CMD_MEMORY	md, mm, nm, mw, cp, cmp, crc, base, loop, mtest
CONFIG_CMD_MFSL	Microblaze FSL support
CONFIG_CMD_MG_DISK	Mflash support
CONFIG_CMD_MII	MII support
CONFIG_CMD_MISC	Miscellaneous functions, such as sleep
CONFIG_CMD_MMC	MMC support
CONFIG_CMD_MTDPARTS	Support for managing MTD partitions
CONFIG_CMD_NAND	NAND support
CONFIG_CMD_NET	bootp, tftpboot, rarpboot

TABLE B-1   Continued

Command Set	Commands
CONFIG_CMD_NFS	NFS support
CONFIG_CMD_ONENAND	Support for OneNAND subsystem
CONFIG_CMD_PCI	pciinfo
CONFIG_CMD_PCMCIA	PCMCIA support
CONFIG_CMD_PING	Ping support
CONFIG_CMD_PORTIO	Port I/O
CONFIG_CMD_REGINFO	Register dump
CONFIG_CMD_REISER	Reiserfs support
CONFIG_CMD_RUN	run command in environment variable
CONFIG_CMD_SAVEENV	Save environment command
CONFIG_CMD_SAVES	Save S record dump
CONFIG_CMD_SCSI	SCSI support
CONFIG_CMD_SDRAM	SDRAM DIMM SPD info printout
CONFIG_CMD_SETEXPR	Set environment variable from eval expression
CONFIG_CMD_SETGETDCR	DCR support on 4xx
CONFIG_CMD_SNTP	SNTP support
CONFIG_CMD_SOURCE	Run script (source) from memory
CONFIG_CMD_SPI	SPI utility
CONFIG_CMD_TERMINAL	Start terminal emulator on a port
CONFIG_CMD_UNIVERSE	Tundra Universe support
CONFIG_CMD_UNZIP	Unzip a memory region
CONFIG_CMD_USB	USB support
CONFIG_CMD_VFD	VFD support (TRAB)
CONFIG_CMD_XIMG	Loads part of multi-image

Appendix C

BusyBox Commands

BusyBox has many useful commands. Table C-1 lists the commands documented in a recent BusyBox snapshot.

TABLE C-1   Documented BusyBox Commands

Command	Description
adduser	Add a user
adjtimex	Read and optionally set system timebase parameters
ar	Extract or list FILES from an `ar` archive
arp	Manipulate the ARP cache
arping	Send ARP requests/replies
ash	Small shell, usually the default
basename	Strip directory path and suffixes from FILE
bbconfig	Print the config file that built BusyBox
bbsh	The bbsh shell (command interpreter)
blkid	Print UUIDs of all filesystems
brctl	Manage Ethernet bridges
bunzip2	Uncompress FILE
busybox	Hello world!
bzcat	Uncompress to stdout
bzip2	Compress FILE(s) with bzip2 algorithm
cal	Display a calendar
cat	Concatenate FILE(s) and print them to stdout
catv	Display nonprinting characters as ^x or M\-x
chat	Useful for interacting with a modem connected to stdin/stdout
chattr	Change file attributes on an ext2 fs
chcon	Change the security context of each FILE to CONTEXT
chgrp	Change the group membership of each FILE to GROUP
chmod	Change permissions on a file
chown	Change the owner and/or group of each FILE to OWNER and/or GROUP
chpasswd	Read user:password information from stdin and update /etc/passwd accordingly
chpst	Change the process state and run PROG
chroot	Run COMMAND with root directory set to NEWROOT

TABLE C-1   Continued

Command	Description
chrt	Manipulate real-time attributes of a process
chvt	Change the foreground virtual terminal to /dev/ttyN
cksum	Calculate the CRC32 checksums of FILES
clear	Clear screen
cmp	Compare FILE1 to stdin if FILE2 is not specified
comm	Compare FILE1 to FILE2, or to stdin if - is specified
cp	Copy SOURCE to DEST, or multiple SOURCE(s) to DIRECTORY
cpio	Extract or list files from a cpio archive, or create a cpio archive
crond	Daemon to execute scheduled commands
crontab	Maintain crontab files for individual users
cryptpw	Output a crypted string
cttyhack	Print selected fields from each input FILE to standard output
date	Display time (using +FMT) or set time
dc	Tiny RPN calculator
dd	Copy a file with converting and formatting
deallocvt	Deallocate unused virtual terminal /dev/ttyN
delgroup	Delete group GROUP from the system or user USER from group GROUP
deluser	Delete USER from the system
depmod	Manage devfs permissions and old device name symlinks
devmem	Read/write from a physical address
df	Print filesystem usage statistics
dhcprelay	Relay DHCP requests from client devices to server device
diff	Compare files line by line and output the differences
dirname	Strip a nondirectory suffix from FILENAME
dmesg	Print or control the kernel ring buffer
dnsd	Small static DNS server daemon
dos2unix	Convert FILE from DOS to UNIX format
dpkg	Install, remove, and manage Debian packages
dpkg-deb	Perform actions on Debian packages (.debs)
du	Summarize disk space used for each FILE and/or directory
dumpkmap	Print a binary keyboard translation table to standard output
dumpleases	Display DHCP leases granted by udhcpd
e2fsck	Check ext2/ext3 filesystem
echo	Print the specified ARGs to stdout
ed	Eject the specified DEVICE (or default /dev/cdrom)
env	Print the current environment or run a program after setting
envdir	Set various environment variables as specified by files

TABLE C-1   Continued

Command	Description
envuidgid	Set $UID to account's UID and $GID to account's GID and run PROG
ether-wake	Send a magic packet to wake up sleeping machines
expand	Convert tabs to spaces, writing to standard output
expr	Print the value of EXPRESSION to standard output
fakeidentd	Provide fake ident (auth) service
FALSE	Return an exit code of FALSE (1)
fbset	Show and modify frame buffer settings
fbsplash	Splash image
fdflush	Force floppy disk drive to detect disk change
fdformat	Format floppy disk
fdisk	Change partition table
fgrep	Search for files
findfs	Find a filesystem device based on a label or UUID
fold	Wrap input lines in each FILE (standard input by default)
free	Display the amount of free and used system memory
freeramdisk	Free all memory used by the specified ramdisk
fsck	Check and repair filesystems
fsck.minix	Check MINIX filesystem
ftpget	Retrieve a remote file via FTP
ftpput	Store a local file on a remote machine via FTP
fuser	Find processes that use FILEs or PORTs
getenforce	Parse command options
getsebool	Get SELinux boolean value(s)
getty	Open a tty, prompt for a login name, and then invoke /bin/login
grep	Search for PATTERN in each FILE or standard input
gunzip	Uncompress FILEs (or standard input)
gzip	Compress FILEs (or standard input)
halt	Halt the system
hd	hd is an alias for hexdump
hdparm	Get/set hd device parameters
head	Print first ten lines of each FILE to standard output
hexdump	Display file(s) or standard input in a user-specified format
hostid	Print a unique 32-bit identifier for the machine
hostname	Get or set hostname or DNS domain name
httpd	Listen for incoming HTTP requests
hush	Query and set hardware clock (RTC)
id	Print information about USER or the current user

TABLE C-1 Continued

Command	Description
ifconfig	Configure a network interface
ifdown	Take down a network interface
ifenslave	Configure network interfaces for parallel routing
ifup	Bring up a network interface
inetd	Listen for network connections and launch programs
init	init is the parent of all processes
inotifyd	Spawn user space agent on filesystem changes
insmod	Load the specified kernel modules into the kernel
install	Copy files and set attributes
ip	Show/manipulate routing, devices, policy routing, and tunnels
ipaddr	ipaddr {add	delete} IFADDR dev STRING
ipcalc	Calculate IP network settings from an IP address
ipcrm	Uppercase options MQS remove an object by shmkey value
ipcs	Provide information on ipc facilities
iplink	iplink set DEVICE { up	down	arp	multicast { on	off }
iproute	iproute { list	flush } SELECTOR
iprule	iprule [list	add	del] SELECTOR ACTION
iptunnel	iptunnel { add	change	del	show } [NAME]
kbd_mode	Report or set the keyboard mode
kill	Send a signal (default is TERM) to given PIDs
killall	Send a signal (default is TERM) to given processes
killall5	Send a signal (default is TERM) to all processes outside the current session
klogd	Kernel logger
lash	lash is deprecated, so use hush
last	Show a listing of the last users who logged in to the system
length	Print STRING's length
less	View a file or list of files
linux32	Create a link named LINK_NAME or DIRECTORY to the specified TARGET
load_policy	Load a console font from standard input
loadkmap	Load a binary keyboard translation table from standard input
logger	Write MESSAGE to the system log
login	Begin a new session on the system
logname	Print the name of the current user
logread	Show messages in syslogd's circular buffer
losetup	Set up and control loop devices
lpd	SPOOLDIR must contain (symlinks to) device nodes or directories
lpq	Line printer daemon

TABLE C-1   Continued

Command	Description
lpr	Line printer remote
ls	List directory contents
lsattr	List file attributes on an ext2 fs
lsmod	List the currently loaded kernel modules
lzmacat	Uncompress to stdout
makedevs	Create a range of special files as specified in a device table
makemime	Create MIME-encoded message
man	Format and display a manual page
matchpathcon	Get the default SELinux security context
md5sum	Print or check MD5 checksums
mdev	Mini-udev implementation
mesg	Control write access to your terminal
microcom	Copy bytes for stdin to TTY and from TTY to stdout
mkdir	Create DIRECTORY
mke2fs	Create an ext2/ext3 filesystem
mkfifo	Create a named pipe (identical to mknod name p)
mkfs.minix	Make a MINIX filesystem
mknod	Create a special file (block, character, or pipe)
mkswap	Prepare a block device to be used as a swap partition
mktemp	Create a temporary file
modprobe	Add or remove modules to or from the Linux kernel
more	View FILE or standard input one screen at a time
mount	Mount a filesystem
mountpoint	Check if the directory is a mountpoint
msh	Control magnetic tape drive operation
mv	Rename SOURCE to DEST, or move SOURCE(s) to DIRECTORY
nameif	Rename the network interface while it's in the down state
nc	TCP/IP Swiss army knife
netstat	Display networking information
nice	Run a program with a modified scheduling priority
nmeter	Monitor the system in real time
nohup	Run a command immune to hangups, with output to a non-tty
nslookup	Query the nameserver for the IP address of the given HOST
od	Write an unambiguous representation of FILE
openvt	Start COMMAND on a new virtual terminal
parse	Parse tokens
passwd	Change the user's password

TABLE C-1 Continued

Command	Description
patch	Apply a diff file to an original
pgrep	Display process(es) selected by the regex pattern
pidof	List PIDs of all processes with names that match NAMEs
ping	Send ICMP ECHO_REQUEST packets to network hosts
ping6	Send ICMP ECHO_REQUEST packets to network hosts
pipe_progress	Move the current root filesystem to PUT_OLD and make NEW_ROOT
pkill	Send a signal to process(es) selected by the regex pattern
popmaildir	Fetch content of the remote mailbox to local maildir
poweroff	Halt and shut off power
printenv	Print all or part of the environment
printf	Format and print ARGUMENT(s) according to FORMAT
ps	Report process status
pscan	Scan a host and print all open ports
pwd	Print the full filename of the current working directory
raidautorun	Tell the kernel to automatically search and start RAID arrays
rdate	Get and possibly set the system date and time from a remote HOST
rdev	Print the device node associated with the filesystem mounted at /
readahead	Preload FILE(s) in RAM cache so that subsequent reads for those files do not block on disk I/O
readlink	Display the value of a symlink
readprofile	Read kernel profiling information
realpath	Return the absolute pathnames of a given argument
reboot	Reboot the system
reformime	Parse a MIME-encoded message
renice	Change the priority of running processes
reset	Reset the screen
resize	Resize the screen
restorecon	Reset security contexts of files in the pathname
rm	Remove (unlink) files
rmdir	Remove the DIRECTORY if it is empty
rmmod	Unload the specified kernel modules from the kernel
route	Edit kernel routing tables
rpm	Manipulate RPM packages
rpm2cpio	Output a cpio archive of the rpm file
rtcwake	Enter a system sleep state until the specified wakeup time
run-parts	Run a bunch of scripts in a directory
runcon	Run a program in a different security context

TABLE C-1   Continued

Command	Description
runlevel	Report the previous and current runlevel
runsv	Start and monitor a service and optionally an appendant log service
runsvdir	Start a runsv process for each subdirectory. If it exits, restart it.
rx	Receive a file using the xmodem protocol
script	Make a typescript of a terminal session
sed	Stream editor for filtering and transforming text
selinuxenabled	Determine if SELinux is enabled
seq	Print numbers from FIRST to LAST, in steps of INCREMENT
sestatus	SELinux status tool
setarch	Change the reported architecture
setconsole	Redirect system console output to DEVICE (default: /dev/tty)
setenforce	Reset file contexts under pathname according to spec_file
setfont	Load a console font
setkeycodes	Set entries into the kernel's scancode-to-keycode map
setlogcons	Redirect the kernel output to console N
setsebool	Change SELinux boolean setting
setsid	Run PROG in a new session
setuidgid	Set uid and gid to account's uid and gid
sh	Print or check SHA1 checksums
showkey	Show keys pressed
slattach	Attach network interface(s) to serial line(s)
sleep	Delay for a specified amount of time
softlimit	Set soft resource limits, and then run PROG
sort	Sort lines of text
split	Split a file into pieces
start-stop-daemon	Start and stop system daemon programs
stat	Display file (default) or filesystem status
strings	Display printable strings in a binary file
stty	Change and print terminal line settings
su	Change user ID or become root
sulogin	Single user login
sum	Checksum and count the blocks in a file
sv	Control services monitored by runsv supervisor
svlogd	Read log data from standard input, optionally filter log messages, and write the data to one or more automatically rotated logs
swapoff	Stop swapping on DEVICE
swapon	Start swapping on DEVICE

TABLE C-1   Continued

Command	Description
switch_root	Switch to another filesystem as the root of the mount tree
sync	Write all buffered filesystem blocks to disk
sysctl	Configure kernel parameters at runtime
syslogd	System logging utility
tac	Concatenate FILE(s) and print them in reverse
tail	Print last ten lines of each FILE to standard output
tar	Create, extract, or list files from a tar file
taskset	Set or get CPU affinity
tc	Show/manipulate traffic control settings
tcpsvd	Create TCP socket, bind it to ip:port, and listen
tee	Copy standard input to each FILE, and also to standard output
telnet	Connect to telnet server
telnetd	Handle incoming telnet connections
test	Check file types, compare values, and so on. Return a 0/1 exit code.
tftp	Transfer a file from/to the TFTP server
tftpd	Transfer a file on the TFTP client's request
time	Run programs and summarize system resource usage
top	Provide a view of process activity in real time
touch	Update the last-modified date on the given FILE(s)
tr	Translate, squeeze, and/or delete characters
traceroute	Trace the route to HOST
TRUE	Return an exit code of TRUE (0)
tty	Print filename of standard input's terminal
ttysize	Print dimension(s) of standard input's terminal
tune2fs	Adjust filesystem options on ext[23] filesystems
udhcpc	Very small DHCP client
udhcpd	Very small DHCP server
udpsvd	Create UDP socket, bind it to ip:port, and wait
umount	Unmount filesystems
uname	Print system information
uncompress	Uncompress .Z file(s)
unexpand	Convert spaces to tabs, writing to standard output
uniq	Discard duplicate lines
unix2dos	Convert FILE from UNIX to DOS format
unlzma	Uncompress FILE
unzip	Extract files from ZIP archives
uptime	Display the time since the last boot

TABLE C-1   Continued

Command	Description
usleep	Pause for N microseconds
uudecode	Uudecode a file
uuencode	Uuencode a file to stdout
vconfig	Create and remove virtual Ethernet devices
vi	Edit a FILE
vlock	Lock a virtual terminal
watch	Execute a program periodically
watchdog	Periodically write to watchdog device DEV
wc	Print line, word, and byte counts for each FILE
wget	Retrieve files via HTTP or FTP
which	Locate a COMMAND
who	Show who is logged on
whoami	Print the username associated with the current effective user ID
xargs	Execute COMMAND on every item given by standard input
yes	Output a string repeatedly until killed
zcat	Uncompress to stdout
zcip	Manage a ZeroConf IPv4 link-local address

Appendix D

SDRAM Interface Considerations

In This Appendix

- D.1 SDRAM Basics   572
- D.2 Clocking   574
- D.3 SDRAM Setup   575
- D.4 Summary   580

At first glance, programming an SDRAM controller can seem like a formidable task. Indeed, there are numerous Synchronous Dynamic Random Access Memory (DRAM) technologies. In a never-ending quest for performance and density, many different architectures and modes of operation have been developed.

We will examine the AMCC PowerPC 405GP processor for this discussion of SDRAM interface considerations. You might want to have a copy of the User's Manual to reference while we explore the issues related to SDRAM interfacing. This document is referenced in the last section of this appendix.

D.1 SDRAM Basics

To understand SDRAM setup, you must understand the basics of how an SDRAM device operates. Without going into the details of the hardware design, an SDRAM device is organized as a matrix of cells, with a number of address bits dedicated to row addressing, and some dedicated to column addressing, as shown in Figure D-1.

Inside the memory matrix, the circuitry is quite complex. A simplified example of a read operation is as follows: A given memory location is referenced by placing a row address on the row address lines and then placing a column address on the column address lines. After some time has passed, the data stored at the location addressed by the row and column inputs is made available to the processor on the data bus.

The processor outputs a row address on the SDRAM address bus and asserts its Row Address Select (RAS) signal. After a short preprogrammed delay to allow the SDRAM circuitry to capture the row address, the processor outputs a column address and asserts its Column Address Select (CAS) signal. It is the SDRAM controller that translates the actual physical memory address into row and column addresses. Many SDRAM controllers can be configured with the row and column width sizes, and the PPC405GP is one of those examples. Later you will see that this must be configured as part of the SDRAM controller setup.

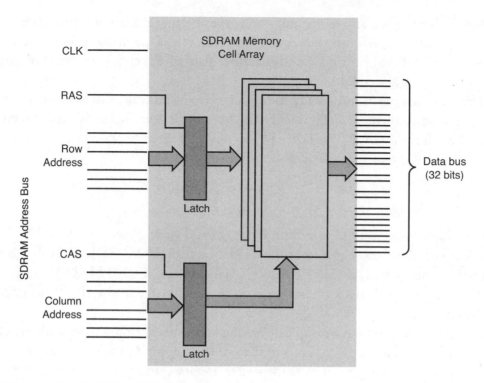

FIGURE D-1   Simplified SDRAM block diagram

This example is much simplified, but the concepts are the same. A burst read, for example, reads four memory locations at once and outputs a single RAS and CAS cycle. The internal SDRAM circuitry automatically increments the column address for the subsequent three locations of the burst read, eliminating the need for the processor to issue four separate CAS cycles. This is but one example of performance optimization. The best way to understand this is to absorb the details of an actual memory chip. The last section of this appendix mentions an example of a well-written data sheet.

D.1.1   SDRAM Refresh

An SDRAM is composed of a single transistor and a capacitor. The transistor supplies the charge, and the capacitor's job is to retain (store) the value of the individual cell. For reasons beyond the scope of this discussion, the capacitor can hold the value for only a short time. One of the fundamental concepts of dynamic memory is that the capacitors representing each cell must be periodically recharged to maintain their value. This is called SDRAM refresh.

A refresh cycle is a special memory cycle that neither reads nor writes data to the memory. It simply performs the required refresh cycle. One of the primary responsibilities of an SDRAM controller is to guarantee that refresh cycles are issued in time to meet the chip's requirements.

The chip manufacturers specify minimum refresh intervals, and it is the designer's job to guarantee them. Usually the SDRAM controller can be configured directly to select the refresh interval. The PowerPC 405GP presented here has a register specifically for this purpose. You will read about this shortly.

D.2   Clocking

The term synchronous implies that the data read and write cycles of an SDRAM device coincide with the clock signal from the CPU. Single data rate (SDR) SDRAM is read and written on each SDRAM clock cycle. Dual data rate (DDR) SDRAM is read and written twice on each clock cycle—once on the rising edge of the clock and once on the falling edge.

Modern processors have complex clocking subsystems. Many have multiple clock rates that are used for different parts of the system. A typical processor uses a relatively low-frequency crystal-generated clock source for its primary clock signal. A phase-locked loop (PLL) internal to the processor generates the CPU's primary clock (the clock rate we speak of when comparing processor speeds). Since the CPU typically runs much faster than the memory subsystem, the processor generates a submultiple of the main CPU clock to feed to the SDRAM subsystem. You need to configure this clocking ratio for your particular CPU and SDRAM combination.

The processor and memory subsystem clocks must be correctly configured for your SDRAM to work properly. Your processor manual contains a section on clock setup and management. You should consult this section for proper setup of your particular board design.

The AMCC 405GP is typical of processors because of its feature set. It takes a single crystal-generated clock input source and generates several internal and external clocks required of its subsystems. It generates clocks for the CPU, PCI interface, Onboard Peripheral Bus (OPB), Processor Local Bus (PLB), Memory Clock (MemClk), and several internal clocks for peripherals such as the timer and UART blocks. Table D-1 shows what a typical configuration might look like.

TABLE D-1   Sample Clock Configuration

Clock	Rate	Comments
Crystal reference	33MHz	A fundamental reference supplied to the processor.
CPU clock	133MHz	Derived from the processor's internal PLL. Controlled by hardware pin strapping and register settings.
PLB clock	66MHz	Derived from the CPU clock and configured via hardware pin strapping and register settings. Used for internal processor local bus data interchange among its high-speed modules.
OPB clock	66MHz	Derived from the PLB clock and configured via register settings. Used for internal connection of peripherals that do not need high-speed connection.
PCI clock	33MHz	Derived from the PLB clock and configured via register settings.
MemClk	100MHz	Drives the SDRAM chips directly. Derived from the CPU clock and configured via register settings.

Decisions about clock setup normally must be made at hardware design time. Pin strapping options determine initial clock configurations upon application of power to the processor. You often can get some control over derived clocks by setting divider bits accessible through processor internal registers dedicated to clock and subsystem control. In the example we present here based on the 405GP, final clock configuration is determined by pin strapping and firmware configuration. It is the bootloader's responsibility to set the initial dividers and any other clock options that can be configured via processor register bits very early after power is applied.

D.3   SDRAM Setup

After the clocks have been configured, the next step is to configure the SDRAM controller. Controllers vary widely from processor to processor, but the end result is always the same: You must provide the correct clocking and timing values to enable and optimize the performance of the SDRAM subsystem.

As with other material in this book, there is no substitute for detailed knowledge of the hardware you are trying to configure. This is especially true for SDRAM. It is beyond the scope of this appendix to explore the design of SDRAM, but you need to understand some basics. Many manufacturers' data sheets on SDRAM devices contain helpful technical descriptions. You are urged to familiarize yourself with the content of these data sheets. You don't need a degree in hardware engineering to understand what you must do to properly configure your SDRAM subsystem, but you need to achieve some level of understanding.

We will examine how the SDRAM controller is configured on the 405GP processor as configured by the U-Boot bootloader we covered in Chapter 7, "Bootloaders." Recall from Chapter 7 that U-Boot provides a hook for SDRAM initialization from the assembly language startup code found in `start.s` in the 4xx-specific CPU directory. Refer to Section 7.4.5, "Board-Specific Initialization," in Chapter 7. Listing D-1 shows the `sdram_init()` function from U-Boot's `.../cpu/ppc4xx/sdram.c` file.

LISTING D-1   *ppc4xx sdram_init()* from U-Boot

```
01 void sdr7am_init(void)
02 {
03         ulong sdtr1;
04         ulong rtr;
05         int i;
06
07         /*
08          * Support for 100MHz and 133MHz SDRAM
09          */
10         if (get_bus_freq(0) > 100000000) {
11                 /*
12                  * 133 MHz SDRAM
13                  */
14                 sdtr1 = 0x01074015;
15                 rtr = 0x07f00000;
16         } else {
17                 /*
18                  * default: 100 MHz SDRAM
19                  */
20                 sdtr1 = 0x0086400d;
21                 rtr = 0x05f00000;
22         }
23
24         for (i=0; i<N_MB0CF; i++) {
25                 /*
26                  * Disable memory controller.
27                  */
28                 mtsdram0(mem_mcopt1, 0x00000000);
29
30                 /*
31                  * Set MB0CF for bank 0.
32                  */
33                 mtsdram0(mem_mb0cf, mb0cf[i].reg);
```

LISTING D-1 Continued

```
34                    mtsdram0(mem_sdtr1, sdtr1);
35                    mtsdram0(mem_rtr, rtr);
36
37                    udelay(200);
38
39                    /*
40                     * Set memory controller options reg, MCOPT1.
41                     * Set DC_EN to '1' and BRD_PRF to '01' for 16 byte PLB Burst
42                     * read/prefetch.
43                     */
44                    mtsdram0(mem_mcopt1, 0x80800000);
45
46                    udelay(10000);
47
48                    if (get_ram_size(0, mb0cf[i].size) == mb0cf[i].size) {
49                            /*
50                             * OK, size detected -> all done
51                             */
52                            return;
53                    }
54            }
55 }
```

The first action reads the pin strapping on the 405GP processor to determine the design value for the SDRAM clock. In this case, we can see that two possible values are accommodated: 100MHz and 133MHz. Based on this choice, constants are chosen that will be used later in the function to set the appropriate register bits in the SDRAM controller.

Starting on line 24, a loop is used to set the parameters for each of up to five predefined memory sizes. Currently U-Boot has logic to support a single bank of memory sized at one of 4MB, 16MB, 32MB, 64MB, or 128MB. These sizes are defined in a table called mb0cf in .../cpu/ppc4xx/sdram.c. The table associates a constant with each of these memory sizes, based on the value required in the 405GP memory bank configuration register. The loop does this:

```
for (i = each possible memory bank size, largest first) {
    select timing constant based on SDRAM clock speed;
    disable SDRAM memory controller;
    configure bank 0 with size[i], timing constants[i]
```

```
    re-enable SDRAM memory controller;

run simple memory test to dynamically determine size;
   /* This is done using get_ram_size() */
if ( tested size == configured size )
     done;
}
```

This simple logic simply plugs in the correct timing constants in the SDRAM controller based on SDRAM clock speed and configured memory bank size from the hard-coded table in U-Boot. Using this explanation, you can easily correlate the bank configuration values using the 405GP reference manual. For a 64MB DRAM size, the memory bank control register is set as follows:

```
Memory Bank 0 Control Register = 0x000a4001
```

The PowerPC 405GP User's Manual describes the fields shown in Table D-2 for the memory bank 0 control register.

TABLE D-2   405GP Memory Bank 0-3 Configuration Register Fields

Field	Value	Comments
Bank Address (BA)	0x00	Starting memory address of this bank.
Size (SZ)	0x4	Size of this memory bank—in this case, 64MB.
Addressing Mode (AM)	0x2	Determines the organization of memory, including the number of row and column bits. In this case, Mode 2 equals 12 row address bits, and either 9 or 10 column address bits, and up to four internal SDRAM banks. This data is provided in a table in the 405GP User's Manual.
Bank Enable (BE)	0x1	Enable bit for the bank configured by this register. The 405GP has four of these memory bank configuration registers.

The designer must determine the values in this table based on the memory module in use on the board.

Let's look at a timing example to see more details on the timing requirements of a typical SDRAM controller. Assuming a 100MHz SDRAM clock speed and 64MB memory size, the timing constants selected by the sdram_init() function in Listing D-1 are selected as follows:

```
SDRAM Timing Register       = 0x0086400d
Refresh Timing Register     = 0x05f00000
```

The PowerPC 405GP User's Manual describes the fields shown in Table D-3 for the SDRAM Timing Register.

TABLE D-3   405GP SDRAM Timing Register Fields

Field	Value	Comments
CAS Latency (CASL)	0x1	SDRAM CAS latency. This value comes directly from the SDRAM chip specifications. It is the delay in clock cycles required by the chip between the time the read command is issued (CAS signal) and the time the data is available on the data bus. In this case, the 0x1 represents two clock cycles, as seen from the 405GP User's Manual.
Precharge Command to Next Activate (PTA)	0x1	The SDRAM Precharge command deactivates a given row. In contrast, the Activate command enables a given row for subsequent access, such as during a burst cycle. This timing parameter enforces the minimum time between Precharge and a subsequent Activate cycle, and it is dictated by the SDRAM chip. The correct value must be obtained from the SDRAM chip specification. In this case, 0x1 represents two clock cycles, as determined from the 405GP User's Manual.
Read/Write to Precharge Command Minimum (CTP)	0x2	This timing parameter enforces the minimum time delay between a given SDRAM read or write command to a subsequent Precharge command. The correct value must be obtained from the SDRAM chip specification. In this case, 0x2 represents three clock cycles, as determined from the 405GP User's Manual.
SDRAM Command Leadoff (LDF)	0x1	This timing parameter enforces the minimum time delay between assertion of address or command cycle to bank select cycle. The correct value must be obtained from the SDRAM chip specification. In this case, 0x1 represents two clock cycles, as determined from the 405GP User's Manual.

The final timing parameter configured by the U-Boot example in Listing D-1 is the refresh timing register value. This register requires a single field that determines the refresh interval enforced by the SDRAM controller. The field representing the interval is treated as a simple counter running at the SDRAM clock frequency. In the example here, we assume 100MHz as the SDRAM clock frequency. The value programmed into this register in our example is 0x05f0_0000. From the PowerPC 405GP User's Manual, we determine that this will produce a refresh request every 15.2 microseconds. As with the other timing parameters, this value is dictated by the SDRAM chip specifications.

A typical SDRAM chip requires one refresh cycle for each row. Each row must be refreshed in the minimum time specified by the manufacturer. In the chip referenced in the final section of this appendix, the manufacturer specifies that 8,192 rows must be refreshed every 64 milliseconds. This would require generating a refresh cycle every 7.8 microseconds to meet the specifications for this particular device.

D.4   Summary

SDRAM devices are complex. This appendix presented a simple example to help you navigate the complexities of SDRAM controller setup. The SDRAM controllers perform a critical function, and they must be set up properly. There is no substitute for diving into a specification and digesting the information presented. The two sample documents referenced in this appendix are an excellent starting point.

D.4.1   Suggestions for Additional Reading

AMCC 405GP Embedded Processor User's Manual
AMCC Corporation
www.amcc.com/Embedded/

Micron Technology, Inc.
Synchronous DRAM MT48LC64M4A2 Data Sheet
http://download.micron.com/pdf/datasheets/dram/sdram/256MSDRAM.pdf

Appendix E

Open Source Resources

This appendix brings together a number of useful resources for open source developers. Source repositories and mailing lists are included. News and information sources are also listed.

Source Repositories and Developer Information

Linux development is centered at several locations on the web. Here is a list of the most important ones for the various architectures and projects:

Home of the Linux kernel and many related projects
www.kernel.org

Primary kernel GIT repository
http://git.kernel.org/

MIPS-related developments
www.linux-mips.org

ARM-related Linux development
www.arm.linux.org.uk

Primary home for a huge collection of open source projects
http://sourceforge.net

Mailing Lists

Hundreds, if not thousands, of mailing lists cater to every aspect of Linux and open source development. Here are a few to consider. Make sure you familiarize yourself with mailing list etiquette before posting to these lists.

Most of these lists maintain searchable archives. This is the first place you should consult. In a great majority of the cases, your question will have already been asked and answered.

Start your reading here for advice on how to best utilize the public mailing lists:

The Linux Kernel Mailing List FAQ
www.tux.org/lkml

List Server serving various Linux kernel-related mailing lists
http://vger.kernel.org

Linux Kernel Mailing: very high volume; kernel development only
http://vger.kernel.org/vger-lists.html#linux-kernel

Linux News and Developments

These web resources can help you keep track of the rapidly moving landscape in the open source communities:

LinuxDevices.com
www.linuxdevices.com

PowerPC News and other information
http://penguinppc.org

General Linux News and Developments
Linux Weekly News
www.lwn.net

Open Source Legal Insight and Discussion

This website presents information and education focusing on intellectual property law as it applies to open source:

Open-Bar website
www.open-bar.org

Sample BDI-2000 Configuration File

```
; bdiGDB configuration file for the UEI PPC 5200 Board
; Revision 1.0
; Revision 1.1  (Added serial port setup)
; --------------------------------------------------------
; 4 MB Flash (Am29DL323)
; 128 MB Micron DDR DRAM
;
[INIT]
; init core register
WREG    MSR         0x00003002  ;MSR  : FP,ME,RI
WM32    0x80000000  0x00008000  ;MBAR : internal registers at 0x80000000
                ; Default after RESET, MBAR sits at 0x80000000
                ; because its POR value is 0x0000_8000 (!)

WSPR    311         0x80000000  ; MBAR : save internal register offset
                                ; SPR311 is the MBAR in G2_LE

WSPR    279         0x80000000  ;SPRG7: save internal memory offsetReg: 279

; Init CDM (Clock Distribution Module)
;  Hardware Reset config {
;      ppc_pll_cfg[0..4] = 01000b
:      XLB:Core -> 1:3
:      Core:f(VCO) -> 1:2
:      XLB:f(VCO) -> 1:6
;
;      xlb_clk_sel = 0 -> XLB_CLK=f(sys) / 4 = 132 MHz
;
;      sys_pll_cfg_1 = 0 -> NOP
;      sys_pll_cfg_0 = 0 -> f(sys) = 16x SYS_XTAL_IN = 528 MHz
;  }
;
;  CDM Configuration Register
WM32    0x8000020c  0x01000101
          ; enable DDR Mode
          ; ipb_clk_sel = 1 -> XLB_CLK / 2 (ipb_clk = 66 MHz)
          ; pci_clk_sel = 01 -> IPB_CLK/2

; CS0 Flash
WM32    0x80000004  0x0000ff00  ;CS0 start = 0xff000000 - Flash memory is on CS0
WM32    0x80000008  0x0000ffff  ;CS0 stop  = 0xffffffff

; IPBI Register and Wait State Enable
```

```
WM32    0x80000054  0x00050001 ;CSE: enable CS0, disable CSBOOT,
                               ;Wait state enable\
                               ; CS2 also enabled

WM32    0x80000300  0x00045d30 ;BOOT ctrl
               ; bits 0-7: WaitP  (try 0xff)
               ; bits 8-15: WaitX  (try 0xff)
               ; bit 16: Multiplex or non-muxed (0x0 = non-muxed)
               ; bit 17: reserved (Reset value = 0x1, keep it)
               ; bit 18: Ack Active (0x0)
               ; bit 19: CE (Enable) 0x1
               ; bits 20-21: Address Size (0x11 = 25/6 bits)
               ; bits 22:23: Data size field (0x01 = 16-bits)
               ; bits 24:25: Bank bits (0x00)
               ; bits 26-27: WaitType (0x11)
               ; bits 28: Write Swap (0x0 = no swap)
               ; bits 29: Read Swap (0x0 = no swap)
               ; bit 30: Write Only (0x0 = read enable)
               ; bit 31: Read Only (0x0 = write enable)

; CS2 Logic Registers
WM32    0x80000014  0x0000e00e
WM32    0x80000018  0x0000efff

; LEDS:
;  LED1 - bits 0-7
;  LED2 - bits 8-15
;  LED3 - bits 16-23
;  LED4 - bits 24-31
;  off = 0x01
;  on  = 0x02
; mm 0xe00e2030 0x02020202 1 (all on)
; mm 0xe00e2030 0x01020102 1 (2 on, 2 off)

WM32    0x80000308  0x00045b30  ; CS2 Configuration Register
                       ; bits 0-7: WaitP  (try 0xff)
                       ; bits 8-15: WaitX  (try 0xff)
                       ; bit 16: Multiplex or non-muxed (0x0 = non-muxed)
                       ; bit 17: reserved (Reset value = 0x1, keep it)
                       ; bit 18: Ack Active (0x0)
                       ; bit 19: CE (Enable) 0x1
                       ; bits 20-21: Address Size (0x10 = 24 bits)
                       ; bits 22:23: Data size field (0x11 = 32-bits)
```

```
                              ; bits 24:25: Bank bits (0x00)
                              ; bits 26-27: WaitType (0x11)
                              ; bits 28: Write Swap (0x0 = no swap)
                              ; bits 29: Read Swap (0x0 = no swap)
                              ; bit 30: Write Only (0x0 = read enable)
                              ; bit 31: Read Only (0x0 = write enable)


WM32   0x80000318  0x01000000     ; Master LPC Enable


;
; init SDRAM controller
;
; For the UEI PPC 5200 Board,
;   Micron 46V32M16-75E (8 MEG x 16 x 4 banks)
;   64 MB per Chip, for a total of 128 MB
;   arranged as a single "space" (i.e 1 CS)
;   with the following configuration:
;       8 Mb x 16 x 4 banks
;       Refresh count 8K
;       Row addressing: 8K (A0..12) 13 bits
;       Column addressing: 1K (A0..9) 10 bits
;       Bank Addressing: 4 (BA0..1) 2 bits
;   Key Timing Parameters: (-75E)
;           Clockrate (CL=2) 133 MHz
;           DO Window 2.5 ns
;           Access Window: +/- 75 ns
;           DQS - DQ Skew: +0.5 ns
;           t(REFI): 7.8 us MAX
;
; Initialization Requirements (General Notes)
;   The memory Mode/Extended Mode registers must be
;   initialized during the system boot sequence. But before
;   writing to the controller Mode register, the mode_en and
;   cke bits in the Control register must be set to 1. After
;   memory initialization is complete, the Control register
;   mode_en bit should be cleared to prevent subsequent access
;   to the controller Mode register.

; SDRAM init sequence
;   1) Setup and enable chip selects
;   2) Setup config registers
;   3) Setup TAP Delay
```

```
; Setup and enable SDRAM CS
WM32      0x80000034   0x0000001a   ;SDRAM CS0, 128MB @ 0x00000000
WM32      0x80000038   0x08000000   ;SDRAM CS1, disabled @ 0x08000000


WM32      0x80000108   0x73722930 ;SDRAM Config 1 Samsung
                       ; Assume CL=2
                       ; bits 0-3: srd2rwp: in clocks (0x6)
                       ; bits 507: swt2rwp: in clocks -> Data sheet suggests
                       ;   0x3 for DDR (0x3)
                       ; bits 8-11: rd_latency -> for DDR 0x7
                       ; bits 13-15: act2rw -> 0x2
                       ; bit 16: reserved
                       ; bits 17-19: pre2act -> 0x02
                       ; bits 20-23: ref2act -> 0x09
                       ; bits 25-27: wr_latency -> for DDR 0x03
                       ; bits 28-31: Reserved


WM32      0x8000010c   0x46770000 ;SDRAM Config 2 Samsung
                         ; bits 0-3: brd2rp -> for DDR 0x4
                            ; bits 4-7: bwt2rwp -> for DDR 0x6
                            ; bits 8-11: brd2wt -> 0x6
                            ; bits 12-15: burst_length -> 0x07 (bl - 1)
                            ; bits 16-13: Reserved


; Setup initial Tap delay
WM32   0x80000204   0x18000000   ; Start in the end of the range (24 = 0x18) Samsung

WM32      0x80000104   0xf10f0f00 ;SDRAM Control (was 0xd14f0000)
                            ; bit 0: mode_en (1=write)
                            ; bit 1: cke (MEM_CLK_EN)
                            ; bit 2: ddr (DDR mode on)
                            ; bit 3: ref_en (Refresh enable)
                            ; bits 4-6: Reserved
                            ; bit 7: hi_addr (XLA[4:7] as row/col
                            ;   must be set to '1' 'cuz we need 13 RA bits
                            ;    for the Micron chip above
                            ; bit 8: reserved
                            ; bit 9: drive_rule - 0x0
                            ; bit 10-15: ref_interval, see UM 0x0f
                            ; bits 16-19: reserved
                            ; bits 20-23: dgs_oe[3:0] (not sure)
                            ;  but I think this is req'd for DDR 0xf
                            ; bits 24-28: Resv'd
```

```
                                  ; bit 29: 1 = soft refresh
                                  ; bit 30 1 = soft_precharge
                                  ; bit 31: reserved


WM32    0x80000104  0xf10f0f02 ;SDRAM Control: precharge all
WM32    0x80000104  0xf10f0f04 ;SDRAM Control: refresh
WM32    0x80000104  0xf10f0f04 ;SDRAM Control: refresh


WM32    0x80000100  0x018d0000  ; SDRAM Mode Samsung
                        ; bits 0-1: MEM_MBA - selects std or extended MODE reg
0x0
                        ; bits 2-13: MEM_MA (see DDR DRAM Data sheet)
                        ; bits 2-7: Operating Mode -> 0x0 = normal
                        ; bits 8-10: CAS Latency (CL) -> Set to CL=2 for DDR
(0x2)
                        ; bit 11: Burst Type: Sequential for PMC5200 -> 0x0
                        ; bits 12-14: Set to 8 for MPC5200 -> 0x3
                        ; bit 15: cmd = 1 for MODE REG WRITE


WM32    0x80000104  0x710f0f00 ;SDRAM Control: Lock Mode Register (was 0x514f0000)

; *********** Initialize the serial port ***********
; Pin Configuration
WM32    0x80000b00   0x00008004  ; UART1


; Reset PSC
WM8     0x80002008   0X10           ; Reset - Select MR1


WM16    0x80002004   0              ; Clock Select Register - 0 enables both Rx &
Tx Clocks
WM32    0x80002040   0              ; SICR - UART Mode
WM8     0x80002000   0x13           ; Write MR1 (default after reset)
                                    ; 8-bit, no parity
WM8     0x80002000   0x07           ; Write MR2 (after MR1) (one stop bit)


WM8     0x80002018   0x0            ; Counter/Timer Upper Reg (115.2KB)
WM8     0x8000201c   0x12           ; Counter/Timer Lower Reg (divider = 18)


; Reset and enable serial port Rx/Tx
WM8     0x80002008   0x20
WM8     0x80002008   0x30
WM8     0x80002008   0x05
```

```
;
; define maximal transfer size
TSZ4     0x80000000  0x80003FFF  ;internal registers
;
; define the valid memory map
MMAP      0x00000000  0x07FFFFFF  ;Memory range for SDRAM
MMAP      0xFF000000  0xFFFFFFFF  ;ROM space
MMAP      0xE00E0000  0xE00EFFFF  ; PowerPC Logic
MMAP      0x80000000  0x8fffffff  ; Default MBAR
MMAP      0xC0000000  0XCFFFFFFF  ; Linux Kernal


[TARGET]
CPUTYPE    5200          ;the CPU type
JTAGCLOCK  0             ;use 16 MHz JTAG clock
WORKSPACE  0x80008000    ;workspace for fast download
WAKEUP     1000          ;give reset time to complete
STARTUP    RESET
MEMDELAY   2000          ;additional memory access delay
BOOTADDR   0xfff00100
REGLIST    ALL
BREAKMODE  SOFT   ; or HARD
POWERUP    1000
WAKEUP     500
MMU        XLAT
PTBASE     0x000000f0


[HOST]
IP         192.168.1.9
FORMAT     ELF
LOAD       MANUAL       ;load code MANUAL or AUTO after reset
PROMPT     uei>


[FLASH]
CHIPTYPE   AM29BX16        ;Flash type (AM29F | AM29BX8 | AM29BX16 | I28BX8
 | I28BX16)
CHIPSIZE   0x00400000    ;The size of one flash chip in bytes
BUSWIDTH   16            ;The width of the flash memory bus in bits (8 | 16 | 32)
WORKSPACE  0x80008000    ;workspace in internal SRAM
FILE       u-boot.bin
FORMAT     BIN 0xFFF00000
ERASE      0xFFF00000    ;erase a sector of flash
ERASE      0xFFF10000    ;erase a sector of flash
```

```
ERASE        0xFFF20000    ;erase a sector of flash
ERASE        0xFFF30000    ;erase a sector of flash
ERASE        0xFFF40000    ;erase a sector of flash

[REGS]
FILE         $reg5200.def
```

Index

Symbol

\ (UNIX line-continuation character), 119

A

"A Non-Technical Look Inside the EXT2 File System" website, 259
Abatron website, 410
access rights, 26
add-symbol-file command, 403
addr2line utility, 361
adduser BusyBox command, 562
adjtimex BusyBox command, 562
Almesberger, Werner, 157
AltiVec, 41
AMCC
    Power Architecture processors, 50-53
    Yosemite board kernel debugging example, 381-382
announcement of Linux, 64
applications, multithreaded, 438-441
ar BusyBox command, 562
architecture
    device drivers, 204
    embedded systems, 12
        init user space process, 19
        kernel, booting, 16-18
        kernel initialization, 18-19
        setup, 13-14
        target boards, starting, 15-16
    setup routine, 114
    specific targets, 193
ARM
    Corporate Backgrounder website, 56
    processors, 55
        additional companies, 59
        Freescale, 58-59
        TI, 56-57
    website, 59

arp BusyBox command, 562
arping BusyBox command, 562
ash BusyBox command, 562
ATCA hardware platforms, 60-61
autoconf.h file, 82-83
automating root file system builds, 137
autotools.bbclass class, 461

B

backtrace command, 330
basename BusyBox command, 562
bbconfig BusyBox command, 562
bbsh BusyBox command, 562
BDI-2000 configuration file sample, 586-592
BeagleBoard, 57, 62, 513
big kernel locks (BKLs), 473
binary tools
    addr2line, 361
    ldd, 362-363
    nm, 363-364
    objcopy, 360-361
    objdump, 359
    prelink, 364
    readelf, 355-359
    resources, 365
    strings, 362
    strip, 361
BIOS, 11
BitBake Hello World recipe processing, 458-459
BitBake (OpenEmbedded), 137, 456
BKLs (big kernel locks), 473
blkid BusyBox command, 562
board-specific initialization, 181-184
boot blocks, 21-22
booting
    from disks, 174
    kernel, 16-18
    KGDB enabled with U-Boot, 373-374

messages, 106-109
troubleshooting, 417-420
"Booting Linux: The History and the Future," 157
bootloaders, 11
    challenges
        DRAM controllers, 161-162
        execution context, 165
        image complexity, 162-165
        storage, 162
    debugging, 441
    GRUB, 195-196
    initial serial output, 15
    initrd support, 148-150
    Lilo, 194-195
    Micromonitor, 197
    Redboot, 197
    roles, 160-161
    selecting, 197
    startup tasks, 11
    U-Boot
        booting from disks, 174
        BOOTP client/server handshakes, 171
        commands, 169-170
        configuring, 167-169
        DHCP target identification, 172-173
        DTBs on boot sequence, 187-188
        Ethernet interface support, 170
        finding, 166
        image formats, 185-186
        porting, 174-185
        reference website, 198
        storage subsystems, 173
        website, 166
bootm command, 17
BOOTP (Bootstrap Protocol), 171
    servers, configuring, 313-316
    U-Boot bootloader support, 171
    website, 198, 323
bootstrap loaders, 105-106
bottom-half processing, 468
brctl BusyBox command, 562
breakpoints
    KGDB, 376
    target memory, 383
Broadcom SiByte processors, 54-55
building
    file systems, 256-257
    JFFS2 images, 240-242
    UBIFS images, 284-287
build numbers, 109
Buildroot, 137, 451
    configuring, 451-452
    installing, 451

output, 452-454
website, 464
build systems
    benefits, 446-447
    Buildroot, 451-454
    kernel
        autoconf.h file, 82-83
        configuration editors, 80-82
        custom configuration options, 91-94
        dot-config file, 78-80
        final sequence example, 101
        Kconfig files, 89-91
        makefiles, 95
        makefile targets, 83-89
    OpenEmbedded, 454-463
    Scratchbox, 447-450
bunzip2 BusyBox command, 562
BusyBox
    applets, 302-303
    commands, listing of, 563-570
    configuring, 291-293
    cross-compiling, 293
    default startup, 298
    description, 295
    launching, 293
    mdev, 545-547
    output example, 294-295
    overview, 290-291
    rcs initialization script, 299-300
    symlinks, 300-302
    system initialization, 297-299
    target directory structure, 295
    toolkit, 135
    website, 304
busybox command, 562
bzcat BusyBox command, 562
bzImage targets, 83
bzip2 BusyBox command, 562

C

C function with local variables listing, 163
cable assemblies (USB), 494
cal BusyBox command, 562
carrier-grade, 6
cat BusyBox command, 562
catv BusyBox command, 562
cbrowser utility, 335-336, 365
CDC (Communications Device Class) drivers, 512-515
cell write lifetimes (Flash memory), 22
CFI (Common Flash Interface), 270

chat BusyBox command, 562
chattr BusyBox command, 562
chcon BusyBox command, 562
checking file system integrity, 233-235
chgrp BusyBox command, 562
chipsets, 41-43
chmod BusyBox command, 562
chown BusyBox command, 562
chpasswd BusyBox command, 562
chpst BusyBox command, 562
chroot BusyBox command, 562
chrt BusyBox command, 563
chvt BusyBox command, 563
cksum BusyBox command, 563
classes (OpenEmbedded metadata), 461-462
clear BusyBox command, 563
clocks, configuring, 574-575
cmp BusyBox command, 563
coldplug processing (udev), 537-538
command-line
    options, 341-342
    partitions, 273-274
    processing, 115-116
        code listing, 119-121
        parameters, 115-116
        setup macro, 116-118
commands. See also utilities
    add-symbol-file, 403
    backtrace, 330
    bootm, 17
    BusyBox, listing of, 563-570
    connect, 393
    continue, 382
    dd, 257
    detach, 443
    e2fsck, 233-235
    GDB user-defined, 392-393
    git, 166
    i shared, 432
    iminfo, 186
    kgdboc, 380
    kgdbwait, 380
    ldd, 139, 362-363, 432-433
    make distclean, 78
    make gconfig, 81
    make menuconfig, 291
    mkcramfs, 242
    mkfs.ext2, 257
    mkfs.jffs2, 241
    modinfo, 539
    modprobe, 532-533
    mount, 232

shutdown, 156
stop-on-solib-events, 432
tftp, 17
ubiformat, 286
U-Boot bootloader supported, 169-170
U-Boot configurable, 558-560
udevadm, 523-524, 543-544
commBusyBox command, 563
commercial distributions, 33
Common Flash Interface (CFI), 270
Common Flash Memory Interface Specification, 288
Communications Device Class (CDC), 512-515
CompactPCI hardware platform, 60
companion chipsets, 41-43
compiling
    DTBs, 192-193
    dtc, 192-193
    kernel, 70-72
    native compilation, 30
components required, 97
composite kernel image
    architecture objects, 104
    boot messages, 106-109
    bootstrap loaders, 105-106
    constructing, 100-102
    final build sequence example, 101
    Image object, 103
    piggy assembly file, 104
configuration descriptors, 491
configuration editors, 80-82
configuring
    board-specific MTD partitions, 276-278
    BOOTP servers, 313-316
    Buildroot, 451-452
    BusyBox, 291-293
    busybox mdev, 547
    clocks, 574-575
    device drivers, 205-208
        ARM system example, 208
        directory, creating, 206
        makefile, editing, 208
        menu items, adding, 206-207
        output, 208
    DHCP servers, 313-316
    DRAM controllers, 161-162
    inittab file, 143-144
    KGDB
        kernel, 371
        runtime, 380-381
    MTD, 263, 267
    NFS kernel support, 247
    NFS servers, 316-318

OpenEmbedded, 462-463
Scratchbox environment, 449
SDRAM controllers, 575-579
   memory bank control register, 578
   timing requirements, 578-579
   U-Boot sdram_init() function, 576-577
TFTP servers, 312-313
UBIFS, 284
U-Boot
   bootloader, 167-169
   build tree, 177-178
   makefile targets, 176-177
udev rules, 533-535
USB, 495-497
   core makefile, 496-497
   Freescale Semiconductor iMX31 Applications
      Processor example, 496
   volume of options, 495
connect command, 393
connections
Ethernet, 512-515
KGDB, 374-375
connectors (USB), 492-493
contexts (execution), 26
continue command, 382
controllers (SDRAM), configuring, 575-579
core dumps, debugging, 327-329
cp BusyBox command, 563
cpio BusyBox command, 563
cpp search directories, 309
cramfs file system, 242-244
cramfs project README file website, 259
crond BusyBox command, 563
crontab BusyBox command, 563
cross-compiling
BusyBox, 293
targets, 448-450
cross debugging, 424
cross-development environments, 30-31
default cross-search directories, 310
flexibility, 307
Hello World program, 307-309
hosts, 306
layout, 307
overview, 306
targets, 306
cross-strip utility, 426-427
cross tools, distributions, 33
cryptpw BusyBox command, 563
cttyhack BusyBox command, 563
customizing
initramfs, 154-155
udev, 540

D

Das U-Boot. *See* U-Boot bootloader
dateBusyBox command, 563
dc BusyBox command, 563
dd BusyBox command, 563
dd command, 257
DDD (Data Display Debugger), 333-335
debug session, 335
invoking, 334
resources, 365
deallocvt BusyBox command, 563
debugging
booting, 417
   early serial debug output, 417
   KGDB trapping crashes on panic, 420
   printk log buffer, dumping, 417-419
bootloaders, 441
cbrowser, 335-336, 365
core dumps, 327-329
cross, 424
DDD, 333-335, 365
dmalloc, 365
Flash code, 441
GDB, 326
   backtrace command, 330
   core dumps, 327-329
   debug sessions, 331-333
   invoking, 329-331
   resources, 365
   sessions, 331-333
   stack frames, 330
   website, 422
hardware-assisted. *See* JTAG probes
with JTAG probes, 413-417
kernel. *See* kernel debugging
multiple processes, 435-438
multithreaded applications, 438-441
real time kernel patch, 473-475
   features, 475-476
   O(1) scheduler, 476
   preemption modes, 474-475
   real-time processes, creating, 477
remote. *See* remote debugging
shared libraries, 429
   events, 431-434
   finding, 433
   initial target memory segment mapping, 430-431
   invoking ldd command, 432-433
   locations, 433
   </proc/pid>/maps memory segments, 434
   requirements, 430
   viewing, 432

target, 424
USB, 516-518
   device driver support, 518
   Ethernet dongle insertion debug output
     example, 516
   platform-specific options, 517
   usbmon utility, 517-518
delgroup BusyBox command, 563
deluser BusyBox command, 563
Denx, Wolfgang, 166
depmod BusyBox command, 563
depmod utility, 214-215
"Design and Implementation of the Second
  Extended Filesystem" website, 259
detach command, 443
/dev directory, 522
development
  cross-development environments. *See*
    cross-development environments
  hosts
    BOOTP/DHCP servers, configuring, 313-316
    NFS servers, configuring, 316-318
    requirements, 311-312
    target NFS root mount, 318-321
    TFTP servers, configuring, 312-313
  setup, 13-14
device drivers
  architecture, 204
  build configuration, 205-208
  debugging, 402-406
    init code, 406-407
    initializing, 403-404
    loopback breakpoints, 405
    sessions, initiating, 404-405
    symbolic debug information, accessing, 402
  dependencies, 214-215
  dynamic, 80
  ext3 and jbd relationship, 213-214
  GPL, 224
  information, viewing, 216
  installing, 209-210
  listing of, viewing, 213
  loading/unloading, 203, 210, 528
  methods
    device nodes, 220-221
    file system operations, 217-220
    numbers, allocating, 220
  minimal example, 204-205
  out-of-tree, 223-224
  parameters, 211-212
  platform, loading, 538-539
  removing from kernels, 215-216

resources, 226
running kernels, adding, 212
USB support, debugging, 518
user space application example, 222-223
utilities
  depmod, 214-215
  insmod, 212
  lsmod, 213
  modinfo, 216
  modprobe, 213-214
  rmmod, 215-216
devices
  descriptors, 490
  discovery, 523-524
  loopback, 256
  nodes, 220-221, 522
  persistent naming, 541-545
  trees
    blobs. See DTBs
    compiler, 192-193
    loading, 17
    source, 189-192
    website, 199
devmem BusyBox command, 563
df BusyBox command, 563
DHCP (Dynamic Host Configuration
  Protocol), 171
  servers, configuring, 313-316
  U-Boot bootloader support, 172-173
  website, 198
dhcprelay BusyBox command, 563
diff BusyBox command, 563
directories
  /dev, 522
  root file systems, 134
  runlevels, 142
  top-level kernel source, 69
dirname BusyBox command, 563
disassembled object code, viewing, 359
discovering devices, 523-524
distributions
  commercial, 33
  components, 97
  cross tools, 33
  defined, 32
  do-it-yourself, 33-34
  file sizes, 239
  installing, 33
  packages, 32
  targets, 33
dmalloc utility, 350-353
  libraries, generating, 350
  log output example, 351-352

requirements, 350
resources, 365
dmesg BusyBox command, 563
dnsd BusyBox command, 563
do-it-yourself distributions, 33-34
dongles, 515
dos2unix BusyBox command, 563
dot-config file, 78
  code snippet listing, 79-80
  customizations, 93-94
  deleting, 78
  hidden, 78
downloading kernel, 68
dpkg BusyBox command, 563
dpkg-deb BusyBox command, 563
DRAM (Dynamic Random Access Memory),
  161-162, 198
drivers
  device. *See* device drivers
  Flash chips, 276
  g_ether, 513
  KGDB I/O, 379-380
  mapping, 274-276
  platform device, loading, 538-539
  sd-mod, adding, 509
  USB
    CDC, 512-515
    HID class support, 511
    host controller, installing, 498
  usb_storage, 508
DTBs (device tree blobs), 187
  architecture-specific targets, 193
  boot sequence role, 187-188
  compiling, 192-193
  device tree source, 189-192
dtc (device tree compiler), 192-193
DTS (device tree source), 189-192
du BusyBox command, 563
dumpkmap BusyBox command, 563
dumpleases BusyBox command, 563
dynamically loadable modules, 80
Dynamic Host Configuration Protocol. *See* DHCP
Dynamic Random Access Memory (DRAM),
  161-162, 198

E

e2fsck BusyBox command, 563
e2fsck command, 233-235
echo BusyBox command, 563
Eclipse Project website, 365
ed BusyBox command, 563

EHCI (Enhanced Host Controller Interface),
  498, 519
ELF files, 356-359
embedded systems
  architecture, 12
    init user space process, 19
    kernel, booting, 16-18
    kernel initialization, 18-19
    setup, 13-14
    target boards, starting, 15-16
  characteristics, 10-11
endpoints, 489-491
Enhanced Host Controller Interface (EHCI),
  498, 519
env BusyBox command, 563
envdir BusyBox command, 563
envuidgid BusyBox command, 564
EP405 U-Boot port, 175-176
erase blocks, 21
Ethernet
  connectivity (USB), 512-515
  interfaces, 170
ether-wake BusyBox command, 564
events
  locations, 433
  shared library, 431-434
exbibytes, 237
execution contexts, 26
expand BusyBox command, 564
expr BusyBox command, 564
ext2 file systems, 257
ext3 file systems, 235-237
ext4 file systems, 237
external bus controller initialization listing, 181-182

F

fakeidentd BusyBox command, 564
FALSE BusyBox command, 564
fbset BusyBox command, 564
fbsplash BusyBox command, 564
fdflush BusyBox command, 564
fdformat BusyBox command, 564
fdisk BusyBox command, 564
fdisk utility, 229-230
fgrep BusyBox command, 564
FHS (File System Hierarchy Standard), 133, 226
File System Hierarchy Standard (FHS), 133, 226
"File System Performance: The Solaris OS, UFS,
  Linux ext3, and Reiser FS" website, 259

files
    autoconf.h, 82-83
    BDI-2000 configuration, 586-592
    device trees, loading, 17
    dot-config file, 78
        code snippet listing, 79-80
        customizations, 93-94
        deleting, 78
        hidden, 78
    ELF, 356-359
    GDB initialization, 393
    GRUB configuration, 196
    inittab, configuring, 143-144
    Kconfig, 89-92
    kernel-parameters.txt, 115
    linuxrc, 150-151
    main.c, 113-114
    makefiles
        targets, 83-89
        U-Boot configuration target, 176-177
        uImage target wrapper script, 185
        USB core, 496-497
        Vega and Constellation example, 95
    object
        formats, converting, 360
        symbols, viewing, 363-364
    piggy assembly, 104
    size distribution, 239
    system.map, 70
    systems
        building, 256-257
        cramfs, 242-244
        ext2, 257
        ext3, 235-237
        ext4, 237
        Flash, 24
        integrity, checking, 233-235
        JFFS2. See JFFS2
        journaling, 235
        mounting, 232-233
        NFS, 244-248
        partition relationship, 229
        pseudo. See /proc file system; sysfs file system
        ramfs, 255-256
        ReiserFS, 238
        resources, 259
        root. See root file systems
        sysfs, 252-255, 500-502
        tmpfs, 256
        UBI, 284
        UBIFS, 284-287, 500-502
        USBFS, 502-504
    ubinize configuration, 285

    versions, 109
    vmlinux, 70-72
        image components, 73-76
        listing, 72-73
find_next_task macro, 400
find_task macro, 394-395
findfs BusyBox command, 564
finding
    kernels, 96
    shared libraries, 433
    U-Boot bootloader, 166
Flash, 24
    chip drivers, 276
    code, debugging, 441
    device listing, 232
    memory. *See* memory, Flash
flash_erase utility, 280
flashcp utility, 280
flashing, 280
flat device tree websites
    references, 199
    syntax, 192
flow of control, 109-111
    architecture setup, 114
    head.o module, 111-113
    startup file, 113-114
fold BusyBox command, 564
fork() function, 435-437
founder of Linux, 6
free BusyBox command, 564
freedom versus free, 4-5
freeramdisk BusyBox command, 564
Freescale processors
    ARM, 58-59
    MPC7448, 40-41
    Power Architecture, 44-48
        PowerQUICC I, 45-46
        PowerQUICC II, 46-47
        PowerQUICC II Pro, 47
        PowerQUICC III, 48
    QorIQ, 48-50
    Semiconductor iMX31 Applications Processor
        USB example, 496
        bus topology, 507
        configuration options, 496
        device node, creating, 510
        host controller drivers, installing, 498
        partition, mounting, 510
        sysfs file system output, 500-502
        usbview output, 504-507
        website, 62
free versus freedom, 4-5
fsck BusyBox command, 564

fsck.minix BusyBox command, 564
ftpget BusyBox command, 564
ftpput BusyBox command, 564
Ftrace utility
　　interrupt off timing measurements, 484
　　kernel performance analysis, 478-479
　　preemption off measurements, 479-481
　　wakeup latency measurements, 481-483
functions. *See also* methods
　　fork(), 435-437
　　gethostbyname(), 432
　　prepare_namespace, 151
　　pthread_create(), 438
　　sdram_init(), 576-577
　　setup_arch(), 114
　　start_kernel(), 114
fuser BusyBox command, 564

G

g_ether driver example, 513
Garzik, Jeff's git utility website, 68
GCC website, 323
GDB (GNU Debugger), 326. *See also* KGDB
　　backtrace command, 330
　　bootloaders, 441
　　core dumps, 327-329
　　cross debugging, 424
　　debug sessions, 331-333
　　detach command, 443
　　Flash code, 441
　　invoking, 329-331
　　multiple processes, 435-438
　　multithreaded applications, 438-441
　　remote debugging
　　　　file stripping, 426-427
　　　　gdbserver utility, 427-429
　　　　sample program ELF file debug information,
　　　　　　425-426
　　remote serial protocol, 382-385
　　resources, 365, 444
　　shared libraries, 429
　　　　events, 431-434
　　　　finding, 433
　　　　initial target memory segement mapping,
　　　　　　430-431
　　　　invoking ldd command, 432-433
　　　　locations, 433
　　　　</proc/pid>/maps memory segments, 434
　　　　requirements, 430
　　　　viewing, 432
　　stack frames, 330
　　website, 444

gdbserver utility, 427-429
General Public License. *See* GNU, GPL
getenforce BusyBox command, 564
gethostbyname() function, 432
getsebool BusyBox command, 564
getty BusyBox command, 564
git command
　　kernel downloads, 68
　　U-Boot bootloader, 166
GNU
　　Compiler Collection documentation website, 130
　　Debugger. *See* GDB
　　GPL (General Public License), 3-4, 550
　　　　device drivers, 224
　　　　exact reproduction, 550-556
　　　　website, 550
　　linker website, 130, 198
　　Press website, 422
grep BusyBox command, 564
growth of embedded Linux, 2
GRUB (Grand Unified Bootloader), 195-196, 199
gunzip BusyBox command, 564
gzip applet, 302
gzip BusyBox command, 564

H

halt BusyBox command, 564
hard real time, 467
hardware-assisted debugging, 312
hardware-debug probe. *See* JTAG probes
hardware platforms, 60-61
hd BusyBox command, 564
hdparm BusyBox command, 564
head BusyBox command, 564
head.o module, 111-113
Hello World program, 28-29
　　cross-development environments, 307-310
　　　　cpp search directories, 309
　　　　default cross-search directories, 310
　　　　listing, 307-308
　　OpenEmbedded version, 457-459
　　Scratchbox example, 449
hexdump BusyBox command, 564
HID (Human Input Device), 511-512
hosted BusyBox command, 564
hostname BusyBox command, 564
hosts
　　controllers, 489
　　cross-development environments, 306
　　mode (USB), 494

requirements, 311-312
target boards
    BOOTP/DHCP servers, configuring, 313-316
    NFS root mount, 318-321
    NFS servers, configuring, 316-318
    TFTP servers, configuring, 312-313
httpd BusyBox command, 564
hush BusyBox command, 564

I

i shared command, 432
IBM 970FX processor, 39
id BusyBox command, 564
ifconfig BusyBox command, 565
ifdown BusyBox command, 565
ifenslave BusyBox command, 565
ifup BusyBox command, 565
images, 103
    bootloader complexities, 162-165
    composite kernel
        architecture objects, 104
        boot messages, 106-109
        bootstrap loaders, 105-106
        constructing, 100-102
        final build sequence example, 101
        Image object, 103
        piggy assembly file, 104
    initrd, 148
        creating, 152-153
        decompressing, 151
    JFFS2, building, 240-242
    OpenEmbedded recipes, 463
    U-Boot bootloader format, 185-186
    UBIFS, building, 284-287
    vmlinux file, 73-76
iminfo command, 186
inetd BusyBox command, 565
init BusyBox command, 565
initcall_debug parameter, 127
initcall macros, 122-126
initialization
    board-specific, 181-184
    details, viewing, 127
    flow of control, 109-111
        architecture setup, 114
        head.o module, 111-113
        startup file, 113-114
    inittab file, 143-144
    kernel, 18-19
        creating, 125-126
        details, viewing, 127

    final boot steps, 127-129
    flow of control, 109-114
    initcall macros, 126
    user space process, 19
    library dependencies, resolving, 139
    processors, 178-180
    runlevels, 141-142
    startup scripts, 144-145
    subsystems, 122-124
    System V Init. *See* System V Init
    udev setup, 535
        coldplug processing, 537-538
        default static device nodes, 536
        startup script, 535-536
    USB, 499-500
        host controllers, 498-499
        usbcore module, loading, 497
    user space process, 19
    user-specified, 140
    web server startup script example, 145-146
initramfs, 153
    customizing, 154-155
    file specification, 154
    initrd, compared, 153
    kernel build directory contents, 153
initrd root file system, 146
    booting, 147-148
    bootloader support, 148-150
    images, 148
        creating, 152-153
        decompressing, 151
    initramfs, compared, 153
    linuxrc file, 150-151
    mounting, 151
inittab file, configuring, 143-144
inodes, 231
inotifyd BusyBox command, 565
insmod BusyBox command, 565
insmod utility, 212
install BusyBox command, 565
installing
    Buildroot, 451
    device drivers, 209-210
    distributions, 33
    Scratchbox, 447-448
integrated SOC processors, 43
    AMCC Power Architecture, 50-53
    ARM, 55-59
    Broadcom SiByte, 54-55
    Freescale. *See* Freescale processors
    MIPS, 53-55
    Power Architecture, 44

Intel processors
Atom, 40, 62
Pentium M, 39-40
XScale website, 62
interfaces
descriptors, 491
Ethernet, 170
interrupt context, 28
interrupt off timing measurements, 483-484
interrupt service routine (ISR), 467
invoking
configuration editors, 81
DDD, 334
GDB, 329-331
ps macro, 395-396
ioctl() method, 217-219
ipaddr BusyBox command, 565
ip BusyBox command, 565
ipcalc BusyBox command, 565
ipcrm BusyBox command, 565
ipcs BusyBox command, 565
iplink BusyBox command, 565
iproute BusyBox command, 565
iprule BusyBox command, 565
iptunnel BusyBox command, 565
ISR (interrupt service routine), 467

J

JFFS: The Journaling Flash File System website, 259
JFFS2 (Journaling Flash File System 2), 24, 239-240
directory layout, 241
Flash memory limitations, 239-240
images, building, 240-242
mkfs.jffs2 command, 241
mounting on MTD RAM drive, 265-266
journaling, 235
JTAG (Joint Test Action Group) probes, 410
debugging, 413-417
Flash, programming, 411-413
setting up, 411

K

kbd_mode BusyBox command, 565
Kbuild documentation website, 98
Kconfig files, 89-92
kernel
booting, 16-18
build system
autoconf.h file, 82-83
configuration editors, 80-82

custom configuration options, 91-94
dot-config file, 78-80
final sequence example, 101
Kconfig files, 89-91
makefiles, 95
makefile targets, 83-89
command-line processing, 115-116
code listing, 119-121
parameters, 115-116
setup macro, 116-118
compiling, 70-72
composite image
architecture objects, 104
boot messages, 106-109
bootstrap loaders, 105-106
constructing, 100-102
final build sequence example, 101
Image object, 103
piggy assembly file, 104
context, 19, 26
debugging. See kernel debugging
documentation, 96
downloading with git utility, 68
final boot
messages, 18
steps, 137-138
finding, 96
GDB. See KGDB
HOWTO website, 98
initialization, 18-19, 125
creating, 125-126
details, viewing, 127
final boot steps, 127-129
flow of control, 109-114
initcall macros, 126
user space process, 19
KGDB configuration, 371
NFS configuration, 247
oops, 353-355
parameters.txt file, 115
preemption, 469
challenges, 469-471
checking for, 471-472
concurrency errors, 470
critical sections, locking, 470
latency sources, 473
models, 471-472
off measurements, 479-481
real time patch modes, 474-475
SMP, 472
real time patch, 473-475
features, 475-476
O(1) scheduler, 476

preemption modes, 474-475
real-time processes, creating, 477
real time performance analysis, 478
   Ftrace, 478-479
   interrupt off timing measurements, 483-484
   preemption off measurements, 479-481
   soft lockup detection, 484
   wakeup latency measurements, 481-483
source repositories, 65-68
subdirectory, 77-78
subsystem initialization, 122-124
top-level source directory, 69
versions, 66-67
vmlinux file, 72-76
website, 65
kernel debugging, 368-369
   JTAG probes, 410
      debugging, 413-417
      Flash memory, programming, 411-413
      setting up, 411
   KGDB, 369
      booting with U-Boot, 373-374
      breakpoints, 376
      connections, 374-375
      console serial port, sharing, 377-379
      debug session in progress, 377
      early kernel code support, 379-380
      enabling, 372
      kernel configuration, 371
      loadable modules, 402-406
      logic, 372
      macros, 393-402
      optimized code, 385-392
      platform-specific code, 381-382
      remote, 382-385
      runtime configuration, 380-381
      serial ports, 372
      setting up, 370
      trapping crashes on panic, 420
      user-defined commands, 392-393
      websites, 422
   Magic SysReq key, 409-410
   optimized kernel code, 389
   printk, 407-409
   resources, 422
KERNELRELEASE macro, 67
KGDB (Kernel GDB), 369
   booting with U-Boot, 373-374
   breakpoints, 376
   connections, 374-375
   console serial port, sharing, 377-379
   debug session in progress, 377

early kernel code support, 379-380
enabling, 372
I/O drivers, 379-380
kernel configuration, 371
loadable modules, 402-406
   init code, 406-407
   initializing, 403-404
   loopback breakpoints, 405
   sessions, initiating, 404-405
   symbolic debug information, accessing, 402
logic, 372
macros, 393-402
   find_next_task, 400
   find_task, 394-395
   ps, 395-397
   task_struct_show, 398-399
optimized code, 385-392
platform-specific code, debugging, 381-382
remote serial protocol, 382-385
runtime configuration, 380-381
serial ports, 372
setting up, 370
trapping crashes on panic, 420
user-defined commands, 392-393
websites, 422
kgdb8250 I/O driver, 379-380
kgdboc command, 380
kgdbwait command, 380
kill BusyBox command, 565
killall BusyBox command, 565
killall5 BusyBox command, 565
klogd BusyBox command, 565
Kroah-Hartman, Greg, 504
ksoftirqd task, promoting, 476

L

lash BusyBox command, 565
last BusyBox command, 565
latency
   interrupt off timing, 483-484
   kernel preemption sources, 473
   preemption off measurements, 479-481
   real time, 467-468
   wakeup measurements, 481-483
layout
   cross-development environments, 307
   root file systems, 133-134
ldd command, 139, 362-363, 432-433
Lehrbaum, Rick, 3
length BusyBox command, 565
lessBusyBox command, 565

Library Optimizer Tool website, 136
Lilo
    bootloader, 194-195
    website, 199
linker command scripts, 163
linux32BusyBox command, 565
Linux
    Allocated Devices website, 548
    Documentation Project, 96, 157
    Foundation, 6-8
    news and developments resources, 583
    Standard Base, 5, 8
LinuxDevices.com, 3
linuxrc file, 150-151
listings
    architecture-specific targets, 193
    autoconf.h file, 82-83
    backtrace command, 330
    BDI-2000 configuration file, 586-592
    booting with DTBs, 187-188
    bootloaders, initial serial output, 15
    boot messages on IPX425, 106-108
    Buildroot output directory, 453
    BusyBox
        build options, 291
        default startup, 298
        gzip applet, 302
        library dependencies, 292
        mdev startup script, 546
        output, 294-295
        rcs initialization script, 299-300
        root file system example, 297
        root file system installation, 301
        target directory structure, 295
    C function with local variables, 163
    command-line MTD partitions, 273
    cramfs file system, 242-243
    device drivers
        build configuration, 206-208
        file system operations methods, 217-219
        loading/unloading, 210
        lsmod output, 213
        minimal example, 204
        modinfo output, 216
        modprobe configuration file, 214
        parameter example, 211
        user space application, 222-223
    DHCP
        exchange, 314
        server configuration, 315
        target identification, 172
    dmalloc utility, 351-352

dot-config file, 79-80
DTBs, 189-192
ext2 file system, 257
ext3 file system, 236
file system check, 233-234
find_next_task, 400
find_task macro, 394
Flash device, 232
fork(), 435-437
GDB
    core dump analysis, 328
    debug sessions, initiating, 332
    initialization file, 393
    stack frames, 330
gdbserver utility
    invoking, 429
    starting on target board, 427
    target board connection, 427-428
GRUB configuration file, 196
Hello World, 28-29, 307-308
    cpp search directories, 309
    default cross-search directories, 310
init process, 125-126
initcall macros, 123-124
initramfs
    build directory, 153
    file specification, 154
    minimal contents, 155
initrd
    boot sequence, 148-150
    images, creating, 152
inittab file, 143
JFFS2
    booting as root file system, 283
    copying to root partition, 282
    directory layout, 241
    mkfs.jffs2 command, 241
JTAG, 412-414
Kconfig file for ARM architecture, 90
kernel
    booting, 16-17
    build output, 70-72
    command-line processing, 119-121
    .config file customizations, 93-94
    final boot messages, 18
    final boot steps, 127-129
    final build sequence example, 101
    IXP4xx-specific Kconfig file, 92
    loading with TFTP servers, 320
    makefiles example, 95
    oops, 353
    preemption, 470-472

subdirectory, 77-78
top-level ARM Kconfig file, 92
vmlinux file, 72-73
KGDB
  booting with U-Boot, 373-374
  breakpoints, 376
  connecting, 374-375
  console serial port, sharing, 378-379
  debug session in progress, 377
  runtime configuration, 380-381
  trapping crashes on panic, 420
Lilo bootloader, 194
linker command script, 163
linuxrc file, 150-151
loadable modules
  debug sessions, initiating, 404-405
  debugging init code, 406-407
  initializing, 403-404
ltrace utility, 343
makefiles
  targets, 83-89
  U-Boot configuration, 176
minimal root file system, 134-135
mstrace utility, 349
MTD
  configuring, 263
  JFFS2file system, mounting, 265-266
MTD partitions
  board-specific configuration, 276-278
  Flash partition mounting, 280
  kernel partition list, 279
  PQ2FADS Flash mapping driver, 274-276
mtrace utility, 348
multithreaded applications, debugging, 438-439
NFS
  exports configuration file, 244, 317
  root mount, booting, 320
  target example, 246
nm utility output, 363
objdump utility, 359
OpenEmbedded
  autotools.bbclass example, 461
  BitBake Hello recipe processing, 458-459
  recipe example, 457
  tasks, 460
optimized kernel code, debugging
  code, 385-386
  disassemble command, 387-389
  local variable output example, 391
  source file, 389-390
partitions
  formatting, 230-231
  information, viewing, 229-230

piggy assembly file, 104
platform-specific kernel debugging, 381-382
preemption off measurements, 480
printk log buffer, dumping, 418-419
/proc file system, 249-251
processes, listing, 345
ps macro, 395-397
ramfs file systems, 255
readelf utility, 356-358
real time, 476-477
Redboot partitions
  creating, 272
  detecting, 270
  Flash partition listing, 269
  Flash partitions, 271
  new partition list, 272
  power-up messages, 269
remote debugging
  continue command, 382
  ELF file debug information, 425-426
  file stripping, 426-427
  target memory breakpoints, 384
resetvec source definition, 164
runlevels, 141-142
Scratchbox, 448-449
SDRAM controllers, configuring, 576-577
setup macro, 117-118
shared libraries
  debugging, 430-431
  event alerts, 431
  invoking ldd command, 432-433
  </proc/pid>/maps memory segments, 434
startup scripts, 144-145
strace utility
  profiling, 341
  web demo application example, 337-340
subsystem initialization, 122
sysfs file system, 252-255
task_struct_show, 398-399
TFTP configuration, 313
top utility default configuration, 347
UBIFS images, building, 284-286
U-Boot bootloader
  4xx startup code, 179
  build tree, configuring, 177
  configuration header file, 168-169
  EP405 port summary, 184
  external bus controller, 181-182
  iminfo command, 186
  uImage target wrapper script, 185
udev
  default static device nodes, 536
  device discovery, 523-524

device nodes, creating, 525-526
mouse device example, 529
persistent device naming, 541
platform device driver, loading, 538
rules configuration, 533-535
rules example, 528
startup script, 535-536
udevadm device query, 543-544
uevents emitted on USB mouse insertion,
  530-531
uevents for USB interface 1-1:1.0, 531
uevents on four-port hub insertion, 525
USB automounting, 540-541
USB
  core makefile, 496-497
  device node, creating, 510
  direct host and peripheral links, 513
  Ethernet dongle insertion debug output, 516
  host controllers, 498-499
  lsusb utility, 507
  partition, mounting, 510
  sd-mod driver, adding, 509
  sysfs file system output, 500-502
  usb-storage module, 509
  USBFS directory listing, 502
  usbmon utility, 517
  usbview utility output, 504-507
wakeup latency measurements, 481-483
web server startup script, 145-146
load_policy BusyBox command, 565
loadable modules. *See* **device drivers**
loading
  device drivers, 210, 528
  platform device drivers, 538-539
loadkmap BusyBox command, 565
logger BusyBox command, 565
login BusyBox command, 565
logname BusyBox command, 565
logread BusyBox command, 565
loopback devices, 256
losetup BusyBox command, 565
lpd BusyBox command, 565
lpq BusyBox command, 565
lpr BusyBox command, 566
lsattr BusyBox command, 566
LSB (Linux Standard Base), 5, 8
ls BusyBox command, 566
lsmod BusyBox command, 566
lsmod utility, 213
lsusb utility, 507-508
ltrace utility, 343-344
lzmacat BusyBox command, 566

M

macros
  initcall, 122-126
  KERNELRELEASE, 67
  KGDB, 393-402
    find_next_task, 400
    find_task, 394-395
    ps, 395-397
    task_struct_show, 398-399
  setup
    command-line processing, 116-121
    console setup code snippet, 117
    family definitions, 118
  used, 119
Magic SysReq key, 409-410
mailing list resources, 582
main.c file, 113-114
make distclean command, 78
make gconfig command, 81
make menuconfig command, 291
makedevs BusyBox command, 566
makefiles
  targets, 83-89
  U-Boot configuration target, 176-177
  uImage target wrapper script, 185
  USB core, 496-497
  Vega and Constellation example, 95
makemine BusyBox command, 566
man BusyBox command, 566
mapping drivers, 274-276
marketplace momentum, 3
mass storage class (USB), 508-511
  device node, creating, 510
  mounting, 510
  partition, mounting, 510
  SCSI support, 508
  sd-mod driver, adding, 509
  usb_storage driver, 508
  usb-storage module, 509
matchpathcon BusyBox command, 566
md5sum BusyBox command, 566
mdev BusyBox command, 566
memory
  analysis tool. *See* dmalloc utility
  cross-development environments, 30-31
  DRAM, 161-162, 198
  execution contexts, 26
  Flash, 20-22
    boot blocks, 21-22
    cell write lifetimes, 22
    erasing, 239

file systems, 24
lifetime, 240
NAND, 22-23
programming, 411-413
typical layouts, 23
writing to/erasing, 20-21
layout, 25-26
leaks, detecting, 349
MMUs, 26
process virtual, 28-30
translation, 26
virtual, 26-30
Memory Management Units (MMUs), 26
Memory Technology Devices (MTD), 262
mesg BusyBox command, 566
methods. *See also* functions
   device drivers
      device nodes, 220-221
      file system operations, 217-220
      numbers, allocating, 220
   ioctl(), 217-219
   open(), 217-219
   release(), 217-219
microcom BusyBox command, 566
Micromonitor bootloader, 197
mini connectors, 493
minimal device driver example, 204-205
minimal root file systems, 134-136
MIPS processors, 53-55, 67
mkcramfs command, 242
mkdir BusyBox command, 566
mke2fs BusyBox command, 566
mkfifo BusyBox command, 566
mkfs.ext2 utility, 230-231, 257
mkfs.jffs2 command, 241
mkfs.minix BusyBox command, 566
mkimage utility, 185
mknod BusyBox command, 566
mkswap BusyBox command, 566
mktemp BusyBox command, 566
MMUs (Memory Management Units), 26
Moblin (Mobile Linux Initiative), 7
MODALIAS field, 532-533
modinfo utility, 216, 539
modprobe BusyBox command, 566
modprobe utility, 213-214, 532-533
more BusyBox command, 566
mount BusyBox command, 566
mount command, 232
mounting
   dependencies, 249
   file systems, 232-233

initrd, 151
root file systems, 18
USB, 510-540-541
USBFS, 502
mountpoint BusyBox command, 566
mount points, 151, 232
mouse device udev example, 529
msh BusyBox command, 566
MTD (Memory Technology Device), 262
   CFI support, 270
   configuring, 263-267
   JFFS2 file systems, mounting, 265-266
   overview, 262-263
   partitions, 267-268
      board-specific configuration, 276-278
      command-line, 273-274
      configuring, 267
      Flash chips, 276
      kernel partition list, 279
      mapping drivers, 274-276
      Redboot, 269-273
   resources, 288
   services, enabling, 263-265
   utilities, 279-283
      flash_erase, 280
      flashcp, 280
      JFFS2, 282-283
      kernel MTD partition list, 279
      MTD Flash partition, mounting, 280
mtrace utility, 348-349
multiple processes, debugging, 435-438
multithreaded applications, debugging, 438-441
mv BusyBox command, 566

N

nameif BusyBox command, 566
NAND Flash, 22-23
native compilation, 30
nc BusyBox command, 566
netstat BusyBox command, 566
NFS (Network File System), 244-246
   configuration file, 244
   kernel configuration, 247
   mounting workspace on target embedded system, 245-246
   restarting, 141-142
   root file system, 246-248
   servers, configuring, 316-318
   targets
      example, 246
      root mount, 318-321
   website, 259

nice BusyBox command, 566
nm utility, 363-364
nmeter BusyBox command, 566
nohup BusyBox command, 566
northbridge chips, 42
nslookup BusyBox command, 566

O

objcopy utility, 360-361
objdump utility, 359
objects
    disassembled code, viewing, 359
    formats, converting, 360
    Image. *See* images
    piggy, 104
    symbols, viewing, 363-364
od BusyBox command, 566
On-The-Go (OTG) USB, 495
open() method, 217-219
open source legal insight website, 583
OpenEmbedded, 454
    benefits, 454
    BitBake, 456
    configuring, 462-463
    image recipes, 463
    metadata, 456
        classes, 461-462
        recipes, 456-459
        tasks, 460
    website, 137, 454, 464
openvt BusyBox command, 566
optimized kernel code, debugging, 385-392
    code example, 385-386
    disassemble command, 387-389
    local variable output example, 391
    source file, 389-390
options. *See* parameters
OTG (On-The-Go) USB, 495
out-of-tree drivers, 223-224

P

packages, 32
parameters
    command-line, 115-116
    device drivers, 211-212
    initcall_debug, 127
    rdinit=, 155
parse BusyBox command, 566
partitions, 229
    file system relationship, 229
    formatting, 230-231

information, viewing, 229-230
    MTD. *See* MTD, partitions
passwd BusyBox command, 566
patch BusyBox command, 567
performance, real time analysis, 478
    Ftrace, 478-479
    interrupt off timing measurements, 483-484
    preemption off measurements, 479-481
    soft lockup detection, 484
    wakeup latency measurements, 481-483
persistent device naming, 541-542
pgrep BusyBox command, 567
pidof BusyBox command, 567
PIDs (process IDs), 250
piggy assembly file, 104
ping BusyBox command, 567
ping6 BusyBox command, 567
pipe_progress BusyBox command, 567
pkill BusyBox command, 567
platforms (hardware), 60-61
    device drivers, loading, 538-539
    specific kernel debugging, 381-382
popmaildir BusyBox command, 567
populating root file systems, 137
porting U-Boot bootloaders, 174
    board-specific initialization, 181-184
    build tree, configuring, 177-178
    EP405 board, 175-176
    makefile configuration targets, 176-177
    processor initialization, 178-180
    summary, 184-185
Power Architecture processors, 44, 62
Power.org website, 62
poweroff BusyBox command, 567
PowerPC 64-bit architecture reference manual
    website, 62
PowerQUICC processors, 44
    PowerQUICC I processor, 45-46
    PowerQUICC II processor, 46-47
    PowerQUICC II Pro processor, 47
    PowerQUICC III processor, 48
PQ2FADS Flash mapping driver, 274-276
preemption. *See* kernel, preemption
prelink utility, 364
prepare_namespace() function, 151
printenv BusyBox command, 567
printf BusyBox command, 567
printk debugging, 407-409
printk log buffers, dumping, 417-419
/proc file system, 249-252
    common entries, 252
    debugging with maps entry, 251

mount dependency, 249
original purpose, 249
process IDs, 250
virtual memory addresses, 251
website, 259
process IDs (PIDs), 250
processes
bottom-half processing, 468
context, 28
init. *See* initialization
listing, 345
multiple, debugging, 435-438
real-time, creating, 477
user space. *See* user space, processes
virtual memory, 28-30
processors
initializing, 178-180
integrated SOCs, 43
additional ARM, 59
AMCC Power Architecture, 50-53
ARM, 55
Broadcom SiByte, 54-55
Freescale ARM, 58-59
Freescale Power Architecture, 44-45
Freescale PowerQUICC, 45-48
Freescale QorIQ, 48-50
MIPS, 53-55
TI ARM, 56-57
stand-alone
companion chipsets, 41-43
Freescale MPC7448, 40-41
IBM 970FX, 39
Intel Atom M, 40
Intel Pentium M, 39-40
overview, 38
program dependencies, 32
protocols
BOOTP
servers, configuring, 313-316
U-Boot bootloader support, 171
website, 198
DHCP
servers, configuring, 313-316
U-Boot bootloader support, 172-173
website, 198
gdb remote serial protocol, 382-385
TFTP
servers, configuring, 312-313
website, 198
ps BusyBox command, 567
ps macro, 344-346
invoking, 395-396
output, 396-397

pscan BusyBox command, 567
pseudo file systems. *See* /proc file system;
sysfs file system
pthread_create() function, 438
pwd BusyBox command, 567

Q – R

QorIQ processors, 45-50

raidautorun BusyBox command, 567
ramfs file system, 255-256
rcs initialization scripts, 299-300
rdate BusyBox command, 567
rdev BusyBox command, 567
rdinit= parameter, 155
readahead BusyBox command, 567
readelf utility, 355-357
ELF file debug information, 357-359
section headers, 356
readlink BusyBox command, 567
readprofile BusyBox command, 567
real time
hard, 467
kernel patch, 473-475
features, 475-476
O(1) scheduler, 476
preemption modes, 474-475
real-time processes, creating, 477
kernel performance analysis, 478
Ftrace, 478-479
interrupt off timing measurements, 483-484
preemption off measurements, 479-481
soft lockup detection, 484
wakeup latency measurements, 481-483
kernel preemption, 469
challenges, 469-471
checking, 471-472
concurrency errors, 470
critical sections, locking, 470
latency sources, 473
models, 471-472
SMP, 472
latency, 467-468
processes, creating, 477
scheduling, 467
soft, 466
realpath BusyBox command, 567
reboot BusyBox command, 567
recipes (OpenEmbedded metadata), 456-459
BitBake Hello World processing, 458-459
Hello World example, 457
images, 463

Red Hat's New Journaling File System: ext3
  website, 259
Redboot
  bootloaders, 197
  partitions, 269-273
    CFI support, 270
    creating, 272
    detecting, 270
    Flash partitions, 269-271
    new partition list, 272
    power-up messages, 269
  user documentation website, 288
reformime BusyBox command, 567
refreshing SDRAM, 573
Reiser4 File System website, 259
ReiserFS file system, 238
release() method, 217-219
remote debugging
  file stripping, 426-427
  gdbserver utility, 427-429
  kernel, 382-385
  running processes, connecting, 442-443
  sample program ELF file debug information,
    425-426
  serial ports, 442
renice BusyBox command, 567
requirements
  dependencies, 32
  development, 13-14
  distribution components, 97
  hosts, 311-312
reset BusyBox command, 567
resize BusyBox command, 567
resources
  binary tools, 365
  Buildroot, 464
  BusyBox, 304
  cbrowser, 365
  DDD, 365
  device drivers, 226
  dmalloc, 365
  file systems, 259
  GDB, 365, 444
  kernel debugging, 422
  Linux Kernel Development, 3rd Edition, 485
  Linux news and developments, 583
  mailing lists, 582
  MTD, 288
  open source legal insight, 583
  OpenEmbedded, 464
  Scratchbox, 464
  SDRAM, 580

source repositories, 582
  udev, 548
  USB, 519
restorecon BusyBox command, 567
rm BusyBox command, 567
rmdir BusyBox command, 567
rmmod BusyBox command, 567
rmmod utility, 215-216
roles
  bootloaders, 160-161
  DTBs in boot sequences, 187-188
root file systems
  automated build tools, 137
  defined, 132
  directories, 134
  embedded challenges, 136
  FHS, 133, 226
  layout, 133-134
  minimal, 134-136
  mounting, 18
  NFS. See NFS
  populating, 137
  UBIFS as, 287
root hubs, 489
route BusyBox command, 567
rpm BusyBox command, 567
rpm2cpio BusyBox command, 567
rtcwake BusyBox command, 567
rules (udev), 527-530
  configuring, 533-535
  cumulative, 534
  distribution-specific attributes/actions, 534
  event-driven, 535
  example, 528
  loading device drivers example, 528
  MODALIAS field, 532-533
  mouse device example, 529
  storage location, 527
  uevents, USB, 530-531
run-parts BusyBox command, 567
runcon BusyBox command, 567
runlevel BusyBox command, 568
runlevels, 141-142
runsv BusyBox command, 568
runsvdir BusyBox command, 568
Rusty's Linux Kernel Page website, 226
rx BusyBox command, 568

S

sb-menu utility, 448
SCCs (Serial Communication Controllers), 45
scheduling real time, 467

Scratchbox, 447
    cross-compilation targets, creating, 448-450
    environment, configuring, 449
    Hello World example, 449
    installing, 447-448
    menuconfig, 449
    remote shell feature, 450
    website, 449, 464
script BusyBox command, 568
scripts
    linker command, 163
    rcs initialization, 299-300
    startup, 144-146
    uImage target wrapper, 185
sd-mod driver, adding, 509
SDRAM (Synchronous Dynamic Random Access
    Memory), 572
    clocking, 574-575
    controllers, configuring, 575-579
        memory bank control register, 578
        timing requirements, 578-579
        U-Boot sdram_init() function, 576-577
    operation basics, 572-573
    refresh, 573
    resources, 580
sdram_init() function, 576-577
sed BusyBox command, 568
selinuxenabled BusyBox command, 568
seq BusyBox command, 568
Serial Communication Controllers (SCCs), 45
Serial Management Controllers (SMCs), 45
serial ports
    KGDB, 372
    remote debugging, 442
    sharing console with KGDB, 377-379
servers
    BOOTP, 313-316
    DHCP, 313-316
    NFS
        configuring, 316-318
        target root mount, 318-321
    TFTP, 312-313
Service Availability Forum, 7
services
    MTD, enabling, 263-265
    NFS, restarting, 141-142
sestatus BusyBox command, 568
setarch BusyBox command, 568
setconsole BusyBox command, 568
setenforce BusyBox command, 568
setfont BusyBox command, 568
setkeycodes BusyBox command, 568

setlogcons BusyBox command, 568
setsebool BusyBox command, 568
setsid BusyBox command, 568
setuidgid BusyBox command, 568
setup_arch() function, 114
setup macro, command-line processing, 116-118
    code listing, 119-121
    console setup code, 117
    family definitions, 118
sh BusyBox command, 568
shared libraries
    debugging with, 429
        events, 431-434
        initial target memory segment mapping, 430-431
        invoking ldd command, 432-433
        locations, 433
        </proc/pid>/maps memory segments, 434
        requirements, 430
    finding, 433
    viewing, 432
showkey BusyBox command, 568
shutdown command, 156
shutting down, 156
slattach BusyBox command, 568
sleep BusyBox command, 568
SMCs (Serial Management Controllers), 45
SMP (Symmetric multiprocessing), 472
SOCs (system on chips), 43
    AMCC Power Architecture, 50-53
    ARM, 55
        additional companies, 59
        Freescale, 58-59
        TI, 56 57
    Broadcom SiByte, 54-55
    Freescale Power Architecture, 44-45
        PowerQUICC I, 45-46
        PowerQUICC II, 46-47
        PowerQUICC II Pro, 47
        PowerQUICC III, 48
    Freescale QorIQ, 48-50
    MIPS, 53-55
soft lockup detection, 484
soft real time, 466
softlimit BusyBox command, 568
sort BusyBox command, 568
source repositories, 67-68, 582
southbridge chips, 42
split BusyBox command, 568
stack frames (GDB), 330
stand-alone processors
    companion chipsets, 41-43
    Freescale MPC7448, 40-41

IBM 970FX, 39
Intel, 39-40
overview, 38
standards
carrier-grade, 6
Linux Foundation, 6-7
LSB, 5
Moblin, 7
Service Availability Forum, 7
start_kernel() function, 114
startup
scripts, 144-146
tasks, 11
stat BusyBox command, 568
stop-on-solib-event command, 432
storage
bootloaders, 162
cross-development environments, 30-31
execution contexts, 26
memory. *See* memory
MMUs, 26
U-Boot bootloader support, 173
udev rules, 527
strace utility, 337
command-line options, 341-342
profiling, 341
web demo application example, 337-340
strings BusyBox command, 568
strings utility, 362
strip utility, 361
stty BusyBox command, 568
subdirectories (kernel), 77-78
su BusyBox command, 568
subsystems (USB), 508
CDC (Communications Device Class) drivers,
512-515
HID (Human Input Device), 511-512
initializing, 122-124
mass storage, 508-511
device node, creating, 510
mounting, 510
partition, mounting, 510
SCSI support, 508
sd-mod driver, adding, 509
usb_storage driver, 508
usb-storage module, 509
sulogin BusyBox command, 568
sum BusyBox command, 568
sv BusyBox command, 568
svlogd BusyBox command, 568
swapoff BusyBox command, 568
swapon BusyBox command, 568

switch_root BusyBox command, 569
symlinks, 300-302
Symmetric multiprocessing (SMP), 472
sync BusyBox command, 569
Synchronous Dynamic Random Access Memory. *See*
SDRAM
syntax
command-line parameters, 116
flat device tree, 192
sysctl BusyBox command, 569
sysfs file system, 252-255
browsing, 253
directory structure, 252-253
systool output example, 253-255
USB devices, 500-502
syslogd BusyBox command, 569
system initialization, 297-299
system.map file, 70
system on chips. *See* SOCs
System V Init, 140
inittab file, 143-144
runlevels, 141-142
startup scripts, 144-145
web server startup script example, 145-146
website, 157
systool utility, 253

T

tac BusyBox command, 569
tail BusyBox command, 569
tar BusyBox command, 569
target boards
BOOTP/DHCP servers, configuring, 313-316
NFS
root mount, 318-321
servers, configuring, 316-318
starting, 15-16
TFTP servers, configuring, 312-313
targets
architecture-specific, 193
bzImage, 83
cross-compilation, 448-450
cross-development environments, 306
debugging, 424
DHCP identification, 172-173
distributions, 33
makefile, 83-89
memory breakpoints, 383
U-Boot makefiles, 176-177
zImage, 83

task_struct_show macro, 398-399
tasks
    ksoftirqd, 476
    OpenEmbedded metadata, 460
    startup, 11
taskset BusyBox command, 569
tc BusyBox command, 569
tcpsvd BusyBox command, 569
tee BusyBox command, 569
telnet BusyBox command, 569
telnetd BusyBox command, 569
test BusyBox command, 569
Texas Instruments (TI) ARM processors, 56-57
TFTP (Trivial File transfer Protocol), 171
    servers, configuring, 312-313
    website, 198, 323
tftp BusyBox command, 569
tftp command, 17
tftpd BusyBox command, 569
time BusyBox command, 569
TI (Texas Instruments) ARM processors, 56-57
tmpfs file system, 256
Tool Interface Standard (TIS) Executable and
    Linking Format, 98
tools. See utilities
top BusyBox command, 569
top-level kernel source directory, 69
topologies (USB)
    logical, 490-491
    physical, 488-490
top utility, 346-348
Torvalds, Linus, 6, 64
touch BusyBox command, 569
tr BusyBox command, 569
traceroute BusyBox command, 569
tracing and profiling tools
    dmalloc, 350-353
    kernel oops, 353-355
    ltrace, 343-344
    mtrace, 348-349
    ps, 344-346
    strace, 337
        command-line options, 341-342
        profiling, 341
        web demo application example, 337-340
    top, 346-348
Trivial File Transfer Protocol. See TFTP
troubleshooting. See debugging
TRUE BusyBox command, 569
tty BusyBox command, 569
ttysize BusyBox command, 569
Tundra chip, 42
tune2fs BusyBox command, 569

U

U-Boot bootloader
    booting from disks, 174
    commands, 169-170, 558-560
    configuring, 167-169
    debugging with JTAG probes, 414
    DTBs on boot sequence, 187-188
    finding, 166
    image formats, 185-186
    KGDB enabled booting, 373-374
    network support
        BOOTP client/server, 171
        DHCP target, 172-173
        Ethernet interfaces, 170
    NFS root mount example, 320-321
    porting, 174
        board-specific initialization, 181-184
        build tree, configuring, 177-178
        EP405 board, 175-176
        makefile configuration targets, 176-177
        processor initialization, 178-180
        summary, 184-185
    reference website, 198
    storage subsystems, 173
    website, 166
ubiformat command, 286
UBIFS (Unsorted Block Image File System), 284
    as root file system, 287
    configuring, 284
    images, building, 284-287
ubinize configuration file, 285
udev
    busybox mdev, 545-547
    customizing, 540
    devices
        discovery, 523-524
        nodes, creating, 525-526
    initial system setup, 535
        coldplug processing, 537-538
        default static device nodes, 536
        startup script, 535-536
    persistent device naming, 541-542
        /dev directory contents, 541
        helper utilities, 542-545
    platform device drivers, loading, 538-539
    resources, 548
    rules, 527-530
        configuring, 533-535
        cumulative, 534
        distribution-specific attributes/actions, 534
        event-driven, 535

example, 528
loading device drivers example, 528
MODALIAS field, 532-533
mouse device example, 529
storage location, 527
uevents emitted on USB mouse insertion, 530-531
uevents for USB interface 1-1:1.0, 531
uevents on four-port hub insertion, 525
USB automounting, 540-541
"Udev: A Userspace Implementation of devfs" website, 548
udevadm command, 523-524
udevadm info command, 543-544
udhcpc BusyBox command, 569
udhcpd BusyBox command, 569
udpscd BusyBox command, 569
uevents, 523-524
    device discovery, 523
    four-port hub insertion, 525
    USB, 530-531
umount BusyBox command, 569
uname BusyBox command, 569
uncompress BusyBox command, 569
unexpand BusyBox command, 569
uniq BusyBox command, 569
Universal Serial Bus. *See* USB
unix2dos BusyBox command, 569
UNIX line-continuation character (\), 119
unlzma BusyBox command, 569
Unsorted Block Image File System. *See* UBIFS
unzip BusyBox command, 569
uptime BusyBox command, 569
USB (Universal Serial Bus), 488
    automounting, 540-541
    bus topology, 507
    cable assemblies, 494
    configuring, 495-497
        core makefile, 496-497
        descriptors, 491
        volume of options, 495
    connectors, 492-493
    debugging, 516
        device driver support, 518
        Ethernet dongle insertion debug output example, 516
        platform-specific options, 517
        usbmon utility, 517-518
    device descriptors, 490
    EHCI, 498
    endpoints, 491

Ethernet connectivity, 513-515
file system, 502-504
Freescale Semiconductor iMX31 Applications Processor example. *See* Freescale processors, Semiconductor iMX31 Applications Processor USB example
initializing, 499-500
    host controllers, 498-499
    usbcore module, loading, 497
interface descriptors, 491
modes, 494-495
resources, 519
revisions, 491
subsystems, 508
    CDC drivers, 512-514
    HID, 511-512
    mass storage, 508-511
sysfs file system, 500-502
tools
    lsusb utility, 507-508
    USBFS, 502-504
    usbview utility, 504-507
topologies
    logical, 490-491
    physical, 488-490
    usbfs, viewing, 504
usb_id utility, 542-543
usb_storage driver, 508-509
USB-USB direct networking example, 513
usbcore module, loading, 497
USBFS (USB File System), 502-504
usbmon utility, 517-518
usbview utility, 504-507
used macro, 119
user space
    context, 26
    processes
        dependencies, resolving, 139-140
        first user space program, 139
        init, 19, 140
        initial RAM disk method. See initrd
        initramfs, 153-155
usleep BusyBox command, 570
utilities. *See also* commands
    addr2line, 361
    automated root file system builds, 137
    bitbake, 137
    buildroot, 137
    busybox, 135
    cbrowser, 335-336, 365
    cross, 33

cross-strip, 426-427
DDD, 333-335, 365
depmod, 214-215
dmalloc, 350-353
    libraries, generating, 350
    log output example, 351-352
    requirements, 350
    resources, 365
fdisk, 229-230
Ftrace
    interrupt off timing measurements, 484
    kernel performance analysis, 478-479
    preemption off measurements, 479-481
    wakeup measurements, 481-483
GDB, 326
    backtrace command, 330
    core dumps, 327-329
    debug sessions, 331-333
    invoking, 329-331
    resources, 365
    stack frames, 330
gdbserver, 427-429
git, 68
insmod, 212
kernel oops, 353-355
ldd, 139, 362-363
Library Optimizer, 136
lsmod, 213
lsusb, 507-508
ltrace, 343-344
Magic SysReq key, 409-410
mkfs.ext2, 230-231
mkiage, 185
modinfo, 216
modprobe, 213-214
MTD, 279-283
    flash_erase, 280
    flashcp, 280
    JFFS2 as root file system, 283
    JFFS2 images, copying, 282
    kernel MTD partition list, 279
    MTD Flash partition, mounting, 280
mtrace, 348-349
nm, 363-364
objcopy, 360-361
objdump, 359
prelink, 364
printk, 407-409
ps, 344-346
readelf, 355-357
rmmod, 215-216
sb-menu, 448

strace, 337
    command-line options, 341-342
    profiling, 341
    web demo application example, 337-340
strings, 362
strip, 361
systool, 253
top, 346-348
udev helper, 542-545
USB
    lsusb utility, 507-508
    USBFS, 502-504
    usb_id, 542-543
    usbmon, 517-518
    usbview, 504-507
uudecode BusyBox command, 570
uuencode BusyBox command, 570

V

vconfig BusyBox command, 570
versions (kernel), 66-67
vi BusyBox command, 570
viewing
    disassembled object code, 359
    kernel initialization details, 127
    .modinfo sections, 539
    shared libraries, 432
virtual memory, 26-30
vlock BusyBox command, 570
vmlinux file, 70-72
    image components, 73-76
    listing, 72-73

W

wakeup measurements, 481-483
watch BusyBox command, 570
watchdog BusyBox command, 570
wc BusyBox command, 570
wear leveling, 240
web demo application, 337-340
websites
    A Non-Technical Look Inside the EXT2 File
        System, 259
    Abatron, 410
    ARM Technologies, 56, 59
    BeagleBoard, 62
    binary tool resources, 365
    Booting Linux: The History and the Future, 157
    BOOTP, 198, 323
    buildroot utility, 137, 464

BusyBox, 304
cbrowser utility, 365
Common Flash Memory Interface
    Specification, 288
CompactPCI, 60
cramfs project README, 259
DDD resources, 365
Debugging with GDB, 422
"Design and Implementation of the Second
    Extended Filesystem," 259
device trees, 199
DHCP protocol, 198
dmalloc utility, 365
DRAM, 198
dtc compiler, 189
Dynamic Host Configuration, 323
Eclipse Project, 365
EHCI, 519
"File System Performance: The Solaris OS, UFS,
    Linux ext3, and Reiser FS," 259
Filesystem Hierarchy Standard, 226
flat device trees
    references, 199
    syntax, 192
Freescale Semiconductor, 62
FSH, 157
Garzik, Jeff's git utility, 68
GCC, 323
GDB: The GNU Project Debugger, 444
GDB resources, 365
GNU
    Compiler Collection documentation, 130
    linker, 130-198
    Press, 422
GPL, 550
GRUB, 199
Intel, 62
JFFS: The Journaling Flash File System, 259
Kbuild, 98
kernel, 65
    debugging resources, 422
    HOWTO, 98
KGDB, 422
Library Optimizer Tool, 136
Lilo, 199
Linux
    Documentation Project, 96, 157
    Foundation, 8
    news and developments, 583
    Standard Base Project, 8
LinuxDevices.com, 3
mailing lists, 582

MIPS architecture, 67
Moblin, 7
MTD resources, 288
NFS, 259
open source legal insight, 583
OpenEmbedded, 137, 454, 464
Power Architecture, 62
Power.org, 62
PowerPC 64-bit architecture reference manual, 62
/proc file system, 259
"Red Hat's New Journaling File
    System: ext3," 259
Redboot user documentation, 288
Reiser4 File System, 259
Rusty's Linux Kernel Page, 226
Scratchbox, 449, 464
SDRAM resources, 580
Service Availability Forum, 7
source repositories, 582
System V init, 157
TFTP protocol, 198, 323
Tool Interface Standard (TIS) Executable and, 98
U-Boot, 166, 198
udev, 548
USB resources, 519
wget BusyBox command, 570
which BusyBox command, 570
who BusyBox command, 570
whoami BusyBox command, 570
wrapper script, 185
"Writing udev Rules" website, 548

X–Z

xargs BusyBox command, 570

yes BusyBox command, 570

zcat BusyBox command, 570
zcip BusyBox command, 570
zImage targets, 83

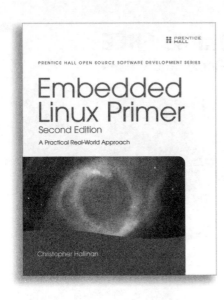

FREE Online Edition

Your purchase of **Embedded Linux Primer** includes access to a free online edition for 45 days through the Safari Books Online subscription service. Nearly every Prentice Hall book is available online through Safari Books Online, along with more than 5,000 other technical books and videos from publishers such as Addison-Wesley Professional, Cisco Press, Exam Cram, IBM Press, O'Reilly, Que, and Sams.

SAFARI BOOKS ONLINE allows you to search for a specific answer, cut and paste code, download chapters, and stay current with emerging technologies.

Activate your FREE Online Edition at
www.informit.com/safarifree

> **STEP 1:** Enter the coupon code: FWGFQGA.

> **STEP 2:** New Safari users, complete the brief registration form.
> Safari subscribers, just log in.

If you have difficulty registering on Safari or accessing the online edition, please e-mail customer-service@safaribooksonline.com